FINANCE & ACCOUNTING
New 2ND Edition

RICHARD GILES

eynsford College

First Floor
37-39 Oxford Street London W1D 2DU
Tel: +44(0)207 734 1722   Fax: +44(0)207 734 7774
www.eynsfordcollege.co.uk

FINANCE AND ACCOUNTING

NEW 2ND EDITION

Richard Giles

Created by Richard Giles & John Capel

© Richard Giles
First published 1996, 2001,
New format 2005, 2008

Published by
The Institute of Commercial Management
PO Box 125
Christchurch
Dorset BH23 1YP
United Kingdom
Tel: +44 (0)1202 490 555
Fax: +44 (0)1202 490 666
Email: info@icm.ac.uk
Web: www.icm.ac.uk

Produced by Brian Quinn
Printed and bound by Thanet Press Ltd, Kent

Preface

This book can be used with confidence because it is designed to be student-friendly, interesting to read and to stimulate learning by the use of clear examples. It has numerous wide-ranging questions. It will benefit you in your examinations. The courses for which the text will be suitable include:

> Association of Accounting Technicians (AAT)
> Chartered Institute of Purchasing and Supply (CIPS)
> Institute of Commercial Management (ICM)
> General Certificate of Education Advanced Level
> Higher National Diploma/Certificate (HND, HNC)
> Foundation Degree in Accounting/Business/Computing/Tourism

Throughout the text masculine pronouns have been used for the sake of simplicity: no offence is intended.
The more work and effort you put into all your studies, the greater the chance of success. Be determined, have a positive attitude and all the very best in your future courses and exams.

Acknowledgements

I would like to take this opportunity to thank the members of staff in the Business, Computing and Tourism Department at Bournemouth & Poole College for all their kind assistance and guidance and, in particular, John Capel, Chris Brookes, Christine Freer, Brian Garraway, David Griffin, Sara Holloway and Robert Giles (IT input) for their assistance, thoughtful ideas and encouragement.

Also, my thanks to the Examining Boards, who have kindly allowed me to use their questions, particularly the Association of Accounting Technicians (AAT). Others include the Institute of Commercial Management (ICM), the Chartered Institute of Purchasing & Supply (CIPS), the Associated Examining Board (AEB), the Royal Society of Arts (RSA), the London Chamber of Commerce & Industry (LCCI), the Chartered Institute of Management Accountants (CIMA) and the Chartered Association of Certified Accountants (ACCA). I would also like to thank SAGE for the format used in the computerised accounting sections.

The Author

Richard Giles has many years of lecturing and accounting experience and was recently the head of the AAT (Association of Accounting Technicians) at Bournemouth & Poole College in Dorset, England. He has written several books on finance that have been continuously published for over 20 years. Richard is also a business moderator for EDI (Education Development International) and has been an advisor for teaching accounting in overseas countries including the Far and Middle East.

FINANCE AND ACCOUNTING

How to use this book

Part I (Chapters 1 to 4): An Introduction to Accounting

Provides you with and insight to the world of accounting and explains its role in various business organisations. Chapter 3 introduces the basic principles of the profit and loss accounts and the balance sheet. Although the book introduces this at an early stage, it is useful to see why it is essential to record financial information in order to calculate a business's profit or loss and also state its financial position in the balance sheet.

Part II (Chapters 5 to 16): The Accounting Model

Encompasses the main body of recording financial information and is in effect, the bookkeeping process. Chapters 5 to 16 discusses the accounting model from the principles of recording double entry transactions in the ledgers and the use of the prime books of entry, that is, the day books, cash books and the journal. This section provides the essential introduction and context for the rest of the book. It is the foundation for building up the accounting model and the basic principles of accounting itself. With this understanding, students will grasp individual skills and the role they play more rapidly and effectively.

Part III (Chapters 17 to 21): Supply Information for Management Control

Introduces you to some basic costing techniques for use by management. Chapters 17 to 21 deals with basic information for management control and discusses the key elements of costing and how this assists management in its decision making.

Part IV (Chapters 22 to 30): The Construction of Financial Statements

Concentrates on the key issues relating to the preparation of final accounts, (the profit & loss account and the balance sheet). It begins with the basic principles that relate to sole traders, then takes you on to more detailed areas, such as adjustments to the final accounts at the end of an accounting period. These then allow further consideration of partnership and limited company accounts including cash flow statements and the accounts of clubs and societies.

Part V (Chapters 31 to 40): Using Accounting Information

Concerns the use of accounting information and includes some attention to the interpretation and decision-making techniques used by cost and management accounting. Chapters 31 to 38 provides a relatively detailed account of the use of accounting ratios and covers some further significant areas of marginal costing, budgeting and capital investment appraisal.

Part VI Solutions to Questions

The final section is the Solutions to Questions that includes abbreviated and full answers to all questions in the text. It will help you to check your work and to see if you are on the right track..

Glossary

This includes a comprehensive list of accounting terminology that helps to explain and understand key accounting words.

Contents

Part IV: The Construction of Financial Statements

Part V: Using Accounting Information

Glossary

Part VI: Solutions to Questions

Index

PART I   AN INTRODUCTION TO ACCOUNTING

Chapter 1

What is Accounting?

INTRODUCTION

The word *'account'* has various meanings to different people. It can refer to identifying and recording something or to measuring or explaining it. The widely accepted definition of accounting produced by the American Accounting Association stated:

Accounting is the process of identifying, measuring and communicating economic information in order to permit informed judgements and decisions by users of that information.

All of us do some sort of accounting in our daily lives. We earn and spend money. As we do this, we identify and record what we are spending, perhaps by jotting it down on scraps of paper or perhaps we are more organised and record it on a notepad. When the bank statement arrives from the bank, we might check the expenditure items with our cheque book counterfoils. This organisation of our money helps us to identify spending patterns and we check this against our income to avoid getting into debt. This is a form of domestic accounting.

Business enterprises are made up of commercial transactions. They are all involved with buying and selling their goods or services. To do this requires money. The business must be adequately financed to both commence and continue in business in order to survive.

For example, the local shop needs to purchase its goods to sell. It also requires other things to buy such as light, heat, power, labour, stationery, equipment and so on. It will sell its goods for a higher price than what it purchased them for, thereby making a profit. This is what business is all about, making profits.

Finance

The word "finance" can conjure up a number of thoughts and meanings both as a noun and verb. Finance is about having sufficient money in business in order to trade. Accounts, business, economics and commerce, financial affairs, investments, funding, capital, are just some of the words which may be associated with finance. Essentially, it is about money. The management of money, the control of it, the raising and spending of it and of course, the making of it. From a business's point of view, the word finance is important because it wants to know two things:

- Where it gets its money from, that is, the sources of its finance;
- What happens to its money. How it is used and whether or not the business is making a profit.

Accounting

Is a derivative of the word "account" and this provides us with the commercial definition of what it is. Accounting books, to compute, charge, balance accounts, to maintain records of finances, etc. Every business organisation needs to maintain accurate accounting records to help it manage and control its finances more efficiently. Records must be kept by all businesses so that they can be run properly. Without day to day records, it would be difficult to know if it was making a profit or loss, or whether it was worth keeping the business going. If a business continued to make losses, then it might as well cease trading altogether.

Bookkeeping

The bookkeeping side of a business is to ensure that financial records such as cash receipts and payments, sales, purchases and expenses, are maintained accurately so that it then becomes possible to know what prices to charge for goods or services. From these figures, it's just a short step away to work out how profitable a business is.

Records are also vital in business because they are needed for Taxation and VAT purposes. The HMRC (Her Majesty's Revenue & Customs) will need to know what profits a business has made in order to assess the liability for tax and if you are registered for VAT, you are obliged to keep a record of a VAT account to see how much money is owed to them.

Accounting is a further onward step from bookkeeping in that it is used for communicating financial information to interested parties such as owners, managers and banks. This also includes preparing financial statements at the end of an accounting period, for example after one year.

Financial statements

Financial statements, that is, the *profit and loss account* and the *balance sheet,* represent the two key reports that help both owners and managers in business to understand how the business has performed. The profit and loss account, as the name suggests, shows how much profit (or loss) a business has made. Whether it is a success or failure. The balance sheet indicates the value of a business's resources (its *assets*) and how these assets are financed by the owner's *capital* and borrowed money (its *liabilities*).

It is a function of accounting to provide those interested parties such as owners, managers, banks, Tax and VAT Offices, with the appropriate financial information which will indicate important aspects such as profit or loss, VAT, and the creditworthiness of a business.

Types of accounting

There are different types of accounting which need to be briefly explained.

Fig. 1.1

Financial accounting

This concerns the recording of financial information and is the bookkeeping side of the business, that is, maintaining and monitoring daily financial records. It also includes the preparation of financial statements. The better the quality of accounting records, the better control the business has. A business needs to record every financial transaction that occurs in the business. How it does this will largely depend upon the size and nature of the business.

The larger and more complex a business, the more it will need in terms of extensive and computerised accounting systems in order to give it the information and control it wants. On the other hand, a small business, like the local shop, which has most of its transactions by cash, may only require a cash book and any supporting invoices when it pays for any goods and services.

Cost accounting

This is largely required to support management in their decision making which concerns how much things cost to produce. How much will something cost, for example, to make a television set, in terms of materials, labour and overheads? Will it cost the same to produce 100 sets a week as it would 1,000 a week? How many sets need to be produced for a business to cover all its costs (break-even)? It's not going to do a business any good if it sells it's televisions for £150 each only to discover they actually cost £175 to make! This is vital information for management to know, particularly in the manufacture of products.

Management accounting
All Information in the form of financial reports, can assist management to arrive at better, more informed decisions. Financial and cost accounting will be used in management accounting to provide the business with essential information so that it can target its aims and objectives more effectively. If the aim of a business is to expand and achieve a growth rate that can expect a good return of profit, what must it do to get it? The objectives sets out how this may be done and management accountants will be expected to provide the reports to do it. Planning, control and the forecasting of results will be an important role of management accounting.

Who needs accounting Information?
Systems set up in accounting help to provide the answers to a number of questions posed by various groups of people. These are what are called 'the interested parties' of accounting information. The list of people who are interested in this information include owners, managers, employees, investors, banks and other financial instructions, customers, suppliers and the government. Owners of businesses largely want to know how much profit they are making.

- **Managers** of business need to have all kinds of information at their finger tips and accounting is essential in providing it for them. They want to know sales figures, levels of stock held, day to day cost of overheads and other expenses, whether there is enough cash in the bank, how much they owe their creditors and so forth. They also want to know how profitable a business is.

- **Government** can ask many questions of a business. The Inland Revenue needs to look at the profits made in order to calculate the right level of tax. The VAT Office is responsible for ensuring Vat is paid and require businesses to keep VAT records. They also require all sorts of statistical information from companies. For example, the number of employees they have, the number of accidents that may have occurred, the number of hours due to sickness and many other facets of information so that an analysis of these can be made for the nation.

- **Banks** and other financial institutions also want accounting information of businesses. It may want a business to supply them with financial statements such as the profit and loss account and the balance sheet. From these records, a bank can assess the level of profitability and liquidity of the business. If it wants to borrow money or extend its overdraft facilities, a business must have the potential to pay off loans and interest otherwise the bank might as well throw their money away.

- **Customers** will need accounting information such as stock and price lists, sales catalogues and other marketing information so that they can buy the right goods at the right price. The business needs to send the customer invoices and statements so that the customer will know precisely what is owed and how much time there is to pay. The business needs to keep customers fully informed of both existing and new products, trade and cash discounts, terms of trade and any other marketing and sales information both parties can take advantage of.
- **Suppliers** also need accounting information about the business to whom they are selling so as to check that it has the ability to pay for their goods and services and that they are reliable in paying their bills on time.

- **Employees** can also take interest in accounting information. They would feel more secure knowing that sales orders were booming and the business was making profits. If it was losing money, then they would be more anxious about their jobs and perhaps understand if the management demanded more effort from them in order to get back to profitability.

- **Investors** and potential shareholders in a limited company will also want to know how well a business is doing and what it is worth so that they can assess what value their shares will be worth and calculate the return on their investment. They could then compare the performance of one company against another and it may help them to decide whether to keep or sell their shares.

In conclusion, accounting is about recording financial transactions that occur on a daily basis. This is the book-keeping element that requires the recording of all the relevant accounts of a business. Financial statements, that is, the profit and loss account and the balance sheet, can then be prepared periodically from these accounting records.

Although *financial accounting* uses historical records that have already occurred, it is *cost accounting* that can be more dynamic in that it uses information not only to determine how much something might cost, but also to try and forecast what might happen in the future. In this way it assists management in helping them to arrive at the right decisions.

KEY POINTS OF THE CHAPTER

Finance:	Management of money, raising, spending and making money
Bookkeeping:	Recording financial information
Accounting:	Using financial information from bookkeeping records, preparing financial statements
Financial statements:	The profit & loss account and balance sheet
Financial accounting:	Recording financial information, preparing financial statements
Cost accounting:	Assists management in finding out how much goods/services cost
Management accounting:	Cost accounting provides the foundation of management accounting to forecast, control and evaluate costs
Interested parties:	All those who need accounting information, owners, managers, banks, creditors, HMRC, etc.

QUESTIONS

1. How would you define the meaning of finance?
2. What is the function of bookkeeping?
3. How does bookkeeping assist in providing information for accounting?
4. What is meant by the term *financial statements*?
5. From 'Who needs accounting information' answer the following:
   a) Who wants to know whether the business is profitable?
   b) Who is concerned with taxes and VAT?
   c) Why does management need accounting information?
   d) Why would a bank want accounting information?
6. Why are customers and suppliers interested in accounting information?
7. How do financial statements assist owners and managers in business?
8. How does the role of financial accounting differ from that of cost and management accounting?

Chapter 2

Business Organisations and Sources of Finance

INTRODUCTION

The United Kingdom is a mixed economy whereby the production of goods and services is provided by both the private and public sectors of business. The private sector is defined as *"economic activity in the hands of individuals"* as distinct from that of the public sector, described as "economic activity in the hands of the State". The state being of course, the Government. The private sector is trade conducted by individuals in the form of sole traders, partnerships, and companies, both private limited and public limited companies (plc's). These forms of businesses produce the majority of our goods and services particularly since the government has privatised so many of the nationalised industries, the public sector's contribution has diminished.

Clubs and societies are mainly the non-profit organisations set up for a specific purpose such as social, sporting, political or other interests, for example, the local tennis or cricket club. Economic activity in the private sector of business will be discussed first.

Business organisations

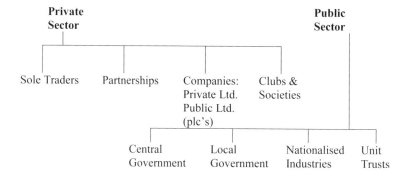

Fig. 2.1 Types of business organisations

The private sector of business

In the private sector of business, as distinct from the public sector, there are three basic types of organisations that are primarily profit-motivated:

- A sole trader;
- A partnership;
- A limited company (private or public limited).

The essential difference between these lies in the *size* of the business. This is directly related to the initial investment in the business - that is, the provision of capital, the most important ingredient in determining the size of a business enterprise.

The sole trader is a one-man business unit. Capital is raised by the private resources of one person. This person may also borrow from banks, building societies or other financial institutions.

Partnerships may have as many as twenty partners and subsequently have greater potential to raise more capital if each partner contributes a share. The more partners, the more capital is available for use in the business.

Limited companies are basically of two types. They are either public limited or private limited companies. Although there is no restriction on the number of shareholders who can contribute capital in either type of company, the private limited company may only sell its shares privately (that is, without resort to advertising) and therefore the number of shareholders is likely to be limited, shares being sold within the boundaries of family, friends and business acquaintances.

A public limited company has no such restriction and can raise its capital by issuing a prospectus (an invitation to the public to buy its shares). A merchant bank or issuing house can act on behalf of the company and make the necessary arrangements for the sale. In this way, very large amounts of capital can be raised and public companies can take credit for being responsible for stimulating growth in capital investment during the last 100 years. For a public company, at least £50,000 of share capital must be registered with the company, of which at least 25% must be issued and paid for before it can start operating.

Shareholders are part owners of their companies. The reward for owning shares may come from the payment of dividends from company profits, or from the increase in value of the shares (capital gain). Dividends are paid on the nominal value of shares (their face value) and not their market value. Dividends are usually determined as so much in the £; for example, 12p/£ would gain £12 per 100 shares.

Limited companies have *'limited liability'*, and sole traders and partnerships are disadvantaged by not having this. This means that in the event of a company's collapse, shareholders are protected against the debts of the company up to the value of their paid-up capital, but nothing more. Sole traders or partnerships are unlimited, which means they are personally liable for all debts. This could involve the selling of personal possessions in order to settle business debts.

Sources of finance
To commence a business takes money. How much money depends upon the nature and size of the business. To start up a large industrial manufacturing business, for example, would require millions of pounds and this would most likely be financed by shareholders of a public limited company. On the other hand, a florist's shop on the High Street may only need a few thousand pounds financed by a sole trader.

Finance can be a scarce resource particularly if you need it quickly. Government, businesses and individuals all want money to satisfy their financial needs. Most financing is either of a short- or long-term nature. For day-to-day operations, there is a need for a business to have sufficient **cash flow** that is, having sufficient resources to pay all its commitments, to pay for the basic things such as purchases of stock, wages and working expenses.

Often, to support cash flow, a business needs to have an overdraft facility with the bank. On a longer-term basis, financing may be required to buy fixed assets such as land, plant and machinery, equipment or motor vehicles. For these items of what is called *capital expenditure* there may be a need to call on a specific long-term loan from the bank, or other forms of financing such as leasing, or the hiring of fixed assets.

Whether on a short or long-term basis, every type of business organisation needs to be adequately financed. One of the major causes of business failure is lack of *solvency*, which means not having sufficient liquidity (cash) to be able to pay debts when these fall due. A business is said to become 'insolvent' when it cannot pay its creditors. This could quickly turn to bankruptcy and the owners will probably lose their capital and their business, while employees will lose their jobs and suppliers will lose what is due to them. In fact, it's a sad story and everyone loses out. A business must always maintain adequate cash flow and keep a tight control of its finances in order to survive the cut and thrust that makes up business life in general.

It is not surprising, therefore, that when a new business starts up and goes to the bank to ask for money, the bank wants to know as much as it can about how the business is to be financed. It would also like to see some kind of planning (that is, a business plan) concerning what is involved in the set-up of the new venture in terms of where the money is coming from and where it is going.

When finance is needed, management must consider three significant facts: how *long* the finance is required, how much it will *cost* to repay including interest charges and whether monthly *repayments* can be met adequately.

The major sources of finance are:
- the owner's capital;
- loan capital;
- bank overdraft;
- debenture issues;
- profits;
- leasing/hiring of fixed assets;
- leaseback of assets;
- mortgages;
- factor finance;
- creditors;
- government funds.

The owner's capital
When a business enterprise begins, the owner(s) put resources into the business, representing the capital. The capital may be in the form of money, equipment, tools, premises or indeed any other resource. The total value of these resources will be expressed in monetary terms and will establish the initial capital (or net worth) of the owner at the commencement of business. Capital may stay the same or may increase or decrease depending on how successful the business is and what the owner decides to do with any profit that is made.

Limited companies have shareholders who have subscribed share capital and are therefore part-owners of a business. The more shares they own, the more of the business they own. A shareholder of a public limited company whose shares are listed on the Stock Exchange may sell his shares if he wishes. Shares listed are 'marketable' securities and may be bought or sold by shareholders or by new investors to the market. Private limited companies are not listed on the Stock Exchange and are therefore not marketable securities. Transfer of shares is restricted to those members who can sell their shares privately.

A company must register with the Registrar of Companies at Companies House, Cardiff, and state the amount of capital it wants to raise. This is known as the *authorised capital.* The shares issued and purchased by shareholders are known as *issued and paid-up capital,* which may be less than the authorised capital. A company may wish to issue further shares at a later date when it may require more capital for future investment and growth.

Classes of shares

There are basically two distinct classes of shares:

Ordinary shares. These are the most common type of shares and are often referred to as *equities.* The rate of dividend depends on how much profit the company has made, and how much the directors decide to pay out as dividends and how much they want to retain in the company (in what is known as *reserves).* Ordinary shareholders are paid last, after preference shareholders, the rate of dividend depending on how much the directors recommend. Large companies may pay an 'interim' dividend half-way through the financial year and a final dividend at the end of the financial year.

Preference shares. These entitle shareholders to a fixed rate of dividend (for example, 8% preference shares). These shares may be more suitable to the investor who wants a regular and fixed dividend and a more reliable investment than that offered by ordinary shares. However, the vast majority of companies only have ordinary shares representing their equity capital. Preference shares represent a very minor holding and have barely any influence on the total capital held by limited companies.

A *'rights issue'* is a situation where a company wants to expand its share capital and where the existing shareholders are invited to buy the new issue first, being offered shares in proportion to their existing shareholding at a favourable price: for example, the offer may be two shares for every five held. If the existing shareholders do not take up the offer, then the shares may be sold via prospectus on the open market. Shareholders are part-owners of a company and represent ownership capital and not loan capital.

Borrowing: loan capital

Bank loans may come from a variety of different sources but the most significant source is the bank. The commercial (or High Street) banks are generally recognised as the 'Big Four' - Barclays, National Westminster, Lloyds TSB and HSBC.

A loan may be short-term (for example, within one year) like a bank overdraft, or a medium-term to long-term loan (for example, two to twenty years), used for specific capital purposes.

Loans on short-term credit are usually required to finance the day-to-day running of the business - for example, to purchase materials, to pay wages, to pay for overhead costs. It is unlikely that a long-term loan would be negotiated to finance short-term expenditure. An overdraft arrangement with the bank usually allows a person or business to reach a certain fixed limit in the current account - for example, £5,000 'in the red'. If the limit is exceeded, the bank may take steps to reduce the overdraft facility or even cancel it. Interest is charged on a daily basis and is usually a percentage above what is termed the bank's *base rate.*

A business bank loan is for a specific period of time with arrangements to repay by regular instalments over the period of the loan. For medium-term to long-term loans, the loan capital may be required for specific projects: for example,

- to purchase machinery or equipment
- to mortgage buildings or land
- to develop new products
- to finance an export campaign

Bank overdraft

An overdraft from the bank is another form of loan but it is generally considered to be short term because the bank could call it in at any time, particularly if the borrower were to default in payments or exceeded their overdraft limit, for example, a sum of up to £500 could be overdrawn before the bank stopped any further cheques by the borrower.

The overdraft has flexibility and interest is only paid on the amount that is overdrawn, charged on a day to day basis. It is considered to be the most important source of short term finance by most business organisations. Indeed, many of them would suffer a severe liquidity problem without it. It must be noted that overdrafts should not be considered to finance long term investment in fixed assets. This should be by a long term loan, normally at a fixed rate of interest.

Debentures

Debentures represent *loan capital*. Debentures may be issued by companies for the purpose of raising finance over a specific period of time (for example, 5, 10, 15 years). Interest payment to creditors (debenture holders) is a fixed percentage of the nominal value of the stock and is payable even if profits are not made. They are usually secured on the assets of the company in that if the company goes into liquidation, the debenture holders can be paid from the proceeds of the asset sales. These are often known as *mortgage debentures*.

The nominal value of a 'block' of debenture stock is £100 and it is this figure which is paid back to the stockholder when the debenture matures. However, it is possible to sell one's stock via the Stock Exchange before the maturity date - that is, they are marketable just like shares. But, unlike shares, the value of debentures is not dependent on the current and expected profits of the company.

Their value is primarily determined by the rate of interest paid on the stock in relation to current rates of interest elsewhere, say, in a bank; generally, if interest rates are 'high' in relation to the rate paid on the stock, then the market value will be below £100. When interest rates fall, therefore, the value of the stock can rise to £100 or some times even more if interest rates are very low.

Profits

The profits of a business can be one of the most important sources of business finance and is an *internal source* that comes from the business itself. For sole traders and partners, most of the profits may be withdrawn by the owner or owners from the business throughout the financial year as part of their income. This is referred to as their *drawings*.
Companies need to pay corporation tax to the Inland Revenue and dividends to shareholders. Any profit that is left can be *ploughed back* into the business to finance its expansion or to provide for specific projects or replacement of assets like machinery, equipment and plant.

Companies who retain their profits may transfer them to what is known as *reserves*: that is, leave it to accumulate in the profit and loss account. Reserves are **not cash** however, but represent the cumulative profit retained over the years in the business. It represents part of the company's capital and the equation capital = assets less liabilities. The more reserves built up, the more the net assets of the business will grow.

Leasing/hiring of fixed assets

A fixed asset is part of a business's capital expenditure and includes assets such as premises, equipment, plant and machinery, motor vehicles, etc. A business does not need to purchase its fixed assets outright but can either lease them or buy them on hire purchase.

There are two basic forms of lease: a finance lease, or an operating lease. A finance lease gives virtually the full advantages of acquiring an asset but without the legal ownership of them.

Depreciation and interest charges can be written off against profits. An operating lease, however, is merely a form of rental and the fixed asset is hired for a fixed charge paid, say, quarterly which is also written off against profits. The firm that leases the assets is known as the lessor, and may be a bank or finance house or the actual manufacturer or supplier of the asset. The firm acquiring the use of the asset is known as the lessee.

Leasing contracts can also have the advantage of servicing arrangements so that the maintenance and regular servicing of assets is the responsibility of the lessor. Leasing can also be an advantage if the fixed asset leased is not required for a long period of time. Indeed, leasing should not really be considered if the asset were to be used for a long period of time. Better to try and purchase it otherwise the cost of leasing could be very high. Both leasing and hire purchase finance can help the cash flow of a business, giving it more funds at its disposal to finance other operations.

Hire purchase can be an expensive form of credit and, although it can ease the acquisition of buying a fixed asset outright, it only becomes the legal property of the business when the last payment is made. The interest and depreciation charges of acquiring an asset under a hire-purchase agreement may be written off against profits.

Leaseback of assets
It may be an advantage to some businesses that own property to sell it to raise the necessary finance and then lease it back from the buyer. The business can then continue to use the asset and rent it back throughout the term of the lease. However, if property value increases, the business would have to forfeit any future capital gains it could have had. A further disadvantage could be that the lease may not be renewed in the future or the lease charge could increase substantially. The business may then have to seek alternative premises at more reasonable charges.

Mortgages
A mortgage is a form of long term loan used to purchase property. A mortgage is generally obtained from either a bank or building society and has the advantages of being long term, usually up to 25 years and that interest rates are lower. The lender will ensure that the mortgage will be secured on the value of the property so that any default in payment can lead to the sale of the asset and the lender reimbursed with the value of the loan. An advantage is also to be gained by *re-mortgaging* the property to obtain extra funds if fixed assets need to be purchased in the long term.

Factor finance
This has become a very popular way by which firms can ensure an adequate cash flow and thus short-term finance coming into the business to meet current expenditure. It involves a firm employing a debt factoring company. The firm employing the company passes all its invoices (trade debts) on to the factoring company that pays a major percentage of their value immediately and the rest when the debt is paid. In this way the firm has immediate funds (liquidity) because its funds (or a major part of them) are not tied up in debtors. The factoring company charges interest on the sum advanced until the debt is cleared; administration charges are payable too. A considerable number of financing arrangements are 'without recourse' - that is, the factoring company bears any losses occurring as a result of bad debts. Both large and small firms will employ factoring companies on a fairly continuous basis; the kind of financing provided can be a 'lifeline' to small firms who are experiencing cash-flow problems because of slow debtors.

Creditors
Suppliers of goods and services to business enterprises provide firms with an important source of short-term finance or *trade credit*. If credit facilities are granted to a business for the purpose of buying goods or services allowing, say, two months to pay, the two months' credit is a short-term

loan without interest charged. Some suppliers of equipment or other fixed assets will also allow businesses to purchase these on credit and may charge interest. However, they may not provide the actual term of payment to be as long as a bank or building society. The term of payment may be restricted to short term only, say up to two or three years.

Government funds

Investors in Industry was originally set up in 1945 as two separate bodies - the Industrial and Commercial Finance Corporation, and the Finance Corporation for Industry. In 1975 the two companies were merged and renamed *Finance for Industry*, and in 1983 that name was changed to Investors in Industry.

The whole purpose of this body is to sponsor small, medium-sized and large companies who are seeking 'venture capital' for projects that are not likely to yield a profitable return for many years to come. Backed by the English and Scottish clearing banks and the Bank of England, Investors in Industry has sufficient capital backing to take the longer-term view - lending money for periods of up to fifteen years. It thus plays an essential role in helping the development of British industry, especially in the highly competitive world of computer technology.

In conclusion, there is a wide variety of finance available to a business entity. The larger the organisation, the more capital it will require to finance itself. The major source of external finance is borrowed capital, usually obtained from a bank. For small businesses wishing to start up new ventures, there are a number of helpful schemes available, which are often open to young people, whereby grants and loans are on offer to those with energy, ideas and a determination to succeed.

Public finance

Public finance refers to Government (or State) finances. It involves the raising of money through taxation and borrowing for the purpose of spending money on public goods and services such as health, social security, education, the environment and defence. Public finance is either in the hands of central government or local authorities. Increasingly, however, it is central
Government which exercises greater control of the public purse and which has taken over much of the spending power of councils to prevent them from over-spending.

The Government has the power to cap any local authority if it overspends its budget limits. For example, if a district has a budget of, say, £80 million and wants to spend £90 million, the Government will cut its financial support in the form of grants or other measures, and force the district to cut back to within the budget level imposed. Most of the money spent by councils comes from council tax based on the value of peoples' homes.

The local authorities provide many community services and include a complex mixture of spending between county, district and parish council services. The county councils provide the majority of services including the heavy costs of local education, police, transport and highways. The district councils provide services for their own areas, including council houses, environmental health, recreation and leisure amenities and the maintenance of parks, libraries, roads and other features unique to their district. Parish councils spend relatively little in proportion to the finances they receive and spend money on projects such as a new sports pavilion or a Girl Guides' hall.

Raising Government finance

The majority of central government finance comes from taxation in one form or another, including National Insurance Contributions (NIC). Any short-fall in raising Government finance is made up by borrowing money. The Treasury is the Government department responsible for the control of public finance.

The Bank of England acts in the capacity of financial adviser to the Treasury as well as functioning as the Government's bank, keeping the records of its receipts and expenditure in what is called the *'Exchequer Account'*. The finance raised is used to pay for the vast programme of public spending as mentioned above.

Since 1997 the Bank of England has been really responsible for the Government's monetary policy and is an independent body that can either increase or decrease interest rates in relation to public demand for goods and services. For example, if house prices were spiralling upwards at too great a pace, the Bank could increase interest rates to curb the demand for mortgages and loans.

Direct taxes like income tax and NIC are those that are levied directly on our pay packets, or corporation tax which is levied directly on a company's profits. Indirect taxes are those on which we pay when we buy goods and services such as VAT and Customs and Excise duties.

The Budget
The aim of the Government is to control public expenditure and borrowing as a proportion of national output, so that expenditure is held more or less level in real terms to the income raised.
When the Government needs to borrow money to balance its budget, mainly from the Post Office National Savings accounts, it is known as the PSBR (*Public Sector Borrowing Requirement*). When the Government repays this debt it is referred to as the PSDR (*Public Sector Debt Repayment*).

The figures below relate to the amount of revenue collected and expenditure incurred by the country in a typical budget year, although figures could vary depending on the Chancellor's decisions. The budget forecast for 2008 spending was between £590 to £600 billion.

The figures are expressed *as pence in the £* so that income tax, for example, brings in over a quarter of all the Government's income (27%) and VAT about half of this figure, (14%). Social security on the other hand, accounts for just more than a quarter of its expenditure (28%) and the National Health Service including various other health services (22%) making both of them account for half of our total public spending, amounting to something approaching nearly £300 billion for the year.

Government revenue and expenditure forecast:

REVENUE Where money comes from:	Pence/£	EXPENDITURE Where money is spent:	Pence/£
Income tax	27	Social Security	28
Business Corporation tax	9	Health Service	22
NIC	16	Education	13
Other Inland Revenue	14	Defence	5
VAT	14	Law & Order	6
Excise Duty	7	Housing & other services	4
Council Tax	4	Transport	3
Business Rates	4	Trade, industry,	
Borrowing	5	Agriculture & employment	4
		Debt interest	5
		Other expenditure	10
	100		**100**

Source: *HM Treasury*: Budget forecast spending of £600 billion

KEY POINTS OF THE CHAPTER

Private sector:	Economic activity in the hands of individuals
Public sector:	Economic activity in the hands of government
Sole-trader:	One-person owner in business
Partnership:	Usually 2-20 partners share ownership
Limited companies:	Shareholders as part-owners in ratio to shares held
Ordinary shares:	Equities, with voting rights, dividends depend on level of profits
Preference shares:	Fixed dividend rate, no voting rights
Rights issue:	Expansion of company share issue
Debentures:	Type of loan capital of companies
Leasing:	Usually to acquire the use of fixed assets without ownership
Hire-purchase:	Buying fixed assets on credit basis
Bank overdraft:	Short term and flexible method of borrowing from bank
Leaseback of assets:	Sale of property and renting back from the buyer
Mortgage:	Long term borrowing secured on value of property
Factor finance:	Invoices traded for immediate cash advance
Council tax:	Local authority charge to residents based on value of home-owner's dwellings
PSBR:	Public sector borrowing requirement
PSDR:	Public sector debt repayment
The Budget:	Government's *fiscal and economic policy* by raising taxes and spending, where the money comes from and where the money goes.

QUESTIONS

1. How does the function of book-keeping differ from the function of accounting?
2. Why does the provision of capital influence the size of a business?
3. What do you consider the main sources of finance are for:
   a) a sole trader
   b) a plc (public limited company)?
4. What is the essential difference between the private sector of business and the public sector?
5. How does a local authority finance its expenditure programme?
6. How does central government raise its finance? What is meant by PSBR?
7. Name the main sources of central government revenue and expenditure
8. What are the economic objectives of the government? With regard to taxation, what is the difference between direct and indirect tax?
9. Clearly differentiate between ordinary and preference shares.
10. Why should a company want to *lease* its fixed assets rather than purchase them? Compare this method of raising finance with the *leaseback* of fixed assets.
11. Use the Budget forecast on the previous page and answer the following:
    a) If education spending is 13p and law and order 6p (or 13% and 6% of Budget) how much is this in actual total spending for each of these departments?
    b) If VAT and excise duty revenue is 21p (21% of Budget) how much should the Government receive?
12. What is one of the main functions of the Bank of England?

Chapter 3

Introducing Financial Statements:
The Profit and Loss Account and The Balance Sheet

INTRODUCTION

A business may have many different accounts, for example, sales, purchases, wages, advertising and rent accounts, yet accounting has only FIVE distinct accounting groups:

- **Revenue**
- **Expenses**
- **Capital**
- **Assets**
- **Liabilities**

A business may have hundreds of accounts recorded in its ledgers (where accounts are recorded), but all of them can be classified into one of these five groups. For example, sales is a revenue account, advertising and wages are expenses, premises come under assets and creditors under liabilities. If you think of the word **"RECAL"** this should help you to remember each one of the five accounting groups. A definition for each of these is as follows:

Revenue
Refers to the income earned by a business when it sells its goods or services. The majority of revenue comes from cash sales or sales on credit, although other revenue could come from sources such as rent received or bank interest earned.

Expenses
These refer to the day to day expenses a business incurs such as purchases of stock, wages, advertising, motor expenses, light and heat, etc. The difference between revenue and expenses is either a profit or a loss. If revenue is more than expenses, the business would make a profit. However, if expenses exceed revenue, the business will make a loss.

Capital
This represents the owner's personal investment in the business, usually from savings. Capital is needed to start a business off to buy the things is needs to begin trading, such as goods to sell or premises to use. Capital may grow if the business makes profits and is successful. The owner's capital is his "net worth" in the business, that is, how much he is worth in terms of the value of his assets less his liabilities.

Assets
These are things of value which the business owns such as its premises, equipment, stock, cash, bank, and debtors (customers who owe money).

- Fixed assets (non current assets) like premises and equipment are used on a more permanent basis in the business.
- Current assets, like stock, cash and bank which are used for *trading* purposes and constantly circulate when buying and selling goods, from stock to customers, to cash or bank and then back to stock to start the trading cycle again.

Liabilities
These are things of value that the business owes.

- Current liabilities are those debts that are owed to creditors, or to the bank for an overdraft. They are expected to be repaid within a period of a year.
- Long-term liabilities are debts owed to creditors that are expected to be repaid over a period that is longer than a year, such as loans, hire purchase finance and mortgages.

The five accounting groups can be used to prepare the financial statements of a business at the end of an accounting period:

Revenue)   These two groups are used for
Expenses)   the profit & loss account

Capital)   These three groups are used for
Assets   )   the balance sheet
Liabilities)

In a very simplified example, if a business had the figures listed below, it would have made a profit of £5,000 because revenue was greater than expenses. The owner's capital would be worth £20,000 because it is the difference in value between assets and liabilities.

Profit & Loss	**Balance Sheet**
Revenue £65,000	Assets £72,000
less	less
Expenses £60,000	Liabilities £52,000
Profit = £5,000	*Capital* =£20,000

Introducing the profit and loss account
Remember that in business, there are two key financial statements:

- The profit and loss account
- The balance sheet.

The profit and loss account is a business's statement of its earnings over a period of time. It shows its income less its expenses. If you have taken a look at the five accounting groups you will immediately realise that matching revenue with expenses will determine whether a business has made a profit or a loss.

Note that expenses do **not** include the purchase of any fixed assets like motor vehicles or equipment, it only refers to the day to day running or operational costs of a business.

Profit = Revenue - Expenses
Starting a business is all about making profits. If an enterprise fails to do this, it will soon cease to be a business. If income is greater than expenses, a profit is made. If the reverse happens and expenses are greater than income, then a loss is the result. The regular calculation of the profit and loss account is absolutely quintessential to the organisation and should be prepared at least once a month. If you wait until the end of the year to calculate profit, it could be too late to realise that things had been going wrong. Calculated on a monthly basis, there is time to take any corrective

action if things are not going to plan. A simplified version of this account is shown below in the accounts of businessman, G Harrison.

Example 1

G Harrison profit & loss account for the year ended 31 December:

	£	£
Sales		75,000
less		
Cost of sales		50,000
Gross profit		25,000
less		
Expenses (overheads)		
wages	10,800	
advertising	2,100	
light, heat	850	
business rates	900	
stationery	400	
motor costs	2,150	
insurance	1,200	
telephone	550	
accountant's fees	700	
general expenses	350	20,000
Net profit		5,000

Note that profit is divided into two parts:

- gross profit   (sales-cost of sales)
- net profit   (gross profit-expenses)

The **gross profit** measures the trading profitability of buying or producing the business's goods or services.   The cost of sales (£50,000) is the actual expense of purchasing goods, usually a combination of opening stock plus purchases, less the value of closing stock.   If it was a manufacturing business, the cost of sales would include the actual factory cost of producing the goods rather than just the purchase of goods. The margin of gross profit is very significant because it must be sufficient to cover all the overhead costs otherwise a loss will result.

The **net profit** measures the final outcome of profit after all other expenses are deducted from the gross profit, (gross profit less all other expenses). Net profit is a distinct measure of a business's performance.

The gross and net profit margins can vary quite significantly between one organisation and another and will depend upon the nature of the business and its volume of sales. For example, a large supermarket can afford to have a small gross margin of say 10% because its sales could run into billions of pounds per annum and still make a substantial amount of profit. The profit and loss account is discussed in greater detail in Chapter 22.

When the balance sheet is prepared, you will see that the net profit (or loss) *is transferred to the capital account.* A profit increases capital and therefore net assets (assets less liabilities) and a net loss has the reverse effect of reducing both the capital and the net assets of a business.

Example 2

Study the following profit and loss account of Roberta James and then try to answer the questions that follow:

Profit & Loss Account for the year ended 31 December:

	£	£
Sales		148,000
less		
Cost of Sales:		
stock (1/1)	4,200	
purchases	72,000	
	76,200	
- stock (31/12)	(3,100)	73,100
less		
Expenses:		
motor expenses	3,150	
rent, rates	6,250	
post. telephone	1,440	
wages, salaries	28,340	
insurance	1,210	
petty cash expenses	990	
loan interest	1,760	
accountant's fees	800	
legal costs	450	
depreciation	950	
overheads	2,100	
advertising	5,100	52,540

Questions
a) Calculate the gross profit for the period ending 31 December.
b) State the cost of sales figure.
c) Calculate the net profit for the period ending 31 December.
d) How would you describe the cost of sales?
e) Which expense (other than cost of sales) reduced profit the most?
f) Where will the net profit be transferred at the year end?

Check your answers:
a) £74,900
b) £73,100
c) £22,360
d) The cost of purchases for the period which includes the opening stock value, add purchases less closing stock value.
e) Wages and salaries.
f) Capital account in the balance sheet.

Introducing the balance sheet

The balance sheet is a major financial statement and lists the assets, liabilities and capital of a business. It is a snapshot of a business that indicates what it owns less what it owes. The assets represent what it owns and shows the resources of the business. The liabilities show what it owes. The difference between assets and liabilities represents the owner's capital.

The assets are therefore financed by the owner's capital and any monies borrowed (liabilities). The balance sheet is seen as a more elaborate statement of the accounting equation:

Capital = assets less liabilities.

A balance sheet should always balance because irrespective of the number of business transactions which may occur, the value of its assets will always equal the value of its capital and liabilities.

Example 1: A simplified balance sheet

G Harrison Balance Sheet as at 31 December:

ASSETS	£	£
premises	50,000	
equipment	2,500	
motor van	7,500	60,000
stock	8,000	
debtors	2,500	
bank	1,400	
cash	100	12,000
Total assets:		**72,000**
less		
LIABILITIES		
creditors	5,700	
bills unpaid	300	6,000
mortgage	41,000	
bank loan	5,000	46,000
Total liabilities:		**52,000**
Net assets: (A - L)		20,000
FINANCED BY		
capital: G Harrison		20,000

NOTE

1 Debtors are customers who money to the business in contrast to creditors to whom the business owes money.
2 Net assets = assets less liabilities and is equal to what the owner, G Harrison is worth £20,000.
3 The accounting equation:

$$C = A - L$$
$$20,000 = 72,000 - 52,000$$

The accounting equation
You can see a very simple rule that links capital, assets and liabilities. The owner in a business is worth the value of assets less the value of liabilities. The above equation is taken from the owner's point of view. For example if G Harrison owned ALL the assets of the business:

Capital = Assets
72,000 = 72,000

Alternatively, the accounting equation can emphasise the business's point of view from the value of its assets:

Assets = Capital + Liabilities
72,000 = 20,000 + 52,000

In this example, a business's assets, £72,000 is financed by a combination of the owner's capital, £20,000 plus what is owed in liabilities, £52,000.

Profits, drawings and capital
If G Harrison made a profit of £5,000 at the end of the financial year, this would increase net assets by £5,000. The accounting equation becomes:

Capital = Assets - Liabilities
25,000 = 77,000 - 52,000

If G Harrison withdrew £4,000 as personal drawings throughout the year for his own use, then this would result in his capital being reduced by the same figure:

Capital = Assets - Liabilities
21,000 = 73,000 - 52,000

Note therefore that while profits increase capital, personal drawings reduce it. G Harrison's capital would have increased by £1,000 at the end of the financial year as a result of profit £5,000 less drawings £4,000.

Horizontal presentation of the balance sheet
The balance sheet may be presented in two basic ways, either vertically or horizontally. The vertical presentation will be used in the text because it is by far the most widely used in business. The horizontal format would emphasise the alternative accounting equation: assets = capital + liabilities.

G Harrison Balance Sheet as at 31 December:

ASSETS	£	LIABILITIES	£
premises	50,000	creditors	5,700
equipment	2,500	bills unpaid	300
motor van	7,500	mortgage	41,000
stock	8,000	bank loan	5,000
debtors	2,500		52,000
bank	1,400	CAPITAL	
cash	100	G Harrison	20,000
	72,000		72,000

The profit and loss account and balance sheet together:
The following example will show a basic profit and loss account and a balance sheet taken from a set of accounts in a business owned by Alan Skene:

Accounts of Alan Skene as on 31 December:

	£
sales	200,000
cost of sales	124,500
rent, rates	11,000
light, heat	2,150
wages	29,850
printing, stationery	2,250
bank & interest charges	650
insurances	1,000
general expenses	350
capital	29,900
drawings by Skene	11,450
premises	50,000
furniture & fittings	2,000
equipment	2,500
motor vehicle	6,000
stock at 31/12	11,500
debtors	8,400
bank	1,500
creditors	5,200
bank loan	30,000

NOTE
These accounts are in *RECAL* order so that if we took the accounts starting with sales and ending with general expenses (revenue and expenses) we can prepare the trading and profit and loss account. This leaves us with assets, liabilities and capital to prepare the balance sheet.

Solution

A Skene
Trading and Profit and Loss account for year ending 31 December:

	£	£
SALES		200,000
Cost of sales		124,500
Gross profit		75,500
EXPENSES		
rent, rates	11,000	
light, heat	2,150	
wages	29,850	
printing, stationery	2,250	
bank & interest charges	650	
insurances	1,000	
general expenses	350	47,250
Net profit		28,250

Alan Skene
Balance Sheet as at 31 December:

	£	£
ASSETS		
premises	50,000	
furniture, fittings	2,000	
equipment	2,500	
motor vehicle	6,000	
stock	11,500	
debtors	8,400	
bank	1,500	81,900
less		
LIABILITIES		
creditors	5,200	
bank loan	30,000	35,200
		46,700
CAPITAL	29,900	
+Net profit	28,250	
	58,150	
-Drawings	11,450	46,700

Here you can see the accounting equation in action:

Capital	=	Assets	-	Liabilities
£46,700	=	£81,900	-	£35,200

NOTE
Where net profit has the effect of increasing the owner's capital, drawings by the owner (generally cash) has the opposite effect and *reduces* his capital.

In horizontal format:

Alan Skene
Balance sheet as at 31 December

	£		£	£
ASSETS		LIABILITIES		
premises	50,000	creditors	5,200	
furniture, fittings	2,000	bank loan	30,000	35,200
equipment	2,500			
motor vehicle	6,000	CAPITAL	29,900	
stock	11,500	net profit	28,250	
debtors	8,400	drawings	(11,450)	46,700
bank	1,500			
	81,900			81,900

As you can see from this format, the accounting equation can be swapped round. This is to show the value of a business's assets to equal the financing of these assets by the owner's capital and any borrowed money (liabilities):

Assets   = Liabilities + Capital
£81,900 = £35,200   + £46,700

The dual effect of business transactions

For every transaction that occurs in business there is always a double entry in that one account is affected in equal measure by another. For example:

If Alan Skene paid £1,000 to his creditors (suppliers), his bank account would decrease from £1,500 to £500. He would owe his creditors £1,000 less falling from £5,200 to £4,200. At the same time, if his debtors (customers) were to pay him £500 from what they owed to him, then his bank account would increase from £500 to £1,000. His debtors would decrease from £8,400 to £7,900.

Irrespective of how many transactions that occur, the balance sheet would still balance because of this dual effect and the equation would still show that assets equal capital plus liabilities. In chapter 5 the double entry principle is discussed in further detail as accounts are recorded in the ledger system of a business.

Categories of assets and liabilities

The two main categories of *assets* are:

Fixed assets	those more or less used permanently in the business: premises, equipment, fixtures and fittings, motor vehicles. Also referred to as non-current assets.
Current assets	those assets used for *trading purposes* and constantly circulating from cash, bank, stock and debtors. Current assets have a higher liquidity than fixed assets because they can be converted into cash more quickly.
Intangible assets	those assets not included above which tend to be 'invisible'. For example, *goodwill* - a business willing to pay to purchase another business may have to include a sum for the reputation or good name of that business.
Investments	when a business buys property, stocks or shares in other business enterprises.

There are two main categories of *liabilities*:

Long-term liabilities	the long-term debts of a business, for example, bank loans, mortgages and hire-purchase, to be repaid longer than the business's financial year (that is, creditors *after* 12 months).
Current liabilities	the short-term debts of a business, for example, creditors, bank overdrafts, bills still outstanding, debts to be repaid within the business's financial year (that is, creditors *within* 12 months).

Example

The following accounts represent the assets and liabilities of H Brown, a retail proprietor, as on 1 January:

	£
ASSETS	
land & buildings	15,000
bank account	2,500
stock at cost	3,000
equipment	1,800
motor van	750
debtors	150
cash	100
fixtures	1,750
LIABILITIES	
mortgage on land & buildings	10,000
bank loan (4 years)	2,000
creditors	1,850
bills outstanding	120

Required:
a) Place the above in their appropriate categories.
b) Calculate the net worth (or capital) of H Brown.

Solution:

a)

Assets			Liabilities	
Fixed	Current	Long-term	Current	
Land and buildings	Stock	Mortgage	Creditors	
Equipment	Debtors	Bank loan	Bills outstanding	
Fixtures	Bank			
Motor van	Cash			

b) Net worth: the owner's capital C = Assets - Liabilities
£11,080 = £25,050 - £13,970

KEY POINTS OF THE CHAPTER

RECAL:	The code word for the 5 accounting groups: revenue, expenses, capital, assets and liabilities
P & L account:	Profit & loss account that matches revenue with expenses
Gross profit:	Sales less cost of sales
Net profit:	Gross profit less all other expenses
Balance sheet:	Lists assets, liabilities and capital, a 'snapshot' of the financial position of a business
Accounting equation:	C = A - L or alternatively, A = C + L
Net assets:	Assets less liabilities
Drawings:	Owner takes cash or stock etc. for personal use, reduces capital
Dual effect:	Each transaction has a 'double-entry' affecting one account equally against another

QUESTIONS

1. When preparing the financial statements of a business how are the five groups of accounts used?

2. a) What is the purpose of the profit & loss account?
   b) Write down the formula for calculating both the gross and net profit.

3. A motor vehicle is purchased for £4,000 and is marked up by 25%.
   If repairs costing £125, advertising £35, wages £100 and general overheads came to £240, calculate the gross and net profit.

4. The accounts of a sole trader, Peter Jackson as at 30 April were:

	£
sales	48,850
cost of sales	32,420
wages	5,280
motor expenses	3,624
light, heat	2,100
rates, insurance	3,400
advertising	456
telephone	195
stationery	100
general costs	485

Required:
a) Prepare a profit & loss account of Peter Jackson as at 30 April.
b) What do you think links the profit & loss account with the balance sheet?

5. Show these assets and liabilities of J Smith, hardware merchant, in the form of a balance sheet.

shop	8,000		
equipment	1,500	bank mortgage	7,000
motor van	900	creditors*	115
bank	120	Loan from insurance company	500
cash	35		
		capital:	
stocks	1,175	J Smith	4,335
debtors*	220		

* Debtors represent people who owe Mr Smith money; creditors represent people to whom Mr Smith owes money.

a) Illustrate Mr Smith's figures by means of the accounting equation.
b) Which party holds the most claim on the business's assets?
c) If Mr Smith paid off his creditors by cheque, how would this affect his balance sheet?
d) Could he buy £125 worth of stock without money in the bank? How could the transaction be financed?
e) Prepare a new balance sheet incorporating the changes in (c) and (d) above.

6. The following accounts represent the financial interests of M Crooks on 1 June. He runs a small business associated with the building trade.

	£
premises	33,500
machinery & equipment	12,500
tools	1,500
motor vehicle	4,200
furniture in the office	1,500
stocks (at cost)	15,000
debtors	1,275
cash	100
bank overdraft	1,750
creditors for supplies	13,450
bills outstanding	750
interest payments due	125
mortgage on premises	22,500
hire-purchase loan on motor vehicle (2 years)	1,000
bank loan (5 years)	10,000
capital account: M Crooks	20,000

Required:
a) Group the above accounts in their appropriate categories - for example, current asset, fixed asset, etc.
b) Prepare the balance sheet of M Crooks as at 1 June.
c) Show the accounting equation which would emphasise the ownership of M Crooks.
d) The liabilities of the owner look rather excessive.
   Has he sufficient funds to meet his current debts?
e) Crooks must find at least £2,000 by the end of the month to pay off bills and creditors outstanding. Suggest how he could pay them.

7. Complete the following table. Enter the figures in the appropriate columns.

		Assets		Liabilities		Capital
		Current £	Fixed £	Current £	Long £	£
Proprietor's capital:	£					
Robert David	13,985					
plant, equipment	4,000					
premises	12,000					
debtors	3,725					
creditors	4,630					
loan from P Jackson	3,500					
building society loan	8,000					
drawings *	2,000					
stocks	6,500					
bank	1,850					
cash	40					

*Drawings are a *deduction* from proprietor's capital. Anything taken from the business for *personal* use reduces the owner's capital.

Required:
Prepare a balance sheet on 1 June for the proprietor, Robert David.
(The loans from P Jackson and the building society are both longer than 12 months and therefore are to be treated as long term.)

8. a) *Redraft* the balance sheet below of Harry Smith as at 30 June in vertical form: it is a poor presentation which needs adjustment.

Capital	£	£	Assets	£
H Smith		12,000	premises	25,500
LIABILITIES			motor vehicles	4,500
Loan from Frank		24,000	drawings of Harry	1,000
Overdraft		1,505	office equipment	3,000
Creditors	4,500		cash	100
- debtors	3,490	1,010	stocks	3,780
gas bill due		55	fixtures & fittings	1,050
HP on vehicles				
Outstanding (1 year)		360		
		38,930		38,930

b)   Briefly comment regarding the extent of liabilities in relation to Harry's own capital. (The loan from Frank is over a period of 5 years.)

c)   Give an opinion as to whether Harry's cash resources are adequate.

d)   Comment on Harry's capital tied up in fixed assets relative to capital tied up in his trading assets (current assets).

e)   Show the appropriate figures in the accounting equation illustrating C = A - L.

9.   The following represents the financial figures of R. James as at year ended 30 June.

ASSETS	£	LIABILITIES	£
land & buildings	25,000		
furniture & fittings	5,500	mortgage	15,500
equipment	7,000	bank loan (5 years)	10,500
motor van	6,500	interest owing	750
bank	2,500	creditors	4,500
cash	50	bills outstanding	1,000
debtors	1,450		
stock	8,000	Capital account	?
PROFIT FROM TRADING	8,250		
Proprietor's personal expenses	4,500		

Required:
Prepare the balance sheet of R James as at 30 June.

10. a)   Why is the profit and loss account and the balance sheet both useful financial statements to both owners and managers of business?

b)   Which figure links the profit and loss account with the balance sheet?

c)   Use the figures obtained in question 9 to write the accounting equation from the owner, R James's point of view.

Chapter 4

The Role of the Accountant and the Accounts Office

INTRODUCTION

The accountant's work is often varied and interesting, as well as far reaching. Many people think they have a boring job to do, recording figures all day long and checking the work of others. Accountants do this of course as part of their work but, more importantly, they are managers of finance whether they work in private practice or in an organisation where accounting is one of a number of departments like sales, marketing, production and personnel. Not only are they concerned with recording financial information, they are also interested in planning and forecasting results.

They are financial consultants helping other managers to decide the way ahead, playing a critical part in evaluating business problems and being part of a team which plans, controls and takes decisions in an organisation. Accountants, when qualified, may take on different roles. There are four main accounting qualifications:

- The Institute of Chartered Accountants (letters ACA);
- The Chartered Association of Certified Accountants (letters ACCA);
- The Chartered Institute of Public Finance and Accountancy (letters CIPFA);
- The Chartered Institute of Management Accountants (letters ACMA).

An ACA may work in a private practice; providing auditing and financial accounting services, such as preparing annual accounts for clients, and advising on taxation matters. In fact, the large professional firms of accountants engage in a whole range of financial consultancy work. Many ACA's work as senior accountants in industry and commerce. An ACCA may similarly work in a private practice and is qualified to provide the same services as an ACA. Probably, a higher proportion of ACCA qualified accountants work in industry and commerce than do so in private practice.

A CIPFA accountant will mainly work for local authorities, where a specialist knowledge of public sector financial accounting is required. An ACMA is not qualified to audit; consequently most ACMA's work in industry and commerce as management accountants, concerned with assisting management to assess business performance and cost-effectiveness. However, some ACMA's are employed in private practice as management consultants. Much of the management accountant's work is involved with assessing future performance.

The purpose of auditing accounts
An audit is an examination of the accounts to check that everything is as it should be. Accounts are subject to annual audits by professional accountants like ACA's or ACCA's. The purpose is to ensure that records and statements give a true and fair view of the accounts. The role of the auditor is to examine a fair sample of the accounting books, documents, vouchers and statements of an organisation in order to state that in their opinion, the accounts are a true and fair view of the company's affairs. A typical Auditors' Report concerning the accounts of a public limited company would appear in the Annual Report and Accounts as:

We have audited the financial statements on pages 28 to 39 of the Annual Report & Accounts in accordance with Auditing Standards.

In our opinion, these financial statements give a true and fair view of the state of affairs of the Company and of that of the Group as at 31 December 20.. and of the profit and cash flow statement of the Group, for the year then ended and have been prepared in accordance with the Companies Act, 1985.

RIVERS & WESSEX
Chartered Accountants
and Registered Auditor

In the case of limited companies, the audit is a legal obligation Auditors act as 'watchdogs' over the shareholders' interests. There is no provision laid down for small businesses (such as sole traders and partnerships) to have their accounts audited although, if an owner wanted verification of the accounts, an auditor could be appointed to act on their behalf.

Every auditor is not only entitled to examine the books of a company, but may also ask for further papers or documents, or call in the directors of the company to add to, or clarify, any information he requires. If, in his opinion, there is insufficient data to make a valid examination, this would be stated in his report. If the auditor is unsatisfied with any aspect of the accounts or with any explanations or returns made by the directors of the company, these would also be stated in the Auditors' Report.

The 1985 Companies Act states that limited companies must appoint an auditor (except small companies) to examine the books and accounts. This is so to express an opinion as to the financial statements being *'true and fair'*, to the shareholders of the company (see Chapter 27, Company Accounts, and the 1985 and 1989 Companies Acts).

The general role of an accountant either in private practice or working in an organisation may be listed as:

- the collection and recording of financial data;
- the organisation of financial data into books of account;
- the control of cash resources;
- the preparation of financial statements, such as profit and loss account and balance sheet;
- the assessment of financial performance through the analysis and evaluation of accounting reports;
- the examination of accounts in the role of auditor;
- the preparation of budgets to forecast estimation of expenditure against income for planning, control and evaluation of trading performance;
- the preparation of costing estimates, including marginal costing and break-even;
- the preparation of cash flow to ensure that sufficient cash is available to meet day-to-day expenditure;
- the arrangements and negotiations necessary for raising capital including loans or overdraft facilities;
- the role of a financial adviser or consultant.

The accounts office

The recording of financial information is the key function of an accounts office. Customers' and suppliers' records must be accurately recorded by the sales and purchase (bought) ledger clerks, information for these records coming from business documents like the invoice and credit note as well as from the receipts and payments of cash. Stock must be recorded either on stock record cards or using a stock program on the computer, showing both the quantity and type of stock in balance as well as its value.

The cashier is responsible for all matters involving the receipt and payment of money and the checking of statements with the business's bank account records. There may be a junior clerk delegated to take care of petty cash payments. A suggested accounts office may be organised as seen below in Figure 4.1:

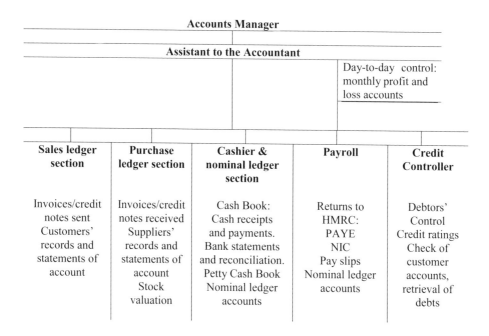

Fig. 4.1 jobs and responsibilities in a typical accounts office

Wages must also be calculated for each of the firm's employees, including payments for overtime or bonus schemes. Appropriate deductions need to be made for taxation, National Insurance and other stoppages from pay.

The accountant and his assistant will have overall control of the staff and be responsible for preparing monthly statements of profit and loss as well as the final accounting reports at the end of the financial period. They may also be involved in the preparation of budget accounts which are used to forecast and control income and expenditure figures for all departments of the business.

The computer is playing an important role in the recording of financial information. Computer programs are available for sales and bought ledgers, stock control, payroll and the preparation of final accounts. The accounts clerk will tend to type in data on a computer keyboard rather than traditionally writing the information in the accounting books.

Finance is one of the most important aspects of an organisation because the whole operation is dependent on its expertise. The preparation of accounts helps to explain what is happening in the business: whether it is successful or not, whether it has sufficient cash to pay its way, whether it should make this decision or that.

KEY POINTS OF THE CHAPTER

Accountant:	Qualified person responsible for maintaining and communicating financial records
ACA:	Institute of Chartered Accountants
ACCA:	The Chartered Association of Certified Accountants
CIPFA:	The Chartered Institute of Public Finance and Accountancy
ACMA:	The Chartered Institute of Management Accountants
Auditing:	An examination of a business's accounts in order to express an opinion on whether the financial statements give a 'true and fair view' of a company's performance and financial position
1985 Companies Act:	Limited companies must appoint an auditor to examine the books of the company although some smaller limited companies may be exempt
Accounts office:	Responsible for maintaining all financial records

QUESTIONS

1. People often think that an accountant's job is boring.
   Could you offer an alternative adjective(s)?

2. One of the accountant's functions is to act as an auditor.
   Find out what this service is.

3. What would be the difference in working for an accountant in private practice or working in an organisation which has its own accounting department?

4. In an accounts office, what may be considered a key function?

5. If you were employed as a wages clerk, find out what the following abbreviations mean: HMRC, PAYE, NIC. Why do you think returns of PAYE and NIC are made to HMRC?

6. What advantages do you think are evident in the use of computerised accounts?

PART II   THE ACCOUNTING MODEL

Chapter 5

Recording Financial Transactions:
The Ledger System and Trial Balance

INTRODUCTION

If you study the diagram of 'The accounting system' on the following page, it will give you an idea of the basic structure of bookkeeping and how financial transactions are processed into the accounts of the ledger. The ledger is the integral part of the accounting system where business transactions are posted from documents into accounts. For example, a sales invoice to a customer is first recorded in the sales day book before it is posted to the customer's account and to the sales account. In this way a business can keep track of what is owed to them from debtors and also the value of overall sales.

Financial transactions are basically divided into TWO categories: those on credit terms and those by cash. By credit terms we mean that payment for goods is delayed until a later point in time, therefore a record is made at the point when the goods are sold and when they have been paid for.

The day books: transactions on credit
The day books are used to record credit transactions. The day books help to organise transactions before they are posted to the ledgers. A sale on credit for example, means that an invoice sent to customer is first recorded in the sales day book then posted to the debtor's account and sales account in the ledger.

When goods are purchased on credit, the supplier's invoice is first recorded in the purchases day book before being posted to the creditor's account and purchases account in the ledger. Further discussion of the day books is to be found in Chapters 7 to 10 and the journal in Chapter 16.

The cash book: transactions by cash
The cash book is used for recording cash and bank transactions. When money is received or paid for in the form of cash, cheques, credit cards, or directly through the banking system, a cash book can be used. For example, cash sales are recorded on the debit side of the cash book then posted to the credit side of sales account in the ledger. Further discussion of the cash book and bank reconciliation can be found in Chapters 12 and 13. The recording of petty cash expenses is found in the following section, Chapter 14.

The trial balance is a device that checks the arithmetic accuracy of the double-entry system. It lists the balances of each account and total debits must equal total credits. From these figures the profit and loss account and balance sheet can be prepared.

FINANCIAL TRANSACTIONS

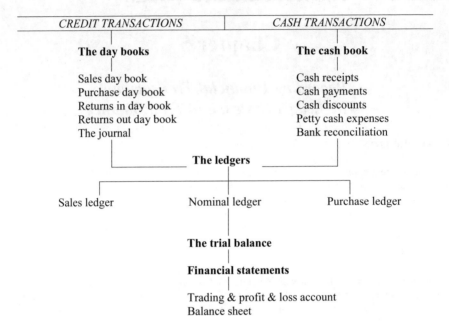

Fig. 5.1 The accounting model

The ledger system
In this chapter we will focus entirely on the ledger system so that you can understand how the principle of double entry bookkeeping operates. In other words, we will temporarily by-pass the day books and cash book and concentrate on how double entry recording actually works.

The ledger is used to record the financial transactions of a business. These transactions are recorded in date order and provide the basis of maintaining accounting records. It is from these records that the financial affairs of the business can be revealed, monitored and controlled.

What is an account?
This is a record of related transactions, for example, the sales account informs us of the value of all sales, whether on credit or directly through cash sales. Note that the left-hand side of an account is the debit side and the right-hand side of an account is the credit side. Look at the following accounts and state what you think is the value in each of them:

Debit	*Account No. 1*	Credit		Debit	*Account No. 2*	Credit
200						400
125						150
50						325

Debit	*Account No. 3*	Credit		Debit	*Account No. 4*	Credit
200		100		75		300
300		200		25		440
50						125

Check your answers:

Account No. 1	£375	DEBIT
Account No. 2	£875	CREDIT
Account No. 3	£250	DEBIT
Account No. 4	£765	CREDIT

The 'debit' is the left-hand side of an account. The 'credit' is the right-hand side. When there are entries on both sides of an account, the 'balance' is the difference between them.

The recording process is based on the principle of double entry in that every transaction has **TWO ASPECTS** to record of equal value and both of these must be recorded, otherwise the accounts will fail to balance and we would also have incomplete information in the accounting system.

The key point in recording accounts in the ledger is:

Debit: when an account RECEIVES money or value
Credit: when an account GIVES (or supplies) money or value

Example of business transactions:

If we were to buy a motor van for £3,000 paying by cheque, the van is RECEIVED and therefore the van account is the debit entry. Money is GIVEN, therefore the bank account will be the credit entry. The double entry is:

Debit: Motor van account
Credit: Bank account

Debit	Motor van account		Credit
Bank	3,000		

	Bank account		
		motor van	3,000

This is the **principle of double** entry bookkeeping and is the essence of recording accounts. The above accounts are in the 'T' account format and is the traditional layout of the ledger. In the following chapter you will come across the 'running balance' format as an alternative layout.

If the motor van had been purchased on credit from Henley Ford Ltd. The double entry is:

Debit: Motor van account
Credit: Henley Ford Ltd account

Debit	Motor van account		Credit
Henley Ford Ltd	3,000		

	Henley Ford Ltd account		
		motor van	3,000

If you have now grasped this basic principle, we can look at more detailed rules for deciding which account is debited and which is credited.

Recording the FIVE accounting groups

The table below will help you to decide how to record transactions, showing each group of account and when they are debited or credited. Note that it is in **RECAL** order.

Recording transactions

Account Group	Type of *balance* the account has	To *increase* *value* in the account	To *decrease* *value* in the account
Revenue	credit	credit	debit
Expenses	debit	debit	credit
Capital	credit	credit	debit
Assets	debit	debit	credit
Liabilities	credit	credit	debit

Note that revenue accounts have a *credit* balance and then the groups follow alternatively, *debit, credit, debit* and finally *credit* with liabilities.

Therefore, if a transaction includes an asset or an expense account that is to be increased in value, the entry must be DEBITED. If their value is to be decreased, then the entry is CREDITED. The reverse applies for revenue, liabilities and capital accounts. These are CREDITED when the accounts are to be increased in value and DEBITED when they are to be decreased in value.

Examples using the table:

1 Started business with £2,000 which was deposited at the bank.
   Debit: bank account   (asset increase)
   Credit: capital account (capital increase)

Debit	Bank account		Credit
Capital	2,000		

	Capital account		
		Bank	2,000

2 Purchased goods for resale £1000 cheque.
   Debit: purchases account   (expense increase)
   Credit: bank account   (asset decrease)

Debit	Purchases account		Credit
Bank	1,000		

	Bank account		
Capital	2,000	Purchases	1,000

3 Cash sales £500 paid into the bank.
   Debit: bank account (asset increase)
   Credit: sales account (revenue increase)

Debit	Bank account		Credit
Capital	2,000	Purchases	1,000
Sales	500		

	Sales account		
		Bank	500

4 Purchased goods on credit £800, from F James (supplier)
    Debit: purchases account (expense increase)
    Credit: F James account   (liability increase)

Debit	Purchases account		Credit
bank	1,000		
F James	800		

	F James account		
		Purchases	800

5 Paid a cheque, £150 for shop rent.
    Debit: rent account (expense increase)
    Credit: bank account (asset decrease)

Debit	Rent account		Credit
bank	150		

	Bank account		
capital	2,000	purchases	1,000
sales	500	rent	150
		balance c/d	1,350
	2,500		2,500
balance b/d	1,350		

NOTE
1 The balance c/d (carried down) is the difference between the debit and credit entries (£2,500-£1,150)
2 This makes both sides equal £2,500, totals on the same line.
3 The balance b/d (brought down) is made under the totals on the opposite side of the account with a commencing balance of £1,350 in the bank account.

The trial balance
The purpose of the trial balance is to test the *arithmetical accuracy of the double entry principle.* It is a list of balances taken from the ledger and placed in either the debit or credit column depending upon whether the account balance itself is a debit or credit.

If each transaction has been recorded correctly, then the total debit balances must equal the total credit balances. The trial balance may be drawn up at any time to check the accuracy of the bookkeeping system. If we check the 5 previous entries we made the debit entries ought to equal the credit entries. Study the following trial balance:

Trial balance

	Debit	Credit
	£	£
R sales		500
E purchases	1,800	
E rent	150	
C capital		2,000
A bank	1,350	
L F James (creditor)		800
	3,300	3,300

NOTE

The presentation of the above accounts in the trial balance is in RECAL order. This organises the accounts into a system and helps in the preparation of the profit and loss account and balance sheet when required.

The totals are the same so the double entry principle was followed and there is a good chance that the entries were correct.

Example: ledger entries and trial balance

The following information refers to the accounts of Ann Rogers, a retailer in the high street:

Balances on 1 May: £

		£
Debtors:	R David (Debit)	500
	L Jones (Debit)	230
Creditors:	J Robert (Credit)	150
	C Andrew (Credit)	200
Bank account (Debit)		270
Capital account (Credit)		650

Transactions occurring during the month of May	Dr Entry	Cr Entry
May 3 Sold goods to R David £300 on credit.	R David	Sales
3 Sold goods to L Jones £250 on credit.	L Jones	Sales
3 Bought goods on credit from J Robert, £600.	Purchases	J Robert
5 Bought goods on credit from G Andrew, £850.	Purchases	G Andrew
10 R David settled his account of 1 May, cheque £500.	Bank	R David
12 Sent a cheque £150 to J Robert and £200 to G Andrew.	J Robert G Andrew	Bank
15 Paid for shop rent, £300 cheque.	Rent	Bank
17 Paid assistant's wages, £125 cheque.	Wages	Bank
20 L Jones sent a cheque £200 on account.	Bank	L Jones
25 Sold goods to L Jones on credit, £180.	L Jones	Sales
27 General overheads paid by cheque, £70.	Overheads	Bank
28 Bought goods on credit from J Robert, £50.	Purchases	J Robert
30 Sold goods to R David, £280 on credit.	D David	Sales
31 Bought shop equipment on credit from Joe Brown, £750.	Equipment	J Brown
31 Cash sales into bank £275	Bank	Sales

Required:

a) Enter all the above information in the ledger of Ann Rogers for the month of May.

b) Extract a trial balance as on 31 May.

Solution

[Dates relate to May]

Capital Account

			1	Balance	650

Bank account

1	Balance	270	12	Robert	150
10	David	500	12	Andrew	200
20	Jones	200	15	Rent	300
31	Sales	275	17	Wages	125
			27	Overheads	70
			31	Balance c/d	400
		1245			1245
	Balance b/d	400			

David Account

1	Balance	500	10	Bank	500
3	Sales	300	31	Balance c/d	580
30	Sales	280			
		1,080			1,080
	Balance b/d	580			

Jones Account

1	Balance	230	20	Bank	200
3	Sales	250	31	Balance c/d	460
25	Sales	180			
		660			660
	Balance b/d	460			

Robert Account

12	Bank	150	1	Balance	150
31	Balance c/d	650	3	Purchases	600
			28	Purchases	50
		800			800
				Balance b/d	650

Andrew Account

12	Bank	200	1	Balance	200
31	Balance c/d	850	5	Purchases	850
		1,050			1,050
				Balance b/d	850

Brown Account

			31	Equipment	750

Purchases Account

1	Robert	600			
5	Andrew	850			
28	Robert	50			
		1,500			

Sales Account

	3	David	300
	3	Jones	250
	25	Jones	180
	30	David	280
	31	Bank	275
			1,285

Rent Account

15	Bank	300	

Wages Account

17	Bank	125	

Overheads Account

27	Bank	70	

Equipment Account

31	Brown	750	

Trial Balance as on 31 May

	Debit £	Credit £
David	580	
Jones	460	
Robert		650
Andrew		850
Brown		750
Capital		650
Bank	400	
Purchases	1,500	
Sales		1,285
Rent	300	
Wages	125	
Overheads	70	
Equipment	750	
	4,185	4,185

The recording of stock and returns inward and outward

Stock
When goods are purchased and then sold the stock account is not affected. Instead all purchases of stock during an accounting period are recorded in the purchases account at cost price and all stock sold is recorded in the sales account (at selling price).

At the end of an accounting period, the value of any unsold stock is recorded in the stock account. For example, if on 31 March the accounting period ended and the value of unsold stock was say £2,100, this would be recorded in the stock account.

In the new accounting period commencing on 1 April, the next day, the closing stock of one period then becomes the opening stock of the next. Therefore the new opening stock value would also be £2,100.

Stock can generally be identified in three forms: *raw materials, work in progress* and *finished goods.* These are discussed further in manufacturing accounts, Chapter 35. All stock is valued at cost price or at the net realisable value (whichever figure is the lower). For example, if stock cost £10 per unit but because it had been damaged was reduced to £5 to sell, then any unsold stock is valued at £5 per unit.

When calculating the closing stock of goods, note that the higher the value of stock, the greater the gross profit because stock reduces the cost of sales figure.

Returns

If goods are sold on credit to a customer an invoice is raised for the sale. If a customer returns goods or is overcharged on an invoice, this is the basis of returns. The credit note is the document that is raised to process the return. From the business's point of view there are two kinds of returns to consider:
- returns inward (sales returns) from customers
- returns outward (purchases returns) to suppliers.

The double entry for returns inward is:
   Debit: returns inward account;
   Credit: the customer's (debtor's) account.

The double entry for returns outward is:
   Debit: the supplier's (creditors) account;
   Credit: returns outward account.

Example using stock and returns:
The following accounts are to be recorded in the ledger for the month of January:

January			£	Debit	Credit
1	Opening balances:	Stock	1,500	Stock	
		Bank	700	Bank	
		Capital	2,200		Capital
5	Purchased stock from Brown		1,000	Purchases	Brown
10	Cash purchases, paid by cheque		400	Purchases	Bank
12	Sold stock to Jackson		250	Jackson	Sales
17	Purchased stock from Brown		1,750	Purchases	Brown
18	Sold stock to Jackson		485	Jackson	Sales
27	Cash sales into bank		1,250	Bank	Sales
28	Returned goods to Brown		100	Brown	Returns out
31	Jackson returned goods to us		50	Returns in	Jackson
31	Cash sales into bank		1,150	Bank	Sales

Note: All transactions are assumed to be on a *CREDIT* basis unless specified by the words:
        Paid by cash or paid by cheque, or cash sales.

Solution

Debit		Capital account		Credit
		1/1 balance b/d		2,200

Stock account

1/1	balance b/d	1,500	

Bank account

1/1	balance b/d	700	10/1 purchases	400
27/1	sales	1,250	31/1 balance c/d	2700
31/1	sales	1,150		
		3,100		3,100
1/2	balance b/d	2,700		

Purchases account

5/1	Brown	1,000	
10/1	Bank	400	
17/1	Brown	1,750	
		3,150	

Sales account

		12/1 Jackson	250
		18/1 Jackson	485
		27/1 bank	1,250
		31/1 bank	1,150
			3,135

Returns Inward account

31/1	Jackson	50	

Returns Outward account

		28/1 Brown	100

Brown account (supplier)

28/1	returns out	100	5/1 purchases	1,000
31/1	balance c/d	2,650	17/1 purchases	1,750
		2,750		2,750
			1/2 balance b/d	2,650

Jackson account (debtor)

12/1	sales	250	31/1 returns in	50
16/1	sales	485	balance c/d	685
		735		735
1/2	balance b/d	685		

Trial balance as on 31 January

	Debit £	Credit £
sales		3,135
returns inward	50	
purchases	3,150	
returns outward		100
capital		2,200
stock	1,500	
bank	2,700	
Jackson	685	
Brown		2,650
	8,085	**8,085**

NOTE
It is preferable to open separate returns accounts so that at any time, the value of either returns in from customers, or returns out to suppliers, can be readily seen. However, returns inward could be debited to sales account and returns outward credited to purchases account as an alternative.

KEY POINTS OF THE CHAPTER

Accounting model:	Chart showing how transactions are recorded; day books, cash book, ledgers, trial balance, financial statements
RECAL:	The 5 accounting groups
Account:	Where transactions are posted
Account format:	Traditionally in 'T' account or 'running balance'
Double entry:	Principle where for every transaction, there is an equal debit entry to corresponding credit entry
Double entry rule:	In general, the debit account receives, the credit account gives. The 5 accounting groups also determine when to debit or credit
Balancing:	The difference taken between debit values and credit values
Trial balance:	An arithmetical check of the double entry principle applied to ledger recording
Returns inward:	Sales returns: Dr inward account, Cr debtor's account
Returns outward:	Purchases returns: Dr creditor's account, Cr returns outward account
Stock:	The value of any unsold goods

QUESTIONS

1. a) What is the purpose of the ledger in business?
   b) Why are sales and purchase ledgers used in some businesses?
   c) What basic principle does the recording of accounts follow? What could happen if this principle was ignored?

2. a) What is the purpose of the trial balance?
   b) If it failed to balance, what would you assume?

3. The following accounts are to be recorded in the ledger of J Bannister, for the month of January:

January			Debit £	Credit £		
1	Opening balances:	Bank	£2,200			
		Equipment	£1,300			
		Capital		£3,500		
5	Purchased stock from Brown	£1,000			Purchases	Brown
10	Cash purchases, paid by cheque	£400			Purchases	Bank
12	Sold stock to Jackson	£250			Jackson	Sales
17	Purchased stock from Brown	£1,750			Purchases	Brown
18	Sold stock to Jackson	£485			Jackson	Sales
27	Cash sales into bank	£1,250			Bank	Sales
28	Returned goods to Brown	£100			Brown	Return out
29	Paid advertising by cheque	£320			Advertising	Bank
29	Paid rent by cheque	£480			Rent	Bank
31	Cash sales into bank	£1,150			Bank	Sales
31	Jack drew a cheque for himself	£500			Drawings	Bank
31	Paid cheque to Brown	£900			Brown	Bank

Note: All transactions are assumed to be on a *CREDIT* basis unless specified by the words: *Paid by cash or, paid by cheque or, cash sales.*

Required:
a) Prepare the above transactions in the ledger of Jack Bannister. Balance each account at the end of the month and bring down the balance on 1 February.
b) Extract a trial balance as on 31 January.

4. Balance the following accounts on 31 January; bring down the balances the next day:

R Green account (creditor)

Jan. 10	bank	500	Jan. 22	balance	1,180
30	bank	1,830	20	purchases	1,000
			27	purchases	150

Bank account

Jan. 1	balance	3,500	Jan. 3	ABC Ltd	850
3	R Smith	500	4	Southern Gas	275
			8	Rent	85
			10	R Green	500
			12	Wessex Water	125
			30	R Green	1,830
			31	purchases	200

Purchases account

Jan. 1	balance	250		
20	R. Green	1,000		
27	R. Green	150		
31	Bank	200		

5. The balances of D Andrew were taken from the ledger on 30 June. You are to prepare a trial
    balance as at 30 June.

Account	£
Bank	3,305
Stock	750
Equipment	4,000
Motor van	1,750
Sales	2,095
Purchases	1,115
Wages	880
Rent	565
General overheads	480
Debtors	955
Creditors	1,560
Bank loan	1,250
Bills outstanding	55
Capital: D Andrew	8,840

6. The following accounts are to be recorded in the ledger of Alan Titchmarch:

January		£
1	Value of opening stock	2,500
1	Bank balance (Dr)	1,200
1	Equipment	300
1	Capital (Cr)	4,000
5	Purchased stock from Smith	2,000
10	Cash purchases, by cheque	1,400
12	Sold stock to James	250
17	Purchased stock from Smith	1,550
18	Sold stock to James	785
27	Cash sales into bank	1,250
28	Returned goods to Smith	130
31	James returned goods to us	35
31	Cash sales into bank	1,250
31	Purchased goods from Smith	800
31	A cheque was received from James	215
31	A cheque was sent to Smith	1870
	Rent was paid by cheque	320
31	Titchmarch took goods for his own private use	80
31	Bought equipment by cheque	650

Note: purchases from Smith and sales to James are on a credit basis

Required:
a)   Balance each account in the ledger as on 31 January.
b)   Extract a trial balance as at this date.

7. The following balances were taken from the books of P McCartney on 1 June:

		£
Bank	Dr. Balance	1,240
Stock	Dr. Balance	2,150
Motor vehicle	Dr. Balance	1,175
J Jones	Dr. Balance	248
N Diamond	Cr. Balance	152
B Manilow	Cr. Balance	502
Capital account	Cr. Balance	4,159

Enter the six accounts in Mr McCartney's ledger. The transactions below relate to the month of June. Make appropriate entries in McCartney's ledger. *(Assume transactions to be on a credit basis unless other wise stated)*

			£
June	2	Bought stock from N Diamond	258
	4	J Jones paid on account	100
	5	Bought stock from B Manilow	374
	10	The proprietor paid N Diamond the balance owing 1 June	
	15	Sold vehicle receiving the full book value to Harry Belafonte on credit	
	18	Paid by cheque 10% deposit on a new vehicle costing (The balance is on credit from Jake's Garage)	2,750
	20	Paid a cheque to B Manilow 33⅓% of his outstanding balance	
	28	Paid N Diamond on account	158
	30	Paid cheque for new stereo equipment to be used on premises	399

Required:
a) Balance each of the above accounts on 30 June. Ensure that after entering 'balance c/d' that totals are on the same line.
b) Bring down the balances on 1 July to begin the new month's transactions.
c) Extract a trial balance as at 30 June.

8. The following represents the ledger accounts of Jack Jones on 1 April:

Debtors:
Smith	£250
Lillee	£115
Thomson	£25

Creditors:
May	£85
Cowdrey	£172

Capital a/c: Jack Jones £18
Bank a/c: £115 [balance overdrawn]

Transactions occurring during April
April	2	Sold goods to Lillee £287 and to Smith £415
	5	Bought goods from Cowdrey £150
	10	Sold goods to Thomson £37
	15	Settled May's account of 1 April

17   Smith settled his account of 1 April
21   Paid £75 to Cowdrey on account
22   Sold goods to Thomson £156
25   Thomson paid £62 on account
26   Bought goods from May £195
29   Paid Cowdrey a further £95 on account
30   Received £201 cheque from Lillee

Required:
a) Enter all the above information in Jack's ledger.
b) Extract a trial balance for the month ending 30 April.

9. Mrs M Ward decided to commence business by opening a small retail shop in the High Street
    on 1 May. Her finances on that day were: cash, £2,500, and a motor van valued at £1,500.
    Hire purchase still outstanding on the vehicle was £1,000. Calculate Mrs. Ward's capital
    as at 1 May.

During her first month's trading, the following transactions took place:

May   1   Deposited £2,000 into the business bank account, retaining £500 in cash.
       2   Rented shop premises paying £250 cheque in advance.
       4   Cash purchases of goods for resale £300.
       5   Purchased £550 goods from Arthur Daley on credit.
       7   Paid £40 cash on stationery items.
      10   Cash sales £120.
      12   Sold goods on credit to Jack Smith £180.
      14   Purchased £750 goods on credit from Donna Steele.
      16   Paid motor expenses £30 cheque.
      17   Cash sales £235 into bank.
      18   Returned goods to Arthur £150 as stock damage.
      19   Paid £100 cheque on the hire purchase of van.
      20   Bought equipment on credit from Land Supplies Ltd £1,800, paying an initial
            25% deposit by cheque, the balance on credit.
      24   Cash sales £130 into bank.
      26   Paid general expenses by cash £80.
      27   Received 50% of the sum due from Jack Smith, by cheque.
      28   Sold goods on credit to David Wheelbarrow £330.
      30   David Wheelbarrow returned 10% of goods to us as being unsuitable.
      31   Cash sales £225 into bank.
      31   Paid Donna Steele £500 on account.
      31   Paid Land Supplies Ltd on account £270 by cheque.

Required:
a) Enter all the above information in the ledger of Mrs M Ward for the month of May.
b) Extract a trial balance as on 31 May.

Chapter 6

The Running Balance Method of Recording

INTRODUCTION

In the traditional style of recording ledger transactions, debit entries were separated from credit entries by the centre line of the page. The balance of each account was determined by finding the difference between the two columns of entries.

For example, in the ledger of P Jackson, the bank account had a balance of £5,000 on 30 June as a result of debits = £13,340 and credits = £8,340. The 'running balance' account is shown below.
The running balance method adopts a style that is like a *bank statement* with debit, credit and balance columns adjacent to each other. The principal advantage of this style of recording is that, after each transaction, the balance is calculated, revealing an immediate up-date of the account.

The traditional method, while clearly dividing debits and credits, does not give an immediate balance after each entry. There is the need to go through the balancing procedure at frequent intervals in order to determine the balance of each account.

Example: P Jackson's bank account in running balance format

Date	Details	Debit	Credit	Balance
1/6	Balance	9,000		9,000 Debit
10	Purchases		2,000	7,000
13	Sales	1,840		8,840
14	Rent		400	8,440
15	Wages		520	7,920
18	Stationery		280	7,640
20	Sales	1,800		9,440
24	Purchases		2,600	6,840
27	R Jones	700		7,540
30	H Bates		2,540	5,000

Different types of ledger

We have already discussed that the ledger is the main book of account in which individual accounts are recorded from business transactions. For smaller businesses, there may not even be a ledger in use. A trader could simply use a type of cash book where receipts are entered on one side and payments on the other.
For larger organisations that may have hundreds or even thousands of accounts, there is a need to have more than a single main ledger. In business, three types of ledger are in general use:

Sales ledger: all customer accounts are recorded here so that we can track what individual debtors owe us.

Purchase ledger: all supplier accounts are recorded here so that a business can track how much individual creditors are owed. Also known as bought ledger.

Nominal ledger: this is used to track ALL other accounts, revenue expenses, capital, assets and liabilities. It is the main ledger and is also known as the *general* ledger.

Definitions:

Personal accounts
Are the individual debtors and creditors found in the sales and purchase ledgers.
Nominal accounts
Are the impersonal accounts of the business, that is, all revenue and expense accounts.
Real accounts
Are the assets of the business such as premises, equipment, stock, etc.

Example: the running balance method of recording using three types of ledger:

On 1 January, W Williams had the following balances in his ledgers:

Sales ledger:	J Brown	£200 Debit
	D Jones	£150 Debit
Purchase ledger:	R Smith	£350 Credit
	J Jackson	£400 Credit
Nominal ledger:	Bank	£400 Debit

Transactions occurring during January were:			**Debit**	**Credit**
January	5	Sold goods to Brown, £230.	Brown	sales
	7	Sold goods for cash £55 into bank.	bank	sales
	10	Bought goods from Smith £150.	purchases	Smith
	14	Returned goods to Smith £25 as faulty.	Smith	returns out
	15	Bought goods from Jackson, £280.	purchases	Jackson
	17	Sold goods to Jones £300.	Jones	sales
	18	Brown returned goods to us £35.	returns in	Brown
	19	Cash purchases £80 by cheque.	purchases	bank
	21	Sold goods to Brown £115.	Brown	sales
	25	Paid Smith £350 by cheque.	Smith	bank
		Paid Jackson £300 by cheque.	Jackson	bank
	30	Received cheques from Brown, £200	bank	Brown
		and from Jones, £150.	bank	Jones

Required:

Enter all the above information in the books of W Williams for the month of January and extract a trial balance as on 31 January. The solution is on the following page.

Solution

Sales ledger

		Debit	Credit	Balance
Brown Account				
1/1	balance			200 Dr
5	sales	230		430
18	returns in		35	395
21	sales	115		510
30	bank		200	310
Jones Account				
1/1	balance			150 Dr
17	sales	300		450
30	bank		150	300

Purchase ledger

		Debit	Credit	Balance
Smith Account				
1/1	balance			350 Cr
10	purchases		150	500
14	returns out	25		475
25	bank	350		125
Jackson Account				
1/1	balance			400 Cr
15	purchases		280	680
25	bank	300		380

Nominal ledger

		Debit	Credit	Balance
Sales Account				
5/1	Brown		230	230 Cr
7	bank		55	288
17	Jones		300	585
21	Brown		115	700
Purchases Account				
10/1	Smith	150		150 Dr
15	Jackson	280		430
19	bank	80		510
Returns Inward Account				
18/1	Brown	35		35 Dr
Returns Outward Account				
14/1	Smith		25	25 Cr

Bank Account

1/1	Balance			400 Dr
7	sales	55		455
19	purchases		80	375
25	Smith		350	25
	Jackson		300	275 Cr
30	Brown	200		75 Cr
	Jones	150		75 Dr

Trial Balance of W Williams as on 31 January

Account	Debit £	Credit £
Brown	310	
Jones	300	
Smith		125
Jackson		380
Sales		700
Purchases	510	
Returns in	35	
Returns out		25
Bank	75	
	1,230	**1,230**

NOTE

The main reason for dividing the ledger is that it makes it easier to organise the accounts if all customers and all suppliers were recorded in separate ledgers, particularly if they were quite numerous in number.

KEY POINTS OF THE CHAPTER

Running balance:	An alternative method of recording ledger accounts where a balance is up-dated after each transaction has taken place
Sales ledger:	The accounts of individual customers only
Purchase ledger:	The accounts of individual suppliers only
Nominal ledger:	The main ledger that records all other accounts, including the total of debtors and creditors
Personal accounts:	The accounts of customers and suppliers found in the sales and purchase ledgers
Nominal accounts:	All nominal revenue and expense accounts, eg. wages, sales, purchases, etc. found in the nominal ledger
Real accounts:	The accounts of tangible assets such as premises, equipment, bank, cash, etc. found in the nominal ledger.

QUESTIONS

1. The following information refers to the accounts of Susan Jameson, a retailer in the High Street who had just started business on 1 May:

Balances on 1 May:	£
Bank account (Debit)	650
Capital account (Credit)	650

Transactions occurring during the month of May

May
1   Sold goods to R Donald £300 on credit.
3   Sold goods to L Jackson £250 on credit.
4   Bought goods (stock) on credit from J Robinson, £600.
5   Bought goods on credit from G Arthur, £850.
10   R Donald settled his account of 1 May, cheque £300.
12   Sent a cheque £150 to J Robinson and £200 to G Arthur.
15   Paid for shop rent, £300 cheque.
17   Paid assistant's wages, £125 cheque.
20   Received a cheque from Jackson £120 on account.
25   General overheads paid by cheque, £70.
31   Bought equipment on credit from Joe Brown, £750.
31   Paid a deposit of 20% on the equipment to Joe Brown
31   Cash sales into bank £375
31   The owner took £250 for self by cheque
31   Jackson returned £50 goods to as being slightly damaged stock.

Required:
a) Enter all the above information in the nominal ledger of Susan Jameson for the month of May. Balance each account at the end of May.
b) Extract a trial balance as on 31 May (in RECAL order).

2.   Roger Lee has the following accounts in his ledger on 1 May:

	£	
Jackson, P	336	Dr
Newman, J	450	Cr
Sales	1,755	Cr
Purchases	1,565	Dr
Bank	525	Dr
Capital: R. Lee	221	Cr

The transactions below took place during the month of May. Enter them in the ledger using the running balance method of recording: £

May	3	Paid a cheque to Newman on account	275
	5	Sold goods to Jackson	122
	8	Jackson paid on account	168
	10	Cash sales	375
	12	Bought goods from Newman	227
	15	Sold goods to Jackson	210
	16	Cash sales	280
	21	Bought goods, paying by cheque	187
	23	Bought further goods from Newman	156

25	Paid Newman a cheque on account	125
28	Received a cheque from Jackson which	
	would leave £250 outstanding in his account	
30	Cash sales	156
	Cash purchases paid by cheque	450
	New account opened. Sold goods to R Fanshawe	300

Required:

a) Enter the opening accounts in the ledger or R. Lee on 1 May.

b) Enter the above transactions in Lee's ledger for the month of May and also extract a trial balance as at 31 May. Assume transactions of personal accounts are on credit unless otherwise stated.

3. Freddy Smith had the following ledger balances on 1 January.

Premises (cost)	20,000	Dr
Motor van	1,875	Dr
Stock	1,900	Dr
Bank	850	Dr
Debtors:		
Rollin	420	Dr
Vines	268	Dr
Mortgage on premises	16,750	Cr
Creditors:		
Boston	1,950	Cr
Turner	350	Cr

The transactions for the month of January were as follows:

		£
January		
1	General expenses paid by cheque	35
2	Cash sales	125
4	Goods from Boston	2,000
5	Sold to Rollin goods	500
7	Cash sales	225
9	Insurance by cheque	84
11	Purchases by cheque, goods	100
14	Rollin settles account balance of 1 January, by cheque	
15	Cash sales	585
16	Paid cheque to Boston on account	1,000
18	Bought from Turner, goods	750
22	Paid general expenses, cheque	80
24	Sold goods to Vines	450
26	Cash sales	378
27	Vines paid cheque to clear balance owing on 1 January	
30	Cash sales	225
31	Paid Turner on account	500

Required:

a) Extract a trial balance as on 1 January for Freddy Smith, including your calculation of his capital account. Enter the balances in his ledger.

b) Enter the above transaction in the ledger of Freddy Smith using the running balance method.

c) Extract a trial balance for Freddy Smith as at 31 January.

4. On January 1, Jack Briggs's financial position was as follows:

	£	
Premises	17,000	Dr
Fixtures	1,500	Dr
Stocks	1,200	Dr
Bank (overdraft)	675	Cr
Cash	150	Dr
Debtors		
J Collins	1,100	Dr
D Smith	925	Dr
Creditors		
R Jones	1,200	Cr

Required:
a) Find the capital account of J Briggs and enter the figure in his ledger.
b) Enter all other accounts in the ledger listed above.
c) Enter the transactions listed below in the ledger of J Briggs.
d) Extract a trial balance as at 31 January.

Transactions during January

January	3	Sold goods to Collins £2,850
	5	Cash sales £1,300 into bank
	8	Purchased goods from Jones £1,605
	12	Paid salaries by cheque £300
	13	Owner withdrew £20 cash for personal use (drawings account)
	14	Paid £260 cheque for general repairs
	16	Cash sales £455. Banked £400
	19	Sold goods to Smith £720
	26	Paid salaries by cheque £300
	27	Cash purchases £90
	29	Received cheques from: Collins and Smith in settlement of their accounts of January 1
	30	Paid Jones by cheque £1,750 on account
	31	Paid purchases of goods by cheque £175
	31	Sold £500 of fixtures cash

5. On 1 July the following balances were extracted from the books of George Harrison, record shop owner.

	£	
Capital George Harrison	1,860	Cr

As represented by:

	£	
Cash/bank	1,812	Dr
Lloyd, C	440	Dr
Jones, D	168	Dr
Bloggs, H	560	Cr

Required:

a) You are required to enter the above information in George's ledger.

b) Enter the transactions listed below in the ledger for the month of July. Use the running balance method of recording.

c) Extract a trial balance as at 31 July.

Transactions during July

July	1	Cash sales £140
	2	General expenses cheque £30
	3	Harrison drew a cheque for personal use £40
	6	Sold to Lloyd £250 goods on credit and to Jones £156 goods on credit
	7	Purchased from Bloggs £400 goods on credit
	8	Cash sales £160
	9	Paid for purchases of goods by cheque £215
	10	Purchased a motor vehicle £350 cash
	15	Paid by cheque:

      Salaries   £85

      General expenses   £27

      Insurance   £54

	21	Cash sales £85
	22	Sold further goods to Jones on credit £44-
	24	Cash Sales £80
	26	Paid by cheque Bloggs account - settled 1 July balance
	27	Received cheques from:

      Lloyd having settled the 1 July balance

      Jones £100 on account

	28	Paid Bloggs another £150 on account
	29	Bought goods on credit from T. Jones £580 (new account)
	30	Paid salaries by cheque £80

6. Mr Les Dawson commenced business on 1 January with capital of £30,000. He put £28,000 into a business bank. account and kept the remainder in a cash account as cash in hand. During the first two weeks in January the following business transactions occurred:

January	1	Credit purchases: Green & Co. £4,000 Black & Co. £2,500
	2	Purchased. fixtures and fittings £6,200, paying by cheque
	5	Paid by cheque £56, advertising in the local paper
	6	Paid rent six months in advance £6,000 by cheque
	7	Cash sales £400. Credit sales: Redhill & Co. £3,500
	8	Wages paid by cheque £86
	9	Paid insurance premium for 12 months £400, by cheque
	12	Credit purchases: Green & Co. £3,000
	13	Paid postage and stationery by cash £38
	14	Withdrew cash £500 for personal use
	15	Paid Green & Co. 50% of his outstanding balance
		Wages paid by cash £84
	16	Cash sales £880. Credit sales: Redhill & Co. £4,600 Shaw Ltd £2,100
	17	Redhill & Co. send a cheque £5,000 on account
	18	Paid Black & Co. in full, by cheque

Required:

a)   Open appropriate ledger accounts for the business, recording the above transactions. Extract a trial balance as at 18 January.

b)   Why is it necessary to have more than a single ledger system for different types of business organisations?

7.   Jack Jones started in his own business on 1 March having the following:

£1,000	in cash which he deposited in his new business bank account
£1,800	motor van which he will use in the business
£550	equipment
£1,150	is on hire purchase from XYB Garages Ltd over two years

Your task is to assist Jack set up a ledger to record the day to day transactions as they occur.
Calculate Jack's capital as on 1 March and enter the above information in the accounts required in the ledger.
The following transactions occurred during March:

March	3	Purchased goods on credit from D Guest £350 and J Good £245
	4	Bought some office furniture, paying by cheque £150
	5	Sold goods on credit to M Bright £180
	8	Cash sales £125, into bank
	10	Bought further goods from J Good £300
	11	Sold goods on credit to M Bright £85
	12	Bought goods from Cash & Carry Warehouse, £220 by cheque
	14	Sold goods to C Taylor, on credit £300
	19	Paid general overheads by cheque £115
	20	20% of the goods bought on the 10th were returned to J Good as unsatisfactory (debit J Good, Credit Returns Outward)
	22	Sold goods on credit to M Bright, £125
	26	Cash sales into bank £190
	27	M Bright returned £40 goods to us which he had purchased on the 22nd (debit Returns Inward, Credit M Bright)
	29	Paid general overheads by cheque £135
	29	C Taylor sent a cheque £150 on account
	30	Drew a cheque for £200 for personal use
	30	Bought goods by cheque £480
	30	Cash sales into bank £400
	31	Purchased further equipment for £1,200, paying a deposit of 20% by cheque. The balance outstanding is on credit from Rawlings Ltd.
	31	Paid off the account outstanding to D Guest and also paid a further cheque to J Good £250 on account.
	31	Received a cheque £225 from M Bright on account.

Required:

a)   Enter all the above information in the ledger of J Jones.

b)   Prepare a trial balance as on 31 March.

Chapter 7

Recording Transactions on Credit: The Sales Day Book

INTRODUCTION

The selling of goods or services is the *life blood* of a business because without sales no business can survive. It is important for a business to research its market thoroughly if it wishes to maximise its sales and profits. Marketing attempts to find out what consumers want to buy and at what price so that it can satisfy consumer demand. That is, making the right product, at the right time, at the right price.

A business needs to advertise and promote its goods in order to attract customer attention. Small businesses may be able to afford the local newspaper but larger companies need to investigate all channels of communication in order to attract a much wider audience.

Quotations

Some customers may require a quotation for the goods they want to purchase. A quotation is a letter of response to a customer's inquiry and is an offer to sell its goods at the prices and terms stated.

Example: Quotation to Frederick Smith

In reply to your recent inquiry dated 15 March, we are pleased to offer the following:

Code No.	Qty	Details	Price	Cost	VAT
2421	50	J's cricket balls	4.00	200.00	17.5%
258	20	J's cricket pads	12.50	250.00	17.5%

Terms:　15% trade discount
　　　　Prices above exclude VAT
　　　　Carriage paid

If Fred Smith were to accept the quotation the sales office would convert it to a **sales order** ready to be processed. The sales office would be responsible for raising the invoice or hand it to the accounts office to prepare.

When orders are received from customers, some of them often like a confirmation that the order will then be accepted and processed in due course.

On the following page, the *accounting model*, Fig. 7.1, illustrates the structure of credit and cash transactions, with the sales day book being the first to be discussed.

FINANCIAL TRANSACTIONS

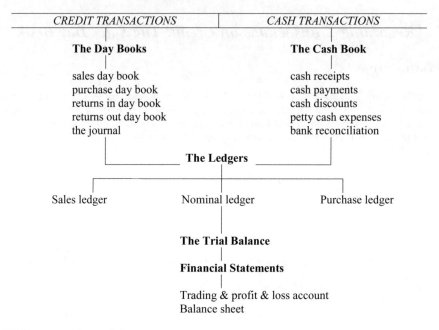

CREDIT TRANSACTIONS		*CASH TRANSACTIONS*

The Day Books

sales day book
purchase day book
returns in day book
returns out day book
the journal

The Cash Book

cash receipts
cash payments
cash discounts
petty cash expenses
bank reconciliation

The Ledgers

Sales ledger   Nominal ledger   Purchase ledger

The Trial Balance

Financial Statements

Trading & profit & loss account
Balance sheet

Fig. 7.1 The accounting model

The use of day books
One of the major functions of the day books (also called *journals*), is to help classify and summarise information from data such as invoices and credit notes. This makes it easier to transfer details to the ledgers.

For example, a batch of sales invoices sent to the customers of G Harrison in January would first be recorded in the sales day book before posting to the ledgers. This provides a prime source of entry for sales on a credit and the key figures of each invoice would be recorded on a day-to-day basis.

The sales day book

Date	Customer's Account	Invoice No.	Net Sales Account	Vat Account	Total Debtors
4/1	Jones, J	2501	200	35	235
5/1	Smith, R	2502	150	26.25	176.25
6/1	Taylor, C	2503	128	22.40	150.40
8/1	Lewis, D	2504	360	63.00	423.00
			838	146.65	984.65

Ledger posting:

Debit: Debtor's account
Credit: Sales and VAT accounts

Each customer's account would be debited in the sales ledger with the invoice total. The credit entries would be the totals for sales account £838 and Vat account (if charged) for £146.65 which would be posted to the nominal ledger.

Daily, weekly or even monthly figures (depending on the frequency of transactions), could be summarised and totalled in the day book and then subsequently posted to the appropriate accounts in the ledgers. It has often been suggested that day books in the accounting system are superfluous and not really required, particularly when computer programs are available to key in the document details.

Someone however still needs to prepare and check documents such as invoices in some sort of systematic order, prior to ledger posting. These figures could be entered on a control form that is attached to a batch of invoices. This becomes a day book or 'journalising' function, that is, preparing information from business documents before ledger posting. The day books are also referred to as the books of prime entry which help to 'feed' information to the ledgers.

The 5 major day books are:

- Sales day book: Records credit sales from invoices sent to customers.
- Purchases day book: Records credit purchases from suppliers' invoices received.
- Returns inward day book: Records sales returns from customers from credit notes sent to them.
- Returns outward day book: Records purchases returns to suppliers from credit notes received from them.
- The Journal: Records transactions that are *outside the scope* of those above, for example, to correct errors or writing off bad debts.

The Invoice

It has already been stated that the invoice is a bill of sale from a supplier to a customer. A supplier would normally give a certain number of days to settle the bill. This could be up to say 30 days and depends upon the supplier's terms of sale.

When a customer receives an invoice, it must be checked for accuracy to ensure that all details are correct including terms for any trade or cash discounts and VAT calculation. If the invoice is satisfactory and the goods have been received in good condition, then it will be passed to the accounts section for processing and future payment. An invoice from G Harrison to M Jones is shown on the following page.

VAT

Value added tax is an indirect form of taxation charged on many of our goods and services. The standard rate is 17.5% based on the net value of any goods or services which is to be charged.

For example, if goods were sold for £200 (gross value) but were subject to a 20% *trade discount,* then VAT on the invoice would be charged on the net value of goods:

	£
Gross value of goods	200
Less 20% trade discount	(40)
Net value of goods	160
VAT (£160 X 17.5%)	28
Total value of invoice	188

If a *cash discount* was also offered for prompt payment of invoice, then the amount offered is also deducted from the value of the invoice to reduce the net value even further and the VAT charged would be less. However, the discount could only be taken if the invoice was paid *within the specified time* stated on the invoice.

For example, if a 5% cash discount was available on the above invoice, the net value for VAT purposes, would be reduced to £152, (£160 less 5%). The VAT charge would be £152 X 17.5% = £26.60. The invoice value would then amount to £186.60: goods £160 + VAT £26.60.

The sales invoice

INVOICE 44572

G Harrison
214 Poole High Street
POOLE
DORSET

VAT Reg. No.	76 48424 23
Telephone	01202 684120
Date	24 March, 2008

To: M Jones
     Ashley Stores
     14 The Parade
     Wareham
     DORSET

Your Order No. 1038/08   dated 8 March, 2008

Quantity	Details	Code No.	Price per Unit	Cost	Vat Rate	Vat Amount
20	Empire bats	Z133	14.16	283.20	17.5	
150	Empire balls	Z128	2.28	342.00	17.5	
10	Senior batting pads	Z342	21.00	210.00	17.5	
				835.20		
	Less trade discount 10%			83.52		
				751.68		131.54
	Add VAT			131.54		
				883.22		

Terms: net cash within 30 days of above invoice date.
Delivery: our vehicle to your store, carriage paid.
E&OE

NOTE:

1 The trade discount of 10% is deducted from the gross sum of £835.2 to arrive at net sales of £751.68. VAT at 17.5% is added to the net sales taking the total value of the invoice to £883.22.

2 Net cash within 30 days simply means that the supplier expects to be paid £883.22 within a month from the invoice date. Check all the above calculations to see if you agree that the invoice is correct.

Terms of payment

Trade discount: A sum allowed to the buyer of goods off the usual list price. The discount rate varies usually in proportion to the amount of goods purchased. There is no double entry with trade discount, the net sum payable is recorded, not the gross sum.

Cash discount: A sum allowed to the buyer to encourage prompt payment, perhaps 2.5% or 5% if invoiced paid within a specific number of days. Cash discount is recorded as part of the double entry.

Bulk discount: This is a trade discount given on bulk purchases, that is, a larger trade discount could be made available if more is purchased.

Carriage forward: The buyer pays for the delivery of goods. This is referred to as carriage inwards and is part of the cost of sales in the trading account.

Carriage paid: The seller pays for the delivery of goods to the buyer's destination.

Cash on delivery: Payment is made when the goods are handed over.

E&OE   Errors and omissions excepted. This indicates that the supplier has every right to correct any error or omission on an invoice.

Ex stock   Goods will be supplied from stock.

Ex works   The buyer is normally responsible for the delivery cost from the factory.

VAT   Value added tax (an indirect form of tax) charged by the Government's HMRC (Her Majesty's Revenue & Customs) on many of our goods and services. The current standard rate is 17.5%. There are also zero rates and exempt tax discussed more fully in Chapter 10.

The invoice set

The invoice usually comes in sets of, say, five or six copies, or even more, because each copy has a specific function in helping to administer the sale and despatch of goods.

An example of copies required:

1 **Top copy**:   the customer's bill of sale, showing details of prices and terms of sale.
2 **Sales copy**:   the sales office copy for filing (also used to make a record of sales, etc.).
3 **Delivery note**:   usually accompanies the delivery of goods and signed by the customer as evidence of receiving order.
4 **Advice note**:   the customer may be advised when the goods are to be despatched.
5 **Accounts copy**:   required as evidence of transaction and for recording in sales day book and ledgers.
6 **Stores copy**:   recording the despatch and entering details on a stock record card.
7 **Transport copy:**   this may be an extra copy on the delivery note to be retained by the transport department as evidence of delivery.

Example 1 A simplified sales day book (with no VAT charge)

Date	Customer's Account	Invoice No.	Amount
1 May	J Smith	1285	300 Dr
5 May	R Jones	1286	255 Dr
7 May	F Brown	1287	100 Dr
15 May	J Smith	1288	125 Dr
15 May	F Brown	1289	120 Dr
		Credit sales	**900**

Sales Day Book

Ledger Posting

Date	Details	Debit	Credit	Balance
J Smith a/c				
1 May	Sales	300		300 Dr
15 May	Sales	125		425
R Jones a/c				
5 May	Sales	255		255 Dr
F Brown a/c				
7 May	Sales	100		100 Dr
26 May	Sales	120		220
Sales a/c				
31 May	Debtors		900	900 Credit

NOTE:

The double-entry:

- Each individual customer (debtor) is debited.
- The total sales for the month are credited.

Example 2: *VAT and the sales ledger control account*

The following information relates to the accounts of G Harrison as at 1 June:

G Harrison's ledger balances as at 1 June

Sales Ledger	£	Nominal Ledger	£
Thomson	45 Dr	Sales a/c	8,500 Credit
Simpson	110 Dr	VAT a/c	350 Credit
Jackson	180 Dr	Sales Ledger control a/c *	335 Dr
	335		

- The sales ledger control account represents the total value of debtors in the sales ledger. The three customers owe the business £335, the same figure that is in the control account.

- The control account is used as a cross- checking devise to ensure that at any time, it equals the total value of debtors' balances. The purchase ledger control account does the same job as a cross checking devise to ensure that it equals the total value owed to suppliers. This is demonstrated in the next chapter.

Sales invoices sent in June:

	Invoice No.	Date	Net sales £	VAT £
Thomson	1136	4/6	180	
Simpson	1137	10/6	200	
Thomson	1138	11/6	100	
Jackson	1139	15/6	360	
Simpson	1140	20/6	160	

Cheques received from customers at the end of June were:

> Thomson   £300
> Simpson   £450
> Jackson   £500 £1,250

Required:
a) Prepare the Sales Day Book for June, calculating the VAT.
b) Enter the opening balances on 1 June in the ledgers of G Harrison.
c) Post from the day book to the appropriate ledgers.
d) Enter the cheques received in the appropriate accounts, including the control account.
e) Prepare a schedule of debtors to cross-check with the sales ledger control account.

Solution:

Sales Day Book: Harrison

Folio No. 25*

Date	Customer's a/c	Invoice No.	Sales a/c £	VAT A/c £	Total debtors £
4/6	Thomson	1136	180	31.5	211.50 Dr
10/6	Simpson	1137	200	35	235 Dr
11/6	Thomson	1138	100	17.5	117.50 Dr
15/6	Jackson	1139	360	63	423 Dr
20/6	Simpson	1140	160	28	188 Dr
			1,000	175	1,175
			(Cr)	(Cr)	(Dr)

Sales Ledger: Harrison

Date	Particulars	Folio	Debit £	Credit £	Balance £
Thomson a/c					
1/6	Balance				45 Dr
1/6	Sales & VAT	*S 25	211.50		256.5
11/6	Sales & VAT	S 25	117.50		374
30/6	Bank			300	74
1/7	Balance				74 Dr
Simpson a/c					
1/6	Balance				110 Dr
10/6	Sales & VAT	S 25	235		345
20/6	Sales & VAT	S 25	188		533
30/6	Bank			450	83
1/7	Balance				83 Dr
Jackson a/c					
1/6	Balance				180 Dr
15/6	Sales & VAT	S 25	423		603
30/6	Bank			500	103
1/7	Balance				103 Dr

* Folio cross-reference to the page number of the day book.

Nominal Ledger: Harrison

Date	Particulars	Folio	Debit	Credit	Balance
Sales a/c			£	£	£
1/6	Balance				8,500 Cr
30/6	Debtors	S 25		1,000	9,500
1/7	Balance				9,500 Cr
VAT a/c					
1/6	Balance				350 Cr
30/6	Debtors	S 25		175	525
1/7	Balance				525 Cr
S/L Control a/c *					
1/6	Balance				335 Dr
30/6	Sales	S 25	1,000		
	VAT		175		1,510
30/6	Bank			1,250	260
1/7	Balance				* 260 Dr

NOTE:

- The key figures from the invoice are entered in the day book – invoice number, sales, VAT and total cost.
- Debtors' accounts are debited with their individual totals in the Sales Ledger.
- Total for Sales and VAT accounts are credited in the Nominal Ledger.
- Total debtors in the sales day book will be debited to the S/L Control account. The Control account is a means of cross checking the total individual balances in the Sales Ledger with the total debtors' balance in the Nominal Ledger.

*Sales Ledger Control account: Balance as at 30 June £260 Debit. The control account is also referred to as *debtors' control.*

Schedule of Debtors in Sales Ledger as at 30 June:

Name	£
Thomson	74 Dr
Simpson	83
Jackson	103
	* 260

The analysed sales day book
The sales day book can be adapted to give businesses more information. Extra columns may be added to provide sales data for different types of product. This type of day book is often referred to as 'columnar' because of the extra columns used.

Large wholesalers and retailers need to know-how various categories of goods are moving. It is inadequate for them merely to have a total of all their sales. Stores such as *Comet* and *Curry's* want to know, for example, how their 'white' goods (washing machines, dishwashers, refrigerators) are selling in contrast with their 'brown' goods (televisions, stereos, videos) because, they need to know how much profit each of their major categories is earning.

This type of information helps management in making decisions. It also helps to keep better control of sales, and therefore purchases and stock levels. If some goods are slow moving, these can be more readily identified and action taken to remedy the situation.

Example of an analysed sales day book

Check the figures down and across for accuracy in the sales day book below.
- Sales ledger posting:
  The total debtors column is used to post individual customer's figures to the debit side of their sales ledger account in the normal way.

- Nominal ledger posting:
  The total of each sales category is posted to the credit side of that account (3 sales accounts). VAT is also posted to the credit side of the VAT account in the normal way. The total of debtors (£3,478) is posted to the debit side of the control account.

Sales day book

Date	Customer's a/c	Invoice No.	Golf a/c	Cricket a/c	Tennis a/c	VAT a/c	Total debtors
7/1	Faldo	3364	400		120	91	611
8/1	Boycott	3365	100	180		49	329
9/1	Woosnam	3366	580	60	140	136.5	916.5
10/1	Bates	3367		130	110	42	282
10/1	Gooch	3368	60	440		87.5	587.5
11/1	Castle	3369	100	126	74	52.5	352.5
12/1	Lyle	3370	240		100	59.5	399.5
			1,480	936	544	518	3,478

Nominal ledger

	Debit	Credit	Balance
Golf Sales a/c			
12/1 Debtors		1,480	1,480 Cr
Cricket Sales a/c			
12/1 Debtors		936	936 Cr
Tennis Sales a/c			
12/1 Debtors		544	544 Cr
VAT a/c			
12/1 Debtors		518	518 Cr
S/L Control a/c			
12/1 Sales, VAT	3,478		3,478 Dr

Computerised Accounts

Many accounting software programs are often supplied with Microsoft Windows that has the advantage of using the mouse to click on to the required icon or command. For example, clicking onto the sales ledger and selecting a function like *batch invoices* so that you can enter details of a customer's account from an invoice directly to the sales day book. Postings will then be automatically entered into the appropriate accounts, that is, debiting the customer's account and crediting sales and VAT accounts.

By using the appropriate code numbers for various types of product for sales, purchases, stock, etc. the computer can give an instant analysis of these accounts. A further advantage is that any account or prime record can be printed off with the instant up-date of the last entry intact so that these can be used as and when required. Invoices, credit notes, customer statements and anything else, may be printed on hard copy by merely pressing the right key.

Before any account can be used, it must be set up and recorded. A customer's account record would obviously include details of name, address, telephone number, e-mail address, contact name, amount of credit allowed, etc.

The account would be provided with an account number and this would be used to access that customer. Notice that when these accounts are printed off, there is far more information provided than on a normal manual accounting system including the time the transaction was recorded.

When entering batch invoices in a sales ledger program, you would enter the customer's account number and the customer's name would be confirmed on the screen. The invoice and its details would be entered including the nominal ledger code number. This is used for analysis purposes so that the movement of various types of sales can be recorded (*N161 sports goods*).
For VAT purposes a code number is provided for example like *T1* that is used to record VAT at the standard rate currently at 17.5% on net goods. *T9* is used if VAT is not applicable to the transaction.

Back-up files and security

In business it is essential to have back-up files whenever information is processed to them. If data is lost, there is nothing worse than trying to reprocess them. It could take hours of additional work. Use labels on the disks so that you can readily identify what you have got on them. It may also be necessary to have passwords before you can process anything to prevent anyone unauthorised accessing confidential information. Accounting information can be very confidential and could be invaluable to other organisations that are in competition with your own place of work.

Computerised Accounts: typical printouts of the sales day book and sales ledger accounts
Date: 06/03/20-
Time: 11.43
Customer from: S01
Customer to: S150

SALES DAY BOOK (CUSTOMERS BATCH INVOICES)

Trans	Type	Date	A/C Ref	N/C	Inv ref	Net	VAT	Gross Amount
9	SI	03/03	S08 Johnson	N161	2642	199.15	34.85	234.00
10	SI	03/03	S09 Kings	N162	2643	198.00	34.65	232.65
11	SI	04/03	S10 Lewis	N162	2644	320.00	56.00	376.00
12	SI	04/03	S11 Smith	N164	2645	300.00	52.50	352.50
12	SI	04/03	S11 Smith	N162	2645	92.00	16.10	108.10
13	SI	05/03	S10 Lewis	N161	2646	356.60	62.76	419.36
14	SI	06/03	S21 Wilson	N164	2647	255.32	44.68	300.00
				Totals		**1721.07**	**301.54**	**2022.61**
						Cr	Cr	Dr s/l control

Note:
Trans: number of transaction to date

Type: sales invoice
N/C: nominal ledger code number
        N160   total sales
        N161   sports goods
        N162   leisure goods
        N163   footwear (men's)
        N164   footwear (ladies')
        N165   miscellaneous goods

SALES LEDGER (CUSTOMER ACTIVITIES)

Account		Name		Contact No.	Telephone			
S10		D Lewis		J. Jennings	01202507891			

Trans	Type	Date	N/C	Inv ref	VAT	Code/details	Value	Debit	Credit
03	J	01/03			T9	o/balance		100.00	
11	SI	04/03	N162	2642	T1	0184 leisure	376.00	376.00	
13	SI	05/03	N161	2646	T1	0230 tennis	419.36	419.36	
37	SR	06/03	N120	23356	T9	bank receipt	100.00		100.00
42	CR	12/03	N162	C391	T1	0184 soiled	16.45		16.45
						Totals		**895.36**	**116.45**

	£	**Balance**	778.91 Debit
Amount outstanding:	778.91		
Amount paid:	100.00		
Credit limit:	5000.00		
Turnover to date:	3242.65		

Note:

Type	J	journal
	SI	sales invoice
	SR	sales receipt
	CR	credit return
VAT		
	T0	VAT at zero rate tax
	T1	VAT at standard rate of tax
	T2	VAT exempt rate tax
	T9	VAT not applicable

The need to check customers

When businesses trade with each, it is accepted practice that sales would be on a credit basis giving the customer time to pay the invoice, often 30 days. The invoice is the bill of sale and is used as the contract between the buyer and the seller.

Credit Control

It is important for a business to try to restrict the outstanding debt of any one customer. A system of credit control is needed to ensure that all customers pay their accounts on time. It would be foolhardy to allow any customer to continue to buy goods without first fully checking how reliable they are with payments. If a customer can show that they are reliable payers, then trust can be built up between the buyer and seller.

A *credit rating* is a device that seeks to find out how good or otherwise a customer is regarding the settlement of debt. For example, a customer with a five star rating could mean that there is 100% reliability that payment will be met. On the other hand, a customer with only a one star rating could mean trouble in the future and that customer would need to be monitored carefully with the amount of sales allowed and ensuring payment is made before further sales are sanctioned.

A *credit controller* in a business has the responsibility of ensuring that new customers are vetted for their reliability and that sales and payments received are carefully monitored to ensure that bad debts are strictly limited. Bad debts are expenses to the business and lower profits. Sometimes the failure of receiving payment from customers who owe large sums of money, can trigger off bankruptcy with the sellers.

New customers need to provide references from previous traders or banks and the controller needs to check these carefully and then come to some decision as to whether business is going to be relatively safe with them. Although sales are the most important aspect of business, it is no use selling goods without payment for them.

Aged debtors' schedule: this refers to how old the customers' debts are in terms on months. A computer program for example, can printout precisely the age of debt owed by a customer in terms of when sales were made and the payment made against these. If some debtors are taking too long to pay, reminders must be sent promptly to them usually by standard letter, asking them to settle their accounts as quickly as possible.

Example of Aged Debtors

Debtor	Current £	1 month £	2 months £	3 months £	3 months + £	Total £
R Andrews			155	180		335
D Baker	148	210				358
A Bartlett		160	50	300		510
W Barstow		351	428			779
D Charleston					880	880
J Durham	120	185				305
	268	906	633	480	880	3167

You can see at a glance that D Charleston is worrying because the debt of £880 is over three months old. Also Andrews and Bartlett have outstanding sums of £180 and £300 that are three months old. Reminders of payment need to be sent and if none are made, then perhaps further sales must be stopped. If customers continue not to pay their bills then it may well be that a solicitor's letter demanding payment or court action is the only final remedy.

Non-trade debtors

Not all customers are of a *trade* type. They may not be buying goods from a business. Instead, they may buy services like insurance or advertising or they may rent property from a business. If a business for example, rented properties to various people or organisations, they could be referred to as tenants rather than customers. Monthly rent would be charged to tenants and on top of this, other charges for light, heat, or services could also be charged to them.

A control account could also be used to check and verify the individual balances of tenants in the same way as debtors control account used for normal trade customers.

Example of non-trade debtors:

Sales ledger: properties division

Tenant: G Harrison account - Property No. 016

1/10	Balance b/d	200	5/10	Bank	200
31/10	Rent receivable	240	31/10	Balance c/d	320
	Services	80			
		520			520
1/11	Balance b/d	320			

Nominal ledger
Rental property control account

1/10	Balance b/d	700	5/10	Bank	1800
31/10	Rent receivable	2400	31/10	Balance c/d	2240
	Services	940			
		4040			4040
1/11	Balance b/d	2240 *			

* Schedule of tenant properties as at 31 October:

	£	£
G Harrison	320	
J Peters	400	
D Rogers	525	
J Jordon	595	
K Jacques	400	2240

KEY POINTS OF THE CHAPTER

Day books:	Books of prime entry to record invoices and credit notes to facilitate ledger posting
Sales day book:	Records invoices sent to customers
Invoice:	A bill of sale from supplier to customer
Trade discount:	A deduction to the buyer from the list price usually expressed in percent terms
Cash discount:	A further deduction from the value of goods to encourage prompt payment usually expressed in percent terms
VAT:	Value added tax, standard rate, zero rate and exempt rate, charged on the value of goods or services
S/L control a/c:	Sales ledger control a/c (in the nominal ledger) used as a cross-check with debtors' balances in the sales ledger
Analysed sales day:	The sales day book using extra columns in order to provide sales data
Computerised accounts:	The use of a computer program to input financial data
Credit control:	The need to check customers for their reliability in settling their debts.
Aged debtors:	A list of debtors showing how 'old' their accounts are in months
Non-trade debtors:	Debtors for services rendered such as rental of property.

QUESTIONS

1. a) What is an invoice?
   b) Why do businesses need to prepare more than a single copy?
2. a) Briefly define the difference between trade and cash discounts.
   b) When Vat is charged, is it calculated on the gross or net amount?
3. a) Look at the invoice sent by Harrison to M Jones at the start of this chapter.
      Which figures from the invoice are entered in the sales day book?
   b) Is the invoice arithmetically correct?
   c) After entry in the sales day book, how would the figures be posted to the ledgers?

4. The credit sales of Royston Carlton were listed for the week ending 8 June. You need to calculate the VAT (17.5%) for each of them:

	Customer's account	Invoice No.	No 27 Amount £
4/6	Thomson	1136	180
5/6	Jackson	1137	200
6/6	Brown	1138	380
7/6	Warren	1139	300
7/6	Thomson	1140	420
8/6	Wilson	1141	60
8/6	Jones	1142	150

Required:
a) Prepare the sales day book for the week ending 8 June.
b) What ledger are the individual debtors posted to? On which side of their account?
c) What ledger are the totals of the day book posted to? On which side of the relevant account is each of the totals posted?
d) What purpose has the sales ledger control account?

5. Debtor's balances on 1 June in G. Harrison's sales ledger were:

	£	
Arthur	100	Dr
Brian	120	Dr
Colin	150	Dr

During the month of June, Harrison sold on credit:

		Invoice	£
5/6	Arthur	421	250
8/6	Brian	422	160
15/6	Arthur	423	200
20/6	Colin	424	280

On 28 June, Harrison received cheques from Arthur, Brian and Colin settling their accounts as stated on 1 June.

Required:
a) The sales day book for the month of June.
b) Sales ledger accounts of Arthur, Brian and Colin for June.
c) The sales account as it would appear in the nominal ledger (opening balance £1,240 Cr).

6. The balances on 1 May in the sales ledger of Brian Garraway were:

	£	
Debtors:		
Bremner W	575	Dr
Lorimer P	255	Dr
Jones M	250	Dr
Gray E	100	Dr
Sales ledger control account	1,180	

The sales invoices issued for the month of May were as follows:

	Customer	Invoice Amount No.	VAT 17.5%
1 May	Bremner	2742	200
6 May	Gray	2743	280
14 May	Bremner	2744	450
18 May	Jones	2745	180
21 May	Lorimer	2746	800
22 May	Giles (New account)	2747	100
24 May	Bremner	2748	300
28 May	Jones	2749	150

Required:
a) Prepare the sales day book for the month of May.
b) Prepare the individual debtor's accounts in the sales ledger.
c) Prepare the debtors control account for the month of May.

7. The following represents the sales day book of Graham Whitehall for the month of June:

Customer	Total	Bats	Balls	Pads
	£	£	£	£
Brearley, M		172	12.50	35.00
Botham, I		60	4.25	20.50
Boycott, G		250	43.75	55.80
Bailey, T		78	12.50	70.00
Benaud, R		195	38.75	61.50

Required:
a) Complete the totals for the sales day book for the month of June (no VAT).
b) Enter the opening balances in XYZ's sales ledger for each of the following (1 June):

Brearley	£200.96
Botham	£15.00
Boycott	£66.30
Bailey	£27.88
Benaud	£40.25

c) Post the additional transactions for June to the personal accounts of the above.
d) Make the necessary postings to the general ledger using a *separate* sales account for each of the above items. The debtors control balance 1 June 21 was £350.39 (debit).
e) Check the individual debtors' total with the debtors control as at 30 June.

8. On 1 July, the sales ledger balances of Gill Grant were:

	£
Goldney	220 Dr
Woods	150 Dr
Capel	400 Dr
Carlton	300 Dr

S/L control account 1,070 Dr

Sales invoices sent to customers during July were:

Customer's Accoount	Invoice No.	Value + VAT 17.5%
		£
5/7 Goldney	4005	360
9/7 Capel	4006	160
14/7 Carlton	4007	100
18/7 Capel	4008	180
18/7 Woods	4009	240
25/7 Carlton	4010	200

On 30 July, Goldney, Capel and Carlton all settled their account balances as on 1 July, paid by cheque.

Required:
a) The sales journal for the month of July.
b) The preparation of the sales and nominal ledger accounts including the control account.

9. The following information represents the sales day book of Dawson's Ltd, a seller of furniture in three grades, basic, standard and deluxe models. All sales are charged with the standard rate of VAT at 17.5%.

Customer	Basic Model	Standard model	Deluxe model	Total sales	VAT account	Total debtors
Jackson	200	420	160			
Thompson	125	500	365			
Illingworth	0	0	660			
Rowcastle	280	400	820			
James	320	640	1,040			

Required:
a) Complete the totals of the sales day book for the week ended 7 April (across and down).
b) The following balances are to be entered in the sales ledger on 1 April:

	£
	£
Jackson	740.50 Debit
Thompson	356.76 Debit
Illingworth	125.50 Debit
Rowcastle	1,040.50 Debit
James	1,360.00 Debit

c) Post the transactions from the sales day book for the week ended 7 April to the sales ledger. Cheques received included £1,000 from Jackson and £2,000 from James.
d) Post the sales figures and VAT to the nominal ledger using separate sales accounts for each grade of furniture (assume balances are zero on 1 April).
The S/L control account on 1 April was £3,623.25 Dr. Cross-check the control account with the sales ledger.

10. The accounts in the sales ledger of Jones Enterprises Ltd on 1 January were:

Davies, J   £800.00 Dr
Smith, P   £450.00 Dr
Forbes, B   £100.00 Dr

During January, the following invoices were sent to these customers:

		Invoice number	Amount	Sales code
5/1	Davies	2334	200 + VAT	S161
12/1	Smith	2335	80 + VAT	S162
17/1	Davies	2336	120 + VAT	S162
21/1	Forbes	2337	400 + VAT	S163
28/1	Smith	2338	300 + VAT	S161
30/1	Forbes	2339	160 + VAT	S163
31/1	Davies	2334	340 + VAT	S161

On 31 January, cheques were received from Davies (£1,000), Forbes (£250) and Smith (£544). VAT is charged at a rate of 17.5%.

Required:
a) Prepare the sales day book for January, using separate columns to record each type of sales.
b) Prepare the sales ledger account for each customer.
c) How would the sales and VAT accounts be posted to the general ledger?

Chapter 8

The Purchases Day Book

INTRODUCTION

The purchase day book has an identical role in summarising and listing invoices received from suppliers before posting to the purchase and nominal ledgers. For example, a batch of purchase invoices received from the suppliers of G Harrison in January would be recorded in the purchase day book as follows:

Purchases day book

Date	Supplier's account	Invoice number	Net Purchase account	Vat account	Total creditors
5/1	Metro	7845	200	35	235
7/1	Slazenger	367339	280	49	329
7/1	Auto	1995	400	70	470
8/1	Slazenger	367443	160	28	188
			1,040	182	1,222

Ledger posting

Debit: Purchases and VAT accounts
Credit: Creditor's account

Posting these details to the ledger accounts, each supplier's account would be credited in the purchase ledger with the invoice total, for example, Metro £235 credit. The double entry would be completed with debit entries to the purchases account £1,040 and VAT £182, in the nominal ledger.

Checking documents
The purchasing of stock is of great importance to businesses that need to buy and sell goods. The right amount of stock must be bought at the right price, at the right time.

If a business spent too much of its money on stock, it could find itself short of money to pay for alternative things such as wages and overheads and be short of what is called 'working capital', that is, having enough money to pay for day to day trading.

If too much stock was purchased, there may be problems of storage. If too little stock was acquired the business may run out of certain items and valuable orders could be lost. Businesses therefore, need to pay close attention to the way they record supplies so that they can track stock levels and ensure that what they spend is exactly the amount they want and the invoices for the goods agree with the terms and conditions of the order.

Delivery and goods received notes
When stock is delivered, it must always be thoroughly checked to ensure that the correct items have been received. The driver of the vehicle would have a delivery note to be signed once the goods have been checked in. A copy of the note should be retained by the person that receives and signs for the goods. If there were any discrepancies between the actual goods and the delivery note, the

note should state what the discrepancy is, for example, only three parcels checked in not four. Many businesses prepare a goods received note which records details taken from the delivery note once the goods have been checked. A copy of the goods received note (GRN) would then be sent to the buying office to confirm with the supplier's invoice that the goods charged on invoice had been received in store.

Checking for errors

Only correct invoices are passed through for payment. This is the key concept for the responsible person who is given the task of checking invoices thoroughly against the purchase order with either the goods received note or the delivery note.

If an invoice agrees with the purchase order and the goods received note, then the invoice is passed to the accounts office for recording and can be authorised for payment. Errors that could occur on an invoice could include:

- The invoice itself is arithmetically wrong;
- The invoice fails to agree with the terms of the purchase order, such as incorrect trade discount;
- The goods received note does not comply with the invoice because there is a discrepancy between actual quantities received and quantities charged.

Action must be taken to solve discrepancies that may have been found. It may be the firm's policy to return to the supplier any invoice that is incorrect. Alternatively, the buying office may telephone, fax, or e-mail the supplier explaining the nature of the error and come to some mutual agreement in solving the problem, for example, it may be more convenient for the supplier to send the shortfall of goods later, or alternatively, a credit note.

Calculating VAT on an invoice offering trade and cash discounts

For the purpose of VAT calculation, both trade and cash discounts can be deducted from the gross value of an invoice so that the VAT charge is reduced. For example, an Invoice No. 442 for £800 had a trade discount of 20% and also offered 5% cash discount if the bill was paid within 14 days. Calculate the value of the invoice and show the amount of cash discount offered:

Invoice No. 442
Date: 15 November 20 -

	£	
Gross value of goods	800	
Trade discount 20%	(160)	
Net goods value	640	
+ VAT 17.5%	106.40	(calculated on £640 – 5% = £608 X 17.5%)
Total invoice value:	746.40	

Terms:

If the invoice is paid within 14 days of the invoice date, deduct £32 (5% of £640) from the total. If the date has elapsed, then net payment of £746.40 within 30 days is payable.

NOTE:

Whether or not the customer pays the invoice on time, the VAT of £106.40 does not change.
Check the VAT calculation on the invoice on page 80 to see if you agree.

Procedure for purchases on credit:

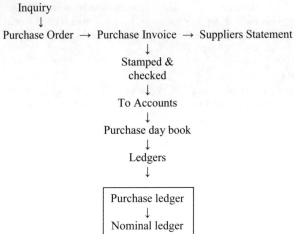

Fig. 8.1 Purchases on credit

The documentation procedure illustrated above could commence with an initial inquiry to a prospective supplier about the terms and conditions of their goods on offer.

A purchase order would follow if the buyer is satisfied with the terms and conditions of sale, for example, prices, discounts, delivery etc.

The invoice, once checked for correctness, will then be the source document for entry in the accounting books, that is, the purchase day book and subsequent posting to the two ledgers.

The buyer of the goods will receive a statement from the supplier, usually monthly, to indicate the transactions which have occurred and the amount of money which is owed.

Procedure for invoice control

The responsibility for checking the correctness of the invoice normally lies with either the buying office or the accounts office. If it is the buying office, it should tie in with the copies of the purchase order raised for the goods in the first place. Copies of the delivery note or GRN can then be sent to the buying office to check the physical goods that came in.

The invoices are stamped with the control grid (see Figure 8.2) to ensure that a full check on each invoice is made. The control grid should have checks for goods received, price terms and calculations. Each check should be initialled by the person who is authorised to do so. Any major errors arising from these checks may require the supplier to be contacted and the discrepancies solved. The invoice is stamped with a control grid such as that shown in Figure 8.3. When a full check is completed and is found to be satisfactory, the invoice can then be passed to the accounts office for entry into the purchases day book and be authorised for payment.

CONTROL GRID	INITIALS
date invoice received	
internal reference number	
order price check	
Extensions check	
goods received check	

Fig 8.2 Invoice control grid

An example of the grid can be seen on the invoice from ROCCO Sports in Figure 8.3 below:

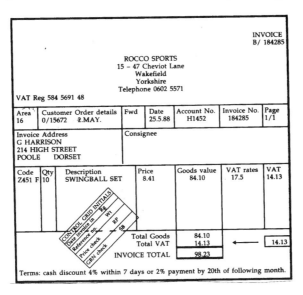

Fig 8.3   Invoice: *ROCCO Sport*s

Example 1:   A simplified purchases day book (without VAT)

Date	Supplier's Account	Invoice No.	Amount £
4 May	R Bates	415	155 Cr
12 May	J Snow	0276	276 Cr
15 May	R Bates	627	359 Cr
20 May	J Sorrell	A253	180 Cr
28 May	J Sorrell	A322	190 Cr
		Purchases Dr Supplier's Cr.	1,160

Ledger posting

Date	Particulars	Debit	Credit	Balance
R Bates account				
4 May	Purchases		155	155Cr
15 May	Purchases		359	514
J Snow account				
12 May	Purchases		276	276Cr
J Sorrell account				
20 May	Purchases		180	180Cr
28 May	Purchases		190	370
Purchases account				
31 May	Creditors	1,160		1,160Dr

Example 2: *Using VAT and the purchase ledger control account*
The following information relates to the accounts of G Harrison on 1 June:

Balances on 1 June:

			£
Nominal Ledger:	Purchases account	(debit)	3,576.50
	VAT account	(credit)	421.25
	Purchase Ledger control account	(credit)	5,646.50
Purchase Ledger:	Decca	(credit)	3,465.00
	EMI	(credit)	1,572.50
	Jacksons	(credit)	609.00

G Harrison's purchases day book   Page 42

Date	Supplier	Invoice no.	Purchases £	VAT £	Total Creditors £
June 4	Decca	4,242	450	78.75	528.75 Cr
8	Decca	5,789	200	35.00	235.00 Cr
15	EMI	687	360	63.00	423.00 Cr
22	Jacksons	1,425	120	21.00	141.00 Cr
			1,130.00	197.75	1,327.75
			Dr	Dr	Cr P/L control

Required:

a) Enter the above balances on 1 June in the ledger of G Harrison.

b) Post the month's details from the day book to the appropriate ledger accounts. The purchase ledger control account [P/L control] is also referred to as the creditors' control account.

c) Enter the payment details: all cheques paid on 30 June.
   £1,500 to Decca on account
   £1,000 to EMI on account
   £200 to Jackson's on account.

Solution:

Nominal ledger

Date	Particulars	Folio	Debit £	Credit £	Balance £
Purchases account					
June 1	Balance				3,567.50 Dr
30	Creditors	P 42	1,130.00		4,697.50
VAT account					
June 1	Balance				421.25 Cr
30	Creditors	P 42	197.75		223.50
P/L Control account					
June 1	Balance				5,646.50 Cr
30	Purchases	P 42		1,130.00	
	VAT			197.75	6,974.25
	Bank		2,700.00		4,274.25

Purchase ledger

Date	Particulars	Folio	Debit £	Credit £	Balance £
Decca records account					
June 1	Balance				3,465.00 Cr
4	Purchase &VAT	P 42		528.75	3,993.75
8	Purchase& VAT	P 42		235.00	4,228.75
30	Bank		1,500		2,728.75
EMI Records account					
June 1	Balance				1,572.50 Cr
15	Purchases	P 42		423.00	1,995.50
30	Bank		1,000		995.50
Jackson account					
June 1	Balance				609 Cr
22	Purchase& VAT	P 42		141.00	750.00
30	Bank		200		550.00

Check the purchase ledger control account with the suppliers in the Purchase Ledger:

June 30   P/L Control account   £4,274.25 Credit

    30   Purchase Ledger schedule: £
           Decca   2,728.75
           EMI   995.50
           Jackson   550.00
                                 £4,274.25 Credit

If the balances failed to agree, then there maybe an error or errors to check both in the purchase ledger and the purchase ledger control account. The control account is also referred to as *creditors control.*

When preparing the trial balance, the control accounts represent the totals of both debtors and creditors. They are useful because if control accounts cross check with personal ledgers it is assumed that double-entry recording is correct. In the event that the trial balance failed to balance, personal accounts need not be checked to locate the error(s) if they already agree with the control accounts.

NOTE:
- The purchase ledger: each creditor account is credited with the purchase + VAT, for example, Decca £528.75
- The nominal ledger: totals for both purchases account and VAT account are debited, £1130 and £197.75
- The total of the purchase day book is credited to the purchase ledger control account, £1327.75
- The purchase ledger is commonly referred to as the *bought ledger* or *creditors' ledger.*

:

Example 3: The analysed purchases day book

The following information relates to the purchases of ABC Shoes Ltd. The day book is in columnar format using separate columns for men's, women's and children's shoes. This will help management analyse how different lines of goods are selling and comparisons can then be made with previous selling periods. Vat is at 17.5%.

Purchase Day Book: ABC Company Shoes Ltd

Date	Supplier	Invoice no.	Men's Shoes £	Women's shoes £	Children's shoes £	VAT £	Total Creditor £
3/2	Footwear Ltd	F2236	120			21.00	141.00
6/2	F H & W	08476			95	16.62	111.62
7/2	Country Casual	04279		75		13.12	88.12
14/2	Footwear Ltd	F2239	210			36.75	246.75
16/2	F H & W	08979			190	33.25	223.25
21/2	Footwear Ltd	F2240	525			91.88	616.88
28/2	Jones Leather	26011		270		47.25	317.25
			855	345	285	259.87	1,744.87

Ledger posting

When posting from the analysed purchase day book, the double entry in the nominal ledger is:

Debit:	Purchase account (men's)	£855
	Purchase account (women's)	£345
	Purchase account (children's)	£285
	VAT account	£259.87
Credit:	Purchase ledger control account	£1,744.87

In the purchase ledger, each supplier's account would be credited as normal, with the total amount due on each invoice, for example, the first entry, Footwear Ltd £141 credit.

The remittance advice

When a payment is made to a supplier, a cheque is prepared or payment could be made directly through the bank by giro credit or there could be an arrangement to pay by direct debit. A remittance advice simply identifies the sender of the payment:

Remittance Advice   No.28

Cheque No.	4456782
Amount:	£480.00
Discount	£20
Invoice No.	4842
Account payee	Metro Sports Ltd.

Computerised accounts

A computerised section was included in Chapter 7 for customers and this basically follows the same principles applying to suppliers. From the main suppliers menu you would click onto *batch invoices* and the invoices received from suppliers would be entered in the purchase ledger program. The supplier's number would be entered and again this would be confirmed by the name coming onto the screen.

The invoice and its details would be entered including the nominal ledger code number used for analysis purposes *(N261 purchase of sports goods)*. The VAT code would also be used. Remember that we used *T1* if goods were charged at the standard rate of tax. Note that greater detail is shown in the supplier's account than that in the manual accounting system.

Computerised Accounts: typical printouts of the purchases day book and purchase ledger accounts

Date: 06/03/20-
Time: 14.32

Supplier from: P01
Supplier to: P150

PURCHASES DAY BOOK (SUPPLIER BATCH INVOICES)

Trans	Type	Date	A/C Ref	N/C	Inv ref	Net	VAT	Gross Amount
22	PI	04/03	P04 Dunlop	N261	12263	120.00	21.00	141.00
23	PI	04/03	P11 Metre	N262	4387	220.00	38.50	258.50
24	PI	04/03	P24 S Gas	N265	209/65	108.00	18.90	126.90
25	PI	05/03	P18 Longs	N265	423	80.00	14.00	94.00
26	PI	05/03	P02 Auto	N263	3353	288.00	50.40	338.40
27	PI	06/03	P04 Dunlop	N261	12298	160.00	28.00	188.00
				Totals		**976.00**	**170.80**	**1146.80**

Note:
Trans: number of transaction to date
Type: purchase invoice
N/C: nominal ledger code number
         N260   total purchases
         N261   purchases sports goods
         N262   purchases leisure goods
         N263   purchases footwear (men's)
         N264   purchases footwear (ladies)
         N265   purchases miscellaneous goods

PURCHASE LEDGER (SUPPLIER ACTIVITIES)

Account		Name		Contact No.	Telephone			
P04		Dunlop Sports		A Sole	0567334582			

Trans	Type	Date	N/C	Inv ref	VAT	Code/details	Value	Debit	Credit
04	J	01/03			T9	o/balance			120.00
22	PI	04/03	N262	12263	T1	0212 sports	141.00		141.00
27	PI	06/03	N261	12298	T1	0230 tennis	188.00	188.00	
45	PP	06/03	N120	23356	T9	bank payment	120.00	120.00	
						Totals		**120.00**	**449.00**
						Balance	329 Credit		

	£
Amount outstanding:	329.00
Amount paid:	120.00
Credit limit:	4000.00
Turnover to date:	1815.70

Confidentiality

Any employee in business must process documents with confidentiality. A fair amount of financial information is of a sensitive or confidential nature and should not be openly discussed with any person who does not need to know the contents either with other internal staff and certainly not with persons outside the business.

This aspect of confidentiality should ensure that the business's records concerning customers, suppliers, employees of the business, financial records should be treated strictly as private. Invoices and statements could be sensitive records and a competitor of the business may find that information in these documents could be very useful to them in terms of prices and conditions of payment.

Any business should always be able to trust its staff with any matter of confidentiality and staff need to be loyal and discreet when handling the business's documents.

KEY POINTS OF THE CHAPTER

Purchase day book:	A book or control sheet listing suppliers' invoices with the key figures
Working capital:	Having sufficient finance to meet day to day costs
Purchase order:	A buyer's request for goods from a supplier
Delivery note:	The driver's record of goods delivered
GRN:	Goods received note records the goods delivered
Statement:	A monthly reminder to the customer showing how much is owed
Control grid:	A stamp on invoices in order to monitor control
Purchase ledger control:	An account to cross check the accuracy of the purchase ledger
Analysed day book:	Columns used to break down different types of purchases and expenses
Computerised accounts:	Using an accounting program to input financial data.

QUESTIONS

1. The following refers to details of invoices received from suppliers. You are to check the value of the VAT at 17.5% and then add up the totals across and down. The carriage is to be paid by the buyer where stated.

Date	Supplier	Invoice	Value	Carriage	VAT	Total
5	Metro	2483	180	10	33.25	
11	Auto	4933	60		10.50	
15	Slazenger	248375	244		42.70	
22	Metro	2978	125	10	23.62	
25	Dunlop	4735	308	15	56.52	

2. Many manufacturers find it essential to complete a goods received note (GRN) from the delivery note. What is a GRN? Explain how it could save the business money.

3. A control grid is stamped on incoming invoices. What is its purpose?

4. The following supplier's invoice No. 2895 is found to be inaccurate when checked. Can you calculate what the real cost should have been? Details are as follows:

INVOICE NO. 2895

Qty	Details	Price/Unit	Gross Purchase	Net Purchase Value
300	Auto Sports kits	4.20	1,260	945.00
			VAT	165.37
				1,110.37

Terms: 25% trade discount.
5% Cash discount is deducted if the account is paid *within* 21 days of the invoice.

5. See Invoice no. 1185 from G Harrison to R Jones. Answer the following questions from the point of view of R Jones receiving the invoice from Harrison.
a) In which book is the invoice entered?
b) Complete the totals across. (Trade discount is 25%.)
c) Calculate the VAT (17.5%). Note 2.5% cash discount is offered.
d) Complete the totals of the invoice at the bottom.
e) How would you complete the postings to the ledgers?

INVOICE 1185

G Harrison
214 The High Street
Poole
Dorset

To: R Jones
14 Ship Road
The Quay
Poole

VAT Reg: 424 28422 56
Invoice No: INV/1185

Date: 10 June   Your Order Ref: 275   Terms: 25% Trade
   Despatch Date: 10 June   Carriage Paid

Code Number	Qty	Description	Unit Price £	Total Price £	Less Trade £	Net £
1042	4	Tennis Rackets (Slazenger) (special edition)	32.00			
1070	10	Squash Rackets (Dunlop)	8.25			

E & OE

TOTAL NET: £
VAT @ 17.5%: £

Delivery Address: as above   TOTAL VALUE: £

Payment within 20 days of invoice date, Cash Discount 2.5%

6. The following represents the transactions of Harry Smith - a retailer - during the month of July:

			Invoice No's
July	1	Bought goods from ABC: 200 units @ £5 units less 25% trade discount	27491
	2	Bought goods from XYZ: 150 units @ £2 units less 20% trade discount	X427
	7	Sold to R Green 100 units @ £7 less 10% trade discount	142
	9	Sold to R Jones 100 units @ £5.50 less 10% trade discount	143
	12	Bought goods from ABC: 500 units @ £4 unit less 25% trade discount	9278
	14	Sold goods to F Smith 100 units @ £3.50 trade discount nil	144
	17	Bought goods from XYZ: 200 units @ £2 unit less 20% trade discount	X588
	21	Sold to R Green 150 units @ £7 less 10% trade discount	145
	26	Bought from ABC: 500 units @ £4.50 less 25% trade discount	10429

Required:
a) Enter the above in Harry Smith's purchases and sales day books (no VAT).
b) Post to the ledgers:
    i) Personal ledgers for individual debtors and creditors
    ii) Nominal ledger for total sales and total purchases.

7. The personal accounts in Harry Smith's ledger on 1 May were as follows:

1 May balances

	£
R Mellows	200 Credit
Paterson Brothers	150 Credit
J Hudson	95 Credit
D Moorcroft	24 Credit

The following invoices were received from the above suppliers during May:

		Invoice No	Net Purchase £	VAT (+17.5%) £
May				
3	Mellows	2784	200.00	
7	Hudson	149	150.00	
10	Paterson Bros.	87632	400.00	
14	Hudson	251	180.00	
20	Mellows	3219	350.00	
21	Hudson	267	225.00	
26	Moorcroft	4929	100.00	

On 30 May Harry Smith **paid off** by cheque, the *opening balances* of each creditor.

Required:
a) The purchases day book for the month of May, you need to calculate the VAT at 17.5% on each purchase.
b) The personal ledger accounts of Smith as they would appear on 31 May.

8. The supplier account balances in the books of R Pearce on 1 September, were:

	£
Metro	800 Credit
Auto	500 Credit
Dunlop	420 Credit
p/l control account	1,720 Credit

During September, Pearce received the following invoices from his suppliers:

Supplier	Invoice No.	Amount + VAT 17.5%
8/9 Metro	2275	1,200
12/9 Auto	4489	680
17/9 Auto	4777	600
23/9 Dunlop	12278	300

On 30 September, Pearce sent cheques to:

	£
Metre	1,000
Auto	1,000
Dunlop	420

Required:
a) The purchase journal for September.
b) The preparation of the purchase and nominal ledgers including the control account. (Purchases and VAT account can commence with a zero balance).

9. The sales and purchase ledger balances of Tom Van Vollenhoven on 1 February were:

£

Sales ledger

Green	420 Debit
Smith	2,155 Debit
Jones	215 Debit
s/l control account	2,790 Debit

Purchase ledger

ABC Co.	475 Credit
Hollins	423 Credit
Jenkins	812 Credit
p/l control account	1,710 Credit

The sales and purchase journal information for 5 February were as follows:

Sales Journal		£
5/2 Green	1271	200 + VAT 17.5%
5/2 Smith	1272	720
5/2 Jones	1273	360
5/2 Green	1274	80

Purchases Journal		
5/2 ABC Co.	14371	1,200 + VAT 17.5%
5/2 Hollins	2269	800
5/2 ABC Co.	14495	480
5/2 Jenkins	7813	200

On 10 February, cheques received from customers:

	£
Green	420
Smith	500
Jones	423

On the same date, cheques were sent to suppliers:

	£
ABC Co.	475
Jenkins	812

Required:
a) Open all personal accounts in the sales and purchase ledgers as on 1 February.
b) Prepare the two journals, including adding VAT.
c)   Post all appropriate figures to the three ledgers, including the control accounts.
     Other accounts in the nominal ledger to commence with zero balances.

10. The following information concerns the analysed purchase day book of Harriet Prince for the first fortnight of January:

Date	Supplier account	Invoice number	Footwear account	Leisure account	Sports account	VAT account	Total account
7/1	Foulkes Ltd	48735	850	70			
8/1	Johnson	564133		350			
9/1	Foulkes Ltd	49822	436	164	80		
10/1	Hardcastle	3388	200		325		
11/1	Johnson	648/33	236	164			
12/1	Douglas Ltd	4422		346			
	Just Sport	1889	140		825		

Required:
a)   Complete the totals across including the calculation of VAT at the 17.5% standard rate.
b)   Total the figures down and cross-check for accuracy.
c)   Explain how the individual accounts are posted.
d)   Post the totals to the nominal ledger.

11. The following suppliers are to be found in the purchase ledger of Eric Lockwood:

	£	
N Fox	315	credit
A Skene	1,040	credit
H Poynton	220	credit
K Holliday	100	credit

Purchase ledger control £1675 credit (Nominal ledger)

During the month of November, the following invoices were received:

		Invoice No.	Amount + VAT 17.5%
			£
4/11	Fox	3345	520.00
10/11	Skene	21219	740.00
12/11	Poynton	98942	180.00
14/11	Holliday	1057	1,240.00

Goods were returned to Neil Fox because of damage valued £40 plus Vat on 18/11 (enter this in the purchase day book as a *negative* entry, deducting from totals). On 28/11 cheques were sent to the following suppliers:

	£
N Fox	315
A Skene	640
K Holliday	100

Required:
a) Prepare the purchase day book for November.
b) Prepare all suppliers' accounts in the purchase ledger.
c) Prepare all appropriate nominal ledger accounts and assume that purchases and VAT accounts have a zero balance on 1 November.

Chapter 9

The Returns Day Books

INTRODUCTION

The two books to record returns are:

- the returns inward day book - to record sales returns from customers (debtors);
- the returns outward day book - to record purchases returns to suppliers (creditors).

Situations arise in business where goods may be returned to the seller for a variety of reasons. They may have been damaged in transit, the wrong type may have been sent, or the buyer may have changed his mind and sent them back. The invoice could have been added incorrectly and over-charged. There may be bottles, crates or barrels involved where a credit is given for their return.

The *credit note* is the documentary evidence for any return or allowance. It signifies that a reduction is to be made from the account where the credit note is sent.

The returns inward day book
The credit notes sent to customers to cover their returns are listed in sequence (numerically) and in date order. Posting to the ledgers will include:

a) the sales ledger. *Credit* the debtor's account with the value of the return + VAT (if charged).
b) the nominal ledger. *Debit* the returns inward account and *debit* the VAT if VAT is charged.

Where a control account is used, *credit* the total value of returns, plus VAT if charged, to the sales ledger control account.

The returns outward day book
Credit notes received from suppliers cover the return of purchases to them. The credit notes are listed in date order. Posting to ledgers will include:

a) the purchase ledger. *Debit* the creditor's account with the value of the return + VAT (if charged).
b) the nominal ledger. *Credit* the returns outward account and *credit* VAT if charged.

Where a control account is used, *debit* the total value of returns + VAT if charged, to the purchase ledger control account.

The credit note is the documentary evidence for returns and allowances. A credit note sent to a customer has the effect of reducing the customer's account. The credit note on the following page will show a credit of £28.20. Mr Smith's account will be credited by £28.20.

On the following page is the example of a credit note sent by George Harrison to one of his customers, Tommy Smith.

Credit Note			
From	G Harrison 214 High Street Poole Dorset		Credit No.: B/ 427
To	T Smith 56-57 Ringwood Road Poole		

Credit in respect of		Date 7 May
☒ Returned Goods ☐ Error		Inv 253
☐ Discount ☐ Over Charge		Order 67231
☐ Shortage ☐		Ref

Date	Details		£	p
June 15	200 Tennis Balls (poor quality)		32	00
Less	25% Trade		8	00
			24	00
Plus	17.5 VAT		4	20
		Total Credit:	£ 28	20

Fig. 9.1 Credit note from G Harrison to a customer

Example 1: The returns inward day book

The debtor's balances in G Harrison's Sales Ledger on 1 June were:

J Jones	£156 Dr
T Smith	£385 Dr
T Dooley	£224 Dr

Returns inward day book (June)

Date	Customer's Account	C/N No.	Returns Inward a/c	VAT a/c	Total debtor's a/c	
			£	£	£	
June 15	T Smith	427	24	4.20	28.20	Cr
23	T Dooley	428	60	10.50	70.50	Cr
30	T Jones	429	10	1.75	11.75	Cr
			94	16.45	110.45	
			(Dr)	(Dr)	(Credit S/L control a/c)	

Example 2: The returns outward day book

The creditor's balances in G Harrison's Purchase Ledger on 1 June were:

Dunlop Sports	£96.21	Credit
Sondico	£124.62	Credit
Arena Sports	£150.00	Credit

Returns outward day book (June)

Date	Supplier's Account	C/N No.	Returns Outward a/c	VAT a/c	Total creditor's a/c
			£	£	£
June 4	Dunlop Sports	142	16.82	2.94	19.76 Dr
18	Sondico	234/C	10.86	1.90	12.76 Dr
26	Arena	67	24.60	4.30	28.90 Dr
			52.28	9.14	61.42
			(Cr)	(Cr)	(Debit P/L control a/c)

The posting from the two returns day books to the sales, purchase and nominal ledgers was as follows:

Sales ledger

Date	Particulars	Folio	Dr	Cr	Balance
J Jones a/c					
June 1	Balance				156.00
30	Returns In	RI 4		11.75	144.25 Dr
T Smith a/c					
June 1	Balance				385.00 Dr
15	Returns In	RI 4		28.20	356.80
T Dooley a/c					
June 1	Balance				224.00 Dr
23	Returns In	RI 4		70.50	153.50

Purchase ledger

Date	Particulars	Folio	Dr	Cr	Balance
Dunlop Sports a/c					
June 1	Balance				96.21 Cr
4	Returns Out	RO 2	19.76		76.45
Sondico a/c					
June 1	Balance				124.62 Cr
18	Returns Out	RO 2	12.76		111.86
Arena a/c					
June 1	Balance				150.00 Cr
26	Returns Out	RO 2	28.90		121.10

Nominal ledger

Date	Particulars	Folio	Dr	Cr	Balance
Returns Inward a/c					
June 1	Balance				
30	Debtors	RI 4	94.00		94.00 Dr
VAT a/c					
June 1	Balance				
30	Debtors	RI 4	16.45		16.45 Dr
30	Creditors	RO 2		9.14	7.31
Sales Ledger Control a/c					
June 1	Balance				765.00 Dr
30	Returns In + VAT	RI 4		110.45	654.55
Returns Outward a/c					
June 1	Balance				
30	Creditors	RO 2		52.28	52.28 Cr
Purchase Ledger Control a/c					
June 1	Balance				942.50 Cr
30	Returns Out + VAT	RO 2	61.42		881.08

Analysed returns

Remember that in many businesses, management would want to know specific details about what they buy and sell. With larger organisations it is essential for them to have access to information which tells them which lines are selling and which are slow movers. The same principle applies to returns. Management would need to know the type of goods returned from customers and also the type of goods returned to suppliers.

Example 3: Analysed returns books

An analysed returns outward day book of a business called ABC Co Ltd is shown below. It buys 3 major products – footwear, leisurewear and sporting items and the figures below indicate the returns made to suppliers during January:

Returns outward day book

Date	Supplier account	Credit Note Number	Footwear Returns	Leisure Returns	Sports Returns	VAT a/c	Total creditor
7/1	James Ltd	C35	50	70		21.00	141.00
8/1	Johnson Ltd	C33			20	3.50	23.50
10/1	Harden Co.	C88	200			35.00	235.00
11/1	Douglas Ltd	C122	130			22.75	152.75
			380	70	20	82.25	552.25

NOTE:

- footwear has most of the returns. These figures are for one week in January. Is it a common pattern that footwear has the most returns or is it just an irregular figure due to the post-Christmas season?
- The double entry:
  Debit each supplier's account; credit each category of goods and VAT account.

Statement to the customer
Statements are normally sent to customers once a month to remind them of their outstanding balances. In Figure 9.2, T Smith owes Harrison £163.80 at the end of June. This balance should cross check with Smith's sales ledger account balance. A debit note was sent on 24 June because Invoice No. 1156 was incorrectly valued by £23, due to the omission of an item.

STATEMENT

G Harrison
214 The High Street
Poole
DORSET

T Smith

Telephone: 674221
VAT Registration No.
42428422

56, 57 Ringwood Road
Poole
DORSET

All accounts are rendered
are due for settlement
within 30 days

Account No. S025

Date	Details	Debit	Credit	Balance
1 June	Balance			385.00
15	C/n 427 Returns		28.20	356.80
21	Invoice 1156 Sales	160.00		
	VAT	24.00		540.80
24	Debit Note	20.00		
	VAT	3.00		563.80
28	Cash – thank you		400.00	163.80
30	Balance now due			163.80

Fig. 9.2 Statement from G Harrison to Tommy Smith

Checking statements with ledger accounts
When statements are received from creditors they are checked with the purchases ledger account to see if balances agree. If they do and all details are correct, the statement is passed on to the Cashier for payment.

If statements do not agree with the ledger accounts, they must be checked and reconciled before they are passed on for payment. For example, G Harrison received a statement from Dunlop Sports Ltd. The balance owing was £3.08. The date of the statement was 16 June.

On checking the ledger account, it was found that the Dunlop balance had been settled.
Dunlop Sports Ltd had not taken cash discount into account, whereas Harrison had deducted 4% for payment within 7 days. If the statement is believed to be in error it must be settled with the supplier in order to solve the problem. Either the discount is valid or it is not. Did Harrison pay on time or was it an error by the accounts section at Dunlop's?

Dunlop confirm by telephone that the discount should have been deducted in Harrison's favour, so the reconciliation of account is shown below:

Balance as per statement:	£3.08
Less cash discount received	£3.08
	———
Balance as per purchases ledger	0

Purchase ledger

Dunlop	Sports Account	Dr	Cr	Balance
June 1	Balance			96.21 Credit
4	Returns out	19.76		76.45
6	Bank	73.37		
	Discount Received	3.08		0

Document check

Purchase order	the buyer issues it to the seller listing what is to be bought in terms of goods or services required
Delivery note	accompanies the delivery of goods to the buyer and signed by the customer as evidence of receiving the order
Goods received note	itemises the goods checked in to store, copy sent to buying office
Invoice	A bill of sale for goods or services sent from the seller to the buyer
Control grid	used to stamp incoming invoices as a way of checking their authenticity and correctness
Pro forma invoice	used for special cases such as cash on delivery where goods must be paid for by the buyer before they are handed over
Credit note	a document sent by the seller to the buyer usually to reduce the amount of an original invoice due to an overcharge or return of goods
Statement	a document sent by the seller to the buyer indicating the amount due to be paid on goods or services rendered over a period of time, usually monthly
Trade discount	given by the seller to the buyer in a trading situation to reduce the list price of goods by a specific percentage, for example, 20% off the gross value.
Bulk discount	the same thing as trade discount but a larger percentage could be offered based on the bulk purchased, the more bought, the larger trade discount offered
Cash discount	settlement discount to encourage the buyer to settle the debt within a shorter period of time
Batch control	a computerised accounting term, *batch data entry,* indicates the entry of the same type of transaction, for example, a batch of purchase invoices to enter.

KEY POINTS OF THE CHAPTER

Credit note:	Documentary evidence of returns/allowances from a supplier to a customer
Debit note:	Sent to a customer when an invoice is undercharged
RIDB:	Returns inward day book used to list credit notes from customers
RODB:	Returns outward day book used to list credit notes from suppliers
Analysed RDB:	Analysed returns day book used in the same way as analysed sales or purchases day books providing further information for management
Customer statement:	A monthly account sent to a customer giving details of transactions for the period and the amount to be paid.

QUESTIONS

1. Debtor's balances on 1 June in the books of G Harrison were:

Sales ledger	£
Arthur	100 Dr
Brian	120 Dr
Colin	150 Dr

Nominal ledger	£
Returns inward a/c	257 Dr
VAT a/c	125 Dr
Sales ledger control a/c	370 Dr

Harrison sent credit notes to customers who had returned goods during June
(VAT at 17.5%).

		£	Credit Note No
12/6	Brian	60 + VAT	261
20/6	Arthur	20 + VAT	262
24/6	Colin	50 + VAT	263

Required:
a)   The returns inward day book for June.
b)   Sales ledger accounts of Arthur, Brian and Colin for June.
c)   Nominal ledger accounts for June.

2. Creditor's balances on 1 June in the books of G. Harrison were:

Bought ledger	£
Dick	280 Cr
Eric	100 Cr
Fred	120 Cr

Nominal ledger	£
Returns outward a/c	352 Cr
VAT a/c	125 Dr
Bought ledger control a/c	500 Cr

Harrison received credit notes from suppliers for returns outward during June
(VAT at 17.5%).

		£	Credit Note No
13/6	Dick	80 + VAT	42
20/6	Eric	48 + VAT	215
26/6	Fred	60 + VAT	88

Required:
a)   The returns outward day book for June.
b)   Bought ledger accounts of Dick, Eric and Fred for June.
c)   Nominal ledger accounts for June.

3. The books of G. Harrison:

Suppliers' Summary of Invoices 31 May

Date	Supplier	Invoice No	Quantity	Unit Price £
May 7	Dunlop Sports	3427	100	5.95
			250	4.50
10	Sondico	84521	500	1.25
			100	3.25
			50	10.65
15	Dunlop Sports	3692	200	4.50
24	Metre Sports	895	100	6.75
			50	8.50
27	Sondico	85971	150	3.25
			50	10.65
31	Metre Sports	1052	125	6.50
			200	8.50
31	Dunlop Sports	4573	100	4.50
			50	6.00

Terms:

Dunlop and Sondico allow Harrison a 10% trade discount.

Metre Sports allow a 20% trade discount. VAT 17.5%.

On 31 May, Harrison returned goods, Dunlop Sports [invoice 3692] 100 units @ £4.50 and Sondico [invoice 85971] 150 units @ £3.25 and received credit notes for them.

Required:
a) The appropriate day books to record the above information.
b) The individual accounts of Dunlop, Metre and Sondico as on 31 May.

4. The balances in the bought ledger of *Freddy Smith* (outfitter) as on 1 June were:

	£	
Trueman, F S	1,090	Cr
Statham, B	250	Cr
Tyson, F	975	Cr
Snow, J	340	Cr
Illingworth, R	420	Cr
P/L Control a/c	3,075	Cr

Invoices were received during June from the following:

	Invoice No	Supplier	Amount	VAT
6/6	27481	Truman, F S	£580	+17.5%
8/6	4278W	Snow, J	520	+17.5%
15/6	992	Illingworth, R	210	+17.5%
22/6	52833	Statham, B	330	zero-rate
25/6	888	Tyson, F	360	+17.5%
30/6	A998	Old, C	580	+17.5%

Credit notes were received from:

Illingworth	No. C447	29/6	£ 6.30 +VAT 17.5%
Tyson	No. 42/82	30/6	£90.00 +VAT 17.5%

Required:
a) The purchases day book of Smith, for the month of June.
b) The individual suppliers' accounts in the bought ledger.
c) A separate returns outward day book.
d) The purchase ledger control account for the month of June.

5. M Crooks has the following accounts in his ledgers on 1 May [VAT at 15% in this question]:

Sales ledger:
J Hunt	£600	Dr
R Speedie	£240	Dr
J Milton	£400	Dr

Purchase ledger:
R Ball	£500	Credit
J Carlson	£400	Credit
D Smith	£150	Credit

Invoices issued during May:

	£	
Hunt	130	+ VAT
Milton	200	+ VAT
Speedie	180	+ VAT

Invoices received during May:

	£	
Ball	250	+ VAT
Smith	120	+ VAT
Carlson	360	+ VAT

Credit note received during May:
Carlson	£200	+ VAT

Cheques received during May:
Hunt	£580	in settlement of account of 1 May
Milton	£390	in settlement of account of 1 May
Speedie	£200	on account

Cheques paid during May: Settled all creditors accounts due 1 May less 2.5% cash discount.

Required:
a) Enter the opening personal accounts in the ledgers of M Crooks.
b) Post all the above transactions to these ledger accounts and balance off at the end of the month.

6. On 1 June personal accounts in J Smith's ledger had the following balances:

	£	
R Morton	175	Credit
W Pierce	184	Credit
L Appleby	150	Dr
T Shuttleworth	210	Dr
M Vincent	145	Dr

The following transactions took place during the month of June:

			£
June	3	Sold goods on credit to T Shuttleworth	150
	4	Sold goods on credit to M Vincent	210
	8	Bought goods on credit from R Morton	470
		Paid R Morton by cheque	175
	9	T Shuttleworth settled his account to date by cheque	
	11	Bought goods on credit from W Pierce	197
	12	Returned goods to R Morton	10
		Sold goods on credit to L Appleby	240
	15	Sold goods on credit to T Shuttleworth	160
		L Appleby returned goods	10
	19	Returned goods to W Pierce	15
	25	Paid W Pierce by cheque	184
	26	L Appleby paid by cheque	150
		Sold goods on credit to M Vincent	310
	29	Bought goods on credit from W Pierce	180
	30	Sold goods on credit to T Shuttleworth	160
		M Vincent returned goods	14
		Paid W Pierce by cheque	182

Required:

From the information given above write up the *personal accounts* in J Smith's ledger. To obtain full marks the accounts should be of the three-column type, with columns headed debit, credit and balance.

As an alternative to this question, all sales and purchases could be subject to VAT at 17.5%. Why not redo the question again, adding VAT as suggested?

[Royal Society of Arts)

Chapter 10

VAT and VAT Returns

INTRODUCTION

VAT is a charge on most of our goods and services in the United Kingdom and represents an indirect source of tax for the Government. The collection of this tax which is charged between traders, eventually falls to us, the consumers, who purchase the product. Businesses, therefore, are the collectors of tax whilst we, the consumers, pay for it.

Basically, a business which charges VAT on sales (output tax), deducts what it pays on purchases and other expenses (input tax) and the balance between these two figures is paid quarterly to HMRC (Her Majesty's Revenue & Customs).

Registration for VAT is compulsory if taxable sales exceed a certain annual limit that the *Chancellor of the Exchequer* sets each budget year. For example, if the sales (or turnover) of taxable goods and services exceeds say £60,000, then a business must register with the local VAT Office.
If a taxable business has registered and sales are expected to fall below the prescribed limits, then it can de -register and opt out of charging VAT or claiming VAT on inputs.

Those businesses who are VAT registered, that is, they have received the Certificate of Registration from HMRC (from the department responsible for the collection of VAT), are given a VAT registration number and the date of their tax period which in most cases, is a quarterly return. The VAT account is therefore normally settled on a three-month basis although other arrangements can be made with the VAT Office.

Supplies of goods and services may be at the standard rate, zero rate or exempt. The current standard rate of VAT charged is 17.5% on most of our goods and services. The Chancellor of the Exchequer, responsible to the Government for deciding taxation rates, has over recent years, imposed the standard rate on a wider area of products.

VAT calculations
When we purchase goods or services, we do not pay a separate sum for VAT, it is part of the price paid. Businesses charge VAT on goods sold (these are VAT outputs) and are themselves charged on goods purchased (VAT inputs). The total VAT received in a tax period less the total VAT paid, is completed on the traders form VAT 100, the difference between the two being the balance due to the VAT Office.

Example:
Sales in the quarter £4,230 (inclusive of VAT). Purchases in the quarter £3,290 (inclusive of VAT). How much VAT is due to the VAT Office?

$$\text{VAT Outputs (on sales)} = \frac{4,230 \times 7}{47} = £630$$

$$\text{VAT Inputs (on purchases)} = \frac{3,290 \times 7}{47} = £490$$

The difference between VAT outputs and inputs (630-490) = the tax due £140 payable to the VAT office. This would be payable to the VAT Office along with the tax return for VAT 100. If the inputs of VAT had been £630 and the outputs of VAT £490 because more goods had been purchased in a tax period than sold, then the VAT office would owe the business £140 for that period. Most tax periods are payable quarterly although some traders prefer to have monthly tax periods, particularly if they are likely to get refunds because they deal with zero rated supplies.
The trader must make the return within one month of the end of the tax period. Other traders can have annual tax periods.

The cash accounting scheme
The cash accounting scheme allows traders the advantage of accounting for their VAT on the basis of receiving and paying cash, rather than on the normal invoice dates which are taken as the date of the tax point. In other words, the VAT return is prepared from the cash receipts (VAT outputs) less the cash payments (VAT inputs) in the given tax period.

The turnover threshold of this scheme is currently for those traders whose taxable turnover, not including VAT, is less than £1,350,000 per annum. A businessman who uses this scheme would use his record of cash receipts and payments in his cash book to prepare returns.

The annual accounting scheme
The annual accounting scheme allows businesses to make a VAT return just once per year, coupled with an agreed monthly direct debit payments to HMRC. Again, there is a turnover threshold and is intended for those traders having a turnover (excluding VAT) of less than £1,350,000 per annum.

Traders must pay at regular monthly intervals and are directed to make 9 monthly direct debit payments on account to the VAT office throughout the year and a final 10th payment with the annual return on the amount due.

Businesses exempt
These are businesses that are NOT registered for VAT because they sell exempt supplies or are under the turnover threshold because they are a small business. At the time of writing, the turnover threshold was £67,000 per annum so that a business with a turnover that is less than this figure does not need to account for VAT or keep records for VAT purposes. Taxable supplies may either be at the standard rate subject to 17.5% tax or at the zero rate (most foods) are subject to a 0% rate of tax. Zero rated and exempt supplies are listed later in this chapter. SSAP 5 (Accounting for VAT), is the standard dealing with this topic. For further details read Chapter 32, Accounting Standards.

Foreign trade
Goods and services imported to the UK are subject to the same rules and regulations when these same goods are available here at home. Since the Single European Market came into force on 1 January 1993, the idea of imports and exports between the member states of the European Union has been disbanded. Instead of 'imports' the term is 'acquisition'. When a buyer from the UK acquires goods or services from a member state, he will account for VAT on the form VAT 100 in the normal way under VAT inputs.

If goods are imported from a non-EU country, the importer will have to account for them with HMRC at the port of entry. Customs will provide a certificate as evidence that goods were imported and this can then be treated as a taxable input on the importer's next return on form VAT 100. The export of goods from the UK is at the zero rate of tax. The exporter must retain evidence of exports such as shipping or airport documentation.

Input tax

For registered traders, input tax offsets the amount deductible to the VAT office. Most of the business's capital and revenue expenditure is allowable for VAT inputs if they are wholly for business purposes. Not all expenditure items are allowable however and a business cannot reclaim all of its input tax. These concern the following:

- motor cars (unless it is for stock resale by a business buying and selling vehicles, or for taxi, car hire, driving school, or other purposes where the vehicle generates income);
- non business expenses incurred by the organisation on items such as entertainment, meals, private use of facilities, etc. where the Vat office does not see these as business-related.
- the purchase of what may be seen as luxury items used for business promotions, for example, racehorses, power boats, etc.

In such cases as these, the full charge for the expense (including VAT) can be made in the annual profit and loss account. If there is any doubt as to what can be claimed as an input, traders must contact their local VAT Office.

Output tax

Output tax is collected on sales or any other form of taxable supplies. Zero rated and exempt items are excluded. However, other sales may also include:

- goods that are taken for the proprietor's own use (VAT calculation at the cost price).
- any sales to staff.
- sales of any business assets where VAT is charged.

Bad debts

If bad debts occur when a trader is registered for VAT, bad debt relief may be claimed as a VAT input in the case where a customer's debt has been owing for a minimum period of 6 months and the debt written off as bad in the accounting books. If at a later point, the customer repays the debt (bad debts recovered), the VAT Office must b repaid with the input tax. For example, to claim VAT relief on a customer who's outstanding debt was £235 (Vat inclusive) on 30 June, the earliest claim for the £35 relief would be after 31 December of that year.

Example 1

Assume that a business is registered with Customs & Excise. The end of the VAT quarter is 28 February and it will need to complete the VAT Form 100 and send it off with the sum payable (if any), not usually later than the 20th day of the following month.

In February, the quarter totals of sales and purchases figures were:

net sales (less returns in)	£60,000 (excluding VAT)
net purchases (less returns out)	£40,000 (excluding VAT)
sales (output tax)	£60,000 x 17.5% = £10,500
purchases (input tax)	£40.000 x 17.5% = £7,000

In addition to these figures, we have £800 of allowable expenses on which VAT of £140 was charged. This is an input tax in the same way as purchases.

On 28 February, the VAT account shows a credit balance of £3,360, indicating that this sum is payable to the IIMRC, VAT Central Unit not later than 20 March.

Solution:

Nominal ledger

	Debit £	Credit £	Balance £
Sales account			
28/2 Balance			60,000 Cr
Purchases account			
28/2 Balance			40,000 Dr
Vat account			
28/2 Debtors		10,500	10,500 Cr
28/2 Creditors	7,000		3,500
28/2 Expenses	140		3,360

VAT at standard, zero rate and exempt
Remember that VAT is paid on most of our goods and services and is a charge on consumer expenditure. It is also collected on imports as well as domestic business transactions and is an indirect source of tax, payable to HMRC.

A taxable element is an individual, firm or company that is, or is required to be, registered for VAT. If traders are registered with HMRC and buy and sell taxable supplies of goods or services, it means that they must account for VAT. When sales are made, VAT is charged at the standard rate and is the output tax. On purchases of goods or services supplied to the trader, the VAT is the input tax.

The VAT account records these outputs (sales) as credit entries, and inputs (purchases) as debit entries. If outputs in a given tax period are greater than inputs, then the difference in VAT is owed to the VAT office. Conversely, if inputs are greater than outputs, the VAT office will need to pay the trader the difference.

Zero-rated supplies
Most business transactions are at the *standard rate,* currently 17.5%, or the *zero rate,* which is nil. Zero-rated supplies include:

- most food items (but not catering which includes meals in restaurants, cafes, etc.);
- books and newspapers;
- young children's clothing and footwear;
- the export of goods;
- prescription charges;
- the construction (or long leasing) of new houses and some other buildings but not existing buildings;

Zero-rated supplies of goods or services cannot charge VAT on sales but a firm can recover its VAT charges on purchases or any other business expenses. From the date on which a trader is first required to be registered, all taxable supplies, either at the standard or zero rate, are liable for VAT.

The Chancellor of the Exchequer is often forced to consider charging the standard rate on food and children's items as a way of raising more taxes particularly if the budget looks to be heavily in deficit.

Exempt supplies
Exempt supplies are transactions on which VAT is not charged. If a trader is exempt from VAT, he must not charge VAT on the supplies of goods or services to customers. At the same time, the trader is not allowed to reclaim any VAT he may have paid on purchases or other business expenses.

Those traders with a small turnover (below that set by the Chancellor's threshold), are exempt and need not keep VAT records. The taxable turnover is the value of all taxable supplies which are either at the standard rate or zero-rated, made in the UK. Note that the turnover does not include any supplies that are exempt. Exempt supplies also include:

- insurance;
- betting, gaming and lotteries (but not gaming machines, club subscriptions and admission to premises);
- certain education and training;
- the services of doctors, dentists, opticians;
- membership benefits provided by trade unions and professional bodies;
- entries to certain sports competitions;
- the letting, leasing and sales of most land and buildings (but not hotel and holiday accommodation or garages and parking spaces);
- the provision of credit services including the operation of bank accounts.

If a trader supplies mostly zero-rated goods, he or she may be exempt from VAT registration, particularly if the input tax would normally exceed the output tax. However, once exempted, the trader cannot recover VAT paid on purchases of goods or services.

On the other hand, a trader could still register for VAT even though his or her turnover may be under the required threshold. Before applying, however, a trader needs to think carefully whether registration would gain benefit, because once registered all outputs and inputs of VAT must be accurately accounted for, including the formality of sending VAT returns regularly to the VAT offices.

The return is normally on a quarterly basis (on Form VAT 100). The period covered by the return is called the tax period and details of supplies made and received in that period will need to be entered on the form.

Tax invoices
All documents relating to VAT, including credit and debit notes, must be filed and retained in order to reclaim input tax. The invoice date is usually taken as the tax point when the supply is made. A business must comply strictly with the requirements as outlined by HMRC as to the preparation of invoices, including:

- the business's name, address and VAT registration number;
- date of supply;
- customer's name and address;
- the description of the goods or services supplied;
- the total cost of the goods or services (excluding VAT charged);
- the rate of any trade or cash discounts offered;
- the total VAT payable;
- the total amount of the invoice.

A business's VAT details

To provide you with an example of inputs and outputs of VAT, the information relates to a business's activity for the quarter from January to March inclusive. Assume that on 1 January the VAT account had a balance of £1,480 credit and this had been settled with the VAT office on 14 January.

Business activity January-March

	£ (inc. VAT)	£ VAT
Sales (outputs)	61,428.0	9,148.85
Purchases (inputs)	47,700.0	7,104.26
Motor expenses	1,245.0	185.43
Telephone	380.0	56.60
Advertising	587.5	87.50
Accounts fees	493.5	73.50
General expenses	263.2	39.20
Total inputs	50,669.2	7,546.49
	Outputs	9,148.45
	Inputs	7,546.49
Total VAT payable:		1,601.96

Note: To calculate the VAT at 17.5% when it is *inclusive,* multiply by 7 and divide by 47.

VAT account 31 March

VAT account	Debit £	Credit £	Balance £
1/1 Balance			1,480.00 Cr
14/1 Bank	1,480.00		
31/3 Outputs		9,148.45	9,148.45 Cr
31/3 Inputs	7,546.49		1,601.96 Cr

KEY POINTS OF THE CHAPTER

VAT:	Value added tax, paid by consumers, collected by traders as a form of indirect tax
Output tax:	Tax collected on sales
Input tax:	Tax paid to suppliers on purchases and other expenses
VAT account:	A record of VAT outputs and inputs, the balance paid to the VAT Office (if credit) or due from VAT Office (if debit)
Zero-rated tax:	On items listed where VAT is not charged, eg. books and newspapers
Exempt supplies:	On items listed where VAT is not charged. If a trader only had exempt supplies, he cannot register for VAT
VAT imports:	Subject to the same VAT regulations as in UK
VAT exports:	Exports from the UK are classed as zero rated
Bad debts:	VAT charged can be reclaimed where 6 months have elapsed since the date of sale
Tax point:	The date when liability for output tax arises. Usually the date of the invoice or when goods have been delivered
HMRC	Her Majesty's Revenue & Customs.

QUESTIONS

1. Answer the following questions in brief:
   a) Although VAT is normally collected on a quarterly basis, what are some of the other methods allowed by the VAT office?
   b) At what date is the tax point normally identified?
   c) How would EC imports normally be dealt with if they were taxable items?
   d) When can bad debts relief be taken as a taxable input?
   e) Are all expenses by a business allowable for taxable input?
   f) How does a business, which is exempt from VAT, record VAT when it is charged against them?
   g) How does a business that is zero rated deal with VAT in its accounts?

2. Assume you have a business registered with the VAT office. The end of the first quarter is on 31 March and the trade details are as follows:

Sales (outputs)	£70,500	(VAT inclusive)
Purchases (inputs)	£47,000	(VAT inclusive)
Allowable general expenses	£940	(VAT inclusive)

   Required:
   Prepare the sales, purchases, general expenses and VAT account for the quarter ending 31 March.

3. Janet Jones provides you with the following information for her last quarter for VAT purposes:

   Sales (taxable outputs) £393,390 (inclusive of VAT at standard rate);
   Purchases (taxable inputs) £281,060 (inclusive of VAT at standard rate).

   During this period, Janet paid £9,875 in settlement of the previous quarter's return. (Open the VAT account with this as a credit.) Draft the VAT account to record these entries for the quarter.

4. The following data refers to the accounts of Susan Brambles Ltd for the VAT tax period April-June. Note that all the figures are *inclusive* of VAT.

	£
Sales	14,570
Purchases	11,327
Credits allowed to customers	940
Credits received from suppliers	799
Equipment purchases	987
New motor car for finance chief	8,850
Operating expenses allowable by VAT office	846

   There was also an over-payment made to the VAT office of £62 in the previous period. Note that credits refer to returns inward and outward.

   Required:
   a) Produce the VAT account for the period to 30 June.
   b) The-sales and purchase figures to June (returns inclusive in these).
   c) The amounts that will be posted to equipment, vehicles and operating expenses accounts.

5. The following transactions have been recorded in the company's books during one week's trading:

	£
Trade purchases (list price)	4,500
Credit sales (list price)	6,000
Purchase of a van	10,460
Entertaining expenses	360
Purchase of sales representative car	8,600

On the sales, a settlement discount of £300 is available and all figures exclude VAT at 17.5%.

Required:
If the balance on the VAT account was £2,165 credit at the beginning of the week, what is the balance at the end, after the above transactions took place?

6. A business registered for VAT incurred the following transactions during the year 31 March:

taxable sales at standard rate	£500,000
taxable sales at zero rate	£25,000
sales exempt tax	£75,000
expenses subject to input tax	£300,000*

*There were also purchases of a motor vehicle for £8,000 and a deliver van for £10,000. All figures given are excluding VAT. VAT cannot be reclaimed on the motor vehicle but can on the delivery van.
Where standard, zero-rated and exempt goods are sold, input tax in some schemes may only be claimed on proportionate basis, for example standard goods to total goods sold. In this question it would be 5/6.

Required:
a) How much input tax can be reclaimed by the business?
   (Note that the input tax reclaimed will be the proportion of standard sales/total sales).
b) Calculate what the balance on the VAT account should be.

Chapter 11

Banking Services

INTRODUCTION

The major clearing banks in England and Wales are: Barclays, Lloyds TSB, National Westminster and HSBC. In Scotland, the Bank of Scotland, the Royal Bank of Scotland and the Clydesdale Bank are the main banks.

The banks deal mainly with receiving deposits of money on one hand and providing overdrafts and loans, on the other. The clearing banks also provide a numerous list of services for their customers which includes: providing home mortgages, foreign currency, night safe deposit, insurance schemes, pension plans, act as trustees, investment brokers, financial consultants and a wide range of other services.

Increasingly, they have taken interest in providing loans for housing and are in direct competition with building societies. The societies too, have been able to provide more intense competition against the banks because of the Financial Services Act (1986), giving them greater scope to provide many banking services to their customers such as the use of cheques and various payment facilities through the society. The clearing banks provide TWO major types of accounts: the deposit account and the current account.

Deposit accounts
The deposit account (or investment account) money can safely be invested earning interest at various rates depending on how much is deposited and how much notice is given to the bank on withdrawals of cash.

Current accounts
Current accounts are used in operating cheques and making payments through the bank. By having a cheque account, you can arrange to have your bills paid through the bank. The bank can arrange payments by direct debit or standing order to pay for regular expenses such as insurance premiums, rates, gas and electricity and so forth. Increasingly, the banks are providing current accounts which pay interest on balances that are in credit, making them more attractive to customers.

It is essential for all businesses to have a business current account particularly for the payment of bills by cheque assists the business in organising its finances more professionally and with greater security.

The banks also act as important business advisors and are the first stopping place for overdrafts and loan facilities when money is needed to keep the business afloat or to give it adequate liquidity (money it can use to keep on trading). It is inconceivable to imagine any business conducting its affairs without having a bank account of any kind.

Bank services

The clearing banks offer a wide range of facilities for its customers, some have been already mentioned. A more comprehensive list is as follows:

- The banks provide a safe place for the deposit of money, encouraging savings and paying interest on deposit, investment and even current accounts.
- It provides the current account that operates the cheque system. An essential account for all businesses.
- Night safe deposits allow customers to bank out of business hours enabling them to deposit money for safe keeping.
- Cash dispensers placed just outside the bank, allows customers with cash facilities, day or night.
- The bank will arrange payments on your behalf through the bank, such as standing orders, direct debits and bank giro.
- The bank provides overdraft and loan facilities.
- A bank can arrange for its customers to buy or sell stocks and shares from the Stock Market.
- The bank can offer financial advice both to the individual and to businesses.
- The bank can arrange for foreign currency and travellers cheques for customers going abroad.
- It can arrange insurance schemes and pension plans.
- The bank provides mortgages for homes and businesses.
- It will act as executor, trustee and tax advisor, making financial decisions on the deceased estate.
- It will assist businesses on foreign exchange transactions including arranging and receiving payment for the export and import of goods.
- Credit and debit cards are provided by banks, for example, Barclays Visa and Connect cards or Halifax's Classic Visa and debit cards.

The banks have increasingly been involved in international banking and have considerably widened their service activities, particularly in lending more money for house purchase. The Financial Services Act, 1986, has made competition between banks and building societies more intense, each trying to offer their customers the greatest benefit for depositing and borrowing money and for providing the best all-round banking services.

Going to the bank

In many businesses, particularly shops, it is important not to hold too much cash on the premises. This can only invite possible theft or burglary. It is not surprising therefore, to find a large number of traders visiting their banks daily to deposit cash, cheques and other valuables, to be credited to their accounts.

When money is to be transferred to the bank, it should be properly organised into convenient bundles so that the bank assistants can quickly and efficiently count and dispose of it.

Notes should be carefully counted and be in their proper denominations, the Queen's head preferably appearing on the right hand side. Coins should be placed in the appropriate bags in their right denominations: 50p, 20p, 10p etc. All monies, including cheques and sales vouchers, should be taken in security bags which must not be obviously displayed to the public. You must always be careful and discreet.

Example: if you took the following money to the bank:

				£
10	x	£20	notes	200.00
30	x	£10	notes	300.00
35	x	65	notes	175.00
42	x	£1	coins	42.00
11	x	50p	coins	5.50
20	x	20p	coins	4.00
28	x	10p	coins	2.80
		60p	bronze	.60
Total cash				729.90
Cheques				151.65
				881.55

You would be carrying over £700 in cash to deposit at the bank. You would therefore take alternative routes and not go the same identical way each time. For very large sums of money, the business would need to make security arrangements and may hire a security van to make these deposits.

A bank form, the paying-in-slip, is used to enter details of cash and cheques deposited at the bank. An example for the above amount is shown below:

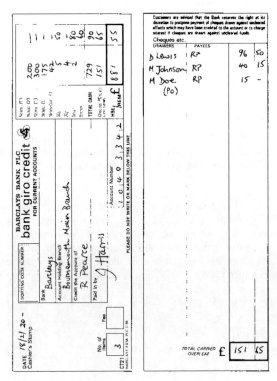

Fig. 11.1 Bank giro credit [paying in slip]

Recording procedure

Before going to the bank to deposit money, it must first be recorded in the business's books. The cashier or other person responsible for banking, would count up the sales for the day and enter the figures on a form which may be referred to as a 'Daily Sales Sheet' or other suitable title. The figures below are the sales for the week ending to 22 February:

DATE	CHEQUES/PO	CREDIT CARD VOUCHERS	CASH	BANK
18/2	151.65	0	729.90	881.55
19/2		87.50	325.60	413.10
20/2	195.00	55.00	473.00	723.00
21/2	210.60	21.00	480.00	711.60
22/2		32.60	525.00	557.60
TOTALS	557.25	196.10	2,533.50	3,286.85

Daily Sales Sheet: week ending 22 February

The cashier, or other person responsible, would sign the receipts abstract once it has been checked as correct.

A bank paying-in-slip for the cash, cheques and credit vouchers would be completed. A voucher summary form for the credit card vouchers, would also be completed and taken to the bank so that the business bank account can be credited. Note that the total amount received from credit card vouchers can also be included with the total amount of cheques on the same paying-in-slip. For example, on the 21 February the total amount banked £711.60 can be entered on the slip showing £480 in cash and £231.60 in cheques and vouchers.

In the accounts of the business, these daily entries would be recorded in the bank account or cash book on the debit side (receipts). An example of cash book receipts is shown below. If we make sales inclusive of VAT we need to extract the VAT by using the fraction 7/47 in order to calculate the sales (excluding VAT) and the VAT amount:

Cash book receipts				Debit
Date	Details	Sales	VAT	Bank
18/2	sales	750.26	131.29	881.55
19/2	sales	351.57	61.53	413.10
20/2	sales	615.32	107.68	723.00
21/2	sales	605.62	105.98	711.60
22/2	Sales	474.55	83.05	557.60
		2,793.32	489.53	3,286.85

When posting these figures to the nominal ledger, the sales account and the VAT account will be credited with £2,797.32 and £489.53 respectively. The bank receipts are debits.

Authorisation of cheques

When cheques are to be prepared for payment, not just any person can sign a cheque in business. Only those persons authorised to do so. This may be delegated to the cashier or someone with sufficient responsibility to prepare cheques up to a certain figure, for example, £500 or £5,000.

It maybe necessary to have two signatures on a cheque for larger sums of money. The greater the value of money, the higher the authorised signature required. It maybe that for sums in excess of say, £5,000, that a director of the company needs to also co-sign the cheque before it can be posted to the creditor.

All cheques are now crossed, that is, they have two parallel lines an the words 'account' or 'a/c payee' in the centre. This instructs the receiving bank that the cheque must be paid into a bank account and therefore cannot be exchanged for cash over the bank counter.

Payments through the bank

Remember that the bank can arrange a great many payments to suppliers and other creditors. The principle means of payment through the bank, other than by cheque, or by debit and credit cards are:

- standing orders
- direct debits
- credit transfer (bank giro credit).

If you have experienced paying telephone, gas, electricity and other bills at a bank, the bank stamp the bill, give you the top half as evidence of payment, and retain the tear off bottom slip, the credit transfer. The bank then automatically pays the creditor and debits your account with the sum to be paid.

Standing orders, direct debits and credit transfers are methods of payment where bills to creditors will be paid by the bank. These methods are very similar in that the payers' account will be debited by the bank when the bills are due to be paid and the sum credited to the creditor. When the bank statement is received, the cash book or bank account must be updated with these entries.

Standing orders

A customer may request the bank, using a standing order form, to pay on his or her behalf, any sum due to a creditor that occurs on a regular basis. It authorises the bank to make such payments on the dates due and to debit the customer's account. The sum to be paid is usually a fixed amount although this may be altered on the advice of the customer. Ideally, regular payments such as house mortgage, insurance premiums, rates or any other expenditure can be arranged by standing order. It is both safe and of utmost convenience to the customer as he does not need to send any money through the post to meet these bills.

Direct debits

This is a similar system to the standing order with the main difference being that it is the creditor that claims the amount due from the customer. The supplier initiates the direct debit with the customer by asking him to complete and sign a direct debit form that will instruct the bank to pay the amount agreed on the dates required. The amounts may be fixed or at varying rates, depending on what is agreed between the customer and supplier. Payments for gas, electricity, insurance premiums, rates, goods from suppliers, can all be arranged by this method and is particularly useful when dates or amounts tend to vary. Standing orders are more convenient if the dates and amounts to be paid are on a fixed basis.

The supplier sends the direct debit forms he has agreed with his customers, to his bank, who will credit his account with the total amount due. The direct debits are sent to the customer's banks where the amounts will be debited against their accounts. The bank statement will indicate all standing orders, direct debits and bank giro credits that have been placed through the bank for payment.

The credit transfer system (BGC)

Clearing banks in this country operate the *bank giro credit system* (BGC) where payments can be made between debtors and creditors. Many household bills can be paid directly through the bank by completing the giro credit slip that is torn off and retained by the bank. The bank debit your account and credit the account of the payee, British Gas, British Telecom, or whoever it might be.

In business a firm can also pay its employees in this way by sending a list of names to their bank indicating the wages to be paid to each employee, the branch and sorting codes of their banks and the time to credit their accounts. Each employee will also receive a payment advice informing them of their gross and net pay and how much will be credited to their bank account. If an employee wishes to be paid through a post office or building society, the same procedure applies.

Trade creditors of the business can also be paid in this way. The firm simply gives the bank a list of its creditors to be paid, indicating the amount, branch and sorting codes of their banks. With the list, credit slips are provided for each payment to a supplier so that he will know where the payment is from. This system saves an enormous amount of time and effort because separate cheques will not be required. All that really happens is that the debtor's account is debited with the total amount to be paid, whilst each creditor's account is credited with the sum due to him. The total debit value equals the total value of credits. The credit transfer system makes for a very safe and convenient way of making payments for staff wages and to suppliers of goods and other creditors.

Bank withdrawals

Many banks have attracted their customers to use various debit and credit cards that saves them writing out a cheque when paying for purchases or other bills. All you do is hand over your card, sign the sales voucher or receipt and what you spend is deducted from your current account. Details of the transaction will appear on the sales voucher or receipt and can be checked against the bank statement. When a bill is paid, the sum will be directly debited to the customer's current account.

When a debit or credit card is used, tills which are linked to EFTPOS (electronic funds transfer at the point of sale), traders have the payment of goods or services automatically debited to the customer's current account and credited to their own account. The banks usually take within three working days to transfer funds from one account to the other. An instant double entry in accounting, no money or cheques passing hands, just an immediate transfer of funds between the buyer and seller!

Bank overdrafts

A trader can apply for a bank overdraft that lets him have money an credit. This means that he can spend more money than he has in his current account. Most banks offer up to £2,000 on a personal current account that enables you to overdraw up to this figure. But beware, interest is charged on a daily basis on the outstanding balance, usually a number of percentage points above the bank's base rate, which can be very expensive.

For business accounts, the bank can arrange for much larger borrowing requirements. Many firms are dependent on overdraft facilities to enable them to meet their day to day expenses, without which they would run into serious cash shortages. Overdrafts are simple to arrange but the bank will normally put a limit on the amount of credit.

Unauthorised overdrafts could be charged at higher rates of interest or worse, the cheques could "*bounce*", that is, they could be stopped by the bank and the payee would not be paid. These cheques would be marked R/D – refer to drawer and would be a serious problem for the business.

The bank statement

A bank statement is a document issued by the bank to its customers, often at monthly intervals, to indicate the sums of money credited (receipts) and debited (payments) to their accounts. Note that this is the opposite way round to recording transactions in the bank account at the place of work. The bank account with a debit balance means that the business has money in the bank. However on the bank statement this would be shown as a credit balance to indicate that the bank owes money to the business as a *liability*.

Look at the statement of Jackson's Ltd. below. The balance on 8 February shows a sum of £17874.77 credit. This means that in the bank account recorded in Jackson's books, the balance would be shown as a debit because it is an **asset** to the business.

BARCLAYS BANK ACCOUNT
SORT CODE   29 99 93

CURRENT ACCOUNT STATEMENT

Account Name:	JACKSON'S LTD, POOLE
Account Number:	10203119
Branch:	POOLE TOWN BRANCHES

Date	Details	Payments	Receipts	Balance
01/2	Start balance			**276.58 Cr**
02/2	001512	532.87		
02/2	Counter credit		2156.22	
04/2	001511	187.50		
04/2	001514	225.90		
05/2	SWI (insurance)			
	7892234552 DD	165.40		
05/2	001516	75.80		
05/2	Counter credit		4370.91	
06/2	001515	320.87		
06/2	001518	192.65		
06/2	BT			
	0943344578 STO	367.40		
06/2	Counter credit		5045.01	
07/2	001517	123.09		
07/2	British Gas			
	91334442 DD	636.50		
07/2	001501	98.90		
07/2	Bank charges	86.25		
07/2	Counter credit		2990.42	
08/2	Counter credit		6048.76	**17874.77 Cr**

STO	standing order
DD	direct debit
O/D	overdrawn balance
BACS	bankers automated clearing services

The legal relationship between the bank and its customers
When money is deposited at the bank for safekeeping and to earn interest, the relationship is one of debtor and creditor. The bank owes you the money, you are the creditor, the bank the debtor. On the other hand, if you owe the bank money, the situation is reversed, the bank being the creditor and you the debtor.

However, there is a difference between the normal debtor/creditor relationship. When money is deposited at the bank, the bank has absolute responsibility of it and may do what it likes with your money. The significant points of difference include:
- The money deposited is only repaid to the customer when demanded.
- The bank has the responsibility to honour cheques demanded by the customer as negotiated between the customer and the bank (including overdraft limits).
- The bank has a right to charge interest and commission on customer's accounts for example, in cases of overdrafts, loans and handling charges.
- The bank has a duty of discretion, that is, it does not disclose customer's banking details to other sources unless given express permission by the customer or there is a legal requirement to do so.

Inter-bank transfers
BACS (Bankers Automated Clearing Services)
This system, set up by the banks, passes payments through the banking system by computer transfer. It is used in business as an efficient way to make a variety of payments including those to employees for wages and salaries, to creditors and to meet various expenses. These transfer payments are made via the banks' computers and allows payments to go directly from one business's account to another.

For example, if an employee was paid through BACS, the employee's bank account would be credited with net pay as indicated on the payslip and the business's bank account debited. Usually the payments need a minimum of three working days to take effect. Note that this is very similar to the bank giro credit that is a paper order passed to the bank, whereas BACS is an electronic transfer. An *auto pay* system can be set up through BACS where a number of periodic payments to regular suppliers or employees can be made for variable amounts on certain selected days.

CHAPS (Clearing House Automated Payments System)
Again, this is a means of electronic payment using the banks' computers, except it is used for high value transactions such as payment for assets like motor vehicles or expensive equipment. Once a transfer is made the payment cannot be cancelled so it is imperative that all details of a transaction are carefully checked before it goes through.

Bank drafts
This is a bank cheque. If a large payment needs to be made by cheque, a bank draft will guarantee that the cheque is as good as paying by cash. A draft is bought from the bank and a fee is charged for the service.

Debit and credit cards
The number of consumers and businesses who use these cards are enormous and ever increasing. They are both common ways of making payments for goods and services. Most of the larger retailers have signs indicating the various different types of cards they will accept as a means of payment.

Debit cards allow customers to make payments without the use of a cheque. Once the card is swiped through a machine or an electronic till, the payment is directly debited to the customer's account via a computer link up (EFTPOS - electronic funds transfer at the point of sale).

The credit card such as *VISA* operates much in the same way allowing customers to buy goods or services on credit. The cardholder is asked to pay the credit card company monthly on the purchases made. If the balance of the account is paid up, no interest is charged. Interest is charged on any outstanding balances, usually at a significantly high rate. It makes sense therefore to try and settle the balance each month and not pay any interest charges. Retailers pay credit card companies a set percentage charge on sales usually up to 5%.

Using the Internet for payment

Many businesses now use websites (on line facilities, for example, www.promise.co.uk) as a means of selling their goods or services. Customers use their computers to pay for their goods by using their debit or credit cards. Once card numbers are clicked on the computer, the payments are credited to the business's bank accounts and the goods despatched to the customers. The business will also receive a schedule of payments received that can be checked against their bank statement.

This method of trade or *'e-commerce'* is fast growing and many large organisations, including the big supermarkets are using it. The largest user however, appears to be *Amazon*. *eBay* is used by private individuals who buy and sell anything and everything but security has been a problem because of fraud. The authorities are continuously trying to minimize the risk taken by traders.

Other banking terms

Cheque:	is an order to the bank, instructing it to pay a specified sum to the *payee*, that is, the person to receive the cheque and is signed by the *drawer* of the cheque. The *drawee* of a cheque is the bank where the cheque is to be paid.
Crossed cheque:	two parallel lines across the cheque indicates that it must be paid into a bank account.
Guarantee card:	a card issued by the bank to customers that will guarantee payment to a recipient up to a certain amount, for example, £50 or £100.
Cheque requisition form:	a request to authorise the use of a cheque or cheques for a specific purpose such as the purchase of fixed assets.
Bank statement:	sent by a bank to its customers at regular intervals stating how much has been received (credits) and how much has been paid (debits) into a customer's account.
R/D:	referred to drawer; where a cheque has literally *bounced*, and not accepted by the bank usually due to insufficient funds held by the drawer of the cheque. Debit the customer's account and credit the cash book.
Remittance advice:	a document sent with a cheque or other means of payment, to the seller of goods or services, indicating that payment is made.

KEY POINTS OF THE CHAPTER

Clearing bank:	A commercial bank offering services to both individuals and businesses
Deposit account:	Used by savers to safeguard their money and to earn interest on their accounts
Current account:	Used for operating cheques and making payments through the bank. Accounts can be overdrawn
Paying-in-slip:	A deposit slip used to record money, cheques, postal orders, credit card vouchers, etc. deposited at the bank and credited to an account
Standing order:	An order to the bank to authorise regular payments to a creditor example, paying a monthly mortgage or insurance premium
Direct debit:	Similar to the standing order although the creditor initiates the payment and can vary the monthly amount

Bank giro:	The credit transfer system that facilitates payments between debtors and creditors
Bank overdraft:	Used on current accounts where the bank offers credit, that is, you can spend more than you've got in your account
BACS	Bankers Automated Clearing Services: transfer of payments by banks using computers
CHAPS	Clearing House Automated Payments System: as for BACS but for high value transactions
Bank draft	A bank cheque - more secure than a normal cheque
Debit cards	Payments by consumers without using cheques, linking with EFTPOS
Credit cards	Consumers buying on credit without either cash or cheques
EFTPOS	Electronic funds transfer at point of sale
Internet payments	Using the computer to purchase from websites as a method of trade for example, *e-commerce* or *eBay*.

QUESTIONS

1. Briefly describe the main functions of a clearing bank.
2. What is the main difference between a deposit account and a current account?
3. When a cheque is crossed, what does it signify?
4. Make out a paying-in-slip, making up details for the name of the business etc. with the following information:

cheques:	Harry Jones	£123.55
	James Last	£23.87
postal order:	Rod Stewart	£18.50
cash:	2 x £50 notes	
	7 x £20 notes	
	11 x £10 notes	
	23 x £5 notes	
	8 x £1 coins	
	4 x 50p coins	
	17 x 20p coins	
	14 x 10p coins	
	5 x 5p coins	
	36p bronze	

5. Why should you make variations to your journey when going to the bank?
6. What is the difference between a direct debit and a standing order?
7. What advantages are there for a business using the credit transfer system?
8. Briefly explain why a bank overdraft can be more than useful to a business.
9. a) What legal relationship exists between a bank and its customers?
   b) Find out what you can about today's banking world by visiting your local branch, collect their leaflets and booklets and be aware of the variety of services they can offer. Compare and contrast these with what a building society can offer.
10. Explain briefly the similarities and differences of using BACS and CHAPS as banking services.
11. Both debit and credit cards are very popular with consumers.
    Explain how they are different when they are used by shoppers.
12. Why is it possible for some unscrupulous people to defraud others when using e-commerce or eBay?

Chapter 12

The Cash Book

INTRODUCTION

The cash book is used to record all cash and banking transactions. It is an extension of the ledger itself, concentrating only on cash or bank entries. Therefore, instead of having a separate bank and cash account in the nominal ledger as we had before, a cash book can be used to record these cash and bank entries, making it more convenient to keep them together.

Any money paid into the business bank account either in cheques or in cash, using the bank's paying-in-slip as documentary evidence, may be recorded in the bank column of the cash book. Entries that are merely in cash are recorded in the cash column. The example below is a two-column cash book using one for cash and bank receipts in and the other for cash and bank payments out:

Example: 2-column Cash Book

Debit						Credit
Receipts			Payments			
	Cash £	Bank £		Cash £	Bank £	

Recording: Debit - cash or bank in.
 Credit - cash or bank out.

Some businesses also use a petty cash book to pay for small items of expenditure such as office cleaning, refreshments, small items of stationery, postage, newspapers, etc. The form of petty cash book can be seen in Chapter 14. For items of expenditure which may be in excess of, say, £10 or £20, the recording would have to be made in the cash book.

Some organisations may want to analyse their receipts and payments of cash. There may be several extra columns used for this purpose for VAT, debtors and different categories of sales on the receipts side. On the payments side, there could be columns used for VAT, creditors and various types of expenses.

A cash book may be in the form of two separate books: a cash receipts book and a cash payments book, particularly if there are a great number of transactions for both receipts and payments. The three-column cash book has columns to record cash discounts as well as cash and bank columns. Discount allowed is on the left and discount received on the right.

Example: 3-column Cash Book

Debit								Credit
Receipts				Payments				
	Discount Allowed £	Cash £	Bank £		Discount Received £	Cash £	Bank £	
Jones	3		57	Fox	4		76	

Cash discounts

These may take one of two forms:

- Discount Allowed: this is entered on the *left side* of the cash book and is given to debtors for prompt payment of their accounts and is treated as an expense to the business.
- Discount Received: this is entered on the *right side* of the cash book and is received from creditors for prompt payment of debts and is treated as revenue to the business.

In practice, cash books rarely look the same because they are adapted to suit the needs of the business. Some businesses may prefer a number of columns for receipts and payments because they may want to analyse various aspects of the business, such as different categories of sales, VAT, or different types of expenses.

Example 1 **Cash Book transactions for G. Harrison:**

January	Debit	Credit
1 Balances in cash £25, bank £900.	cash £25	
	bank £900	
4 Paid stationery, by cash £20.	stationery £20	cash £20
5 Cash sales £72.	cash £72	sales £72
13 Paid rates £125 by cheque.	rates £125	bank £125
15 Cash sales £15.	cash £15	sales £15
25 Paid cash to creditor, James £115 on account.	James £115	cash £115
26 Cash sales £80.	cash £80	sales £80
28 Paid Fox, another creditor, a cheque £76,	Fox £80	(bank £76
in settlement of an £80 account (£4 discount received		(disc. recd £4.
28 Received £57 cheque from Jones (debtor)	(bank £57	Jones £60
in settlement of a £60 account (£3 discount allowed .	(discount allowed £3	
29 Received from Smith (debtor) cheque for £152	(bank £152	Smith £160
in settlement of £160 owing (£8 discount allowed.	(discount allowed £8	

Balancing G Harrison's Cash Book (see solution)

    a) The cash balance c/d 31 January:

total cash in debit column	£192
less total cash out in credit column	(£135)
	£57

    b) Bank balance c/d 31 January:

total bank in debit column	£1,109
less total bank out in credit column	(£ 201)
	£ 908

Ledger posting from Cash Book

To complete the double entry from the cash book, the *'opposite side'* rule applies. Entries on the debit side of the cash book are posted on the credit side of the respective ledger account.
Entries on the credit side of the cash book are posted to the debit side of the respective ledger account. However, when posting cash discounts to the nominal ledger, the totals posted remain on the *same* side.

Discount Allowed   £11 Debit   Discount Received   £ 4 Credit

Solution:

Cash Book

PageNo.42

Dr   Cr.

Date	Details	Disc. Alld.	Cash	Bank	Date	Details	Disc Recd.	Cash	Bank
1 Jan	Balance b/d		25	900	4 Jan	Stationery		20	
5 Jan	Sales		72		13 Jan	Rates			125
15 Jan	Sales		15		25 Jan	James		115	
26 Jan	Sales		80		28 Jan	Fox	4		76
28 Jan	Jones	3		57					
29 Jan	Smith	8		152	31 Jan	Balance c/d		57	908
		11	192	1,109			4	192	1,109
1 Feb	Balance b/d		57	908					

Note:
The double entry is completed when entries in the cash book are posted to their corresponding accounts in the ledger.

For example, cash sales: Debit: Cash column as above (Asset +)
                            Credit: Sales a/c in the ledger (Revenue +)
            Rates: Credit: Bank column as above (Asset-)
                            Debit: Rates a/c in ledger (Expense +)

Nominal ledger

Date	Details	Folio	DR £	CR £	Balance £
Sales a/c					
1/1	Balance				0
5/1	Cash	C 42		72	72 Cr
15/1	Cash	C 42		15	87
26/1	Cash	C 42		80	167
Stationery a/c					
1/1	Balance				0
4/1	Cash	C 42	20		20 Dr
Rates a/c					
1/1	Balance				0
13/1	Bank	C 42	125		125 Dr
Discount Allowed a/c					
1/1	Balance				0
31/1	Sundries	C 42	11		11 Dr
Discount Received a/c					
1/1	Balance				0
31/1	Sundries	C 42		4	4 Cr

NOTE:
The folio C 42 refers to the Cash Book page number and is used as a cross- reference to the source of information.

Sales ledger

Date	Particulars	Folio	DR £	CR £	Balance £
J Jones a/c					
1/1	Balance				60 Dr
28/1	Bank	C 42		57	
	Discount Allowed	C 42		3	0
R Smith a/c					
1/1	Balance				160 Dr
29/1	Bank	C 42		152	
	Discount Allowed	C 42		8	0

Purchase ledger

Date	Particulars	Folio	DR £	CR £	Balance £
N Fox a/c					
1/1	Balance				80 Cr
28/1	Bank	C 42	76		
	Discount Received	C 42	4		0
R James a/c					
1/1	Balance				115 Cr
25/1	Cash	C 42	115		0

Example 2: *An analysed cash book and ledger posting*

The advantages of using extra columns include:

- totals are available to show *where* the money is received and *where* it is paid out;
- it facilitates ledger posting in total; for example, sales £494.57 is posted to the credit side of sales a/c in the nominal ledger.

Example 2: An analysed cash book and ledger posting

CASH BOOK

Date	Particulars	Discount Allowed	Debtors	Cash sales	Bank
1 May	Balance b/d				124.16
1	Sales			114.78	114.78
2	Sales			122.17	122.17
3	Sales			75.49	75.49
4	Jackson, P	5.79	109.93	107.75	217.68
5	Thompson, J	3.27	60.90	74.38	135.28
6	Balance c/d				376.02
		9.06	170.83	494.57	1,165.58

Date	Particulars	Discount received	Creditors	Wages	Misc. expenses	Bank
1 May	Wages			186.48		186.48
2	Light & Heat				44.54	44.54
2	Dunlop Co	24.10	482.16			482.16
3	Gold Ltd.	18.02	322.40			322.40
4	Petty cash				48.00	48.00
5	Slazenger	-	82.00			82.00
		42.12	886.56	186.48	92.54	1,165.58
7	Balance b/d					376.02

Sales ledger

Date	Particulars	Folio	DR £	CR £	Balance £
Jackson, P a/c					
1 May	Balance				364.86 Dr
4	Bank			109.93	
	Disc. All.	CB 17		5.79	249.14 Dr
Thomson, J a/c					
1 May	Balance				64.17 Dr
5	Bank			60.90	
	Disc. All.	CB 17		3.27	0

Purchase ledger

Date	Particulars	Folio	DR £	CR £	Balance £
Dunlop & Co					
1 May	Balance				846.82 Cr
2	Bank		482.16		
	Disc. Recd	CB 17	24.10		340.56 Cr
Gold Ltd.					
1 May	Balance				340.42 Cr
3	Bank		322.40		
	Disc. Recd	CB 17	18.02		0
Slazenger					
1 May	Balance				482.00 Cr
5	Bank	CB 17	82.00		400.00 Cr

Nominal ledger

Date	Particulars	Folio	DR £	CR £	Balance £
Sales a/c					
1 May	Balance				8,424.10 Cr
6	Cash	CB 17		494.57	9,418.67
Wages a/c					
1 May	Balance				511.22 Dr
6	Bank	CB 17	186.48		697.70
Misc. Expenses a/c					
1 May	Balance				54.20 Dr
6	Bank	CB 17	92.54		146.74
*Discount a/c**					
1 May	Balance				26.50 Dr
6	Sundries	CB 17	9.06	42.12	6.56 Cr
S/L Control a/c [debtors]					
1 May	Balance				1,215.90 Dr
6	Bank			170.83	
	Disc. Alld.	CB 17		9.06	1,036.01

P/L Control a/c [creditors]				
1 May	Balance			2,927.75 Cr
6	Bank		886.56	
	Disc. Recd.	CB 17	42.12	1,999.07

*Using the same account for both discount allowed and received.
- Discount allowed is regarded as an expense £9.06   debit
- Discount received is regarded as revenue   £42.12 credit

Example 3: Analysed cash receipts book and analysed cash payments book
The following is an example of recording cash receipts separately from cash payments:

Date	Details	Pay-in Slip No.	Total	VAT	Debtors	Discount Allowed	Cash Sales	Sundry Receipts
			£	£	£	£	£	£
1/5	balance b/d		325.00					
3/5	Lewis	27	426.50		426.50	20.00		
3/5	Johnston	27	300		300			
3/5	cash sales	27	752	112			640	
5/5	cash sales	28	940	140			800	
6/5	rent received	29	125					125
6/5	cash sales	29	846	126			720	
			3714.50	378	726.50	20.00	2160	125
	less Payments (below)		(2755.00)					
	balance b/d		959.50					

Posting to nominal ledger accounts:
All credits except discount allowed account.
VAT £378, S/l control £726.50 and discount allowed £20, sales £2160 and rent received £125 all credits. Discount allowed account £20 debit.

Analysed cash payments book

Date	Details	Cheque Number	Total	VAT	Creditors	Discount Received	Sundry Expenses
1/5	Metro	12455	385		385		
3/5	Slazenger	12456	960		960	40	
5/5	stationery	12457	470	70			400
7/5	light, heat	12458	94	14			80
7/5	Ariel	12459	705		705		
7/5	insurance	12460	141	21			120
			2755	105	2050	40	600

Posting to nominal ledger accounts:
All debits except discount received account.
VAT £105, P/l control £2050 and discount received £40, stationery £400, light, heat £80 and insurance £120 all debits. Discount received £40 Credit.

Computerised Accounts

The bank account below is taken from an accounting program (SAGE). Its nominal ledger code number *N120*. If any customer receipts are to be entered you need to select the bank account then click onto customer receipts.

The date and details of the cheque received will then be entered and these can clear any particular invoice that it matches either in full or in part. Any discount taken by the customer can also be entered in a discount column provided for the purpose.

The same procedure applies to supplier payments. Where receipts and payments are not related to customers or suppliers, then bank receipts and bank payments are chosen instead. For example, if we wanted to pay a telephone bill we would select bank, then bank payments and enter the details of how we are to pay this bill, by cheque, standing order, direct debit, or by any other means.

Computerised Accounts: print outs of the cash book (bank account) and other ledger accounts:

NOMINAL LEDGER - BANK ACCOUNT

Account			Name			Account Balance		
N120			Bank Current Account			1783.50 Dr		
Trans	**Type**	**Date**	**Ref**	**VAT**	**Ledger / details**	**Value**	**Debit**	**Credit**
04	J	01/03		T9	O/balance	1342.50	1342.50	
37	SR	04/03	23356	T9	S10 Lewis	100.00	100.00	
58	SR	06/03	237892	T9	S21 Wilson	250.00	250.00	
59	PP	06/03	100022	T9	P04 Dunlop	120.00		120.00
61	BP	06/03	100023	T1	N150 telephone	117.50		117.50
62	SR	06/03	224	T1	N160 cash sales	164.50	164.50	
63	BP	06/03	SO	T1	N145 rent	188.00		188.00
64	BP	06/03	100025	T1	N130 petrol	18.50		18.50
65	J	07/03	100024	T9	N123 petty cash	50.00		50.00
69	SR	07/03	749344	T9	S09 Kings	285.00	285.00	
70	SR	07/03	963200	T9	S08 Johnson	140.00	140.00	
85	BP	07/03	100026	T9	P02 Auto	396.00		396.00
86	BP	07/03	CC	T9	N125 bank charges	18.75		18.75
87	SR	07/03	225	T1	N160 cash sales	282.00	282.00	
88	BP	07/03	100027	T1	N148 advertising	23.50		23.50
89	SR	08/03	226	T1	N160 cash sales	376.00	376.00	
90	BP	08/03	SO	T2	N151 insurance	224.25		224.25
					Totals		**2940.00**	**1156.50**
					Balance		1783.50	DEBIT

Note:

Type	J	journal
	SR	sales receipt
	PP	purchase payment
	BP	bank payment

VAT		
	T0	VAT at zero rate tax
	T1	VAT at standard rate of tax
	T2	VAT exempt rate tax
	T9	VAT not applicable

Account	Name				Account Balance		
N110	Sales Account				13048.80 Cr		

Trans	Type	Date	Ref	VAT	Ledger / details	Value	Debit	Credit
04	J	01/03		T9	O/balance	12348.80		12348.80
09	SI	03/03	2642	T1	S08 Johnson	199.15		199.15
10	SI	03/03	2643	T1	S09 Kings	198.00		198.00
11	SI	04/03	2644	T1	S10 Lewis	320.00		320.00
12	SI	04/03	2645	T1	S11 Smith	300.00		300.00
12	SI	04/03	2645	T1	S11 Smith	92.00		92.00
13	SI	05/03	2646	T1	S10 Lewis	356.60		356.60
14	SI	06/03	2647	T1	S21 Wilson	255.32		255.32
62	SR	06/03	224	T1	N120 bank	140.00		140.00
87	SR	07/03	225	T1	N120 bank	240.00		240.00
89	SR	08/03	226	T1	N120 bank	320.00		320.00
					Totals	13048.80		13048.80
					Balance			13048.80 CREDIT

Account	Name				Account Balance		
N130	Motor Expenses Account				461.75 Dr		

Trans	Type	Date	Ref	VAT	Ledger / details	Value	Debit	Credit
04	J	01/03	Balance	T9	O/balance	421.50	421.50	
64	BP	06/03	100025	T1	N120 bank	15.74	15.74	
113	BP	07/03	100035	T1	N120 bank	24.51	24.51	
					Totals	461.75	461.75	
					Balance		461.75 DEBIT	

NOTE:

The revenue and expense accounts *exclude* any VAT charged when posting to the nominal ledger because the VAT sum will have been posted to the VAT account.

KEY POINTS OF THE CHAPTER

Cash book:	A separate book for recording cash and bank transactions
Discount allowed:	Given to the customer for prompt receipt
Discount received:	Received from the supplier for prompt payment
Cash book posting:	'Opposite sides' rule with the exception of discounts which remain on same sides
Analysed cash books:	More columns used for analysis purposes, providing management with more relevant information
Control accounts:	Totals in the debtors and creditors columns including discounts, posted to control a/c's, debit for p/l control and credit for s/l control
Computerised accounts:	Using an accounting program for data input, like SAGE, TETRA OR PEGASUS
Revenue & expenses:	Those accounts that include VAT and entered in the cash book must be posted *excluding* VAT when posting to their respective ledger accounts.

QUESTIONS

1. Explain why there may be a variety of different cash books in use.
2. Why, when posting entries from the cash book, do cash discounts remain on the same side in their respective nominal ledger accounts?
3. a) If a customer paid off her account of £640 less a cash discount of 5%, how would this transaction be posted from the cash book to both the sales and nominal ledgers?
   b) If we paid a supplier to whom we owed £200 less 2.5% cash discount, how would this be posted from the cash book to the purchase and nominal ledgers?

4. The following balances were brought down from the cash book of Harry Palmer on 1 July:
   Cash £747 Dr   Bank £1,022 Dr
   The transactions that took place during July were as follows:

			£
July	1	Paid rent by cheque	44
		General expenses by cheque	32
	3	Cash sales	156
	4	Paid a cheque of £95 to H Smith, having been allowed £5 discount	
	6	Paid shop assistant's wages, cash	60
	10	Cash sales	188
	12	Paid for general expenses, cash	14
	15	Paid an advertising bill, cheque	35
	17	Cash sales	204
	18	Transferred to bank [contra entry] (Dr bank, Cr cash columns)	500
	20	Paid cheque to J Jones £185, having been allowed a £15 discount	
	22	Received £98 cheque from A Knott in settlement of £100	
		Received £296 from P May in settlement of £300	
	24	Cash sales £156 directly paid to bank	
	26	Paid shop assistant's wages, cash	60
	28	Received a cheque from C Daley on a/c	140
	30	Paid rent by cheque	44
	31	Paid a cheque to J Johnson of £180 in settlement of £200 owing	

Required:
a) Prepare the Cash Book of Harry Palmer for the month of July, bringing down the balances the next day.
b) If Harry operated two personal ledgers and a nominal ledger, indicate how posting from the Cash Book to these would be done, using four of the above as examples.

5. On 1 July ABC Co has the following balances in its cash book:

    Cash in hand   £484
    Bank   £276

During the month the transactions were as follows:

		£		£
Cheques Received:			Discount Allowed:	
2/7	Jackson & Son	186		14
3/7	Chappell Ltd	250		18.75
12/7	Clogg & Co	100		-
28/7	Hughes, K	358		17.90
Cheques Issued:			Discount Received:	
2/7	Mitre Sports	500		12.50
4/7	Arena	160		8.00
22/7	Dunlop	80.50		-
28/7	Slazenger Sport	172.00		7.50
Cash Received:				
Week ending				
6/7	Shop takings	258.75	Paid £200 into Bank	
13/7	Shop takings	196.80	Paid £150 into Bank	
20/7	Shop takings	220.00	Paid £175 into Bank	
27/7	Shop takings	187.75	Paid £150 into Bank	
Cash Paid Out:				
6, 13, 20, & 27/7	Assistant salaries	£56.75 (each date)		
22/7	Advertising	£42.24		
23/7	Delivery expenses	£14.75		
25/7	Petty expenses	£8.00		
29/7	Delivery expenses	£10.50		

Required:

a) Enter the above transactions in *date order* for the month of July. Balance as on 31 July and bring down the new balances.

b) Ledger accounts for nominal accounts only. Assume balances are nil on 1 July.

6. The following personal accounts were in P Land's ledger on 1 January:

	£	
Smith, J	220	Dr
Jones, S	84	Dr
Bloggs, H	2 80	Credit

The following transactions took place during January:

			£	
Jan	1	Balances b/d Cash	25	Dr
		Bank	381	Dr
	2	Cash sales	140	
	3	General expenses - cash	15	
		- cheque	27	
	5	Personal drawings cheque	40	
	8	Cash sales	185	
	15	Salaries – cheque	85	
	16	Insurance premium – cheque	54	
	21	General expenses – cash	27	
	24	Cash sales	80	
	26	Smith pays a cheque to settle a/c *less* 5% discount		
	28	Jones pays a cheque to settle a/c *less* 5% discount		
	29	Cash sales paid directly into bank	285	
	31	Paid salaries – cheque	85	
		General expenses – cheque	54	
		Paid Bloggs sum owing and was allowed 2.5% discount		

Required:
a) Prepare the Cash Book of P Land for the month of January and balance on 31 January.
b) Write up the personal accounts of P Land using the running balance method, as they would appear in January.
c) Write up the nominal accounts in P Land's ledger as they would appear in January.

7. On 1 January, D Dawson had the following balances in his books:
£

Cash	142	Dr
Bank (overdrawn)	150	Cr
R Smith	200	Dr
J Green	160	Dr
D Land	200	Cr
A Land	80	Cr
J Jones	300	Cr

During the month of January, his cash/bank transactions were as follows:
Cheques paid
January 3   To D Land £195 in settlement of his a/c
9   To A Land £76 in settlement of his a/c
17   To Jones, £150 on account
22   Withdrew from bank for personal use £100
Cheques received
January 16   From R Smith £195 in settlement of a/c
23   From J Green £152 in settlement of a/c
Cash Received
January 5   Cash sales for the week £125, £100 in bank
12   Cash sales for the week £200, £100 in bank
19   Cash sales for the week £150, £125 in bank
26   Cash sales for the week £135, £100 in bank

Cash Paid
January   5   Shop assistant's wages £45 per week for the month (to 26 January)
          22   To Southern Gas, cash £55
          27   General expenses £27
          29   Petty expenses £3

Required:
a)   Prepare the Cash Book for D Dawson for the month of January, balancing on 31 January.
b)   Show the personal accounts of D Dawson in his ledger to appear as on 31 January.

8.   Jack Jones used a modified cash book in his music shop. All payments were made by cheque and shop sales were banked daily.
    On the receipts side of his Cash Book he used columns for the following:
    Discount   *Debtors*   *Record*   *Other*   *Bank*
    allowed   sales   sales
    On the payments side:
    Discount   *Creditors*   *Assistant's*   *Other*   *Bank*
    received   wages   expenses/
                                                        drawings

Jack's bank balance on 1 May was £850.55 (Dr). During May the transactions were:
a)   *Cheques issued*
    May 2   To J Brown £95 in settlement of £100 debt.
        2   To wages for assistant £56 per week to 30 May.
        4   To F Smith £1,150 on account.
        8   To A Jackson £190 in settlement of £200 debt.
        12   Delivery expenses £27.
        15   Jack withdrew for personal use £150.
        22   To Wimborne DC for business rates £196.
        24   To British Telecom for telephone £77.
        26   Delivery expenses £42.
        28   Jack withdrew for personal use £125.
        30   Petty cash expenses £85.

b)   *Cash sales and cheques received from debtors*

	£
May 5 shop sales for week ending amounted to	227.75
12 shop sales for week ending amounted to	187.00
19 shop sales for week ending amounted to	245.60
26 shop sales for week ending amounted to	310.25
31 shop sales for week ending amounted to	156.20
(All banked the same day.)	

Cheques from debtors
May 7 From G Chappell £142.50, discount allowed £7.50
    10 From D Waiters £50 on account
    18 From R Benaud £285, discount allowed £15
    25 From D Lillee £25 on account
Sales: for the purpose of analysis only, you are to take 'record sales' to be 20% and all other sales to be 80% of the total sales figures provided above.

Required:
Draw up the Cash Book of J. Jones for the month of May, balancing at the end of the month.

9. A wine shop owned by R Lees kept an analysis Cash Book using columns for wine, beer and lager, spirits, other sales, total sales, VAT and bank.
The daily takings are banked each day at the local branch. The cash register calculates the VAT separately when a sale goes through the till. The takings over four days were as follows:

June		Wine	Beer & lager	Spirits	Other Sales	Total sales	Bank
		£	£	£	£	£	£
2	Takings	200	250	80	30		
	VAT	30	37.5	12	4.5		
3	Takings	150	200	50	20		
	VAT	22.5	30	7.5	3		
4	Takings	180	240	60	24		
	VAT	27	36	9	3.60		
5	Takings	300	340	100	60		
	VAT	45	51	15	9		

Required:
a) Prepare a suitable Cash Book using the above columns to analyse the different sale categories.
b) Post the sales and VAT to the ledger.
c) Why is it sometimes useful to make analysis columns?

10. ### NOMINAL LEDGER - BANK ACCOUNT

Account				Name		Account Balance		
N120				Bank Current Account		1783.50 Dr		
Trans	Type	Date	Ref	VAT	Ledger / details	Value	Debit	Credit
04	J	01/03		T9	O/balance	1342.50	1342.50	
37	SR	04/03	23356	T9	S10 Lewis	100.00	100.00	
58	SR	06/03	237892	T9	S21 Wilson	250.00	250.00	
59	PP	06/03	100022	T9	P04 Dunlop	120.00		120.00
61	BP	06/03	100023	T1	N150 telephone	117.50		117.50
62	SR	06/03	224	T1	N160 cash sales	164.50	164.50	
63	BP	06/03	SO	T1	N145 rent	188.00		188.00
64	BP	06/03	100025	T1	N130 petrol	18.50		18.50
65	J	07/03	100024	T9	N123 petty cash	50.00		50.00
69	SR	07/03	749344	T9	S09 Kings	285.00	285.00	
70	SR	07/03	963200	T9	S08 Johnson	140.00	140.00	
85	BP	07/03	100026	T9	P02 Auto	396.00		396.00
86	BP	07/03	CC	T9	N125 bank charges	18.75		18.75
87	SR	07/03	225	T1	N160 cash sales	282.00	282.00	
88	BP	07/03	100027	T1	N148 advertising	23.50		23.50
89	SR	08/03	226	T1	N160 cash sales	376.00	376.00	
90	BP	08/03	SO	T2	N151 insurance	224.25		224.25
					Totals		**2940.00**	**1156.50**
					Balance		1783.50	DEBIT

Required:
From the above computerised bank account, post all revenue and expense accounts to the nominal ledger. Note that sales, telephone, petrol (motor expenses) and advertising are all *inclusive* of VAT.

Chapter 13

The Bank Reconciliation Statement

INTRODUCTION

The cash book's bank balance needs to be confirmed with the bank statement at frequent intervals to check that its receipts and payments are in line with the banks recording of these.

Bank reconciliation is a method of bringing together the bank balance as shown on the bank statement with the balance as shown in the cash book. These balances may not agree at any specific time because:

- items in the cash book may not yet have been paid at the bank in time for these to be entered in the bank statement, or
- items in the bank's statement may not yet be in the cash book. Some examples are:

Items in the cash book not yet recorded in the bank statement:

- Cheque payments entered on the credit side of the cash book but not yet presented for payment at the bank – these are 'un-presented cheques';
- Cheques, cash entered on the debit side of the cash book, but not yet deposited at the bank – these are 'un-deposited cheques, cash'.
  These items will then be recorded in the bank reconciliation statement.

Items in the bank statement not yet recorded in the cash book:
a) Payments and charges made by the bank and charged against the business:

- Standing orders
- Direct debits
- Interest and bank charges
- Cheques R/D (referred to drawer, due to insufficient funds).
  These items will be entered on the *credit* side of the cash book, the payments side.

b) Receipts by the bank on the business's behalf and not yet recorded in the cash book:

- Cheques from customers paid through Bank Giro
- Interest received on deposits at the bank
- Dividends received from investments
  These items will be entered on the *debit* side of the cash book, the receipts side.

Procedure for bank reconciliation

Checking must be made in some systematic order. Have the appropriate cash book pages ready to be compared with the latest batch of bank statements.

1. *Tick* those items that appear on *both* sets of records – for example, the receipts side of the cash book with the receipts side of the statement. Also check the payments side of both records. If entries do appear on both sets of records, then no further action is required. Only those items that are not ticked on both sets of records need action to be taken.
   Also check the *opening balances* in the cash book and bank statement for any differences because if there are these also need action to be taken.

2. If there are any *un-ticked items* on the bank statement, such as bank charges, standing orders, direct debits or interest received, these need to be first entered in the cash book.
The cash book balance will then have been updated. Once the cash book has been adjusted the final stage is set for the reconciliation – that is, preparation of a simple bank reconciliation statement. This is composed of those items left un-ticked in the cash book.

3. The Bank Reconciliation Statement is then prepared usually in this format:

- Balance as per bank statement (end of month balance)
- *Add* any *un-deposited* cheques/cash (from debit side cash book)
- *Deduct* any *un-presented* cheques (from credit side cash book)
- This should equal the balance as per cash book.

Example 1: *The Bank Reconciliation Statement of K McDonald*

National Bank plc							
K. McDonald Statement of Account							
Date	Details	Debits		Credits		Balance	
		£		£		£	
Oct 30	Balance					841	✓
Oct 31	606218	23	✓			818	
Nov 5	Sundry Credit			46	✓	864	
Nov 7	606219	161	✓			703	
Nov 9	Direct Debit	18				685	
Nov 12	606222	93	✓			592	
Nov 15	Sundry Credit			207	✓	799	
Nov 19	606223	246	✓			553	
Nov 19	Bank Giro Credit			146	✓	699	
Nov 20	Bank Giro Credit			246		945	
Nov 21	606221	43	✓			902	
Nov 21	Sundry Credit			63	✓	965	
Nov 22	Bank Giro Credit			79	✓	1,044	
Nov 23	Loan Interest	391				653	
Nov 26	606220	87	✓			566	
Nov 26	Deposit A/C Interest			84		650	
Nov 27	606226	74	✓			576	
Nov 28	Sundry Credit			88	✓	664	
Nov 30	606225	185	✓			479	

Her cash book showed the following details:

		£				Cheque No.	£	
Nov 1	Balance b/d	818	✓	Nov 2	Rent	219	161	✓
Nov 5	B Mason	46	✓	Nov 5	H Gibson	220	87	✓
Nov 8	K Dean	146	✓	Nov 7	G Wise	221	43	✓
Nov 14	G Hunt	207	✓	Nov 8	T Allen	222	93	✓
Nov 16	C Charlton	79	✓	Nov 12	Gas	223	246	✓
Nov 19	D Banks	63	✓	Nov 15	F Chaucer	224	692	
Nov 26	P Perry	88	✓	Nov 19	M Lewis	225	185	✓
Nov 28	A Palmer	29		Nov 23	G Bridges	226	74	✓
Nov 30	J Dixon	17		Nov 29	L Wilson	227	27	
Nov 30	Balance c/d	206		Nov 29	P Brown	228	91	
		1,699					1,699	

Required:

a) Bring the Cash Book balance of £206 (overdrawn) up to date as at 30 November.

b) Draw up a bank reconciliation statement as at 30 November.

Solution:

The cash book is brought up-to-date by entering the un-ticked items taken from the bank statement:

Cash Book

Dr					Cr
Dec 1	Deposit interest	84	Dec 1	Balance b/d	206 (o/d)
	Bank giro credit	246		Direct debit	18
	Balance c/d	285		Loan interest	391
		615			615
				Balance b/d	285

Bank reconciliation statement as at November 30

		£	
1	Balance as per bank statement (30/11)		479 Credit
2	Add deposits not yet credited:		
	Palmer	29	
	Dixon	17	46
			525
3	Less un-presented cheques:		
	Chester	692	
	Wilson	27	
	Brown	91	
			(810)
4	Balance as per cash book		285 (o/d)

Example 2: Using a previous bank reconciliation statement

On 1 August Alan Simons had an overdraft of £33.65 in his Cash Book. The previous bank reconciliation statement on 31 July is shown below. First check these items with the new bank statement on 16 August show on the next page:

Bank reconciliation statement as on 31 July:

		£	
Balance as per bank statement		149.25	
Add			
Deposits not yet credited:		440.00 ✓	
		589.25	
Less			
Un-presented cheques:			
05625	37.50		
05634	133.20 ✓		
05637	98.80 ✓		
05651	200.00 ✓		
05653	153.40 ✓	622.90	
Balance as per cash book		33.65 (overdrawn)	

Cash Book – A Simons to 16 August

4/8	Sales	300 ✓	1/8	Balance b/d	33.65		(overdrawn)
15/8	Sales	500 ✓	7/8	Rent	77	✓	
16/8	D Adams	345	8/8	Purchases	123.5	✓	
			9/8	A Jones	48	✓	
			11/8	SEB	108.5		
			12/8	petty cash	95		
			16/8	insurance (DDR)	35	✓	
			16/8	balance c/d	624.35		
		1,145			1,145		

Bank Statement – A Simons to 16 August

			Dr	Cr	Balance
Aug	1	Balance			149.25
	2	Credit		440 ✓	
	3	05634	133.20 ✓		
	4	credit		300 ✓	
	7	05637	98.80 ✓		
	10	05651	200 ✓		
	10	05653	153.40 ✓		
	11	05654	77 ✓		
	11	05659	123.50 ✓		
	13	05663	48 ✓		
	14	DDR (Insurance)	35 ✓		
	16	Credit		500 ✓	
	16	Closing balance			520.35

Have you checked these figures? The deposits of £440 and all cheques except 05625, £37.50, from the previous bank reconciliation statement on 31 July, can be ticked off against the same entries on the bank statement above.

The figures for August in the cash book can then be cross-checked against the remainder of the bank statement for August in the usual way. The reconciliation up to the 16 August is shown below:

Bank reconciliation as on 16 August:

	£
Balance as per statement	520.35
Add deposits not yet credited:	345.00
Less un-presented cheques:	865.35
37.50	
108.50	
95.00	241.00
Balance as per cash book	624.35

Cheques dishonoured by the bank

The bank statement may include cheques received from customers that have been lodged as deposits then at a later date, refused to be paid by the debtor's bank usually because of insufficient funds in the debtor's account. The entry would be first made as a credit at the bank then, once the cheque had been refused payment, a debit entry would be made on the statement.

If this occurs, the customer's account would have to be re-debited with the amount of the cheque and the bank account credited with the same figure: for example, if a customer, Mr. Smith's cheque for £141 had "R/D" (refer to drawer) and was therefore dishonoured by the bank:

Sales ledger

			Debit	Credit	Balance
Smith account					
May	1	Balance			141 Dr
	9	Bank		141	0
June	10	Bank (R/D)	141		141 Dr

Cash book (extract)

		Payments	(credit)
June	10	Smith (R/D cheque)	141

Overdrafts

Remember that a bank overdraft is shown as a debit balance in the bank statement and is a credit balance in the bank account or cash book.

When preparing the bank reconciliation statement therefore, the additions and subtractions work in the opposite way:

Bank reconciliation as on 31 August:

	£	
Balance as per statement	450	Dr
Less deposits not yet credited:	210	
	240	
Add un-presented cheques:	425	
Balance as per cash book	665	(overdrawn)

Cheques

If a customer sends a cheque, remember that it must be correct in all detail, including signature, date, figures matching with words etc. A cheque that is over 6 months old is referred to as a *"stale"* cheque and will not be accepted by the bank. Remember that there may also be arithmetic or other errors in the cash book and the bank itself is not immune to making errors. Therefore, there may be questions which will include all types of omissions and errors as well as the 'run of the mill' un-presented cheques and sums not yet credited.

KEY POINTS OF THE CHAPTER

BRS:	Bank reconciliation statement used to reconcile the bank statement with the cash book
Bank statement:	The bank account prepared by the business's bank recording deposits and payments through the bank
Bank terms:	Direct debits, standing orders, bank giro, bank charges, R/D, etc.
Bank overdraft:	The bank account overdrawn because payments are in excess of receipts
Cheque dishonoured:	Bank will not accept cheque because the payee has insufficient funds
Undeposited sums:	Those un-ticked items on the debit side of the cash book that have not yet been recorded at the bank and not on statement
Unpresented cheques:	Those un-ticked cheques on the credit side of the cash book that have not yet been cleared by the bank and not on statement.

QUESTIONS

1. The information given below refers to the books of John Lloyd for the month of January:

Cash Book – John Lloyd (Bank columns)

			£				£
Jan	1	Balance	93	Jan	1	Jack Jones	52
	4	Sales	88		8	Office Expenses	24
	7	Tom Jones	87		9	Harry Smith	141
	16	A Knott	228		10	Gas, Electricity	34
	18	J Snow	74		12	Freddy Smith	108
	21	Sales	255		17	Rates	46
	28	A Clarke	54		21	Salaries	84
	31	R Wilson	36		30	George Fame	116
						Balance c/d	?
			915				915

Bank Statement – John Lloyd – for month of January

			Debit £	Credit £	Balance £
Jan	1	Balance			93 Cr
	4	Sundries		88	181
	8	Sundries		87	268
	11	452	52		
		453	24		192
	12	SO	55		137
	14	DD	18		119
	16	Sundries		228	347
	17	455	34		313
	18	456	108		205
	19	Sundries		74	279
	21	Sundries		255	534
	22	457	46		488
	24	458	84		404
	29	Dividend		16	420

Notes: SO = Standing Order
DD = Direct Debit

Required:
a) Adjust the cash book with the appropriate entries from the bank statement and bring the new balance down.
b) Prepare the bank reconciliation statement for the month of January.

2. The following represents the Cash Book and bank statement figures of J Jones for the month of June:

Cash Book (bank columns only)

		£				£
1/6	Balance b/d	469	6/6	Jones, F		130
14/6	Doyle, C	393	9/6	Singleton, S		63
17/6	Cronin, A	200	20/6	Jackson, J		292
28/6	Smith, W	205	27/6	Hemming R		78
		___		Balance c/d		?
		___				___

Bank of education Statement of J Jones – for month of June

		Dr	Cr	Balance
		£	£	£
1/6	Balance			469 Cr
5/6	Credit		393	862 Cr
12/6	123971	130		732 Cr
19/6	123972	63		669 Cr
20/6	Credit		200	869 Cr
26/6	Credit			
	Smith, R		100	969 Cr
28/6	SO			
	Leicester BSC	86		883 Cr
29/6	Charges	19		864 Cr

Required:

a) Bring down the balance of J Jones's Cash Book and check both sets of records and action any un-ticked items.

b) Adjust the Cash Book.

c) Prepare the bank reconciliation statement as at 30 June.

3. The unbalanced Cash Book of P Bentley in the 1st and 2nd weeks of May appeared as follows:

			£				£
May	1	Balance		2,300	May 2	Harrison	168
	3	Smith	125		4	Rent, Rates	154
		Jones	217	342	8	Wages	218
	6	Sales	115		10	Jackson	517
		Jones	13	128	12	Robson	26
						Balance c/d	?
	10	Fox	259				
		Sales	175	434			
	12	Knott	189				
		Sales	215	404			

Bank statement to 12 May was as follows:

			Dr £	Cr £	Balance £
May	1	Balance			2,300 Cr
	1	Counter Credit		342	2,642
	5	449	168		2,474
	6	Credit transfer			
		R White		435	2,909
	6	Counter Credit		128	3,037
	7	450	218		2,819
	9	SO (AB Soc.)	125		2,694
	10	Counter Credit		434	3,128
	12	Direct Debit (SEB)	44		3,084

Required:
a) Adjust the Cash Book with the appropriate entries. Balance on 12 May.
b) Prepare the reconciliation statement on 12 May.

4. The Cash Book and bank statement of Janet Jones was as follows:

Dr		Bank £			Bank £	Cr
1/5	Balance b/d	850.55	2/5		95.00	
5/5		227.75			56.00	
7/5		142.50	4/5		1,150.00	
10/5		50.00	8/5		190.00	
12/5		187.00	9/5		56.00	
18/5		285.00	12/5		27.00	
19/5		245.60	15/5		150.00	
25/5		25.00	16/5		56.00	
26/5		310.25	22/5		196.00	
31/5		156.20	23/5		56.00	
					77.00	
			26/5		42.00	
			28/5		125.00	
			30/5		85.00	
					56.00	
					25.00	
			31/5	Balance c/d	37.85	
		2,479.85			2,479.85	
1/6	Balance b/d	37.85				

Details	Payments £	Receipts £	Balance £	
Balance forward			850.55	Cr
2741	56.00		795.55	
CC		227.75		
CC		142.50	1,164.80	
2742	95.00			
2743	1,150.00		80.20	Dr
CC		50.00	30.20	Dr
2746	56.00		86.20	Dr
CC			100.80	Cr
2744	150.00	187.00		
2745	27.00		76.20	Dr
CC		285.00		
CC		245.60		
Bank Giro		200.00	654.40	Cr
(R Smith)				
CC		25.00	679.40	
2747	56.00		623.40	
CC		310.25	933.65	
2748	56.00			
Charges	31.50			
Lillee R/D	25.00			
2749	196.00		625.15	Cr

Required:
a) Check the Cash Book entries with Janet Jones's bank statement and bring it up to date.
b) Prepare the reconciliation statement for the month end 31 May.

5. The following information refers to a summary of Rebecca David's Cash Book as at the month ended 31 May.

Receipts		£	Payments	£
May 1	Balance b/d	2,706	General expenses	7,225
	Cash sales	11,142	Creditors	6,955
	Debtors	3,100	Wages	2,580
	Commission	2,152	Office equipment	1,000

The bank statement dated 31 May received by Rebecca David had an overdrawn balance of £893 (Dr). When checking with the Cash Book records the following facts were revealed:

- A payment of £420 to a supplier had been entered as a receipt.
- Bank commission of £19 and administrative charges and interest payment of £23 had not yet been entered in the Cash Book records.
- A cheque of £215 from a customer of R David had been dishonoured by the bank and marked 'R/D'.
- A credit transfer of £426 from an R David customer had been directly paid through the bank.
- Cheques of £375, £410, £72 and £95 had not yet been presented to the bank for payment.
- The opening Cash Book balance of £2,706 was b/d in error and should have read £2,607.

- A request to transfer £850 from deposit to current account, and entered in the Cash Book, had been misinterpreted by the bank and the transfer had been made the opposite way round. Cash Book to be corrected.
- Cash sales of £11,142 were under-cast in error and should have read £11,642.
- The final paying-in-book deposit of £1,215 had not yet been credited by the bank.

Required:
a) Reconstruct the Cash Book incorporating the information above and bring down the balance on 31 May.
b) Prepare the bank reconciliation statement for the month ended 31 May.
c) Why is there a need to reconcile banking transactions?

6. The following information relates to the cash ledger of Alan D. Robert for the month of 19 June.

	£		£
1/6 Balance b/f	2,870	General expenses	2,420
Debtors	8,755	Creditors	10,455
Cash sales	6,420	Salaries	2,815
Other receipts	895	Rental charges	400

The bank statement received by the business on 30 June showed a balance of £1,935 (credit).

When the proprietor checked his records with those of the statement, the following facts were revealed:
- The bank's commission and other charges amounted to a total of £79.
- A customer's cheque, which had been sent to Robert, had been marked 'R/D' and dishonoured by the bank. The cheque was for £1,353.
- A receipt of £300 from a customer of Robert had been wrongly entered as a payment in his cash ledger.
- The opening cash ledger balance of £2,870 was brought forward in error and should have been £2,780.
- Several cheques signed by Robert and presented for payment, had not yet been cleared by the bank. The cheques were for £315, £455, £170 and £595.
- Wages of £200 had been under-cast in error and had not been recorded in the cash ledger.
- A credit transfer of £420 from a Robert customer had been directly paid into the bank.
- Other entries in the statement included £122 paid to Robert as a dividend from ACY Ltd, and a direct debit relating to an insurance premium for £70.
- The final paying-in-book deposit of £1,800 had not yet been credited by the bank.

Required:
a) Reconstruct the cash ledger for the month of June, bringing down the balance on 30 June.
b) Prepare the bank reconciliation statement for the month ending 30 June.

7. The bank reconciliation statement for H & J Smith as on 24 May is shown below:

	£
Balance as per bank statement	589.00
Add Deposits not yet credited	420.00
	1,009.00

Less Un-presented cheques:		
05625	137.50	
05634	233.00	
05637	108.00	
05651	310.00	
05653	152.00	940.50
Balance as per Cash Book		68.50

The cash book of H & J Smith to 31 May was as follows:

Cash Book – H & J Smith

24/5	Balance b/d	68.50			
24/5	Sales	300.00	24/5	Purchases	300.15
25/5	Sales	500.00	25/5	General expenses	77.00
26/5	D Adams	345.00	26/5	Purchases	123.50
			27/5	A Jones	48.00
			27/5	SEB	208.85
			28/5	Petty cash	195.00

Bank Statement to 31 May – H & J Smith

		Dr	Cr	Balance	
				£	
May 24	Balance			589.00	Credit
25	Credit		420.00		
26	05634	233.00			
27	Credit		300.00		
28	05637	108.00			
30	05671	310.00			
30	05653	152.00			
31	05654	77.00			
31	05659	123.50			
31	05663	48.00			
31	DDR Star Insurance	35.00			
	(No. 445/5689)				
31	STO Power Gen				
	(No. 8331/98)	120.00			
31	Credit		500.00		
31	Closing balance			602.50	

Required:
a) Bring the cash book up to date on 31 May and balance at this date.
b) Prepare the bank reconciliation statement as on 31 May.

(Association of Accounting Technicians)

8. According to the cash book of JB Wentworth Ltd. the company's account with the bank had an overdrawn balance of £1,689 on 30 April. Subsequently, the company received its bank statements for April and the following discoveries were made:

- The following cheques recorded in the cash book for April were un-presented for payment in the bank:

No. of cheque	Amount
326	£223
329	£1,137
343	£5
364	£894

- A dividend of £142 received from a company called Randle plc, was credited directly to the bank account via bank giro.
- A standing order on 16 April £46 for gas had not been entered in the cash book
- A cheque for £144 received from a customer, J Browning, was returned by the bank R/D – refer to drawer, the drawer had insufficient funds in the bank.
- The bank had charged the company £164 for bank charges and a further £310 in bank interest payments.

The following items recorded by JB Wentworth Ltd. as receipts in the cash book had not yet been credited by the bank:

- Timber Production plc   £438
- Hedge & Gate Ltd.   £362
- In the company's cash book for April, discount received £8 had been included in error in the bank payments column.
- A cheque No. 986 NOT drawn by the company for £1,040 (but by another company by the name of Went-Wright plc had been debited in the bank statement and the bank has now accepted that this was their error.

Required:
Prepare a corrected cash book to show the up-dated balance as on 30 April and prepare the company's bank reconciliation statement as on the same date.

(Association of Accounting Technicians)

Chapter 14

The Petty Cash Book

INTRODUCTION

The Petty Cash Book is a subsidiary of the cash book and is primarily used to record small payments of cash as an alternative to the credit side of the cash book. In this way, numerous small cash payments need not interfere with the main channels of cash entries. It uses a voucher system as evidence that cash payments have been made. These must be countersigned by an authorised person before money can be released. It is based on using a 'float' such as £100 per month from which these petty cash payments are made. When this sum is used up, it is reimbursed from further cash received through the cash book. Analysis columns can be used in the petty cash book to identify the different areas of payments.

The advantages of having a Petty Cash Book include:

- The handling of work can be subdivided between a number of employees. The cashier who is responsible for the cash book may delegate petty cash control to a junior accounts clerk.
- It frees the cash book from too many small and less significant figures.
- The style of the petty cash book allows for the analysis columns to be used, which facilitates easier ledger posting.

The Petty Cash Book is also known as the 'imprest system' because it uses a float or 'imprest'. To make payments for minor expenses such as travel, office cleaning, office refreshments, stationery and so forth. When the float or imprest is used up after a set of period of time, it is reimbursed by a further payment made on the credit side of the cash book. Reimbursements may be made weekly, monthly or whenever it is appropriate to the business.

A petty cash voucher is a document used for paying out petty cash. Petty cash vouchers must be signed by any person who receives a cash payment and also by a person authorised to make the payments, such as the cashier or office manager. Vouchers are numbered consecutively and any receipts given when spending petty cash, are attached and filed with vouchers because they will be required for audit purposes.

Control of petty cash

Each payment should be supported by a petty cash voucher. The voucher shows why the petty cash is required and who has authorised the payment. The petty cashier should always support the giving of petty cash by the signature of the person taking the cash. On some items of spending VAT maybe reclaimable that is why it is important to attached any receipts as evidence of money spent. An example of a petty cash voucher is given in Figure 14.1.

Random checks can be made on the petty cashier. At any particular time, the total sum of the number of vouchers used in the month – that is, their total value – added to the balance of petty cash should equal the petty cash float. For example, if the petty cash float was £50:

Petty cash balance	£ 4.25
Vouchers used	£45.75
Float =	£50.00

PETTY CASH VOUCHER	No.: **1**	
	Date: **2 June**	
Description	Amount	
Office refreshments:		
Coffee	1	12
Buns		38
	1	50
Signature: **John Jones**		
Authorisation: **P P Smith**		

Fig. 14.1 A petty cash voucher

Double-entry with cash book
When any sum for petty cash is to be withdrawn from the Cash Book and entered in the Petty Cash Book, the double-entry is:

    Debit the Petty Cash Book
    Credit the Cash Book

In the following example the petty cash float is £125 per month. During May, £87.25 was used for petty cash expenses leaving a balance brought down on 1 June of £37.75. A reimbursement of £87.25 is required to give the Petty Cash Book its float of £125. The double entry is:

    Debit Petty Cash Book   £87.25
    Credit Cash Book   £87.25

The calculation of VAT
VAT is an indirect source of taxation charged by the Government on most of our goods and services. Some goods are not yet subject to VAT, such as most of our food, books, children's clothing and postage.

The standard rate of tax is currently 17.5% and goods and services that are at the standard rate must be charged at this percentage rate. The responsibility for collecting this money lies with HMRC (Her Majesty's Customs & Revenue). The tax charged on sales is called an 'output tax' and tax charged on purchases or expenses is called an 'input tax'.

Where some items are purchased by petty cash, which include VAT, the amount of VAT included is recorded as a separate sum in the petty cash records because it can be recovered as 'input tax' and must be recorded in the VAT account.
Examples:
Envelopes and typing paper inclusive of 17.5% VAT £5.17
Cleaning materials inclusive of 17.5% VAT £9.40

If a payment is given which is inclusive of VAT, it is still necessary to calculate the VAT charged (the fraction 7/47 equals the VAT charged):

$$\frac{7 \times 9.40}{47} \quad = £1.40 \quad \text{(cleaning £8.00, VAT £1.40)}$$

$$\frac{7 \times 5.17}{47} \quad = £0.77 \quad \text{(stationery £4.40, VAT £0.77)}$$

Example: Petty Cash Book of R Taylor

R Taylor uses a Petty Cash Book in his business. He uses small sums of cash frequently for items such as office refreshments, packing materials, travel expenses, postage and telegrams, sundry expenses and VAT. [See petty cash book on following page].

Petty Cash float: £125 month
Balance brought forward from previous month, 31 May: £37.75

The entries for the month of June were:

June		Amount £	VAT £	Voucher No.
1	Petty cash reimbursement	87.25		
2	Office refreshments	1.50		1
5	Taxi fares	5.00		2
6	Packing materials	15.44	2.32	3
7	Petrol	5.45	0.82	4
12	Postage	8.50		5
14	Replacement glass	17.17	2.57	6
16	Telegrams	4.20		7
18	Office refreshments	2.12		8
21	Packing materials	14.43	2.17	9
22	Petrol	3.03	0.45	10
24	Miscellaneous expenses	16.21		11
28	Refreshments and taxi fares	15.50		12

NOTE: See R Taylor's petty cash book is on the following page:

• After entering the opening balance of £37.75, the receipt of £87.25 on 1 June, is entered on the debit side of the petty cash book to make up the float to £125 for the new month.

• The payments are entered on the credit side. The total sum is entered first, then placed in the appropriate analysis column for example, office refreshments £1.50 on 2 June.

• Each payment should be accompanied by a voucher number which acts as evidence for the money paid out of petty cash.

• The petty cash book is totalled as often as is convenient, in this example, at the end of the month. At the end of June, £116.88 was spent leaving a balance carried down of £8.12 which must equal the cash left in the petty cash box.

• The balance of £8.12 is then brought down under the receipts side (debit), ready for reimbursement in July to £150 (increasing the float by £25). Petty cash payments in July can then be entered.

The Petty Cash Book

Debit £	Date	Details	No.	Credit Total £	Office refresh. £	Packing materials £	Travel expenses £	Post and telegrams £	Sundries £	VAT £
37 75	1/6	Balance b/d								
87 25	1	Cash book (reimbursement)								
	2	Office refreshments	1	1 50	1 50					
	5	Taxi fare	2	5 00			5 00			
	6	Packing materials	3	17 76		15 44				2 32
	7	Petrol and oil	4	6 27			5 45			0 82
	12	Postage	5	8 50				8 50		
	14	Replacement glass	6	19 74					17 17	2 57
	16	Telegrams	7	4 20				4 20		
	18	Office refreshments	8	2 12	2 12					
	21	Packing materials	9	16 60		14 43				2 17
	22	Petrol and oil	10	3 48			3 03			0 45
	24	Miscellaneous costs	11	16 21			14 40	1 26	0 56	
	24	Office refreshments, taxi	12	15 50	5 50		10 00			
				116 88	9 12	29 87	37 88	13 96	17 72	8 33
	30	Balance c/d		8 12						
125 00				125 00						
8 12	1/7	Balance b/d								
141 88	1	Cash book (reimbursement)								
150 00										

Posting from the petty cash book to the ledger:

Nominal Ledger: G Harrison

Date		Folio	Debit £	Credit £	Balance £
Office Refreshments a/c					
June 1	Balance				20.15 Dr
30	Petty Cash	PC 42	9.12		29.27
Packing Materials a/c					
June 1	Balance				50.10 Dr
30	Petty Cash	PC 42	29.87		79.87
Travel Expenses a/c					
June 1	Balance				40.06 Dr
30	Petty Cash	PC 42	37.88		77.94
Postage and Telegrams a/c					
June 1	Balance				15.24 Dr
30	Petty Cash	PC 42	13.96		29.20
Sundry Expenses a/c					
June 1	Balance				12.20 Dr
30	Petty Cash	PC 42	17.72		29.92
VAT a/c					
June 1	Balance				12.15 Dr
	Petty Cash	PC 42	8.33		20.48
Petty Cash Control a/c					
June 1	Balance				125.00 Dr
30	Petty Cash	PC42		116.88	8.12
July 1	Receipts	CBR5	141.88		150.00

NOTE:
- Each of the analysis columns identifying the petty cash expenses is posted from the credit side of the Petty Cash Book to the debit side of its respective ledger account.
- The petty cash control account identifies the total petty cash expenditure, £116.88 and the cash book reimbursement of £141.88 to make up the petty cash float back to £150.

Computerised Accounts

A computerised cash book was included in Chapter 12 and the same principle applies to entering details in the petty cash book. For entering money from the bank account to petty cash a bank transfer can be made using the *bank menu*. In the case below a sum of £50 was transferred from the bank current account N120 to the petty cash account N123.

When entering expenditure details the menu *bank* is selected then click on *payments* making sure the correct nominal account code of N123 is used for petty cash. Voucher numbers and details are entered along with the correct expenditure nominal code, for example N135 is used for postage account and N130 petrol is posted to motor expenses account.

Computerised Accounts: typical printouts of the petty cash book and ledger accounts

NOMINAL LEDGER - petty cash

Account		Name			Account Balance		
N123		Petty Cash Book			45.34 Dr		

Trans	Type	Date	Ref	VAT	Ledger / details	Value	Debit	Credit
66	J	05/03	100023	T9	N120 bank/petty cash	50.00	50.00	
71	CP	06/03	PCV23	T1	N130 petrol	7.50		7.50
72	CP	06/03	PCV 24	T2	N135 stamps	1.70		1.70
73	CP	06/03	PCV 25	T2	N135 parcel postage	3.90		3.90
74	CP	07/03	PCV 26	T1	N142 cleaning	10.20		10.20
75	CP	07/03	PCV 27	T1	N150 telephone	5.40		5.40
76	CP	07/03	PCV 28	T2	N135 stamps	3.90		3.90
77	CP	07/03	PCV 29	T0	N137 tea, coffee	2.20		2.20
78	CP	08/03	PCV 30	T1	N139 bleach, etc	2.96		2.96
79	CP	08/03	PCV 31	T1	N142 cleaning	12.00		12.00
80	J	08/03	100028	T9	N120 bank/petty cash	50.00	50.00	
81	CP	08/03	PCV 32	T2	N135 stamps	4.90		4.90
					Totals		100.00	54.66
					Balance		45.34 DEBIT	

Account		Name			Account Balance		
N135		Postages Account			62.95 Dr		

Trans	Type	Date	Ref	VAT	Ledger / details	Value	Debit	Credit
04	J	01/03	Balance	T9	O/balance	48.55	48.55	
72	CP	06/03	PCV 24	T2	N123 petty cash	1.70	1.70	
73	CP	06/03	PCV 25	T2	N123 petty cash	3.90	3.90	
76	CP	07/03	PCV 28	T2	N123 petty cash	3.90	3.90	
81	CP	08/03	PCV 32	T2	N123 petty cash	4.90	4.90	
					Totals	62.95	62.95	
					Balance		62.95 DEBIT	

NOTE:
All expense accounts exclude VAT because any VAT charged is posted to the VAT account.

KEY POINTS OF THE CHAPTER

Petty cash book:	A separate book from the cash book to record small items of expenses
Petty cash float:	The 'imprest' system where a sum of money is reimbursed back to the original sum or the sum required
Petty cash control:	Check cash unused with vouchers issued to see if it equals the imprest
Petty cash voucher:	A form used as evidence that petty cash has been paid to someone authorised to take it. Any receipts should be attached
VAT:	Receipts with VAT must be retained and the input VAT recorded in the petty cash book
Posting:	Petty cash expenses are posted to the debit side of their corresponding accounts in the nominal ledger
Reimbursement:	The float is reimbursed by debiting the petty cash book and crediting the cash book or the bank account with the sum required
Petty cash control:	Records the total payments credited and the reimbursements debited to make up the petty cash float in the nominal ledger.

QUESTIONS

1. Why is the petty cash book part of the accounting system?
2. What kind of procedures should be in place to ensure the petty cash book is secure?
3. How would handling petty cash be useful to a trainee accounts person?
4. The following petty cash transactions from the accounts of Harry Palmer for the month of May are shown below. Your analysis columns should be for cleaning, stationery, postage and sundry expenses. The agreed amount of the imprest is £100.

		£
1	Balance of cash on hand	14.50
3	Cash received from cashier to make up total of imprest	
3	Postage	2.85
4	Envelopes	1.40
5	Cleaner's wages	5.65
6	Bus fares	2.50
7	Gummed paper	1.30
10	Postage stamps	2.60
11	Cleaner's wages	5.65
12	Rail fares	4.82
13	Cleaning materials	1.85
14	Typing paper	12.26
18	Cleaner's wages	6.65
19	Paper clips, etc.	1.60
20	Postage	1.80
24	Typing paper	14.75
25	Cleaner's wages	5.65
28	Bus fares	2.28
31	Cleaning materials	2.14
31	Parcel post	1.10
31	Received cash from cashier to make up total of the float.	

Required:

a) Prepare the petty cash book for Harry Palmer for the month of May and balance as at the end of the month.

b) Post the totals of the analysis columns to the nominal ledger and commence each petty cash expense with a 'nil' balance on 1 May.

5. Prepare a Petty Cash Book from the balance brought down in question 4. The float is £100. You will need to add *two* further columns: packing materials and VAT. Transactions for the month of June were as follows:

		£
June	1 Computer paper, pencils	10.50
	2 Taxi fares	5.75
	3 Postages, telegrams	6.55
	5 Cleaner's wages	5.65
	7 Bus fares	2.25
	10 Miscellaneous stationery	15.15
	12 Packing materials	8.00
	VAT	1.20
	16 Cleaner's wages	8.21

		£
17	Taxi fares	11.50
18	Received a further £50 to increase float to £150	
19	Packing materials	16.00
	VAT	2.40
20	Computer paper	12.00
21	Parcel post	4.50
23	Postage	6.75
25	Cleaner's wages	8.21
26	Packing materials	8.00
	VAT	1.20
28	Pens, pencils etc.	2.25
July 1	Received cash from cashier to make up the float	

6.   ABC Co uses its bank for all significant receipts and payments of cash. All cash payments under £10 come out of the petty cash. The imprest is £100 and is reimbursed every month by a cheque payment from the Cash Book.

The headings used by ABC Co are as follows: cleaning, travelling expenses, stationery, Post Office, refreshments, general and VAT. The balance of the petty cash on 30 June was £15.65. The firm uses the voucher system and all vouchers begin from No. 1 on the first of the month. The transactions for July were as follows:

		£
July 2	Reimbursement from Cash Book	
2	Cleaning materials	1.50
	VAT	0.22
3	Stamps and parcel post	8.68
6	Window cleaning	6.00
	VAT	0.90
8	Pens, pencils, computer paper	10.00
	VAT	1.50
11	Newspapers	0.85
12	Tea, coffee, and sugar	3.76
15	Envelopes, ribbons	2.40
	VAT	0.36
19	Telegrams	4.60
20	Taxi fares	3.85
23	Charity donations	1.50
27	Bus fares	4.50
28	Window cleaning	6.00
	VAT	0.90
29	Floor polish and dusters	2.80
	VAT	0.42

Required:
a)   Draw up a Petty Cash Book using the appropriate columns. Bring the imprest balance up to date on 2 July.
b)   Enter the above transactions and balance the book on 31 July. Bring down the balance and make the appropriate reimbursement on 1 August.
c)   Post the analysis totals to the nominal ledger on 31 July, commencing with a 'nil' balance for each of the petty cash expenses on 1 July.

7. The following details refer to J Smith's petty cash. He keeps the amount of imprest at £50 per
    month. The balance on hand, 1 January, is £8.42 and the necessary reimbursement is made.
    VAT is at 15%. [3/23 of price when inclusive of VAT].

			£
January 7	Voucher No. 1	Petrol and oil	8.05 (VAT inc.)
10	2	Stationery	4.50 (VAT inc.)
14	3	Cleaning materials	2.20 (VAT inc.)
25	4	Refreshment supplies	4.85
26	5	Postage stamps	3.00
27	6	Envelopes and typing Paper	7.60(VAT inc.)
29	7	Cleaning materials	2.80(VAT inc.)
30	8	Petrol and oil	7.20(VAT inc.)

Required:
Draw up a Petty Cash Book for J Smith and balance on 31 January.

8. Gill Graham runs her petty cash on the imprest system, having a float of £200 per month. She
    uses analysis columns for VAT, postage, travel, cleaning, refreshments, stationery and sundries.
    At the end of August, she had £28.75 to carry forward to the new month. During the first three
    weeks of September, the following transactions occurred:
    September

1	Enter the balance brought down from August in the Petty Cash Book.
2	Cashier reimburses Gill to bring up to required float.
3	Purchased stamps £12.50.
5	Rail fares to Bristol, £13.60.
6	Typing paper, biros, etc., £14.10 (inc. VAT 17.5%).
8	New kettle and cups £18.80 (inc. VAT 17.5%).
11	Window cleaner £10.50.
12	Postage stamps £8.75.
15	Taxi expenses £7.80.
16	Repairs to typewriter £12.80 + VAT 17.5%.
18	Window cleaner, £10.50.
20	Donation for Poppy Appeal £2.00.
20	Milk money £6.25.
21	Tea, coffee, etc., £4.80.

    For the remainder of September, there are eight further vouchers to record.

Required:
a) Enter the above petty cash transactions in the Petty Cash Book for Gill Graham.
   and record the remaining eight petty cash vouchers overleaf.
b) Balance the petty cash book as at 30 September.
   Post the individual expense columns to the nominal ledger.

PETTY CASH VOUCHER	Folio: *13* Date: *22/9*	
For what required	Amount	
	£	p
Stationery items	*1*	*80*
VALUE ADDED TAX	*0*	*32*
	2	*12*
Signature: Authorisation:		

PETTY CASH VOUCHER	Folio: *17* Date: *27/9*	
For what required	Amount	
	£	p
Taxi fare	*11*	*40*
VALUE ADDED TAX	*-*	*-*
	11	*40*
Signature: Authorisation:		

PETTY CASH VOUCHER	Folio: *14* Date: *24/9*	
For what required	Amount	
	£	p
Coffee, Tea, etc.	*4*	*24*
VALUE ADDED TAX	*-*	*-*
	4	*24*
Signature: Authorisation:		

PETTY CASH VOUCHER	Folio: *18* Date: *28/9*	
For what required	Amount	
	£	p
Magazines, newspapers	*3*	*40*
VALUE ADDED TAX	*-*	*-*
	3	*40*
Signature: Authorisation:		

PETTY CASH VOUCHER	Folio: *15* Date: *25/9*	
For what required	Amount	
	£	p
Milk	*8*	*20*
VALUE ADDED TAX	*-*	*-*
	8	*20*
Signature: Authorisation:		

PETTY CASH VOUCHER	Folio: *19* Date: *28/9*	
For what required	Amount	
	£	p
Stamps, envelope	*6*	*86*
Cards	*1*	*50*
VALUE ADDED TAX	*-*	*-*
	8	*36*
Signature: Authorisation:		

PETTY CASH VOUCHER	Folio: *16* Date: *27/9*	
For what required	Amount	
	£	p
Window cleaning	*10*	*50*
VALUE ADDED TAX	*-*	*-*
	10	*50*
Signature: Authorisation:		

PETTY CASH VOUCHER	Folio: *20* Date: *30/9*	
For what required	Amount	
	£	p
Stationery	*4*	*24*
VALUE ADDED TAX	*0-*	*74*
	4	*98*
Signature: Authorisation:		

Chapter 15

Capital and Revenue Expenditure

INTRODUCTION

A business spends money on two types of expenditure. One concerns the purchase of fixed assets such as vehicles and equipment, and the other concerns money spent on running the business with expenses such as purchases of stock, wages and salaries, light and heat, stationery, etc.

Capital expenditure
Capital expenditure, therefore, is money which is spent on fixed assets or money spent on improving their value. For example, if a second-hand vehicle was purchased for £3,500, and later required a new engine costing £1,000 which was seen as better than the one before, then the value of the vehicle under fixed assets should be £4,500. This is capital expenditure rather than revenue expenditure.

Revenue expenditure
On the other hand, all aspects of expenditure in running the vehicle for business purposes, including petrol, repairs and maintenance, car tax and insurance, depreciation of the vehicle, replacement tyres, etc., would be treated as revenue expenditure. That is, it would be seen as part of the day-to-day running of the business.

Capital expenditure on fixed assets must also include any cost which is involved in bringing their value in to the business. If premises were purchased, the value capitalised would include solicitor's and estate agent's fees, land registry fees and any other cost involved with the purchase. If new plant and machinery were to be installed in a factory, the capital cost would include the carriage of it to the premises and all costs in the installation.

In the financial statements all capital expenditure is listed in the balance sheet under fixed assets, whereas all revenue expenditure appears as expenses in the trading and profit and loss account. Any unsold stock is also entered under current assets.

It is extremely important, therefore, to make the distinction between these two expenditure types, otherwise serious errors will arise when the financial statements are prepared. For example, if machinery was purchased for £5,000 and it was wrongly treated as purchases under revenue expenditure, this would have the effect of under-stating the value of fixed assets and over-stating the value of chargeable expenses. Result: profits are under-stated and fixed assets are under-stated. The Inland Revenue would also be displeased and would require an adjustment to the accounts because it would reduce the tax payable on profits.

Cableduct Ltd
An article recently published in the *Daily Mail,* 'The roof falls in and upsets the taxman', is a case in point. The problem concerned the repairing of a roof and whether or not it was repairs or improvement to the roof, the subtle difference being that it can cost companies many more thousands of pounds in the payment of tax.

According to the Inland Revenue, repairs to fixed assets are allowable against tax whereas improvements to them are not. A company called Cableduct fell foul of the tax office when they had part of their factory roof replaced. In this case, the old roof was made of asbestos and corrugated iron and its replacement was excellent metal sheeting. The tax office said that this was an improvement in roof covering because the roof had a different covering from that of the original. In other words, it should have been treated as a capital item, not revenue expenditure.

This would have been a big blow to Cableduct because the roof cost £55,000. It was very old and although they had temporary repairs, the lot had to come down and be replaced. Thus the problem was the tax office regarding something to be replaced in its entirety as improvement and therefore a capital cost.

At the time, the company was struggling hard to break even and the tax office's decision was an additional burden it could have done without. The accountants of the company argued that a roof was only part of a building and that profile metal sheeting was not available when the original roof was built.

Fortunately for Cableduct, their accountants won the case, saving the company £13,750 in tax. The purchase of fixed assets is made on the assumption that they will benefit the business over a number of accounting periods, whereas when money is spent on day-to-day expenses their value is consumed within the accounting period. There are some exceptions to this, such as painting or repairs and maintenance of buildings that could last far longer than the financial period. However, as a general rule this is treated as revenue expenditure.

Check the table below to see how capital and revenue expenditure maybe treated:

Capital and revenue expenditure

Transaction	Revenue expenditure Profit and loss account	Capital expenditure Balance sheet
1 New computer £2,500		2,500
2 Installation of computer £1,000		1,000
3 Gas and electricity £450	450	
4 Modernisation of premises £8,000		8,000
5 Office buildings painted (every 5 years) £6,000	6,000	
6 Wages and salaries £17,500	17,500	
7 New vehicle for manager £9,500		9,500
8 Stock for resale £3,200	3,200	
9 Motor expenses £800	800	
10 Purchase of land £20,000		20,000
11 Solicitor's fees for purchase £550		550
12 Running costs of computer £600	600	

The distinction between capital and revenue income
When fixed assets are sold, the sale value of them is referred to as *capital income*. The profit or loss from the disposal of them will depend on how much they are sold for and this will be recorded in the profit and loss account. If a profit on the sale of a fixed asset is made:

Other revenue:
profit on sale of fixed asset
If a loss is made on the sale:
Expenses:
loss on sale of fixed asset.

Revenue income refers to the normal trading activities of the business when it sells its goods or services, including further income from rent, interest, commission received, etc.

KEY POINTS OF THE CHAPTER

Capital expenditure: Funds spent on the purchase or improvement of fixed assets, for example, premises, equipment, motor vehicles, etc.

Revenue expenditure: Funds spent on day-to-day costs, for example, wages, advertising purchases, rent, etc.

Capital income: Sale of fixed assets above book value

Capital loss: Sale of fixed assets below book value

Revenue income: Income from normal trading activities, that is, sales

QUESTIONS

1.   Classify the following items as to whether they are capital or revenue expenditure:
   a)   The purchase of a new IBM computer for the office.
   b)   Cost of software for the use of the new computer.
   c)   Cost of computer paper.
   d)   A refit of the stockroom with new shelving.
   e)   The payment of gas and electricity bill.
   f)   The purchase of stock for resale.
   g)   Discounts allowed on the sale of stock.
   h)   The acquisition of a new motor vehicle for the supervisor's use.
   i)   The road tax and insurance of the vehicle.
   j)   The repairs and maintenance of the motor vehicle.
   k)   The cost of new floppy disks for the use of the computer.
   l)   The complete decoration of the offices to last a number of years.

2.   In the setting-up of a new business for Jack Ramsgate, classify the following between capital and revenue expenditure:
   a)   The purchase price of premises.
   b)   The estate and solicitor's fees.
   c)   The cost of a computer system.
   d)   The cost of delivery charges and installation fees of the new computer.
   e)   The cost of training of personnel on the computer system.
   f)   Running repairs to the computer.
   g)   Oil and petrol for the motor vehicle.
   h)   An extension built on the premises.
   i)   The extension is painted on completion.
   j)   The extension is repainted six months later.
   k)   Improved roofing of the premises is installed two years later.
   l)   The cost of an advertising campaign which is expected to benefit a number of accounting periods.

3.   a)   Why is it important to make the distinction between capital and revenue costs as those stated in the two previous questions?
   b)   If the cost of a computer, £2,800, was recorded in the purchases account and the cost of the vehicle insurances (£480) was recorded in the motor vehicles account, what effect, if any, would it have on the final account?

Chapter 16

The Trial Balance, Journal and Suspense Accounts

INTRODUCTION

The trial balance is used to check the arithmetical accuracy of the double-entry system. At frequent intervals, ledger account balances are listed to see if total debits equal total credits. If the trial balance fails to balance, the ledger accounts need to be checked to locate the errors and to correct them. The trial balance is not a fool-proof system because some types of error will not be disclosed:

- Errors of compensation
- Errors of principle
- Errors of omission
- Errors of commission
- Errors of original entry
- Errors of reverse entry.

The following entries are examples of errors made in the ledger where the use of a trial balance has failed to disclose them.

An error of compensation
This refers to an error where the *same* mistake has been made to both sides of a transaction.

8 June: A cheque of £451 was received from a debtor, T Smith, but was entered incorrectly as £415 in the records:

Entry: Debit Cash Book £415
                 Credit Smith account (Sales Ledger) £415

Both debit and credit entries have recorded the same error and the trial balance would fail to disclose it and therefore would still balance.
Correction of error:
                 Debit Cash Book £36
                 Credit Smith account   £36
This makes up the under-stated £415 to the correct £451.

An error of principle
This refers to an error where a transaction has been posted to the wrong group of accounts. An asset account incorrectly posted as an expense is a good example.

10 June: Office equipment bought on credit from ABC Suppliers Ltd, at £2,500, was incorrectly posted to the purchases account instead of office equipment:

Entry: Debit Purchases account £2,500
                 Credit ABC Suppliers Ltd £2,500
Correction of error:
                 Debit Office Equipment account £2,500
                 Credit Purchases account £2,500
This will clear the over-stated purchases of £2,500 and correctly increase the asset by £2,500.

An error of omission
This refers to an error where a transaction has been omitted altogether – a sales or purchase invoice mislaid, a gas or electricity bill neglected or missing. No transaction would be entered in the books and the trial balance would fail to disclose the omission and still balance, of course.

14 June: A sales invoice £235 inclusive of VAT to J Jackson had been misplaced and no entries were made in the books:
Entry: Debit J Jackson account (Sales Ledger) £235
                Credit Sales account £200, VAT account £35
This is the correction of error because there was no previous entry.

An error of commission
This refers to an error where a transaction has been posted to the wrong account, but to the same group of accounts – a nominal account like a gas bill incorrectly posted to another nominal account like office expenses. The trial balance would still balance because both are debit entries to the expense account.
26 June: A gas bill of £185 had been incorrectly entered in office expenses instead of light and heat account:
Entry: Debit Office Expenses account £185
                Credit Cash Book £185
Correction of error:
                Debit Light and Heat account £185
                Credit Office Expenses account £185
This clears the over-stated office expenses by £185 and correctly increases the light and heat account by £185.

An error of original entry
This refers to an error which has been made on an original document, such as an invoice or credit note which may have omitted or miscalculated something. The trial balance would still balance because the wrong figures would be used for both debit and credit entries.

30 June: An invoice for £380 + VAT sent to F Jones, a customer where VAT had been calculated at 15% instead of 17.5%:
Entry: Debit F Jones £380 + VAT £57 = £437.000
                Credit Sales £380 , VAT £57
Correction of error:
                Debit F Jones £9.50
                Credit VAT £9.50
VAT had to be increased by £9.5, 17.5% of £380 = £66.50.

An error of reverse entry
This error refers to making an entry the opposite way round to what it should be.

30 June: If cash sales £480 had been entered on the credit side of the cash book.
Entry: Debit Sales £480
                Credit Bank £480

Correction of error:
                Debit Bank £960
                Credit Sales £960
Doubling the sum of £480 then provides the correct balance in each account.

The location of errors

All these types of error will **not** be disclosed by the trial balance because both debit and credit entries are equal and therefore the total columns will also be equal. If the trial balance fails to balance, then the error or errors must be located and correcting entries made. It may be necessary to comb through the ledgers carefully to check for any arithmetical inaccuracies or any obvious double entry error (for example, posting two debits or two credits for the same transaction).

The journal

The journal is used for those transactions that are normally outside the scope of the other subsidiary books. When the book-keeping system was in its early stages of development, the journal acted as the only subsidiary book in use. All transactions were entered in the journal prior to ledger posting. Later on, as the book-keeping system developed, it was found that the use of the journal as the only book of original entry was inadequate. There were so many repetitious entries to be made that separate subsidiary books were soon in use.

The journal has now a different role. It is left with the function of *providing some original entry for those miscellaneous types of transaction* that do not quite 'fit in' to the other subsidiary books. The journal is ideal to use when making correction of errors.

The previous six errors have been journalised as:

Journal		Debit	Credit
June		£	£
8	Bank	36	
	T Smith		36
	Error of compensation, £451 cheque entered as £415		
10	Office equipment	2,500	
	Purchases		2,500
	Error of principle, asset recorded as an expense		
14	J Jackson	235	
	Sales		200
	VAT		35
	Error of omission, invoice No. 2176 had been omitted		
26	Light & heat	185	
	Office expenses		185
	Error of commission, gas bill entered in office expenses		
30	F Jones	9.50	
	VAT		9.50
	Error of original entry, sales VAT charged at 15%, instead of 17.5%		
30	Bank (cash book)	960	
	Sales		960
	Error of reverse entry, cash sales £480 entered as debit in bank		

Error correction: sales ledger

	Folio	Dr £	Cr £	Balance £
T Smith account				
June 1 Balance				451 Dr
2 Bank	CB 5		415	36
8 Bank	J2		36	0
J Jackson account				
June 1 Balance				50 Dr
14 Sales	J2	235		285
F Jones account				
June 1 Balance				120 Dr
15 Sales, VAT		437		557
30 VAT	J2	9.5		566.50

Error correction: nominal ledger

	Folio	Dr £	Cr £	Balance £
Office Equipment account				
June 1 Balance				1,000 Dr
10 Purchases	J2	2,500		3,500
Purchases account				
June 1 Balance				2,850 Dr
10 Office equipment	J2		2,500	350
Light and heat account				
June 1 Balance				350 Dr
26 Office expenses	J2	185		535
Office Expenses account				
June 1 Balance				595 Dr
26 Light and heat	J2		185	410
VAT account				
June 1 Balance				40 Cr
14 Sales	J2		35	75
15 Sales			57	132
30 Sales	J2		9.5	141.50
Sales account				
June 1 Balance				590 Cr
14 Jackson	J2		200	790
15 Jones			380	1,170
30 Bank		480		690
30 Bank	J2		960	1650

The journal is commonly used in the following circumstances:

- The correction of errors;
- the opening entries in a new accounting period;
- the transfer of balances between accounts including revenue and expenses to trading and profit and loss;
- the writing-off of bad debts;
- the purchase or sale of fixed assets;
- providing adjustments to the final accounts such as depreciation, accruals, pre-payments, provision for bad debts;
- making any other adjustments to accounts which are outside the scope of other subsidiary books, for example, transfer of balances from one account to another.

Examples of journal entries recorded on 31 December:

- The writing off of a bad debt. Harry Smith for £600;
- providing for depreciation of motor vehicles £450 for the year ended;
- the purchase of a motor vehicle on credit £7,800 from Ford Motors Ltd.
- contra entry of F Baggins £950 to be transferred to his sales ledger account from his purchase ledger account.

Journal		Debit	Credit
		£	£
December			
31	Bad debts	600	
	Harry Smith (debtors control)		600
	Smith written off as bad due to bankruptcy,		
	Debtors control also credited		
31	Profit & loss account	450	
	Provision for depreciation of vehicles		450
	Motor vehicles depreciated 25% per annum		
31	Motor vehicles	7,800	
	Ford Motors Ltd.		7,800
	Purchased on credit over 5 years, invoice 44765		
31	F Baggins (purchase ledger)	950	
	F Baggins (sales ledger)		950
	Contra entry : transfer of purchase debt to customer's		
	account in the sales ledger		

The suspense account and the correction of errors

The purpose of using a suspense account is to balance the trial balance temporarily. When errors are made which produce an incorrect trial balance because the totals disagree, a suspense account may be entered in the trial balance by inserting the difference between the trial balance totals. A suspense account is opened in the nominal ledger and is written off when the error or errors are located. The journal is used to make the appropriate corrections.

Example:

Extract of trial balance taken from the books of G Harrison 30 June

Account	Dr £	Cr £
Sales		18,600
Purchases	12,500	
Furniture and fittings	4,200	
General expenses	150	
Discount		35
Returns	750	
	87,160	86,500
Suspense		660
	87,160	87,160

The following errors were located in the books of G Harrison:
- sales were under-cast by £100 in cash sales when posted to sales account;
- general expenses of £40 had not been posted from the Cash Book to the nominal ledger;
- the purchase of furniture of £300 was wrongly debited to the purchases account;
- discount received of £100 had not been posted to the discount account in the nominal ledger.
- returns outward £250 had in error been recorded as returns inward.

Required:
- Open a suspense account in the nominal ledger on 30 June with an opening balance of £660 Credit.
- Make the appropriate journal entries to correct the errors.
- Adjust the accounts in Harrison's nominal ledger.
- If Harrison had a net profit of £8,500 on 30 June, how would the above errors affect net profit?

Solution:

Journal		Debit	Credit
		£	£
June			
30	Suspense	100	
	Sales		100
	Sales understated in nominal ledger		
	General expenses	40	
	Suspense		40
	Double entry not completed		
	Furniture & fittings	300	
	Purchases		300
	Error of principle		
	Suspense	100	
	Discount received		100
	Double entry not completed		
	Suspense	500	
	Returns inward		250
	Returns outward		250
	Returns out posted as returns in		

Harrison's nominal ledger

	Folio	Dr £	Cr £	Balance £
Suspense account				
June 30 Trial balance			660	660 Cr
Sales		100		560
General Expenses			40	600
Discount		100		500
Returns		500		0
Sales account				
June 30 Balance				18,600 Cr
Suspense			100	18,700
General Expenses account				
June 30 Balance				150 Dr
Suspense		40		190
Furniture and Fittings account				
June 30 Balance				4,200 Dr
Purchases		300		4,500
Purchases account				
June 30 Balance				12,500 Dr
Furniture and fittings			300	12,200
Discount Received account				
June 30 Balance				35 Cr

Suspense	100	135

Returns account		
June 30 Balance		750 Dr
Suspense	500	250

How profit is affected

If the trading and profit and loss account had already been prepared before the errors were located, the correction of the above would have changed the value of net profit:

Net profit (before errors)			£8,500
Add	Sales (under-cast)	£100	
	Discount received	£100	
	Purchases	£300	
	Returns	£500	£1000
			£9,500
Less	General expenses	£40	(40)
Net profit (after errors)			£9,460

Computerised Accounts

The setting up of journal entries is found in the nominal ledger menu and clicking onto the journal function. The correct nominal ledger code is used to display the name of the account required. The debits must equal the credits, if it does not, then an error has been made. Usually the balance between debits and credits is shown on the screen and when it is at zero then the two columns equal. The correction of errors can be made using this function.

Computerised Accounts: journal entries

Date: 01/03/20-
Time: 10.55
Period: Month 1

JOURNAL ENTRIES

N/C	Name of account	Debit	Credit
N120	Bank	1342.50	
N300	Premises	45200.00	
N305	Equipment	3455.00	
N310	Motor vehicles	10340.00	
N312	O/stock	1560.00	
N320	Debtors	2874.50	
N330	Creditors		3845.80
N350	Bank loan		8900.00
N355	VAT		1328.20
N360	Mortgage on premises		29243.00
N360	Capital		21455.00
	Totals	64772.00	64772.00

Opening entries in new accounting period

Note: the computerised journal is virtually looks the same as the manual system

KEY POINTS OF THE CHAPTER

Trial balance:	An arithmetical check of the double entry system
Error of compensation:	Same error that affects both debit and credit entries
Error of principle:	Error where transaction posted to wrong group of accounts
Error of omission:	Transaction completely omitted from books
Error of commission:	Error where transaction posted to wrong account but correct group
Error of original entry:	Error on original document
Error of reverse entry:	Double entry the opposite way round
Location of errors:	Investigation of where errors could have been made in the accounting system
Journal:	Book of prime entry to record miscellaneous transactions eg correcting errors
Suspense account:	A temporary device to ensure trial balance balances until errors located and corrected
Profit adjustment:	Where errors have affected profit calculation and profit amended
Computerised accounts:	Using a computer program to input data

QUESTIONS

1. a) If the trial balance balances does this mean that the nominal ledger is correct? Explain briefly.
    b) Why is the journal used in relation to errors?

2. a) If a suspense account was listed in the trial balance, what kind of errors could be disclosed?
    b) What kind of errors could be made when using a computerised system of accounting?

3. Make the appropriate journal entries to correct the following errors:

▪ an amount of £300 had been included in the salaries account for a job which involved repairing the proprietor's garage (J Jones);
▪ a cheque of £350 from P Smith had been credited to R Smith in error;
▪ the purchase of a computer for the office staff, costing £925, had been posted to the purchases account;
▪ an invoice for rates owing to the local District Council for £178 had been mislaid.

4. On 1 January, Tom Jones had the following assets and liabilities:

	£
Premises	20,000
Vehicle	500
Equipment	2,100
Stock	1,860
Debtors	675
Mortgage on premises	15,000
Bank (overdrawn)	450
Creditors	1,155

You are asked to prepare an opening journal entry of 1 January showing Tom Jones's assets, liabilities and capital as at this date. Note that capital is assets less liabilities.

5. An extract of Harry's trial balance:

	Debit £	Credit £
Suspense account		247
	20,534	20,534

Subsequently the following errors were found:
- goods £285 to R Smith had been posted to J Smith in error
- accounting equipment sold for £600 credited to sales account
- cash discount of £8 allowed to J Jones and credited to him, but no entry was made to the discount account
- the addition of the sales day book was under-cast by £200
- salaries accrued £55 at the end of the previous year had not been brought forward to the new accounting period
- a sales invoice of £275 had been misplaced. No entries had been made

Required:
a) Journal entries to correct the books.
b) The suspense account entries.

6. The accounts of a business were extracted on 30 June as follows:

	£	£
Bank account	1,245	
Capital account		34,900
Stock	3,400	
Premises	20,000	
Furniture and fittings	900	
Wages and salaries	15,400	
Office expenses	1,060	
Purchases	13,900	
Sales		21,900
Drawings	3,800	
Debtors	2,600	
Creditors		3,230
	62,305	60,030

It was subsequently discovered that the following errors had been made in the listing of the balances:
- The bank account was overdrawn £1,245
- A sum of £200 drawn out by the owner for his personal use had been included under 'office expenses'
- Purchases on credit totalling £1,000 had not passed through the books
- The balance of the discount allowed account, £160, had been omitted
- £2,400 included under wages and salaries and £600 included under purchases represented extensions to premises
- Office cash of £55 had been omitted from the list of balances

Required:
a) A suspense account in the ledger.
b) A corrected trial balance for the month ending 30 June.

7. You work as a senior accounts clerk for R Underwood, and have been assisting in the preparation of the final accounts. The trial balance as at 30 April did not agree, and a suspense account was opened for the difference. The following errors have now been traced:

    - The total of the returns outward book, £248, had not been posted to the ledger
    - An invoice received from a supplier, A Biggs, for £200 had been mislaid, so entries for this transaction had not been made
    - A payment for repairs to vehicles, £72, had been entered in the vehicle repairs account as £70
    - When balancing the account of G Bradford in the ledger, the debit balance had been brought down in error as £28, instead of £82
    - £100 received from the sale of office equipment had been entered in the sales account
    - A private purchase of £230 by R Underwood had been included in the business purchases
    - The purchase day book was understated by £92

    Required:
    a) Show the requisite journal entries to correct the errors.
    b) Write up the suspense account showing the correction of the errors
    c) If the originally calculated profit was £10,500, show your calculation of the correct figure.
    d) State four types of errors that do not affect the agreement of the trial balance, giving an example of each.

8. Hawkers & Peters have produced a trial balance for the year ended 31 March, which does not balance. A suspense account of £507 Cr was opened for the difference. An examination of the firm's books disclosed the following errors:
    - An invoice from R Pitman, amounting to £300 for goods purchased, has been omitted from the purchase day book and posted direct to the purchases account in the nominal ledger but not entered in the purchase ledger
    - The sales day book has been under-cast by £450
    - Discount allowed for the month of March, amounting to £242, has not been posted to the nominal ledger
    - A cheque, amounting to £540, for the purchase of furniture and fittings had been correctly entered in the Cash Book but entered in the nominal ledger account as £450
    - A sales invoice, amounting to £730, sent to J Knight, has been omitted from the books completely
    - A payment, amounting of £233, for heating and lighting had been correctly entered in the Cash Book but posted, in error, to the motor expenses account at £322
    - An invoice regarding the purchase of a new printer included £180 in respect of computer stationery; the total invoice value had been posted to the equipment account.

    Required:
    a) Write up the journal entries, where necessary, to correct the errors.
    b) Draw up the suspense account.
    c) If the net profit for the year excluding the seven errors was £22,031, produce a statement showing the corrected profit figure.

9. The draft trial balance of James McLippie & Son as at 30 April did not agree and the difference was posted to a suspense account with a debit balance £1,352. Subsequent investigation of the accounts revealed the following errors:

    - The discount received column in the cash book had been over-cast by £100

- J Stanley, a customer, had not been credited with £8 discount although this had been correctly entered in the Cash Book
- The sales book had been over-cast by £900
- An invoice made out (correctly) for £45 in respect of sales made to H Purcell had been recorded in the sales book as £54 (this is quite apart from the error in the sales book referred to above)
- The purchases book had been under-cast by £360
- Goods returned from J Blow, a customer, had been recorded in the returns inward book as £108; in fact, the value of the goods returned had been subsequently agreed with the customer at £88 but no adjustment had been made in the accounting records
- VAT (at 15%) amounting to £15 collected on cash sales of £100 had not been entered in the VAT column in the Cash Book; instead the sales had been recorded in the cash column as £115

Required:
a) Prepare journal entries to show how the above errors would be corrected.
b) The suspense account entries.
c) If the profit had been calculated at £13,564 before the errors were disclosed, what is the profit for the year after correcting the above errors?

[Association of Accounting Technicians]

10. The trial balance of J. Sharp, a retailer, does not balance. You are asked to look through his accounts and subsequently you do find the errors below. The trial balance of the proprietor on 30 June was as follows:

	Dr £	Cr £
Premises	20,000	
Motor van	500	
Equipment	2,100	
Stock	1,860	
Debtors	675	
Creditors		1,155
Capital, J Sharp		12,500
Bank		455
Sales		35,750
Purchases	20,195	
General expenses	1,250	
Wages	3,970	
Suspense		690
	50,550	50,550

Errors found were:
- A piece of equipment worth £500 had wrongly been posted to purchases account
- A gas bill of £85 had been paid but had not gone through any of the books
- Discount allowed, £68, had not been posted to the ledger
- Sales were under-cast by £800
- A cheque from a debtor (R Smith), £150, had been recorded as £105 in his account but correctly in the corresponding account
- The total from the returns inward account, £87, had not been posted to the ledger

Required:

a) Prepare suitable journal entries to correct the above errors and write up the suspense account.

b) Prepare the corrected trial balance of J Sharp as on 30 June.

c) State which of the above errors would not be found by the trial balance.

FOUNDATION ACCOUNTING

A revision section

1 Write down the accounting equation

2 Briefly explain the principle of double entry

3 How would the following be recorded in the nominal ledger:
Cash sales into bank
Purchased goods on credit from XYZ Ltd.
Owner takes cash for his own use
A debtor pays off his balance outstanding (4 marks)

4 How are transactions processed either on credit terms or by cash through an accounting system to the ledgers?

5 State the posting procedure from the sales journal, including VAT

6 State the posting procedure from the returns outward journal

7 Calculate an invoice that has goods gross £800 less trade discount 30% + VAT

8 Calculate an invoice that has goods gross £1200 less trade discount 25% and offers 5% cash discount for early payment (2 marks)

9 What is the basic rule applied when posting from a cash book to the ledgers?

10 If the total cash paid to creditors was £1860 and discount received was £40 how is this posted to the control account? How is the discount posted? (2 marks)

11 How are the following accounts classified under RECAL:
returns in, returns out, drawings,
discount received, discount allowed and cash (2 marks)

12 When a bank statement arrives from the bank, why does it rarely agree with the business's cash book? (2 marks)

13 Briefly explain the procedure to prepare a bank reconciliation (2 marks)
On a bank statement, which side would record DD's, STO's and bank charges and how would these be recorded in the cash book?

14 Why is it an advantage to use multi-columns in journals and cash book records? (2 marks)

15 Write down two functions of the journal (2 marks)

16 Explain the following briefly:
Error of principle
Error of commission
Error of compensation
Error of original entry (4 marks)

17 Provide two reasons why control accounts are used (2 marks)

18 When using the petty cash system:
How is a reimbursement recorded?
How are analysis columns posted to the ledger?
What kind of evidence is required before giving out petty cash?
What is the difference between petty cash and petty cash expenses? (4 marks)

19 When is the stock account recorded in the ledger?
When stock is purchased or sold or goods returned, which accounts are used? (2 marks)

20 How is a bad debt written off?

21 What is the basic function of a trial balance? Explain why it is not fool-proof (2 marks)

Total = 40 marks

AAT PROCESSING QUESTION

The following transactions take place on 1 June and have yet to be entered in the ledger system.
The bank statement was received on 2 June but contains some items for the bank account relating to 1 June.
You work as an accounts assistant for Motormart Ltd. and have been made responsible for keeping the
ledgers up to date and producing the trial balance. The following entries are for you to process.

Sales invoices sent:

Customer	Total	VAT	Net Sales
	£	£	£
Auto Ltd.	5492	818	4674
Salfords Ltd.	3396	506	2890
Ford Motors Ltd.	6156	917	5239
Other customers	22696	3380	19316
	37740	**5621**	**32119**

Purchase invoices received

Supplier	Total	VAT	Net purchases
	£	£	£
Carmart Ltd.	8371	1247	7124
Lombards Ltd.	7727	1151	6576
Lucas & Co.	5820	867	4953
Other suppliers	12676	1888	10788
	34594	**5153**	**29441**

Credit note issued

Customer	Total	VAT	Net return
	£	£	£
Ford Motors Ltd.	168	25	143

Journal

	Debit	Credit
	£	£
Creditors control account	1450	
Debtors control account		1450

Transfer of balances (relating to other customers/other suppliers)

Cheques issued £

Lombards Ltd.   2817
(full repayment of debt for £2958)
Cash purchases   1363
(inclusive of £203 VAT)

Cheques received £

Ford Motors Ltd.   1472
(full repayment of debt for £1550)

Bank statement received

The only items relating to 1 June were:

Bank interest received	£122
Bank charges	£210

The following balances are available to you at the start of the day on 1 June:

	£
Sales ledger	
Auto Ltd.	24,617
Salfords Ltd.	41,561
Ford Motors Ltd.	27,124
Other customer balances	627,341
Purchase ledger	
Carmart Ltd.	28,413
Lombards Ltd.	56,987
Lucas & Co.	33,792
Other supplier balances	492,853
Nominal ledger	
Purchases	2,652,194
Sales	3,122,786
Returns in	6,225
Bank (debit)	4,120
Bank charges	261
Bank interest received	103
VAT (credit)	71,089
Discount allowed	21,408
Discount received	15,194
Debtors control	720,643
Creditors control	612,045
Other debit account balances	1,431,500
Other credit account balances	1,015,134

Task 1
Draw up the sales and purchase ledger accounts (including other customer and supplier account balances) and balance at the end of the day 1 June.

Task 2
Draw up the nominal ledger accounts and post all relevant data from the prime books. Balance at the end of the day 1 June. Ensure that your sales and purchase ledger totals equal your control account balances.

Task 3
Prepare a trial balance as at 1 June (include other debit and credit balances).

(Association of Accounting Technicians)

PART III SUPPLY INFORMATION FOR MANAGEMENT CONTROL

Chapter 17

The Purpose of Management Information

INTRODUCTION

What does management need to know? They want to know the right information to assist them to make the right decisions about running their business. For example, they would want to know:

- How sales figures were doing.
- Whether production output was up to capacity.
- How much their products cost to make in terms of labour, materials and overheads.
- Whether marketing needs were adequately met.
- Whether they had sufficient money to pay their bills.

A great deal of this information can be obtained from internal accounting records and marketing and sales offices. External information can also be obtained from newspapers, trade journals, government and trade statistics and of course, the Internet.

It's not only the quantity of information that is important, it is also the quality that matters in terms of what is relevant, reliable and timely. Information that is relevant, reliable and up-to-date are three qualities of good management information.

For example, if government statistics estimated that the economy was set to grow by say 3% in the coming year, how would this affect the business? It could mean that the market for their products might increase and therefore they would need to estimate sales and output figures to take this into account when planning their production and marketing figures.

In our economy, there are a wide diversity of different types of businesses which require all kinds of information. Even the sole trader operating a small corner shop must have a knowledge of how sales are moving and the type of costs that his business incurs. In larger organisations and particularly in factories making a whole range of products, it becomes even more important to feed management with how much products cost to produce in order to assist them in making the right decisions at the right time.

In the manufacturing account discussed in Chapter 35, we need to find out the different type of direct and indirect costs which make up the factory cost. From these figures we were able to calculate the factory cost per unit given the output produced. If we add the further indirect costs of the profit and loss account (office and distribution overheads) to the factory cost this will give us the total cost price of a unit. This total cost is known as the absorption cost.

It is essential for management to know how the cost of a product is made up in both direct and indirect costs because it assists them to decide what mark-up of profit could be added in order to arrive at the selling price.

Example, to produce a kitchen table may cost:

	£
Direct costs:	
direct materials (wood)	20.00
direct labour (3 hours x £8 per hour)	24.00
Indirect costs:	
factory overheads	12.50
Factory cost:	56.50
office overheads	21.00
Total cost:	77.50
+ 20% mark up (profit)	15.50
Selling price =	93.00

There is also a need to break down costs into fixed costs and variable costs in order to make further calculations such as finding the break even point in production, that is, the point where all costs are covered and profit is then available at the point above break-even.

This is a marginal costing technique. It for example, the monthly output of tables was 1,000 units, how many must be produced to cover all costs? This is a key factor which management need to know because once the break-even point is passed, profits can be made.
For example, if we assume that all direct costs are variable and all overheads (factory and office) are to be relatively fixed, how can we calculate the break-even point and other key facts?
First of all we need to calculate the *contribution* to profit:

Contribution	=	selling price	-	variable cost	
£49.00	=	£93.00	-	£44.00	(labour & materials)

$$\text{Break-even point} = \frac{\text{fixed costs}}{\text{contribution per unit}}$$

$$\frac{£33,500*}{£49} = 684 \text{ units (rounded up to nearest unit)}$$

This means that at an output of 684 units, all costs will be covered but no profit yet made. However on the next unit, some profit will occur.

* Fixed costs £33.50 X 1000 output

Estimated Profit (based on 1000 units)

$$= (\text{output X contribution}) - \text{fixed costs}$$

1000 X £49   - £33,500 = £15,500

Note that if a profit of £15.50 is made per unit, then an on output of 1000 will produce a profit of £15,500. For each unit above the break-even point, an estimated profit of £49 should be made, that is, the value of contribution. Therefore:
How much estimated profit will be made on 100 units above break-even?   £4,900 (100 X £49)
How much estimated loss will be made on 100 units below break-even?   £4,900 loss
For further information read marginal costing later in this section and also Chapter 36.

The uses of costing

Management need to have all kinds of information at its fingertips so that it can organise and control the organisation both in the short term on a day by day basis and also in the long term where planning and forecasting is involved. The control aspect of costing involves making decisions at various levels. For example, at a supervisory level it may be the factory foreman ensuring that the quality of production is maintained.

At a higher level, the production controller will need to monitor and co ordinate all aspects of production including materials and labour and ensuring that the right products are produced at exactly the right time. At top management level it may be necessary to make a decision as to whether or not to close down a plant because it simply fails to make profits. The type of questions costing helps to answer include the following:

- How much will the new product cost?
- How many units do we need to produce and sell to break even?
- What is the estimated monthly profit on an output of 2,500 units?
- Is it possible to reduce the selling price and still make a profit?
- How many must we sell to cover the advertising campaign?
- Can we afford to employ more labour?
- Can we sell a special order at 25% less than normal selling prices? How do the actual figures for materials and labour compare to those forecast?

Where managers need information, costing helps to provide it. It is not surprising therefore, that cost accounting is sometimes referred to as management accounting because of the information it supplies to help management make better, more informed decisions.

One of the most common costing questions which arises is simply "How much does it cost to make?" This involves costing principles and the techniques or methods used to find out that information. For example, if management wanted to know the full cost of making a specific unit, the technique of absorption costing will be used. If it wanted to know the break-even point of the product, then marginal costing would be used. If management wanted information concerning the future plans of the business in terms of what the costs are planned to be and be able to compare them with what actually happens, then this is the technique of what is called budgetary control.

If it wanted to compare predetermined costs of materials, labour and overheads against actual costs, this is a technique of standing costing. Therefore, whatever the question costing principles exist to help supply the answers to these types of questions.

Cost Information

Absorption Costing	Marginal Costing	Budgeting	Standard Costing

Fig. 17.1 Costing techniques

Absorption costing

A product or service absorbs all the costs in terms of labour, materials and overheads. Both fixed and variable costs are included in absorption. The distinction between these types of cost is important to understand:

Fixed costs such as rent, rates and insurance costs are relatively insensitive to output change. If the number of units produced or sold varied in output, generally speaking, the fixed costs do not change in relation to the level of activity. The technique of absorption costing ensures that a fair proportion of fixed costs are charged to the unit cost of the product.

Variable costs on the other hand are those that are sensitive to output change and do vary with the level of activity. Direct materials and direct labour and other variables such as power will increase if there is greater output or decrease if the output level falls.

With absorption costing all costs are charged to a specific cost unit so that profit can be estimated per unit. For example, the tables on the previous page, were produced at a cost of £77.50 each in terms of labour, materials and overheads. The profit mark up was 20% so that profit per unit is £15.50. If 1,000 tables were produced and sold, the estimated profit would be £15,500.

However, if output were to change, the total cost per unit would also change because of the impact of fixed costs. If output were to increase to say 1,100 tables then the fixed costs would be diluted over a larger number of units making the unit cost less. Management need to consider this key factor when making pricing decisions on the output they produce.

Marginal costing
This refers to variable costs and is really seeking to answer "How much EXTRA cost is involved in producing one more unit". Under this system the cost of a product is linked to the variable costs of production, as the key element of cost. Fixed costs are relatively 'fixed' irrespective of the volume of output. It stands to reason therefore, that the greater the output, the more diluted the fixed costs per unit will-be, enabling the cost of the product to become cheaper (achieving economies of scale).

The relevance of such an approach is seen for example, if a decision is to be made whether or not to accept a special order at a lower selling price than normal. Unless the special order requires more facilities of production, the fixed costs should not be affected too much, only the variable costs. Therefore a special price may well be acceptable.

Budgeting
Budgeting has been described as a management tool to help form future plans. For example, if from market research it becomes known that 1,000 units a month of a particular product can be sold, management can then plan how much it would cost to produce in terms of materials, labour and overheads.

Costing then becomes a key factor of planning for the future. The plan is then used to compare the forecast of results with the actual results when they occur. In this way, a yardstick is provided for management to see if things are going according to their plan. If things do not go as planned, they must find out why and then try to do something about it. This gives management what is called its "budgetary control".

Standard costing
Standard costing is part of the absorption costing technique and assists management in providing predetermined costs that are linked to budgetary control. It will help them control business costs.
Management calculates what each element of cost should be, in terms of materials, labour and overheads and this becomes the *'standard'* cost. The standard cost for a product can therefore be estimated in advance and then be compared with the actual costs when they are incurred. The difference between the standard cost and actual cost is the *'variance'*. For example:

	Standard Cost Per Unit	Actual Cost Per Unit	Variance Per Unit
Direct labour	2.40	2.50	10p Adverse
Direct materials	5.25	5.00	(25p) Favourable
Factory overheads	8.75	9.35	60p Adverse
Administration overheads	12.55	12.90	35p Adverse

For reasons of budgetary control, managers will want to know why the variances occurred. From our example, labour and all overheads were more than planned but materials were 25p less per unit. In this way, costs become more accountable and any corrective action can be taken in those areas where problems such as inefficiency of material or labour might occur.

The analysis of variances is another key element of costing and will assist management in finding out why costs behaved from what they had predicted. If you look at the costs above, where the variance is a plus because actual cost is more than the standard cost, it is referred to as *'adverse'* and where the cost is a minus, it is referred to as *'favourable'* (costs are less than the standard). Therefore, labour and all overhead costs are seen as adverse variances, whereas the materials cost is a favourable variance because it is less than the predicted standard cost.

The reporting of these costs is very significant for management because the performance of a business can be measured against any previous accounting periods as well as the forecast of results with actual results. Management can then discover whether a certain trend is emerging and if costs are being maintained and controlled.

The coding of costs
In modern industry where the use of computers is wide-spread, all costs have a number which is used to code and classify the item of expenditure. The type of system used will be determined by the type of organisation that uses it. For example, UNIPART would use an extensive coding system for its stock of materials, having literally thousands of parts to classify. Almost all coding is based on a numerical system whereby the break-down of numbers relate to a specific element of the location, type and description of the item coded. For example:

Code No. 07244501	07	=	Cost Centre – Workshop A:
	24	=	Stationery
	45	=	Stock record cards
	01	=	Revenue Expenditure

This code number 07244501 identifies that the expense of stock record cards has been charged to a cost centre, Workshop A. For example, a specific factory area producing a specific product could be designated a cost centre. Although this appears to look rather tedious, once various costs have been coded then each cost centre can be charged with the appropriate costs to that centre, helping to improve the monitoring and control of various costs to different sections or departments.

Coding should have a basically simple structure so that codes can be logical and easy to follow. It needs to be flexible and capable of adapting to change such as making additions or reductions to the system. Any duplication of numbers and meanings should be prevented. (The following chapter deals with coding in more detail)

Costing methods

Methods of costing are determined by the type of information an organisation needs. For example, if a business was involved in the construction of buildings it would require contract costing. If it was producing large quantities of similar products such as computer parts it may require batch costing methods. If the essence of a job was from specific customers who needed individual aspects of production, then a job costing method is required. If it were producing tins of paint or cans of beer, it would probably use the method of process costing. The main costing methods are:

Cost Information

| Job Costing | Batch Costing | Contract Costing | Process Costing |

Fig. 17.2 Costing methods

Job costing
Used to satisfy individual customers who have their own specifications of what they require. For example, the Royal Navy may want specific pumps or compressors which may require more materials or parts or different measurements than those from the normal run of production.

Batch costing
This method is used to produce quantities of output for similar or identical products. It may be a batch of 50 electric motors all basically identical for a particular customer. To find the unit cost of one motor, the total cost of the batch is divided by the output of the batch. Any waste or scrap units should not be included as part of the unit cost of the batch.

Contract costing
This would normally be a large job, costly to produce and take some reasonable length of time to complete. For example, a builder could be constructing a number of new homes where he would organise a number of individual contractors to organise bricklayers, plumbers, electricians, plasterers, etc. The contract price would usually be estimated in advance and often have built-in clauses that allow the contractor to make any additional charges where conditions changed.

Process costing
This is where a series of continuous production processes take place. At each stage of production, the output of one process goes on to form the input of the next process. If we were producing barrels of beer or gallons of paint, the method of process costing would be ideal. By dividing the costs of one process by the number of units produced, the average cost of that process is calculated. The number of units and the cost of these is then transferred to the following process until all processes are completed finally arriving at the total cost of finished goods with the total output produced.

The classification of costs

Management need to know where money is being spent and by how much. For example, how much would it cost to make a pair of cotton jeans? Direct costs are those directly involved in producing a product including materials and labour costs. Indirect costs are largely production factory overheads such as factory rent, rates and insurance, indirect labour and indirect materials.
Profit and loss expenses are also indirect costs but not factory overheads but rather office or administration overheads.

Example of cost classification: the unit costs of a pair of jeans

	£	£
Direct materials		
cotton	1.40	
zip	.30	
embroidery	.20	1.90
Direct labour		
machinists	.20	
cutters	.15	
assemblers	.05	0.40
prime cost		2.30
Indirect costs		
factory indirect wages	.12	
rent, rates, insurance	.03	
depreciation of plant	.20	
factory general expenses	.10	
factory overheads		.45
production cost		2.75
Profit & loss expenses		
admin. & distribution overheads		1.25
Total cost		**4 .00**

In our example, the unit cost of one pair of cotton jeans is £4.00 in terms of direct and indirect factory costs, £2.75 that represents the production cost. A further £1.25 represents the office overheads. If management wanted to make a profit of 25% on the total cost (a mark-up) the selling price would be £5.00 per unit. (£4.00 + £1 profit). This is an example of cost plus pricing policy that many producers use when determining a selling price considered to be what consumers might be willing to pay.

Direct costs are those more easily traceable to a product. Direct labour and materials can be more readily identified to a unit cost. Indirect costs are more difficult to trace. For example, how much in rent and rates can be identified on a pair of jeans?

There is a real need in industry to classify all costs carefully in their own categories so that the precise nature of what something costs can be estimated in terms labour, materials and overheads. However, nothing is certain in business, not all things go to plan. You might plan to produce 5,000 units of something at a cost of £15 each but things could easily go wrong. Materials might suddenly increase in cost due to shortages, a new competitor might come onto the market offering a lower price product. Management would have to think again and come up with alternative plans of action. Good costing information is essential for survival and making adequate profits.

KEY POINTS OF THE CHAPTER

Costing:	Part of the management process of collecting data in order to calculate costs and assist decision making
Absorption costs:	The total cost of a unit in terms of labour, materials and overheads
Marginal costs:	Identifying the extra (marginal) cost in relation to output levels
Standard costs:	Establishing predetermined costs in order to compare actual with standard results
Budgeting:	Planning or forecasting results for the future
Budgetary control:	Management tool to monitor costs, comparing actual results with those planned

Coding of costs:	Numbers and or letters to identify specific costs and where they have been allocated
Job costing:	A specific Job cost to suit a customer
Batch costing:	The cost of a batch of similar or identical products
Contract costing:	For larger-scale cost programmes, duration often over long periods
Process costing:	Continuous process of production where the cost of one is passed onto the next process.
Cost classification	The categories of cost, the areas where money is spent.

QUESTIONS

1. Why is there a need for cost accounting?
2. Basically, how would you explain the difference between absorption and marginal costing?
3. What is meant by budgetary control?
4. Briefly explain what standard costing attempts to do.
5. The following information concerns a small manufacturing business:

	£
direct wages	40,000
direct materials	60,000
business rates	1,600
advertising	1,500
administration	18,500
rent and insurance	6,200

   a) If it was estimated that 8,000 units were to be produced, calculate the total (absorption cost) per unit.
   b) Which of the above would you consider as being the variable costs?
   c) What would be the total fixed costs?

6. Contract costing is said to be used for high cost programmes taking a considerable time to produce. How would it differ from job or batch costing?
7   Why does it appear essential to code costs in a large manufacturing organisation?
   Provide an example of how you would cost an electric motor charged to a specific cost centre
8   How would you classify the following costs of a car manufacturer?
   a) component parts
   b) factory foreman's wages
   c) assembly worker
   d) sheet metal body worker
   e) factory rent, rates and insurance
   f) salesmen's salaries
   g) administration officer's wages
   h) lubricants for plant & machinery
   i) warehouse costs
   j) manufacturing cleaner's wages

9 a) Why do you think it is important to have a cost classification system?
   b) What elements make up the prime cost?
   c)   What are the 3 main elements of cost?
10 A batch of 5000 units are produced and you have been asked to calculate costs:

	£
materials & components	8,000
direct wages	7,500
factory overheads	4,200
sales & distribution expenses	6,250
administration expenses	4,650

   You have been asked to calculate: the direct cost per unit, the factory overheads per unit, the production cost per unit and the total cost per unit. Only materials and wages are variable. If a mark-up of 20% was added, what is the unit selling price? What is the break-even point?

Chapter 18

The Use of Cost Centres and Coding of Costs

INTRODUCTION

The use of cost centres provides management with information concerning the location of expenses. It is something that incurs costs. An organisation can be divided into appropriate sections which could be used to allocate and apportion costs and thereby identify the cost of activities in various departments of a business. For example, the cost of stationery can be directly attributed to a number of different sections in a business. The monitoring of these costs to those sections that use them will help maintain a better control of costs and assist management with their budgetary programmes. In a college it would be useful to know how much a business studies department is costing to operate compared to say an engineering department.

The Institute of Cost and Management Accountants have basically defined a cost centre as:

'A production or service location, function or activity whose costs maybe attributed to cost units'.

A cost centre can therefore be anything that incurs a cost, most often it is a place like a department or section in an organisation. A unit cost is the cost of either a product or a service that has certain costs attributed to it. This could either be a single unit or a batch of units.

To find the unit cost of anything, the *direct costs* can normally be traced to a cost centre quite easily. The *indirect costs* such as rent, rates, insurance, light and heat may not be so easily traceable and may benefit a number of cost centres. It is important therefore to have a sound and fair basis of apportioning these overheads to various cost centres so that a justifiable cost can be attributed to them.

A cost centre can be a production or service centre. Any service centre that incurs costs in terms of its overheads can then be apportioned to production centres in order to find the total overheads chargeable to a specific production centre.

The allocation and apportioning of costs

The allocation of cost applies where the costs incurred can be identified to a specific cost centre. Direct costs such as direct labour and direct materials should be a straightforward allocation of costs. Some indirect costs like indirect labour or indirect materials could also be easily identified and charged to specific cost centres in the same way as direct costs. For example, it would be quite straight forward to allocate direct labour to a specific cost centre if the employee specifically works in that centre.

The apportioning of costs applies when a cost is incurred for the benefit of two or more cost centres. Overheads such as rent, rates and insurance are typical indirect costs that require a fair apportionment of costs because they are likely to benefit more than one centre.

Example:
Business rates of £24,000 are charged to a business that operates three distinct production centres and one service centre. It was decided to apportion this cost to the four centres in relation to the *floor area* occupied by each of the centres.

Production Centres	Area (in square metres)
Production centre 1	1,400 square metres
Production centre 2	2,600 square metres
Production centre 3	1,000 square metres
Service centre 4	3,000 square metres

Total area for all centres   8,000 square metres

The apportionment of rates will then be charged to each cost centre on the basis of floor area in relation to the ratio of the cost centre's area to the total area.

Centre 1	1,400/8,000 metres X £24,000 =	£4,200	
2	2,600/8,000 metres X £24,000 =	£7,800	
3	1,000/8,000 metres X £24,000 =	£3,000	
4	3,000/8,000 metres X £24,000 =	£9,000	£24,000

Bases of apportionment

The bases of apportionment includes a number of various facilitators that could be used so that overheads are divided between cost centres as fairly as possible. Some of these are:

Cost type	*Bases of apportionment*
rent, rates	floor area
insurance (buildings)	floor area
insurance (employees)	number of employees
light, heat, power	floor area or metered units
canteen expenses	number of employees
wages office expenses	number of employees
distribution costs	value of sales

For example, if the canteen expenses of a factory were say £150,000 and using the four cost centres above there were:

Centre 1	50 employees
Centre 2	30 employees
Centre 3	10 employees
Centre 4	10 employees

How much should be apportioned to each of the cost centres? Check your answer:

Centre 1	£75,000	
Centre 2	£45,000	
Centre 3	£15,000	
Centre 4	£15,000	£150,000

The coding of accounts for income and costs

Each income and cost account needs to have a code number so that it can be properly classified into its own specific area or location. By using a range of code numbers for various categories of sales, purchases, stocks, overheads and any other type of account used by a business, an integrated accounting system, using computerised software, can be built up. This provides a record of each account in its own specific location and provides us with an analysis of any figures when we require them.

For example, a retailer like *Comet or Curry's* selling a wide range of electrical goods could use a system of code numbers for their products like this:

Code No.	Description	Brand Name
20	sales: washing machines	Hoover
21	sales: washing machines	Indesit
22	sales: washing machines	Creda
23	sales: washing machines	Bosch
24	sales: washing machines	Hotpoint
30	sales: fridges	Bosch
31	sales: fridges	Indesit
32	sales: fridges	Whirlpool

So, every time a sale is keyed in by the sales assistant and the appropriate code number entered, an analysis of sales for each category is recorded. The bar *code system* operates in exactly the same way. This will assist management in their planning and decision making because they will realise which models are the best sellers and which are the slow movers. Marketing strategies can then be developed in line with sales figures.

In our modern economic society the use of computers is widespread and essential because there is often an urgent need for information to be reliable, up-to-date, relevant and instant. If things are not going as scheduled, then alternative plans need to be made quickly in order to rectify situations. Do we need to advertise certain goods more? Should we offer some form of special discount? Interest free credit? Should we offer *'Buy one, get one free'*? Good management information needs to be reliable and relevant to the needs of the business. It also needs to be accurate and up-to-date.

Each account in the nominal, sales and purchase ledgers should have a code number to identify the type of account its is. All nominal ledger accounts could have a number allocated to them. For example:

0 - 250	sales ledger accounts
251 - 750	purchase ledger accounts
751 – 1000	nominal ledger accounts

These numbers would depend upon how large a business is and the number of accounts it needs to operate. Almost all coding of accounts is based on a numerical system whereby the break-down of numbers used relates to specific elements such as location, type and description of item coded. Where cost centres are used, the first two numbers often identify the location of the centre, for example:

code number 01445502
Is identified as:

01	cost centre 1 administration
44	stationery
55	photocopying paper
02	revenue expenditure

code number 02314002 is identified as:

02	cost centre 2 production shop: pumps & compressors
31	direct cost - paint
40	10 litres blue - deluxe
02	revenue expenditure

A coding system needs to be basically simple and easy to use and easy to recognise. It needs to follow certain principles of simplicity, flexibility, unambiguous and controllability. It should be simple in its structure and logical. It needs to be flexible to be able to meet any changes or new additions to the system. It should also be unambiguous to avoid any duplication of numbers. The coding system should also be properly documented and authorised by the appropriate person in charge of coding.

KEY POINTS OF THE CHAPTER

Cost centre:	a location, function, or an activity where costs may be attributed to it
Unit cost:	the cost of a product or service
Batch:	a number of units
Allocation:	cost can be identified to a specific centre
Apportion:	cost is incurred and benefits two or more centres
Coding:	identifies and locates any type of account
Coding principles:	simplicity, flexibility, unambiguous and controllable

QUESTIONS

1. Define a cost centre.

2. Define a cost code.

3. What are the qualities of good management information?

4. How do cost centres assist management?

5. Why are overheads more difficult to apportion than direct costs?

6. a) What advantage is gained from coding different sales categories?
   b) Why is it essential to have a good coding system when using a computer?
   c) Why are codes important when a business has cost centres?

7. The floor area of 4 production centres are:

   Centre A   150 sq metres
   B   75 sq metres
   C   25 sq metres
   D   50 sq metres

The cost of rent and rates is £240,000. How could this be apportioned to the 4 centres?

8. You work in a retail store as an accounting assistant and you are responsible for the preparation of invoices sent to customers. The code and prices that you use are listed as follows:

Code No.	Item	List Price
184	hockey sticks (girls)	7.80
185	hockey sticks (ladies)	8.95
186	hockey sticks (men's)	10.50
190	hockey balls (light)	1.50
191	hockey balls (heavy)	2.00
195	hockey shin pads (girls)	5.00
196	hockey shin pads (ladies)	5.40
197	hockey shin pads (men's)	6.00
200	rugby balls (boys light)	15.00
205	rugby balls (men's heavy)	17.50
210	rugby jerseys (small/med)	15.80
211	rugby jerseys (large)	20.80
212	rugby shorts (small/med)	12.10
213	rugby shorts (large)	14.00
220	rugby boots (sizes 2-5)	8.60
221	rugby boots (sizes 6-15)	12.00
222	squash racquets (light)	9.80
223	squash racquets (medium)	11.00
224	squash racquets (heavy)	12.40
240	tennis racquets (light)	7.50
241	tennis racquets (medium)	8.50
242	tennis racquets (heavy)	9.50

Terms: All prices are Excluding VAT.
            10% trade discount on all orders of £500 or more
            Delivery charges add £8.00 per order + VAT

The following orders have been placed:
Order No. 238 dated 31 July
40 hockey sticks (girls)
12 hockey balls (light)
30 sets of hockey shin pads (girls)
20 tennis racquets (light)
20 tennis racquets (medium)

Order No. 239 dated 1 August
8 rugby balls (light)
8 rugby balls (heavy)
15 rugby jerseys (6 medium, 9 large)
15 rugby shorts (6 medium, 9 large)

Required:
You are to prepare two suitable invoices using the correct code numbers and prices listed.
In a computerised accounting system why would it be essential to quote the appropriate code numbers?

Chapter 19

Providing Comparisons on Costs and Income

INTRODUCTION

What is a budget? From a personal point of view it is making some sort of action plan where you try to match your expenditure against your income. For example, if you are earning £800 a month (after tax) then your spending should be budgeted towards a figure which is less than £800 a month otherwise you would soon be in financial difficulties.

From a business's point of view the purpose of preparing a budget is to try and ensure that its financial resources are used in the best possible way. A business needs to know where its resources are coming from and how these resources are used. Budgets are a management tool used to establish a business's aims and objectives. It helps them to set up targets for the future and goals for management to achieve. For example:

Can a sales target of £100,000 per week be achieved?
How many products do wee need to produce in a given period?
How much will labour, materials and overheads be?
Can we afford to increase our marketing budget?
Can we afford to buy more fixed assets?

Plans are made, objectives are agreed. Budgets can help management by providing them with a yard stick which assists them to measure performance. How will the budget figures compare with the actual results when then occur? Will theses be better or worse than the forecasts? How do the results compare with those of its main competitors? Is the business increasing its market share or is it losing it? Budgets can be used to help monitor and control expenditure but more importantly, they are used to plan for the business's future by setting realistic targets for management to achieve.

Budgetary control

Budgetary control is a management tool where the key element is to set realistic performance targets and then monitoring results to see whether or not the business is on the right course. It it isn't, then management must decide on the best course of action to adjust or modify its plans to make sure the business is on the right track. The stages of control are:

- Forming budgets for each department or cost centre including sales, production, stock, capital and cash flow.
- To communicate these budgets to all personnel involved with them and to ensure they understand their nature and importance.
- To monitor actual results against the budget forecasts, usually on a monthly basis, comparing what was planned against what actually occurred.
- When results are compared with the budget, any key differences are disclosed *(variances)* and possible reasons for these differences discussed.
- Appropriate action taken where necessary to try to keep the business on target.

Using budgetary control

In the following example, management has forecast the monthly cost of producing 2000 units of an electronic component in terms of labour, materials and overheads:

Total Cost	£	Cost per unit £
direct labour	11,340	5.67
direct materials	47,620	23.81
factory overheads	15,100	7.55
admin overheads	23,340	11.67
total costs	97,400	48.70

In the first month, the actual results of the business having an output of 2000 units were:

Total Cost	£	Cost per unit £
direct labour	11,120	5.56
direct materials	47,700	23.85
factory overheads	15,400	7.70
admin overheads	23,400	11.70
total costs	97,620	48.81

When comparing the budget figures with actual results the differences between the two sets of figures are the *'variances'*. When the actual figures are less than the budget costs they are said to be *favourable*. If the actual figures are more than the budget the position is said to be *adverse*. From the example, you can see that the difference between the forecast and actual figures was only £220 adverse overall. If we break these figures down and look at each specific cost:

	Budget £	Actual £	Variance £	
direct labour	5.67	5.56	0.11p	Favourable
direct materials	23.81	23.85	(0.04p)	Adverse
factory overheads	7.55	7.70	(0.15p)	Adverse
admin overheads	11.67	11.70	(0.03p)	Adverse
total costs	48.70	48.81	(0.11p)	Adverse

Comparing results

From the above figures, direct labour shows a favourable 11p per unit cost whilst the other three costs are all adverse, direct materials 4p, factory overheads 15p and administration overheads 3p. Management need to investigate the reasons behind these variances and to try to determine why they occurred particularly if the variance was excessive.

Was labour more efficient in producing the 2000 units and took less hours to make them? Or was it that a pay settlement was lower than anticipated? Direct materials were 4p per unit more and this could simply be an increase in the purchase price or it could mean that there was more wastage than usual in production.

Factory overheads were distinctly the most adverse by 15p per unit. Could it have been a higher cost in factory rent, rates and insurance? Or could it be with factory indirect labour increasing higher than expected? The budget figures need to be rechecked to find out what caused this difference.

The administration overheads were only 3p per unit adverse but nevertheless, we still need to know what caused this difference.

The term *'exception'* reporting refers to the reporting of those variances which appear excessive and exceed a certain amount or percentage. Factory overheads could be one of these and the report would concentrate upon why the actual figure exceeded the forecast by as much as 15p in this case.

Some variances are controllable and this means that it is probably an internal problem that managers can rectify. For example, how much in bonuses to pay labour or the amount of materials to use in a production process. Some variances are non-controllable and these are due to external factors which management would find difficult to control, for example, the rate of price inflation or a new competitor introducing goods at a lower price, or the price of oil suddenly increasing due to any uncertainties in supply.

The comparison of profit and loss
The trading performance of businesses is very important to management and the comparison between trading results over previous year's performances is essential in order to check whether a business is improving, deteriorating or staying at a consistent level. Management is also interested in how the business is performing against its major competitors.

Example:
Arrow Ltd. recorded the following figures over a 3-year period:

	Year 1	Year 2	Year 3
	(£000's)	(£000's)	(£000's)
sales	120	180	270
cost of sales	80	135	216
gross profit	**40**	**45**	**54**
Less expenses:			
distribution costs	18	27	30
administration expenses	10	10	20
net profit	**12**	**8**	**4**
net profit %	**10%**	**4.44%**	**1.48%**
(net profit/sales)			

At a glance it can be seen that while gross profit has steadily increased the net profit has fallen steeply from £12,000 in year 1 to only £4,000 in year 3. In percentage terms this fall is quite substantial in that year 1 it was 10% of sales and a very low 1.48% of sales in year 3. Perhaps you can see that the major reason for this was the doubling of administration expenses in year 3.

Management would need to investigate and identify precisely why the administration expenses doubled in value to £20,000 in the third year and then take what action is necessary. It could be a rather simple explanation in that an extra employee was hired by the business and this has had an adverse affect on profits.

If Arrow's major competitors were averaging say 12.5% per annum, then they are seriously adverse in comparison. Although its sales figures have increased by a large 50% each year it has suffered because it has not been able to control its costs. The cost of sales has grown proportionately more than the sales figures hence the gross profits are not as improved as they should be. If this pattern was to follow in year 4 the business would possibly make a loss and its future would be uncertain.

KEY POINTS OF THE CHAPTER

Budgets:	a forecast of where resources come from and where they go
Budgetary control:	a management tool to assist in their decision-making
Variances:	the differences between forecasts and actual results
Direct costs:	mainly labour and materials
Indirect costs:	factory, distribution and administrative overheads
Exception reporting:	reporting excessive variances
Profit/loss:	the difference between revenue and expenses
Gross profit:	the difference between sales and cost of sales
Net profit:	the difference between gross profit and other expenses

QUESTIONS

1 How would you define a budget?
2 A key aspect of budgetary control is to monitor progress. What does this mean?
3 What is meant by the term 'variance' including those found to be favourable and adverse?
4 Management often make comparisons between actual data and other forms of data. Name some of the financial comparisons that management make.
5 What is reporting by exception? Provide an example to clarify.
6 Provide examples of external factors which would be out of management's control.

7 Study the following figures based on a production output of 5000 units:

Budget	£	Actual £
direct labour	24,000	24,350
direct materials	32,500	32,250
fixed overheads	28,500	28,250

Required:
Based on costs per unit, calculate the 3 elements of cost for both the budget and actual figures.
Compare the 2 sets of figures calculating the appropriate variances
Provide possible explanations to these variances which could assist management.

8 The trading results between two companies in the same line of business were as follows:

	Big Ltd. (£000's)	Little Ltd. (£000's)
sales	300	360
cost of sales	200	240
distribution costs	45	48
administration expenses	35	40
interest charges	3	10

Required:
Compare the performance of the two companies in terms of revenue and costs and provide a brief explanation of which company has performed the better of the two.

Chapter 20

A Brief Introduction to Wages

INTRODUCTION

Wages and salaries are a reward for labour. Most people have to work for a living and the income they earn is a result of having to go out to work for five or more days a week. Wages are usually paid on a weekly basis whereas salaries are generally associated with staff who are often as not paid monthly. Pay is also referred to as *'remuneration'*. Many people also work on a part-time basis and are paid on an hourly rate of pay.

There are two distinct ways in which pay maybe calculated:
* Time rates
* Payment by results

Time rates
This is by far the most common way of being paid. Some people are paid a certain sum of money to do a certain number of hours work. For example, 37.5 hours a week, basic pay £250. Any hours worked over the basic hours could be paid at a premium rate at say time and a half or time and a third. For example, if week worked a basic week of 40 hours at a basic rate of £5.00 per hour and any overtime after 40 hours was paid at time and a quarter, the premium rate would be paid at £6.25 per hour (£5 X 1.25).

The rates for overtime vary from one business to another. Some businesses do not pay a premium rate for overtime worked, the same basic rate is paid. Some employers may offer time and a quarter for any overtime hours worked in a weekday from Monday to Friday and more for week-end work.

Example:
Harry works a basic 40 hours per week and is paid a premium for overtime, Monday to Friday is time and a third. Saturday work is rewarded with time and a half and any Sunday work gets paid at double time. If Harry worked an extra 6 hours throughout the week and an extra 4 hours on Saturday morning and 3 further hours on Sunday morning, how much would his gross earnings be? His basic rate of pay is £6.00 per hour.

Basic Pay: 40 hours X £6.00 per hour = £240.00

Overtime:
Mon-Fri	6 hours X £8.00 per hour	=	£48.00	
Saturday	4 hours X £9.00 per hour	=	£36.00	
Sunday	3 hours X £12.00 per hour	=	£36.00	£120.00

Total gross pay   £360.00

Payment by results

This alternative method of payment offers an incentive to workers to work harder for more pay. Sales people on commission will earn more if they sell more. Factory workers who can produce more output will receive more pay. Piece work is a method where a factory worker is paid for greater productivity and is particularly suitable where the work is of a repetitive nature.

Example 1:

A worker gets £1.00 for every 100 units he produces. If he produces 15000 units in a week he would earn £150.

Example 2:

Another worker is paid a retainer of £80 per week (a basic wage for going to work) and is on piece work where he gets 2p per unit on 501 - 5000 units, and a further 4p per unit on units above 5000. In a week where he produces 8000 units, how much would he earn?

Basic retainer		£80.00
Piece rates:		
501 - 5000	= 4500 X 2p	£90.00
5001 - 8000	= 3000 X 4p	£120.00
Total pay		£290.00

Example 3:

A sales representative earns a flat retainer of £100 per month and a commission is also paid at 2.5% of total sales. If his sales in one month was £18,000, how much would he earn?

Basic retainer	£100.00
Commission £18,000 X 2.5% =	£450.00
Total pay	£600.00

Gross and net pay

The gross pay of an employee refers to the examples shown above. It refers to all earnings before any deduction from pay is made. The net pay refers to gross pay less all deductions from pay. There are two basic types of deductions, voluntary and statutory.

Statutory deductions

These are those deductions that are legally required by the Government and refer to income tax and National Insurance Contributions (NIC). Both these are collected automatically from your pay if you are an employee. If you are self-employed and run your own business, then you are required to send your personal tax return to the local tax office at the end of your trading period.

Income Tax

Income tax in the UK is a progressive tax that means that the more you earn, the more you pay. The amount to be deducted is decided by the Chancellor of the Exchequer and it is presented to Government in the Budget each year. At the time of writing there were **two tax bands** based on the taxable pay of an employee (that is, after personal tax allowances have been deducted from gross pay):

- the basic rate at   20% (say up to £38,500 per annum, taxable income)
- the higher rate at   40% (from £38,500 upwards per annum, taxable income)

These figures are not calculated on gross pay but on a person's *taxable pay,* that is, *after personal tax allowances have been deducted from gross pay.* A single person with a basic personal allowance of £5,400 per annum would pay no tax on the first £5,400 of his earnings. HMRC (Her Majesty's Revenue & Customs) provides you with a tax code, for example, 5405L would identify your personal tax allowance of £5,400 per annum.

Example:
If you earned a gross annual pay of £18,500 how much tax would you pay? (Assume a personal tax allowance of £5,400 per annum). Also if your pay was £48,500 per annum, what is paid?

Remember that the basic rate of tax is at 20% per annum and this is charged after the tax allowance has been deducted from gross pay. The higher rate band will be charged at 40% and will be payable on taxable pay above £38,500 per annum. This is not applicable here.

	£	£	£
Gross pay	18,500	48,500	
Less tax allowance	(5,400)	(5,400)	
Taxable pay	13,100	43,100	
Basic rate X 20% =	2,620	38,500 X 20% = 7,700	
		4,600 X 40% = 1,840	
		9,540	
Income tax per week:	£2,620/52 = £50.38	£9,540/52 = £183.46	

National Insurance Contributions
This is yet another form of tax that the employee has to pay but in return, it does provide funds for benefits like unemployment, sick pay, pension, child support and so forth. Both the employer and the employee are charged but at slightly different rates. Those persons on low incomes are not charged NIC. At the time of writing this was about £100 per week so only those above this rate is charged at the current rate of 11%. Therefore if you earned £205 per week you would be charged:

£205 - £100 =   £105 X 11% = £11.55 NIC

Voluntary deductions
These deductions are agreed by the employee and maybe for a voluntary savings scheme, or pension fund, trade union subscriptions, social club funds or anything else which the employee wants to pay from his wages or salaries. Most employees contribute towards the Government's own pension fund paid through NIC and is called SERPS (State Earnings-Related Pension Scheme). Some businesses operate their own pension plans for the benefit of their employees and payment towards these funds depends upon how much the business pays and how much the employees have to pay.

Example of net pay:	£	£
Gross pay for the week		288.00
Less deductions:		
Taxation	40.70	
NIC	20.68	
Pension fund	7.12	
Trade Union subs	.50	69.00
Net pay		219.00

Recording payroll details in the nominal ledger

When recording payroll data in the nominal ledger, the entries could include the use of a wages control account that has the function of ensuring that all relevant entries are recorded. It is a cross-checking device to make sure that all double entry transactions are recorded. The control account debit entries should balance with the credit entries when all entries are completed.

The payroll details below are posted to the ledger, month ending 31 October, the double entries when using a control account are:

Gross Pay	Tax	Employee NIC	TU Subs.	Pension Funds	Employer NIC	Net Pay
£25,915	£4,585.70	£3,971.6	£130	£400	£4,927.85	£16,827.70

The double entry for the payroll

Gross pay and employer's NIC are debited and credited respectively to wages and wages control accounts:

Debit
Wages account:
  Wages £25,915
  Employer's NIC £4,927.85

Credit
Wages control account:
  Wages account £25,915
  Employer's NIC £4,927.85

The payments due to the tax office (Inland Revenue) are credited to the Inland Revenue account and debited to the wages control account:

Wages control account:
  Tax £4,585.70
  Employee's NIC £3,971.60
  Employer's NIC £4,927.85

Inland Revenue account:
  Tax £4,585.70
  Employee's NIC £3,971.60
  Employer's NIC £4,927.85

The bank account is credited with net wages to be paid and debited to wages control account:

Wages control account:
  Net pay £16,827.70

Bank account:
  £16,827.70

The pension fund and trade union subscriptions accounts are credited with the sums due to them and the wages control account debited:

Wages control account:
  TU subscriptions £130
  Pension funds £400

TU Subscriptions and Pension Funds accounts
  TU subscriptions account £130
  Pension funds account £400

Nominal Ledger:

Wages account

31/10	payroll	25,915.00	
	NIC (employer)	4,927.85	
		30,842.85	

Inland Revenue account

31/10	tax	4,585.70
	NIC (employer)	4,927.85
	NIC (employee)	3,971.60
		13,485.15

TU Subscriptions account

31/10	payroll	130.00

Pension funds account

31/10	payroll	400.00

Bank account

31/10	payroll	16,827.70

Wages Control account

31/10	tax	4,585.70	31/10	wages	25,915.00
	NIC (employer)	4,927.85		NIC	4,927.85
	NIC (employee)	3,971.60		(employer)	
	TU subscriptions	130			
	Pension funds	400			
	bank (net pay)	16,827.70			
		30,842.85			**30,842.85**

KEY POINTS OF THE CHAPTER

Time rates:	usually a basic rate of pay plus a premium for overtime
Payment by results:	incentives offered to workers to produce more and get paid for it
Gross pay:	earnings before deductions
Net pay:	earnings after deductions
Statutory deductions	those legally to be deducted, tax and NIC
Voluntary deductions	employees decide what to pay for example, savings schemes
Tax rates:	starter, basic and higher rates of tax
NIC rates:	paid above a threshold for example, £100 week, at a percentage based on the gross pay
Wages control account:	to ensure that all payroll entries are recorded in the nominal ledger.

QUESTIONS

1. Calculate the following gross weekly wages for Harry, Jack and Fred:
   a) Harry Jones has a basic week of 36 hours paid at a flat rate of £4.00 per hour. Overtime is at time and a half. How much will he earn working 39 hours in a week?
   b) Jack works 46 hours and Fred 43 hours per week at only £2.80 per hour. Overtime starts after 38 hours and is paid at time and a quarter. Calculate their gross pay.
2. There are 3 employees, Tom, Dick and Harry. You are required to calculate their gross pay.
   Tom 40 hours, Dick 38.5 hours, Harry 45 hours
   The basic working week is 36 hours at a low rate of £3.00 per hour. Overtime is time and half.
3. Charlie is on piece work where the attendance retainer is £1.25 per hour. The piece work is at the following rates:
   0 - 1000 units 2p unit; 1001- 1500 units 3p unit; over 1500 units 2.5p unit
   How much will he earn during a 42 hour week in which he produces 1825 units?
4. A sales representative is paid a basic salary of £400 per month and he also earns 10% commission on sales over £5000. In a month where his sales were £9,850 how much did he earn?
5. Pamela earns £150 per week and is paid an additional 8 hours overtime at £4.75 per hour. Tax is £32.55 and NIC £13.70. Calculate both her gross and net pay.
6. On the pay sheet of 3 employees, work numbers 10, 11 and 12, their hours per week plus overtime were:
   No.10 35 hours basic plus 5 hours week-days and 4 hours Saturday
   No. 11 35 hours basic plus 2 hours week-days and 3 hours Saturday
   No.12 35 hours basic plus 6 hours week-days and 3 hours Saturday and 3 hours Sunday
   The rates are £4.20 per hour basic time, time and a quarter for week-days, time and a half on Saturdays and double time on Sundays. Calculate their gross pay.
7. Calculate Arthur's net pay for the week: Gross pay £226.80
   Deductions: Pension fund £14 tax free; NIC £16.34; Tax to be deducted.
   Arthur has £110 per week as his personal tax allowance on top of his tax free pension. The basic rate of tax is 20% and there is £3 to be deducted to take account of the lower starter rate. (Calculate the tax on whole £'s only).
8. The details from the month's payroll week ending 31 December, 20- were:

Gross Pay	Tax	Employee NIC	Pension Funds	Employer NIC	Net Pay
£138,815	£18,981.55	£12,500.40	£1,055	£13,000.55	£106,278.05

   Your supervisor has asked you are to enter the details from the month's payroll, ending 31 December, 20- in the nominal ledger.
9. Explain clearly what is meant by *statutory deductions* from pay.

10. The following information relates to the time sheet of Julie Harris:

	Basic time	*Overtime*
Monday	8 hours	1.5 hours
Tuesday	8 hours	0.5 hours
Wednesday	8 hours	2.5 hours
Thursday	8 hours	2.0 hours
Friday	6 hours	0.5 hours
Saturday		3.0 hours
Sunday		2.0 hours

   Julie earns a basic rate of £4.80 per hour and is paid time and a quarter for week-days, time and a half for Saturdays and double time on Sundays. Calculate Julie's gross pay for the week.

Chapter 21

Control Accounts: Sales and Purchase Ledger Control

INTRODUCTION

We have already indicated in chapters 7 and 8 the role of the sales and purchase ledger control accounts. These accounts are recorded in the nominal ledger and represent the totals of debtors' and creditors' balances. These are cross-checked against the sales and purchase ledgers to ensure that they agree. For example, if the total debtors' balances in the sales ledger was £36,500 at the end of a certain month, then the sales ledger control account should also equal the same amount. The sales ledger control account is commonly referred to as the *debtors' control account* whilst the purchase ledger control account is known as the *creditors' control account.*

If a computer program is used, the nominal ledger would provide immediate access to the control accounts and these would tally with the sales and purchase ledger programs under the menu often referred to as *Aged debtors' and creditors' balances*.

For management purposes, it is essential to know how much is owed by debtors of the business as well as how much is owed to creditors. When can a business expect to receive its cash? When can it be in a position to pay its creditors? These two vital questions affect the future cash flows of the business and the amount of working capital that will be available for trading operations.

Once the two control accounts have verified the correctness of the sales and purchase ledger account balances, these control accounts will represent the totals for debtors and creditors in the trial balance. (It is not necessary to show all individual customers and suppliers).

The location of errors

If either of the control accounts do not verify the total balances of the sales and purchase ledgers, a detailed check is required to locate any errors. Both the individual balances of customers or suppliers need to be checked for errors as well as the control accounts. It could simply be that a balance of an account is arithmetically wrong or an entry has been made on the wrong side of an account, for example, recording returns inward on the debit side of a debtor's account instead of the credit side.

Another likely source of error could be as simple as an incorrect addition of figures in say the sales or purchases day books and these would then be posted as incorrect figures to the ledgers. Note the error below in the sales day book:

Example: sales day book

	Sales a/c	VAT a/c	Total debtors a/c
	£	£	£
D Smith	200	35	235
S Holloway	420	73.5	493.5
M Plummer	500	87.5	587.5
	1,120	196	1,216
	Credit	Credit	Dr s/l
	Sales	VAT	Control

Posting sums to the debit side of the sales ledger would be correct for each customer. However, when posting to the nominal ledger, the sales and Vat accounts would be correct but not the sales ledger control account.

If the sales ledger control account is debited with £1,216 (check the sum, it should = £1,316) an error of £100 would show the control account £100 less than it should be. When cross-checking the sales ledger with the control account there would be a difference of £100. This error would have to be located and corrected by a journal entry.

The control accounts may be prepared either in the traditional 'T' account format or the running balance format. In most exams, the traditional method of recording is favoured because the debit and credit entries are more distinct and perhaps they are a little easier to assess.

Terms used with control accounts:
Some entries in the control accounts may need some clarification:

- Cheques dishonoured refer to customers' cheques that have been stopped by the bank, usually because the customer has insufficient funds to pay the debt. These are debited in the sales ledger control account as well as debited in the individual customer's account.
- Contra entries are sums offset between debtors' and creditors' balances when a business both sells and buys goods from the same person or organisation. The entry is to debit purchase ledger control and credit sales ledger control accounts as well as debiting the individual accounts in the purchase ledger and crediting them in the sales ledger.
- Bills receivable are notes from customers promising to pay at a future date. They are treated like a post-dated cheque and are *credited* to the sales ledger control account.
- Bills payable are the reverse of bills receivable in that the business promises to pay its suppliers at a future date. These are *debited* to the purchase ledger control account.

Example 1: Sales Ledger Control (Debtors control account)
The following are balances from the ledgers of ABC Company:

	£
Sales ledger Dr. balances at 1 June	7,300
Credit sales (June)	12,500
Cash sales	2,840
Cash/cheques received from debtors	11,500
Returns from customers	400
Discounts allowed to Customers	280
Debtors' cheques returned from bank marked 'R/D'	
- cheques dishonoured	330
Sales ledger Dr balances at 30 June	7,950

Debtors control account

		Dr	Cr	Balance
June 1	Balance			7,300 Dr
30	Sales	12,500		19,800
	Bank/cash		11,500	8,300
	Discounts		280	8,020
	Returns inward		400	7,620
	Cheques dishonoured	330		7,950

NOTE:

- The 30 June balance from the sales ledger £7,950 is verified with the S/L control account balance as above, the balances agree.
- The cash sales £2,840 are **not** included in the control account because they are not associated with selling goods to debtors. For the same reason, cash purchases are not included in the purchase ledger control account.

Example 2: **Purchases Ledger Control (Creditors Control account)**

	£
Purchases ledger Cr. Balances at 1 June	12,500
Credit purchases for June	19,750
Cheques paid to supplies	18,200
Discounts received	478
Returns to suppliers	545
Debit note from suppliers, resulting from under-charge	50
Credit balances from purchases ledger at 30 June	13,427

Creditors control account

		Dr	Cr	Balance
June 1	Balance			12,500
30	Purchases		19,750	32,250
	Bank	18,200		14,050
	Discounts received	478		13,572
	Returns outward	545		13,027
	Debit note, under-charge		50	13,077

NOTE:
There is a discrepancy of £350 between the purchase ledger (£13,427) and the control account above, (£13,077). Somewhere in the accounts, an error has occurred and records must be checked until it is found and corrected.

Any transaction which affects either a debtor (in the sales ledger), or a creditor (in the purchase ledger) must be reflected in the appropriate control account. The control accounts represent the totals of respective debtors and creditors.

Note that sometimes it happens that a debtor might *overpay* his account or, conversely, a creditor is *overpaid*, and this temporarily gives rise to a debtor's account with a credit balance, or a creditor's account with a debit balance

Correcting errors
In the purchase ledger control account above, a discrepancy of £350 occurred between the purchase ledger balances of £13,427 credit and the purchase ledger control account of £13,077 credit.

The errors located were found to be:

- A cheque to a supplier £200 had not yet been recorded in the purchase ledger but the total cheques payable to suppliers had been posted to the p/l control account.
  Correction: debit supplier's account £200

- A supplier's balance brought forward £75 debit (due to our overpayment) had been incorrectly brought forward as £75 credit.
  Correction: debit supplier's account £150

Reconciliation between purchase ledger control account and purchase ledger:

	£	£
Purchase ledger balances		13,427 credit
Less		
Cheque to supplier	200 debit	
Balance brought forward	150 debit	(350)
Balance as per p/l control account		**13,077**

KEY POINTS OF THE CHAPTER

S/L control account:	Sales ledger control account used to verity the correctness of customer accounts in the sales ledger
P/L control account:	Purchase ledger control account used to verify the correctness of supplier accounts in the purchase ledger [or bought ledger]
Location of errors:	Where discrepancies occur between the control accounts and the sales and purchase ledgers, errors must be found and corrected
Contra entries:	Sums set off between debtors and creditors balances
Dishonoured cheques:	Cheques from customers that are not accepted by the bank and debited to s/l control account
Bills receivable:	These are promises by customers to pay on a certain date and are credited to the s/l control account
Bills payable:	These are promissory notes to suppliers to pay them on a certain date and are debited to the purchase ledger control account
Verify balances:	Cross checking the control accounts with the sales and purchase ledgers to make sure that they agree.

QUESTIONS

1. From the following details for the month of January, prepare Fred Smith's sales ledger control account and purchases ledger control account as they would appear in the nominal ledger. The opening balances in the purchase ledger and sales ledger were: £4,420 credit and £2,420 debit respectively that agreed with the control accounts.

	£
Credit purchases from suppliers	36,480
Credit sales to customers	30,500
Cash paid to creditors	36,840
Receipts from trade debtors	26,175
Discounts received	825
Discounts allowed	720
Purchase returns	815
Debit note to debtor	119
Bad debt written off	730
Credit balances in purchases ledger transferred to sales ledger	180
Returns inward	414

On 31 January, the purchase ledger had a balance of £2,240 and the sales ledger £5,080. Check these figures with your two control accounts in the nominal ledger.

Required:
Prepare the sales and purchase ledger control accounts for the month of January. Check for any discrepancies between the control accounts and the subsidiary ledgers.

2. The following information has been taken from the books of Harry Jones relating to the month ended 31 January:

	£
Sales ledger control balance 1 January	2,246
P/L control balance 1 January	1,608
Transactions for the month:	
Credit sales	38,127
Cash sales	9,750
Purchases on credit	27,121
Receipts from customers	27,560
Payments to suppliers	19,422
Discount allowed	810
Dishonoured cheques from customers	925
Returns outward	316
Returns inward	1,427

Required:
Prepare the sales and purchase ledger control accounts for the month ended 31 January.

3. The following figures for the month of May relate to the accounts of George Harrison:

Balances brought forward from:	£
1 May sales ledger control	13,740 Dr
31 May sales ledger balances	16,996
Sales	12,450
Returns inward	150
Cash from customers	9,208
Discounts allowed	245
Bad debts	222
Cheques returned from bank marked	
Insufficient funds	442
Cash sales	4,173
Debit notes to customers	154
Interest charged to customers	
(on overdue accounts)	58
Contra: balances in sales ledger	
transferred to purchases ledger	42

Required:
a) Prepare the debtors control account for the month of May.
b) From the figures you have prepared, what conclusions do you arrive at?

4. You work as an account's assistant for a manufacturing company, Rock Ltd, and have to write up the control accounts for the month of February. Details of transactions are as follows:

	£
February 1 P/L control (credit balance)	26,100
Sales ledger control (debit balance)	51,400
Total transactions in the month of February:	
Bad debts written off	420
Credit purchases	37,590
Cash purchases	5,200
Returns outwards	510
Returns inwards	1,480
Cheques paid to creditors	24,270
Cheques received from debtors	47,360
Contras between s/l & p/l	800
Dishonoured cheques (from debtors)	140
Credit sales	74,900
Cash sales	9,250
Discount allowed	1,840
Discount received	960
Cheque received from a supplier	460

Required:

a) Prepare the sales ledger control account for February. [The sales ledger schedule total was £74,540]

b) Prepare the purchase ledger control account for February. [The purchase ledger schedule total was £37,510]

c) i Describe one other system of internal check which can be used to ensure accuracy of posting.

ii Which of the two control accounts agreed?

iii How much was the discrepancy in the control account which failed to balance?

[Institute of Bankers]

5. You work as an account's assistant for a wholesale company by the name of Zarak Ltd, and have to write up the control accounts for the month of August. Details of transactions are as follows:

	£
August 1 Sales ledger control (debit balance)	48,000
Purchase ledger control (credit balance)	24,200
Total transactions in the month were:	
Credit sales	61,740
Credit purchases	34,720
Cash purchases	3,905
Discount allowed	760
Discount received	980
Returns inwards	1,750
Returns outwards	430
Cheques received from debtors	51,720
Cheques paid to creditors	23,890
Dishonoured cheques (from debtors)	880
Contras between s/l and p/l	750

Required:

a) Prepare the sales ledger control account for August. [Sales ledger schedule total was £55,790]

b) Prepare the purchase ledger control account for August. [Purchase ledger schedule total was £32,870]

c) Briefly explain why control accounts are used. Which of the two control accounts did not balance with the schedule?

PART IV   THE CONSTRUCTION OF FINANCIAL STATEMENTS

Chapter 22

Financial Statements: The Calculation of Profits

INTRODUCTION

This chapter continues from the first introduction of these accounts discussed in chapter 3. The preparation of the trading and profit and loss account (abbreviated as the profit and loss account), usually follows after the extraction of the trial balance from the accounts in the nominal ledger. Whether the accounts are for sole traders, partnerships or companies, the trial balance is generally the first step. Financial statements states what has occurred in a business's financial period. Has it made a profit or has it suffered a loss? Is the business financially secure? Is it in a position to pay the bills demanded from its creditors?

The financial period
A financial period is usually seen as the business's financial year, that is, when trading commenced and when it finished. This could be from 1 January to 31 December or indeed, any twelve month period. If trading commenced 1 April it would end 31 March and so on. Once this period is recognised, then an exact matching between revenue earned and expenses incurred must take place in order for profit or loss to be calculated.

The need to make profits
All business organisations need to calculate profit or loss on a frequent basis for management purposes, therefore an accounting period could be seen as monthly rather than annually. If a forecast of monthly profit is prepared, then the actual figures can be compared with them to see if there is any corrective action to be taken. Is the amount of profit satisfactory? Are sales targets being met? Are expenses under control? Making profits is the most significant part of any business, without profits there is no return on the owner's investment and the business would have difficulty surviving.

Note that for a VAT registered business, both revenue and expenses must be recorded *excluding* VAT because it belongs to HMRC. Any VAT owing (a credit balance) is recorded in the balance sheet as a current liability. If VAT is a debit balance, then it is shown as a current asset because the Tax Office would owe the business any sums overpaid in tax.

Remember back to Chapter 3 that first discussed financial statements. *Profit* is basically the difference between revenue and expenses found in the profit and loss account. On the other hand, the balance sheet identified a business's assets, liabilities and capital.

The link between these two statements is profit. Profit increases capital and therefore net assets (assets less liabilities). On the other hand, a loss would decrease capital and net assets.

The trading and profit and loss account
The following simplified figures have been taken from the trial balance of G Harrison as at the month end, 31 January. The unsold stock as at this date had a value at cost, of £750. The closing

stock is an important figure because it is deducted from the cost of sales and therefore affects the calculation of gross profit.

Example 1

G Harrison
Trading and profit and loss account for month ended 31 January

	£	£
Sales	2,900	
returns inward	(85)	2,815
Cost of sales:		
stock (1 January)	680	
purchases	1,800	
returns outward	(35)	
stock (31 January)	(750)	1,695
Gross profit		1,120
Expenses:		
Wages		
light and heat	480	
printing and stationery	70	
telephone	85	
carriage outwards	80	
advertising	30	
overheads	75	
discount allowed	40	
motor expenses	15	
interest charges	70	
	10	955
Other revenue:		165
Commission received	65	
discount received	20	85
Net profit		250

NOTE:
- The gross profit = sales less cost of sales, ie. the selling prices less the cost prices of goods. This is the trading account section.
- The net profit = gross profit less expenses + other revenue. This is the profit and loss account section.
- The cost of sales is the buying price of goods sold and is a combination of opening stock + purchases, less closing stock
- Returns inward (sales returns) is deducted from sales whilst returns outward (purchases returns) is deducted from purchases.

In the second example, we will calculate George Harrison's final accounts from a trial balance as at the year end, 31 December. These are simplified figures so that you get to learn the basics of preparing the profit and loss account and the balance sheet without any adjustments to the accounts.

Adjustments such as depreciation of fixed assets or accrued expenses will have a bearing on the matching concept between revenue and expenses so as to arrive at a 'true and fair' calculation of profit or loss. These are discussed in the immediate chapters that follow.

Example 2

G Harrison's trial balance as on 31 December

Account	£	£
Capital: G Harrison		10,000
Drawings	2,600	
Premises	12,000	
Fixtures and Fittings	2,000	
Equipment	3,000	
Motor Van	1,250	
Building Society Mortgage		8,000
Bank Loan		1,000
Stock (1 January)	1,000	
Bank/cash	400	
Debtors	850	
Creditors		950
Sales		11,000
Returns Inward	250	
Purchases	5,000	
Returns Outward		350
Salaries	850	
Light and Heat	300	
Printing and Stationery	100	
Telephone	155	
Delivery Expenses	125	
Advertising	300	
Packing Materials	340	
Discount Allowed	65	
Rates and Water	285	
Motor Expenses	500	
Interest Paid	140	
Discount Received		125
Commission Received		85
	31,510	31,510

NOTE: The value of unsold stock on 31 December was £1,500.

Required:
a) Prepare the trading and profit and loss account of G Harrison for the year ended 31 December.
b) A balance sheet as at that date, 31 December.

Solution:

G Harrison
Trading and profit and loss account for the year
ended 31 December

	£	£
Sales	11,000	
- Returns inward	250	10,750
Less cost of sales		
Stock (1/1)	1,000	
+ Purchases	5,000	
	6,000	
- Returns outward	350	
	5,650	
- Stock (31/12)	1,500	
		4,150
Gross profit		6,600
Less other expenses		
Salaries	850	
Printing and stationery	100	
Telephone	155	
Delivery expenses	125	
Advertising	300	
Packing materials	340	
Discount allowed	65	
Rates and water	285	
Motor expenses	500	
Interest paid	140	
Light and heat	300	3,160
		3,440
Add other revenue		
Discount received	125	
Commission	85	210
Net Profit		3,650
(transferred to Capital account)		

NOTE:
The value of the closing unsold stock on 31 December is also entered in the
balance sheet as a current asset.

G Harrison
Balance sheet as at 31 December

	£	£	£
Fixed Assets (at cost)			
Premises	12,000		
Fixtures and Fittings	2,000		
Equipment	3,000		
Motor Van	1,250		18,250
Current Assets			
Stock (at cost) 31.12	1,500		
Debtors	850		
Bank/cash	400	2,750	
Less Current Liabilities			
Creditors	950	950	
Working Capital *			1,800
Capital Employed			20,050
Less Long-term Liabilities			
Mortgage (Building Society)	8,000		
Bank Loan	1,000		9,000
Net assets			11,050
Financed by:			
Capital: G Harrison (1/1)	10,000		
+ Net Profit	3,650	13,650	
- Drawings		(2,600)	11,050

NOTE:
- Working Capital *   Current Assets - Current Liabilities
         £1,800   = £2,750   -   £950
- Capital Employed   Fixed Assets   +   Working Capital
         £20,050   = £18,250   +   £1,800

* Working capital is also referred to as *net current assets*

Transfer of nominal ledger accounts to trading and profit and loss
All revenue and expense balances are transferred to the trading and profit and loss account at the end of an accounting period. Once profit and loss has been calculated, revenue and expense accounts will start the new accounting period with new zero balances.

The stock account will also be transferred to trading and the unsold stock value at the end of the year will be entered in the stock account as the new stock value. The nominal ledger of G Harrison is shown on the following page after the transfer of revenue and expenses to trading and profit and loss accounts.

Nominal ledger of G Harrison

	Details	Dr £	Cr £	Balance £
Sales account				
31 December	Balance			11,000 Dr
	Trading	11,000		0
Purchases account				
31 December	Balance			5,000 Dr
	Trading		5,000	0
Returns Inward account				
31 December	Balance			250 Dr
	Trading		250	0
Returns Outward				
31 December	Balance			350 Cr
	Trading	350		0
Stock account				
1 January	Balance			1,000 Dr
31 December	Trading		1,000	0
31 December	Trading	1,500		1,500 Dr
*1 January	Balance			1,500 Dr
Salaries account				
31 December	Balance			850 Dr
	Profit and Loss		850	0
Printing and Stationery account				
31 December	Balance			100 Dr
	Profit and Loss		100	0
Telephone account				
31 December	Balance			155 Dr
	Profit and Loss		155	0
Delivery Expenses account				
31 December	Balance			125 Dr
	Profit and Loss		125	0
Advertising account				
31 December	Balance			300 Dr
	Profit and Loss		300	0
Packing Materials account				
31 December	Balance			340 Dr
	Profit and Loss		340	0

NOTE:
- The remaining revenue and expense accounts will also be transferred to Profit and Loss Account.
- All other accounts (that is, assets, liabilities and capital) are not affected in the same way and their balances are carried forward to the new accounting period, 1 January.
- Stock(end) £1,500 becomes stock beginning in the new accounting period, 1 January *.

Working capital (net current assets)
The calculation for working capital is the total value of current assets less the total value of current liabilities. Working capital is part of the balance sheet presentation because it indicates how well a business might be able to cover its short-term debts. Every business needs to have adequate working capital to pay for its day-to-day trading activities.

A business needs to have sufficient liquidity (cash or near cash) to pay its bills when they fall due. If current liabilities were to be in excess of current assets, the business would technically be insolvent, that is, it would not have the ability to pay its short-term creditors.

Working capital ratio (net current ratio)
The minimum working capital ratio should therefore not fall below a figure of 1:1 (although large companies like the big supermarkets often run on negative working capital without difficulty). This is calculated by dividing current assets by current liabilities, for example G Harrison's ratio is:

$$\text{Working capital ratio} = \text{current assets/current liabilities}$$
$$2.9 = \frac{£2750}{£950}$$

In this case, for every £1 of current debt, there is £2.90 in current assets to cover it, a very good liquidity position to be in. Accounting ratios are discussed more fully in Chapter 31.

KEY POINTS OF THE CHAPTER

RECAL:	The 5 accounting groups: revenue, expenses, capital, assets, and liabilities
Profit and loss account:	Matches revenue with expenses for profit (loss) calculation
Cost of sales:	Opening stock + purchases - closing stock
Gross profit:	Sales less cost of sales
Net profit:	Gross profit less expenses + other income
Balance sheet:	A list of assets, liabilities and capital
Accounting equation:	Capital = assets - liabilities
Fixed assets:	The more permanent, less liquid assets of the business, eg. premises
Current assets:	The trading or circulating assets eg. stocks, debtors, bank and cash
Current liabilities:	Short term debts repayable within 12 months
Long term liabilities:	Debts repayable after 12 months
Working capital:	Current assets - current liabilities, a business must have sufficient to meet day to day costs; also referred to as net current assets
Working capital ratio:	Current assets/current liabilities, a business should normally have a minimum ratio of 1:1, also referred to as net current ratio
Capital employed:	Fixed assets + working capital, the employable capital tied up or invested in assets; can also be expressed as total assets less current liabilities.

QUESTIONS

1. A car costs £5,000 and is marked up by 25% to sell. If £125 was spent on advertising, £250 on repairs and overheads were £325 per car.
   Calculate the gross and net profit on its sale.

2. What is the basic difference between the gross and net profit?

3. Why is sufficient working capital important to the well being of a business?

4. Complete the following accounting equations:

	C	=	A	-	L
a)	8,000		96,000		
b)	1,500				22500
c)	14,700		104,500		
d)			16,740		14,340
e)	100				1,000

5. The following represents the trial balance of J Wright on 30 June:

Account	Dr £	Cr £
Capital: J Wright		25,000
Premises	19,000	
Bank	1,250	
Equipment	4,075	
Motor vehicle	2,250	
Drawings: J Wright	1,750	
Stock (1/7) beg.	1,250	
Debtors	1,000	
Creditors		2,100
Sales		50,000
Returns inward	200	
Returns outward		550
Purchases	44,500	
General expenses	650	
Salaries	1,125	
Administration expenses	450	
Rates and insurance	300	
Interest received		150
	77,800	77,800

   Note: At the year ended 30 June, the value of unsold stock was £3,750.

   Required:
   a) A trading and profit and loss account for the year ended 30 June.
   b) A balance sheet as at that date. Show working capital.

6. The following represents the trial balance of Jack Armstrong as at 31 December.

	Dr £	Cr £
Premises	27,000	
Motor van	2,000	
Fixtures and fittings	5,300	
Bank	4,250	
Cash	250	
Stock (1 January)	8,000	
Debtors	3,100	
Mortgage on premises		20,000
Interest owing		1,000
Creditors		9,000
Capital: J Armstrong		7,000
Sales		71,000
Discount		300
Returns outward		1,000
Rates and water	500	
Motor and travel expenses	2,500	
Purchases	34,000	
Returns inward	2,250	
Light and heat	600	
Advertising	590	
Wages	16,500	
Insurance	360	
General expenses	2,100	
	109,300	109,300

Note: The value of closing stock on 31 December was £4,200 at stock-taking.

Required:

a) Prepare the trading and profit and loss account of J Armstrong for the period ended 31 December.

d) Prepare the balance sheet as at 31 December, and clearly show working capital.

7. The following relates to Freddie Smith, small retailer, as at year ended 31 December:

	Dr £	Cr £
Capital		2,000
Shop premises	1,950	
Fixtures	750	
Stock 1 January	320	
Debtors	1,020	
Creditors		1,245
Sales		6,950
Purchases	4,050	
Returns inward	100	
Outward		150
Rent	250	
Wages and salaries	600	
General expenses	75	
Light and heat	355	
Bank	875	
	10,345	10,345

Note: Closing stock at 31 December was £650.

Required:
a) Enter all the above accounts in the ledger of Freddy Smith as they would appear on 31 December. Transfer all revenue and expense accounts to the trading and profit and loss account. Adjust for stock end.
b) Prepare the trading and profit and loss accounts for the year ending 31 December and a balance sheet as at that date.

8. The following balances were taken from the books of Fred White as at 30 September:

	Dr £	Cr £
Capital: F White		12,730
Drawings: F White	1,200	
Purchases	8,400	
Sales		12,900
Stock (beg.)	1,358	
Debtors	1,889	
Creditors		2,184
Commission received		1,033
Water, rates, insurance	664	
Wages	3,173	
General expenses	125	
Equipment	1,500	
Motor van	410	
Cash	528	
Overdraft at bank		2,400
Premises	12,500	
Returns inward	153	
Returns outward		653
	31,900	31,900

Note: Stock value on 30 September was £2,415.

Required:

a) Prepare the trading and profit and loss account of F White for the year ended 30 September and a balance sheet as at that date.

b) Why are some accounts transferred to the trading and profit and loss account and not others? Explain, giving examples.

9. James Robert has a small business enterprise. The following trial balance was extracted from his ledgers at the financial year end 30 April:

	Dr £	Cr £
Capital: J Robert		18,000
Drawings	2,800	
Bank overdraft		725
Premises	15,700	
Motor van	1,000	
Equipment	1,400	
Debtors	2,900	
Creditors		3,850
Stock (beg.)	3,500	
Purchases	28,400	
Sales		42,650
Rent received		750
Wages	8,500	
Rates and insurance	270	
Light and heat	195	
Administrative expenses	325	
Selling and distribution costs	500	
VAT	275	
Returns inward	400	
Returns outward		190
	66,165	66,165

Note: Stock unsold on 30 April was valued £5,280.

VAT is not an expense. HMRC owe the money to J Robert and is entered as a current asset in the balance sheet.

Required:

a) The trading and profit and loss account for the year ended 30 April.

b) A balance sheet as at this date.

Chapter 23

Adjustments: Accruals, Prepayments and Drawings

INTRODUCTION

The financial acumen of any business needs to be tested at periodic intervals to see whether it has been profitable. For many large businesses, it is often necessary for management purposes to prepare financial statements at regular monthly intervals in order to keep a check on the pulse of the business and to calculate how much profit (or loss) is made in different areas of the organisation. For example, large retail organisations like Sainsbury's, Tesco's and Marks & Spencer, would want to know which of their products are making them the most money and those that are not.

Adjustments

Adjustments to the final accounts are required because any transaction which specifically belongs to an accounting period, whether paid or incurred (due to be paid), must be included within the accounts of that period. This is part of what is called the *"accruals"* concept in accounting that is discussed in Chapter 32. For example, if a business owed wages of £2,500 at the year end, this sum must be included in the accounts for the year. Similarly, if an expense was paid in advance of the accounting period, the sum prepaid would be deducted from the accounts at the year end.

These adjustments are part of the *matching concept* in accounting which attempts to match as exactly as possible the revenue earned in one period with the expenses incurred in the same period, in order to arrive at a 'true and fair' assessment of profit (or loss).

Types of adjustments

In this section, we will look at 6 major adjustment types that are usually indicated as notes to the accounts after the trial balance:

:	1 Closing stock	(value of stock still unsold)
	2 Accrued expenses	(expenses still owing)
	3 Prepaid expenses	(expenses paid in advance)
	4 Revenue accrued	(income owed to the business)
	5 Revenue prepaid	(income paid in advance)
	6 Owners drawings	(value taken for personal use such as stock).

Each of these adjustments will have a **TWO-FOLD** effect on the final accounts:
- they are included in the trading and profit and loss account, because they affect the profit or loss for the period,
- they are included in the balance sheet because they affect the value of assets, liabilities or capital.

How do these adjustments affect the profit & loss account and balance sheet?

Type of adjustment	Profit and loss account	Balance sheet
▪ Closing stock	reduced cost of sales	current asset
▪ Accrued expenses	increase expenses	current liability
▪ Prepaid expenses	reduce expenses	current asset
▪ Revenue accrued	increase revenues	current asset
▪ Revenue prepaid	reduce revenues	current liability
▪ Owner's drawings	reduce expenses	reduce capital

Closing stock

At the end of a financial period, if the business has any unsold stock, it needs to be valued, the practice is to value it at its cost price. If any stock has fallen below that of its cost value (it may be obsolete or damaged) the rule is to take its lower value (chapter 34 discusses this more fully – stock is valued at cost, or if lower, at its net realisable value).

As we saw in the previous chapter, any unsold stock is deducted from the cost of sales in the trading account. This is part of the matching process between revenue and expenses. Any unsold stock is not an expense in the current accounting period but is an expense as the opening stock in the new period, when it is part of the new period's cost of sales.

In George Harrison's accounts as at 31 December, his closing stock value was £1,500. The cost of sales would be reduced by this sum and it would also be included under current assets in the balance sheet, as was indicated in the previous chapter.

Adjustments as at 31 December

- the value of closing stock was £1,500
- accrued expenses: gas owing £54, salaries owing £34
- prepaid expenses: rates and water £40, stationery unused £20, packing materials unused £60
- revenue accrued: commission due £120, rent received in advance £240
- revenue prepaid: commission paid in advance £25
- drawings: owner takes £500 stock and £50 for personal telephone calls.

G Harrison's trial balance as on 31 December

	£	£
Capital: G Harrison		10,000
Drawings	2,600	
Premises	12,000	
Fixtures and Fittings	2,000	
Equipment	3,000	
Motor Van	1,250	
Building Society Mortgage		8,000
Bank Loan		1,000
Stock (1 January)	1,000	
Bank/cash	400	
Debtors	850	
Creditors		950
Sales		11,000
Returns Inward	250	
Purchases	5,000	
Returns Outward		350
Salaries	850	
Light and Heat	300	
Printing and Stationery	100	
Telephone	155	
Delivery Expenses	125	
Advertising	300	
Packing Materials	340	
Discount Allowed	65	
Rates and Water	285	
Motor Expenses	500	
Interest Paid	140	
Rent Received		125
Commission Received		85
	31,510	31,510

Accrued expenses

These are expenses incurred during the financial period but not yet paid for. Any outstanding expenses must be charged to the profit and loss account for the year in which they were used. Even if an invoice for the telephone, gas or electricity account, has not yet been received for the period, an estimate of the cost can still be included in the accounts.

This could mean looking at previous figures for the same quarterly bills or estimating the number of units consumed in the period. The estimated charge due to be paid would be included in the profit and loss account and also as a current liability in the balance sheet.

We will use the same trial balance of G Harrison, to illustrate these adjustments. The example below shows that G Harrison, as at 31 December had:

- a gas bill   £54 owing
- salaries   £34 owing

Profit & loss account and balance sheet (extract)

	£	£
Profit & loss account		
Light & heat	300	
Accrued expense	54	354
Salaries	850	
Accrued expense	34	884
Balance sheet		
Current liabilities:		
Accrued expenses	88	

Nominal ledger – accrued expenses

			Dr	Cr	Balance
Light & heat account					
	31/12	Balance			300 Dr
		Accrued	54		354
		Profit & loss		354	0
	1/1	Accrued		54	54 Cr
Salaries account					
	31/12	Balance			850 Dr
		Accrued	34		884
		Profit & loss		884	0
	1/1	Accrued		34	34 Cr

NOTES:
- The accrued expense is brought down as a credit entry in the new accounting period 1/1 as owing.
- It indicates that these expenses are still to be paid in the new accounting period.
- If for example, salaries £34 were paid on 10/1 by cheque, the double entry is:
- Debit: salaries account £34, Credit: bank account £34

Prepaid expenses (prepayments)

These are expenses that are paid in advance of the current financial period. Some expenses that are likely to be paid in advance are rent, rates, insurance premiums and advertising. Unused stocks of stationery or packing materials etc. can also be classified as prepaid if the value of them is sufficiently material enough. (If there was only £10 stationery unused it may not be worth bothering about).

Any payment in advance of the financial period must be deducted from the appropriate expense in the profit and loss account and the figure included as a current asset in the balance sheet. On 31 December, G Harrison had the following expenses prepaid:

- water and rates £40
- stock of stationery unused £20
- packing materials unused £60

Profit & loss account and balance sheet (extract)		
	£	£
Profit & loss account		
Rates & water	285	
Prepaid	(40)	245
Printing & stationery	100	
Prepaid	(20)	80
Packing materials	340	
Prepaid	(60)	280
Balance sheet		
Current assets:		
Prepaid expenses	120	

Nominal ledger - recording prepaid expenses				
		Dr	Cr	Balance
Rates & water account				
31/12	Balance			285 Dr
	Prepaid		40	245
	Profit & loss		245	0
1/1	Prepaid	40		40 Dr
Printing & stationery account				
31/12	Balance			100 Dr
	Prepaid		20	80
	Profit & loss		80	0
1/1	Prepaid	20		20 Dr
Packing materials account				
31/12	Balance			340 Dr
	Prepaid		60	280
	Profit & loss		280	0
1/1	Prepaid	60		60 Dr

NOTES:
- The prepayment is brought down as a debit entry in the new period 1/1
- This indicates that expenses of £120 belong to the new financial period.

Journal entries

The journal entries for these adjustments at the period end are the *prime entry* to enable the double entry to take place in the ledger. The entries for the above are:

		Debit £	Credit £
Dec.31	Light, heat	54	
	Salaries	34	
	Accrued expenses		88
	Prepaid expenses	120	
	Rates, water		40
	Printing, stationery		20
	Packing materials		60
	Being adjustments at period end		

Journal (table title)

Revenue accrued

If any income is owing to the business (other than normal sales) at the end of the financial period, then this must be included in the same way as in the previous adjustments. If for example, a trader owed us money for commission because we sold his goods in our shop, the sum owing must be added to the income already earned on commission during the period. Other income could come from rent received from tenants or interest receivable due from the bank.

Revenue accrued (or accrued income) is therefore added to the appropriate revenue account in the profit and loss account and is also included as a prepayment in the balance sheet. On 31 December G Harrison had the following revenue due to him:

- commission due £120
- sub-let of premises (as rent received) £240

Profit & loss account and balance sheet (extract)

	£	£
Profit & loss account		
Other income:		
Commission	85	
revenue accrued	120	205
Rent received accrued		240
Balance sheet		
Current assets:		
prepaid expenses		120
revenue accrued		360

Nominal ledger – recording revenue accrued

		Dr	Cr	Balance
Commission received account				
31/12	Balance			85 Cr
	Revenue accrued		120	205
	Profit & loss	205		0
1/1	Revenue accrued	120		120 Dr
Rent received account				
31/12	Balance			125 Cr
	Revenue accrued		240	365
	Profit & loss	365		0
1/1	Revenue accrued	240		240 Dr

Note:
The revenue accrued is brought down as a debit entry in the
new financial period to indicate that this sum is still due to be paid.

Revenue prepaid

Revenue prepaid is the exact opposite to revenue accrued. In this case, income is paid in advance of the current accounting period and should therefore be *deducted* from the income already received.
For example, it we had already been paid some commission in advance of £25 which will be earned in the following period, this sum would be deducted from commission received and appear as a current liability in the balance sheet. In the ledger, the double entry is:

Debit: commission received £25 (revenue decrease)
Credit: revenue prepaid £25 (current liability)

Nominal ledger – recording revenue accrued

		Dr	Cr	Balance
Commission received account				
31/12	Balance			85 Cr
	Revenue accrued		120	205
	Revenue prepaid	25		180
	Profit & loss	180		0
1/1	Revenue accrued	120		120 Dr
	Revenue prepaid		25	95 Dr

Note that when £120 is received for commission, the balance will then become £25 in credit

The owner's drawings

We have already noted that when the owner of the business takes out cash for his own benefit, the sum withdrawn is debited to the drawings account and the bank or cash account is credited. The same principle applies if the owner takes anything of value away from the business for his/her own personal use.

This could include any value in stock, anything that benefits him by way of using his motor vehicle for personal use, or insurance, telephone bills, repairs or building on his personal premises. Indeed, any value that is personal as distinct from any business value. This is the principle of the owner being a separate entity from that of the business. The double entry would be:

Debit: drawings
Credit: the corresponding account.

On 31 December, G Harrison had the following drawings:
- £500 stock for his own use
- £50 of the telephone account were for private calls

The journal entries for these adjustments at the period end enable the double entry to take place in the ledger as we saw with accrued and prepaid expenses. The entries for the above adjustments are:

Journal		
	Debit £	Credit £
Dec.31 Accrued revenue	360	
Commission received		120
Rent received		240
Commission received	25	
Prepaid revenue		25
Drawings	550	
Purchases		500
Telephone		50

Preparing the final accounts of G Harrison with all adjustments

All the adjustments shown above will now be used to prepare the profit and loss account and balance sheet of George Harrison.

The following two pages will illustrate G Harrison's profit and loss account and balance sheet for the year ended 31 December:

George Harrison: Trading & Profit & Loss Account
Year ended 31 December

	£		£
Sales	11,000		
Returns inward	(250)		10,750
Less			
Cost of sales:			
Stock	1,000		
Purchases	5,000		
Returns outward	(350)	5,650	
Stock drawings		(500)	
		5,150	
Stock (31 December)		(1,500)	3,650
Gross profit			7,100
Expenses:			
Salaries	850		
+ accrued	34	884	
Light & heat	300		
+ accrued	54	354	
Rates & water	285		
- prepaid	(40)	245	
Print & stationery	100		
- prepaid	(20)	80	
Packing materials	340		
- prepaid	(60)	280	
Telephone	155		
- drawings	(50)	105	
Delivery expenses		125	
Advertising		300	
Discount allowed		65	
Motor expenses		500	
Interest paid		140	3,078
			4,022
Other revenue:			
Rent received	125		
+ revenue accrued	240	365	
Commission received	85		
+ revenue accrued	120		
- revenue prepaid	(25)	180	545
Net profit			4,567

G Harrison Balance sheet as at 31 December

Fixed Assets (at cost)	£	£	£
Premises	12,000		
fixtures and fittings	2,000		
equipment	3,000		
motor van	1,250		18,250
Current Assets			
Stock	1,500		
Debtors	850		
bank/cash	400		
prepayments	120		
revenue accrued	360	3,230	
Current Liabilities			
Creditors	950		
Accruals	88		
revenue prepaid	25	1,063	
Working Capital			2,167
Capital Employed			20,417
Long-term Liabilities			
Mortgage	8,000		
bank loan	1,000		(9,000)
			11,417
Financed by			
capital: G Harrison	10,000		
+ net profit	4,567		
drawings	14,567		
cash	(2,600)		
stocks	(500)		
telephone	(50)		11,417

NOTE:
If working capital was a negative figure, then the term used is 'net current liabilities' and would be deducted from fixed assets of £18,250.

Examples of adjustments and ledger entries
The following examples concern some questions that examine how these adjustments affect the accounts in the nominal ledger:

Example 1
The light & heat account had a balance brought down of £1,895 and the figure to profit and loss account was £1,520 that had included an electricity prepayment of £375. This was an error because the prepayment was in effect, an accrued expense of £375. What effect did this have on the account? What would be the entry to correct the error? The account would have appeared as:

Light & heat account			
31/12 balance b/d	1,895	31/12 prepaid	375
		31/12 profit & loss	1,520
	1,895		1,895
1/1 prepaid b/d	375		

The correct figure to be transferred to profit and loss account should be £2,270 (£1895 add £375 accrual). The easiest way to correct this error is to double the £375 as a credit entry of £750 to profit and loss account (£1,520 + £750 = £2,270). This provides the correct debit balance of £375 accrued that is then the accrued expense brought down. The account should have read:

Light & heat account

31/12	prepaid b/d	375	1/1	profit & loss	750
	accrued c/d	375			
		750			750
			1/1	accrued b/d	375

Example 2

A company makes its accounts up to 31 December 20-2. The following information relates to the telephone account:

Charges paid to date for 31 December 20-2	£2,144
Rental charges paid 15 November to 15 February 20-3	£428
Incurring dialled calls 1 December to 1 March 20-3	£856

Prepare the telephone account for the period ended 31 December 200-2

Telephone account

31/12	balance	2,144	31/12	prepaid	214
	rental	428		profit & loss	2,643
	accrued calls	285			
		2,857			2,857
1/1	prepaid b/d	214	1/1	accrued b/d	285

In this case half the rental is paid in advance to 15 February and one third of the calls are still to be charged for to the year ended 31 December.

KEY POINTS OF THE CHAPTER

Accounting period:	Normally 12 months but may be broken down more frequently for profit calculation particularly for larger organisations
Adjustments:	Required for the matching process between revenue and expenses, eg. closing stock, accrued expenses, prepaid expenses
Accrued expense:	An expense owing
Prepaid expense:	An expense paid in advance
Revenue accrued:	Income still to be received
Revenue prepaid:	Income paid in advance
Drawings:	Taken from the business for the owner's personal use
Final accounts:	The profit and loss account and balance sheet
Financial statements:	The profit and loss account and balance sheet.

QUESTIONS

1. If adjustments were not included in the financial statements at the year end, what effect would it have on the accounts?
2. When a number of adjustments are made at the foot of a trial balance at the financial year end, what should be remembered when entering them in the final accounts? Give examples to clarify your answer.
3. If you received a gas bill in November for £360 which included power used in the previous 3 months and you expected to receive approximately the same sum for the next quarter, how would this affect the accounts if the year end was 31 December? The light & heat account balance prior to the November bill was £1,855, prepare the ledger account to record the above information at the year end.
4. The following accounts were taken from the books of Harry Wright for the financial year ended 31 December:

	Debit £	Credit £
Capital: H Wright		16,000
Drawings	4,200	
Stock 1 January	12,890	
Purchases	22,430	
Sales		32,300
Premises	12,000	
Equipment	760	
Motor van	2,250	
Debtors	23,220	
Creditors		33,600
Returns inward	250	
Returns outward		540
Rates and water	850	
Wages	4,480	
Advertising	250	
Office expenses	280	
Discount received		350
General expenses	820	
Bank overdraft		1,890
	84,680	84,680

Note: At 31 December:
   a) The value of stock £10,500.
   b) Wages owing £42.
   c) Rates pre-paid £30.
   d) At invoice for office stationery still unpaid £55.

Required:
Prepare the trading and profit and loss account of H Wright for the year ended 31 December, and a balance sheet as a that data. (Show working capital).

5. You work as an accounts clerk for a company which is preparing its first year's accounts. You are in the process of writing up various expense accounts and transferring amounts into the profit and loss account and balance sheet, for the year ending 31 December.

Rent of £600 is payable quarterly in arrears and the following payments have been made: 1 April £600; 5 July £600; 20 October £600.

Insurance: After a few months of trading the company realised that it had not insured against a number of possible risks. Details of policies taken out were as follows:

1 January   Annual premium of £700 paid in respect of occupiers' and employers' liability.
1 April   Annual premium of £600 paid on building insurance.
1 July   Stock insured and an annual premium of £800 paid.

Required:
a) Write up the rent account for year ended 31 December clearly showing the amount transferred to the profit and loss account.
b) Write up the insurance account for year ended 31 December clearly showing the amount transferred to the profit and loss account.
c) What amount in respect of rent and insurance would you include as accruals/prepayments in the balance sheet?

6. Jones started a new business on 1 December 20-4 and made the following transactions regarding insurance for the business:

1/12/20-4	Took out cover for occupiers' liability	Annual premium paid £1,000
1/2/20-5	Took out cover on buildings	Annual premium paid £1,200
1/5/20-5	Took out cover on stock	Annual premium paid £800

Write up the insurance account in the ledger, clearly showing the amount to be transferred to the profit and loss account for the year ending 30/11/20-5.

7. Trial Balance of Peter Jackson as on 30 June:

	Debit £	Credit £
Sales		77,615
Purchases	56,470	
Returns Inward	205	
Rent received		1,545
Returns Outward		315
Opening stock	3,345	
Insurance, telephone	430	
Light, heat	446	
Postage, stationery	450	
Discount allowed	75	
Motor expenses	1,060	
Wages	4,785	
Discounts received		86
Cash	200	
Bank overdraft		420
Premises	20,000	
Equipment	1,600	
Motor Vehicle	500	
Debtors	2,400	
Creditors		2,560
Loan (Long term)		4,925
Capital		4,500
	71,966	71,966

The following additional information was available on 30th June:
a) Unsold stock was valued £2,580.
b) Accrued expenses: Wages £145, gas & electricity bills £182, telephone £95.
c) Prepayments: Insurance premiums £105, unused stationery £55.
d) Rent of £360 per quarter to 31 July, was still unpaid.

Required:
a) Prepare the trading and profit and loss account for the period ended, 30th June.
b) Prepare the balance sheet as on 30th June.

8. Trial Balance of H Andrews as on 30 November

	Debit £	Credit £
Sales		57,615
Purchases	36,470	
Returns inward	1,205	
Commission received		1,520
Returns outward		1,315
Opening stock	2,355	
Carriage inwards	442	
Drawings	4,238	
Maintenance & rates	998	
Insurance & telephone	334	
Light & heat	546	
Postage & stationery	350	
Discount allowed	175	
Motor expenses	560	
Wages	6,285	
Cash	520	
Bank overdraft		1,850
Equipment	30,502	
Motor vehicles	2,500	
Debtors	12,400	
Creditors		12,560
Loan (long term)		6,160
Capital		18,860
	99,880	99,880

The following additional information was available on 30th November:
a) Unsold stock was valued £3,800.
b) Accrued expenses: Wages £185, gas & electricity bills £190.
c) Prepayments: Insurance premiums £80, unused stationery £110.
d) The owner took stock for his own use valued £80 per week for the whole year.
e) Of the commission received 10% of it is earned in advance for December.

Required:
Prepare the trading and profit and loss account for the period ended, 30 November and the balance sheet as on that date.

Chapter 24

Adjustments: Bad Debts and Provisions for Debtors

INTRODUCTION

Any business that offers credit to its customers and therefore creates debtors must make every effort to ensure that debts are paid. This, for larger businesses particularly, means having an effective credit control section which has the responsibility of ensuring debtors pay their bills in reasonable time as guided by the invoice date.

Accounts must be monitored on a regular basis and customers chased up if they are late in meeting their payments. Inevitably, a large number of businesses do have to write off some of their customers at one time or another. This is costly to the business because a debtor (asset) has to be written off as an expense. The double entry to write off the debtor is:

Debit: bad debts account (expenses +)
Credit: debtor's account   (asset -)

If a sales ledger control account is used in the nominal ledger, the control account is also credited. As an example, G Harrison decided to write off one of his customers, James Hunt as a bad debt, value £75:

Sales ledger

		Dr	Cr	Balance
J Hunt account				
1/12	Balance			75 Dr
31/12	bad debts		75	0

Nominal ledger

		Dr	Cr	Balance
Bad Debt account				
1/12	Balance			110 Dr
31/12	J Hunt	75		185
	profit & loss		185	0
S/L control account				
31/12	balance			925 Dr
31/12	J Hunt		75	850

Types of adjustments
In this section, we will look at adjustments made in relation to debtors' accounts:

- Provisions for bad debts
- Recovery of bad debts
- Provisions for cash discounts

Each of these adjustments affect the profit and loss account and the balance sheet:

	Type of adjustment	profit & loss	balance sheet
1	Create provision for bad debts	increase expense	debtors – provision
2	Increase provision for bad debts	increase expense	debtors – provision
3	Reduce provision for bad debts	reduce expense	debtors – provision
4	Recovery of bad debts	reduce expense	increase bank
4	Create provision for discounts	increase expense	debtors – provision
5	Increase provision for discounts	increase expense	debtors – provision
6	Reduce provision for discounts	reduce expense	debtors – provision

Note that to create a provision refers to making a start and entering a provision account in the nominal ledger. Thereafter, these provisions can be increased or decreased according to the level of debtors and the amount to be provided. When a provision for bad debts or discounts is reduced, the expense is reduced, thereby reducing the sum to be deducted from debtors in the balance sheet.

Provisions for bad & doubtful debts
Accountants are said to be prudent in that they are cautious when it comes to valuing a business's assets. This follows the accounting concept of prudence discussed further in Chapter 32, accounting standards. If some customers in the sales ledger are slow in paying their bills and look in some way doubtful as to settling their accounts, it is a normal procedure to make a sufficient allowance against debtors in the event that they will fail to pay their debts.

Example
On 31 December, it was decided to make a 10% provision for bad debts against G Harrison's debtors figure of £850. This creates an expense charged against the profit & loss account and a new account is opened in the nominal ledger. The double entry is:

Debit: profit & loss account £85 (expense increase)
Credit: provision for bad debts account £85 (asset decrease)

Profit & loss account and balance sheet (extract) Year 1		
	£	£
Profit & loss account		
Expenses:		
Provision for bad debts		85
Balance sheet		
Current assets:		
Debtors	850	
- provision for bad debts	(85)	765

Nominal ledger			
	Dr	Cr	Balance
Provision for bad debts account			
Year 1			
31/12 profit & loss		85	85 Cr
Year 2			
1/1 Balance			85 Cr

At the year end 31 December in Year 2, Harrison had the following information:

- bad debts written off £135
- debtors £1,550
- 10% provision for bad debts to be maintained.

Profit & loss account and balance sheet (extract) Year 2

	£	£
Profit & loss account		
Expenses:		
bad debts	135	
provision for bad debts	70	205
Balance sheet		
Current assets:		
Debtors	1,550	
- provision for bad debts	(155)	1,395

NOTE:
10% of debtors = £155 but only £70 needs to be charged to profit & loss account because £85 is *already credited* to that account. In this way the provision for bad debts account is adjusted each year to equal the percentage required against debtors' balances considered to be doubtful or unreliable.

Want?	10% of debtors = £155
Got	£85 in the provision account
Need?	£70 (to make up the total (£85 + £70)

Nominal ledger

		Dr	Cr	Balance
Bad debts account				
Year 2				
31/12	Balance			135 Dr
	profit & loss		135	0
Provision for bad debts account				
Year 2				
1/1	Balance			85 Cr
31/12	profit & loss		70	155
Year 3				
1/1	Balance			155 Cr

If on 31 December, in Year 3 the debtors of G Harrison were £1,450 and the 10% provision was still maintained, how much would the charge be against the profit & loss account?

Want?	£1,450 x 10% provision = £145
Got	£155 in the provision account
Need?	£10 less in the provision account

In this case, the provision account is *reduced* and would be debited with £10 and the profit & loss account credited with £10. The double entry:

Debit: Provision for bad debts account £10
Credit: Profit & loss account £10 (expense reduced)

Provision for bad debts account

		Dr	Cr	Balance
Year 3				
1/1	Balance			155 Cr
31/12	profit & loss	10		145
Year 4				
1/1	Balance			145 Cr

Transfer of bad debts to provision for bad debts

Alternatively, the bad debts account can be transferred to the provision for bad debts account at the end of the period. After all, the provision account is a sum set aside to cover any bad debts that might occur in the future so it would be logical to make this transfer. If we return to the end of year two:

Nominal ledger

		Dr	Cr	Balance
Bad debts account				
Year 2				
31/12	Balance			135 Dr
	provision bad debts		135	0
Provision for bad debts account				
Year 2				
1/1	Balance			85 Cr
31/12	bad debts	135		50 Dr
	profit & loss		205	155 Cr

Profit & loss account – Year 2
Expenses:
   Provision for bad debts   205

NOTE:

Exactly the same sum has been charged to the profit and loss account using this alternative method. A 10% provision equalling £155 is made by charging the profit and loss account with £205 because of the £50 *debit balance* remaining, after bad debts had been transferred into the provision account. The balance sheet would remain exactly the same (debtors £1,550 – provision £155 = £1,395).

The journal entries to record the above adjustments for Year 2:

Journal

		Debit	Credit
Year 2		£	£
Dec.31	Provision for bad debts	135	
	Bad debts		135
	Profit & Loss account	205	
	Provision for bad debts		205
	Being adjustment of provision to equal 10% debtors		

The Recovery of Bad Debts

In the event of a customer paying back a debt which had previously been written off, either in part-payment or in full, the debt must first be reinstated in the customer's sales ledger account. It is important to do this because the record will then show that the customer did in effect, honour the debt at some future point in time. Once the cheque has been received and banked, the posting to the ledger account clears the debt. The procedure for this type of transaction is therefore as follows:

1 Reinstate the debt:
    Debit: the customer's account (and sales ledger control account) with amount recovered;
    Credit: the bad debts account

2 Bank the amount received:
    Debit: bank account
    Credit: customer's account (and sales ledger control account).

Example:
If J Hunt, the bad debt of Harrison, previously written off for £75, repaid his account in full on 30 November, year 2, the ledgers would show the following:

Sales Ledger

		Debit	Credit	Balance
J Hunt account				
Year 1				
1/12	Balance			75 Dr
	bad debts		75	0
	BAD DEBT WRITTEN OFF			
Year 2				
30/11	bad debts	75		75 Dr
	bank		75	0

The nominal ledger entries are:

Nominal Ledger

		Debit	Credit	Balance
Bad debts account				
Year 3				
1/11	balance			120 Dr
30/11	J Hunt		75	45
Sales ledger control account				
Year 2				
1/11	balance			1,440 Dr
30/11	J Hunt	75		1,515
30/11	bank		75	1,440
Bank account				
Year 2				
1/11	balance			745 Dr
30/11	J Hunt	75		820

NOTE:

- Remember that the sales ledger control account must reflect in total, what affects the individual accounts in the sales ledger. Both the debt recovered and received in J Hunt's personal account must also be recorded in the control account, otherwise the schedule of debtors would not reconcile with the sales ledger control account.
- In effect, it makes no difference to the sales ledger control balance, but the record must still show the reinstatement and clearance of the debt.

Credit control

It is important for a business to try to restrict the total of outstanding debts due from their customers. A system of internal control is needed to ensure that all customers pay their accounts on time, and particularly if the economy starts to take a downturn and liquidity becomes a problem for many businesses.

It would be foolhardy to allow just any customer to buy any amount of goods they wanted without first fully checking how reliable they were. If a customer shows that he can regularly pay his outstanding debts, then trust is built up between the buyer and seller. Where some customers take their time about paying and their debts are outstanding over a long period of time (say, beyond a period of three months), then firm action needs to be taken to recover the debts.

It is essential in business to have an *'aged debtors list'* that is, a list which clearly establishes how old the debts of customers are. For example, a firm has debtors who owe a total of £18,500. The 'aged' list of debtors might be as shown in the table below. It would seem that those debts which are 3 months old or more ought to be investigated to see what measures could be taken to expedite payment.

Aged list of debtors

		£
60%	Are current (1 month)	11,100
20%	are 2 months old	3,700
15%	are 3 months old	2,775
5%	are over 3 months old	925
	Total customers' debts	18,500

From this schedule of aged debtors, a business can make an estimate of the percentage debt that might be doubtful. The percentage provision for doubtful debts could be on the basis of:

Current (up to a month)	1.5%
One-two months	2.0%
Two-three months	2.5%
Over three months	5.0%

Therefore:	£11,100 x 1.5%	£166.50	
	£3,700 x 2.0%	£74.00	
	£2,775 x 2.5%	£69.38	
	£925 x 5.0%	£46.25	£356.13

A provision of £356 on a total debt of £18,500 = 1.92%, or approximately 2.0% overall. This could then be the figure in the final accounts for the provision for bad and doubtful debts.

The credit controller

A business may employ a credit controller with the responsibility of chasing up the older debts. A thorough and continuous system is required to ensure that customers do not exceed their credit limits and that they pay their bills on time.

A *credit rating* is a device that seeks to inform the credit controller how good or bad a customer is when paying his bills. For example, a 5-star rating might indicate an absolute top mark rating for those customers showing great reliability. At the other end of the scale, a 1-star rating would indicate that the customer needs close attention and that the value of sales would have to be closely monitored to make sure payment is made. A credit limit is made on customers that will indicate the limit of their purchases. In this way, payment must be made before further sales are made to the customer.

Credit ratings of customers can change, depending on whether they become more or less reliable. The credit rating also gives guidance as to the value of sales allowed to a customer. The higher the rating, it follows that the higher the sales value a customer is given.

The credit controller can make up the ratings according to past experiences with customers. With new customers, assistance can be gained from organisations like Dun & Bradstreet that make evaluations of company performance and estimate their ability to pay debts. A new customer would normally be expected to give references from other suppliers or from their bank.

The provision for debtors discounts

If it is the policy of a business to allow customers to have cash discounts on their sales, it may be seen as prudent to make an appropriate provision for it in the same way as providing for bad and doubtful debts. The amount of provision for discount is therefore:

Debit: profit and loss account (an expense)
Credit: provision for discounts allowed account (negative asset)

The provision for discounts must always be calculated on the net value of debtors: that is, after deducting the provision for bad debts. The balance sheet will then indicate the gross debtors' figure, less both provisions for discounts and bad debts.

The provision for discounts allowed to customers may then be adjusted each year in relation to the amount of discounts allowed and the provision for bad debts.

Exampl:e

George Harrison has £800 credit as the opening balance (1 January year 1) in the provision for bad debts account. He decides to provide a 2.5% provision for discounts at the year end. The following figures relate to the two years ended 31 December:

Year 1 Debtors £16,800   Bad debts written off £785
Year 2 Debtors £18,000   Bad debts written off £700.
Provision for bad debts 5%
Provision for discounts 2.5%

Solution:

Nominal ledger

		Dr	Cr	Balance
Provision for Bad Debts account				
Year 1				
1/1	Profit & Loss account			800 Cr
31/12	Bad debts	785		15
	Profit & Loss account		825	840
Year 2				
31/12	Bad debts	700		140
	Profit & Loss account		760	900
Provision for Discounts Allowed account				
Year 1				
31/12	Profit & Loss account		399	399 Cr
Year 2				
31/12	Profit & Loss account		29	428

Profit & Loss Account year ended 31/12		£	£
Year 1	Provision for bad debts	825	
	Provision for discounts	399	
Year 2	Provision for bad debts	760	
	Provision for discounts	29	

Balance Sheet as on 31/12				
Year 1	Debtors			16,800
-	Provision for bad debts		840	
	Provision for discounts		399	1,239
				15,561
Year 2	Debtors			18,000
-	Provision for bad debts		900	
	Provision for discounts		428	1,328
				16,682

NOTE:	Year 1	Year 2
Provision for bad debts:	£	£
Want	840	900
Got	(15)	(140)
Need (P & L)	825 Cr	760 Cr

Provision for discounts:

Want	2.5% of £16800 - £840 provision	2.5% of £18,000 - £900 provision
Need	= £ 399	= £428, got £399 need = £29

KEY POINTS OF THE CHAPTER

Bad debt:	A debtor which is written off as unable to pay
Provision for bad debts:	A charge against profits to cover any possible future bad debts
Bad debts recovered:	A former bad debtor who pays either the full sum or part sum which was previously written off
Provision for discounts:	A charge against profits to cover any cash discounts offered to debtors, always made after the provision for bad debts deducted from debtors
Credit control:	Internal control of debtors to ensure their bills are paid within target date
Aged debtors list:	A list of debtors indicating age of debts, usually in month order
Credit rating:	Indicates how reliable a customer is in relation to paying debts

QUESTIONS

1. It has been said that if a customer is written off as 'bad' it is recognised that an asset has changed to an expense.
   Explain and use the double entry principle to clarify your point.
2. At the end of a financial year, the balance of bad debts account could be transferred to the provision for bad debts account.
   Would this have an effect on what is transferred to profit and loss account ?
3. Explain the double entry principle on the occasion that a custom once written off as a bad debt, repays half the sum which was owed.
4. Given a business has a high value of debtors, why should the accountant be prudent and on what basis would he/she make his/her calculations?
5. The following information represent the accounts of James Hunt on 31 December:

Account	£
Capital: J Hunt	8,000
Drawings	2,500
Cash	100
Bank	400
Equipment	400
Motor vehicle	1,500
Stock (1/1)	4,800
Debtors	2,500
Creditors	3,130
Sales	12,200
Purchases	7,000
Returns outward	250
Rent	160
Discount received	20
Stationery	90
Wages	3,000
General expenses	1,000
Rates	150

Adjustments: 31 December
- Stock unsold £4,300.
- Rates pre-paid £38.
- A provision for bad debts is to be made to equal 5% of debtors.
- Wages outstanding £120.
- Stationery unused £40.

Required:
a) A trading and profit and loss account for the year ended 31 December.
b) A balance sheet as at that date.

6. You work for a firm of accountants and have to prepare the final accounts for a client, S Waugh. The following trial balance was extracted on 29 February 20-5.

	Dr £	Cr £
Capital		60,000
Loan from A Boarder [long-term]		25,000
Premises	39,000	
Drawings	15,000	
Stock at 1/3/20-4	26,500	
Motor vans (at cost)	35,000	
Carriage outwards *	4,000	
Fixtures (at cost)	15,000	
Purchases and sales	173,200	319,200
Debtors and creditors	21,400	14,200
Returns inwards and outwards	1,200	800
Discounts allowed and received	4,000	2,100
Motor expenses	9,200	
Rent and rates	12,400	
Postage and telephone	3,100	
Wages and salaries	49,800	
Insurance	6,100	
Interest paid	2,000	
Advertising	4,200	
Bank/Cash	200	
	421,300	421,300

* A profit and loss expense

Notes at 29/2/20-5:
- Stock at cost £31,000.
- A provision for bad debts is to be created to equal 4% of debtors.
- Rent is prepaid (£850).
- There is £140 still outstanding on interest payments.
- Advertising paid in advance is £146.

Required:
a) Prepare the trading and profit and loss account for the year ended 28 February 20-5.
b) Prepare the balance sheet as at 28 February 20-5.

[Institute of Commercial Management]

7. The following trial balance was extracted from the accounts of A Farney on 30 November:

	Dr £	Cr £
Bad debts written off in year	400	
Cash in hand	250	
Cash at bank	6,250	
Purchases/sales	23,500	80,000
Motor vehicles	12,500	
Rent and rates	1,250	
Light and heat	600	
Carriage outwards	350	
Opening stock	18,750	
Commissions received		1,350
Capital		75,740
Drawings	8,500	
Returns	1,650	2,000
Office salaries	25,000	
Debtors creditors	23,600	5,650
Provisions for bad debts		1,860
Fixture and fittings	8,000	
Land and buildings	46,000	
Bank Loan (long-term)		10,000
	176,600	176,600

Notes at 30 November:
- Closing stock £19,500.
- £800 owing on office salaries.
- Rates had been paid £150 in advance.
- £100 is owed for heating.
- Provision for bad debts is to be increased to 10% of the debtors.
- Interest on loan of £1,000 is still outstanding.
- It was decided to create a provision for discounts for customers at a rate of 1.25% pa.

Required:
a) Prepare. the trading and profit and loss account for the year ended 30 November.
b) Prepare the Balance sheet as at 30 November.

[Institute of Commercial Management]

8. During the financial period ending 31 December, Charcoal Ltd wrote off bad debts totalled £6,420. The company rather surprisingly, also received £850 from a customer previously written off as a bad a few years ago.
On 31 December, its debtors were 'aged' as follows::

No. of days outstanding	Debtors £	
Over 90 days	4,210	
90 days	7,560	
60 days	20,800	
30 days	56,440	89,010

The company had an opening provision for bad and doubtful debts of £6,400.
When the customers of over 90 days' debt were investigated, it was decided to write off £800 as bad. The company's policy concerning the provision for bad debts is to use a percentage sliding scale off (round up to nearest £:

Over 90 days	75%
90 days	50%
60 days	10%
30 days	0%

Required:

As on 31 December:

a) The bad debts account.
b) The provision for bad debts account. (Bad debts to be transferred to this account.)
c) The figure to be transferred to the profit and loss account and the debtors' presentation in the balance sheet.
d) Explain briefly the double-entry procedure when a bad debt is recovered.

[Association of Accounting Technicians]

9. Bradshaw Limited produced the following aged debtor analysis as at the end of the financial year:

	Balance	Current	One month	Two months	Three months and over
	£	£	£	£	£
Debtors at 31/12/20-4	120,000	50,000	30,000	30,000	10,000
Debtors at 31/12/20-5	180,000	90,000	60,000	25,000	5,000

In both years the provision for bad debts account is made up by providing for bad debts at:

20%	on debtors over 3 months
10%	on debtors aged 2 months
2%	on debtors aged 1 month
0.5%	on current debtors

Required:

a) i) Calculate the provision for bad debts as at 31/12/20-4.
   ii) Calculate the provision for bad debts as at 31/12/20-5.
b) Prepare the provision for bad debts account over the two years. Note provision as at 1/1/20-4 was £4,900 CR).
c) Briefly state with reasons if you think Bradshaw's credit control has improved over the two years.
d) If a provision for discount allowed was created to equal 2% of net debtors, show how the debtors would be shown in the balance sheet as on 31/12/20-5.

[Institute of Commercial Management]

Chapter 25

Depreciation of Fixed Assets

INTRODUCTION

Fixed assets lose their value over periods of time. For example, if equipment was purchased at the beginning of the financial period for £2,000 would it be worth the same sum at the end of the period? It may only be worth £1,500 and therefore its value would have depreciated by £500.
The concept of depreciation is that fixed assets lose their value over periods of time and that loss is recorded as an expense, charged to the business in the profit and loss account.
Two key points to note are:

- Depreciation is a measure of the wearing out of fixed assets through use, time or obsolescence,
- Depreciation charges should be made as equitably as possible over the useful life of an asset so that charges directly relate to the benefit gained from using it.

There are various reasons why a fixed asset should lose its value. Fixtures, fittings, equipment and motor vehicles all wear out over periods of time due to the continuous use of them.
Equipment, particularly in computer technology, can soon become obsolete and need replacement. This is because competition in the market place often demands that the business with the most cost effective goods and services will win a larger share of the market. Therefore equipment needs to be replaced even though it could still be relatively new.

Other fixed assets deplete in value because their resources are used up. Quarries and mines become exhausted due to output of minerals etc. The extraction of the resource in effect, becomes the charge for depreciation as we will demonstrate later on in the section.

Depreciation is therefore a charge against the purchase of fixed assets spread over their 'useful life'. The measurement of the actual charge each year is not an exact science because it is too subjective. To calculate how much depreciation to charge on an annual basis will depend upon:

- The type of fixed asset purchased.
- The method chosen to depreciate it.
- An estimation of how long the fixed asset will last over its useful life.
- An estimation of how much the residual (or scrap) value of the fixed asset will be when it is disposed of.

Fixed assets are normally depreciated after each financial period and should be calculated on an equitable and consistent basis. Once a suitable method has been adopted to depreciate a particular asset, or the same group of assets, the *same* method should be used throughout its useful life.

Methods of depreciation
Although there are a number of various ways to depreciate fixed assets there are two major methods:
- The straight line method (or fixed instalment).
- The reducing balance method (or diminishing balance method).

The straight line method

This method charges the same amount of depreciation each year because a fixed percentage is calculated on the *cost price*. Many businesses might choose this method to depreciate the value of furniture, fixtures and fittings, or the leasing of premises, because for these, the same depreciation charge is seen as an equitable method. The formula to calculate this is:

$$\text{Straight line} = \frac{\text{Cost - Residual value}}{\text{Estimated life (years)}}$$

For example, if furniture was purchased for £2,000 and was to be used over a period of 4 years with an estimated £200 residual value:

Cost of asset	£2,000
Estimated residual value	£200
Sum to be written off	£1,800

Depreciation to be charged annually:

$$\frac{£2,000 - 200}{4} = £450 \text{ per annum}$$

This represents a 22.5% annualised charge based on the cost of the fixed asset (£450/£2,000). If there was no scrap value the annual charge would have been 25% (£500/£2,000).
The effect it would have on the annual value of furniture is shown below:

Year	Depreciation per annum	Cumulative Depreciation	Net book value (NBV)
	£	£	£
0			2,000
1	450	450	1,550
2	450	900	1,100
3	450	1350	650
4	450	1800	200
			(residual value)

The method charges the same £450 depreciation on furniture for each year over the 4 years of its estimated life. When it is disposed of, the sum received may or may not equal £200. If the scrap value for example was zero, then a further charge of £200 is made to the profit and loss account as *'loss on disposal of fixed asset £200'*. If it were sold for £300, then the result would be *'profit on disposal £100'*, (£300 - net book value £200).

Profit & loss account	£
Year 1	
Expenses:	
Depreciation of furniture	450
Year 2	
Depreciation of furniture	450
Year 3	
Depreciation of furniture	450
Year 4	
depreciation of furniture	450

Balance sheet

Fixed assets	Cost	Depreciation	Net Book Value
	£	£	£
Year 1	2,000	450	1,550
Year 2	2,000	900	1,100
Year 3	2,000	1,350	650
Year 4	2,000	1,800	200

Note that in the profit and loss account, the depreciation charge is for that particular year. In the balance sheet, the cumulative (total) depreciation is shown after each year. The cost of a fixed asset less its cumulative depreciation equals its *net book value*.

The reducing balance method

If this method was applied to the furniture, a fixed percentage rate would be applied on the net book value of the asset each year, this means that the depreciation charge gets less over the life of the asset. This provides more depreciation in the early years and less depreciation in the later years. How is the rate % calculated?

Cost of asset	£2,000
Estimated residual value	£400
Sum to be written off	£1,600
Estimated 'life'	4 years

Formula for rate %:

$$\text{Rate \%} = 1 - \sqrt[N]{\frac{\text{residual value}}{\text{cost of asset}}}$$

(N = number of years)

$$1 - \sqrt[4]{\frac{400}{2,000}}$$

$$= 1 - \quad 0.669$$
$$= 0.331 \text{ or } 33\% \text{ per annum on the net book value}$$

Check your answer:

Residual Value of asset $= \text{Cost} (1-R)^N$
$= £2,000 (1-33\%)^4$
$= £2,000 (0.67)^4$
$= £403$

The effect the reducing balance method would have on the annual value of furniture:

Year	Depreciation per annum	Cumulative depreciation	NBV
	£	£	£
0			2,000
1	660	660	1,340
2	442	1102	898
3	296	1398	602
4	199	1597	403
			(residual value)

If the straight line method had been chosen, then £400 per annum would be charged to the profit and loss account. Compare this figure with the reducing balance method and see the affect it would have on the annual profit and loss account.

Recording depreciation in the ledger
The double entry for recording depreciation in the ledger is:

Debit: profit & loss account (expense +)
Credit: provision for depreciation of asset account (asset -)

If we use the above example of the furniture using the reducing balance method of depreciation, the nominal ledger accounts, in the 'T' format would appear as:

Nominal ledger

Debit						Credit
		Furniture account				
Year 1						
1/1	Bank	2,000				

		Provision for depreciation of furniture account				
				Year 1		
31/12	Balance c/d	660		31/12	profit & loss	660
				Year 2		
				1/1	balance c/d	660
31/12	Balance c/d	1,102		31/12	profit & loss	442
		1,102				1,102
				Year 3		
31/12	Balance c/d	1,398		1/1	balance b/d	1,102
				31/12	profit & loss	296
		1,398				1,398
				Year 4		
31/12	Balance c/d	1,597		1/1	balance b/d	1,398
				31/12	profit & loss	199
		1,597				1,597
				Year 5		
				1/1	balance b/d	1,597

Profit & loss account years ending 31 December:

Year	Less expenses	£
1	depreciation of furniture	660
2	depreciation of furniture	442
3	depreciation of furniture	296
4	depreciation of furniture	199

Balance sheet as at Year 4

	Cost	Depreciation	NBV (net book value)
Fixed Assets	£	£	£
furniture	2,000	1,597	403

Which method to depreciate?
The most *equitable* charge should be made. This would allocate the cost of depreciation in the fairest way over the useful life of the asset in relation to the benefits it brings. If the benefit of using a fixed asset is highest in the earlier years and less so in the later years, then depreciation should be greater during those earlier periods and less in the later.

The reducing balance method would probably be the most suitable in this case and could apply to plant, machinery, equipment and motor vehicles. On the other hand, if the asset brings benefit more or less equally throughout its useful life, then depreciation charges should reflect this and the straight line method adopted. Furniture, fixtures and fittings are likely to have this method applied when calculating the depreciation charge for the period.

The cost of some fixed assets notably motor vehicles, plant, machinery and equipment, includes not only depreciation charges but also the cost of maintenance and repairs. As these fixed assets become older and more wear and tear occurs, it is argued that they will cost more to service and maintain. Reducing depreciation in the latter years will then allow for further costs on repairs, making the overall cost of operating the asset more evenly throughout its useful life.

Both methods are the major forms of depreciation used in practice. A business could use the straight line method to depreciate its furniture, fixtures and fittings, whilst adopting the reducing balance method for its vehicles and equipment. Other methods like the machine hour rate may also be adopted and these are discussed later in the chapter.

Disposal of fixed assets
When an asset is sold or scrapped, the fixed asset account and its corresponding depreciation can be transferred to a *'disposal of fixed asset'* account.

Let us assume that the furniture was sold at the end of year 4 for £350 and the reducing balance method had been used to depreciate. The net book value came to £403, therefore a loss of £53 would have been incurred. The double entries require to transfer these details are:

Year 4 – *Disposal of furniture:*

Debit: Disposal of fixed asset account £2,000
Credit: Furniture account £2,000

Debit: Provision for depreciation of furniture account £1,597
Credit: Disposal account £1,597

Debit: Profit & loss account £53 (loss on disposal)
Credit: Disposal account £53

Debit: Bank account £350 (receipt on sale)
Credit: Disposal account £350

Nominal ledger

Debit					Credit
Furniture account					
Year 4					
31/12	Balance b/d	2,000	31/12	disposal account	2,000

Provision for depreciation of furniture account

31/12	Disposal account	1,597	31/12	balance b/d	1,597

Disposal of fixed asset account

31/12	Furniture	2,000	31/12	Depreciation	1,597
				Bank	350
				profit & loss	53
		2,000			2,000

NOTE:
- The loss on disposal of £53 is shown on the credit side of the disposal account
- The net book value of furniture is £403 [2,000-1,597] and it was sold for £350 which incurred the loss of £53.
- If the furniture had been sold for say £450, a gain of £47, the disposal account would be debited by £47, the profit & loss account credited by £47.

The journal
Is used for transactions such as the sale and purchase of fixed assets, depreciation and other adjustments and the corrections of errors. If we were to journalise the above disposal entries in year 4, the journal would appear as:

Journal

Date	Details	Dr	Cr
Year 4			
31/12	Disposal account	2,000	
	Furniture		2,000
	Provision for depreciation of furniture	1,597	
	disposal account		1,597
	bank	350	
	disposal account		350
	Being disposal of furniture		
	profit & loss account	53	
	disposal account		53
	Being loss on disposal of furniture		
	profit & loss account	199	
	provision for depreciation of furniture		199
	Being annual depreciation of furniture		

NOTE:
The debit entry is recorded first, the credit entry is slightly indented and a brief narrative is used to describe the transaction.

Example: depreciation of equipment

A business depreciates its equipment at the rate of 20% per annum, based on the **straight-line method**, applied on a month by month basis. The residual value is nil. Its financial period commences 1 January. The following information relates to the purchase, depreciation and disposal of the equipment over a period of three years:

Year 1   purchased equipment code A300 costing £4,800 on 1 January.
             purchased equipment code A310 costing £3,600 on 1 October.
Year 2   purchased equipment code A320 costing £2,400 on 1 July.
Year 4   on 1 October, traded in the equipment bought on 1 January Year 1 for £1,500 and purchased new equipment coded A330 for £8,000 from Jackson & Turner Ltd on credit, on the same date.

It was decided that the remaining economic life of the equipment code A320 purchased in July Year 2 should be reduced and written off in total by 30 June Year 5.

Required:
a) Prepare the equipment account, provision for depreciation of equipment account and disposal of equipment account over the four years, ending 31 December.
b) Show the appropriate journal entries which are required for year 4.
c) Prepare an extract of the profit and loss account for each of the four years for the period ending 31 December.
d) Prepare an extract of the balance sheets as at the end of each of the four years as on 31 December.

Solution:

Equipment account

Details	Debit £	Credit £	Balance £
Year 1			
1/1 Bank A300	4,800		14,800 Dr
1/10 Bank A310	3,600		8,400
Year 2			
1/7 Bank A320	2,400		10,800
Year 4			
1/10 Disposal A300		4,800	6,000
1/10 J & T Ltd A330	8,000		14,000

Provision for depreciation of equipment account

			Debit £	Credit £	Balance £	
Year 1						
31/12	Profit and Loss	A300		960		
		A310		180	1,140	Cr
Year 2						
1/1	Balance b/d				1,140	Cr
31/12	Profit and Loss	A300		960		
		A310		720		
		A320		240	3,060	Cr
Year 3						
1/1	Balance b/d				3,060	Cr
31/12	Profit and Loss	A300		960		
		A310		720		
		A320		480	5,220	Cr
Year 4						
1/1	Balance b/d				5,220	Cr
1/10	Profit and Loss	A300		720	5,940	Cr
31/12	Disposal a/c	A300	3,600*[1]		2,340	
	Profit and Loss	A310		720		
		A320		1,120*[2]		
		A330		400	4,580	Cr
Year 5						
1/1	Balance b/d				4,580	Cr

Calculation of depreciation:

A300 £960 per annum x 3years = £2,880
      + £960 x (3/4 year)   = £ 720
                                   £3,600*[1]

A320 £1680 depreciation left for 1.5 years, therefore 1 year:

$$= £1,680/1.5 = £1,120*[2]$$

Disposal of fixed asset account

	Details	Debit £	Credit £	Balance £	
Year 4					
1/10	Equipment A300	4,800		4,800	Dr
	Provision for depreciation		3,600	1,200	
31/12	J & T (trade in)		1,500	300	Cr
	Profit and loss (profit)	300		0	

Journal

Date	Details	Folio	Debit £	Credit £
Year 4				
1/10	Equipment A330		8,000	
	Disposal A300			1,500
	J & T Ltd			6,500
	Being purchase of new equipment A330			
	using A300 as part-exchange			
1/10	Disposal A300		4,800	
	Equipment A300			4,800
	· Provision for depreciation		3,600	
	Disposal			3,600
	Being disposal of old equipment, A300			
31/12	Disposal		300	
	Profit and loss			300
	Being profit on disposal of A300			
31/12	Profit and Loss account		2,960	
	Provision for depreciation			
	of equipment			2,960
	Being depreciation of equipment for			
	the year [720 + 720 + 1,120 + 400]			

An *alternative* method of showing the disposal of A300 in the journal that by-passes the disposal account is:

		Debit £	Credit £
Year 4			
1/10	Provision for depreciation	3,600	
	J & T Ltd.	1,500	
	Equipment		4,800
	Profit and Loss account		300
	Being disposal of old equipment A300 and Profit on disposal		

(Note that it has fewer entries yet has the same function as the above for the disposal of the A300).

Extract of profit and loss accounts for years ended 31 December

Year	Expenses	£
Year 1	Depreciation of Equipment	1,140
Year 2	Depreciation of Equipment	1,920
Year 3	Depreciation of Equipment	2,160
Year 4	Depreciation of Equipment	2,960
	Other Revenue:	
Year 4	Profit on disposal of fixed asset	300

Extract of balance sheets as at year ended 31 December

	Fixed assets	Cost £	Depreciation £	Net book value £
Year 1	Equipment	8,400	1,140	7,260
Year 2	Equipment	10,800	3,060	7,740
Year 3	Equipment	10,800	5,220	5,580
Year 4	Equipment	14,000	4,580	9,420

The use of a fixed assets register

The purchase of capital transactions can cost a business large sums of money. It may have a fleet of motor vehicles or extensive factory equipment, plant and machinery, office equipment, etc. The journal, as we have already pointed out, can be used as a book of prime entry to record the buying of these fixed assets. Yet is this sufficient to record and control what happens to them? There could be a whole list of valuable fixed assets housed in various departments or factory floors, and occasionally some of these would be scrapped or sold off and replaced by new ones. What is required, therefore, is a fixed asset register which lists all these assets of a business, together with other important facts about each of them, such as:

- the date of purchase;
- description of the asset;
- internal control number or other number for identification;
- the location of the asset;
- the cost of the asset;
- the method of depreciation used;
- the estimated scrap/sale value;
- the estimated useful life of the asset;
- its disposal date and authorisation of disposal;
- the proceeds, if any, on disposal.

The fixed asset register is not part of the double entry system; it is simply used for the purpose of internal control. The register can be used to make physical checks for the location of fixed assets and the person (the supervisor or manager) who is in charge of them. The register should also be reconciled with the fixed asset accounts in the nominal ledger to ensure that all aspects match. In other words, if an asset is sold off, this should be properly authorised, the asset released, the register completed and the necessary entries made in the journal and ledger accounts.

If any discrepancies do arise as a result of checks between the ledger accounts and the register, these must be investigated to find out why there are differences. It could be that there is a delay in sending the appropriate authorisation form when an asset has been disposed of. It could, of course, be far more serious in that theft could have occurred. Whatever the cause of any discrepancy, a solution should be found and the appropriate action taken.

The type of register for fixed assets will vary from one business to another. Some may have an individual page devoted to each type of fixed asset. Others may have columns across the page for various headings and list the assets in an organised way (for example, by department, or by the type of asset it is).

In the first example shown below, a list of fixed assets is recorded giving details of individual items, although not in the same depth as in the first. This is an example of a single page of a fixed asset register which, in the practice of this particular business, carries on for several pages, identifying a large number of individual fixed assets at a total cost value of £886,540. There is a great amount of investment capital tied up in the purchase of them and a tight control of the details concerning each fixed asset is required.

Example 1

Register of Fixed Assets as on 31 December

	£
Compaq 386N	
Code No. 025	
Cost as at 1/1/1995	2,600
Depreciation (straight-line) at 20%pa:	520
Net Book Value	2,080
Location: General Office: Expected residual value: 10% cost	

	£
Electronic Typewriter 4572	
Code No. 030	
Cost as at 30/3/1995:	360
Depreciation (straight-line) at 20%pa:	54
Net book value	306
Location: Technical Office: Expected residual value: scrap 0	

	£
Amstrad Computer 1428	
Code No. 028	
Cost as at 30/6/1994:	780
Depreciation (straight-line) at 20%pa:	234
Net book value:	546
Location: General Office: Expected residual value: scrap 0	

	£
Motor Vehicle: Peugeot GLA 242X	
Cost as at 30/04/1994:	10,800
Depreciation (reducing-balance) at 25%pa:	3,881
Net book value:	6,919
Location: Sales Director (RCP): Expected residual value £2000	

Example 2: A register identifying the motor vehicles of a business

Register of fixed assets as on 30 September. 20-4

Description of Vehicles	Depn. Method	N/L A/C	Date of Purchase	Cost	Depn. for year	Cum Depn.	NBV	Disposal Date	Auth. No.	Disposal Value	P& L a/c
Rover E676	S-L	N255	1/10/01	32,000	6,400	19,200	12,800				
Peogeot E932	S-L	N255	1/04/02	(36,000)	7,200	(18,000)	(18,000)	25/09/04	033	16,500	(2,500)
Rover F778	S-L	N255	1/01/04	24,000	3,600	3,600	20,400				
Rover G800	S-l	N255	1/04/04	28,000	2,800	2,800	25,200				
Totals				**84,000**	**20,000**	**25,600**	**58400**				**(2,500)**

NOTE:

The cost, cumulative depreciation and net book value (NBV) would be represented in the balance sheet under fixed assets.

The depreciation for the year, £20,000 and the loss on disposal £2,500 would be charged to the profit and loss account for the period ended 30 September, 20-4.

Example of final accounts with all adjustments

Robert Harden: trial balance as on 31 October, 20-8

	Dr	Cr
Cash at bank/in hand	6,500	
Purchases/sales	26,000	75,100
Motor vehicles	12,500	
Provision for depreciation (motor vehicles)		5,000
Rent and rates	1,400	
Light and heat	700	
Carriage inwards	500	
Carriage outwards	400	
Opening stock	18,300	
Commissions received		1,500
Drawings	9,000	
Returns	1,800	1,400
Office salaries	26,000	
Debtors/creditors	24,000	6,000
Provision for bad debts		2,000
Fixtures and fittings	8,000	
Provision for depreciation (fixtures and fittings)		2,400
Land and buildings	50,000	
Bank loan		10,000
Interest on loan (10%pa)	1,000	
Capital		82,700
	186,100	186,100

Notes: 31 October
a) Closing stock £21,000.
b) Revenue accrued: £420 still to be received on commission.
c) Rates had been paid £200 in advance.
d) £120 is owed for electricity (heating and lighting).
e) Provision for bad debts is to be increased to 10% of the debtors.
f) Provision for depreciation of 10%pa on cost is to be made on fixtures and
    fittings.
g) Provision for depreciation of 20%pa on book value of motor vehicles.
h) During the financial year, Robert Harden took goods for own use from
    the business which cost £800.

Required:
Prepare the trading and profit and loss account of Robert Harden for the year ended 31 October,
20-8 and a balance sheet as at that date, 31 October, 20-8.

Solution:

Robert Harden:

Trading and profit and loss account for year ending 31 October, 20-8

	£	£	£
Sales			75,100
Less returns inwards			1,800
			73,300
Less Cost of Sales:			
Opening stock		18,300	
Purchases	26,000		
add carriage inwards	500		
less returns outwards	(1,400)		
less stock for own use	(800)	24,300	
		42,600	
Closing Stock		(21,000)	21,600
Gross profit			51,700
Rent and rates paid	1,400		
Rent and rates in advance	200	1,200	
Light and heat paid	700		
Light and heat owing	120	820	
Carriage outwards		400	
Office salaries paid		26,000	
Interest on loan		1,000	
Increase in provisions for bad debts		400	
Provision for depreciation			
– fixtures & fittings		800	
Provision for depreciation – vehicles		1,500	32,120
			19,580
Add other revenue –			
Commissions received	1,500		
Add Accrued	420		1,920
Net profit			21,500

Robert Harden: balance sheet as at 31 October, 20-8

	£	£	£
	Cost	Cumulative Depreciation	Net book value
Fixed Assets			
Land and buildings	50,000	-	50,000
Fixtures and fittings	8,000	3,200	4,800
Motor vehicles	12,500	6,500	6,000
	70,500	9,700	60,800
Current Assets			
Stock	21,000		
Debtors	24,000		
- provision for bad debts	(2,400) 21,600		
Pre-payments	200		
Bank/cash	6,500		
Revenue accrued	420	49,720	
Current Liabilities			
Trade creditors	6,000		
Accruals	120	6,120	
Net current assets			43,600
Capital employed			104,400
Long Term Liabilities			
Bank loan			10,000
			94,400
Financed by.			
Capital	82,700		
Add net profit	21,500	104,200	
Less drawings (9,000 + 800)		9,800	94,400

Other alternative methods of depreciation
Apart from the main two methods already outlined, the straight line and the reducing balance, there are other ways in which to depreciate which may be more appropriate for certain types of fixed assets. These other methods are:

- revaluation
- machine hour rate
- unit rate
- depletion rate

Revaluation
This method could be suitable for fixed assets that may not have a high unit value. The hotel, catering and tourism industry could adopt this method against such items as crockery, cutlery, bedding, kitchen utensils etc. The assets are valued at the beginning of the year, any purchases throughout the year are added and at the end of the year the assets are re-valued in order to calculate depreciation.

Example:

Hotel Truro		£
1 January	value of kitchen equipment	3,250
	cost of new equipment during period	850
		4,100
31 December	revaluation of kitchen equipment	(3,500)
	depreciation charges for the year	**600**

Property revaluation

A further example of revaluation of fixed assets could involve an increase in value of land and buildings. For example, if premises were valued £10,000 at cost then after a number of years, the owner decided to re-value them to £100,000, this would represent an increase of £90,000.

If the land was worth £50,000 (land is not normally depreciated, only the value of buildings), this leaves £50,000 of property that could be depreciated. The double entry for the increase is:

Debit: premises £90,000
Credit: fixed asset revaluation account £90,000
(Recorded in the *'financed by'* section of the balance sheet)

If the owner wanted the premises depreciated over say 25 years, the annualised depreciation charge would be £2,000 per annum:

$$\frac{£50,000 \quad \text{(buildings)}}{25 \quad \text{(years)}}$$

= £2,000 per annum depreciation

Machine hour rate

Where plant and machinery is used, the number of operative or productive hours a machine performs over the accounting period could be the basis of adopting this method.

Example, if a machine costing £40,000, having a scrap value estimated at £5,000, had the capacity to operate for a total of 2,500 hours and is expected to use 750 hours in its first year, the depreciation charge would be:

$$\frac{\text{(Cost of fixed asset} - \text{scrap value)} \times \text{Number of period hours used}}{\text{Estimated total number of hours operated}}$$

$$= \frac{(40,000-5,000) \times 750}{2,500 \text{ units}}$$

= £10,500 depreciation for the year

Unit rate

This method is virtually identical to the machine hour rate but uses the number of units of output a machine could produce instead of the number of hours operated. If we substituted the number of units produced (the output), the depreciation charge would be the same. For example:

$$\frac{\text{(Cost of fixed asset} - \text{scrap value)} \times \text{Number of period units}}{\text{Estimated total output of units}}$$

$$= \frac{(40,000-5,000) \times 750 \text{ units}}{2,500 \text{ units}}$$

= £10,500 depreciation

Depletion rate
Again a similar method is used. For example, if a quarry was purchased on lease for £800,000 and it was estimated that a total of 10,000 tons of a resource could be extracted with and 1,500 tons taken in the first year:

Cost of fixed asset x Tonnage taken in period
            Estimated total output of units

= 800,000 x 1,500
       10,000

= £120,000 depreciation charge for the year

A business could use any of the methods discussed in this chapter. The key point is that the method should be the most equitable for a particular fixed asset, depreciation being in proportion to the benefit given by the asset over its useful life.

KEY POINTS OF THE CHAPTER

Depreciation: The loss in value of fixed assets charged against profits
Provision for depreciation: An account recording depreciation charges
Straight-line method: Where the same sum is depreciated each year and calculation based on cost
Reducing-balance: Where depreciation reduces each year and calculation based on net book value
Disposal of fixed asset a/c: Used to transfer fixed assets when sold or disposed of
Journal: A record of prime entry to record fixed assets and depreciation, etc.
Fixed asset register: A record of fixed assets monitoring location, depreciation, disposal, etc.
Alternative methods: Other depreciation methods including revaluation, machine hour rate, depletion rate.

QUESTIONS

1. a) Identify the factors which can cause fixed assets to depreciate.
   b) Using these factors which depreciate fixed assets, which of them do you consider significant in the following:
      i   a new high-tech machine capable of increased productivity;
      ii the purchase of a motor vehicle;
      iii the mining of minerals;
      iv the purchase of land;
      v   a new long-term lease of a fleet of vehicles.

2. a) What purpose does the journal serve relating to capital transactions?
   b) Outline the need for a business to maintain a fixed asset register.

3. A machine in the manufacturing industry has cost £3,500,000 and it is estimated that it will be used for five years.

    a) Prepare a depreciation schedule for the machine based on the equal instalment method and assume that it has a scrap value of £100,000.
        Your schedule should show for each of the five years, the annual depreciation, the accumulated depreciation and the net book value at the end of the year.

    b) Express the total depreciation as a percentage of the original cost.

    c) Prepare a depreciation schedule for the machine based on the reducing balance method, assuming an annual depreciation rate of 51%. Your schedule should show, for each of the five years, the annual depreciation, the accumulated depreciation and the net book value at the end of the year.

                                                                        (LCCI)

4. Another machine in the factory costs £225,000 and it is also estimated that it will last five years. It is estimated to have a scrap value of £7,500.

    a) Using the equal instalment method, calculate the percentage of the cost that must be written off in five years.

    b) The percentage of the cost written off each year.

    c) Prepare a schedule of depreciation that shows the annual depreciation for each year, the accumulated depreciation each year and the net book value at the end of each year.

    d) Using the reducing balance method, calculate the annual rate of depreciation.

    e) Using the reducing balance method, calculate the net book value of the machinery after it has been in use for four years.

                                                                        (LCCI)

5. The following accounts relate to Arthur Jones, a local businessman, as at year ended 31 December. You are to prepare a trading and profit and loss account for the year ended 31 December and balance sheet as at that date, from the information below:

Trial Balance as on 31 December

	Dr £	Cr £
Capital – A S Jones		71,000
Premises	57,500	
Equipment	23,000	
Provision for depreciation of equipment		6,000
Motor van	8,000	
Provision for depreciation of motor van		2,000
Stock (January 1)	8,300	
Purchases and sales	30,800	66,600
Returns inward	700	
Returns outward		900
Wages	16,500	
Carriage inwards *	500	
Carriage outwards	400	
Commission received		500
Bank interest	350	
Lighting and heating	1,650	
Postage and stationery	600	
Insurance	1,200	
Telephone	500	
Rent receivable		750
Debtors, creditors	7,000	11,750
Bank	1,950	
Discount	100	
Bad debts	450	
	159,500	159,500

Adjustments to be taken into account 31 December:
a) Unsold stock valued at cost £9,500.
b) Wages due to be paid £550.
c) Jones, the proprietor, takes goods for own use valued at cost £800.
d) Pre-paid stationery – unused stock valued £95.
e) Rent receivable still outstanding £180.
f) Depreciation: Motor van rev-valued to £4,500.
          Equipment depreciated 20% on net book value.
g) Provision for bad and doubtful debts to equal 10% of debtors.

Required:
Prepare the profit and loss account for the period ended 31 December and a balance sheet as at that date.

6. The trial balance of ABC Co. as on 31 December was as follows:

Account	Dr £	Cr £
Premises (cost)	24,000	
Fixtures and fittings (cost)	4,000	
Motor vehicle (cost)	5,000	
Bank	3,305	
Stock	5,750	
Debtors	20,500	
Creditors		24,220
Loan (3 years) 10%pa		15,500
Capital: ABC Co		18,000
Sales		21,274
Commission received		485
Discount		557
Salaries	2,864	
Light and heat	122	
Petty cash expenses	44	
General expenses	268	
Purchases	14,090	
Returns outward		484
Returns inward	577	
	78,520	78,520

The following information is to be taken into account as on 31 December:
- The value of unsold stock £6,259.
- Gas bill still outstanding £42.
- Under general expenses, stationery unused was £70.
- The owner took stock for his own use £2,100.
- Depreciation: Furniture and fittings 10% on cost.
                 Motor vehicle re-valued to £3,750.
- Provision for bad debts 5% of debtors.
- 6 months interest on loan unpaid.

Required:
a) Prepare the trading and profit and loss account of ABC Co. for the year ended 31 December.
b) A balance sheet as at that date, showing working capital and capital employed.
c) Calculate the working capital ratio (current assets/current liabilities). Is it adequate?

7. Mavron plc, owned the following motor vehicles as on 1 April 20-6:

Registration No.	Purchase date	Cost	Estimated residual value	Estimated life (years)
AAT	1/10/20-3	£8,500	£2,500	5 years
DJH	1/04/20-4	£12,000	£2,000	8 years

Mavron's policy is to provide at the end of each financial year, the straight line method of depreciation, applied on a month-by-month basis on all of it motor vehicles. During the financial year to 31 March 20-7, the following transactions occurred:

- On 30 June 20-6 the AAT vehicle was traded in and was replaced by vehicle registered KGC that cost £15,000. Its residual value was estimated £4,000 and estimated life 5 years. The trade in value was £5,000 and the balance due was paid in cash £4,000 and the remainder on credit from Pinot Finance Ltd.
- The estimated remaining economic life of the DJH vehicle was to be reduced from 6 years down to 4 years with no change in its residual value.

Required:
a) Prepare the motor vehicles, provision for depreciation, Pinot Finance Ltd. and the disposal of fixed asset accounts, up to and including the year ended 31 March, 20-7;
b) Show the necessary journal entries to give effect to the above transactions during the financial year ended 31 March 20-7;
c) Show the extracts of the profit and loss account and the balance sheet for the period end to 31 March 20-7;
d) Prepare an appropriate fixed asset register to show the above information to the period ended 31 March 20-7.

8. The following trial balance was extracted from the accounts of Harry Gallagher on 31 December. You are to prepare the trading and profit and loss account for the period ended 31 December and a balance sheet as at that date.

Trial Balance H Gallagher as on 31 December

	Dr £	Cr £
Sales		37,615
Purchases	26,470	
Returns	1,205	1,315
Stock (1/1)	2,355	
Carriage inwards	442	
Carriage outwards	580	
Drawings	2,560	
Maintenance and rates	998	
Insurance, telephone	334	
Light, heat	546	
Postage, stationery	350	
Bad debts	175	
Motor expenses	560	
Wages	6,285	
Provision for bad debts		300
Provision for discounts		65
Cash	500	
Bank overdraft		3,005
Equipment (cost)	21,600	
Provision for depreciation of equipment (1/1)		2,160
Motor van (cost)	2,500	
Provision for depreciation of van (1/1)		500
Debtors, creditors	12,420	12,560
Bank loan [Long term]		3,500
Capital: Gallagher		18,860
	79,880	79,880

Additional information was available on 31 December:

- Unsold stock was valued £3,895.
- Accrued expenses: wages £185, electricity bill £90.
- Pre-payments: stock of unused stationery £110, insurance £80.
- The bad debts provision is to be adjusted to equal 5% of debtors.
- The provision for discounts is to be adjusted to equal 1.5% of debtors.
- Depreciation: the van at 20% on the reducing balance method. Equipment at 10% of cost.
- Gallagher took £800 stock for personal use.

9. a) Jim Barlow is the owner of a taxi business and his financial year runs from 1 July to 30 June. On 1 July 20-5 he had two vehicles, one a Ford purchased on 10 January 20-3 for £10,000 and the other, a Toyota, purchased on 12 August 20-3 for £8,000.

During November 20-5, Jim Barlow decided to replace the Ford and trade it in for a new Mercedes costing £15,500. Jim took delivery of the new car on 4 November 20-5. The garage accepted the Ford together with a cheque for £9,500 in payment.

Vehicles are depreciated at 10% per annum on the reducing balance method (alternatively the diminishing balance), with a full year's depreciation charged in the year of purchase and no depreciation charged in the year a vehicle is disposed of.

Required:
i) Calculate the net book value of the Ford and Toyota vehicles as on 1 July 20-5.
ii) Write up the journal entries and draw up the appropriate ledger accounts for motor vehicles, provision for the depreciation of motor vehicles and the disposal of motor vehicles accounts for the year ended 30 June 20-6. Show clearly any transfers to the profit and loss account and the balance sheet.
iii) If depreciation was applied on a month by month basis (in the final year only), how would it affect the ledger accounts on the trade-in and purchase of the new Mercedes in November 20-5? How would the final account be affected?

b) When a fixed asset is purchased, a business will use depreciation as a means to set aside cash each year so that it eventually has the funds to purchase a replacement when it becomes necessary. Comment briefly on this statement.

[Association of Accounting Technicians]

10. You are employed in the accounts department of Jackson, Jackson & Walker, a small family-run partnership. You have been asked to make the appropriate calculations for depreciation and entries for the preparation of the final accounts for the period ending , 31 December 2003.

EQUIPMENT DETAILS
Since 1 January 1999, the company has purchased the following equipment:

Description Code No.	A/C Code	Purchase Date	Cost	Estimated Residual Value	Estimated Life (YEARS)
W2431	N200	1/01/99	£8400	£800	5
W2500	N200	1/04/00	£10800	£600	6
W3010	N200	1/04/01	£10400	£800	6
W3250	N200	2/07/03	see invoice	£800	6

Further information includes:

i) The company's policy on its equipment is to provide depreciation at the end of each financial year using the straight-line method, applied on a monthly basis.

ii) The equipment code W2500 purchased on 1 April 2000 proved unreliable and was traded in for the W3250 from ROTHWELL SUPPLIERS LTD. on credit on 2 July 2003 as per invoice. (Vat charge is treated as a purchase input to Vat account).

iii) The company has a contract with Legal & General Insurance under which the W3250 is insured at an annual premium of £720, the first premium is paid at the time the equipment is purchased.

TASK 1

Prepare the following accounts for each of the years as above up to the year ended
31 December 2003, in the books of the company:

		Account Code
▪	the equipment account (use a single account for all equipment purchases)	N200
▪	the provision for depreciation of equipment;	N210
▪	the fixed asset disposal account	N220
▪	the equipment insurance account (for the W3250 fork lift truck only).	N230
▪	the Rothwell Suppliers Ltd. Account	N440
▪	the VAT account	N550

TASK 2

Write up the appropriate journal entries for the purchase, disposal and depreciation accounts, that are necessary to give effect to the above for the periods 2 January and 31 December, 2003 Show as an extract to the profit & loss account and the balance sheet the relevant figures for depreciation.

TASK 3

Prepare a fixed asset register with columns for details, purchase date, cost, depreciation for final period, cumulative depreciation and net book value of the individual items of equipment as at 31 December 2003. The total of your register should equal the figures in the financial statements.

SUPPLIER'S INVOICE FROM ROTHWELL SUPPLIERS LTD.
INVOICE NO. 221

ROTHWELL SUPPLIERS LTD.
CHESSEL BEACH HIGH ROAD
ABBOTSBURY, DORSET DH23 2PO
VAT Reg. No.   762 5842441
Telephone   01502 985150
Date/Tax Point: 2 JULY 2003

To: JACKSON, JACKSON & WALKER   Order No. 643/03 dated 15 June 2003

Quantity		Code	Cost	Amount
	Equipment:			£
ONE	Fork lift truck	W3250		9,200
	VAT 17.5%			1,610
	Total			10,810
Less part-exchange (W2500)				(5,000)
Balance due				**5,810**

Chapter 26

Partnership Accounts

INTRODUCTION

A partnership is defined as two or more persons in business with a view to making a profit. There is little legal constraint and most partnerships can be formed without complex documentation or procedure. As far as the law is concerned, the 1890 Partnership Act and 1907 Partnership Act apply, the former to all partners and the latter to limited partners. A limited partner is one who has limited liability and has no control in the partnership because he is not involved in any decision-making in the business. Only general partners have the right to control the partnership. However, general partners do not have the advantage of limited liability and are therefore liable to the debts of the enterprise, even up to the extent of their personal wealth.

It is advisable that a *written agreement* should exist between partners (rather than merely a verbal arrangement) so that, if disagreements arise between the partners, the written agreement can be referred to in a court of law. A 'Deeds of Partnership' is such an agreement, where a contract is signed by each partner and witnessed, preferably by a member of the legal profession, outlining the proposed agreements by the partners. Agreements between partners usually include the following important items:
- the amount of capital to be contributed by each partner;
- how profits and losses are to be shared (for example, equally, or by some specific ratio);
- whether salaries are to be paid;
- whether interest is to be paid on capital or charged on partners' drawings from the business;
- whether loans by partners to the business are to be paid interest and at what rate;
- the level of control to which each partner is entitled;
- the length of time the partnership is to exist;
- the procedure to be followed in the event of a new partner being admitted or an existing partner leaving;
- the procedure to be followed in the event of the partnership being dissolved (wound up).

In the event of non-agreement between partners, where a Deeds of Partnership does not exist, the 1890 Partnership Act applies. Under Section 24, the Act states:

- profit or loss is to be borne *equally* between partners;
- no interest is to be paid on capital or charged on drawings;
- no partnership salaries are to be paid;
- loans by partners are to be paid interest at 5% per annum.

Partnership appropriation account

The final accounts of a partnership are prepared identically to those of other business units as far as the calculation of profit and the preparation of a balance sheet are concerned because the principles applied are exactly the same.

The partnership does have, however, an *'appropriation account'* to show how profits (or losses) are shared between partners. This account is follows immediately after the profit/loss account.

Example 1:
Peter and Jane agreed to share profits of £7,500 equally. Other items such as salaries £1500 each, 5% interest paid on capital accounts (£5000 capital each) and interest charged on drawings £200 for Peter and £150 for Jane, are to be accounted for first, leaving a residue of £4,350 to be divided equally. The partner's salaries and interest on capital accounts are deductions from profit but interest on drawings is added .

Profit and loss appropriation account of Peter & Jane year ended 31 December

		£	£	£
Net Profit				7500
Less:				
Salary:	Peter	1,500		
	Jane	1,500	3,000	
Interest on Capital (5%):				
	Peter	250		
	Jane	250	500	3,500
				4,000
Add:				
Interest charged on Drawings:				
	Peter	200		
	Jane	150		350
				4,350
Share of Profits:				
	Peter	2,175		
	Jane	2,175		4,350

Partners' current accounts
A current account is a record of a partner's personal finances in the business. Items recorded in this account include additions such as partner's share of profits, interest paid on capital, salary awarded and any other money deposited by the partner. Deductions from the current account are mainly drawings of cash or stock and the interest charged on drawings.

The appropriation account at the end of the accounting period acts as a source of entry to the current account (in effect, being part of the *double-entry*):

Nominal ledger

		Dr	Cr	Balance
Current Account: Peter				
December 31	Balance			200 Cr
	Salary		1,500	1,700
	Interest on Capital		250	1,950
	Profit		2,175	4,125
	Drawings	2,000		2,125
	Interest charged	200		1,925 Cr
Current Account: Jane				
December 31	Balance			500 Dr
	Salary		1,500	1,000 Cr
	Interest on Capital		250	1,250
	Profit		2,175	3,425
	Drawings	1,500		1,925
	Interest charged	150		1,775 Cr

NOTES:

- A debit balance in the partner's current account indicates that the partner has overdrawn on his account and owes that sum to the business.
- A partnership salary is part of the appropriation account and not an expense in the profit & loss account, in the same way as an employee.

Balance sheet (extract) of Peter & Jane as at 31 December . . .

	£	£	£
Net Assets			13,700
Financed by:			
Capital accounts:			
Peter	5,000		
Jane	5,000	10,000	
Current accounts:			
Peter	1,925		
Jane	1,775	3,700	13,700

Example 2

Jim, Julie and Jake are in partnership, sharing profit and losses in the ratio of **2:2:1** respectively. During the financial year ended 31 December the net profit was £16,810.
The partners' drawings for the year were:

Jim   £3,150
Julie   £3,000
Jake   £1,800

The interest charged on drawings:

Jim   £320
Julie   £300
Jake   £275

These charges were based on average drawings over the year. Interest is to be paid on partners' capital accounts at the rate of 5% per annum. Only Julie is entitled to a salary of £1,500 per annum because of her extra duties working in the business.

Balances in the partners' accounts

Partner	Capital accounts	Current accounts
Jim	£10,000	£700 Cr
Julie	£10,000	£450 Dr
Jake	£5,000	£350 Dr

Required:

a) Prepare the partners' profit and loss appropriation account and partners' current accounts for year ended 31 December.
b) Prepare an extract of the 'financed by' section of the partners' balance sheet as at 31 December.
c) What is the difference between a general partner and a limited partner?

Solution:

Profit and loss appropriation account year ended 31 December

		£	£	£
Net Profit				16,810
Salary:	Julie		1,500	
- Interest on capital:				
	Jim	500		
	Julie	500		
	Jake	250	1,250	2,750
				14,060
+ Interest changed on drawings:				
	Jim	320		
	Julie	300		
	Jake	275		895
				14,955
Share of capital:				
	Jim		5,982	
	Julie		5,982	
	Jake		2,991	14,955

NOTE:

After contingencies of salary, interest paid and interest charged, the residue was £14,955. This was divided in the ratio agreed by the partners of 2:2:1 respectively.

Partners' current accounts as shown in the nominal ledger

		Dr £	Cr £	Balance £
Current Account: Jim				
December 31	Balance			700 Cr
	Interest on Capital		500	1,200
	Profit		5,982	7,182
	Drawings	3,150		4,032
	Interest charged	320		3,712
Current Account: Julie				
December 31	Balance			450 Dr
	Interest on Capital		500	50 Cr
	Salary		1,500	1,550
	Profit		5,982	7,532
	Drawings	3,000		4,532
	Interest charged	300		4,232
Current Account: Jake				
December 31	Balance			350 Dr
	Interest on Capital		250	100 Dr
	Profit		2,991	2,891 Cr
	Drawings	1,800		1,091
	Interest charged	275		816

Balance sheet extract of Jim, Julie & Jake as at 31 December . . .

		£	£	£
Net Assets				33,760
Financed by:				
Capital:				
	Jim	10,000		
	Julie	10,000		
	Jake	5,000	25,000	
Current account's:				
	Jim	3,712		
	Julie	4,232		
	Jake	816	8,760	33,760

c) A *general partner* has a right to share in the decisions that affect the partnership and therefore shares in the control of the business. He is not protected by limited liability and therein he is liable for the debts of the business, even up to his own personal wealth.

A *limited partner* is one who has registered as a limited partner with the Registrar and is protected with limited liability. This means that, in the event of bankruptcy and debt, he is only liable to the extent of his capital contributed to the business and not his personal wealth. However, he must never be part of partnership decisions and holds no control or active part in the business. Retired partners sometimes wish to remain a part of the partnership, at the same time relinquishing control, and hence apply to become limited partners.

Goodwill

The term *'goodwill'* may arise in a business because it may have earned itself a good name or reputation built up over a period of time through its business activities. The value of goodwill can be calculated on certain factors like average sales over a period of time, or profits earned over a number of accounting periods.

When a business is sold, the net value of the assets is assessed and a value may then be paid towards goodwill. If, for example, a business has an average turnover (sales) of £30,000 per annum based on the last three years' sales, the vendor (the seller) may want something in the region of 10-20% for goodwill or even more. The buyer and seller may agree on any amount depending on how much the buyer wants to buy and how much he can afford.

If a new partner is admitted to the partnership, he may well have to pay the existing partners a sum for goodwill. For example, two partners A and B decided to admit partner C to help expand the business and also to inject new capital. The three of them mutually agree to the proposal that C is to pay £2,000 as goodwill and that this should be credited to the partners' A and B capital accounts:
Double-entry:

Debit	Bank account	£2,000
Credit	Partner A	£1,000
	Partner B	£1,000

Partner C is to introduce £3,000 of capital into the business that will also be debited to the bank account:
Double-entry:

Debit	Bank account	£3,000
Credit	Partner C	£3,000

Alternatively, if partner C had insufficient money to pay the £2,000 goodwill, a goodwill account may have been debited and partners A and B still credited with the £1,000 to their capital:
Double-entry:

Debit	Goodwill account	£2,000	(an *intangible asset*)
Credit	Partner A	£1000,	
	Partner B	£1,000	

The writing-off of goodwill

It has been standard practice to write off the value of goodwill arising from the purchase or the commencement of a new business partnership. FRS 10 (Financial Reporting Statement 10) *Goodwill and Intangible Assets,* recognised that it is difficult to separate goodwill from the business as a whole, and it is largely a subjective valuation agreed by the partners.

It has not been the practice to recognise goodwill in published accounts. If a value has been placed on a business, or partners come together with an agreed sum for goodwill, it ought to be written off as soon as practicable on the basis of the partners' agreed partnership profit-sharing ratio. If this is not stated, it will be assumed that it is written off equally.

If goodwill is to be written off either immediately or over a period of time, the partners' capital accounts will be debited and the goodwill account credited, thus writing off the goodwill.

Example 3
Tom, Dick and Harry were separate traders for a number of years and now have decided to form a partnership bringing their assets and liabilities into the new business.
Their capital accounts at the time, 1 January, were:

Tom	£18,000	
Dick	£12,000	
Harry	£6,000	£36,000

It has been recognised by Tom, Dick and Harry that a sum for goodwill should be included in the accounts:

Tom	£6,000	
Dick	£8,000	
Harry	£10,000	£24,000

If the goodwill was to remain in the current year's accounts, then the partners would have these sums credited to their capital accounts and the goodwill account would be debited with the total (that is, £24,000) as an intangible fixed asset.

However, if the partners did *not want* a goodwill account to be maintained in the partnership books, then it would be written off in relation to their agreed profit sharing ratio at the time the goodwill was introduced. If the partners, Tom, Dick and Harry, share profits and losses in the ratio of 3:2:1 respectively, then their position would be:

Writing-off a goodwill account			
	Capital Introduced	Goodwill introduced	Goodwill Written off	New balances
	£	£	£	£
Tom	18,000	6,000	(12,000)	12,000
Dick	12,000	8,000	(8,000)	12,000
Harry	6,000	10,000	(4,000)	12,000

What has occurred here is that Harry, who has benefited the most by introducing a greater value of goodwill (he may have brought in more trading customers) and because of the profit-sharing ratio, only loses 1/6 of total goodwill to be written off £24,000/6. On the other hand, Tom has most capital to lose because he takes half the profit share and therefore must apportion half the value of goodwill against his capital account.

KEY POINTS OF THE CHAPTER

1890 Partnership Act:	Rules, conditions relating to general partners
1907 Partnership Act:	Rules, conditions relating to limited partners
Deeds of partnership:	A contract between partners expressing mutual agreements
Appropriation account:	Comes immediately after the profit & loss account and shows how profits are shared
Partner's current account:	Records personal finances of partner
Interest on capital:	Deducted from profits and credited to partners' current accounts
Interest on drawings:	Added to profits and debited to partners' current accounts
Salaries awarded:	Deducted from profits and credited to partners' current accounts
Interest on partners' loan:	An expense in profit & loss account and credited to partners' current account
Goodwill:	Reputation and good name of business and concerns arrival of new partners or retirement of existing partners
FRS 10:	Financial Reporting Statement that concerns the writing off of goodwill.

QUESTIONS

1. Smith and Jones are in partnership, sharing profits and losses in a ratio to their capital accounts. The trial balance as on 31 December was as follows:

		Debit £	Credit £
Premises		23,500	
Furniture and fittings		2,750	
Motor van		2,000	
Provision for bad debts			115
Carriage in		142	
Returns		288	343
Purchases		11,665	
Sales			21,429
Discounts		199	146
Stock (1/1)		3,865	
Debtors, creditors		2,355	3,569
Salaries		5,055	
Rates and insurance		645	
Light and heat		162	
Bank		522	
Capital:	Smith		18,000
	Jones		12,000
Current accounts:	Smith	625	
	Jones	540	
Drawing accounts:	Smith	2,303	
	Jones	1,500	
Rent received			2,514
		58,116	58,116

Note: at 31 December
- The value of unsold stock £4,200.
- Gas bill due for payment £65.
- Rates paid in advance £30.
- Provision for bad debts to be increased to £250.
- Depreciation: Furniture and fittings by 20%
                    Motor van revalued £1,800.
- Jones is awarded a salary of £1,000 for extra responsibilities.
- Interest charged on Drawings: Smith £209, Jones £160.

Required:
a) Prepare the trading, profit and loss and appropriation accounts for the year ended 31 December and balance sheet as at that date.
b) Show the current accounts as they would appear in the ledger.

2. Lee and Crooks are partners sharing profits and losses equally. At the end of the financial year, 31 December, the trial balance extracted from the books was:

Premises		15,000	
Equipment (cost)		3,600	
Provision for depreciation of equipment account			360
Motor vehicle		3,500	
Stock (1/1)		3,742	
Debtors		5,188	
Creditors			3,165
Bank			850
Cash		255	
Provision for bad debts			70
Rates and insurance		450	
General overheads		600	
Wages		6,342	
Carriage in		450	
Carriage out		156	
Discount			440
Bank charges		235	
Advertising		350	
Printing, stationery		285	
Sales			24,565
Returns inward		350	
Purchases		13,080	
Returns outward			2,052
VAT			340
Current accounts:	Lee		300
	Crooks	155	
Drawings:	Lee	3,700	
	Crooks	2,704	
Capital accounts:	Lee		14,000
	Crooks		14,000
		60,142	60,142

Note: at 31 December,
a) The value of unsold stock (at cost) £5,150
b) Crooks took goods for his own use £420.
c) Provision for Bad Debts increased to £500.
d) Depreciation: Equipment 10% on cost.
   Motor vehicle 20% on cost.
e) Partners' charge on drawings: Lee £300
                                  Crooks £249
f) Partners' salaries: Lee £1,500
                                  Crooks £1,000

Required:
Prepare the trading, profit and loss and appropriation accounts for the year ended 31 December, and a balance sheet as at that date.

3. Jones, Smith and Brown are partners in a wholesaling enterprise. They have a warehouse and a small section of offices. Expenses attributed to the warehouse are to be listed under 'Distribution Costs' in the profit and loss account. All other expenses in the profit and loss account are to be listed under 'Administration Expenses'. The accounts extracted for the trial balance at the year ended 31 December were:

Trial Balance of Jones, Smith and Brown as on 31 December

	£	£
Premises (at cost)	35,000	
Fixtures (at cost)	18,500	
Motor Vans (at cost)	12,750	
Bank		2,460
Cash	100	
Equipment (at cost)	11,000	
Stock (1 January)	77,450	
Debtors	18,142	
Creditors		64,800
Purchases/sales	86,257	142,000
Returns	4,150	4,400
Provision for bad debts		180
Rates (3/4 Warehouse)	840	
Wages (1/4 Warehouse)	16,424	
General expenses (1/4 Warehouse)	1,764	
Insurance	283	
Loan (5 years)		27,000
Capital accounts, balances 1 January		
Jones		25,000
Smith		20,000
Brown		5,000
Current accounts, balances 1 January		
Jones		1,242
Smith		1,615
Brown	37	
Drawings for the year:		
Jones	6,000	
Smith	4,000	
Brown	1,000	
	293,697	293,697

The following additional information is to be taken into account: as at 31 December:

- Unsold stock valued at cost £82,427.
- Rates unpaid £120.
- Invoice due on stationery £125 (Administration expense).
- Depreciation: Motor vans re-valued to £11,250 (distribution cost)
  Equipment and fixtures 10% on cost (Administration expense).
- Insurance pre-paid £37.
- Smith was awarded a salary of £2,750.
  Drawings by partners to be charged 5% interest.
  Interest on capital to be paid 6%.
  Profits are shared according to their capital accounts ratio on 1 January (25 : 20 : 5).

Required:
a) Prepare the partners' trading, profit and loss account and appropriation account for the year ended 31 December.
b) Prepare the partners' current accounts as they would appear in the ledger.
c) Prepare the partners' balance sheet as at 31 December.

4. The following information refers to the accounts of Smith, Jones and Rogers who are in partnership and, according to their Deeds, share profits and losses in the ratio of 2:2:1 respectively.
During the financial period ended 31 May 20-5, the net profit of the business was £7,300 and the partners' drawings for the year were:

Smith	£2,000
Jones	£1,900
Rogers	£1,500

Interest on partners' drawings has been calculated as follows:

Smith	£65
Jones	£55
Rogers	£45

As far as the partners' capital accounts are concerned, the agreement states that 6% will be allowed as interest payment.

The partners had agreed that Smith should withdraw £1,000 from his capital account on 1 December 20-4 and that Rogers should contribute the same amount on that date. Jones is awarded a salary of £900 for extra responsibilities. The opening balances on the partners' accounts on 1 June, 20-4 were:

	Capital account £	Current account £
Smith	9,000	600 Cr
Jones	8,000	400 Dr
Rogers	7,000	300 Dr

Other balances on 31 May 20-5 were as follows:

	£
Fixed assets (net)	30,700
Stocks	12,750
Debtors	4,655
Cash	500
Bank (Cr.)	2,995
Creditors	14,560
Accruals	300
Bank loan (5 years)	4,950

Required:
a) Prepare the partnership profit and loss appropriation account and the partners' current accounts for the year ended 31 May 20-5.
b) Prepare the partners' balance sheet as at 31 May 20-5 and show net current assets as part of its construction.
c) Make a brief comment on the partners' financial position as at 31 May 20-5.

[Associated Examining Board]

5. French and Saunders run a business consultancy and have the following account balances in their books on 31 March 20-5:

	£
Capital accounts:	
French	20,000
Saunders	25000
Current accounts: [1/4/20-4]	
French	4200 Cr
Saunders	2060 Dr
Drawings for the year:	
French	12000
Saunders	15000
Premises	60000
Vehicles	6000
Depreciation of vehicles	5000
Bank	3800
Debtors	3210
Creditors	6970
Bank loan 11% [long term]	20000
Net trading profit for year	19800
Interest accrued on loan	
6 months	

Note:
• The partners have agreed on equal sharing of profit/ losses.
• The partners have agreed 8% interest on capital accounts.
• Interest charges on drawings amount to: French £200, Saunders £600.

Required:
a) The profit and loss appropriation account of French & Saunders for the year ended 31 March 20-5 and the current accounts of each partner.
b) The balance sheet of the partnership as on 31 March 20-5.
c) A brief memorandum, addressed to the partners, commenting on the partnership liquidity and suggesting how it could be improved.

d) French has used her own premises for the business partnership and £500 has been agreed for running costs.No entries have been made. What effect would this have on the preparation of the above accounts?

[Higher National Diploma]

6. You work as Accountant for Wooldridge & James, a partnership, and have to prepare their final accounts for the year ended 31 May, 20-5.

	Debit £	Credit £
Capital account balances:		
Wooldridge		50,000
James		30,000
Current a/c balances: [1/6/20-4]		
Wooldridge		1,000
James		2,000
Drawings on 30/11/20-4		
Wooldridge	5,000	
James	8,000	
Drawings on 31/5/20-5		
Wooldridge	8,000	
James	10,000	
Fixed assets (Net)	114,000	
Current assets	80,650	
Deferred liabilities		29,000
Current liabilities		75,000
Profit for the year		38,650
	225,650	225,650

The Partnership agreement between Wooldridge and James stipulates:
- Profits and losses to be shared 60% Wooldridge and 40% James.
- Salaries to be credited Wooldridge £9,000, James £12,000.
- Interest to be paid on capital and current account balances as on 1/6/20-4 at 10% per annum.
- Drawings also to be subject to interest at a rate of 10% per annum calculated on their half-yearly balances.

Required:
a) Prepare the partnership profit and loss appropriation account for the year ending 31/5/20-5. Prepare the partners' current accounts after completion of the profit and loss and appropriation account.
b) Prepare the partnership's balance sheet in its abbreviated form as on 31/5/20-5.
c) Write a memorandum to the partners explaining the situation under Section 24 of the Partnership Act 1890 if no Partnership Agreement existed.
d) Prepare a statement, to be sent with the above memorandum, showing how the profits would be divided if Section 24 of the Partnership Act 1890 applied.

[Higher National Diploma]

7.   Alan and Brenda are in partnership and agree to share profits and losses equally. During the
     year to 31 December, the net profit of the firm was £14,680.
     The partners' drawings for the year were:

                      £
         Alan   4,950
         Brenda   4,565

     Interest charged on drawings is at 10% per annum based on average drawings for the year:

         Average balance of   Alan   £2,500
                              Brenda   £2,100

     Interest is paid on capital of 5% per annum. The balances on the partners' accounts were:

	Capital account (1/1)	Current account (1/12)
	£	£
Alan	12,000	600 Cr
Brenda	12,000	50 Dr
Partners' salaries:		
Alan	3,500	
Brenda	2,500	

Required:

a) Prepare the partnership profit and loss appropriation account and the partners' current
    accounts for the year ended 31 December.
b) An extract of the partners' balance sheet as at 31 December.
c) Alan and Brenda decide to admit a new partner, Charlie. Goodwill is agreed at a value of
    £6,000. This account is to be debited on 1 January, the new financial period. Alan and
    Brenda are to be credited equally with the value of goodwill.

d) Charlie will inject £10,000 of his own capital which will be debited to the business's bank
    account.
    If profits and losses are then to be shared on a capital input ratio, what will be the profit-
    sharing ratio?
    How would the balance sheet be affected on 1 January?

8. Arthur, Belinda and Charlene were in partnership at the year ended 31 March, 2006. The profit sharing ratio was 3 : 3 : 2 in favour of Arthur. It was decided to invite a new partner, Denise, into the business, with effect from 1 April 2006.

Denise was to contribute a sum of £30,000 as her capital and it was agreed that goodwill was valued £90,000. The goodwill account is not to remain in the books. The new profit sharing ratio of the new partnership was mutually agreed at 3: 3: 2:1 still in favour of Arthur.

Capital accounts as on 1 April, 2005:

Arthur	£60,000
Belinda	£50,000
Charlene	£25,000

Current accounts as on 1 April, 2005

Arthur	£500	Credit
Belinda	£160	Debit
Charlene	£180	Credit

Drawings for the year:

Arthur	£28,500
Belinda	£27,000
Charlene	£23,500

The partners were awarded salaries from profits:

Arthur	£15,000
Belinda	£15,000
Charlene	£10,000

6% Interest on capital account balances (as on 1 April, 2005) was to be awarded.

The net profit for the year ended was £81,500.

TASK 1.1
Prepare the partner's capital accounts showing all entries as on 1 April, 2006 and the goodwill account.

TASK 1.2
Prepare the partners' appropriation account for the year ended 31 March, 2006 and the partners' current accounts as at this date.

TASK 1.3
Prepare the partners' capital accounts and the goodwill account as on 1 April, 2006

TASK 1.4
Prepare an extract of the balance sheet as it would appear on 1 April, 2006 for the new partnership. The balances brought forward from 31 March, 2006 were:
Fixed assets (NBV) £142,000, Current assets £67,820 and Current liabilities £41,800.

(Association of Accounting Technicians)

Chapter 27

Company Accounts

INTRODUCTION

Company accounts are regulated by the consolidated 1985 Companies Act and the supplementary 1989 Companies Act. The formation of a limited company needs only a minimum of two founder members who are willing to subscribe share capital. There is no maximum limit. Basically, there are two distinct types of limited company:

- Private Limited Company;
- Public Limited Company (PLC).

A PLC must bear these letters after its name on all correspondence to distinguish it from a private company (for example, Barclays Bank PLC). The word *'limited'* means that shareholders' liabilities are limited to the nominal capital of their shares, in the same way a limited partner is limited to the amount of capital he has subscribed.

The private company can only sell its shares privately. It cannot issue a prospectus inviting the public to buy its shares. This privilege is only permitted to the PLC. A private company, therefore, is restricted in the amount of share capital it can raise because it cannot, by statute, advertise to sell its shares. It is likely to sell its shares to family and friends interested in financing a business venture.

Unlike the private company, the PLC has the potential to raise large sums of capital by offering its shares for public sale. A merchant bank or issuing house can arrange for the issue of shares and, indeed, could buy the shares outright, then offer them to the public for sale via the prospectus.
Most private companies are small business ventures with a limited number of members, and rarely employ more than twenty people. On the other hand, public limited companies like the commercial banks, large retail chains and manufacturing enterprises are big business concerns that have thousands of members and employees. PLC shares may be listed on the Stock Exchange once they have been vetted and accepted by the Stock Exchange Council. Private company shares cannot be listed.

Documentation

The procedure to form a limited company is a little more involved than forming other business units. The sole trader has virtually no legal constraint and partnerships are advised to prepare Deeds of Partnership before starting up in business. A limited company must prepare two important documents that are sent to the Registrar at Companies House for companies to obtain approval before it can proceed. These documents are the *Memorandum of Association* and the *Articles of Association*.

The Memorandum gives the 'external' view of the company to the public, including details of its name, address, registered office, share capital and, most important, its objectives (that is, what it proposes to do).

The Articles give the 'internal' view of the company which relates to the rules and regulations governing the internal organisation of the company, such as voting rights, conduct at meetings, power of directors and so forth.

Once these documents are approved by the Registrar, a limited company is issued a *Certificate of Incorporation* which gives it the status of being a *separate legal entity* from the owners of the business (the shareholders). The company has then the right of its own identity and can proceed under its own name, acting under its own name in the course of its business. A Board of Directors is elected by the shareholders to take control of the company on their behalf. The directors control, the shareholders own.

A private company, on receipt of its Certificate of Incorporation, can commence trading. A PLC must issue its prospectus to sell its shares before it can begin. The directors of the company must state, in the prospectus, the minimum amount of share capital it requires in order to start business and that the share issue has been underwritten (guaranteed) to ensure that the minimum capital is raised. Once this minimum capital is raised, the Registrar can issue the PLC its *Certificate of Trading* – its right to commence business operations.

The preparation of company accounts
The 1985 Companies Act gives guidance as to the preparation of final accounts relating to companies.
The trading and profit and loss account. Now referred to as the *income statement.*
Expenses may be sub-divided into categories like distribution costs and administration expenses. The net profit is shown before and after taxation.

The appropriation account.
This part of the income statement starts with the division of profits before tax. Basically, profits maybe distributed by:
▪ provision for taxation;
▪ dividends to shareholders on the basis of the number of shares issued and paid up on the value of nominal capital;
▪ transfer of any profit to the company reserves (profits retained in the company).

Example 1
James & Harding plc had the following accounts at its year end, 31 December:

	£
Profit (before tax)	80,000
Issued and paid up capital:	
8% £1 preference shares*	200,000
£1 ordinary shares	800,000
Retained profit b/f (1/1)	18,000
8% preference dividend paid (30/6)	8,000

The board of directors recommended on 31 December, the following:
▪ provide £24,000 for corporation tax (30% of net profit),
▪ provide for the remaining dividend balance to be paid to preference shareholders
▪ to provide 5% dividend to ordinary shareholders.

* Note that the vast majority of limited companies only have ordinary shares. At the time of writing, preference shares are only in existence with very few limited companies.

Required:
Prepare the company's appropriation account for the period ended 31 December.
Show an extract of the company's balance sheet indicating appropriate figures to be included for current liabilities and the *'financed by'* section indicating share capital and profit and loss balance.

Solution:
James & Harding plc Profit & Loss Appropriation Account year ended 31 December

	£	£
Profit (before tax)		80,000
Taxation		(24,000)
Profit (after taxation)		56,000

Statement of changes in equity:

	£	£
Retained earnings b/f (1 January)		18,000
Profit for the year		56,000
		74,000
Provision for Dividends:		
8% Preference paid	8,000	
8% Preference due	8,000	
Ordinary shares due	40,000	(56,000)
Retained profit c/f (31 December)		18,000

James & Harding plc Balance sheet as at 31 December (extract only):

	£	£
Current liabilities:		
provision for tax	24,000	
provision for dividends	48,000	72,000
Equity::		
£1 8%preference shares	200,000	
£1 ordinary shares	800,000	
Retained earnings	18,000	1,018,000

NOTE:

- Half the preference dividend £8,000 was paid during the year, 30 June. This is an interim payment. The final provision of £8,000 makes a total of £16,000 (8% of £200,000 shares).
- The 5% dividend to ordinary shareholders is £40,000 (5% of £800,000 shares).
- The retained profit balance (1 January) is brought forward from the previous accounting period and is the starting point for the *statement of changes in equity*..
- The retained profit balance (31 December) is the profit carried forward to the next accounting period. It is also entered in the balance sheet under equity (capital & reserves).
- The provision for dividends and tax are seen as current liabilities because they are due to be paid in the following financial period.

The capital of limited companies

Unlike the capital of sole traders and partners, there are a number of terms relating to a limited company's capital and you need to be able to distinguish each of them. These terms refer to authorised (or nominal), issued, called up and paid up capital.

Authorised capital is the nominal capital of the company and is normally the maximum amount of capital it can issue. It is the company's registered capital and is that sum stated in the company's

Memorandum of Association. A company may set up with share capital of £1 million pounds, some of which may be preference shares (as in the above example). However, it is far more likely that it will be ordinary shares, (known as equities) the most common shares of limited companies.

Issued capital is that nominal capital issued to shareholders and cannot be in excess of authorised capital. If all the authorised capital is issued, then authorised and issued capital will equal the same sum. For example, if the nominal capital was £1 million and £500,000 was issued, there would be a further £500,000 un-issued shares that the company could still sell at a later date.

Called up capital refers to shares which have been allotted to shareholders and have only called up part of the sum due on the shares. The balance due can be called up at a later point of time.
For example, it a company allots £500,000 £1 shares and only calls up 50p a share, it will receive £250,000 as paid up capital. This means that although it has issued £500,000 of share capital, it has only called up half of it. The balance of £250,000 is the uncalled capital.

Paid up capital refers to the issued capital paid for by shareholders. If some shareholders have not yet paid for their shares, they would be debtors to the company until they have paid for them. For example, if only £245,000 had been received for the called up capital, then this leaves £5,000 still to be collected and represents unpaid capital.

Example 2:

	£	£
Authorised capital:		
1 million £1 ordinary shares	1,000,000	
Issued capital:		
500,000 £1 ordinary shares	500,000	
Called up capital:		
500,000 50p ordinary shares	250,00	
Paid up capital	245,000	
Unpaid capital	5,000	250,000

The issued and paid up capital equals £245,000 plus the unpaid called up capital £5,000 equals £250,000 representing the capital of the company at that time of the floating of the shares. On the asset side, the current assets would show the £245,000 banked, plus the £5,000 as debtors still to pay for their shares.

Capital and revenue reserves
Capital reserves are not retained profits as seen in the appropriation account because these are revenue reserves. Capital reserves include the sums transferred to the share premium account which have come from the selling of shares at a higher sum than its nominal value (face value). For example, 1,000 £1 shares sold for £1.50 each means that there is £1,000 share capital and £500 in the premium account.

A further example of capital reserves includes *revaluation* of fixed assets. If premises were valued at cost £100,000 and this was re-valued by the company to £200,000, the company would show an increase of £100,000 in its 'revaluation reserve' account which is part of the capital & reserves in the balance sheet. Fixed assets replacement reserve is another name for the revaluation of fixed assets.

Revenue reserves are retained profits from normal trading activity and any profit retained in the appropriation account could be transferred to the reserves account. Note that this is not actual money but represents an increase in the shareholders' capital and the net assets of a company. Often retained profits are simply held in the profit and loss account balance.

Bonus shares may be issued to a company's shareholders without payment. They are 'free shares' coming out of the revenue reserves. For example, if there was £100,000 share capital and £50,000 in reserves, and shareholders were offered 1 bonus share for every 2 they held, then share capital becomes £150,000 and the reserves would be zero.

Shares and debentures

There are two classes of share capital that may be issued to shareholders, ordinary shares and preference shares. Again, please note that preference shares hardly feature in limited companies today, the majority of shares being *ordinary*. These ordinary shares are by far, the most common and represents the 'true' shares, taking the greater risks. The rate of dividend depends on how much profit is made and how much is to be distributed. These are also referred to as 'equity' shares and are given voting rights – one share, one vote. These votes may be used at annual general meetings but rarely are they exercised in public limited companies because very few shareholders actually attend the meetings.

Preference shares are paid at a *fixed* rate of dividend and shareholders are entitled to be paid first before ordinary shares. The shares do not hold voting rights and are suitable for the less adventurous type of shareholder who wants a more reliable and consistent rate of dividend.

Debentures represent loan capital and not share capital. They are paid at a fixed rate of interest over the specified period of the loan. The interest paid is an expense entered in the profit and loss account, not the appropriation account.

The 1985 Companies Act

Under Part VII of the 1985 Companies Act, and particularly sections 221 and 222, the main points state:

1. Every limited company must keep accounting records, with reasonable accuracy, to disclose the financial position of the company.
2. Financial records must be kept daily including receipts and payments of money, the assets and liabilities of the company, including stocktaking at the year end. These records must be kept for a period of 3 years for a private company and 6 years for a public company.
3. The final accounts of the company must be kept in accordance with the formats laid down in Schedule 4 of the Act. This must include:
   - A profit and loss account
   - A balance sheet, as at the same period
   - An auditors' report
   - A directors' report

Public companies must have at least two directors and a private company, one. Every company must have a secretary. The directors of a company must make a report as part of the annual accounts and must present a fair view of the business's development in its financial year. The directors must indicate the dividend they wish to recommend and also the amount they propose to withhold as reserves.

Annual reports must be filed with the Registrar, Companies House. For companies registered in England and Wales, the address is in Cardiff. For companies registered in Scotland, there is an address in Edinburgh. A company must show its accounts to its members for each accounting period at its annual general meeting. It must ensure that a copy of its accounts is sent to the Registrar within a period of 10 months following the end of the financial period for a private company and 7 months for a public company.

The 1989 Companies Act

The Companies Act, 1989, is a supplementary Act and does not replace the 1985 Companies Act which, in effect, consolidated all previous Acts from 1948 to 1981. The 1989 Act amends and adds to the existing legislation of the 1985 Act.

As far as company accounts go, the provisions of the Act under sections 221 and 222 (Part VII) emphasise the duty of all companies to keep accounting records. Some of the 1989 Act's interesting sections is outlined below:

221

Every company shall keep accounting records, sufficient to:

show and explain the company's transactions with reasonable accuracy at any time and the financial position of the company, and to enable the directors to ensure that the balance sheet and profit and loss account complies with the requirements of the Companies Act.

A company's accounts shall be kept at its registered office or such other place where the directors think fit and shall at all times be open to inspection by the company's officers. Accounting entries shall contain day-to-day records of sums of money received and spent as well as a record of its assets and liabilities.

If a company deals with goods for resale, the accounts must contain statements of the value of stock held at end of the financial year and show sufficient details of buyers and sellers, except by way of ordinary retail trade.

226

It is the duty of the directors to have individual, as well as group, company accounts prepared for each financial period, a balance sheet as at the last day of that period and a profit and loss account for that period. Both these financial reports must give a 'true and fair' view of the state of affairs of the company for the financial period under review.

227

Where a company acts as a parent company and has subsidiary companies, the directors must prepare individual accounts for each company and also consolidated accounts for the group.

238

Persons entitled to receive copies of the annual accounts and director's and auditors' reports are:

- every member of the company;
- every holder of the company's debentures;
- every person entitled to receive notice of general meetings and not less than 21 days before the meeting is held.

Final accounts for internal or external use

As discussed earlier in this chapter, there is little difference in preparing financial statements between private and public limited companies.

Example 3 on the following pages, illustrates the internal accounts of Lowell & Company Ltd. It shows the full complement of the accounts as we would do for sole traders or partnerships. Note that expenses in this example are divided into distribution and administrative costs.

When final accounts are prepared for external use, the Companies Act state that only certain information need be published. The accounts are therefore abbreviated for shareholders or any other interested parties. There may be details within the accounts that a company prefers to remain confidential such as *'directors remuneration'* that refers to the fees directors are paid. A copy of the external accounts must be sent to the Registrar, Companies House, as required by the 1985 Companies Act.

Debenture interest, that is, the interest payable on debenture stock, is listed under 'interest payable' and is an expense to the company and must be paid whether it makes a profit or loss. Dividends provided however, are dependent on how much profit is made.

Example 3:

Company Income Statement for year end 31 December (internal use)

	£00's	£00's	£00's
Continuing Operations			
Revenue			
Sales			100,000
Cost of Sales	4,000		
Stock (1/1)	66,000		
Purchases	70,000		
	(10,000)		
Stock (31/12)			(60,000)
Gross Profit			40,000
Distribution Costs			
Salesmen's salaries	8,500		
Distribution expenses	1,500		
Advertising	2,500		
Motor expenses	1,500		
Depreciation of motors, equipment	2,500	16,500	
Administration Expenses			
Office salaries	7,350		
General office expenses	1,400		
Discount	250		
Bad debts provision	350		
Rates and Insurance	500		
Miscellaneous costs	1,200		
Light and heat	2,450	12,500	(29,000)
			11,000
Other Income			
Bank interest			800
Dividends from other companies			800
Profit from operations			12,600
Finance Costs			
Bank loan interest			(250)
Profit (before tax)			12,350
Tax			(3,150)
Profit *for the period from continuing*			
operations			9,200
Discontinued operations			
Profit (loss) from discontinued			
operations			0
Statement of changes in equity			
Retained earnings (1 January) b/f			400
Profit for the year			9,200
			9,600
Provision for dividends:			(4,600)
Transfer to reserves			(4,000)
Retained earnings (31 December) c/f			1,000

Company Balance Sheet as at year end 31 December

	£00's Cost	£00's Depreciation	£00's Net book value
Non-current assets			
Premises	50,000		50,000
Equipment	35,000	8,000	27,000
Motor vehicles	4,000	1,000	3,000
Investments	10,000		10,000
	99,000	9,000	90,000
Current assets			
Inventories (Stock)	10,000		
Receivables (Debtors)	18,500		
Cash and cash equivalents	3,500	32,000	32,000
Total assets			122,000
Current liabilities			
Payables (Creditors)	16,250		
Provision for dividends	4,600		
Provision for taxation	3,150	24,000	(24,,000)
Net current assets			8,000
Non-current liabilities			
Bank loan	6,000		(6,000)
Total liabilities			30,000
Net assets (A – L)			92,000
Equity			
Share capital (50,000 @ £1)			50,000
Share Premium Account			25,000
Reserves			16,000
Retained earnings			1,000
Total Equity			92,000

NOTE:

1   The share premium account is the amount received in excess of the nominal value of shares when issued. In the above case, the 50,000 shares sold at £1.50 each, a total sum of £75,000 received, £25,000 being the share premium.

2   The retained earnings £1,000 has been carried forward from the *changes in statement of equity*. The reserves of £16,000 is a result of £12,000 in the reserves account and £4,000 transferred from profits.

3   The company balance sheet is using the current international terminology, please see the following page.

FRS 3 Reporting Financial Performance

FRS 3 (Financial Reporting Standard No.3) is recognised as a key standard in accounting for companies because it helps to define the basic components of financial statements in the way they are presented to the public. This is for the benefit of interested parties such as shareholders, potential investors, the Stock Exchange, banks and others. It was first issued in 1992 and has since been the subject of a number of amendments in order that reporting a company's performance is as fair and correct as possible.

The general idea is to focus on the key components of the profit and loss account to assist all users of it in their assessment of financial performance. This includes the results of what is called 'continuing operations' as well as those new operations which may have been acquired or those operations which may have been discontinued in the financial period because they have been subsequently sold or terminated.

The standard applies to all limited company's profit and loss statements and is intended to give a 'true and fair' view of reporting a business's financial performance.

The standard requires a 'layered' format in the profit and loss account to focus attention on important components of the financial statement. These are:

- The results of continuing operations which include the results of any acquisitions.
- The results of any operations which have subsequently been discontinued.
- Profits or losses on the sale or termination of operations including the disposal of fixed assets. These are considered as 'exceptional items'.
- Any items of business deemed to be 'extraordinary'.

The use of international terminology

The financial statements of limited companies are now being asked to be prepared using international terminology rather than the present UK terms. The following is a list of these to be used:

Profit and loss account items:	*International terms:*
Profit and loss account	Income statement
Turnover/sales	Revenue
Taxation	Tax expense

Balance sheet items:	
Fixed assets	Non-current assets
Tangible fixed assets	Property, plant and equipment
Intangible fixed assets	Intangible current assets
Stock	Inventory
Debtors	Receivables
Creditors	Payables
Long-term liabilities	Non-current liabilities
Debentures	Loan stock
Capital & reserves	Equity
Profit & loss account	Retained earnings
Capital & reserves (consolidated accounts)	Equity attributed to equity holders of the parent

Other items:	
Statement of total recognised gains & losses	Statement of recognised income & expense

Example 4
The following financial statements represent Hardcastle, a public limited company, manufacturing a wide range of commodities.

Hardcastle plc: Income Statement for year ended 31 December

	£000's	£000's
Continuing operations		
Revenue	9,100	
acquisitions	169	
	10,269	
Discontinued operations	1,000	11,269
Cost of sales		9,366
Gross profit		1,903
Distribution costs		(305)
Administration expenses		(910)
Profit from operations		
Continuing operations	545	
Discontinued operations	143	688
Profit on sale of properties:		
in continuing operations		25
loss on disposal of fixed assets		(15)
		698
Finance costs (interest payable)		(94)
Profit before taxation		604
Taxation		(173)
Profit for the period attributable to equity holders		***431***

Note:
  EPS (earnings per share) 54p per share
  (£431,000 profit/800,000 ordinary shares)

Statutory books
These are the registers that by law, a company must keep:

- a register of members, that is, the company's shareholders. Their names, addresses and the type of shares they have as well as the transfer of shares from one person to another. For shareholders who have more than a 5% shareholding, a separate register is used. A shareholder is obliged to inform the company if he has more than a 5% holding.
- A register of debenture holders, their names, addresses etc. as in the case of shareholders.
- A register of charges, that is, the company borrowing money from its debenture holders or any other financial institution and the assets where upon the borrowing has been secured.
- A register of directors and company secretaries to indicate who they are.
- A register of directors' interests, that is the holding of shares or debentures they may have in the company.

Hardcastle plc: **Balance Sheet as at 31 December**

	£000's	£000's
Non-Current Assets		
Property, plant & equipment		950
Investments		68
Intangible assets		120
		1,138
Current Assets		
Inventories		975
Receivables		510
Cash & cash equivalents		25
		1,510
Total Assets		**2,648**
Current Liabilities		
Payables		405
Tax liabilities		90
		495
Net Current Assets		1,015
Non-Current Liabilities		
Loan stock		250
Total Liabilities		**745**
Net Assets (A –L)		**1,903**
Equity		
Share capital		800
Share premium account		50
Retained Earnings	622	
+ brought forward	431	1,053
Total Equity		**1,903**

NOTE:

1   The new international terms have been used
2   An alternative format identifies current assets less current liabilities as sub-totals, showing net current assets.

KEY POINTS OF THE CHAPTER

Limited companies:	Shareholders have the advantage of limited liability
1985,1989 Companies Acts:	Regulate what companies must legally do
Memorandum of Association:	External view of company disclosing its share capital and objectives
Articles of Association:	Internal view of company disclosing its own rules & regulations
Certificate of Incorporation:	The company receives its own identity and separate legal status
Certificate of Trading:	Allows a plc to commence trading
Annual reports:	Includes the final accounts, auditors' and directors' reports
Appropriation a/c:	Starts at net profit (b/tax) and shows how company profits are distributed
Ordinary shares:	Known as 'equities', have voting rights dividends vary with amount of profits
Preference shares:	Receive fixed dividend rates but no voting rights
Debentures:	Long term loan capital issued by company
Revenue reserves:	Sums retained from profits, helping expansion and growth
Capital reserves:	Share premium account and revaluation of assets but not trading profits
FRS 3:	Outlines how financial accounts of companies should be reported
Statutory books:	The registers held by the company, shareholders, directors, etc

QUESTIONS

1. XYZ Co Limited had an authorised capital of £200,000 divided into 100,000 ordinary shares of £1 each and 100,000 7.5% preference shares of £1 each. The following balances remained in the accounts of the company after the trading and profit and loss accounts had been prepared for the year ended 31 December.

	Debit £	Credit £
Ordinary share capital: fully paid		80,000
7.5% preference shares: fully paid		50,000
Machinery and plant at cost	95,000	
Provision for depreciation on machinery and plant		19,000
Premises at cost	68,000	
Profit and loss account balance (1 January)		5,000
Net profit (for year ended 31 December)		15,500
Accruals		2,150
Bank		395
Stock	9,750	
Debtors and creditors	3,100	3,955
Pre-payments	150	
	176,000	176,000

- The directors have recommended an ordinary dividend of 10% and wish to provide for payment of the year's preference share dividend.
- A Revenue Reserve is to be created of £2,000.
- Taxation of £3,760 to be provided for.

Required:

a) The profit and loss appropriation account for the year ended 31 December.

b) Prepare the balance sheet at 31 December to show clearly the working capital.

c) Make brief comments with reference to the company's working capital.

2. The following balances remain on the books of ABC Co Ltd after the preparation of trading and profit and loss accounts for the year ended 31 December:

	£	£
60,000 ordinary shares of £1 each fully paid		60,000
Machinery and plant (at cost)	52,500	
Motor vehicles (at cost)	4,000	
Furniture and fittings (at cost)	5,750	
General reserve		30,000
Premises (at cost)	45,000	
Profit and loss balance brought forward (1/1)		5,460
Net profit for year		18,750
Accrued expenses		2,810
Provision for depreciation:		
Machinery and plant		10,500
Motor vehicles		1,500
Furniture and fittings		1,000
Provision for bad and doubtful debts		650
Sundry debtors	10,855	
Sundry creditors		4,900
Stocks	11,985	
Cash in hand	500	
Bank	4,980	
	135,570	135,570

Required:

You are required to prepare a profit and loss appropriation account for the year ended 31 December, and a balance sheet at that date. The following information is available:

a) The directors decided to transfer £10,000 to reserve and to recommend a dividend of 15% on the ordinary shares.

b) The authorised capital of ABC Co Ltd is 100,000 ordinary shares of £1 each.

c) The provision for taxation payable next year is £1,500.

d) Briefly comment on the adequacy of the company's working capital.

3. Bournemouth Trading Company Limited has extracted the following trial balance from its books at the end of the accounting period, 31 December.

	£	£
Issued Share Capital:		
60,000 @ £1 shares fully paid		60,000
6% Debentures		5,000
Share premium account		6,000
Stock (1/1)	20,600	
Purchases	118,940	
Debtors	12,460	
Wages, salaries	10,768	
Directors' fees	2,500	
Debenture Interest	150	

Furniture and fittings (cost)	4,000	
General expenses	1,820	
Insurance	42	
Provision for bad debts		750
Creditors		4,860
Bank overdraft		940
Freehold premises (cost)	52,000	
Sales		149,500
Maintenance and power	5,840	
Provision for depreciation of furniture and fittings		1,500
Returns inward	650	
Cash	80	
Profit and loss balance (1 January)		1,300
	229,850	229,850

You are to take the following into account on 31 December:
a) Unsold stock valued at £22,000.
b) Provision of 15% is to be made for ordinary shares. The outstanding debenture interest is also to be accounted for.
c) Under maintenance and power, there is £76 due to rates and £14 insurance relates to the next financial period.
d) Furniture and fittings to be depreciated 15% on cost.
e) The provision for bad debts is to be adjusted to 5% of the debtors.
f) The figure of £600 is to be transferred to reserve.
g) £500 is to be provided for taxation.

Required:
Prepare the company's trading and profit and loss account and appropriation account for the year ended 31 December and a balance sheet as at that date (show full set of figures as for internal use).

4. The accounts of Robertson and David Co. Ltd were extracted from the books on 30 June year 2

Trial Balance as on 30 June year 2

	Debit £	Credit £
Issued and paid-up capital:		
160,000 ordinary shares @ £1		160,000
40,000 8% preference shares @ £2		80,000
Profit and loss account (1 July year 1)		7,780
General reserve		25,000
7% Debentures		40,000
Premises (cost)	287,910	
Motor vehicles (cost)	32,000	
Plant, equipment (cost)	16,880	
Provision for depreciation of motor vehicles		4,800
Stock (1 July year 1)	49,600	
Bank		11,752
Cash	1,558	
Purchases	535,600	
Sales		696,500
Returns	500	1,600

Wages	65,460	
Rates, water, insurance	3,600	
General expenses	22,536	
Preference dividend paid (31 December year 1)	3,200	
Debtors, creditors'	63,380	53,944
Bad debts	2,150	
Provision for bad debts		3,120
Discount allowed	122	
	1,084,496	1,084,496

Note:

Additional details, 30 June year 2
a) Stock value £39,400.
b) Rates pre-paid £1,000; wages still outstanding £3,360.
c) Invoice unpaid for general expenses £30.
d) Depreciation: Motor vehicles 20% on book valuation
                  Plant and equipment 25% on cost.
e) Adjust the provision for bad debts to equal 5% of debtors.
f) The Directors of the company propose a dividend of 10% for ordinary shares. The
   paid dividend is to be entered in the appropriation account.
   Preference shares to receive their final dividend.
g) No interest has been paid on the debentures.
h) A transfer of £4,000 is to be made to reserve.
i) A provision of £19,200 is to be made for taxation.

Required:

Prepare the trading, profit and loss appropriation accounts for the year ended 30 June year 2,
and a balance sheet as at that date.

[Higher National Diploma]

5. The following trial balance represents the accounts of G Chappell & Sons Ltd as on 31
December:

	£	£
Authorised and paid-up capital		
125,000 @ £1 shares (Equity)		125,000
Share premium		2,500
Premises	110,000	
Furniture and fittings (cost)	4,200	
Profit and loss account (1/1)		1,170
Discounts	422	329
Salaries	7,537	
Rates and insurance	2,333	
Rent received		825
Purchases	90,450	
Returns	782	1,789
Sales		105,411
Stock (1/1)	9,142	
General overheads	2,197	
Provision for bad debts		108
Dividend paid (30/6)	1,000	
Provision for depreciation of furniture and fittings		200
Debtors	9,920	
Creditors		5,226
Bank	6,575	
General reserve		2,000
	244,558	244,558

You are to take the following into account on 31 December:
a) Value of unsold stock £12,498.
b) Rates paid in advance £70.
c) Salaries accrued: £263.
d) Overheads: a bill for gas £103 was still outstanding.
e) Depreciation of furniture and fittings 25% on book value.
f) Provision for bad debts to be adjusted to equal 5% of debtors.
g) The Directors propose to provide for a final dividend of 2.5% and to transfer £2,000 to reserve.
h) Taxation: a sum of £1,250 is to be provided for.

Required:
Prepare trading, profit and loss and appropriation accounts for the period ended 31 December, and a balance sheet as on that date.

6. Harrison's is a small private company producing electrical components. It is a relatively new business and the Board are anxious to do well and hope that the year's final accounts will look promising.
The following information has been extracted from the books:

Trial Balance of Harrison Co. Ltd on 31 December

	£	£
Stock (1 Jan.)	5,760	
Purchases	82,500	
Premises (at cost)	60,500	
Plant and equipment (at cost)	60,000	
Provision for depreciation of plant		18,000
Office equipment (at cost)	15,000	
Provision for depreciation of office equipment		6,000
Bank		2,400
Debtors, creditors	48,750	45,100
Cash	440	
Summary of expenses *	66,550	
Sales		176,000
Finance loan 12.5% (5 years)		40,000
General reserve		2,000
Authorised and paid-up capital:		
50,000 £1 ordinary shares		50,000
	339,500	339,500

* Divide into distribution Costs 60%, administration Expenses 40%.

Additional information available on 31 December:
• The value of unsold stocks (at cost) £6,485.
• Administration expenses: Stationery of stock unused valued £1,250.
  Rates pre-paid £110.
  Office salaries outstanding £260.
• Distribution costs: Salesmen's salaries outstanding £484.
• A provision for bad debts is to be created to equal 10% of debtors (enter under Administration Expenses above).
• Depreciation: both plant and office equipment is depreciated by reduced balance method, 20% on net value (enter under Administration expenses above).
• The Directors have proposed a dividend of 7.5% on ordinary shares.

- Taxation of £3,750 is to be provided.
- There was no profit and loss balance on 1 January.
- The interest on the loan has not yet been paid.

Required:
   a) Prepare the company's trading and profit and loss account, and appropriation account for the year ended 31 December.
   b) A balance sheet as at this date showing clearly working capital.
   c) Prepare a brief report for the directors of the company with regard to working capital.

[Higher National Diploma]

7. You work as an assistant to the Accountant for Jason Limited which has a registered capital of £500,000, divided into 800,000 ordinary shares of 50p each and 200,000 8% preference shares of 50p each. The following balances remained .in the accounts of the company after the trading and profit and loss accounts had been prepared for the year ended 30 November year 2.

	Dr £	Cr £
General reserve		5,000
Ordinary share capital: fully paid		100,000
8% preference shares: fully paid		30,000
Premises at cost	140,000	
Light and heat owing		880
Profit and loss account balance (1 December year 1)		19,200
Bank		8,200
Debtors and creditors	5,800	1,120
Net profit (for year ended 30 November year 2)		40,600
Machinery and plant at cost	50,000	
Provision for depreciation on machinery and plant		30,000
Stock	38,340	
Insurance pre-paid	820	
Cash	40	
	235,000	235,000

Information as on 30 November year 2:
The directors of Jason Ltd have recommended:
- providing payment of the year's preference dividend
- providing for corporation tax of £8,400
- a maximum dividend which would maintain a working capital ratio of 1.5:1, the balance remaining from profits to be transferred to general reserve

Required:
a) The profit and loss appropriation account for the year ended 30 November year 2.
b) The balance sheet as at 30 November year 2.
c) State the number of ordinary and preference shares which can still be issued by the company. Briefly explain the difference between these classes of shares.

[Institute of Commercial Management]

8. You work as Assistant to the Financial Accountant of Compton Ltd, manufacturers of cosmetics, and are working on the annual accounts.

The following balances remain in the ledger of Compton Ltd after the preparation of the profit and loss account for the year ended 31 March year 2.

	£
Stocks and work in progress	98,000
Debtors	87,000
Provision for bad debts	4,000
£1 ordinary shares [Authorised £600,000]	400,000
16% preference shares of £1 each [Authorised £200,000]	100,000
Creditors	74,000
Balance at bank	4,000
Accruals	3,500
Pre-payment	2,500
General reserve account	14,000
Share premium account	20,000
Net profit for the year ended 31/3/year 2	108,000
Profit and loss account balance 1/4/year 1	22,000
Premises (at cost)	300,000
Plant and equipment (at cost)	310,000
Vehicles (at cost)	200,000

The Directors propose the following:
a) To transfer £20,000 to reserves.
b) To propose an ordinary dividend of 12% and to pay the preference dividend.
c) To provide for corporation tax of £30,000.

Depreciation of fixed assets has been calculated as follows:
a) Plant and equipment has a residual value of £30,000 and a 'life' estimated at 10 years. It is five years old and depreciation is based on the straight-line method.
b) The vehicles are valued at current market value of £84,000.
c) There is no depreciation on premises.

Required:
Draw up a profit and loss appropriation account for the year ended 31 March year 2 and a balance sheet as at that date.

[Higher National Diploma]

9. You are an assistant to the accountant at J P Davies plc, which has been in business for several
    years. The trial balance on 30 June year 2 was as follows:

Trial Balance – J P Davies plc as on 30 June year 2

	Dr £	Cr £
£1 preference shares (15%) (Authorised £200,000)		100,000
£1 ordinary shares (Authorised £500,000)		200,000
Revenue reserves		45,000
Debenture stock (12.5%)		100,000
Profit for year ending, 30/6/year 2 (before debenture interest)		80,000
Profit and loss balance (1/7/year 1)		40,000
Stocks	200,000	
Premises	200,000	
Plant and machinery	180,000	
Vehicles	50,000	
Office equipment	90,000	
Provisions for depreciation:		
Premises		10,000
Plant and machinery		70,000
Vehicles		30,000
Office equipment		55,000
Debtors	220,000	
Creditors		190,000
Cash	500	
Provision for bad debts		11,000
Pre-payments	9,500	
Accruals		21,000
Bank overdraft		5,500
Interim preference dividend paid	7,500	
	957,500	957,500

Note:
a) A full year's debenture interest is still to be charged.
b) Corporation tax is to be provided, £20,000.
c) The final dividend on preference shares is to be provided for.
d) To propose an ordinary dividend of 20%.
e) To transfer £25,000 to Revenue Reserves.

Required:
Draw up the company's profit and loss appropriation account for the year ended 30 June year 2
and a balance sheet as on that date.

[Higher National Diploma]

Chapter 28

Cash Flow Statements

INTRODUCTION

Historically, the balance sheet and the profit and loss account were always the most important financial statements of a business organisation. However, during the late 1960's and the early 1970's, it was considered necessary by the Accounting Standards Committee (ASC) representing the accounting profession, to try and highlight a business's cash flow position and they produced SSAP No. 10, The Statement for Sources and Application of Funds in 1975 attempted to indicate where the sources of funds came from and where the funds went.

Statements of Standard Accounting Practice are studied in more detail in Chapter 32.

In August 1990, the ASC was taken over by a new independent body responsible for setting standards, the Accounting Standards Board (ASB). In the September of 1991 they produced their first statement, Financial Reporting Standard No. 1 (FRS 1), The Cash Flow Statement, replacing SSAP No. 10, which is now obsolete.

The major purpose of this new FRS, is basically the same as the old funds flow statement and that is, to emphasise a business's inflow and outflow of cash during the financial year. The cash flow statement may be described as the LINK between:

- Two balance sheets in the financial period, that is, one at the beginning of the year and one at the end.
- The profit and loss account for the year.

In 1996 the cash flow statement was further revised and included a statement which reconciles cash flow to the movement in net debt. FRS 1 was revised in 1996 and stated that cash flows had to be reported under eight standard headings as shown below. However, for the purpose of a number of examinations the preparation of the statement involves three distinct stages.

Operating activities

The first of these is the reconciliation between a company's *operating profit* for the year and the net cash flow from operating activities (the first of the standard headings).

This involves the cash movements of stock, debtors and creditors and also any adjustments for non-cash transactions like depreciation that is added back to operating profit.

Any profit or loss from the disposal of a fixed asset is NOT included. If any profit on a disposal was included in the operating profit, it would have to be deducted. If a loss had been included, then it would be a added back to operating profit.

Note that an *increase* in stocks and debtors reduces cash flow whilst the increase in creditors actually increases cash flow. The reverse is also true. A *decrease* in stocks and debtors actually increases cash flow but a *decrease* in creditors decreases cash flow.

Example of operating activities

	£
operating profit	125,000
+ depreciation charges	35,000
	160,000

+ loss on sale of fixed assets	2,000
- increase in stocks	(40,000)
	122,000
- increase in debtors	(5,000)
	117,000
+ increase in creditors	23,000

| = net cash inflow from operating activities | **140,000** |

The sum of £140,000 would then be the starting figure to the second stage that is to draw up the actual cash flow statement for the period using the eight standard headings.

The final stage is to prepare a *reconciliation of net cash flow* to the movement of net debt.

For example, if the cash flow statement shows a final figure of say £25,000 increase in net cash (the cash/bank increase in the balance sheet) and the increase in net long term debt was £50,000, then the change in net debt would be £25,000 (£50,000 - £25,000).

The cash flow statement is prepared under the following standard headings:

1 Operating activities:
   a) net profit on normal trading activities (before taxation)
   b) non-cash flow expenses like depreciation
   c) adjustments to the movements in working capital.
2 Returns on investments and servicing finance:
   a) interest or dividends received
   b) interest paid.
3 Taxation
4 Capital expenditure and financial investment:
   a) purchase of fixed assets
   b) disposal of fixed assets
5 Acquisitions and disposals:
   a) cash flow from the acquisition of a business
   b) cash flow from the disposal of a business.
6 Equity dividends paid:
   a) dividends paid to equity shareholders (but excluding advanced corporation tax).
7 Management of financial resources:
   a) cash flow from the acquisition or disposal of short-term investments (current assets).
8 Financing:
   a) The issue of shares or debenture stocks
   b) Repayment of shares or debenture stocks
   c) Repayment of other loans.

From these headings, the statement should then balance off in relation to the increase or decrease in cash or the bank for the period. Interested parties, such as owners, managers, shareholders, etc., should be able to see the major inflows and outflows of funds through the financial year. Questions that could be raised include:

- Is enough cash being raised to finance the business's spending?
- Were profits sufficient to pay for tax, interest and dividends?
- Why did the large overdraft occur in the bank?

Example

Duran Ltd: balance sheets as at 31 December

	Year 1		Year 2	
	£	£	£	£
Fixed Assets				
Cost	60,000		100,000	
Less cumulative depreciation	20,000		34,000	
		40,000		66,000
Investments at cost		40,000		20,000
		80,000		86,000
Current Assets				
Stock	40,000		120,000	
Debtors	44,000		96,000	
Bank	2,000		6,000	
	86,000		222,000	
Current Liabilities				
Tax owing	12,000		28,000	
Dividend owing	8,000		10,000	
Creditors	14,000		20,000	
	34,000	52,000	58,000	164,000
		132,000		250,000
Long Term Loans		20,000		28,000
		112,000		222,000
Financed by:				
Ordinary shares		80,000		100,000
Share premium account		-		20,000
Profit/loss account balance		32,000		102,000
		112,000		222,000

Duran Ltd: abbreviated profit and loss accounts for Year ended 31 December

	Year 2 £
Sales	1,500,000
Cost of sales	(1,200,000)
Gross profit	300,000
Total expenses (including depreciation)	(196,500)
Operating profit for year	103,500
Add profit on sale of investments	8,000
Less interest payable	(3,500)
	108,000
Less tax provision	(28,000)
	80,000
Add retained profits	32,000
	112,000
Less proposed ordinary dividend	(10,000)
Retained profits c/f	102,000

NOTE:
No tangible fixed assets were disposed of during the year but £20000 of investments had been sold for £28,000.

Required:
Prepare a cash flow (FRS 1) Statement for the year ended 31 December Year 2

Solution:

Duran Ltd Cash flow statement for the year ended 31 December year 2

	£	£
1 Operating activities *		
cash outflow		(8,500)
2 Returns on investments and servicing finance:		
interest paid		(3,500)
3 Taxation		(12,000)
4 Capital expenditure and financial investment:		
purchase of fixed assets	(40,000)	
sales of fixed assets	28,000	(12,000)
5 Acquisitions and disposals		-
6 Equity dividends paid:		
ordinary shares		(8,000)
7 Management of financial resources		0
		(44,000)
8 Financing:		
issue of ordinary shares	20,000	
share premium account	20,000	
long term loan	8,000	48,000
Net cash inflow		**4,000**

* Calculation of Operating activities:

	£
Operating profit	103,500
+ depreciation charges	14,000
	117,500
Working capital:	
+ stock	(80,000)
+ debtors	(52,000)
	(14,500)
+ creditors	6,000
	(8,500)

NOTE:
- The net increase in cash £4,000 corresponds with the increase in the bank balance in the balance sheet (£2,000 to £6,000).
- The movements in working capital shows that increased spending on stocks (£82,000) or allowing debtors more credit (£52,000) is a cash outflow whilst taking more credit from suppliers £6,000 is a cash inflow.
- Outflows of cash are in brackets indicating deductions.

Other key facts

Dividends and taxation paid: because these are provided for in one period and actually paid in the next, it is the previous year's figures which will be entered in sections 3 and 6.

Fixed assets: when fixed assets are purchased and entered in section number 4, Investing activities, we need to know how much they cost; therefore the difference between the two periods is taken (£60,000 to £100,000), indicating £40,000 cost of new assets acquired.

If the assets were given at their net book values, (that is, after depreciation has been deducted), you must remember to add on any depreciation charges in order to arrive at the cost of purchase.

The net asset value of the two periods (£40,000 to £66,000) indicates an increase of £26,000, add the depreciation charges for the period of £14,000 = £40,000 cost of fixed assets.

In the event that some fixed assets are disposed of during the financial period, any gain or loss on their disposal is not to be included as part of the inflow of cash section number 1.

The actual sum received for the sale of the fixed assets is recorded under section number 4, Investing activities: £20,000 of the investments had been sold off (£40,000 down to £20,000) under fixed assets and the profit and loss account stated a profit of £8,000. Therefore the assumption is that the actual sale of investments brought an inflow of cash of £28,000.

Reserves and profit and loss balances: these figures only represent internal transfers of funds and therefore play no part in the recording of figures in the cash flow statement. In addition to the revised cash flow statement, there is a further requirement that seeks to reconcile the movement in cash flow with the movement of debt within the financial period.

Reconciliation of net cash flow to movement in net debt

	£	£
Increase in net cash flow		4,000
cash from increase in debt (LTL)		(8,000)
(loan 20,000 to 28,000)		
change in net debt		(4,000)
Net debt in year 1		
bank	2,000	
loan	(20,000)	(18,000)
Net debt in year 2		
bank	6,000	
loan	(28,000)	(22,000)
change in net debt		**(4,000)**

Analysis of changes in net debt

	Net debt Year 1	Net debt Year 2	Cash flow Year 2
bank	2,000	6,000	4,000
debt (loan)	(20,000)	(28,000)	(8,000)
	(18,000)	(22,000)	(4,000)

Therefore the net debt for the period to 31 December year 2 has increased by £4,000 as a result of the long-term loan increasing by £8,000, offset by a net cash flow increase of £4,000. The difference being a £4,000 net increase in debt.

KEY POINTS OF THE CHAPTER

Cash flow statement:	A link between the profit & loss account and balance sheets at the start and end of an accounting period.
FRS 1:	Financial Reporting Standard No.1 cash flow statements revised in 1996
Operating activities:	The net operating profit and depreciation and changes to debtors, creditors and stocks.
Reserves:	Any internal transfer of funds does not affect inflow or outflows of cash.
Liquidity:	Cash or near cash funds to cover debts, the working capital of the business.
Movement of debt:	Reconciliation of net cash flow with change in net debt.

QUESTIONS

1. The final accounts of ABC Co Ltd for year ended 31 March were as follows:

Balance Sheet of ABC Co Ltd as at 31 March:

	Year 1 £	Year 2 £
Assets		
Fixed (net)	140,000	195,000
Stocks	23,500	21,550
Debtors	14,725	18,450
Bank	4,150	2,925
Cash	500	500
	182,875	238,425
Liabilities		
Creditors	19,550	26,450
Provision for taxation	12,500	15,000
Provision for dividends (ordinary)	6,000	6,500
Debenture stock	35,000	50,000
	73,050	97,950
Net Assets:	109,825	140,475
Shareholders' Funds:		
Issued and paid-up capital:		
Ordinary shares	75,000	75,000
Preference shares	15,000	25,000
Reserves	15,725	33,725
Profit and loss balance (31/3)	4,100	6,750
	109,825	140,475

Profit and Loss Account of ABC Co Ltd

Year ended 31 March year 2

Operating profit		44,150
(Depreciation charges £8,000)		
Corporation tax		15,000
		29,150
Preference dividends paid	2,000	
Provision for ordinary	6,500	
Reserves	18,000	26,500
		2,650
Profit and loss balance (1/4) year1		4,100
Profit and loss balance (31/3) year 2		6,750

Required:
A cash flow statement for the year ended 31 March year 2.

2. The final accounts of K Bishop Limited for the years ended 31 March year 1 and year 2 were as follows:

Summarised Balance Sheets at 31 March

	Year 1 £	Year 2 £
Assets		
Fixed (net)	420,000	585,000
Stocks	70,500	64,650
Debtors and pre-payments	44,175	55,350
Bank	12,450	8,775
Cash	1,500	1,500
	548,625	715,275
Liabilities		
Trade creditors and accruals	(58,650)	(79,350)
Provision for tax	(37,500)	(45,000)
Proposed final dividend	(18,000)	(19,500)
10% Debenture stock	(105,000)	(150,000)
	(219,150)	(293,850)
	329,475	421,425
Capital and Reserves:		
£1 ordinary shares	225,000	225,000
£1 preference shares (8%)	45,000	75,000
Profit and loss account	59,475	121,425
	329,475	421,425

Note:

There were no disposals of fixed assets during the year.

Summarised Profit and Loss Account for year ending 31 March Year 2.

	£	£
Operating profit		147,450
(after provision for depreciation of £24,000)		
Interest payable		(15,000)
Profit for year before tax		132,450
Provision for tax		(45,000)
Profit for year after tax		87,450
Preference dividend paid	6,000	
Proposed ordinary dividend	19,500	(25,500)
Retained profit		61,950

Required:

a) Prepare a cash flow statement (as set out in FRS 1) for the year ending 31 March year 2.

b) Comment on the changes that have taken place during the year to 31 March year 2.

[Chartered Institute of Purchasing & Supply]

3 The following information refers to the accounts of P Jackson & Co Ltd:

Balance Sheet as at	31 Dec. Year 1 £	31 Dec. Year 2 £
Assets		
Premises (cost)	35,000	45,000
Machinery *	20,000	21,500
Stock	15,000	20,580
Debtors	8,450	12,375
Bank/cash	2,255	1,835
	80,705	101,290
Liabilities		
Creditors	10,150	12,755
Accruals	1,125	955
Taxation due	5,100	6,530
	16,375	20,240
Capital		
Issued @ £1 ordinary shares	50,000	60,000
Profit and Loss account	14,330	21,050
	64,330	81,050

* Machinery	Cost £	Depreciation £	Net £
Balance (31/12/year 1)	25,000	5,000	20,000
Additions year 2	6,000		
	31,000		
Sale of old stock	(3,000)	(2,000)	
Depreciation		3,500	
Balance	28,000	6,500	21,500

Profit and Loss Account, Year Ended 31 December Year 2

Operating profit	12,750
+ profit on sale of machinery	500
	13,250
Corporation tax	6,530
Retained to profit and loss account	6,720

Note:
Any gain or loss on the sale of a fixed asset *is not* included in section 1 as net profit although the actual sum received is included.

Required:
a) A cash flow statement for the year ended 31 December year 2.
b) Comment on the change of working capital over the two periods.

4. Study the following balance sheets of Jones & Rogers plc, and profit and loss account for the year ended 31 May year 2.

Jones & Rogers plc Balance Sheets as at 31 May

	Year 1		Year 2	
	£	£	£	£
Ordinary shares	170,000		200,000	
Share premium account	17,000		20,000	
Profit and loss account	8,000	195,000	10,000	230,000
Fixed Assets (cost)	180,000		260,000	
Depreciation	40,000	140,000	60,000	200,000
Investment (cost)		10,000		5,000
		150,000		205,000
Current Assets:				
Stock	50,000		60,000	
Debtors	30,000		47,000	
Bank	10,000	90,000	18,000	125,000
Current Liabilities:				
Creditors	17,000		18,000	
Provision for tax	16,000		18,000	
Provision for dividends	12,000	(45,000)	14,000	(50,000)
Deferred Liability.				
9% Debentures		-		(50,000)
		195,000		230,000

Jones & Rogers plc Profit & Loss account Year ended 31 May Year 2.

	£
Operating profit	30,000
+ Profit on investment	4,000
	34,000
- Provision for taxation	18,000
	16,000
+ Profit and loss balance (1/6/year 1)	8,000
	24,000
- Provision for dividends	14,000
Profit and loss a/c (31/5/ year 2)	10,000

Required:
a) Calculate the working capital ratio over the two years and briefly comment on the business's liquidity.
b) Prepare a cash flow statement for the year ended 31 May Year 2.

5. The following final accounts relate to Harry Fox Co Ltd for the years ending 31 December year 1, and year 2. Study the figures carefully from the point of view of analysing the firm's performance between the two financial periods.

Profit and Loss account, Harry Fox Co Ltd, Years ended 31 December year 1 and year 2

	Year 1 £	Year 2 £
Retail sales	128,640	196,480
Operating profit	12,850	21,590
Interest payable	0	0
Corporation tax (provision for year)	5,100	9,250
Net profit (after tax)	7,750	12,340
Dividends:		
Ordinary shares	6,500	9,000
Retained profits	1,250	3,340

Note: Depreciation charges for the year were £4,500.

Balance Sheet, Harry Fox Co. Ltd, as at year ended 31 December .

	Year 1 £	Year 2 £
Fixed Assets (net)	28,904	38,244
Current Assets		
Stock	7,288	10,338
Debtors	4,942	8,358
Bank	3,750	1,674
Cash	100	50
Current Liabilities		
Creditors	1,930	2,670
Accruals	550	1,000
Taxation	5,100	9,250
Dividends	6,500	9,000
Deferred		
Bank loan	5,000	2,500
Shareholders' Funds		
Authorised capital		
50,000 @ £1 ordinary shares	50,000	50,000
Issued and paid-up capital @ £1 ordinary shares	20,000	25,000
Reserves	5,904	9,244

Required:
a) Prepare two separate balance sheets at the year ended 31 December for Harry Fox Co Ltd, showing clearly working capital and capital employed.
b) Prepare a cash flow statement for the year ended 31 December year 2.

6. You work in the accounts office of XYZ Ltd and the accountant has provided you with the following information at the end of the financial period, 31 March year 2:

Balance Sheets of XYZ Ltd at 31 March

	Year 1 £	Year 2 £		Year 1 £	Year 2 £
Freehold property at cost	25,000	25,000	Issued Share Capital	30,000	30,000
Equipment *			Profit and loss a/c	27,000	33,000
	18,000	22,200	Corporation tax due:		
Stock in trade	16,400	17,800	1 January	6,000	4,000
Debtors	13,600	14,000	Creditors	12,000	13,000
Bank	2,000	1,000			
	75,000	80,000		75,000	80,000

* Equipment movements during the year ended 31 March year 2 were:

	Cost £	Depreciation £	Net £
Balance at 31 March year 1	30,000	12,000	18,000
Additions during year	9,000		
Depreciation provided during year		3,800	
	39,000	15,800	
Disposals during year	(4,000)	(3,000)	
Balance at 31 March	35,000	12,800	22,200

The company's summarised profit calculation for the year ended 31 March Year 2 revealed:

	Year 1 £	Year 2 £
Sales	95,000	100,000
Profit on sale of equipment		2,500
Less		102,500
Cost of sales and other expenses	84,800	92,500
Net profit before tax	10,200	10,000
Corporation tax on profits of the year	6,000	4,000
Retained profit of the year (after tax)	4,200	6,000

Required:
Prepare a cash flow statement for the year ended 31 March Year 2.

[Institute of Commercial Management]

7. You work for a small limited company and are assisting in the preparation of the annual accounts for year ending 30/5/year 2.

Aspen Limited Balance Sheet as at 30 May

	£	Year 1 £	£	£	Year 2 £	£
Fixed Assets at cost		173,000			243,400	
Less						
Depreciation		57,800	115,200		78,100	165,300
Current Assets:						
Stock		74,400			72,080	
Debtors		97,920			100,020	
Bank		10,880			-	
Current Liabilities:		183,200			172,100	
Creditors	41,440			37,080		
Overdraft	-			2,320		
Provision for tax	17,120			12,400		
Proposed dividend	10,000	68,560	114,640	12,000	63,800	108,300
			£229,840			£273,600
Financed by:						
£1 ordinary shares			200,000			220,000
Reserves			29,840			53,600
			£229,840			£273,600

Aspen Limited, Profit and Loss Account for Year Ended 30/5/year 2

	£
Operating profit for the year	49,160
Interest payable	(1,000)
Profit after interest	48,160
Provision for tax	12,400
Profit after tax	35,760
Proposed dividend	12,000
Profit & loss balance b/f	23,760
Profit & loss balance c/f	53,600

Required:
a) Prepare a cash flow statement of Aspen Limited for the year ended 30 May in Year 2.
b) Calculate the current ratio for both years.

[Institute of Commercial Management]

Chapter 29

Accounts of Clubs and Societies

INTRODUCTION

Most private sector businesses are profit motivated. Goods and services are produced and distributed for the purpose of making money. However, there are non-profit organisations that are not primarily set up to make profits. These are the clubs and societies that are organised for specific purposes - for example, social, sporting, political and other organisations.

In many regions up and down the country, there are local tennis, cricket, football and rugby clubs. There are also amateur dramatic and choral societies as well as political and other associations.
Any finance required, is raised by the members of these organisations in a number of various ways.

Members' subscriptions provide a major source of income, while donations from various bodies and fund-raising activities are ways of raising extra finance. The sources of finance are used to pay for the running and up-keep of the club or society.

Money that comes in and goes out of a social organisation should be properly accounted for in order to safeguard the members' interests. It is therefore necessary to keep some basic records of the accounts in order to know what funds are available at what time.

Most of the social organisations elect honorary members who take on specific responsibilities. The club chairman is usually the spokesman and *figure- head* of the organisation. The club secretary will have the responsibility of taking care of the essential paper work such as letters to members, agendas, minutes of meetings, reports of activities and so forth. The club treasurer will have the responsibility of looking after the accounts.

The Treasurer's accounting reports
Formal accounting methods tend to be uncommon because the treasurer may lack time or expertise or both when it comes to keeping the accounts of the club or society. However, he should be expected to keep a tight control of cash throughout the financial period and be in a position to prepare for members the following financial reports at the end of the club or society's social year:

- a receipts and payments account;
- any specialised accounts such as a bar account, if required;
- an income and expenditure account;
- a balance sheet showing the organisation's state of affairs.

The receipts and payments account
This statement is a summary of all cash receipts and payments of the organisation for the year and is, in effect, a simplified cash book. The purpose of it is to show members where the cash has come from and where it has gone and, significantly, how much is left in balance at the end of the year under review.

The income and expenditure account
This is a statement that is the equivalent of the business's trading and profit and loss account where expenses are matched against income. Adjustments such as accruals, pre-payments and depreciation are also accounted for because they affect the profit or loss for the year.

A social organisation uses the words 'surplus' or 'deficit' to indicate its profit or loss. Some clubs and societies operate a bar or refreshment counter for the benefit of members. The treasurer can prepare a special bar or refreshment account to indicate whether or not such an activity has made a surplus or deficit.

The balance sheet

This statement is prepared in the same way as any other organisation. The net resources of the club or society are financed by the *'accumulated funds'* - that is, the capital or net worth of the social organisation. Accumulated funds represent assets less liabilities in the same way as capital. Any surplus from the income and expenditure account is added to the funds. Any deficit is deducted.

Example 1
Poole Tennis Club begins its social year on 1 April, 2003. Its accumulated funds at this date are £17,704, made up of:

Bank balance	£304
Equipment	£400
Club House	£15,000
Investment	£2,000
	£17,704

At the end of the social year, 31 March 04, the treasurer listed the receipts and payments for the year and prepared the club's receipts and payments account as shown

Receipts and payments account for the period ended 31 March 04

Receipts	£	Payments	£
Balance b/d (1 April 03)	304	Sports equipment	108
Subscriptions	400	Tennis balls	30
Subscriptions in advance	55	Hire of courts	230
Refreshment sales	91	Light and heat	35
Dance tickets	25	General expenses	140
Tournament fees	72	Refreshment purchases	60
Donations	30	Club house improvement	350
		Balance c/d (31 March 04)	24
	977		977
Balance b/d (1 April 04)	24		

Note:
On 31 March 04 the following were to be taken into consideration before preparing the Club's income and expenditure account for the period ended:

- stock of refreshments   £27
- subscriptions owing for current year   £150
- electricity bill owing   £35
- sports equipment to be depreciated by   £58
- bill for refreshment purchases due   £12

Preparing a refreshment or bar account

It may be useful to prepare a separate account to deal with these to show whether a surplus or deficit is made. A surplus or deficit may then be transferred to the income and expenditure account.

Refreshment account Poole Tennis Club

	£	£
Sales		91
Less cost of sales:		
Stock (1 April 03)	0	
+ Purchases	60	
+ Purchases due	12	
	72	
- Stock (31 March 04)	27	
		45
Surplus *		46

* Transferred to the income side of the income and expenditure account.

Poole Tennis Club: Income and expenditure account for the period ended 31 March 04

Expenditure	£	£	Income	£	£
Tennis balls		30	Subscriptions	400	
Hire of courts		230	+ owing	150	550
Light and heat	35		Refreshment surplus		46
+ owing	35	70	Dance tickets		25
General expenses		140	Tournament fees		72
Depreciation of equipment		58	Donations		30
Surplus		195			
(income greater than expenditure)					
		723			723

NOTE:

- The subscriptions owing £150 belong to the current period ending 31 March and are therefore added to income. The subscriptions in advance are not included because they belong to the next period ending 31 March year 3.
- The last financial statement is the balance sheet showing the Poole Tennis Club's resources and the financing of them via the accumulated funds.

Example 2
The following information has been submitted by the Corfe Mullen Social Club, for the year ended 31 March 04.

Corfe Mullen Social Club –
Receipts and payments account, year ended 31 March 04

Receipts	£	Receipts	£
1/4/-03 Balance (bank)	2,000	Insurance, rates	480
Subscriptions	5,575	Wages	5,650
Surplus (bingo)	850	Bar purchases	6,500
Bar takings	10,225	General expenses	275
		Light and heat	480
		New furniture	500
		Club repairs, maintenance	1,275
		31/3/04 Balance (bank)	3,490
	18,650		18,650

Other information:	£	31/3/04	£
1/4/03		Bar stock	850
Club premises at cost	25,000	Subscriptions: in arrears	480
Furniture and equipment	2,000	in advance	50
Bar stock	1,600	Furniture and equipment valued	1,950
Bank balance (as above)	2,000	Bar purchases owing	500
Subscriptions: in arrears	150	Insurance prepaid	35
in advance	100	Light and heat owing	50
Insurance prepaid	80		
Light and heat owing	130		

Required:
a) The club's bar account for the period ended 31 March 04.
b) The club's income and expenditure account for the same period.
c) The club's balance sheet as at 31 March 04
d) The club's subscriptions account for the period ended 31 March 04.

Solution:

Corfe Mullen Social Club –
Bar account, year ended 31 March 04

	£	£
Sales		10,225
- Cost of sales:		
Stock (1/4/03)	1,600	
+ Purchases	6,500	
	8,100	
+ Purchases due	500	
	8,600	
- Stock (31/3/04)	850	7,750
Surplus transferred to income and expenditure account		2,475

Corfe Mullen Social Club – Income and expenditure account, year ended 31 March 04

Expenditure	£	£	Income	£	£
Insurance and rates	480		Surplus from bar		2,475
+ Prepaid (1/4/03)	80		Surplus from bingo		850
	560		Subscriptions	5,575	
- Prepaid (31/3/04)	35	525	+ In advance (1/4/03)	100	
Wages		5,650		5,675	
Light and heat	480		- In arrears (1/4/03)	150	
- Owing (1/4/03)	130			5,525	
	350		+ In arrears (31/3/04)	480	
+ Owing (31/3/04)	50	400		6,005	
General expenses		275	- In advance (31/3/04)	50	5,955
Maintenance and repairs		1,275			
Depreciation of furniture and equipment		550			
Surplus t/f to accumulated Fund		605			
		9,280			9,280

Corfe Mullen Social Club – Balance sheet as at 31 March 04

	£	£		£	£
FIXED ASSETS			Accumulated fund		
Premises	25,000		(1/4/03)	30,600	
Furniture and equipment	1,950	26,950	+ Surplus	605	31,205
			CURRENT		
CURRENT ASSETS			LIABILITIES		
Stock (bar)	850		Stock creditors	500	
Subscriptions (arrear)	480		Light and heat (accrual)	50	
Bank	3,490		Subscriptions (advance)	50	600
Insurance (prepaid)	35	4,855			
		31,805			31,805

NOTES:

1 The Accumulated fund on 1 April 03 was calculated as:

	Assets £	Liabilities £
Premises	25,000	
Furniture and equipment	2,000	
Bar stock	1,600	
Bank account	2,000	
Subscriptions: arrears	150	
advance		100
insurance (prepaid)	80	
Light and heat (owing)		130
	30,830	230

Accumulated fund was £30 830 - £230 = £30 600.

2 Adjustments at the beginning of the accounting year as well as at the end:
When accruals and prepayments appear at the beginning of an accounting year (1 April year 1) they are treated in the **reverse** way as to how they are treated at the end (31 March year 2).

	1/4/03	*31/3/04*
Accrued expenses	deducted	added
Prepaid expenses	added	deducted
Subscriptions: arrears	deducted	added
advance	added	deducted

Subscription account

1/4/03	Accrued b/d	150	1/4/03	Prepaid b/d	100
31/3/04	Prepaid c/d	50	31/3/04	Bank	5,575
	I & E account	5,955		Accrued c/d	480
		6,155			6,155
1/4/04	Accrued b/d	480	1/4/04	Prepaid b/d	50

KEY POINTS OF THE CHAPTER

Clubs & societies a/c's:	Prepared using the same accounting principles as other organisations
Receipts & payments a/c:	A summary of the club's cash book
Income & expenditure a/c:	The club's profit & loss a/c
Bar a/c:	A trading a/c of bar or refreshments indicating surplus/deficit
Adjustments:	Using same accounting principles, adjustments at start of period treated in opposite way to period end
Accumulated fund:	A club's capital a/c (assets less liabilities)
Subscriptions:	Annual fees paid by club's members to support activities

QUESTIONS

1. a) Contrast a club's financial statements with those of other business organisations.
    b) How is the accumulated fund calculated at the commencement of the accounting year?

2. When adjustments appear at the commencement of an accounting period as well as at the end these must be taken into account. During the year to 31 December, subscriptions received amounted to £2,650 of which £150 were paid in advance.

    At the commencement of the period on 1 January there had been £200 of subscriptions in arrear and £75 had been in advance. On 31 December subscriptions still outstanding came to £225. Note that the club has a total of 104 members and the membership fee is £25 each.

    Write up the *subscriptions account* and state the figure to be transferred to the income & expenditure account at the year end 31 December.

3. From the following receipts and payments account of the Parkstone Golf Club and the further particulars provided below, prepare an income and expenditure account for the year ended 31 March, 20-2 and a balance sheet as at that date.

Receipts and Payments Account for the year ended 31 March, 20- 2.

Receipts	£	Payments	£
Balance from last year	1,600	Wages	4,800
Entrance fees	8,400	Payment for new Equipment	3,500
Subscriptions:		Printing and stationery	200
Current year	4,800	Postage	175
In advance	500	Lighting and heating	575
Profits and refreshments	1,160	Insurance	250
Equipment rented to members	750	General expenses	1,850
	17,210	Balance (bank)	5,860
Balance b/d	5,860		17,210

Additional information at 31 March, 20-2:
a) £50 is owing for subscriptions for the year.
b) £15 is owing by members for equipment rentals.
c) Printing and stationery, value £28, is still unpaid.
d) The Club House & equipment appear in the books on 1 April year 1 at a value of £10,000.

4. The Sandal Rugby Club was started on 1 April, 20-1 with a bank balance of £3,300 which was provided by its members. The receipts and payments for the year ended 31 March, 20- 2 were:

	£
Pavilion and other buildings, land	8,150
Equipment	500
Gate money	3,500
Collections at matches	1,642
Donations from members and other	1,585
Refreshment expenses	756
Receipts from refreshments	1,100
Loan from local bank secured on land and buildings (@ 12% per annum)	5,000
Rates, water	185
Light, heat	75
Wages of grounds man (part-time)	800
Match expenses paid	115
Printing and other expenses	125
Advertising	176
General expenses	80
Transport costs	1,050

Notes: 31 March, 20-2.
▪ Rates pre-paid £45.
▪ The interest on loan has not yet been accounted for since 1 July, 20-1.
▪ Wages owing to grounds man £40.
▪ Stocks of catering amounted to £65.
▪ The equipment was to be depreciated by £100.

Required:
a) Prepare the income and expenditure account for the year ended 31 March, 20-2.
b) A balance sheet as at that date.

5. The following is the trial balance of the Broadstone Amateur Rugby Union Club as on 31 December:

	£	£
Accumulated Fund at 1 January		10,500
Club House	18,560	
Club-room equipment	755	
Sports equipment	150	
Sale of refreshments		3,765
Purchase of refreshments	2,400	
Interest accrued		50
Subscriptions received for current year		2,800
Subscriptions in advance		55
Receipts from Club-house games		200
Maintenance of games equipment	500	
Postage	150	
Insurance	850	
Sundry expenses	275	
Printing and stationery	105	
Wages	1,450	
Bank		1,870
Loan from Building Society		5,955
	25,195	**25,195**

Note:
Take into consideration the following:
* Sports equipment is to be depreciated at 10% per annum and club-room equipment at 20% per annum
* £75 subscriptions are due for the current year
* £95 is owing for the purchase of refreshments
* Stock of refreshments on hand at 31 December was £370

Required:
a) An account to show the profit or loss on sale of refreshments.
b) The income and expenditure account for the year ended 31 December.
c) A balance sheet as at 31 December.

6. The following information relates to Broadstone Youth Tennis Club at the beginning of their season 1 April, 20- 1.

	£
Club House	15,000
Equipment	800
Bank	500
Stock (refreshments)	250

A summary of receipts for the year

Subscriptions	1,500
Subs in advance	150
Refreshments	1,855
Dances	550
Fees for tournaments	360
Donations from members	100
Members'' loan (5%pa.)	2,000
Sales of lottery	875

A summary of payments for the year	£
Sports equipment	450
Tennis balls (expense)	50
Lottery tickets, prizes	565
Light and heat	80
General expenses	240
Refreshment purchases	1,255
Club House re-building	1,850
Maintenance of grounds	200
Insurance, rates, water	375

Note:

At the end of the season, 31 March, 20- 2 the following information was available to the Club Treasurer:
- The sports equipment (including additions) was valued at £900.
- Stock of refreshments valued at cost £165.
- Subscriptions owing by members £80.
- A gas bill was still to be paid £18.
- Insurance was pre-paid £25.
- Club House rebuilding is classified as a capital expense, not revenue expense.
- Members' interest on loan had not been paid (from 1 April year 1).

Required:
a) Prepare a receipts and payments account for the year ended 31 March year 2.
b) Prepare the club's income and expenditure account for the year ended 31 March year 2 and a balance sheet as at that date.

7. From the following details and the notes attached relating to the Wiltshire Tennis Club prepare an income and expenditure statement for the year ended 31 December and a balance sheet as at that date.

On 1 January, the club's assets were: freehold club-house, £1,000.00, equipment £70.00; club subscriptions in arrears £8.00; balance at bank £76.00. The club owed £40.00 to Caterer's Ltd for Christmas dance catering.

Summary of Receipts and Payments

Receipts	£	Payments	£
Subscriptions	164.00	Catering-Christmas dance	
Locker rents	10.00	(Caterer's Ltd)	40.00
Receipts from dances and social	139.00	This year's dances and socials	95.00
Sales of used match tennis balls	15.00	Band fees-dances	25.00
Sale of old lawn mower	8.00	New lawn mower	55.00
		Repairs to tennis nets	19.00
		Match tennis balls	31.00
		Match expenses	17.00
		Repair and decoration	
		of Club House	65.00

Note:
a) The book value on January 1 of the old lawn mower sold during the year was £15.
b) The club has 40 members and the subscription is £4.00 per annum. The subscriptions received included those in arrears for the previous year.
c) On 31 December £1 1.00 was owed to James Ltd for tennis balls supplied.
d) Equipment as at 31 December, is to be depreciated by 10%.

8. You have been asked to prepare some accounts for the local golf club. The treasurer of the Redbridge Golf Club has passed on to you all the necessary financial information:

Redbridge Golf Club: Balance Sheet as at 30 June, 20- 1

	Cost £	Depreciation £	Net £
Fixed Assets:			
Club property	120,000	24,000	96,000
Fixtures and fittings	22,000	6,600	15,400
	142,000	30,600	111,400
Current Assets:			
Bar stock		1,420	
Subscriptions in arrears		2,140	
Bank		4,780	
		8,340	
Current Liabilities:			
Creditors for bar supplies			
Subscriptions in advance	575		
	1,165		
		1,740	
			6,600
			118,000
Financed by:			
Accumulated Fund:			113,800
Balance			4,200
Surplus for the year			118,000

Redbridge Golf Club: Receipts and Payments Account for the year ended 30 June, 20- 2

Receipts	£	Payments	£
Bank balance b/d	4,780	Bar purchases	7,248
Subscriptions	18,220	Bar steward's salary	4,926
Bar takings	12,435	General expenses	2,674
		Maintenance expenses	3,749
		Heating and lighting	788
		Bank Balance c/d	16,050
	35,435		35,435

Note:
- The following balances were available at 30 June, 20-2:
  Bar stock   £1,540
- Subscriptions in arrears   £1,875
- Subscriptions in advance £1,450
- Creditors for bar supplies £638
- The club's policy is to provide depreciation annually on fixed assets at the following rates based on their cost:
  Club property 2.5% per annum, Fixtures and fittings 10% per annum.

Required:
a) Showing clearly the profit or loss made on the bar, prepare the club's income and expenditure account for the year ended 30 June, 20-2
b) Explain the difference between the receipts and payments account and the income and expenditure account of a club or an association.

(Association of Accounting Technicians)

Chapter 30

The Extended Trial Balance

INTRODUCTION

The trial balance is an indication or test of arithmetical accuracy of the double entry system. At the end of a financial period, the trial balance is extracted from the accounts of the nominal ledger in readiness for the preparation of the final accounts. All adjustments relating to the end of the period must also be taken into account to ensure the correct matching of revenue with expenses.

The extended trial balance (ETB) is a form of a worksheet where extra columns are provided alongside the trial balance figures in order to accommodate any adjustments or changes which may be required for the preparation of the final accounts. The final two columns of the ETB are the profit & loss account and the balance sheet. The worksheet is then used to prepare the formal financial statements for the client. The ETB may be displayed in a number of various formats.

In general accounting practice there are often a number of extra columns to include bank and cash transactions, accruals and prepayments. In examination questions the format is often shortened to have columns for the trial balance, adjustments, the profit and loss account and the balance sheet.

An abbreviated example of the layout of the ETB including some entries, is as follows:

Details	Trial Balance		Adjustments		Profit and Loss		Balance Sheet	
	Dr	Cr	Dr	Cr	Dr	Cr	Dr	Cr
Sales		95,100				95,100		
Purchases	52,150				52,150			
Telephone	1,325		50		1,375			
Light, heat	1,540		75		1,615			
Stationery	890			100	790			
Wages	14,745		100		14,845			
Motor van	2,450						2,450	
Depreciation of van		490		490				980
Equipment	1,500						1,500	
Depreciation of equipment		150		150				300
Accruals								225
Prepayments							100	
Depreciation of fixed assets			640		640			

NOTE:

- The trial balance column lists all figures concerning the trial balance at the period end.
- The adjustments column is used for making the balance day adjustments including accruals, prepaid expenses, writing off bad debts, making provisions for depreciation, bad debts or discounts and for adjusting any figures for VAT etc.
- The final two columns are used to extend the figures across to either the profit and loss account or the balance sheet. The net profit so far is £23,685 [£95,100 less £71,415].
- The difference between the columns in the profit and loss account will indicate either profit or loss that is then transferred to the balance sheet.

If a net loss occurred, it would be credited in the profit and loss column and debited in the balance sheet column. In some formats, the ETB has *separate* columns for accruals and prepayments as we have in Example 1 that follows. If we had used the abbreviated format as above, these would be recorded under the adjustments column along with other entries for closing stock, depreciation etc.

Example 1

The following accounts relate to Arthur Jones, as at the year ended 31 December. You are required to prepare the extended trial balance and the trading and profit and loss account for the year ended 31 December and a balance sheet as at that date.

Arthur Jones: Trial balance as at 31 December

	Debit £	Credit £
Premises	57,500	
Equipment	23,000	
Provision for depreciation equipment		6,000
Motor van	8,000	
Provision for depreciation van		2,000
Stock (1/1)	8,300	
Purchases/sales	30,800	66,600
Returns	700	900
Wages	16,500	
Carriage inwards	500	
Carriage outwards	400	
Commission received		500
Bank interest charged	350	
Light, heat	1,650	
Postage, stationery	600	
Insurance	1,200	
Telephone	500	
Rent received		750
Debtors, creditors	7,000	11,750
Bank	1,950	
Discount allowed	100	
Bad debts	450	
Capital account		71,000
	159,500	159,500

Adjustments to be taken into account 31 December were:
  a) Closing value of unsold stock £9,500
  b) Wages accrued £550
  c) The owner takes stock of goods for own use valued £800 (cost)
  d) Unused stationery £95
  e) Rent received still due to be paid £180
  f) Depreciation: equipment 20% pa, reducing balance method, motor van is revalued to £4,500
  g) Make a provision for bad & doubtful debts to equal 10% of debtors.

Required:
Prepare the extended trial balance for the period ended 31 December.

Procedure for the extended trial balance
(See the worked example of Arthur Jones on page 322)

1 **Trial balance entries**
   Enter the trial balance data of Arthur Jones in the first two columns of the ETB.

2 **Adjustments**
   The two adjustments columns are used to enter the following transactions:

- Closing stock £9,500 entered in both the debit and credit columns. These are then extended across to the credit side of the profit and loss account and the debit side of the balance sheet.

- Depreciation of equipment (20% reducing balance) £3,400, credit the provision for depreciation account and extended across to the credit side of the balance sheet as £9,400 in total. Debit the depreciation of equipment account £3,400 and extended across to the debit side of the profit and loss account as an expense.

- Depreciation of the motor van (re-valued to £4,500) the same procedure is used, credit the provision for depreciation £1,500 and extended across to the credit side of the balance sheet as £3,500 in total. Debit the depreciation of motor van account £1,500 and extended across to the debit side of the profit and loss account as an expense, (or alternatively, debit depreciation of fixed assets £4,900 in total and extended to the debit side of the profit and loss account).

- Provision for bad debts (10% of debtors), £700 entered in credit column of the provision for bad debts account and extended across to the credit side of the balance sheet. Debit the bad and doubtful debts account £700 and extended across to the debit side of the profit and loss account as an expense.

- Stock drawings £800 credit to purchases account and extended to the debit side of the profit and loss account as £30,000. Debit £700 to capital account (or a separate drawings account) and extended across to the credit side of the balance sheet to = £70,200 capital.

3 **Accruals and prepayments**
   Using the two accruals and prepayments columns to enter the following:

- Wages accrued £550 entered in the accruals column and extended across to the debit side of the profit and loss account to = £17,050.

- Stationery prepaid £95 entered in the prepayments column and extended across to the debit side of the profit and loss account to = £505.

- Rent received accrued £180 entered also in the prepayments column and extended across to the credit side of the profit and loss account to = £930.

- Note that the totals of accruals and prepayments are entered at the bottom of the ETB and extended across to the balance sheet on the opposite sides, accruals on the credit side and prepayments on the debit side.

4 **Extending entries across**

Extend all other trial balance entries across to either the profit and loss account or the balance sheet as appropriate.

For example, expense accounts are debited to the profit and loss account, revenue accounts are credited. Assets are debited in the balance sheet columns whilst liabilities and capital are credited in the balance sheet.

5 **Profit and loss entries**

When all entries are completed, the net profit/loss is calculated by finding the **difference** between the debit and credit columns of the profit and loss account:

> The debits = £67,305, credits = £78,430, the **net profit** therefore = £11,125.
> This is entered on the debit side of the profit and loss account so that both sides total £78,430.

> The net profit is also extended across to the credit side of the balance sheet, effectively making both debit and credit columns = £107,225. See the extended trial balance of Arthur Jones on the following page.

NOTE:

- The adjustments column imposes the double-entry principle. For example, depreciation is debited to profit and loss as an expense and the provision for depreciation is credited in the balance sheet.

- The accruals and pre-payments columns simply list those items to be adjusted and are totalled, then transferred the opposite way round in the balance sheet columns so that accruals are entered on the credit side and prepayments on the debit side.

- The net profit of £11,125 on the debit side of the profit and loss account is the difference between the debit and credit sides of this account. The figure is also entered on the credit side of the balance sheet to indicate an increase in the owner's capital.

- If the expense column of the profit and loss account was more than the revenue   column, then a net loss would be the result. In this case, the loss would be entered as a credit in the profit and loss account column and a debit in the balance sheet column.

The extended trial balance is used widely in accounting practice particularly for client's accounts. As a worksheet, it summarises all the relevant figures that have been calculated either from ledger accounts, or more likely for small traders, from their various business documents provided by the client for the financial year.

Although the extended trial balance does looks a little complicated at first by its multi-columns, once it has been used a number of times, it provides a relevant record of calculations in readiness for the preparation of the year-end final accounts of a business.

Arthur Jones – Extended Trial Balance

Description	Trial Balance		Adjustments		Creditors/ Accruals	Debtors/ Pre-payments	Profit and loss account		Balance sheet	
	Dr	Cr	Dr	Cr			Dr	Cr	Dr	Cr
Premises	57,500								57,500	
Equipment	23,000								23,000	
Prov. For depreciation		6,000		3,400						9,400
Motor van	8,000								8,000	
Prov. For depreciation		2,000		1,500						3,500
Stock (1/1)	8,300						8,300			
Purchases	30,800			800			30,000			
Sales		66,600						66,600		
Returns inward	700						700			
Returns outwards		900						900		
Wages	16,500				550		17,050			
Carriage inward	500						500			
Carriage outwards	400						400			
Commission received		500						500		
Bank interest	350						350			
Lighting, heating	1,650						1,650			
Postage, stationery	600					95	505			
Insurance	1,200						1,200			
Telephone	500						500			
Rent received		750				180		930		
Debtors	7,000								7,000	
Provision for bad debts				700						700
Creditors		11,750								11,750
Bank	1,950								1,950	
Discount allowed	100						100			
Bad debts	450						450			
Capital account		71,000	800							70,200
Depreciation – Equipment			3,400				3,400			
Depreciation – van			1,500				1,500			
Bad and doubtful debts			700				700			
Stock (31/12)			9,500	9,500				9,500	9,500	
Net Profit/loss							**11,125**			**11,125**
Accruals/prepayments					550	275			275	550
	159,500	159,500	15,500	15,500	550	275	78,430	78,430	107,225	107,225

Example 2 The ETB and the suspense account

The trial balance of Arthur Jones did not balance as on 30 June and a suspense account was entered in the ETB as £690 credit. Subsequently the following errors were located:

- Equipment £500 had in error been posted to the purchases account
- A gas bill £85 had been paid but not put through the books
- Discount allowed £68 had not been posted to the ledger
- Sales had been under-cast by £800
- A cheque from a debtor £150 had been recorded as £105 in debtor's account but correctly recorded in the corresponding account
- The total from the returns inward account £87 had not been posted to the ledger account
- Cash sales £900 into bank had in error been posted in reverse.

In addition to these entries above, on 30 June the closing stock value was £2,150 and wages owing were £240. Depreciation of the van and equipment is at 10% per annum and buildings valued £12,000, at 2% per annum.

Required:
a) Make the appropriate corrections first in the journal and then directly in the ETB, entering the suspense account on the opposite side of the adjustments column. This is to offset errors that affect the suspense account.
b) Include the adjustments for stock, wages and depreciation.
c) Extend all figures across as appropriate, calculating net profit/loss.

Solution:

	Journal		
Date	*Details*	*Debit*	*Credit*
June 30	Equipment	500	
	Purchases		500
	Light and heat	85	
	Bank		85
	Discount allowed	68	
	Suspense		68
	Suspense	800	
	Sales		800
	Suspense	45	
	Debtors		45
	Returns inward	87	
	Suspense		87
	Bank	1,800	
	Sales		1,800

NOTE:
In the ETB, those errors that include the suspense account are all offset by the £690 debited in the adjustments column. For example, returns inward £87 is debited in the adjustments column and the corresponding credit is offset in the suspense account of £690.

Solution:

The ETB of Arthur Jones

Details	Trial balance Dr	Cr	Adjustments Dr	Cr	Profit and loss Dr	Cr	Balance sheet Dr	Cr
Premises	20,000						20,000	
Motor vehicle	500						500	
Equipment	2,100		500				2,600	
Opening stock	1,860				1,860			
Debtors	675			45			630	
Creditors		1,155						1,155
Capital		12,500						12,500
Bank		455	1,800	85			1,260	
Sales		35,750		⌈ 800 ⌊1,800		38,350		
Purchases	20,195			500	19,685			
General expenses	1,250				1,250			
Wages	3,970		240		4,210			
Suspense		690	690					
Light and heat			85		85			
Discount allowed			68		68			
Returns in			87		87			
Closing stock			2,150	2,150		2,150	2,150	
Accrued expenses				240				240
Depreciation:								
Van			50	50				
Equipment			260	260				
Buildings			240	240	550			550
Net Profit					**12,695**			**12,695**
	50,550	50,550	6,170	6,170	40,500	40,500	27,140	27,140

KEY POINTS OF THE CHAPTER

ETB:	Extended trial balance, a worksheet to assist in preparing final account's
Format of ETB:	Various methods of presentation some using more columns than others
Adjustments:	Balance day adjustments for example, accruals, prepayments, provision for depreciation
Profit calculation:	The difference between Dr and Cr columns in the Profit and Loss account, t/f to balance sheet
Suspense account:	Used when trial balance fails to balance and may be included in ETB in the adjustments column on opposite side of suspense balance, offset to clear errors.

QUESTIONS

1. The Trial Balance figures as on 31 March for R Westlake Ltd.

	£	£
Premises	130,000	
Equipment and machines	28,120	
Motor vehicle	8,600	
Stocks	4,800	
Bank overdraft		8,390
Petty cash	980	
Debtors and creditors	7,420	5,160
Mortgage and premises		84,000
Loan (8 years)		7,300
Sales		51,000
Purchases	17,400	
VAT		2,740
Wages	16,300	
Lighting and heating	2,280	
Telephone	1,870	
General expenses	370	
Interest	2,300	
Business rates	2,070	
Director's fees	4,600	
Insurance	1,480	
Capital		70,000
	228,590	228,590

Note
- Stocks are valued at £5,350 as at 31 March
- Wages - a bonus of £750 is outstanding on 31 March
- Insurance premium is pre-paid to June (£290)
- Equipment and motor vehicle are to be depreciated by 10%

Required:
a) Prepare an extended trial balance for R Westlake Ltd on 31 March.
b) Prepare the trading and profit and loss account of the firm for the month ended 31 March.
c) Prepare the balance sheet as at that date

2. The following figures have been extracted from the ledgers of Frances Mitchell:

Trial balance as at 30 June:

	Dr £	Cr £
Sales		276,156
Purchases	164,700	
Carriage inwards	4,422	
Carriage outwards	5,866	
Drawings	15,600	
Rent and rates	9,933	
Insurance	3,311	
Postage and stationery	3,001	
Advertising	5,661	
Salaries and wages	52,840	
Bad debts	1,754	
Debtors	24,240	
Creditors		25,600
Returns outwards		131
Cash	354	
Bank	2,004	
Stock	23,854	
Equipment (cost)	116,000	
Capital: E Mitchell		131,653
	433,540	433,540

The following information was available on 30 June:
- Wages are accrued by £420
- Rates have been pre-paid by £1,400
- Stock of unused stationery valued £250
- A provision for bad debts is to be created to equal 5% of debtors
- Unsold stock at the close of business valued at £27,304
- Depreciate equipment 10% of cost

Required:
a) Prepare an extended trial balance for F Mitchell as on 30 June.
b) Prepare the trading and profit and loss account for the year ended 30 June and a balance sheet as at that date.
c) Advise F Mitchell on the position of the working capital of the business.

[Institute of Bankers]

3. The following trial balance has been extracted from the ledger of M Yousef, a sole trader:

Trial balance as at 31 May:

	Dr £	Cr £
Sales		138,078
Purchases	82,350	
Carriage	5,144	
Drawings	7,800	
Rent and rates and insurance	6,622	
Postage and stationery	3,001	
Advertising	1,330	
Salaries and wages	26,420	
Bad debts	877	
Provision for bad debts		130
Debtors	12,120	
Creditors		6,471
Cash on hand	177	
Cash at bank	1,002	
Stock (opening)	11,927	
Equipment		
at cost	58,000	
accumulated depreciation		19,000
Capital		53,091
	216,770	216,770

The following additional information as at 31 May is available:
- Rent is accrued by £210
- Rates have been pre-paid by £880
- £2,211 of carriage represents carriage inwards on purchases
- Equipment is to be depreciated at 15% per annum using the straight-line method
- The provision for bad debts to be increased by £40
- Stock at the close of business has been valued at £13,551

Required:
a) Prepare an extended trial balance for M Yousef as at 31 May.
b) Prepare the trading and profit and loss account for the year ended 31 May and a balance sheet as at that date.

[Association of Accounting Technicians]

4. You work for a firm of accountants and your boss, Mike Walker, has asked you to prepare a draft set of accounts for a client, a sole trader, Harry Andrews, who runs a small shop.

Trial balance of Harry Andrews, a sole trader, as on 31 December, 20-6

	Debit £	Credit £
Sales		67615
Purchases	46470	
Returns inward and outward	1205	1315
Stock (01/01)	3355	
Carriage Inwards	442	
Drawings	2560	
Maintenance and Rates	1578	
Insurance, telephone	334	
Light, heat	546	
Postage, stationery	350	
Bad debts	175	
Motor expenses	560	
Wages	11285	
Provision for b/debts		305
Cash	520	
Bank overdraft		3065
Equipment (cost)	21600	
Provision for depreciation of equipment		2160
Motor van (cost)	7500	
Provision for depreciation of van		3000
Debtors, creditors	12400	12560
Bank loan (long term)		6000
Capital a/c		14860
	110880	**110880**

Additional information was available on 31 December 20-6:

1. Unsold stock was valued £4800.
2. Accrued expenses: Wages £185, electricity bill £190.
3. Prepayments: Stock of unused stationery £110, insurance £80.
4. Bad debts provision is to be adjusted to equal 10% of debtors.
5. Depreciation: The van at 20% on its net book value (reducing balance method) and the equipment at 10% of cost (straight-line method)

Required:
Prepare the extended trial balance of H. Andrews for the period ending 31 December, 20-6.
Prepare the trading & profit & loss account of H. Andrews for the period ending 31 December, 20-6 and a balance sheet as at that date.

[Higher National Diploma)]

5. The following trial balance was extracted from the accounts of Fred Smith on 30 June

	Dr £	Cr £
Sales		27,615
Purchases	16,470	
Returns	205	315
Stock [opening]	2,355	
Carriage inwards	442	
Carriage outwards	580	
Drawings	2,560	
Maintenance and rates	1,998	
Insurance, telephone	334	
Light, heat	546	
Postage, stationery	350	
Bad debts	175	
Motor expenses	560	
Wages	5,285	
Provision for bad debts		65
Cash	200	
Bank overdraft		2,005
Equipment [cost]	11,600	
Provision. for depreciation of equip.		1,160
Motor van [cost]	2,500	
Provision for depreciation of van		1,500
Debtors, creditors	2,420	2,560
Bank loan [deferred]		4,500
Capital: F Smith		8,860
	48,580	48,580

The following additional information was available on 30 June:
- Unsold stock was valued at £2,895
- Accrued expenses: wages, £185; electricity bill, £90
- Pre-payments: stock of unused stationery, £110; insurance, £80
- The bad debts provision is to be adjusted to equal 5% of debtors
- Depreciation: the van at 25% on the reducing balance method; equipment at 10% of cost.

Required:
a) Prepare an extended trial balance for F. Smith as on 30 June.
b) Prepare the trading and profit and loss account of F. Smith for the period ended 30 June
c) Prepare the balance sheet of F. Smith as on 30 June, showing net current assets.
[Higher National Diploma]

6. You work for a firm of accountants, Carter & Cutler, and are asked to prepare a draft of the end of year accounts for a client, P Jackson. The trial balance was extracted from the accounts:

As at 30 June	Dr £	Cr £
Suspense account		549
Bank		6,500
Purchases/sales	46,000	75,250
Motor vehicle	12,500	
Provision for depreciation (Motor vehicles)		5,000

Rent and rates	1,400	
Light and heat	700	
Carriage inwards	500	
Discounts [balance]	400	
Opening stock	6,300	
Commissions received		1,500
Drawings	9,611	
Returns	1,800	1,500
Office salaries	16,000	
Debtors/creditors	24,000	16,000
Provisions for bad debts		2,000
Fixtures and fittings	8,000	
Provision for depreciation		
Fixtures and fittings		2,400
Land and buildings	65,000	
Bank loan (repayable long-term)		10,000
Interest on loan (12.5% pa)	938	
Capital		72,450
	193,149	193,149

Note: as on 30 June

- Closing stock £5,300
- During the financial year P Jackson took goods for own use from the business which cost £2,000
- Revenue accrued: £426 still to be received on commission
- Rates had been paid £200 in advance
- £312 is owed for interest on the bank loan and £540 is due on salaries
- Provision for bad debts is to be increased to 10% of the debtors
- Provision for depreciation of 10% p.a. on cost is to be made on fixtures and fittings
- The motor vehicles are to be re-valued to £6,000

The trial balance as on 30 June, did not balance, so a suspense account had to be opened with a credit balance of £549. However, the following errors were revealed shortly after the accounts had been further scrutinised:

- Credit sales of £1,200 had been omitted from the books (a sales invoice had been found relating to June)
- A receipt of £500 from a debtor had been recorded in the Cash Book only, the posting being omitted
- Discounts received (£376) had been recorded correctly in the purchase ledger, but had in error been posted to the debit side of the discounts account
- Discounts allowed (£224) had also been recorded correctly in the sales ledger, but had in error been posted to the credit side of the discounts account
- Payments made to the firm's supplier totalling £21,257 had been debited as £21,752 in the purchase ledger control account
- Finally, the accountant's bill of £750 had been paid and recorded in the Cash Book but no further entry had been made

Required:
a) Prepare the necessary journal entries to record the above errors and show the suspense account as it would appear after the correction of all the accounting errors.
b) Adjust the relevant accounts in the trial balance affected by the errors.
c) Prepare an extended trial balance for P Jackson as at 30 June.

d) Prepare the trading and profit and loss account of P Jackson for the year ended 30 June.

e) Prepare the balance sheet of P Jackson as on 30 June, showing net current assets.

(Higher National Diploma)

7. The following figures relate to the financial data of Harry Smith. Prepare a draft extended trial balance for the client as well as a set of final accounts.

Trial balance as at 31 May, 20 -	Debit £	Credit £
Premises	50,000	
Equipment	15,100	
Provision for depreciation of equipment		2,500
Motor vehicle	6040	
Provision for depreciation of vehicle		3,480
Debtors	8,800	
Creditors		8,130
Opening stock	10,300	
Bank	7,451	
Mortgage on premises		30,130
Mortgage repayments (inc. interest)	2,460	
Capital		62,500
Purchases, sales	38,058	49,603
Stationery	672	
Light & heat	403	
VAT	885	
British Telecom *	423	
Motor expenses *	1,598	
Wages	10,960	
Maintenance & repairs	935	
General overheads	1,350	
Bank & interest charges	298	
Discounts	445	225
Bad debts	190	
Petty cash float	200	
	156,568	156,568

* VAT is inclusive of these figures and needs to be extracted in the ETB

Further information provided as on 31 May, 20-:

- Stock: the closing value was £15,400
- The owner, Harry Smith, has taken £550 cash per month from sales takings for personal use and this has NOT been recorded in any of the books.
- Depreciation of fixed assets:
  The vehicle is depreciated by 25% on reducing balance, equipment by 20% on cost.
- Gas and electricity bills in arrear amounted to £190, wages £420. Stationery unused was valued £80.
- A provision of 5% for bad or doubtful debts is to be made against debtors.
- Of mortgage repayments, £1,020 was interest charged.
- Harry Smith has rented part of his premises to a client for £900 per annum commencing 1 April. Payment will not be received until 30 June, 20-.

Required:

a) Prepare an extended trial balance from the above information.

b) Prepare a draft copy of the profit & loss account for the period ended 31 May, 20- and a balance sheet as at that date.

PART V   USING ACCOUNTING INFORMATION

Chapter 31

Accounting Ratios and Preparing Reports

INTRODUCTION

An accounting ratio is one figure divided by another expressed in percentage or decimal terms. The numerator (top figure) divided by the denominator (bottom figure). Ratios help to measure the performance of a business and provide important indicators of how well a business is doing. Trends can be identified in areas such as profitability and liquidity and help to make comparisons from one year to another and between different business organisations. In business there are a whole series of ratios that can be calculated to test the relationship of one set of data against another. For example, if sales were £250,000 and net profit was £25,000, the net profit percent relates these two figures together:

$$\text{Net profit \%} = \frac{\text{Net profit x 100}}{\text{Sales}}$$
$$= \frac{25,000 \text{ x } 100}{250,000} = 10\%$$

In other words, for every £1 of sales, 10p is net profit. For £1,000 of sales, £100 is net profit and so forth. Accounting ratios can assist both the owners and managers of business to improve their decision-making. The performance of every business organisation is related to its aims and objectives. Whether the results look good, bad or indifferent, will largely depend upon the objectives of the business.

For example, if a business wanted a 40% return on gross profit and it only achieved 35%, then the report on its performance will be disappointing and questions would be raised as to why the objective was not achieved. On the other hand, if the aim was to achieve a 30% return, then the result would be received far more favourably.

Accounting ratios help owners and managers in business to compare figures over periods of time and also to compare them with their competitors and with industries in the same field as themselves. It will help them to analyse the levels of financial performance being achieved. By preparing these ratios, key questions about the business can be analysed. A ratio in isolation may have little meaning or impact, but ratios that indicate comparisons between accounting periods or with other competitors can say far more about the relative performance of a business.
Is the business becoming more successful or less so? Which factors might be identified to help management decide what to do for the best?

Various groups of accounting ratios
A business's accounting ratios can be analysed into various groups and text books are never consistent about this. The reasons why are:
- there are many different types of business's producing a wide variety of different goods or services;
- accounting ratios are devised to meet a wide variety of different business organisations;
- the calculation of certain ratios can change over periods time.

However, the important thing is to be consistent from one financial period to the next and businesses must try to use the same formula for their calculations within their industry. The comparison of results will then be far more meaningful as a result.

The following are some of the accounting groups to be considered:
- Profitability
- Liquidity (short-term solvency)
- Efficiency
- Liquidity (long-term solvency)
- Investment

There are other groupings too and these should not confuse your basic understanding of how to calculate the ratios and what they are to be used for. In accounting, there are always different ways to say and mean the same thing. For example, under the heading efficiency, asset usage ratios can be expressed as asset turnover, solvency ratio are another way of stating liquidity, the rate of stock turnover is also the stock holding period, etc.

By using key figures from financial statements, accounting ratios can be used to compare a business's performance from one period to another, or used to compare one organisation with another. By using ratios to evaluate financial information, it is possible to compare the performance of different types of organisations, large or small.

A ratio in itself may not provide all that much information about a company, but if a number of years' figures were taken, a trend or pattern emerges. Are things improving or going downhill? If a business is compared to its major competitors, very useful information can be provided; is the business performing at a similar level or doing better or worse?

The commercial banks and other financial institutions provide annual performance comparisons with which to analyse key financial ratios for companies in different sectors of industry, for example, business and professional services, retail and distribution, heavy and light manufacturing. They tend to group the ratios into two categories:

- performance ratios which gives an indication of a company's profitability and efficiency;
- financial ratios which indicates the overall financial position of a company.

These ratios are defined clearly as to how they are calculated and what they are used for and do provide a valuable yardstick to both owners and managers for financial planning purposes.

The following information will be used as an example for the calculation of accounting ratios. The company, *Allied Components, plc*, is a small public company, recently quoted on the Stock Exchange.

Ratios will be used to test for profitability, liquidity, efficiency, structure and investment will be calculated, including a brief evaluation of the results.

Allied Components plc: profit and loss account, year ended 31 December

	£[000s]	£[000s]
Turnover		9,000
Cost of Sales		
Stock (l/ 1)	500	
Purchases	5,650	
Stock (31/12)	(150)	6,000
Gross Profit		3,000
Distribution costs	550	
Administration expenses	850	
Interest payable	400	1,800
Net Profit (before tax)		1,200
Provision for tax		300
Net Profit (after tax)		900
Provision for Dividends:		
8% preference shares	160	
Ordinary shares	300	460
Retained Profits		440

Allied Components plc: balance sheet, as at year ended 31 December

	£[000s]	£[000s]
Fixed Assets (net value)		20,000
Current Assets:		
Stock (31/12)	150	
Debtors	1,080	
Bank cash	2,170	
Pre-payments	100	
	3,500	
Creditors falling within 12 months:		
Trade creditors	1,200	
Accruals	40	
Provision for tax	300	
Provision for dividends	460	
	2,000	
Net Current Assets		1,500
Capital Employed		21,500
Creditors falling after 12 months:		
Debenture stock		6,500
		15,000
Capital and Reserves		
Ordinary Share Capital	3,000	
8% Preference Shares	2,000	
Reserves 9,560		
+ Retained Profits 440	10,000	15,000

Profitability ratios

These ratios are used to measure the trading performance of a business in terms of profit to sales or profit to capital. The ratios in themselves may have little meaning unless they are compared to past performances or with businesses in the same category (for example, supermarkets or electrical appliances).

Allowing for factors such as inflation or other economic indicators which may influence demand, ratio analysis can be useful in detecting trends and the reasons behind them.
The ratios used are not the whole category available but they are amongst the most common:

- The Gross profit % $= \dfrac{\text{Gross profit x 100}}{\text{Net Sales}}$

- The Net Profit % $= \dfrac{\text{Net profit x 100}}{\text{Net Sales}}$

- Return on Capital Employed $= \dfrac{\text{Net profit x 100}}{\text{Capital Employed}}$

- Return on Net Worth $= \dfrac{\text{Net profit x 100}}{\text{Net Worth (Owner's Equity)}}$

- Return on Total Assets $= \dfrac{\text{Net profit x 100}}{\text{Total Assets}}$

The net profit returns may be shown (for a company) as before or after tax, or both. When comparing ratios with other periods, it is important to be consistent. Compare like with like, otherwise distortions will occur and negate the usefulness of any comparison. The profitability ratios of Allied Components are:

The Gross profit % $= \dfrac{£3,000 \text{ x } 100}{£9,000}$
                 $= 33.33\%$

The Net Profit % $= \dfrac{£1,200 \text{ x } 100}{£9,000}$
                 $= 13.33\%$

Return on Capital Employed $= \dfrac{£1,200 \text{ x } 100}{£21,500}$
                 $= 5.58\%$

Return on Net Worth $= \dfrac{£1,200 \text{ x } 100}{£15,000}$
                 $= 8\%$

Return on Total Assets $= \dfrac{£1,200 \text{ x } 100}{£23,500}$
                 $= 5.1\%$

Note: The net profit has been taken *before tax* in the above figures.

Are these profit returns reasonable? With no comparative figures to guide our analysis, it is difficult to make useful comment. However, if the 'norm' for Allied Components within its own industry was, for example, between 35% and 40% gross and between 14% and 18% net, then we could assume that the company's profitability was marginally lower than was expected.

Is the company satisfied receiving around £33 gross per £100 sales and £13 net per £100 sales (before tax)? Could it do any better? Is it buying its materials at optimum prices?

Is its return on capital a reasonable figure? How does it measure up to interest rates? All Allied Components' profits to the balance sheet figures are between 5% and 8%. The return on capital employed, seen by the majority of organisations as *one of the most significant* returns on measuring performance. It is only a low 5.58%. If base interest rates were high, the return on capital is very mediocre. This measures profit to the business resources as a whole, and the directors of the company would need to seek improvement on a miserable 5%.

Is the sales department doing its job effectively? Could an improvement in marketing be the answer? Could some of the expenses be cut without affecting the quality of the product? These are some of the questions management could be asking, to seek ways of improving profits.

Liquidity ratios (short-term solvency)

These ratios indicate the business's ability to have sufficient cash resources to meet current debts. The two most significant ratios are:

- working capital ratio (or current ratio);
- quick asset ratio (or acid test).

$$\text{Working Capital ratio} = \frac{\text{Current Assets}}{\text{Current Liabilities}}$$

$$= \frac{£3,500}{£2,000} = 1.75$$

$$\text{Quick Asset ratio} = \frac{\text{Current Assets (less Stock)}}{\text{Current Liabilities}}$$

$$= \frac{£3,500 - £150}{£2,000} = 1.68$$

Working capital needs to be adequate to enable the business to trade with reasonable 'comfort'. It should be enough to finance short-term debts (those which are due within the financial period). If creditors demand payment, the business should be in a sound enough financial position to meet the demands.

The working capital ratio should not fall normally below 1:1 because then there would be inadequate liquid resources to meet debts. A ratio falling below 1:1 means the business is potentially 'insolvent' that is, it has insufficient liquidity to meet current debt.

Liquidity is just as important as profit earning. A business could be in an attractive profit earning position and yet still fail because it has disregarded its liquidity. Creditors can force a business to pay their debts by taking them to court. If the court ruled that the business must pay up within a specific period of time, it may well mean that it must be 'liquidated' to pay off its outstanding debts.

The quick asset ratio is an immediate test of liquidity because the value of stock is deducted from the total of current assets. Can a business, without relying on its stock, meet its immediate debts? However, the importance of this ratio is also related to the business's rate of stock turnover – the speed with which a business sells its stock. The faster stock is sold, the less important is the quick asset ratio.

A supermarket like *Sainsbury's,* for example, has such a high rate of stock turnover that stock is almost like cash anyway. On the other hand, a manufacturing business making motor vehicles could have a much lower rate of turnover, therefore taking longer to produce and sell its goods and receive its cash. Comparisons need to be made with previous years to check the business's liquidity trend. Sound liquidity, particularly for small businesses, ought to be in the proximity of:

Working Capital ratio   1.5 to 2.5
Quick Asset ratio   0.75 to 1.5

Ideally, the working capital and quick asset ratios should fall somewhere between these ratios, 2:1 and 1:1 respectively, although this depends on the size and nature of the business. As long as there is adequate liquidity to satisfy creditors, that is what is important.

Efficiency ratios (effective resource use)
These ratios are used to try and identify the strengths and weaknesses of a business using a variety of different ratios, including money incurred on expenses, stock turnover, debt collection, the investment of assets to turnover and productivity.

Expense percentages
Each type of expense may be analysed in relation to sales for the purpose of evaluating the significance of different types of expense and how they affect profit:

$$\text{Cost of Sales \%} = \frac{\text{Cost of Sales} \times 100}{\text{Sales}}$$

$$= \frac{£6{,}000 \times 100}{£9{,}000} = 66.66\%$$

$$\text{Distribution Expenses \%} = \frac{\text{Distribution Expenses} \times 100}{\text{Sales}}$$

$$= \frac{£550 \times 100}{£9{,}000} = 6.11\%$$

$$\text{Administration Expenses \%} = \frac{\text{Administration Expense} \times 100}{\text{Sales}}$$

$$= \frac{£850 \times 100}{£9{,}000} = 9.44\%$$

$$\text{Financial Expenses \%} = \frac{\text{Financial Expense} \times 100}{\text{Sales}}$$
[interest payments]

$$= \frac{£400 \times 100}{£9{,}000} = 4.44\%$$

Total Expenses %   =   86.65%
Therefore Net Profit %   =   13.35%
                              100%

These expenses may be related to pence in the £ to indicate an easy break-down of expenses to the number of pence profit in the £.

Relation of expenses to pence/£

	Pence
Cost of sales	67
Distribution expenses	6
Administration expenses	9
Financial expenses	4
	87 total
	13 in the £ profit

Is 13p in the £ an adequate return? How does it compare with previous trading performances? How does it compare with similar organisations trading in similar goods or services?

If 13p is regarded as an insufficient return, investigation is needed in order to find out why the return is low. Is 67p/£ for cost of sales too high? Is the firm inefficient in buying or producing its goods? How do the other expenses compare with previous years? Is the selling price too low? These points need to be analysed and are important in assisting management and owners in making decisions.

The rate of stock turnover

This ratio refers to the number of times the stock is sold within an accounting period. It gives an indication of the business's selling efficiency.

$$\text{Calculation: Rate of Stock Turnover} = \frac{\text{Cost of Sales}}{\text{Average Stock}}$$

$$= \frac{£6,000}{£325} = 18.5 \text{ times per year}$$

This is a reasonably high rate of stock turnover where stock is sold every 2.8 weeks. $\frac{52 \text{ weeks}}{18.5}$

The speed of stock turnover depends on the nature of goods sold. A large supermarket will have a high turnover rate because it sells goods required every day. For goods required less frequently, such as furniture, the stock rate will be less. Because turnover of stock measures the business's selling efficiency, the trend should be carefully checked and deviations from the normal patterns investigated.

If the rate of stock is sold every 2.8 weeks, it is seen as relatively fast compared with another organisation whose rate is, say, every 16 weeks and which sells goods like jewellery or furniture and not supermarket goods.

The stock turnover should be compared with the gross profit percentage (33.3%) to see the effect of selling prices on turnover figures. For example, if the rate of turnover increases, it may indicate a policy by the firm of reducing its selling prices in order to increase turnover and sales. If the gross profit percentage falls but actual gross profit increases, the policy will be seen as successful.

On the other hand, if selling prices are forced down because of intense competition, the gross profit percentage may fall without either an increase in actual gross profit or stock turnover. If stock taking is only carried out at the end of a financial year, the average stock is computed on the basis of adding stock beginning with stock end and dividing by 2:

Stock (1 January)	£500	
Stock (31 December)	£150	£650/2 = £325

If stock levels at the end of the financial period are not an average indication of stock because of seasonal changes, the turnover ratio is likely to be a false representation of the business's true selling efficiency. If this is the case further stock-take figures need to be taken throughout the year.

The collection of debt

This ratio is an indication of the period of credit taken by debtors; in other words, how long it takes them to pay their debts. The ratio has a significant bearing on both the efficiency of credit control and the accuracy of liquidity. If credit control is doing its job properly, the period of credit taken by debtors should be satisfactory. If debtors are paying their bills regularly, the liquidity ratio is more reliable.

$$\text{Average credit taken by debtors} = \frac{\text{Debtors x 365}}{\text{Credit Sales}}$$

$$\text{(all sales in } \textit{Allied's } \text{ accounts} = \frac{£1,080 \text{ x } 365}{£9,000}$$
are credit sales)

$$= \text{ 44 days to collect debts}$$

In general, a monthly invoice can normally take about 40 to 50 days. Some manufacturing organisations which produce and sell highly expensive goods (like motor vehicles, machinery and equipment) may need to give distributors a far longer period of time in which to settle debts, such as 3 to 12 months.

The method of payment may also be far more complex, involving time-payments calculated to suit both buyer and seller. The important thing to remember is that credit control should be constantly checking the reliability of individual debtors rather than merely observing an average collection period as a whole.

Creditors' payment period

This links with the collection of debt from customers. If debtors pay promptly, as in Allied's case, there should be little problem in the payment of creditors if they are approximately in the same proportion. We will assume that all purchases of stock are on a credit basis.

$$\text{Average credit obtained from suppliers} = \frac{\text{Creditors x 365}}{\text{Credit Purchases}}$$

$$= \frac{1,200 \text{ x } 365}{5,650}$$

$$= \text{ 77.5 days to pay debts}$$

It is taking Allied Components about 2.5 months, on average, to pay creditors, and this contrasts with a more rapid response from customers who only take 1.5 months to pay. Obviously, this is a liquidity advantage to the company because it can use the extra funds provided by creditors as a significant source of capital for other projects.

As long as creditors are willing to accept this extended period of credit, then the position is a sound one. If, however, they always press for payment and discounts have been lost as a result, it may be time to review the situation and pay them more promptly.

Asset usage

There are a number of ratios that can be used to identify the amount of investment in assets which will generate turnover (sales). The term for these ratios varies, although asset usage or asset turnover are commonly applied.

$$\text{Asset turnover:} \quad \frac{\text{Sales}}{\text{Capital Employed}}$$

$$= \frac{9,000}{21,500} = 0.42$$

$$\text{Sales /Trading Assets:} \qquad \frac{\text{Sales}}{\text{Current Assets}}$$

$$= \frac{9,000}{3,500} \quad =2.57$$

The commonly used sales: capital employed indicates the type of investment required in operational assets that are needed to produce the appropriate level of turnover. In this case, 0.42:1 may be considered very low because for every £1 invested in capital employed, only 42p is generated in sales. This maybe due to a significant investment in fixed assets required by this type of organisation.

The sales: trading assets ratio is better and indicates that it takes £1 invested in current assets to generate £2.57 in sales. These figures must not be taken in isolation, of course, and comparisons must be made with past performances and with competitors in the same industry.

Productivity
Two ratios may be used to identify productivity in terms of the number employed. If we assume that Allied has a workforce of 200, two ratios may be calculated:

$$\text{Sales: Employees} \qquad = \frac{£9,000,000}{200}$$

$$= \ £45,000 \ \text{turnover/employee}$$

$$\text{Profit (before tax): Employees} = \frac{£1,200,000}{200}$$

$$= \ £6,000 \ \text{profit/employee}$$

Productivity has always been seen to be an important contributory factor to efficiency in business because the greater the productivity, the greater the profit and the more resources are available for distribution. A business can afford to pay its workforce more if productivity increases, without it being inflationary. If productivity falls, the business is seen to be less efficient and employees produce less in terms of units to man-hours. This could be caused by a number of factors, such as the inefficient use of manpower, plant and machinery, or technology may need updating.

Structure ratios (Long-term Solvency)
There are a number of ratios that may be used to identify the relationship between the members' capital and the extent of liabilities. In this sense, the structure only refers to how the business is financed: that is, internally by its owners, or, externally by the extent of its liabilities.

$$\textit{The Owner's Stake} = \frac{\text{Capital (Net Worth)}}{\text{Assets (Total Assets)}}$$

$$= \frac{£15,000}{£23,500}$$

$$= \ 63.8\%$$

$$Interest\ Cover\ =\ \frac{Net\ Profit\ (before\ tax,\ interest)}{Interest\ Payable}$$

$$=\ \frac{1,600}{400}\ =\ 4{:}1$$

The owner's stake identifies how much the owners are worth in the business. In this case 63.8% is in the hands of the company's shareholders. This leaves 36.2% in the hands of its creditors.

The ratio of interest cover (net profit without the interest or tax payable) to the payment of interest signifies the number of times the interest can be paid from profits. Allied can cover the interest payments four times over from its profits. How sound this figure is will depend on the trend (that is, is the proportion better or worse than previous year's figures?).

Capital Gearing
Gearing may be high or low, depending on the level of borrowed capital and preference capital to ordinary share capital. The company which is high-geared has a high proportion of borrowed and preference capital relative to ordinary shares. If ordinary share capital predominates then the company is said to be low-geared.

Gearing plays an influential part in the pay out of ordinary share dividends. If profits are good, the high-geared company can benefit its ordinary shareholders by paying higher dividends.

For example, if borrowing at fixed interest rates is 8% and return on investment is 14.5%, the ordinary shareholders will obviously be delighted because they earn 6% above the fixed interest borrowed. Conversely, if returns are the opposite way around and fixed interest payments are greater than investment, the result may not only be disappointing but also financially precarious because fixed interest must be paid regardless of profits. If creditors hold the balance of financial power they can soon call in their loans and precipitate the collapse of the company.

$$Capital\ Gearing\ =\ \frac{Long\text{-}term\ debt}{Capital\ employed}$$

$$Capital\ Gearing\ of\ Allied\ Components\ =\ \frac{£8,500}{£21,500}$$

$$=\ 39.5\%$$

The capital gearing ratio above, infers that the company's creditors finance about 40% of the business's resources as long term debt. The remaining 60% is financed by the company's shareholders. This may be considered as moderate gearing. If the ratio of creditors' finance exceeded 50% then gearing would be considered relatively high and therefore more risky because the majority of financing would be in the hands of creditors rather than in the hands of the company's shareholders.

Investment ratios

The shares of public limited companies can be bought and sold on the Stock Exchange and these may be listed if the shares or debentures have obtained an official quotation from the Stock Exchange Council. It is these stocks and shares that are published in the daily national newspapers. Some public companies do not necessarily want official listing and may seek to be listed on the alternative Securities Market. This *'second division'* of listing still permits the buying and selling of securities (stocks and shares) but is not under the same strict code of practice demanded of an official listing.

The shares of private limited companies do not appear on any listing of the Stock Exchange simply because securities of private companies must be dealt with privately and not publicly. The major newspapers and particularly the *Financial Times,* list the securities each day, giving information about share prices, their change in value, dividends, yield, cover and price to earnings ratios and other significant reformation about the fluctuating fortunes of the stock market.

The *Financial Times Index* (FTI) is the barometer of the Exchange, and its rise or fall each day indicates how the market responds to the demand for stocks and shares. If the market believes there is confidence in the economy, demand for shares could pick up and the market is said to be 'bullish' and share prices are likely to rise. On the other hand, if confidence falls, demand can dry up and investors may rush out and sell, causing share prices to fall. This is a 'bear' market. The investment ratios all concern ordinary shares (equities) rather than preference shares which are on a fixed rate of dividend.

The following investment ratios of Allied Components are:

- Earnings per Share (EPS)

$$= \frac{\text{Net Profit (after tax)} - \text{Preference Dividend}}{\text{No. of Ordinary Shares}}$$

$$= \frac{£900 - £160}{3,000 \text{ shares}} = 25\text{p per share}$$

- Percentage Dividend

$$= \frac{\text{Sum to Ordinary Shares} \times 100}{\text{Issued \& Paid Up Capital}}$$

$$= \frac{£300 \times 100}{3,000} = 10\text{p share}$$

- Yield Percentage

$$= \frac{\text{Dividend per share} \times 100}{\text{Market Value per Share *}}$$

$$= \frac{10\text{p} \times 100}{125} = 8\% \text{ yield}$$

* Market Value as listed on Exchange for Allied Components, £1.25 (125p per share).

- Cover

$$= \frac{\text{Net Profit (after tax – Preference Dividend)}}{\text{Dividend on Ordinary Shares}}$$

$$= \frac{£900 - £160}{£300} = 2.5 \text{ times}$$

- Price/Earnings Ratio

$$= \frac{\text{Market Price per Share}}{\text{EPS}}$$

$$= \frac{125p}{25p} = 5 \text{ times}$$

The EPS is one of the most publicised ratios when companies report their half-yearly or yearly results. It indicates the earning potential of each ordinary share. Allied has an EPS of 25p per share which may look very attractive to some shareholders, each share literally earning 25p in profit. This does not mean that the dividend is 25p per share, it simply indicates that each share has earned 25p.

The dividend per share is the dividend recommended by the board to its ordinary shareholders. Allied is recommending a 10% (or 10p) per share. This links with the cover. Ordinary shares could have been paid 2.5 times what has been offered. The higher the cover, the greater the sum retained by the company, rather than paid as dividends. If the cover is low, it indicates that the board is offering the shareholders most of the available profit, less being retained by the company as reserves.

The price to earnings (P/E) ratio indicates the market value of a share in relation to the number of years' profits it represents. In other words, a P/E of 5 means that the current market price of £1.25 equals approximately 5 years of current profit earned. Generally speaking, the higher the P/E ratio, the better. It indicates what the market is prepared to pay for them.

The investment ratios concerning Allied PLC may then be analysed and compared with other stocks and shares on the Stock Exchange.

EPS	25p/share
Dividend to Ordinaries	10p/share or 10%
Yield/	8%
Cover	2.47 times
P/E ratio	5 times

A good investment or not? Retain or sell? It is difficult to say. The Stock Exchange is a reliable source as far as the reporting of figures is concerned, yet nothing is certain as to which shares will be successful.

The limitations of accounting ratios and parties interested in financial information

Accounting ratios need to be analysed and interpreted and not merely listed as a set of figures. They need to be compared with the previous year's performances and, where possible, with other similar organisations to investigate and evaluate what the figures indicate.

There have been a number of cases where accounting ratios have indicated a sound financial position but, on closer inspection of the accounts, evidence has revealed that the 'apparent soundness' of the figures is merely an empty shell and the organisation is far from sound.

For example, a liquidity ratio may indicate an 'ideal' situation of 2:1, yet this may be entirely because of a heavy stock position that is old or obsolete and, although measured at cost, in real terms is worth far less and would be difficult to off-load to the market.

It may be that there is a significant amount owing by debtors, who are at best unreliable. This could be responsible for achieving an unrealistic liquidity ratio that looks very sound on paper but in actual terms is precarious, because a certain proportion of debtors should have been written down or written off. What of the 'ideal' 2:1 ratio when the business goes bankrupt or a company is liquidated a few months later?

Accounting ratios can never reveal the whole story about a business because they can never provide all the information needed to make a full evaluation. A business may look fine on paper, but what is it really like? Do the figures reveal anything about the ability of its management or the relationship between the management and the rest of its employees? Is the company dynamic, aggressive, attractive, traditional, bright or dull?

Not all organisations are the same because of the nature, size, structure, management policy and many other aspects that concern the running of a business. This will make it more difficult to compare financial performance between different organisations unless some of these aspects are addressed. The High Street banks do make performance comparisons between companies and bear in mind their size, turnover and nature of the industry being compared.

Not only owners and management are interested in the performance of their organisations. Bankers and creditors who may be asked to lend money to the business need to know if their investment is going to be sound. Accounting ratios may help them to decide whether or not to go ahead. They will also need to be cautious about the reliability of the accounts and the ratios calculated and may wish to make more inquiries to organisations like Dun & Bradstreet who specialise in assessing the 'credit rating' of different business organisations.

Employees may also be interested in the financial performance of their organisations from the point of view of productivity and profits. If the business is successful and productivity is improving, the trade unions have a solid platform when negotiating new pay awards and conditions.
Shareholders of companies and potential shareholders who may not be in a position to know the reliability of firms need investment advice from a bank or other financial institution.

The *Financial Times* share section can also give current information concerning dividends and yields, etc., but professional help is still needed to guide shareholders through the maze of security (shares) dealings.

KEY POINTS OF THE CHAPTER

Accounting ratios:	A numerator divisible by a denominator expressed as a % or as a decimal
Comparability:	Comparing ratios with past figures or with competitors
Profitability ratios:	Those measuring profits to sales or capital
Liquidity ratios (short-term):	Those measuring working capital or acid test
Liquidity ratios (long-term):	Those measuring debt/equity or interest cover
Efficiency ratios:	Measuring stock turnover, expense %, collection of debt, asset usage, etc.
Investment ratios:	Measures investment potential of limited companies, eg, eps, etc
Limitations of ratios:	Cannot inform us of everything about a company eg human factors

QUESTIONS

1. The following trading results refer to the accounts of P Jackson & Co during the last three years, year ending 31 December.

	Year 1 £	Year 2 £	Year 3 £
Trading and Profit and Loss			
Sales:			
Cash	5,000	6,000	8,000
Credit	25,000	30,000	37,000
Cost of sales	20,000	24,000	31,950
Distribution costs	3,000	3,200	4,100
Administration expenses	3,150	3,750	4,275
Stock:			
1 January	1,950	2,050	2,950
31 December	2,050	2,950	5,050
Balance Sheet (extract)			
Debtors	5,000	6,000	9,000
Capital Invested (1 January)	26,500	30,000	31,750

Required:
a) The trading and profit and loss account of P Jackson & Co for each of the 3 years ending 31 December.
b) Accounting ratios to indicate: Gross Profit %, Net Profit %, Expense %, Rate of stock turnover, Credit taken by debtors, Return on capital invested.
c) Brief comments using the accounting ratios to give some indication of the firm's performance over the 3 years.

2. Study the following information regarding companies A and B then answer the following questions below.

Profit and Loss Account	Company A £	Company B £
Turnover	9,000	24,000
Cost of goods	5,000	10,500
Other Expenses		
Selling	500	4,750
Administration	750	2,250
Financial	300	500
Balance Sheet		
Fixed assets	7,000	10,000
Current assets	4,275	6,750
Current liabilities	2,000	3,500

Required:
a) Preparation of profit and loss accounts for the year ended 31 December and balance sheets as at that date.
b) Profitability: Gross Profit %, Net Profit %, Return on Capital
c) Working capital and working capital ratio.
d) A brief comment on the results comparing the two firms.

3. Below are shown the summarised balance sheets of Harry Smith at the end of three consecutive years:

	Year 1 £	Year 2 £	Year 3 £
Creditors	6,480	9,740	12,565
Bank	-	-	1,500
Loan (long-term)	12,500	10,500	10,000
Capital	24,100	24,180	26,220
	43,080	44,420	50,285
Cash in hand	100	100	250
Bank	1,450	1,750	-
Debtors	8,455	7,940	9,165
Stock	4,575	6,230	10,120
Shop fittings	3,500	3,400	5,750
Premises	25,000	25,000	25,000
	43,080	44,420	50,285

Required:
a) To calculate the amount of the working capital at the end of each year;
b) To calculate the ratio of current assets to current liabilities correct to one decimal place at the end of each year;
c) To calculate the acid test correct to one decimal place at the end of each year;
d) Which year do you consider has been the 'safest' as far as Harry's ability to repay debts?

4. The following represents the accounts of XYZ Co for the year ended 31 December

Trading and Profit and Loss account year ended 31 December

	Year 1	Year 2	Year 3
	£	£	£
Sales	50,000	60,000	80,000
Cost of sales	30,000	40,000	48,000
Gross profit	20,000	20,000	32,000
Distribution costs and			
selling expenses	5,000	7,000	12,000
Administration expenses	4,000	5,000	6,000
Net profit	11,000	8,000	14,000

Balance Sheet as at 31 December

Fixed assets	37,000	45,700	55,000
Current assets	20,900	24,000	30,000
	57,900	69,700	85,000
Current liabilities	9,900	18,500	24,000
Long-term liabilities	6,000	3,700	5,500
Net assets	42,000	47,500	55,500
Financed by:			
Capital	31,000	42,000	47,500
Net profit	11,000	8,000	14,000
Drawings		(2,500)	(6,000)
	42,000	47,500	55,500

Required:

a) Use appropriate accounting ratios to evaluate Year 1, Year 2 and Year 3.

b) Compare the performance of the firm over the three years.

[Higher National Diploma]

5   Rocco Bank Ltd and Ball Bearings Ltd are two independent companies in the type of business activity their names suggest. As a young financial adviser, you are asked to assess the situation of both companies:

	Ball Bearings Ltd		Rocco Bank Ltd	
	£000s	£000s	£000s	£000s
Fixed assets (net)	39,000		4,000	
Intangibles	4,000		-	
Investments (long-term)	2,000	45,000	9,000	13,000
Stocks	27,000			
Debtors	25,000			
Advances			21,000	
Cash, liquid assets	-		59,000	
Investments	3,000	55,000	7,000	87,000
		100,000		100,000
Creditors	48,000			
Taxation	1,000		1,000	
Current and deposit accounts			91,000	
Bank	7,000	56,000		92,000
10% debenture stock		33,000		500
Shareholders' Funds				
Ordinary Shares @ £1	10,000		2,000	
Reserves	1,000	11,000	5,500	7,500
		100,000		100,000

Note:

Net Profit (before tax)	2,500	2,600
Proposed ordinary dividends	700	400

Required:

Choose accounting ratios that you consider will reveal the differences between the two companies. Discuss your calculations from the point of view of profitability and financial stability.

[Institute of Bankers]

6. ABC Co Ltd is a small private company in the rag trade. Its first four years trading annually to 31 December were made up as follows:

Year	Sales	Purchases	Increase or decrease of material stocks during year	Selling and Distribution costs	Rent	General Administrative Expenses
	£	£	£	£	£	£
1	36,000	39,000	+ 12,000	900	3,000	4,500
2	54,000	37,500	- 3,000	1,250	3,000	5,250
3	78,000	63,000	+ 4,500	2,500	3,000	6,000
4	120,000	108,000	+ 12,000	4,000	3,500	11,500

Required:

a) Trading and profit and loss accounts in columnar form for each of the four years ending 31 December.
b) Calculate two accounting ratios for each of the four years.
c) A brief discussion of the implication of these figures and the inferences drawn from them.

7. The following figures relate to a retailing organisation that has expanded its business operations. Its premises were converted into a 'self-service' style during the 2nd year:

	Year 1	Year 2	Year 3
	£	£	£
Net sales	120,000	150,000	200,000
Gross profit %	30%	331/3%	35%
Fixed expenses:	20,000	25,000	30,000
Variable expenses: (12% of sales)	?	?	?
Average stock held (cost):	8,000	8,500	10,000
Capital employed:	60,000	105,000	160,000

Required:

Prepare the trading and profit and loss accounts for each trading year, preferably in columnar form and the business profit returns and rate of stock turnover, for each year.

(Association of Accounting Technicians)

8. The accounts of T Carr are as follows:

Trading and profit and loss accounts for years ended 30 September:

	Year 1		Year 2		Year 3	
	£'000	£'000	£'000	£'000	£'000	£'000
Sales						
Less: Cost of sales		120		180		270
Gross profit		80		135		216
Less: Overhead expenses		40		45		54
Variable	18		27		27	
Fixed	10	28	10	37	20	47
Net profit		12		8		7

Balance sheets as at 30 September

	Year 1		Year 2		Year 3	
	£'000		£'000	£'000	£'000	£'000
Fixed assets		30		60		80
Current assets	24		25		40	
Stock	26		40		55	
Debtors	20		10		-	
Balance at bank	70		75		95	
Less: Current liabilities	20		35		45	
Creditors	-		-		10	
Bank overdraft	20	50	35	40	55	40
		80		100		120
Share capital:						
Ordinary shares of £1		50		62		75
Retained earnings		30		38		45
		80		100		120

Required:

Prepare a table of four accounting ratios, each ratio showing a distinctly different aspect of changes in the company during the past three years and a brief report on your findings.

(Association of Accounting Technicians)

Chapter 32

Accounting Standards:
Statements of Standard Accounting Practice and
Financial Reporting Statements

INTRODUCTION

Statements of Standard Accounting Practice and Financial Reporting Statements represent the profession's accounting standards. These statements are prepared for the purpose of standardising the preparation of the final accounts of a business and all accountants are expected to conform to these standards. The statements strongly oblige the accounting profession to accept what is considered the norm for accounting practice. The provisions laid down by the profession must be carried through and if they are not, accountants quite clearly need to state why they have not been adopted. Accounting standards are authoritative statements of how transactions are treated in the profit and loss account and balance sheet, for example, how to deal with depreciation at the year end.

The preparation and publication of the SSAPs had been the responsibility of the six major accounting bodies of the UK (the ASC, Accounting Standards Committee,) and provided both guidance and greater reliability to accountants in preparing the financial statements of a business. One of the principle statements is SSAP 2 (disclosure of accounting policies) issued in 1971, which outlines the basic accounting concepts and could be said to be at the very heart of accounting theory. This has now been superseded by FRS 18.

Largely due to these published statements, there has been far greater conformity in accounting practice and therefore less variation in preparing final accounts. The accounts are then more objective and reliable, rather than subjective and more open to controversy.

Until the publication of the *Dearing* recommendations in 1988 there were some 24 statements which had been published by the ASC. Since Dearing, a new body, the ASB (Accounting Standards Board) was formed in 1990 and now represents the authority that has the task of issuing new accounting standards called FRS's. A number of SSAPs have now been withdrawn or revised such as SSAP 12 (Depreciation) which is now superseded by FRS 15. Both SSAPs and FRSs appear on many courses and examinations and those included in this chapter are:

- SSAP 2 now FRS 18 (Disclosure of accounting policies)
- SSAP   5 (Accounting for VAT)
- SSAP   9 (Stocks and long term contracts)
- SSAP 13 (Accounting for research and development)
- SSAP 12 (now FRS 15 (Accounting for depreciation)
- SSAP 21 (Accounting for leases and hire-purchase contracts)

On 1st August, 1990, the Accounting Standards Committee gave way to the Accounting Standards Board . The ASB commenced operations on this date and is an independent body responsible for setting standards, taking over the functions of the ASC. The new board agreed to adopt the existing SSAPs although it is giving them a fresh overhaul, that is, modifying and changing them for the purpose of improving the presentation of financial statements even further, the accounting standards then become the generally accepted accounting practice (GAAP).

GAAP

What is generally accepted accounting practice'? These are governed by the rules which are handed down to the accounting profession from the accounting bodies and company law, such as the 1985 Companies Act. When these rules, mandatory or otherwise, become consistently adopted by different business organisations, they then become the accepted practice by the accounting profession. GAAP is not something that is static, but is always in flux, changing to new circumstances, primarily imposed by the profession itself or by the government.

Financial reporting exposure drafts (FREDs)

The ASB also agreed that its future agenda was to consider the overall fundamental concepts of accounting and also the exposure drafts issued by the ASC. An exposure draft is all the research and preparation required for the purpose of issuing a future accounting standard. For example, FRED 22 *Reporting Financial Performance* (for limited companies) issued in 1992 proposed:

"that the profit and loss account and the statement of total recognised gains and losses are combined to form a single statement of financial performance. That the statement is divided into three sections: operating; financing and treasury and also other gains and losses".

There is however, no legal obligation to apply to the terms of an exposure draft. With an accounting standard, the accounting profession is obliged to adopt it. With SSAP 2, [now as FRS 18] limited companies are *legally obliged to adopt it* as it comes under the 1985 Companies Act.
The ASB's first standard was published in September, 1991 and was given the new title of Financial Reporting Standard (FRS replacing the former letters, SSAP).

FRS 1 (cash flow statements) was published by the ASB and provides a standard for cash flow reporting as was discussed in a previous chapter. It superseded SSAP 10 (statements of sources & application of funds) which is now obsolete.

SORPS

Apart from exposure drafts and accounting standards, there are also Statements of Recommended Practice (SORPs) which advises the profession on the most suitable practices which could be adopted although they are not obliged to do so. These statements were set up by the ASC in the mid-eighties and made it clear that although companies ought to consider adopting such practices, they were clearly not obliged to do so.

International Accounting Standards Committee

The aim of this committee (IASC) established in 1973, was to attempt to eliminate most of the choices of accounting treatment permitted under International Accounting Standards (IAS) in order to promote greater standardisation in the preparation of financial statements in many areas of the world. Less choice would mean better comparability of statements and more objectivity. A balance sheet therefore, prepared in Europe, in Australia, or the USA, should look like a balance sheet prepared here in the UK and follow exactly the same principles.

Accounting principles

The Accounting Standards Board published its exposure draft 'Statement of Principles' in November, 1995 and it set the framework by which it would develop its future accounting standards, with the aim of ensuring that the preparation of financial statements were as objective and uncontroversial as possible.
Information concerning the profit and loss account and the balance sheet should be as acceptable as possible to a wide range of users including the public, the government, creditors and investors in general. Financial adaptability is a new idea where a business needs to adapt to environmental

change if circumstances warranted. For example, if there was a market upturn, would a business be able to acquire the resources to benefit from an increase in output and therefore economies of scale? Information from the final accounts of businesses need to be reliable and as valid as possible and this may be difficult because of the variety of choices still available within accounting standards.

One of the problems in accounting is the concept of consistency. There is a great need for consistency in preparing reports and evaluating business performance to allow for any decent comparison of results. For example, the calculation of capital gearing (debt/equity) may be undertaken in several different ways which makes comparison between one organisation and another more difficult.

A controversial concept discussed in the draft is that between historical cost and current value accounting where the latter could be more relevant particularly in times of rising prices. Although the ASB favours current values it is experienced enough to know the problems of consistency which can arise if it were adopted.

A key issue of the exposure draft concerned the presentation of financial statements with the need to provide them with supplementary information. One of these was a move to improve recognised gains and losses (SORG – statement of recognised gains and losses), that is, the profit for the year plus any revaluation of assets or exchange rate differences which would affect the level of profit for the financial period.

To summarise, these issues boil down to which approach to financial statements best serves the needs of its users. On the one hand, the traditional historical cost approach where revenue is matched with expenses for the purpose of calculating profit. On the other hand, the balance sheet approach focuses the attention on getting the valuation of the balance sheet correct. By this, the calculation of profit is more in line with the opening and closing capital positions, that is, comparing their values and calculating profit from the difference between them (see current cost accounting below).

The concept of cost
The recording of accounts is traditionally on a historical cost basis which means that the recording of transactions through time is made in relation to what the business paid for them. The advantage of recording at cost is that it does not interfere with more subjective aspects such as "values", that is, what value should we put on stock or motor vehicles, etc. It is much easier and less controversial to record at the cost price of something. For example if we were to value a computer or other asset, what are some of the possibilities?

- at original cost
- at cost less depreciation
- at net realisable value
- at current replacement value
- at present value
- at current purchasing power
- at current cost accounting

Cost price
To value an asset at historical cost price simplifies the recording process. Whatever something cost on invoice or on a cash basis would be recorded at that price at that time.

Cost less depreciation
We have already witnessed in Chapter 25 concerning depreciation that this is how fixed assets are recorded. Each fixed asset group would have a sum calculated as a charge towards depreciation. The difference then, between cost and depreciation becomes the net book value of the asset. This is generally accepted accounting practice. Variations do occur of course, due to the estimations involved in applying the different depreciation methods that businesses may choose to adopt.

Net realisable value
This estimates the value of an asset, usually to stock values, although it can apply to a fixed asset, to estimate what it would sell for less selling expenses involved such as advertising, freight charges, etc. For example, if stock cost £100 and later it was found that it could only sell for £80, the stock should be valued at £80 rather than at its cost. SSAP 9 discusses this concept further.

Current replacement cost
This is as it suggests, that is, the current or market cost of replacing an asset in order to acquire the same service from it. Current replacement prices may come from catalogues or quotations from suppliers. (If an asset is purchased second hand, it would have a second hand replacement value).

Present value
This applies to different investment opportunities with the returns an asset could provide. The earnings from its future production is discounted at the going rates of interest which could be earned. One asset then could be compared with others as to its income or earnings potential, discounted to present day values.

For example, if interest rates were 10% something purchased for £100 today would only be worth £90 next year and approximately £82 the year after. Therefore the asset with the greatest present value, discounted over a number of given years could be the best potential investment. Chapter 38 discusses this further.

Current purchasing power (CPP)
This is related to the cost concept but adjusting the purchasing power to take into account changes to the "buying power of money" by using an index like the retail price or consumer price index. For example, if the cost of an asset was £1,500 and since the date of purchase, the retail price index had risen to 120, then the use of current purchasing power would indicate that to buy the asset again would cost £1,800.

In times of rising prices or high inflation, the index could rise steeply and the use of current purchasing power would markedly increase the value of assets. However, this aspect of inflation accounting was thought to be controversial because of the inconsistencies that could occur by the use of different indices. For example, on various types of assets used by different types of business organisations.

The government set up a committee to investigate CPP and to inquire as to its merits. The *Sandilands Report* (1975) was the outcome of the committee's enquiries at a time when inflation was a serious problem in the United Kingdom. In short, the report stated that CPP "is complicated and likely to be misunderstood unless it is very carefully interpreted by the company".

This of course cast shadows of real doubt as to whether consistent standards could be maintained. The report also criticised CPP that it was conceptually the most difficult method of inflation accounting to implement and therefore had its limitations, particularly as to the unit of measurement to use to bring figures up to date.

Current cost accounting (CCA)

This is a combination of using historical cost and the effect of price changes, due to changes in the retail price index, (RPI) on the level of profit.

For example, if net assets (assets less liabilities) on 1 January were £30,000 and this had increased to £50,000 on 31 December, the profit calculated for the year would be £20,000 if no other factors were involved like addition to or withdrawing of capital.

1 January:	Net assets	£30,000
31 December:	Net assets	£50,000
Net profit		£20,000

On a historical cost basis the profit is £20,000. If however, the annual inflation for the period was 8% then the profit of £20,000 is reduced by £2,400 in real terms:

1 January:	Net assets + 8%	£32,400
31 December:	Net assets	£50,000
Net profit		£17,600

This method brings us to the important concept of what is termed "capital maintenance". Capital maintenance is about comparing the value of net assets in one period to their value in the following period and to see how well off or otherwise a business is at the end of that period.

The theory of capital maintenance is also linked to that of inflation. On a historical cost basis, the calculation of profit does not take into account rising prices or the replacement cost of assets or indeed anything else. Therefore if prices rise due to inflation, we can say again that profits will be overstated by the rate of inflation at the time.

Historical cost is a basic measure of what something costs at the time of purchase. It is simple to use and clearly the most objective method. Historical cost accounting is widely recognised as the generally accepted accounting practice. However, it is not a perfect system, but what is a perfect system? The only difficulty with it, is in times of sharply rising prices. Is it an adequate method to use when preparing financial statements?

Will a profit of £25,000 be sufficiently objective if inflation has risen by 20% in the period in which it was earned? The real danger lies in the distribution of profit. If a company paid most of its profits as dividends, its capital and reserves would diminish because the real net value of its capital would have fallen.

A list of current SSAPs

The following is a list of Statements of Standard Accounting Practice that are currently still in use at the time of writing:

SSAP	4	Accounting for government grants
SSAP	5	Accounting for value added tax (VAT)
SSAP	9	Stocks and long term contracts
SSAP	13	Accounting for research and development
SSAP	19	Account for investment properties
SSAP	20	Foreign currency translation
SSAP	21	Accounting for leases and hire purchase contracts
SSAP	25	Segmental reporting.

The statement: 'true and fair'

It was stated at the beginning of this chapter that the authority for developing accounting standards was taken by the ASC (the Accounting Standards Committee) and since August of 1990 the responsibility then passed on to. the ASB (the Accounting Standards Board). A key point describes why accounts are expected to comply with accounting standards:

> *'Accounting standards are authoritative statements of how particular types of transaction and other events should be reflected in financial statements and accordingly compliance with accounting standards will normally be necessary for financial statements to give a true and fair view'.*

In other words the role of an accounting standard is to identify proper accounting practice for the benefit of those preparing accounts and the auditors of them. The effect of using the standards has been to create a common understanding between the users and persons preparing of accounts as to how particular items should be treated so that a uniform approach is taken by all.

The Companies Act 1989 gives the statutory recognition to the existence of accounting standards and to their beneficial role in the preparation of financial statements. In particular, Section 256 of the Act provides:

> *'In this Part, accounting standards means statements of standard accounting practice issued by such a body or bodies as may be prescribed by regulations'.*

In addition the notes to financial statements must comply with the requirement that it shall be stated whether the accounts have been prepared in accordance with applicable accounting standards and particulars of any material departures from these standards must be given with the reasons why any departures have been made.

The ASB develops its views by considering how its principles of accounting apply to the possible accounting options available for a particular accounting topic, for example, like depreciation. The Board also considers the environment in which its standards are to be applied including the legislation within which standards must apply. The new FRS's must therefore be drafted in the context of current legislation applying to the UK and EC Directives with the aim of ensuring consistency between accounting standards and the law.

At the time of writing, the following Financial Reporting Statements (FRS) have been released by the Accounting Standards Board:

A list of current FRS's

FRS	1	Cash flow statements
FRS	2	Accounting for subsidiary undertakings
FRS	3	Reporting financial performance
FRS	4	Capital instruments
FRS	5	Reporting the substance of transactions
FRS	6	Acquisitions and mergers
FRS	7	Fair values in acquisition accounting
FRS	8	Related party disclosures
FRS	9	Associates and joint ventures
FRS	10	Goodwill and intangible assets
FRS	11	Impairment of fixed assets and goodwill
FRS	12	Provisions, contingent liabilities and contingent assets
FRS	13	Derivatives and other financial instruments: disclosures

FRS 14   Earnings per share
FRS 15   Tangible fixed assets
FRS 16   Current tax
FRS 17   Retirement benefits
FRS 18   Accounting policies
FRS 19   Deferred tax
FRS 20   Share-based payment
FRS 21 * (IAS 10) Events after the balance sheet date
FRS 22   (IAS 33) Earnings per share
FRS 23   (IAS 21) The effects of changes in foreign exchange rates
FRS 24   (IAS 29) Financial reporting in hyperinflationary economies
FRS 25   (IAS 32) Financial instruments: disclosure and presentation
FRS 26   (IAS 39) Financial instruments: recognition and measurement
FRS 27   Life Assurance
         * IAS - International Accounting Standards

The following pages outlines some of the Statements of Standard Accounting Practice and Financial Reporting Statements of interest to candidates studying for various examination bodies:

FRS 18:   Disclosure of accounting policies (superseded SSAP 2)

FRS 18 is based on the former SSAP 2, issued in the November of 1971 that outlined fundamental accounting concepts, policies and bases:

> *"It is fundamental to the understanding and interpretation of financial accounts that those who use them should be aware of the main assumptions on which they are based. The purpose of this statement is to assist such understanding by promoting improvement in the quality of information disclosed. It seeks to achieve this by establishing as standard accounting practice the disclosure in financial accounts in clear explanations of the accounting policies followed in order to give a true and fair view".*

The accounting concepts

All final accounts involve some element of judgement on the part of the accountant who has prepared them. Accountants could easily prepare different final accounts from the same data, and each would conform to fundamental principles. The accounting profession recognised four basic concepts that were to be followed in preparing financial statements. The four fundamental accounting concepts of SSAP 2 were:

- going concern concept;
- accruals concept;
- consistency concept;
- prudence concept.

FRS 18 is a significant accounting statement that effectively up-dated SSAP 2. It provides the objectives of preparing the financial statements of all business entities in order to arrive at a *true and fair view*. The standard defines accounting policies as:

'Those principles, bases, conventions, rules and practices applied by an entity that specify how the effects of transactions and other events are to be reflected in the financial statements through recognising, selecting measurement bases for, and presenting assets, liabilities, gains, losses and changes to shareholders funds.'

Accounting concepts define the process of how financial transactions are reflected in the financial statements. These concepts help to make up the accounting framework and the profession is obliged to conform to them. The first two concepts of *going concern* and *accruals* as stated under SSAP 2, are redefined as 'the bedrock principles of financial concepts'. The concept of *realisation* is also of importance in that it relates to profits earned at the balance sheet date. The other concepts of *consistency* and *prudence* are seen as 'desirable elements' in the preparation of financial statements. The concept of prudence is now treated as an objective of *reliability* and the concept of consistency is treated as an objective of *comparability*. See the section below that outlines these two objectives.

Going concern concept
The value of an organisation's assets is based on the assumption that the firm will continue trading. Businesses tend to value their assets at cost less estimated depreciation. If for any reason (such as lack of working capital) there is a probability of closure because of bankruptcy or liquidation, then the balance sheet would have to reflect the situation – that is, assets would have to be valued at a realistic market valuation and other liabilities may arise, such as redundancy payments.

Accruals concept (or matching concept)
It is taken for granted that a set of final accounts includes all expenses incurred and all income earned, not merely the payment date: for example, if an organisation owed its employees £50,000 in wages at the end of the financial year it would have to include this figure as an accrued expense, otherwise the profits of the firm would appear over-stated. In this concept, the matching of revenue with expenses must include all items pertinent to the period, paid or unpaid.

Realisation concept
Only profits realised at the period end should be included in the income statement. Any income that may not be certain at the financial year end cannot be included in the current profit for the year. For example, a sale can only be processed at the period end, if an invoice has been sent to the customer and not on the basis of a purchase order yet to be processed.

Objectives and constraints in the selection of accounting policies

'Business entities should use those policies that are the most appropriate to their particular circumstance for the purpose of giving a fair view. These policies are determined against the objectives of relevance, reliability, comparability and understandability'.

Relevance
Financial information is only seen as relevant if it has the ability to influence the economic decisions of users. For example, if there was more than a single accounting policy to choose from, then the most relevant to the business entity, would be chosen. This does appear rather obvious but it still needs to be stated as part of the objectivity in the selection of the right accounting policies to be chosen. In identifying that policy, *'a business will consider which measurement basis is the most relevant and how to present information in the most relevant way'*. For example, does a business use the reducing balance or straight line method to depreciate its assets? Which is the most relevant for that type of business?

Reliability
As we have just stated above, without following the basic accounting concepts (or principles), reliability could easily be lost. Financial information is reliable if it can be depended upon by its users to represent somewhat faithfully, what it is supposed to represent. For example, if an equity holder read a company's profit for the year as £1.5 million, then it is assumed that this is the correct figure for the company. If say, another body of accountants prepared the same figures and arrived at a loss of £1 million, then all reliability is lost.

The accounts are assumed to be free of errors or systematic bias and they are prepared with a degree of caution so as not to over value the company's assets. Prudence is required in areas of uncertainty about the value of assets, liabilities, gains or losses. With a large sum for debtors, for example, it would be imprudent not to make an adequate provision for bad and doubtful debts as this could overstate the value of assets. The concept of prudence is therefore applied.

Comparability

Information concerning an entity's financial statements gains more credibility when figures can be compared more readily with other similar organisations. This comparability can be achieved through a consistent approach and disclosure of financial information.

The use of appropriate accounting policies, suitable for the particular purpose of an accounting entity, should result in financial information being presented in a way that all users can observe and evaluate on a consistent basis. Differences and similarities can then be more easily analysed if figures are straight forwardly comparable between one organisation and another. For example, one manufacturer could choose a FIFO system to value its stock of raw materials. If a similar manufacturer also chose this method, then it would be assumed that both would use exactly the same method of measurement in which to calculate stock in the FIFO way.

Understandability

Again, it may seem obvious, but any information provided by financial statements need to be understood by a variety of various users, particularly those with some knowledge of business and economic activity. However, one could argue that any financial information should be reasonably understood by any member of the public given a little guidance to what financial information is supposed to attain. In all, the most significant aspect is to prepare financial statements with a view that is both *true and fair*. The figures have been calculated correctly and that all users should conform to the basic principles of arriving at a profit that is seen as true and fair. Financial statements should be reliable, valid, and comparable with others in the same business environment.

The separate valuation principle

FRS 18 states that the amount attributed to either an asset or a liability must be determined at cost as separate items. The separate figures can then be added together, to arrive at the total stated in the balance sheet.

Accounting policies

Under an accounting policy, the concern is to recognise the use of accounting concepts and select the most appropriate base for a specific business and present these in financial statements as assets, liabilities, gains and losses.

Accounting estimates

An estimate is the method to be used to value assets and liabilities, gains and losses. For example, when estimating depreciation you could choose from a number of various methods and also need to estimate the finite value of a fixed asset as well as its residual value.

Substance over form

A transaction should be accounted for and presented in accordance with their economic substance rather than the legal aspect of it. For example, in the case of hire-purchase of fixed assets, the value of it is recorded in the balance sheet even though there is no legal ownership of it until the last payment is made to the hire-purchase company.

Other concepts

Materiality concept
This is the view that small, insignificant items may be excluded from the normal accounting policy. The *size* of the business enterprise will dictate what is materially relevant. A large organisation may consider a valuation of a fixed asset under £500 as insignificant. The will be treated as an expense item and written off in the year it was bought, irrespective of how long it will last. A smaller organisation may consider £500 as significant and depreciate the asset over a number of accounting periods.

Money measurement concept
Essentially this concept recognises that a set of final accounts will only be the outcome of financial transactions. A profit and loss account or balance sheet cannot possibly measure the value to an organisation of intangibles such as the morale or skill of its employees.

Dual aspect concept (the accounting equation)
The basic accounting equation recognises that assets represent the value of a business entity and that these are financed by the owner's capital and the liabilities of the business, $(A = C + L)$.

SSAP 5:   Accounting for value added tax
This standard aims to achieve uniformity in the treatment of VAT in published accounts. VAT is currently charged at the rate of 17.5% (standard rate) on a wide variety of goods and services. There are also goods that are zero-rated for VAT and exempt from VAT.

Businesses that are registered for VAT (those listed with HM Customs & Excise) are collectors of this indirect form of tax on behalf of the Government. Traders collect VAT on their sales (output tax), offset by what they pay on purchases and other expenses (input tax). The balance between these two figures in the VAT account will either indicate whether a sum is owing to the VAT office or whether the business is owed money from it.

Standard rate supplies
Most of our goods and services are charged at the standard rate. This has been increased from 15% to the current 17.5%. Only those traders registered with Customs & Excise can charge VAT on their goods or services.

Zero-rated supplies
The zero rate is nil which means that traders do not charge VAT on their sales, but they can recover input VAT charges on their purchases and other expenses where VAT has been charged.
Zero-rated supplies, for example, include most of our food (but not catering, which means food in restaurants, hotels, cafes, etc).

Exempt supplies
VAT is not charged on supplies which are exempt in the same way as zero-rated supplies. However, a trader cannot reclaim any VAT paid on purchases or other expenses where VAT has been charged. No VAT account is recorded in the books because there is no registration with HMRC (Her Majesty's Revenue and Customs).

In the preparation of the financial statements, SSAP 5 states that those businesses registered with HMRC should *exclude* VAT on all taxable inputs and taxable outputs. In other words, sales, purchases, taxable expenses and fixed assets are recorded net (excluding VAT). The VAT charges are recorded in a VAT account. At the end of the financial period, any VAT owing would be listed as a current liability (a credit balance), or a current asset (a debit balance) in the balance sheet.

With expenditure that is not VAT deductible, such as tax on motor vehicles or for expenses for which the VAT office will not allow recovery, the full amount will appear in the profit and loss account and balance sheet. The same will apply to those non-registered businesses which are exempt from VAT: all their expenditure will *include* VAT charges in the recording of their accounts as well as in their final accounts.

SSAP 9: Stocks and long term contracts

This standard seeks to establish a broad band of generally accepted accounting techniques in the valuation of stock. There are a number of different ways that stocks can be valued, and this statement was written with a view to limiting the number of options open in valuation. Stocks may be comprised of finished goods, raw materials and partly finished goods; SSAP 9 states that:

'stock should be valued at the lower of cost or its net realisable value'.

Net realisable value is referred to as the selling price of stock less any expenses involved in the selling process. In other words, stock should be valued as a general rule at the cost price, but if for any reason (such as a recession) the selling price is seen to fall lower than that of cost, then the net realisable value should be used. This is the conservatism or prudence in accounting, to be able to foresee possible losses, and not recognising profits until realised.

The statement, in defining cost, states that the purchase cost would include any import duties, carriage inwards, handling charges or other costs in the procurement of goods, less any trade discount which may be offered.

The manufacturing cost should include the cost of direct labour and materials plus factory overheads as a result of what is considered 'normal' output levels. (Any idle or slack production affecting overheads should not be considered as part of the stock valuation.)

A system of costing stocks should be consistently adopted and, once a method or base in valuation has been used, the same system should be kept, otherwise distortion of profits will occur and the final accounts may not be accepted by the firm's auditors as being 'true and fair'. More details concerning the valuation of stocks and work-in-progress can be found in Chapter 33.

SSAP 13: Accounting for research and development

The standard concerns itself with the costs incurred for any research or development carried out by a business entity in the course of its business activity.

The emphasis lies on a key fact: whether the costs incurred are to be classified as revenue expenditure or capital expenditure. Note that *revenue expenditure* relates to expenses charged to the profit & loss account and that *capital expenditure* is a charge to fixed assets in the balance sheet, (to be written off in future accounting periods to the profit & loss account).

The word *research* falls into either pure or applied research. Pure research is seen to be as original research having new scientific principles. The term applied research relates to anything that builds upon the original research.

However, all research, whether pure or applied, is seen as *revenue expenditure* to be written off in the profit & loss account in the period incurred, (because it is difficult to actually divide the benefit gained in future periods from either pure or applied research).

The word *development* relates to improving products from the research stage and may involve testing, modification and building prototypes, before any normal production is carried out.

If future benefits are to be gained, then some development costs can be *capitalised* and spread over a number of periods in the same way as other fixed assets and written off in the same way.
The 1985 Companies Act clearly states this and development costs can be capitalised as long as the project is technically feasible and have earnings potential over future accounting periods.

FRS 15:   Accounting for depreciation (superseded SSAP 12)
Depreciation is defined as the loss of value in fixed assets over periods of, time. The standard defines that:

'Depreciation is the measure of the wearing out of a fixed asset through use, time, or obsolescence and that charges of depreciation should be spread fairly over the fixed asset's life. It is the measure of the cost of the economic benefits of the fixed asset that have been consumed during the period.'

This basically means that if there is greater benefit gained using fixed assets at the beginning of there use and less benefit gained as they become older and more worn out, then the depreciation charges should reflect this. For assets like plant and machinery, motor vehicles and equipment, the *reducing balance method* would be appropriate because less depreciation is charged the older a fixed asset becomes. On the other hand, if there is little change of benefit gained from one period to the next, then an equal measure of depreciation could occur each year and the *straight line method* could be adopted here.

The depreciation charges for the period are written off to the profit and loss account as expenses and the cumulative depreciation to date is deducted from the cost value of fixed assets in the balance sheet. The concept of consistency must apply and, once a method of depreciation has been adopted, the same method should be used until the asset is finally disposed of. Again, if this were not the case, distortion of profits would occur and incorrect figures would be recorded in the profit and loss account and the balance sheet. If it were necessary to make re-valuations in fixed assets that involved changing the method of depreciation, reasons as to why this should occur must accompany the final accounts.

In February 1999, FRS 15 was published to replace SSAP 12. However, despite this new standard, all the key elements of SSAP 12 are still intact and much of it remains. FRS 15 seeks to clarify some points and to make more precise definitions so that there are fewer ambiguities. The principles of depreciation have not changed concerning the cost, the methods used, the estimated useful life and the residual value of fixed assets. Some rules have tightened up and the estimates relating to an asset's useful life and residual value, if any, should be reviewed annually and revised if deemed appropriate to do so.

Because of the concept of materiality it may be that depreciation is not charged. An asset may have a very long useful life or its residual value may be unusually high. The new standard allows this on the condition that such assets are reviewed annually for what is termed *'impairment'*, that is, when an asset's recoverable value falls below that of its net book value.

For example, it the net book value of a fixed asset was £1,500 and its realisable value was only £1,000, then it would be reasonable to assume that further depreciation was appropriate. In this case the asset could then be depreciated and the net book value lowered in proportion to its recoverable value over a period of time the asset is to be used.

The standard states that fixed assets are shown in the balance sheet initially at cost, cost being defined as the purchase price less any trade discounts plus any other costs directly attributing to the bringing of an asset to its operational condition (just as before).

If a fixed asset is constructed rather than purchased, the arbitrary apportionment of indirect overheads should not be included in the overall cost of its production. Neither should any abnormal costs such as wastage time because of industrial disputes or faults or errors in the design or development of an asset.

If there are any financial costs in relation to the funding of an asset, for example, paying interest charges, these could also be regarded as directly attributable to its purchase cost. The new standard gives the option of capitalising these costs as long as there is consistent treatment of these costs. Whichever costs are capitalised, these must stop as soon as the asset is ready for use, even if it is not actually in use. Any further costs after this point are charged as revenue expenditure to the profit and loss account.

If a fixed asset such as premises is to be re-valued, a company must apply a consistent policy of revaluation in that if one asset is re-valued, all others in the same class must be as well. A full valuation is required at least every five years, or whenever evidence indicates a change in value in the interim period.

When an asset has been re-valued the current period's depreciation charge is based on the re-valued amount and the remaining economic useful life of the asset. Thus if a property is re-valued (excluding the land value) from say £50,000 to £100,000 and the remaining economic life is a period of 25 years, then the depreciation charge would be £4,000 per annum over this period of time.

In the disclosures of accounting policies of financial statements, companies should disclose separately for each class of tangible assets:

- the depreciation methods used;
- the useful economic lives or the depreciation rates used;
- the total depreciation charges for the period;
- the financial effect of any changes where material;
- the cost or re-valued amount at the beginning of a financial period and at the balance sheet date;
- the cumulative depreciation or any impairment at the beginning of a financial period and at the balance sheet date;
- a reconciliation of asset movements including acquisitions, disposals, re-valuations, impairments
- the net book values at the beginning of the financial period and the balance sheet date.

Where there has been any change in the depreciation method used, the effect if material, should be disclosed and the reason for the change should be indicated.

SSAP 21: Accounting for leases and hire purchase contracts

The standard defines both operating and finance leases and sets out the appropriate accounting treatment from the point of view of the lessees (the ones taking out the lease) and the *lessors* (the ones providing the lease). When finance leases are taken on by the lessee and there is fairly substantial risk involved , the lease is *capitalised*, that is, it is entered in the balance sheet as a fixed asset and depreciated over its useful life using the straight line method of depreciation (also referred to as *amortisation*).

An operating lease is acquired more on a rental basis rather than a fixed long term contract as is the case for a finance lease. It is therefore seen as a rental agreement and is revenue expenditure rather than capital expenditure. The lessor would normally be expected to take responsibility for repairs and maintenance, insurance and other costs in ensuring that the asset is operable. The rental payment of the lease would be entered in the profit and loss account as an expense.

If a fixed asset is acquired under a hire purchase agreement, it is treated as capital expenditure and entered as a fixed asset in the balance sheet on the purchase date. However, the legal entitlement of it is not normally passed to the buyer until the last payment has been made to the creditor. Any interest charged is entered as an expense in the profit and loss account, as well as any depreciation charges. The outstanding sum owed to the creditor will be entered as a long term liability in the balance sheet.

UITF abstracts (Urgent Issues Task Force)

UITF 's main role is in the general assistance to the Accounting Standards Board (ASB) with any important accounting issues where there is an accounting standard or a provision of companies legislation, or any conflicting interpretation that might exist or might develop. The UITF will then seek to find some form of consensus as to what should be done to resolve the problem. The ASB normally expects to accept the findings of the UITF.

The aim of this body is to try to avoid the development of any unsatisfactory or conflicting interpretations of either law or accounting standards. Over the last few years, a succession of abstracts have been prepared that have helped to clarify a number of Financial Reporting Statements, for example, Abstract 4 dealt with the presentation of long term debtors in current assets and Abstract 23 contributed to the application of transitional rules in FRS 15 that is related to depreciation.

KEY POINTS OF THE CHAPTER

SSAP :	Statements of standard accounting practice
FRS:	Financial reporting statements
ASC:	Accounting standards committee
ASB:	Accounting standards board
GAAP:	Generally accepted accounting practice
FRED:	Financial reporting exposure drafts
SORPS:	Statements of recommended practice
IASC:	International accounting standards committee
IAS:	International accounting standards
Accounting principles:	Principles accepted by the accounting profession.
Statement of principles:	Exposure draft discussion on preparation and use of financial statements
Cost concept:	Traditionally to value at historical cost although there are many alternatives such as NRV, present value, CPP, CCA, etc.
UITF abstracts:	Urgent issues task force.

QUESTIONS

1. If the accounting profession had not drawn up a set of SSAPS, what could have been the effect on the preparation of final accounts for different business organisations?
2. What is meant by:
   a) the concept of entity
   b) the concept of money measurement?
3. Suggest three different methods that may be attributed to the value of an asset in the balance sheet.
4. Present value takes into consideration the future estimated returns.
   Explain what this actually means.
5. FRS 18 are seen to be of fundamental importance to the accounting profession. Why is this the case?
6. The accounting policies of Renton Industries plc, year ended 30 April is as follows:
   "The accounts are prepared under the historical cost convention modified to include the revaluation of investments which are included at their market value.
   Other fixed assets are valued at cost less accumulated depreciation. Stock is valued at the lower of cost and net realisable value. Sales will only be accounted for from the actual date of the invoice. Interest payments and other accruals are to be charged to profit and loss as incurred and if sufficiently material".
   Identify and briefly discuss the underlying concepts of the above accounting policy.
7. Under SSAP 5, if a trader is not registered for VAT, yet has to pay VAT on purchases of goods and expenses, how does this affect his final accounts?
8. If a trader is registered and charges the standard rate of VAT, how are his accounts affected?
9. What do you consider the most significant points in relation to SSAP 9?
10. An historic cost basis is traditionally used in preparing final accounts. In times of inflation, it has been said that these final accounts may mislead users of financial information.
    a) Explain the alternative approaches in the preparation of inflation-adjusted accounts.
    b) The likely effect on the measurement of profits and fixed assets when these alternatives are adopted.
    c) What may be considered as capital expenditure in SSAP 13?
11. In FRS 15 the term 'impairment' arises.
    a) What does this imply as far as depreciation is concerned?
    b) If an asset is to be re-valued what effect has this on the rate of depreciation?

12. Why is it important when preparing financial statements, to comply with accounting standards set by the Accounting Standards Board?

Chapter 33

Accounting for Stocks

INTRODUCTION

The purchase of stock is of great importance to many organisations, particularly in manufacturing or those businesses that need to buy and sell goods. The right amount of stock must be bought at the right price, at the right time. If a business over-spent on stock, it could tie up too much of its working capital on materials.

If too much stock was purchased, there could be problems of storage and some of it may become obsolete or damaged. If too little stock was bought, the business may run out of certain items which could cause hold-ups in production and the loss of valuable orders. The optimum level of stock should be held at all times, neither too much nor too little.

When stock is delivered, it should always be carefully checked to ensure that the correct quantity of items is received. The driver of the goods has a delivery note, to be signed once, the goods have been checked in. If there are two copies, one is retained by the store as a record of delivery, the other copy going with the driver. If the number of parcels or packages do not correspond with the delivery, the delivery note does not need to be signed by the person receiving the goods. A brief statement on the note as to the reason why it isn't signed could be written: for example, five packages received, not six. The signing of incoming goods is a serious business and only authorised persons should be given this responsibility.

Many businesses prepare a GRN, which enters details of the goods once they have been checked in. A copy of this would go to the buying office so that it can be checked against the purchase invoice. The store man would retain a copy and enter the details of the goods on a stock bin card. Each stock item would have its own card to record the quantities of goods received and issued and the balance in stock.

JIT

The ideal situation would be to order the exact amount of stocks to enable a production run to be completed. There would be no direct materials or work in progress left in stock. This is referred to as the *'just-in-time'* (JIT) approach to ordering. You would order all materials just-in-time to match just-in-time production schedules. However there is no ideal world in business. There are always fluctuations in the level of demand for stocks and it is far better to have a certain percentage of stock held in reserve (buffer stock).

This could be vital if you had a sudden large demand for your product or conversely there was a shortage accompanied by a costly delay in delivery. Output could suddenly be at a standstill with bottlenecks occurring in the production process.

Documentation procedure
The accountant may be involved in designing control systems to ensure that materials are:

- properly ordered;
- inspected and received;
- stored in appropriate places;
- issued to production or other departments on request.

In a manufacturing business, the cost of raw materials, work-in-progress and finished goods will require a significant amount of investment in working capital; therefore it is of essential importance that the right level of stock is produced as efficiently as possible. If stock levels fail to be managed properly (for example, a shortfall holds up production), then the costs of idle time can diminish potential profits within a very short period. The procedure for the ordering of materials into a typical manufacturing organisation may be illustrated as follows:

Source documents

Purchase requisition	An internal request for stock items from anyone who may originate the request, the storekeeper or production manager, to those responsible for ordering materials.
Purchase order	The buyer will make out the order to send to the appropriate supplier, bearing in mind price, delivery dates and reliability of supplier.
Progress of deliveries	It is the responsibility of the buyer to ensure that materials are chased up and arrive on time, particularly urgent orders.
Delivery of materials	The document which accompanies the goods on arrival is the delivery note and is signed by the person receiving the goods, usually the store man, as proof of delivery.
Goods received note	The document made out once the goods have been checked in, inspected and signed for. A copy is sent to buying office to check against incoming invoice. The goods are then stored.
Issues to store	Materials issued from stores to production as and when required; the stores issue voucher is an authorisation to release stocks and record of usage.
Stock bin card	Details of goods received and issued for each stock item. Kept with physical stock and helps to control stock movements.

Purchase requisition

This is the internal request for materials to be purchased by the chief buyer or purchasing manager, and proper authorisation must be made before a requisition is signed and goods purchased. The storekeeper in respect of materials, would send requisitions when stock is approaching re-ordering levels.

PURCHASE REQUISITION

DATE   2/1   SERIAL NUMBER   R 2953/9

FROM   H Smith

QUANTITY	DESCRIPTION	CODE NO.	JOB NO.	DEPARTMENT
275	25 mm bolts	17484 TW	0184/95	Stores 3

SIGNATURE   AUTHORISATION

Fig. 33.1 Purchase requisition

Purchase order

The buying or purchasing department will be responsible for sending the purchase order to the suppliers. Price, delivery dates, reliability and quality are all significant elements the buyer must consider before placing orders. However, most orders will tend to be routine and sent to the usual suppliers. Copies of the order may also go to the section which made the requisition, the goods inward section to await the goods, and one for the file.

The goods received note

Once materials have been checked in by the store man and the delivery note signed, the GRN is raised as evidence that the materials have arrived and been placed in stock. The GRN is an essential source document because a company must only pay for materials it actually receives. When the purchase invoice arrives from the supplier, the GRN will be checked against it.

GOODS RECEIVED NOTE				
DATE 8/1		SERIAL NUMBER G364		
SUPPLIER SPALDINGS (Lines)				
QUANTITY	DESCRIPTION	CODE NO.	JOB NO.	DEPARTMENT
275	25 mm bolts	17484/TW	0184/95	Stores
TRANSPORT BY British Geoffrey Diamond Ltd				
DELIVERY ADVICE/NOTE NO. 692/18				
RECEIVED BY H Smith		CHECKED BY PS		

Fig. 33.2 The goods received note

The stores issue voucher

When materials are issued to production, a voucher is raised to authorise the transfer of materials to a specific job or contract. The appropriate stock bin card will record, in the issue column, the materials released from store.

STORES ISSUE VOUCHER				
DATE 10/1		SERIAL NUMBER S 295		
FROM J Davies				
QUANTITY	DESCRIPTION	CODE NO.	JOB NO.	DEPARTMENT
175	25 mm bolts	17484 TW	0184/95	Shop 3
RECEIVED BY L White		AUTHORISED BY HS		

Fig. 33.3 Stores issue voucher

The stores returns voucher

This form reverses the procedure given with the stores issue voucher. If materials are returned to store, the voucher indicates what has been sent back, perhaps because of surplus or wrong stock, and the appropriate stock bin card will enter details in the receipts column.

Bin cards

The store man needs to show movements of individual stock receipts and issues. The bin card (or stores card) is a simple record of stock movements and is kept with each category of stock. Physical checks can be made against the records maintained by the stores or cost office (the stock record card) and a system of control is provided.

The bin card should be designed to give all the information we need concerning each item of stock. This includes, at the top of the card, its description, code number if applicable, unit of storage (such as boxes, packages or single units) and the level of stock required, including maximum, minimum and re-order levels. Once the re-order level is reached, the store man will inform the stock control clerk who will need to make out the purchase requisition to the purchasing department, along with other requests for stock.

The bin card is used to record all inputs and outputs of stock as well as the stock balance. The card helps to control the stock of each item and this will help management to identify stock movements, minimise unnecessary waste, or even stock theft. Under the heading 'Costing of direct materials' on the following pages, the value of the stock held in the bin is also indicated on the stock record card, sometimes referred to as the stores ledger account.

BIN CARD						
ITEM Bolts (25 mm)			MAXIMUM STOCK 750			
CODE No. 17484 TW			MINIMUM STOCK 100			
			RE-ORDER LEVEL 250			
RECEIPTS				ISSUES		
Date	GRN No.	Quantity Received	REQ No.	Quantity Issued	Stock Balance	Notes
8/1	G364	275			275	New stock
10/1			5295	175	100	
21/1	G590	200			300	
28/1			5487	120	180	
1/2	G783	500			680	
27/2			5655	200	480	
4/3	SR24	25			505	Returns

Fig. 33.4 The bin card

Stock control levels

For the purpose of controlling stock movements, each bin card should indicate the following levels of control:

    a) the minimum stock level;
    b) the maximum stock level;
    c) the re-order level.

From time to time a business needs to estimate, for each stock item, the average usage and the anticipated delivery time (lead time), so that as stock levels fall to the re-order level, an order can then be placed to replenish the stock item. In theory, at least, by the time the stock order has come in, the stock item would be at the minimum level.

The difference between the minimum stock held and zero stock is referred to as 'buffer stock', which gives a vital few days to chase up any supplier whose order is delayed. As the optimum level of stock should be carried for each item, it is important to calculate the re-order, minimum and maximum levels required for each stock item. The formulae for these are:

Re-order level   = maximum usage x maximum lead time
Minimum stock level = re-order level less (average usage x average lead time)
Maximum stock level= re-order level + re-order quantity less (minimum usage x minimum lead time)

Example

A business uses the following data for an item of its stock:
Average usage	400 units per day
Maximum usage	500 units per day
Minimum usage	200 units per day
Minimum lead time	15 days
Maximum lead time	25 days
Economic re-order quantity	4,000 units

You are required to calculate the re-order, minimum and maximum levels of stock.

Solution

Re-order level   = 500 x 25   = 12,500 units
Minimum stock level = 12,500, - (400 x 20)   = 4,500 units
Maximum stock level= 12,500 + 4,000 - (200 x 15)= 13,500 units

The economic re-order quantity refers to the optimum order level: that is, the best amount of stock to order at any time the stocks need replenishing to the levels wanted. The formula for the re-order quantity is:

$Q = \sqrt{\dfrac{2AC}{H}}$ Q = the economic re-order quantity
A = the annual demand of the stock item
C = the cost of ordering one consignment
H = the cost of holding 1 unit in stock

The economic re-order level in the above example was 4,000 units which was calculated from:

A = the annual demand: 400 units per day X 240 working days = 96,000 units
C = the cost of ordering one consignment from suppliers, estimated £12.50 on average
H = the cost of holding one unit in stock, estimated at 15p per unit.

$Q = \sqrt{\dfrac{2 \times 12.50 \times 96,000}{0.15}}$

$\sqrt{\dfrac{2,400,000}{0.15}} = \sqrt{16,000,000}$

= 4,000 units.

The re-order quantity of 4,000 units should, then, be sufficient to bring stocks up to no greater than the maximum level once the stock arrives in store.

Continuous stocktaking

Stocktaking refers to the physical counting of stock at any given time, and these figures are checked against balances indicated on stock records. Continuous stocktaking is a system whereby a certain proportion of stock items is checked each day. A sufficient number of items are checked so that, in the course of a year, all items are checked at least once. Those items which have a high value per unit should be checked more frequently to obtain a tighter stock control of them.

Periodic stocktaking

This is in contrast to the above and is usually required on an annual basis, at the end of the accounting period, so that the stock end figure is used in the final accounts. The disadvantage of this is that, due to counting all stock items, disruptions can easily occur and production time may be lost. Discrepancies are also likely to be greater between the stock records and the physical count.

Perpetual inventory

This is a stock recording system whereby the balance is shown on the record for a stock item after every movement, either receipt or issue. With this system the balances on a stock record card (as shown on the following pages) represent the stock on hand and the balances would be used in preparing the periodic accounts. The recording and pricing of stock issues form the basis for the operation of the cost accounting system.

ABC inventory analysis

This system attempts to put the emphasis of stock control on the most significant items in stock: that is, in terms of relative annual cost. The annual cost of each item is established and all items are then ranked in order. In general, about 20% of the stock items often account for about 80% of stock purchasing. It therefore makes some sense to concentrate on checking the top 20% of stock items, due to 80% investment in them.

Stock wastage

It is inevitable that some proportion of stock will be wasted or lost due to several reasons. The wastage of stock must be kept at a minimum otherwise more money is required to keep stock at the right levels. Waste of materials in production can also lead to idle time on the assembly lines, causing costs to increase. Some of the causes of stock wastage are:

- If liquids are purchased, these may be vulnerable to changes in temperature and evaporation losses occur.
- Some units bought in bulk may be difficult to break up accurately, and only estimates are made when the stock is issued.
- Human error may occur, particularly where there may be a high labour turnover and where induction training is poor. Errors may result on different levels of assembly and more stock is scrapped because it fails to meet the appropriate quality.
- In production, plant and machinery can break down, causing more waste of material.
- Facilities for storage of stocks may be inadequate and this may cause premature deterioration and even scrap.
- Obsolescence may result in stock being replaced due to technological, fashion or other factors.

Example
A new trainee was placed on the assembly line collecting roof tiles. It was found that, in the first week, production was 10% less than normal on a specific batch, due to the tiles being broken or smashed when collected off the line. These had no residual value and had to be scrapped.

Normal cost of batch: 2,000 tiles @ 1.20 each   £2,400
Actual tiles produced: 1,800 tiles @ 1.20 each   £2,160
Loss due to 10% scrap   £240

The £240 scrap can be treated as a loss on factory overheads in the manufacturing account.

SSAP No. 9 [Stocks and Work-in-Progress]

This states that stock should be valued at its *cost or, if lower than cost, at its net realisable value* (its expected selling price). In other words, if some stock items are valued lower than their cost because of age or damage, etc, the expected selling price should be stated rather than cost, to give a more realistic assessment of stock value in the financial period under review. See page 360 for further information.

If an organisation uses a computer, there are programs available to maintain stock records which have various functions like keeping up-to-date stock records, minimum and maximum stock levels, re-order levels and current balances of each stock type. Effective stock control should ensure that computer records are checked with actual physical records to avoid cases of fraud or pilfering of stock. The table below gives an example of stock valuation showing 'at cost or lower of net realisable value.

In the final accounts for the year ended 31 December, the figure in the final column, £430, would be taken, along with other stock valuations, as the stock end value. This indicates that the items of stock valued at less than their cost should be taken rather than the cost price of these items.

Lower of cost and net realisable value (Stock valuation at 31 December)

Stock Code	No. in stock	Cost price £	Value at cost £	Net Realisable Value (NRV) £	Lower of cost or NRV £
EO 145	10	5.00	50.00	40.00	40.00
EO 146	20	10.00	200.00	250.00	200.00
EO 147	5	12.00	60.00	60.00	60.00
EO 148	25	5.00	125.00	100.00	100.00
EO 149	10	2.50	25.00	10.00	10.00
EO 150	2	25.5	51.00	20.00	20.00
			511.00	480.00	430.00

Fig. 33.5 Stock valuation at lower of cost

Costing direct Materials

In manufacturing concerns the valuation of direct materials (materials used in producing a product) is usually straightforward in that the quantity used is valued at the supplier's price.

Stocks of materials are normally held in stores and issued to production as and when required. Stock cards or computer records are used to show what has come in and gone out of stock and the balance on hand.

When costly parts (such as car engines or gear boxes) are valued, the cost price of each part is clearly known and used for stock valuation purposes. However, for items of stock having a *low value* and bought frequently in large quantities (such as nuts, bolts, brackets, screws, washers, etc.), it may not be possible or desirable to itemise the value of each item, particularly when costs may vary from time to time.

To cost these low-value items in production there are three distinct methods of valuation which basically consider the stock being issued in a particular order. The three methods are:
- FIFO   First-in, first-out
- LIFO   Last-in, first-out
- AVCO   Average cost of stock

In actual physical terms, the order of movement of stock does not matter. It does matter how the stock is valued.

- FIFO assumes that stock in first is the first stock out
- LIFO assumes that stock in last is the first stock out and
- AVCO takes the weighted average of units in stock

Example

Stock received:	300 @ £1	= £300 January
	200 @ £1.20	= £240 March
Stock issued:	400 between January to March	

Using the three methods of stock valuation, what is the value of the stock still in hand for each method?

FIFO 100 x £1.20 = £120
LIFO 100 x £1.00 = £100
AVCO 100 x £1.08 = £108   (£540/500 = £1.08)

So, for valuation purposes the FIFO method in this case values stock the highest (when prices rise) and LIFO and lowest. AVCO is in between the two. Most organisations tend to use either the FIFO or AVCO methods. LIFO is rarely used because in times of rising prices it values stock the lowest and therefore has the effect of under-stating profit.

Remember an important concept in accounting from Chapter 32? The concept referred to is *'consistency'*. Once a method has been chosen it should be consistently used and in this way stock valuation in one period can be accurately and fairly compared with another.

The following pages illustrate the stock record sheets or cards (see Figures 33.6 to 33.8) of the same item of stock (25 mm bolts) using the three distinct methods of valuation. Note that the stock end on 28 February shows:

- FIFO values the balance in stock at £7,680
- LIFO values the balance in stock at £7,120
- AVCO values the balance in stock at £7,303

Clearly, the prices of the stock item increased because the FIFO valuation is the highest and LIFO the lowest, as one would expect.

Let us assume that, for simplicity purposes, the stock cards showing stock values at FIFO, LIFO and AVCO represented the total value for stock at the end of the period, 28 February. What effect would they have on the trading account?

By using FIFO, the gross profit would be greater than either LIFO or AVCO because it has a higher value of closing stock. LIFO clearly has the lower profit because its stock value is the lowest, particularly in times of rising prices. AVCO has a profit that falls between the other two.

Stock record card: FIFO

STOCK RECORD CARD

UNIT: BOLTS (25mm)   QUANTITY LEVEL: Minimum: 100
CODE: 17484 TW   Maximum: 750
SUPPLIERS: Spaldings (Lincolnshire)   Re-order level: 200

DATE	Received			Issued			BALANCE			
	Qty	Unit Price £	Cost £	Qty	Unit Price £	Cost £	No in Stock	Unit Price £	Value £	
Jan 5	150	12-	1,800				150	12	1,800	
7	125	10-	1,250				125	10	1,250	
							275		3,050	
10				150	12	1,800				
				25	10	250	100	10	1,000	
21	200	14-	2,800				200	14	2,800	
							300		3,800	
28				100	10	1,000				
				20	14	280	180	14	2,520	
Feb 1	500	16-	8,000				500	16	8,000	
							680		10,520	
27				180	14	2,520				
				20	16	320	480	16	7,680	Stock (end) 28/2

Fig. 33.6 Stock record card, FIFO

Stock record-card: LIFO

STOCK RECORD CARD

UNIT: BOLTS (25mm)   QUANTITY LEVEL: Minimum: 100
CODE: 17484 TW   Maximum: 750
SUPPLIERS: Spaldings (Lincolnshire)   Re-order level: 200

DATE	Received Qty	Unit Price £	Cost £	Issued Qty	Unit Price £	Cost £	BALANCE No in Stock	Unit Price £	Value £	
Jan 5	150	12-	1,800				150	12	1,800	
7	125	10-	1,250				125	10	1,250	
							275		3,050	
10				125	10	1,250				
				50	12	600	100	12	1,200	
21	200	14-	2,800				200	14	2,800	
							300		4,000	
28				120	14	1,680	100	12	1,200	
							80	14	1,120	
							180		2,320	
Feb 1	500	16-	8,000				500	16	8,000	
				200	16	3,200	680		10,320	
27							100	12	1,200	
							80	14	1,120	
							300	16	4,800	
							480		7,120	Stock (end) 28/2

Fig. 33.7 Stock record card LIFO

Stock record-card: AVCO

STOCK RECORD CARD

UNIT: BOLTS (25mm) QUANTITY LEVEL: Minimum: 100
CODE: 17484 TW   Maximum: 750
SUPPLIERS: Spaldings (Lincolnshire) Re-order level: 200

DATE	Received			Issued			BALANCE			
	Qty	Unit Price £	Cost £	Qty	Unit Price £	Cost £	No in Stock	Unit Price £	Value £	
Jan 5	150	12-	1,800				150	12	1,800	
7	125	10-	1,250				125	10	1,250	3,050/ 275
10				175	11.09	1,941	275	11.09	3,050	unit
21	200	14-	2,800				100		1,109	price =
							300	13.03	3,909	value div. by stock.
										3,909/ 300
28				120	13.03	1,564	180		2,345	
Feb 1	500	16-	8,000				680	15.21	10,345	10,345/ 680
27				200	15.21	3,042	480	15.21	7,303	Stock (end) 28/2

Fig. 33.8 Stock record card AVCO

The effect on the trading account

Let us assume that for simplicity purposes, the stock cards showing stock values at FIFO, LIFO and AVCO represented the total value for stock at the end of the period, 28 February. What effect would they have on the Trading Account? Look at the difference to gross profit after using the three different stock methods shown below:

Trading account for the period ending 28 February:

	FIFO £	LIFO £	AVCO £
Sales	75,000	75,000	75,000
Cost of sales:			
Stock (1/2)	7,000	7,000	7,000
Purchases	45,000	45,000	45,000
Stock (28/2)	(7,680)	(7,120)	(7,303)
	44,320	44,880	44,697
Gross profit	30,680	30,120	30,303

By using FIFO, the gross profit is greater than either LIFO or AVCO because it has a higher value of closing stock £30,680. LIFO clearly has the lowest profit, £30,120, because its stock value is the lowest, this is particularly so in times of rising prices. AVCO has a profit of £30,303, which falls between the other two stock values.

Although the 1985 Companies Act does not outlaw the use of LIFO, SSAP No. 9, Stocks and Work in Progress, states that it should not be used because it does not provide an up-to-date valuation of stock thereby distorting what should be the true profit. FIFO and AVCO methods are the two methods recommended with the overall proviso that stock should never recognise profit in advance and should therefore be valued at cost, or if lower than cost, at its net realisable value.

When FIFO is the method used, at least it follows the correct chronological sequence for valuation purposes. The stock left at the end of the period being valued at the most current price. If LIFO was used, the closing stock could be understated because values would reflect earlier prices. There could be a situation where earlier prices were more costly than current and you would therefore have a method of costing more in line with FIFO. When using AVCO there is a middle ground between FIFO and AVCO and the weighted average price comes about each time a new stock purchase is made.

Remember that for numerous low-priced material stocks pricing decisions are NOT affected by which stock actually moves in and out of the bin or shelving where the stock is located. This is because such items are used and issued at random. However, it must also be recognised that a closing stock value in one period, becomes the opening value of stock in the next. Thus FIFO's closing stock of £7680, becomes the opening stock value immediately in the next accounting period. This will have the effect of increasing the cost of sales more than either LIFO or AVCO resulting in less gross profit. By virtue of this, the difference in stock values and its effect on profits tend to cancel each other out. What is important is that once a method has been adopted, then it must be used consistently over and over again, to avoid any distortions to profit.

KEY POINTS OF THE CHAPTER

GRN:	Goods received note
Purchase requisition:	Internal request to store for stock items
Purchase order:	Order from buyer to supplier
Purchase invoice:	Bill of sale from the supplier
Store issue voucher:	Authorisation of material transfer from store
Bin card:	Shows movement of a stock item
Minimum stock level:	The minimum amount in stock prior to a new order arriving in store
Maximum stock level:	The maximum amount in stock held after the arrival of a new order
Re-order level:	The quantity of stock ordered sufficient to bring stocks up to their required levels
Economic re-order quantity:	The optimum level of stock to order
Continuous stocktaking:	Proportions of stock are checked day by day
Periodic stocktaking:	Stock checking at the period end, usually on an annual basis
Perpetual inventory:	The stock balance of an item is calculated after each receipt and issue
SSAP 9:	The standard for stocks and work-in-progress
Direct materials:	The materials used in a producing a product
FIFO:	Stock valued on first in first out basis
LIFO:	Stack valued on last in first out basis
AVCO:	Stock valued on average cost basis
Lower of cost & NRV:	Stock valued at the lower of cost and net realisable value basis
Stock record card:	Shows receipts, issues, balance and value of individual stock items

QUESTIONS

1. Make a list of all the significant documents used in the acquisition of materials.
2. Why is it important to have a system of stock control in a large manufacturing organisation?
3. Why is it important to record the stock levels on a bin or stock record card?
4. The following data relates to an item of raw material:

cost of raw material	£10/unit
usage per day *	100 units
minimum lead time	20 days
maximum lead time	30 days
cost of ordering materials	£400 per order
carrying costs	10% of cost per unit of raw material

* Assume that the usage per day is the normal level and includes both maximum and minimum levels. You are also to assume that there is a 5-day, 48-week working year.

Required
a) the re-order level;
b) the re-order quantity;
c) the maximum level;
d) the minimum level.

[Association of Accounting Technicians]

5. You are given the following information regarding material stock code Q242:
   - The average demand for the material is 400 kilos per week, 50 weeks for the year
   - The cost of ordering is £150 per order
   - Q242 costs £6.00 per kilo and carrying costs (holding costs) are 331/3% of this figure for each kilo held
   - The maximum usage in any one week is 600 kilos, the minimum 400 kilos

   On average, the orders take between 1 and 3 weeks to be delivered. Note that these figures are based on weeks rather than days of use.

Required
a) the optimum order quantity to be placed;
b) the re-order level;
c) the minimum stock level;
d) the maximum stock level.

[Association of Accounting Technicians]

6. a) Write short notes which will clearly differentiate between:
   - Continuous stocktaking
   - Periodic stocktaking
   - Perpetual inventory

   b) Calculate the normal stock control levels from the following information:

Economic order quantity	12,000 kilos
Lead time	10-14 working days
Average usage	600 kilos per day
Minimum usage	400 kilos per day
Maximum usage	800 kilos per day.

[ACCA]

7. The goods listed below were in stock at Jack's Store on 31 December.
Record the items on a stock card/sheet and calculate the value of stock at the end of the year, 31 December.

Code no.	Items	Quantity	Cost per unit £	NRV per unit £	Lower of cost or NRV £
427	Jeans	50	10.5	12.5	525
428	Jeans	10	15.20	14	
859/1	Sweaters	120	8.75	7.5	
859/2	Sweaters	60	12.50	15.95	
859/3	Sweaters	15	9.95	12.50	
870	Men's socks	50	1.15	1.50	
870/1	Men's socks	5	3.90	1.00	

8. The stock issues of a manufacturer for the months June to August inclusive were as follows:

Stock Issues – June, July, August

		Quantity (units)	Cost per unit £	Value of stock £
1/6	Balance	200	2.00	400
15/6	Purchases	100	1.95	
30/6	Purchases	200	2.10	
		500		
30/6	Issues	150		
1/7	Balance	350		
21/7	Purchases	200	2.15	
		550		
30/7	Issues	200		
1/8	Balance	350		
10/8	Purchases	150	2.20	
21/8	Purchases	100	2.20	
		600		
31/8	Issues	250		
1/9	Balance	350		

Required:

Write up a stock record card for the months June to August and calculate the value of stock on 1 September in terms of both FIFO and LIFO order issues.

9. Complete the stock record card by entering the 'balance in hand' figure on the right of the card. Calculate the value of stock end if purchases were £2.50 per ream up to 12/9 and £3.00 after 12/9 (use FIFO method).

STOCK RECORD CARD									
						MONTH:		Sept	
Item: Repro Paper – Size A4						Quantities			
Suppliers: 1 ABC Co Ltd						MIN:		100 Ream	
3 XYZ Ltd 4						MAX:		200 Ream	
						Re-order level:			

DATE	ORDERED			RECEIVED			ISSUED		BALANCE
	Supp.	0/No.	Qty	Supp.	0/No.	Qty	Dept.	Qty	130 Reams
Sept 1	1	347	150						
3	2	348	125						
6							P	36	
6							A	20	
9				1	347	150			
10							T	25	
12				2	348	100			
14							B	55	
14							M	60	
16	2	349	100						
18							A	25	
19				2	349	90			
20							P	79	

10. Use FIFO and LIFO methods to value the following stock:

January	1	Balance	50 units @ £3 unit
	10	Purchased	100 units @ £3
	16	Purchased	100 units @ £3.20
	24	Issued	80 units
February	7	Purchased	200 units @ £3.50
	14	Issued	240 units
	20	Issued	80 units
	28	Purchased	50 units @ £3.40

Required:
a) Prepare two stock cards to illustrate FIFO and LIFO methods of stock recording.
b) What effect would these methods have in the trading account?

Chapter 34

Accounting for Incomplete Records

INTRODUCTION

Many small business organisations do not keep a full set of adequate accounting records because they have neither the time nor the necessary accounting experience to do so.

Sole traders, in particular, keep only partial or 'incomplete records' and rely on the services of an accountant to write up their accounts at the end of the financial year. This is required for the purpose of calculating the taxation due to the Inland Revenue and also to have some idea of how the business has performed.

Some financial data are available, of course, because all businesses need to have essential information such as:

- How much they owe suppliers
- How much customers owe them
- How much cash is available
- How much VAT is payable to HMRC (Her Majesty's Revenue and Customs)

Because of these reasons the accountant is able to use the financial information which may be available, like invoices, credit notes, till rolls, bank statements, cheque stubs, receipts for cash, etc., to prepare a set of accounts (that is, the trading and profit and loss account and balance sheet).

From incomplete financial data, therefore, it is still possible to reconstruct accounts by relating and piecing them together in order to prepare the final accounts.

Procedure

The following is a basically simple procedure that helps to piece the accounts together:

- Establish the owner's capital (net worth) at the beginning of the financial year by listing assets against liabilities.
- Prepare a bank/cash summary in the form of a simplified cash book that will identify receipts and payments of money into and out of the business. The accountant would do this from records such as bank statements, till rolls, cheque stubs, etc.
- Establish the sales and purchases for the year. This may need to include a reconstruction of debtors' and creditors' accounts. Financial data available to the accountant would come from documents such as invoices, credit notes, cheque stubs, statements, etc.
- Extract a trial balance.
- Prepare an extended trial balance (if required).
- Prepare the trading and profit and loss accounts including items for adjustments, and a balance sheet for the financial year.

Example 1

You have just completed a business studies course and have been asked by an old school friend, Vic Brown, to have a look at her books. Vic has been running a retailing business for the past year and needs to know what his liability might be for taxation purposes.

His summary cash book for the year ended 31 March 20-8 and his assets and liabilities is as follows:

Summary Cash Book

	£		£
1/4/20-7 Balance b/f	10,000	Payments to suppliers	157,340
Cash sales	50,000	Cash purchases	7,880
Cash received from debtors	219,500	Rent	22,500
		Rates	900
		Salaries	13,080
		Wages	30,500
		General Expenses	22,000
		Drawings	15,000
		31/3 Balance c/f	10,300
	£279,500		£279,500

Assets and liabilities

	£	£
	1 April 20-7	31 March 20-8
Creditors for goods	28,400	30,010
Rent owing	1,000	500
Stock	54,000	53,000
Debtors	46,600	55,700
Pre-paid rates	170	295
Fixtures and fittings	10,000	10,000
Vehicle	7,500	7,500

Note:

In preparing the accounts for the period end 31 March 05, it is decided:

- To depreciate the vehicle by one third
- To depreciate the fixtures and fittings by 10%
- To make a provision for bad debts of 5%
- To assume that Vic has taken £1,000 *worth of goods* from the business for his own use.

Solution:

1 Calculation of capital on 1 April 20-7:

Assets:	£	
stock	54,000	
debtors	46,600	
rates	170	
fixtures	10,000	
vehicle	7,500	
bank	10,000	128,270
Less		
Liabilities:		
creditors	28,400	
rent owing	1,000	29,400
Capital		**98,870**

2 Using the debtors control and creditors control accounts format to establish sales and
purchases for the period:

Debtors control account

1/4 balance b/d	46,600	31/3 bank	219,500
31/3 SALES	228,600	balance c/d	55,700
	275,200		275,200
¼ balance b/d	55,700		

The sales figure of £228,600 is the balancing item between the £275,200 in the credit column and
the £46,600 in the debit column.
Total sales: £228,600 + £50,000 cash sales = £278,600

Creditors control account

31/3 bank	157,340	1/4 balance b/d	28,400
balance c/d	30,010	31/3 PURCHASES	158,950
	187,350		187,350
		1/4 balance b/d	30,010

The purchases of £158,950 is the balancing item between the debit column of £187,350 and the
credit column of £28,400.
Total purchases: £158,950 + £7,880 cash purchases = £166,830

3. **The trial balance of Vic Brown as at year ended 31 March 20-8**

	Debit £	Credit £
Sales		278,600
Purchases	166,830	
Rent (22,500-1,000)	21,500	
Rates (900+170)	1,070	
Salaries	13,080	
Wages	30,500	
General expenses	22,000	
Capital		98,870
Drawings	15,000	
Fixtures, fittings	10,000	
Motor vehicle	7,500	
Opening stock	54,000	
Debtors	55,700	
Bank	10,300	
Creditors		30,010
	407,480	**407,480**

NOTE:
Rates would include £170 prepaid at the beginning of the year, 1 April 20-7 and
rent would be deducted by £1,000 on the same date. Adjustments at the year end
are not included in the figures.

4.   **Vic Brown: trading and profit and loss account for year ending 31 March, 20-8**

	£	£	£
Sales			278,600
Less cost of sales:			
Opening stock		54,000	
Purchases	166,830		
Less goods for own use	(1,000)	165,830	
		219,830	
Closing stock		53,000	166,830
Gross Profit			111,770
Rent (22,500 - 1,000 + 500) *		22,000	
Rates (900 + 170 - 295) *		775	
Salaries		13,080	
Wages		30,500	
General expenses		22,000	
Depreciation: Vehicle		2,500	
Depreciation: Fixtures and fittings		1,000	
Provision for bad debts (5%)		2,785	94,640
Net Profit			£17,130

* Both rent and rates figures have been adjusted in respect of opening and closing accruals and prepayments.

Vic Brown: balance sheet as at 31 March, 20-8

	£ Cost	£ Depn.	£ Net
Fixed Assets			
Fixtures and fittings	10,000	1,000	9,000
Vehicle	7,500	2,500	5,000
	17,500	3,500	14,000
Current Assets			
Stock	53,000		
Debtors	52,915		
Pre-payments	295		
Bank	10,300	116,510	
Current Liabilities			
Creditors	30,010		
Accrued rent	500	30,510	
Working Capital			86,000
			£100,000
Financed by			
Capital			98,870
Add profit			17,130
Less drawings (15,000 + 1,000)			16,000
			£100,000

Example 2: The valuation of stock, following loss through theft or fire

During the night of 17 June, the premises of Match Ltd was damaged by a fire. It also destroyed a quantity of stock and all of the company's stock records. The destroyed stock was covered by insurance against loss by fire and the company wishes to calculate the amount to claim. The following information is available:

	(On 1 January) £000	(On 17 June) £000
Stock at cost	132	
Trade creditors	45	53
Trade debtors	39	47

The following transactions took place between 1 January and 17 June

	£000
Cash purchases	17
Payments to creditors	274
Cash received from debtors	314
Cash sales	80
Discounts received	10
Discounts allowed	8

A physical stock take carried out first thing in the morning on 18 June showed the remaining stock to have a cost of £91 000. Match Ltd earns a gross profit of 30% of selling price on all of its sales.

Required:
Calculate the cost of the stock destroyed by the fire.

Solution:

Match: Finding sales and purchases

Debtors account

1/1	Balance	39,000	17/6	Bank	314,000
17/6	Sales	330,000		Discount	8,000
				Balance	47,000
		369,000			**369,000**
	Balance b/d	47,000			

Creditors account

17/6	Bank	274,000	1/1	Balance	45,000
	Discount	10,000	17/6	Purchases	292,000
	Balance	53,000			
		337,000			**337,000**
				Balance b/d	53,000

Trading account as on 17 June

		£	£	£
Sales:	Credit		330,000	
	Cash		80,000	410,000
Cost of sales:	Stock		132,000	
Purchases:	Credit	292,000		
	Cash	17 000	309,000	
			441,000	
Stock undamaged			(91,000)	
			350,000	
Stock loss			(63,000)	287,000
Gross profit				123,000

NOTE:
Gross profit of 30% sales = £123,000, then working backwards to cost of sales, £287,000 and finally, the difference between £287,000 and £350,000 is the assessment of stock loss.

KEY POINTS OF THE CHAPTER

Statement of affairs:	Calculation of capital from assets – liabilities using the accounting equation: C = A - L
Bank summary:	A list of receipts and payments for the accounting period
Control accounts:	Sales and purchase ledger control accounts constructed to establish sales and purchases for the period
Adjustments (beginning):	Accruals and prepayments treated the opposite way to those at end of period, for example, an accrual at the start of an accounting period is deducted from an expense whilst an accrual at the end is added.

QUESTIONS

1. The balance sheet of Harry Jones, a trader, was as follows on 1 January.

	£		£
Capital	7,000	Equipment	2,900
Creditors	560	Stock	3,100
		Debtors	950
		Balance at Bank	610
	7,560		7,560

The information given below relates to Harry's business transactions for the year to 31 December.

	£
Payments to suppliers	39,950
Payments received from customers	49,645
Bank drawings for private use	2,310
Salaries and wages	4,165
Expenses	2,242
Discounts allowed	150
Discounts received	585

At 31 December the stock in trade was valued at £4,850. Expenses paid in advance amounted to £200, trade debtors to £4,845 and trade creditors to £3,550. Depreciation of equipment is at 15% per annum.

Required:
a) The total account for debtors and the total account for creditors for the year, thus ascertaining the sales and purchases for the year.
b) A summarised bank account for the year.
c) The trading and profit and loss account for the year ended 31 December.
d) The balance sheet at 31 December.

2. The following information relates to Frederick Smith at the commencement of the accounting period 1 January.

	£	
Stock	3,200	debit balance
Debtors	3,850	debit balance
Creditors	2,460	credit balance
Rates in advance	70	debit balance
Capital	6,500	credit balance

Smith did not keep proper books of account but from his cheque stubs it was possible to draw up a summary of his bank details for the year:

	£		£
(1/1) Balance (beg.)	1,840	Rent, rates	1,050
Cash received	68,375	Suppliers for materials, etc.	43,955
from customers		Light and heating	545
Interest from bank	150	Wages, salaries	8,825
		Insurance	490
		Misc. expenses	2,240
		Motoring expenses	1,985
		Advertising	650
		(31/12)	
		balance	10,625
	70,365		70,365

At the end of the year the following balances were extracted:

31 December	£
Stock	4,750
Debtors	8,242
Creditors	5,465
Rates in Advance	55

Note:
Frederick also took £5,000 from the bank for his own Christmas present at the end of the year!

Required:
Prepare a trading and profit and loss account for the year ending 31 December and a balance sheet as at that date.

3. The following information was extracted from the books of Jack Rogue at 31 December.

	£		£
(1/1) Opening balance	1,120	Cash paid to suppliers	40,800
Cash received from		Rent and rates	2,155
credit customers	58,750	Lighting and heating	325
		Salaries	6,450
		Insurance	120
		General expenses	1,145
		Drawings	6,525
		Motor vehicle expenses	875
		Closing balance (31/12)	1,475
	59,870		59,870

Other balances:	1 January £	31 December £
Stock	3,955	4,555
Debtors	3,525	4,625
Creditors	3,410	4,150
Motor vehicle	2,750	2,500
Insurance paid in advance	60	75

Required:
Jack's trading and profit and loss account for the year, and balance sheet as at 31 December.

4. The following balances represent the accounts of Frances Smith, a sole trader who does not keep a full set of accounts:

	1 January £	31 December £
Premises	25,000	25,000
Tools and equipment	2,150	
Motor vehicle	2,500	1,950
Debtors	1,750	2,780
Stock	2,565	3,425
Bank	-	
Mortgage on premises	15,250	13,295
Creditors	3,150	4,825
Overdraft	1,765	-

Smith's receipts and payments for the year were as follows:

	£		£
From credit customers	42,720	Light and heat	350
Cash sales	5,400	Wages to assistant	3,240
		Rates	390
		Insurance	270
		Telephone	120
		Drawings	5,160
		Payments to suppliers	33,470
		New equipment	2,000
		Motor expenses	450
		Miscellaneous expenses	375

Further information
• Discount to customers £545; discount received from suppliers £425
• Tools and equipment to be depreciated 10%, including new purchases
• Debtors are to be provided against going bad by 5% (from 31 December balance)
• Wages to assistant owing £55
• The owner took stock for personal use valued at £750
• The mortgage repayment (£1,955) has not been included under payments for the year

Required:
a) A summarised bank account for the year ended 31 December. (Assume all cash is paid direct into the bank and all payments are by cheque.)
b) A trading and profit and loss account for the year ended 31 December, and a balance sheet as at that date.

5. The following information relates to the books of J Archer, who has been running a retailing business for the past year and who needs to know what his state of affairs is for taxation purposes.

The summary of his receipts and payments for the year ended 31 March 20-5 was:

	£		£
Bank balance (1/4/20-4)	10,000	Payments to suppliers	157,340
Cash sales	50,000	Cash purchases	7,880
Receipts from debtors	219,500	Rent and rates	22,900
		Salaries	13,580
		Wages	30,500
		General expenses	20,500
		Light and heat	1,500
		Telephone	850
		Motor expenses	2,150
		Drawings	12,000
		Bank balance (31/3/20-5)	
			10,300
	279,500		279,500

J Archer's assets and liabilities were:

	1 April 20-4	31 March 20-5
	£	£
Creditors	28,400	30,010
Rent owing		500
Stock	54,000	53,000
Debtors	46,600	55,700
Pre-paid rates		295
Fixtures and fittings	10,000	9,000
Motor vehicle	7,500	6,450

In preparing the accounts it is decided to:
- Depreciate the fixtures by a further 10% of the 31/3/20-5 value
- Make a provision against bad debts of 5%

Required:
a) Prepare a trading and profit and loss account for the year ended 31 March 20-5 and a balance sheet as at that date.
b) Make a brief assessment of Archer's trading performance using any accounting ratios you think are necessary.

6. Jack Jones is a retailer who does not keep a proper set of accounts. He keeps a record of receipts and payments through the bank, and documents (such as invoices and bills) relating to the business.

On 1 January, his statement of affairs showed the following balances (other than his bank account):

	£
Premises	15,000
Fixtures and fittings	2,500
Motor van	1,350
Debtors	2,750
Stock	3,000
Creditors	2,600
Bank loan (5 years)	4,000

His bank account for the financial year was:

Bank balance (January 1)	2,000	Wages (casual)	1,550
Shop sales + receipts		Light and heat	295
from debtors	47,250	Advertising	300
Commission	500	Rates and water	250
		Personal drawings	2,875
		Payments to suppliers	38,550
		Motor van expenses	750
		Shop equipment	1,300
		Telephone	290
		Bank + interest charges	215
		General expenses	500
		Repairs to property	700
		Bank balance (December 31)	2,175
	49,750		49,750

Note: Discount allowed to customers £225. Discount received from suppliers £550.

Further information
- Balances at the end of the financial year, 31 December, other than bank account:
  Debtors   £1,800
  Creditors £2,465
  Stock   £3,815
- The owner took £800 goods for his own use during the year
- Depreciation: the motor van is re-valued to £1,000.
                 fixtures are to be reduced by 20%
                 premises remain at cost
- Rates in advance £40; advertising pre-paid £50; casual wages due to be paid £75
- A provision for bad debts to equal 5% of current debtors is to be made

Required:
a) Prepare a statement of affairs on 1 January to show Jack Jones's financial position.
b) Reconstruct debtors' and creditors' accounts in order to calculate sales and purchases for the financial year.
c) Prepare the trading and profit and loss account for the year ended 31 December; also a balance sheet as at this date.

(Higher National Diploma)

7. You work as a self-employed accountant and are about to draw up the final accounts for a client, D White. D White does not keep a full set of accounts but has kept a receipts and payments book for the year.

Data extracted on 31 December

Summary of Receipts and Payments Book

	£		£
Balance b/f (1/1)	1,488	Cheques to suppliers	148,992
Cheques from debtors	208,500	Salaries and wages	27,800
		Rent and rates	6,700
		Lighting and heating	1,420
		Misc. expenses	5,255
		Drawings	14,900
		Purchase of equipment	4,000
		Balance c/f	921
	209,988		209,988

	1 January	31 December
	£	£
Stock	11,900	12,850
Debtors	15,210	16,930
Creditors (for purchases)	11,840	13,120
Accruals for salaries and wages	490	560
Pre-payment of rates	810	900
Fixed assets	56,000	

Note: Fixed assets are to be depreciated by 15%.

Required:
a) Prepare the trading and profit and loss Account of D White for year ending 31 December.
b) Prepare the balance sheet of D White as on 31 December.

[Institute of Commercial Management]

8. Justin Harris carries on a retail business and does not keep his books on a double entry basis. The following particulars have been extracted from his books.

	1 July 20-7	30 June 20-8
	£	£
Fixtures and fittings	48,000	
Stock in trade	32,000	36,000
Trade debtors	4,000	6,400
Trade creditors	14,000	12,000
Cash in hand	720	1,440
Balance at bank	9,800	8,800

At 1 July 20-7, the only outstanding expense items were lighting accrued, £160, and rates in advance, £400.

At 30 June 20-8, there was £1,000 owing for rent, rates had been paid in advance by £480, wages accrued amounted to £360, and there was a stock of heating fuel valued at £600.

The following cash and bank transactions took place during the year ending 30 June, 20-8:

	£
Carriage inward	3,360
Wages	18,360
Sundry expenses	1,000
Printing, stationery and advertising	2,240
Rent and rates	5,000
Heating and lighting	2,760
Cash received from customers	205,000
Cash paid for purchases	160,400
Cash withdrawn from business for own use	12,160

During the year Harris had taken goods from his business for his own consumption amounting to £30 per week, and had not paid any money into the business for them.

Depreciation of fixtures and fittings to be charged at 10%. There have been no sales or purchases of fixtures and fittings during the year.

Required:

Prepare a trading and profit and loss account for the year ended 30 June 20-8, and a balance sheet at that date.

9. You work for a firm of accountants that prepares the accounts for Murray Limited. During the night of 2nd June, Murray Limited suffered a fire that destroyed all the company's stock records and a quantity of stock. The stock was covered by insurance against loss by fire. You have been asked by your firm to assist with preparing the insurance claim for Murray Limited. You have ascertained the following information:

	On 1 January £000s	On 2 June £000s
Stock at cost	264	?
Trade debtors	78	94
Trade creditors	90	106

The following transactions took place between 1 January and 2 June.

	£000s
Cash purchases	34
Payments to creditors	548
Cash received from debtors	628
Cash sales	160
Discount received	20
Discount allowed	16

The physical stock-take, carried out first thing in the morning on 3 June, showed the remaining stock (undamaged) to have a cost value of £182,000. Murray Limited operate a standard margin of 30%, that is, a gross profit of 30% on selling price.

Required:

a) Calculate the total value of purchases for the period.

b) Calculate the total value of sales for the period.

c) Use the information in tasks (a) and (b) to calculate the cost of the damaged stock.

(Institute of Commercial Management)

10. The assets and liabilities as at the start of business on 1 November 20-7 of Jeanie Patel, retailer, are summarised as follows:

	£	£
Motor vehicles:		
At cost	9,000	
Provision for depreciation	1,800	
		7,200
Fixtures and fittings:		
At cost	10,000	
Provision for depreciation	6,000	
		4,000
Stock		16,100
Trade debtors		19,630
Cash		160
		£47,090
Capital – Jeanie Patel		30,910
Bank overdraft		6,740
Trade creditors		9,440
		£47,090

All receipts from credit customers are paid intact into the business bank account, whilst cash sales receipts are banked after deduction of cash drawings and providing for the shop till cash float. The cash float was increased from £160 to £200 during September 20-8.

The following is a summary of the transactions in the business bank account for the year ended 31 October 20-8:

Receipts	£	Payments	£
Credit sales	181,370	Drawings	8,500
Cash sales	61,190	Motor van (bought	
		1 May 20-8	11,200
		Purchases	163,100
		Establishment and	
Proceeds of sale of		administrative expenses	33,300
Land owned privately		Sales and distribution	
by J. Patel	16,000	expenses	29,100

Additional information for the year ended 31 October 20-8:
- A gross profit of 331/3% has been achieved on all sales
- Bad debts of £530 have been written off during the year
- Trade debtors at 31 October 20-8 reduced by £8,130 as compared with a year earlier
- Trade creditors at 31 October 20-8 amounted to £12,700
- Depreciation is to be provided at the following annual rates on cost:
  Motor vehicles   20%
  Fixtures and fittings   10%
- Stock at 31 October 20-8 has been valued at £23,700

Required:
A trading and profit and loss account for the year ended 31 October 20-8 and a balance sheet as at that date for Jeanie Patel.

(Association of Accounting Technicians)\

Chapter 35

Manufacturing Accounts

INTRODUCTION

There is a wide range of different business organisations in our economic environment which require financial reports. The larger the organisation, the more important it is to provide it with essential information so that management can make objective and sound decisions.

A manufacturing organisation which makes its own products wants to know, among other things, how much it costs to produce its goods and how these costs are divided in terms of costs directly or indirectly related to production. From these figures it is possible to analyse cost types and their effect on production levels and price.

A business needs to know its total production costs for the purpose of setting its selling price. Given a certain production capacity (for example, 10,000 units) and a total cost (absorption cost) of say £100,000, the cost per unit is £10. From this, a selling price can be determined by adding a sum to the cost, a margin considered to be what the market will pay.

The purpose of preparing a manufacturing account is to calculate the cost of production – that is, the factory cost as distinct from other costs in the profit and loss account. The cost of manufacturing a product can be divided into three parts:

Direct Costs:
These are directly involved with the making of the product, including the labour, the materials and any direct expense directly related to production.

   (i)   Direct Labour. The factory wages related to the workers actively involved making the product; such as machinists or assembly workers.

   (ii)   Direct Materials. The raw materials and components specifically used to make the product, such as the tube, frame, stand and electrical/electronic parts of a TV set.

   (iii) Direct Expenses. There are few of these because most of them tend to be indirect and related to factory overheads. Direct expenses include direct power, the hiring or leasing of special equipment or plant for production, or the payment of royalties for patents or trade marks used in production.

The total of **direct costs** = the *PRIME COST*

Indirect Costs.
These refer to the factory overheads and include indirect labour, materials and expenses.

   (i)   Indirect Labour. This relates to the factory employees but excludes direct wages. Factory store men, cleaners, progress chasers, production controllers, engineers and draftsmen are some examples.

   (ii)   Indirect Materials. These may relate to factory lubricants, fluids, stationery, safety clothing and any other materials used in the factory, but excluding direct materials.

   (iii) Indirect Expenses. These relate to any factory overhead but exclude indirect labour and materials. Factory rates, insurance, light and heat, power (if not direct), rent, depreciation of factory equipment and any general factory expenses are examples.

The total of **indirect costs** = the *FACTORY OVERHEAD COST*

> *Work-in-Progress.* This relates to the stock of partly finished goods both at the beginning and end of a financial period, such as televisions partly completed on the assembly line.

The **combined** direct and indirect costs and work-in-progress = FACTORY COST (also referred to as the Production Cost).

Example 1:

A Manufacturing Account (output 20,000 units)

	£	£	£
Direct Costs			
Stock of raw materials (1 Jan.)	2,000		
+ Purchases of raw materials	24,000		
+ Carriage in of raw materials	1,000		
- Stock of raw materials (31 Dec.)	27,000		
	(3,000)	24,000	
Direct manufacturing wages	19,000		
+ Accrued wages	1,000	20,000	
Hire of special equipment		1,000	
Prime Cost			45,000
Indirect Costs			
Safety clothing		1,000	
Indirect factory wages		12,000	
Depreciation of plant		500	
Factory rates, insurance		2,500	
Factory maintenance		4,000	
Factory general expenses		1,000	
Factory Overheads			21,000
			66,000
Work-in-Progress			
+ Stock (January 1)			1,500
			67,500
- Stock (December 31)			(2,500)
Factory cost			**65,000**
(Transferred to Trading a/c)			

The factory cost per unit
The factory's production cost per unit is £3.25 based on an output of 20,000 units, made up of prime cost and factory overheads. It does not include the firm's profit and loss expenses per unit, such as distribution costs and administration expenses.

The factory cost per unit is a guide to the factory to indicate whether the firm is cost-effective in the production of its goods.

Prime cost per unit	= £45,000/20,000 units	= £2.25
Factory overheads per unit	= £21,000/20,000 units	= £1.05

Work-in-progress adjustment = £1,000/2,0000 units   = (0.05)

Factory cost per unit = £65,000/20,000 units   = £3.25

Transfer of factory costs to trading account

	£	£	£
Sales			100,000
Less			
Cost of Sales			
Stock: finished goods (1 Jan.)	5,500		
Add factory cost	65,000		
	70,500		
- Stock: Finished goods (31 Dec.)	(3,500)		67,000
Gross profit			33,000

Example 2

The following figures relate to the accounts of ABC Company Limited, television manufacturing business, for the year ended 31 December:

	£000s
Stocks of raw materials 1 January	3,186
Stocks of raw materials 31 December	4,479
Stocks of finished goods 1 January	4,264
Stocks of finished goods 31 December	9,651
Purchases of raw materials	23,766
Sales of finished goods net	79,695
Rent and rates	3,292
Manufacturing wages	23,463
Manufacturing power	765
Manufacturing heat and light	237
Manufacturing expenses and maintenance	819
Salaries and wages	13,870
Advertising	2,217
Office expenses	786
Depreciation of plant and machinery	745
Hiring of plant	504

One-half of the salaries and wages and three-quarters of the rent and rates are to be treated as a manufacturing charge.

Work-in-Progress (1 January)	1,156
Work-in-Progress (31 December)	£1,066

Required:

Manufacturing, trading and profit and loss accounts for the year to show clearly:
a) the cost of raw materials used;
b) prime cost;
c) cost of factory overheads;
d) factory cost of goods completed;
e) cost of goods sold;
f) gross profit for the year;
g) total of administrative and selling expenses;
h) net profit for the year.

Solution:

ABC's manufacturing account year ended 31 December

		£000's	£000's	£000's
Direct Costs				
Stocks of raw materials (1/1)		3,186		
Purchases of raw materials		23,766		
		26,952		
Less stocks of raw materials (31/12)		4,479		
	(a)	22,473		
Direct wages		23,463		
Direct expenses		504		
	(b)			46,440
Indirect Costs				
Indirect wages and salaries			6,935	
Indirect expenses:				
Depreciation: plant			745	
Manufacturing heat and light			237	
Expenses and maintenance			819	
+ power			765	
+ rent and rates			2,469	
	(c)			11,970
				58,410
Add				
Work-in-Progress (1/1)				1,156
				59,566
Less				
Work-in-Progress (31/12)				1,066
Factory Cost				**58,500**
(transferred to Trading a/c)	(d)			

ABC's trading and profit and lost account year ended 31 December

	£	£	
Sales		79,695	
- *Cost* of *Sales*			
Stocks of finished goods (1/1)	4,264		
Factory cost	58,500		
	62,764		
- Stocks of finished goods (31/12)	9,651	53,113	(e)
Gross Profit		26,582	(f)
- *Other* Expenses			
Rent and rates			
Wages and salaries	823		
Advertising	6,935		
Office expenses	2,217		
	786	10,761	(g)
Net profit		15,821	(h)

Note that the total cost of output is £58,500 + £10,761 = £69,261

The valuation of stock

The unsold stock of finished goods at the end of the financial year may be valued in a number of different ways (see Chapter 33 for further details). For manufacturing organisations, the value of finished goods is at prime cost plus factory overheads at normal output levels. This generally means at the production cost per unit is the most appropriate method. If finished goods were to fall in value below that of cost, then stock would be valued at lower of cost or net realisable value.

The calculation of 'profit' in the manufacturing account

An assessment of profit may be determined in the manufacturing side of the business. This maybe calculated if a *market value* of the goods manufactured is given.

For example, if 250 televisions were to be produced by ABC Company Ltd. at a production cost of £30,000, the cost per unit would be £120. If the televisions could have been purchased externally from *other manufacturers* at £150 each, we can calculate whether it is worth ABC Company Ltd. manufacturing the televisions in the first place or simply purchase the finished goods to sell by adding a mark up on cost.

250 @ £150 market value	=	£37,500
ABC's production cost		£30,000
'Profit' on the manufacturing side		£7,500

If a manufacturer wanted to emphasise the profit made on the production side of the factory, the manufacturing account can include the market valuation of those goods:

ABC's manufacturing account

	£
Cost of production	30,000
Manufacturing profit	7,500
Being market value:	
250 @ £150 each	37,500

ABC's trading account

		£
Sales		47,500
Stocks of finished goods (1/1)	8,500	
Market value of production	37,500	
	46,000	
Stock of finished goods (31/12)	10,950	35,050
Trading profit		12,450
Manufacturing profit		7,500
Gross Profit		19,950

NOTE:

Manufacturing profit	= £7,500	
Trading profit	= £12,450	
∴ Gross profit	£19,950	

Mark-up and margins of profit
The 'mark-up' is usually expressed as a percentage and is *added to* the cost price of goods in order to arrive at to the selling price. ABC Company produced and sold 260 units earning revenue of £79,695:

$$\text{Selling price per unit} \quad = \quad \frac{£79,695}{260} \quad = £306.50 \text{ per unit}$$

$$\text{Total cost price per unit} \quad = \quad \frac{£69,261}{260} \quad = £266.38 \text{ per unit}$$

$$\textit{Profit} \text{ per unit} \qquad = \qquad\qquad £40.12 \text{ per unit}$$

Mark-up percentage
This is always based on the *cost price*

$$= \quad \frac{\text{Profit x 100}}{\text{Cost}}$$

$$= \quad \frac{£40.12 \text{ x } 100}{£266.38} \quad = 15\% \text{ mark-up}$$

The percentage mark-up on cost is the guideline to selling price. How much to mark up may be a problem. How much will the market be prepared to pay? What are the prices of the firm's competitors? What will be the cost of 'follow-up' services? ABC Co. has marked up its stock by 15% at present prices. Will competition in the market place become more intense and force the company to review its mark-up?

Margin percentage
This is always based on the *selling price*

$$= \quad \frac{\text{Profit x 100}}{\text{Selling Price}}$$

$$= \quad \frac{£40.12 \text{ x } 100}{£306.50} \quad = 13\% \text{ margin}$$

The margin percentage is a guideline to profit based on sales. In this case, every £100 sales will produce a profit of £13. Sales of £1,000 produce a profit of £130 and so forth. The margin percentage is a useful indicator of profit calculated on the value of sales.

The relationship between mark up and margins of profit
There is a distinct relationship between these concepts of profit. For example, a 50% mark up is always a 33.333% margin (or one third to be more precise).

If a product cost £4 to manufacture and 50% mark up was added, the selling price would = £6. The margin therefore would = 33.333% (2/6). The following mark up percentages will always equal their respective margin percentages:

Mark Up	*Margin*
100%	50%
50%	33.333%
33.33%	25%
25%	20%
20%	16.666%

KEY POINTS OF THE CHAPTER

Manufacturing account:	An account to find the factory cost
Direct cost:	A cost directly attributable to a specific product eg materials
Indirect cost:	A cost difficult to trace to a specific product eg factory rent
Prime cost:	The direct factory costs
Factory overheads:	The indirect factory costs
Factory cost:	Total production cost
Manufacturing profit:	The difference between the factory cost and the market price
Direct materials:	Raw materials or components
Work-in-progress:	Goods not completed, partly finished
Finished goods:	Goods completed, transferred to the warehouse
Mark-up %:	Profit based on cost price
Margin %:	Profit based on selling price

QUESTIONS

1. From the following information, prepare Fred Smith's manufacturing account, trading and profit and loss account for the year ended 31 December:

	£
Stocks (January 1)	
Raw materials	5,675
Work-in-progress	2,225
Finished goods	7,550
Purchases of raw materials	40,850
Sales	101,255
Returns (Dr.)	7,235
Factory	
Wages (Direct)	18,600
Power	2,675
Depreciation of plant	3,765
Rent and rates	3,720
Insurance	500
Office	
Light and heat	846
Insurance	245
General expenses	170
Wages	6,750
Rent and rates	975
Stocks (December 31)	
Raw materials	6,200
Work-in-progress	2,135
Finished goods	8,225

At 31 December:
- Wages owing: £854 (office)
- Depreciation of office equipment £500
- Rent and rates pre-paid: 15% of both factory and office

2. Harry is a manufacturer. From the following details relating to his business, prepare separate accounts to show for the year ended 31 December:

- the factory cost of goods;
- the manufacturing profit;
- the trading profit;
- the net profit.

	£
Stocks (1 January)	
Raw materials	6,757
Finished goods	10,560
Stocks (31 December)	
Raw materials	5,583
Finished goods	12,565
Wages: factory (Direct)	15,500
Office	12,765
Rent, rates and insurance	4,580
(factory four-fifths; office one-fifth)	
Sales of finished goods	101,500
Purchases of raw materials	40,875
Manufacturing expenses	5,945
Selling expenses	12,855
Administrative expenses	7,400
Depreciation: machinery	2,150
Office furniture	500
Accounting machines (office)	150

Other Information
- (1/1) Stocks of work-in-progress (NIL)
  (31/12) Stocks of work-in-progress (NIL)
- The market valuation of the cost of production is £78,000

Required:
a) Calculate, on the basis of 2,000 units produced in the yea r:
   i) Direct labour cost per unit
   ii) Direct material cost per unit
   iii)Factory overheads per unit
   iv)Production costs per unit

b) Was manufacturing cost-effective?
   Compare the market value per unit cost with production cost per unit.

3. ABC Co Ltd is a manufacturer. From the following details relating to his business prepare separate accounts to show for the year ended 31 December:
   a) the factory cost of goods;
   b) the gross profit;
   c) the net profit.

£

Stocks (1 January)	
Raw materials at cost	4,200
Finished goods at factory cost	7,525
Work-in-progress	5,450
Stocks (31 December)	
Raw materials at cost	4,875
Finished goods at factory cost	9,674
Wages: factory (direct)	27,855
office	15,640
Rent, rates and insurance	3,600
(factory four-fifths; office one-fifth)	
Sales of finished goods	121,565
Purchases of raw materials	45,750
Manufacturing expenses	4,380
Selling expenses	3,895
Administrative expenses	1,675
Depreciation: machinery	4,500
office furniture	1,500
office equipment	350
At 31 December	
Work-in-progress	5,980
Factory wages accrued	255

Based on 10,500 units produced by ABC Co during the year, calculate:

d) the prime cost per unit;
e) the overhead factory cost per unit;
f) production costs per unit;
g) total costs per unit;
h) assuming that 10,000 units were sold during the year, calculate both the mark-up % and margin % applied by the company.

4. Prepare the manufacturing, trading and profit and loss accounts of Fred's Co Ltd for the year ended 31 December. Production output: 10,000 units in year.

	£
Stocks (1 January)	
Raw materials	4,250
Work-in-progress	-
Finished goods (2,050 Units)	10,250
Stocks (31 December)	
Raw materials	5,150
Finished goods: units in balance*	
Valued at production cost per unit	
Work-in-progress	-
Purchases of raw materials	32,600
Sales (10,800 units)	86,500
Factory	
Direct wages	15,255
Power (direct)	1,650
Indirect salaries	4,780
Factory maintenance	1,585
Rates, insurance and general expenses	750
Indirect materials	1,480
Depreciation of plant	1,875
Office	
Rates, insurance and general expenses	455
Selling and distribution costs	2,875
Bad debts	450
Administration expenses	3,450
Discount (Dr.)	375
Depreciation of office equipment	500
Commission received	1,750

At 31 December:

a) Direct wages owing £250.
   Rates in advance (office) £50.
b) A provision for bad debts to be created to equal 5% of debtors (Debtors £7,850).
c) £150 was still due for factory power.

* units in balance:
output	10,000 units	
+ opening stock	2,050	
	12,050	
- sales	(10,800)	
=	1,250	X production cost per unit

5. The following information is taken from the accounts of Peter Jackson, a businessman producing science equipment for colleges:

Trial balance of P Jackson as on 30 June 20-5

	£	£
Stocks (1/7/20-4)		
Raw materials	6,885	
Finished goods	3,500	
Motor vehicle (cost)	8,750	
Premises (cost)	36,900	
Accumulated depreciation of vehicle (2 years)		1,750
Purchases (raw materials)	55,725	
Direct wages	45,780	
Sales		180,344
Discounts	855	1,044
Returns	548	
Salaries (assistants)	18,346	
Overheads (factory)	14,385	
Overheads (office)	7,044	
Creditors		6,755
Debtors	7,400	
Bank		2,045
Cash	400	
Drawings	10,420	
Capital		?

On 30 June, the following additional information was also available:

a) Stocks in hand were valued:
   Raw materials £7,432
   Finished goods £4,200
b) The motor vehicle is depreciated on straight line and is now 3 years old.
c) Of the factory overheads, £240 is pre-paid and £600 is accrued.

Required:
Prepare the manufacturing account, trading and profit and loss account for the year ended 30 June 20-5 and a balance sheet as on that date.

6. XYZ Co Ltd is a company that manufactures electrical components for the car industry. Production is planned for 50,000 units in the financial year ended 31 December.

Trial balance as at 31 December	£	£
Authorised and issued share capital:		
70,000 @ £1 ordinary shares		70,000
Share premium		7,000
Premises (cost)	86,000	
Plant (cost)	12,000	
Provision for depreciation of plant		6,000
Debtors	10,498	
Creditors		58,409
Stock (1 Jan.):		
Raw materials	5,892	
Finished goods (2,500 units)	8,500	
Provision for bad debts		200
Bad debts	528	
Bank/cash	2,910	
Direct wages	56,804	
Raw materials purchases of	156,820	
Sales (48,000 units)		204,000
General expenses (1/2 factory)	2,944	
Profit and loss balance (1 Jan.)		5,830
Rates and insurance (1/2 factory)	610	
Office wages	5,220	
Delivery charges	2,400	
Discount	313	
	351,439	351,439

Further information at 31 December:
- Stocks: Raw materials unused £20,893.
    50,000 units of finished goods were produced. The unsold stock to be valued at production cost/ unit.
- The provision for bad debts to be increased to £750.
- The plant is to be depreciated 10% on net value.
- A taxation provision of £750 is to be made.
- The directors have recommended a 5% dividend on the share capital.
    A revenue reserve is to be created by a transfer of £2,000 in the appropriation account.

Required:
a) Prepare the company's manufacturing, trading, profit and loss and appropriation accounts for the period ended 31 December, and a balance sheet as at that date.
b) Calculate on the basis of the number of units produced, the direct labour, direct materials and total overheads per unit.

[Higher National Diploma)]

Chapter 36

Marginal Costing

INTRODUCTION

Marginal costing is related to those costs that can be directly traceable to a specific unit. These are the variable costs that are sensitive to the level of output. For example, if only one unit was produced, then the variable costs that can be directly traced to producing that unit is a marginal cost. If output increased to two units, then the variable or marginal cost would also increase to two units. Fixed costs on the other hand, such as rent rates do not vary in relation to output levels and are more insensitive to the volume of production. For marginal costing to take place, it is necessary to divide costs into variable and fixed costs.

Variable costs
Variable costs are those direct costs traceable to a unit such as direct materials and direct labour which are sensitive to output change.

Fixed costs
Fixed costs are far less sensitive to output changes and are the indirect costs such as rent, rates, insurance, or other overheads. Therefore, if output was to change, either by increasing or decreasing, it would not really affect the cost of rent or rates but it would affect direct materials or direct labour costs. The terms marginal and variable costs are inter-changeable so that a £10 per unit variable cost is also described as £10 per unit marginal cost.

It is important to make this distinction because the level of activity will have a direct bearing on the amount of profit or loss on a given output of production. In general, the more units produced, the fixed cost per unit will decrease, thereby increasing potential profits. On the other hand, if output levels fall, then the fixed costs per unit will increase, reducing the profit level.

Example 1

Output level:	500 units
Variable cost:	£10.00 per unit
Fixed costs:	£25,000

Cost per unit:

500 x £10 variable cost =	5,000		
Add Fixed costs	25,000	30,000	= £60.00 per unit
		500	

Output level:	600 units
Variable costs:	£10.00 per unit
Fixed costs:	£25,000

Cost per unit:

600 x £10 variable cost =	6,000		
Add Fixed costs	25,000	31,000	= £51.67 per unit
		600	

Therefore, by *increasing* the level of output, fixed costs are "diluted" making the cost per unit cheaper and potentially increasing profits. Conversely, if output was to ***decrease***, the cost per unit would be greater. If only 400 units were produced the cost per unit would increase to £72.50 per unit (check this figure) £29,000/400 units.

The importance of contribution
Contribution is a key element in marginal costing because it is used in a number of formulae to calculate for example, the break-even point and the profit or loss on a given output.

Contribution refers to the selling price less variable costs. The more contribution, the more profit. Fixed costs are deducted from contribution to arrive at the estimated profit.

Contribution = selling price - variable cost

Example 2
A product is sold for £15 a unit. The variable cost is £10 a unit. Fixed costs are estimated to be £12,000. Calculate the estimated profit on an output of 4,000 units and the break-even point (the point at which revenue equals total cost).

Contribution	= selling price	- variable cost
£5	£15	- £10

Estimated profit = (output x contribution) - fixed costs
(4,000 x £5) - £12,000

= £8,000

Break-even point = fixed costs / contribution per unit

= £12,000 / £5
= 2,400 units

From our example, an estimated profit of £8,000 should be made on producing 4,000 units. We can check this by:

Revenue:	4,000 x £15	=	£60,000
less			
Variable costs:	4,000 x £10	=	(£40,000)
Fixed costs:			(£12,000)
Estimated profit:			£8,000

We can also check the break-even point to see if this is correct:

Revenue:	2,400 x £15	=	£36,000
less			
Variable costs:	2,400 x £10	=	(£24,000)
Fixed costs:			(£12,000)
Estimated profit:			£0

As a form of quick calculation, if you wanted to calculate say the profit on 2,410 units (10 above the break-even point) simply multiply by the contribution per unit: 10 x £5 = £50 profit. Or 10 below the break-even point would equal £50 loss.

The contribution to sales ratio may also be used to estimate profit on the sales revenue. If, in the financial year, £76,800 were the sales to date, what profit is estimated on this revenue? Assume fixed costs of £25,000.

Profit = Revenue x Contribution/Sales ratio (C/S ratio) less Fixed costs.

Contribution/Sales ratio = $\dfrac{\text{Contribution}}{\text{Sales}} = \dfrac{5}{15}$

∴ Contribution on estimated revenue = £76,800 x $\dfrac{1}{3}$ =   £25,600

Less fixed costs   £25,000

Estimated profit   =   600

Calculate estimated profit on £89,400 sales revenue . . . £4,800 profit
Calculate estimated profit/loss on £62,400 revenue . . . [£4,200] loss

The break-even chart
The break-even chart is a graphic illustration showing the point at which revenue covers total costs that is, the break-even point. In business it is rarely used because prices constantly change, making it difficult to use the chart effectively. However, the chart is useful because it does show the estimated point at which breakeven takes place, both in units and revenue. In practice, it can be a guide to show a band of break-even rather than a point; for example, instead of 200 units representing break-even, it may be a band between 190 and 210 units. The construction of the chart is shown on the following page.

Fixed costs for the financial period: £2,000

Variable costs per unit: £6.00
Sales price per unit: £10.00

Contribution: £4.00 per unit (£10 - £6)

Break-even point: $\dfrac{\text{Fixed costs}}{\text{Contribution/Unit}}$

$\dfrac{£2,000}{£4}$ = 500 units

Break-even revenue: 500 x £10 unit (selling price)

= £5,000

Fig. 37.1 Chart showing costs only

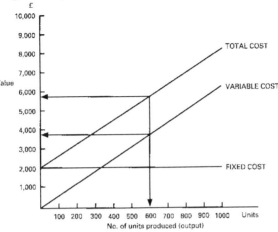

Variable cost: 600 units = £3,600
Total cost: 600 units = £5,600 and these *start at £2,000* because, irrespective of production levels, fixed costs of £2,000 are incurred.

Fig. 37.2 Chart showing break-even point

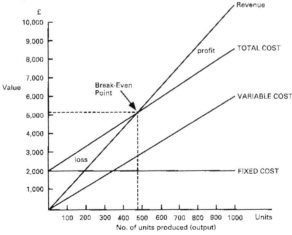

The break-even chart shows the additional line of revenue. Revenue commences at zero because it is dependent on the number of units sold and produced. Check on the chart for:

What sum of revenue is earned on 600 units? 600 x £10 = £6,000

The break-even point is the point where the revenue line crosses the total cost line – that is, at 500 units. Revenue at this point is £5,000. Any point beyond 500 units means profit. Any point below 500 units means loss.

Check on the chart:

	Approximate figures
What is the loss on 400 units?	Check: £400 loss
What is the profit on 600 units?	Check: £400 profit
If revenue was £7,000, what profit?	Check: £800 profit
If revenue fell to £3,500, what loss?	Check: £600 loss

A summary of costing formula

Contribution: Selling price - Variable cost

Profit or Loss: (Output x Contribution/unit) - Fixed costs

Break-even point: $$\frac{\text{Fixed costs}}{\text{Contribution per unit}}$$

% Margin of Safety: $$\frac{\text{(Planned output - Break-even point)}}{\text{Planned output}}$$

Contribution/Sales Ratio: (C/S) $$\frac{\text{Contribution per unit}}{\text{Sales per unit}}$$

Break-even Revenue: $$\frac{\text{Fixed costs}}{\text{Contribution/Sales Ratio}}$$

Estimated Profit from Sales Value: (Sales x Contribution/Sales Ratio) - Fixed costs

Example of marginal costing

As a costing assistant for a manufacturing company, you are asked to make a number of calculations. The company has a plant capacity of 10,000 units per annum, but at present is working only to about 90% capacity. The pricing policy of the enterprise is to add a 20% mark-up to cost.

Costs based on a budget of 10,000 units per annum

	£	
Direct labour	100,000	100% variable
Direct materials	200,000	100% variable
Factory overheads	80,000	£2 per unit variable
Administrative overheads	120,000	fixed costs
Total estimated costs:	500,000	

Required:

a) Prepare a table to show total, fixed and variable costs based on a planned output of 10,000 units per annum.

b) Calculate the contribution per unit.

c) What is the estimated profit on the planned output?

d) i) Calculate the break-even point.
    ii) What is the loss on 10 units below break-even?
    ii) What is the profit on 10 units above break-even?

e) i) Calculate the contribution/sales ratio (profit/volume ratio).
    ii) Calculate the profit or loss on sales of £425,000.

f) If the selling price was reduced by 10% and advertising costs were £20,000, to gain an estimated extra 1,500 units sold, would it be worth going ahead with the project?

g) An improved model is to be launched. Variable costs will increase by £8 per unit. Fixed costs will increase by an estimated £50,000. The selling price to launch the new model is £65. What extra sales are required to cover these costs?

Solution:

a)

Table of costs (10,000 output)

	Total £	Fixed £	Variable £
Direct labour	100,000	-	100,000
Direct materials	200,000	-	200,000
Factory overheads	80,000	60,000	20,000
Administrative overheads	120,000	120,000	-
	500,000	180,000	320,000

b) Contribution per unit: £28
   Selling price £60   -   Variable cost/unit £32

c) Estimated profit on planned output:

10,000 x £28 per unit	£280,000
Less fixed costs	£180,000
Estimated profit	= £100,000

d) Break-even point:

   $$\frac{Fixed\ Costs}{Contribution/Unit} = \frac{£180,000}{28}$$

   = 6,429 units
   (rounded up)

   Loss on 10 units below:
   10 x Contribution/unit = 10 x £28
   = £280 loss

   Profit on 10 units above:
   10 x Contribution/unit = 10 x £28
   = £280 profit

e) Contribution: Sales ratio:

   $$\frac{Contribution/unit}{Sales/unit} = \frac{£28}{£60}$$

   = 0.46667

   Profit/loss on sales of £425,000:

Sales x Contribution: Sales ratio	= £425,000 x 0.46667
Contribution	= £198,335
-Fixed cost	= £180,000
Estimated profit	£18,335

f) Is the project worth going ahead? YES
   New selling price: £60 - 10% = £54
   New contribution/unit: £22 x 1,500 extra units sold:

	= £33,000
less costs for advertising	£20,000
Estimated profit	£13,000

g) Extra sales required:
Selling price £65 - Variable costs £40
New contribution/unit = £25
To cover an extra £50,000 fixed costs:

$$\frac{\text{Fixed costs}}{\text{Contribution/unit}} = \frac{£50,000}{£25}$$
$$= 2,000 \text{ units}$$

The break-even point taken from a profit and loss account

Estimating the break-even point from say the monthly forecast of the profit and loss account can be a useful indicator of the minimum sales required to break-even. Gross profit must be sufficient in order to cover all overhead costs then break-even has been achieved. For example, if overheads were £25,000, then gross profit would need to be at least the same figure to cover costs. If the gross per cent margin was known, then the estimated sales to break-even could be calculated by dividing the margin into the overhead expenses.

Example: estimated sales for March

	£
Sales	80,000
Cost of sales	48,000
Gross profit (40%)	32,000
Less	
Operating expenses	25,000
Net profit (8.75%)	7,000

Estimate the sales required to break-even:

Operating expenses
Gross Margin %
25,000
.40
= £62,500 sales to break-even

Check: Sales £62,500 – Cost of sales £37,500 (60% of sales)
= Gross profit £25,000 – Operating expenses £25,000 = £0 profit

The limiting factor

The amount of contribution per unit a business makes is essential to profit. The greater the contribution, the greater potential to make profits. If a company made two or more products, it may have to decide, in some cases, in what quantities to produce them which would make the most benefit to contribution.

If there was a restriction or constraint in any way, in the production or demand for products, a choice may have to be made on the products that will achieve the greater contribution. The constraint is referred to as the 'limiting factor'.

Example
A business makes two major products, refrigerators and washing machines:

	Product data			
	Refrigerators		Washing machines	
	£	£	£	£
Sales per unit		120		250
Variable costs:				
direct materials	40		100	
direct labour	24		50	
overheads (variable)	10	74	20	170
Contribution/unit		46		80

In terms of contribution per unit, the washing machines are better although we do not know the quantities produced of each product. If an output of 200 refrigerators and 150 washing machines were produced:

   total contribution refrigerators   200 x 46 = £9,200
   total contribution washing machines 150 x 80 = £12,000

Again, the washing machines come out on top. If direct materials were in short supply in a given month, which of the two products makes the better contribution in terms of materials?

$$\frac{\text{Contribution}}{\text{Direct materials}} = \text{contribution to £1 direct materials used}$$

Refrigerators: $\frac{46}{40}$ = £1.15 contribution/direct materials

Washing machines: $\frac{80}{100}$ = £0.80 contribution/direct materials 100

In this case, the refrigerators are the better prospect and perhaps should be given the first priority in production. If only 80% direct materials were available, each product requiring the same type of materials but in different quantities:

Cost of materials:
  Refrigerator: 200 units x £40 per unit = £8,000
  Washing machine: 150 units x £100 per unit = £15,000 £23,000

If only 80% of materials could be purchased: £23,000 x 80% = £18,400

Produce refrigerators first, having the higher material contribution per unit:
  200 x £40 per unit   = £8,000 materials to make 200 units
  which leaves £10,400 for washing machines:
     $\frac{£10,400}{100}$ = 104 units to make

  Total materials: Refrigerators   200 x £40 = £8,000
        Washing machines 104 x £100 = £10,400 £18,400

The contribution to sales ratio
If the sales potential of either product was the same, the C/S ratio could be used to rank the two products:

Refrigerators: $\dfrac{C}{S} = \dfrac{46}{120} = 38.33\%$

Washing machines: $\dfrac{C}{S} = \dfrac{80}{250} = 32\%$

If sales for either product had a potential of £12,000 per week then refrigerators have the greater contribution to profit by £760:

Refrigerators £12,000 x 38.33% = £4,600
Washing machines £12,000 x 32% = £3,840.

In practice, it is never quite as straightforward as it appears. Many other factors come into play, not least the customers, the investment in plant and machinery and the workforce. It is not just a case of figure-crunching: the effect on reliable customers, the morale of workers and the cost of expensive equipment are all influential in deciding what the best course of action might be.

To make or buy?
Another important point in marginal costing is to decide whether to make products or buy them from elsewhere if they look cheaper to purchase. This time we must look at the fixed costs because they play an influential part in making the decision.

If, in producing the refrigerators, the business also made the motors of the these units, costing £22 each, but could buy them from a supplier for £18: (apparently £4 cheaper)

Variable cost of motor/unit £10
Fixed overheads charged £12 £22
Purchase from external supplier £18

Is it a case of down tools, shut the motor shop and buy from outside? Buying 200 motors a week would save the business £800; or would it? Do the fixed costs conveniently disappear once the making of a product is closed down? No. When the existing facilities for production are available for use, the fixed costs still remain and burden the other products with a greater proportion of fixed costs per unit:

Refrigerators:		+ Motor	Total
Variable costs	£64	£10	£74
Fixed Overheads	£24	£12	£36
	£88	£22	£110

If the motor was purchased externally, most of the fixed cost of £12 still remains as part of the product cost. A refrigerator could still incur £36 fixed costs (£24 + £12) and a total absorption cost of £118 per unit if the motor was purchased from suppliers at £18:

Refrigerators:			
Variable costs	£64	£18	£82
Fixed Overheads			£36
Total cost			£118

Therefore, when deciding whether to make or buy, all the costs must be considered, particularly fixed costs that do not go away if a section or a product is closed down.

The use of marginal costing assists management by providing further information with which to improve decisions making, in particular when output levels differ from those planned, or special prices for special orders need to be calculated. In the real world, however, you must remember solutions are not always based on figures alone.

The limiting factor, used to find out which would be the best combination of units to produce, is fine in theory; but in practice, it's the regular and reliable customers who need to be satisfied first, irrespective of the order of contribution made to profits.

KEY POINTS OF THE CHAPTER

Marginal costing:	The extra cost involved in producing 1 or more units (or 1 or more less)
Variable costs:	Sensitive to output change (example, direct materials)
Fixed costs:	Insensitive to output change (example, rent, rates)
Contribution:	Contributes towards profit, the selling price less variable cost
Break-even point:	The point at which revenue equals total costs, no profit, no loss
Calculation of break-even:	Fixed costs divided by contribution/unit
Calculation of profit/loss:	(Output x contribution) – fixed costs
Calculation of C/S ratio:	Contribution/unit divided by sales/unit
Estimated profit from sales:	Sales x C/S ratio – fixed costs
Margin of safety:	Output level – break-even paint
The limiting factor:	Making choices as to which products would achieve the best contribution

QUESTIONS

1. The following costs relate to an output of 2,000 units:

	£	£
Direct labour	25,000	
Direct materials	40,000	
Overheads	35,000	100,000
Variable Costs		
Direct materials		100%
Direct labour		£1.50 per unit
Power (part of overheads)		0.50 per unit
Revenue		
Sales per unit		20% above cost price

Required:
a) A table to show total, fixed and variable costs based on an output of 2,000 units.
b) The contribution per unit.
c) The estimated profit based on 2,000 units.
d) The estimated profit on 2,100 units and on 1,950 units.
e) i) The break-even point.
   ii) The profit on 1 above break-even.
   iii) The loss on 1 below break-even.
f) *Variation.* If sales price per unit were to decrease by 10% and output was to increase by 10%, what is the estimated profit (or loss)?

2. Mr Baldwin's small factory produces jeans. Output per month is 500 units.

Monthly costs	£	Variable Cost
Direct labour	2,000	£0.50/unit
Direct materials	2,000	100%
Overheads (fixed)	1,000	-
Costs per month	5,000	
Selling price:	Mark-up of 25% on cost	

Required:
a) The contribution per unit.
b) The estimated profit per month based on 500 units.
c) i)   The break-even point per month.
    ii)   The break-even revenue per month based on C:S ratio (contribution: sales ratio).
d) If during the first 6 months revenue reached £42,500, what is the estimated profit?
e) If sales in a month were £5,950, what is the estimated profit/loss in the month?
f) Variations due to market changes:
    Propose to reduce the sales price by £1.00 and sales estimated to rise by 20% per month, or increase advertising cost by £2.50 per month and improve the jeans with stronger zip costing £0.30 per unit, with sales estimated to rise by 15% per month.
    Which is the better of the two proposals?
g) If advertising costs increase by £765 during the first year, how many extra units need to be sold to cover this cost? (Treat as a fixed cost and divide by contribution per unit).

3. D. Lillee & G.Thompson produce sports gear under the trade name 'Down Under'. The present year expects costs to be:

	£
Direct labour	48,000
Direct materials	55,000
Production overheads	22,500
Distribution costs	15,000
Administration costs	13,500
Financial and general costs	4,000

Sales revenue: £4 per unit

Variable costs	
Direct labour	75%
Direct materials	100%
Production overheads	10%
Distribution costs	10%

Expected production capacity: 50,000 units.

Required:
a) A table to show the division of total, fixed and variable costs based on a capacity of 50,000 units.
b) Calculate the unit contribution.
c) If an order for 1,000 units was received, what would the extra cost be, based on marginal costing?
d) Could the firm accept the above order at £2.80 per unit?

e) i) Calculate the break-even point.
ii) Calculate the break-even revenue based on the cost: sales ratio.
f) Calculate the loss on 50 units below break-even.
g) What is the estimated profit on 50,000 units?
h) What is the profit/loss on a production of 39,500 units?

4. The following costs relate to a budgeted sales forecast of 30,000 units per year:

Costs	Budgeted £	Fixed £	Variable £
Production cost	287,500	25,000	262,500
Administration	35,000	30,000	5,000
Distribution	95,000	62,500	32,500
	417,500	117,500	300,000
Revenue per unit:	£15.00		

Required:
a) The number of units needed to sell to cover costs.
b) If sales decline to 20,000 units, what is the estimated profit or loss?
c) If £80,000 is spent on advertising, how many extra units need to be sold to cover cost?
d) On sales of £345,750 after 10 months, what is the estimated profit/loss at this point?
e) The following proposals have been made:
   - Spend £2.00 per unit improving the product, expecting sales to rise to 40,000 units
   - Pay £1.00 per unit sales commission, expecting sales to rise to 38,500 units
   - An additional order of 8,000 units at £12.50 per unit for export (export costs £10,000)
   Which of these three proposals do you consider the best?

5. Smith Engineering Ltd has prepared the quarterly budget figures for three months ending 31 March as follows:

	Budgeted forecast total £	Fixed costs £	Variable costs £
Cost of production	115,000	10,000	105,000
Cost of distribution and sales	38,000	25,000	13,000
Administration expenses	14,000	12,000	2,000
	167,000	47,000	120,000

Sales forecast
12,000 units @ £15 each.

As an assistant to the cost accountant you have been asked to calculate the following:
a) What is the minimum number of sales units required to cover costs?
b) If demand was to fall to 8,000 units, what is the effect on the forecast profit?
c) If an additional £16,000 was spent on advertising the product, how many *more* units need to be sold to cover costs?
d) Alternative proposals were to be considered:
   - Redesign and improve packaging costing £1.50/unit (test marketing indicates that sales would increase by 25%)
   - Reduce the selling price by £1 (research indicates that sales would increase by a third)
   Should the company consider one of the above proposals or leave things as they were in the budgeted forecast?

[Higher National Diploma]

6. As a costing assistant you need to prepare budget estimates for the next financial year. At current production levels, the company produces 6,000 units per year and has the capacity to increase this by another 1,000 units. The firm's pricing policy is to mark up by 25% on cost. The estimated costs for the next financial period based on an output of 6,000 units are:

	£
Direct labour	78,000
Direct materials	114,000
Factory overheads:	
Indirect labour	12,000
Indirect expenses	33,000
Office overheads	123,000
	360,000

Your research reveals that direct labour and direct materials are 100% variable.
Indirect labour is 10% variable as a result of sharing a bonus payment scheme.
Power (indirect expenses) is estimated at £1.80 per unit variable.
All other costs are to be considered fixed.

Required:
a) Prepare a suitable table to show total, fixed and variable costs based on an output of 6,000 units.
b) The contribution per unit.
    The break-even point.
c) Prepare a chart based on an output of 6,000 units to illustrate:
    The company's break-even point.
    The profit/loss based on a production of 6,500 units.
    The profit/loss based on a production of 3,500 units.

[Higher National Diploma]

7   As an assistant to the cost accountant of a manufacturing company, you have been asked to prepare some costing information relating to the launch of the company's new product.

Expected output:	10,000 units
Cost per unit	£
Direct materials	30
Direct labour	70
Variable overheads	40

Total fixed costs attributed to the product is £240,000. Selling price per unit: £200.

Required:
a) The contribution per unit.
b) The break-even point.
c) The margin of safety, expressed as a percentage * (see below)
d) The maximum profit on the expected output of 10,000 units and the estimated profit if production fell to 8,500 units.
e) The following proposals have been put forward:
    • By reducing the price to £190 per unit, 12,000 units are estimated to be sold
    • By increasing the price to £210 per unit, 9,500 units are estimated to be sold
    • By retaining the existing price at £200 and an extra £60,000 is spent on advertising, sales being estimated at 11,800 units.   Which of these 3 proposals do you consider is the best? Explain briefly why.

* margin of safety as a % =   Output - break-even point
                           =   Margin of safety x 100
                                Output

8. A firm makes two products, A and B. Their cost data per unit is:

		A		B
Output per week:		50 units		80 units
Sales/unit		100		60
Variable costs:				
materials	40		15	
labour	12	52	20	35
Contribution		48		25
Fixed costs		30		20

a) What different methods can be used to decide the best contribution available on different products?
b) If there is a shortfall of materials and only 80% is available, what would management be advised to do?
c) What factors should management consider before deciding either to keep production going or simply to buy from outside a product which appears cheaper to purchase? (For example, if product B could be purchased for £50 per unit.)

[Higher National Diploma]

9. You work in the Management Accounts Department of a Manufacturing company that makes three products from one basic raw material. Due to a serious accident at the supplier's factory there will be a shortage of the basic raw material next year. Next year's budgeted data is as follows:

Maximum amount of raw materials available – £2,094,000

Product	X	Y	Z
Maximum possible sales (units)	24,000	32,000	25,000
Variable costs per unit:			
Direct material	£24	£32	£38
Direct labour	£32	£21	£23
Overheads	£12	£10	£12
Selling price	£80	£88	£94

Total annual fixed costs are £585,000.

Required:
a) Calculate the maximum profit that the company can make in the next year
b) If there was no shortage of the basic raw material, should the company consider accepting a 'special order' for 5,000 units of Product Y at a price of £74 (the additional costs of handling this order are estimated at £7,500)? What would be the extra profit/loss if the order is accepted.

(Higher National Diploma)

Chapter 37

Budgeting

INTRODUCTION

The budget is a key financial plan of a business that attempts to *forecast* a number of months ahead, how best to use its resources. It is a forecast that tries to find out where the resources are coming from and where they are being used. In a well-structured organisation the budget is at the centre of the financial control system. When budgets are being prepared the responsibility for each main section (or cost centre) is normally allotted to the functional heads of each department, such as the sales manager, production manager, finance manager, and so forth.

The basic purpose of a budget is to control the organisation's expenditure and to plan ahead for the future. Budgets should be communicated to all personnel who need to know in order to involve them in the forward planning of the organisation. Budgets assist those in management by motivating them towards the major objectives of the organisation. Expenditure for the year ahead can be planned, profits estimated and targets set. Actual results can then be measured against the budgeted plans, and differences (variances) may be analysed, discussed and acted upon where appropriate.

Budgets are prepared by management in order to attempt to achieve company policy; their preparation is usually a time-consuming, exercise. The main steps may be summarised as follows:

- the objectives of the organisation should be clearly stated;
- an initial forecast of expenditures and revenues is prepared;
- computations are made in terms of manpower, materials, equipment, overheads, etc;
- the initial budget is reviewed and amended where appropriate until it is accepted.

In order to set realistic objectives, management must obtain as much information as it can in terms of both internal and external factors. Externally, the organisation must consider the economic and political climate and obtain as much information as possible about competitors. Internally, it must assess the strengths and weaknesses of its own structure and consider the alternative plans available in order to compete effectively and gain its optimum share of the market.

The main types of budget are:
- Sales budget
- Production budget
- Personnel budget (or manpower)
- Capital expenditure budget
- Administration budget
- Cash budget
- Operating budget (profit and loss)

The *sales budget* must start with the expected level of sales. Selling is the life-line of an organisation and its cornerstone. Without sales, there is no organisation and therefore it is essential to make an accurate estimation of what sales (for every product) are likely to be. From the sales budget, other budgets should then fall into place.

The *production budget* must ensure that it can meet the demands set by the sales budget. It must take into account the stocks it already holds and be sure it has the necessary materials, labour, machinery and so forth to meet the appropriate sales demand. It is of little use to budget for a 30% sales increase if production cannot cope with even a 10% increase. If management wants a 30% increase, it must prepare, plan and be ready to finance it.

The *personnel budget* must ensure that the organisation has the right manpower at the right time, with the appropriate financial support to meet manpower and training needs.

The *capital expenditure* budget takes into account capital costs and involves the purchase of fixed assets like plant, machinery, equipment, new premises and other items expected to be used in the organisation over the long term. Fixed assets need replacement because they are likely to be worn out eventually or become obsolete. The budget needs to forecast what resources need to be put aside either for replacement or expansion purposes.

The *administration budget* usually takes into account all the overheads of the organisation from the administrative point of view and involves, largely, the fixed costs like rent, rates, stationery, heating, telephone, etc.

The *cash budget* (or cash flow forecast) is often regarded as the *key* budget. It involves all the other budgets in its forecast because it must include all sources of expected revenues in the months ahead (normally six or twelve months) against all sources of expected expenditure. In other words, it shows the forecast of the *flow of cash* into and out of the organisation and affects the monthly bank balance.

An organisation must have sufficient *liquidity* (or cash) to meet its day-to-day needs, otherwise it will run into financial difficulties and may have a cash crisis. If it runs out of money because of poor forward planning, how can it pay for wages, materials and a long list of overhead costs? On the other hand, if it can be foreseen that there may be a cash shortage ahead, management can negotiate, ahead of time, the necessary liquidity it needs and, in so doing, it emphasises the financial soundness of the organisation.

The *operating budget* represents a forecast of the profit and loss account. What will the estimated profit (or loss) be in six or twelve month's time? The business will plan its objectives and aim to make a satisfactory return on capital employed. All other budgets will contribute in preparing the operating budget and the forecast of profit or loss can then be compared against actual results, usually on a monthly basis, to see if activities go according to plan.

The *forecast balance sheet* can also be prepared to show the financial position of the business at the same time as the operating budget.

In summary, a business will want to look ahead and plan for the future. It will want to estimate its potential sales and expenditure and then closely monitor actual results month by month, so a careful comparison can be made between the forecast figures and the actual figures. Any variances between the two sets of figures can then be analysed by management and relevant action taken whenever necessary.

If a budget needs adjustment because circumstances have changed, then forecasts need to be amended to reflect changes. In this way, a budget becomes a very significant management tool to help them make better decisions and improve forward planning.

Example 1: The cash budget
A new company has gathered the following information for the six months from 1 January to 30 June.

- Sales (in units) £40 per unit:
- Jan.   Feb. Mar.   Apr.   May   June
  200   300   200   400   300   400   units
- Production is 300 units per month for the whole 6 months.
- Fixed overhead costs will be £3,000 per month, payable in the month after production.
- Variable overhead costs will be £15 per unit payable in the month of production.
- Direct wages will be £5 per unit payable in the month of production.
- Equipment costing £10,000 will be purchased in February and paid for in March. Once installed, it will allow production to increase to 500 units per month.
- Materials will cost £8 per unit and suppliers will be paid in the month following purchases.
- All sales of units are on credit. Debtors are expected to pay in the *month following* their purchase.
- Cash at bank on 1 January = £10,000.

Required:
A *separate* schedule of payments and a cash budget for the six month period, January to June.

Solution:

Schedule of payments

	Jan. £	Feb. £	Mar. £	Apr. £	May £	June £
Fixed overheads		3,000	3,000	3,000	3,000	3,000
Variable overheads						
(300 x £15)	4,500	4,500	4,500	4,500	4,500	4,500
Direct wages						
(300 x £5)	1,500	1,500	1,500	1,500	1,500	1,500
Equipment			10,000			
Materials						
(300 x £8)		2,400	2,400	2,400	2,400	2,400
	6,000	11,400	21,400	11,400	11,400	11,400

Cash budget

	Jan. £	Feb. £	Mar. £	Apr. £	May £	June £
Bank balance b/f	10,000	4,000	600	(8,800)	(12,200)	(7,600)
+ Receipts*	-	8,000	12,000	8,000	16,000	12,000
	10,000	12,000	12,600	(8,000)	3,800	4,400
- Payments	6,000	11,400	21,400	11,400	11,400	11,400
Bank balance c/f	4,000	600	(8,800)	(12,200)	(7,600)	(7,000)

* Receipts calculated *(a)* £40 unit sales, allowing for one month credit.

Analysis of the cash budget

The cash budget clearly highlights that the company does not have sufficient cash resources to finance the above plan. However, if it could lease the new equipment rather than buy it, or obtain more capital by March, the problem would be solved. If the company had not prepared a cash-flow budget it would have had a deficit from March to June of a proportion it may not have planned. By preparing a cash flow, the organisation can demonstrate it has some control in its financial affairs and is therefore more likely to accommodate the deficit period by negotiation with its creditors.

The cash flow emphasises the common business problem that, in order to finance an increasing level of sales, stocks have to be increased, equipment purchased, etc. Extra expenditure is incurred before the revenue from extra sales comes in.

In conclusion, budgets are both a planning and control tool because they help management to evaluate the financial implications of various courses of action ahead of time and to monitor those plans by comparing actual results with budget plans.

Example 2: Cash and operating budgets

The following information relates to a businessman, D Balfour, who has started business on January with £5,000. He has made a forecast for the next six months concerning receipts and payments of cash:

- Production will involve the making of an electrical component for the computer industry. His plan is to produce 500 units per month in the first six months.
- Sales: each unit has a selling price of £12.50. The sales estimate for six months to 30 June was:

Jan	Feb	Mar	Apr	May	June	
400	480	480	560	640	400	(Units)

- Variable overheads (based on output), will be £1.50 per unit, payable in the month of production
- Fixed costs will be £1000 per month payable after the month of production.
- Production wages (direct) will be £3 per unit payable in the month of production.
- Salaries will be £500 per month until April, but expected to rise by 10% in the following months.
- Equipment costing £8,000 will be purchased in March. A 25% deposit will be paid in March, with the balance to be paid equally in April and May.
- Materials will cost £2 per unit and suppliers will be paid in the month after the purchase.

All unit sales are on credit. Debtors are expected to pay in the month *following* their purchase. £5,000 was deposited in the business bank account on 1 January.

Required:

a) A cash budget covering the six month period from January to June (without a separate cash payments schedule).
b) A brief analysis of the cash budget.
c) An operating budget which will show the trading and profit and loss forecast for the six months to 30 June and a forecast balance sheet as on that date.

Solution:

Cash Budget

	Jan. £	Feb. £	Mar. £	April £	May £	June £	Total £
Receipts							
Sales	0	5,000	6,000	6,000	7,000	8,000	32,000
Payments							
Fixed costs	0	1,000	1,000	1,000	1,000	1,000	5,000
Variable overheads	750	750	750	750	750	750	4,500
(500 x £1.5)							
Production wages	1,500	1,500	1,500	1,500	1,500	1,500	9,000
(500 x £3.0)							
Salaries	500	500	500	500	550	550	3,100
Materials	0	1,000	1,000	1,000	1,000	1,000	5,000
(500 x £2.0)							
Equipment			2,000	3,000	3,000		8,000
	2,750	4,750	6,750	7,750	7,800	4,800	34,600
Net cash flow	(2,750)	250	(750)	(1,750)	(800)	3,200	(2,600)
Bank balance b/f	5,000	2,250	2,500	1,750	0	(800)	5,000
Net cash flow	(2,750)	250	(750)	(1,750)	(800)	3,200	(2,600)
Bank balance c/f	2,250	2,500	1,750	0	(800)	2,400	2,400

Analysis of the Cash Budget

Note the different format of this cash budget. Receipts are matched against payments so that an increase or decrease results. This is then added or subtracted to the opening bank balance to arrive at the bank balance carried forward. In January, a decrease of £2,750 is deducted from the opening bank balance of £5,000, providing a closing bank balance of £2,250.

From the forecast of cash flow, it appears that D Balfour may be a little short of liquidity in the months of April and May. This is not surprising because part of his expenditure is capital expenditure, purchasing equipment in March of £8,000 and finishing the payment for it in May. He could ask the bank to tide him over during these months by arranging for an overdraft facility. He could, if he wanted, finance the asset purchase in other ways, probably by simply extending the period of credit over 12 months or even longer.

In June, however, the cash flow is back in surplus and certainly appears sound. Cash flow forecasts a business's liquidity. Can sales generate sufficient receipts of money to be able to finance labour, materials, overheads and capital expenditure?

Budgets are an important management tool if they are taken seriously. They can help plan and control the business because they assist in management decision making. When actual results are recorded, they can be carefully monitored against the budget forecast. How will D Balfour's budget compare with his first six months trading? Will he have about £2,500 in the bank in June? If he has not, what factors have occurred to have caused the difference?

The operating budget

The operating budget refers to the forecast of the profit and loss account. The sales forecast for the six months to June was:

Total of 2,960 units x £12.5 per unit = £37,000

The first six production months at 500 units per month would cost:

		£
Wages	£3.0 per unit x 3,000 =	9,000
Variable overheads	£1.5 per unit x 3,000 =	4,500
Materials	£2.0 per unit x 3,000 =	6,000
	£6.5 Total cost:	19,500

There was no opening stock because it was a new business and therefore there will be no closing stock carried forward from the previous period. If the closing stock was to be valued at production cost per unit then:

Units produced:	3,000 units
Units sold:	2,960 units
	40 units in stock x production cost per unit

Value of closing stock: 40 x £6.5 per unit [production cost]
= £260

As far as any adjustments are concerned, D Balfour decided to depreciate the equipment by 20% per annum and a full 10% for the six months, even though it was to be purchased in March.

D Balfour - Budgeted trading and profit and loss account for six months ending 30 June			
	£	£	£
Sales			37,000
- Cost of sales:			
Stock (1/1)		-	
Production cost	19,500		
Stock (30/6)	(260)		19,240
Gross profit			17,760
Expenses:			
Fixed costs	5,000		
+ Accrued (1 month)	1,000	6,000	
Salaries		3,100	
Depreciation of equipment		800	9,900
Net profit			7,860

D Balfour			
Budgeted balance sheet as on 30 June			
FIXED ASSETS	£	£	£
Equipment	8,000	800	7,200
CURRENT ASSETS			
Stock	260		
Debtors			
(400 x £12.5)	5,000		
Bank	2,400	7,660	
CURRENT LIABILITIES			
Creditors			
(500 x £2)	1,000		
Accruals	1,000	2,000	
(1 month fixed cost)			
Working capital			5,660
			12,860
FINANCED BY:			
Capital (1/1)	5,000		
+ Net profit	7,860		12,860

D Balfour's prospects look very sound for a period covering the first six months' trading. It may be that his sales forecast is a little optimistic and his expenditure may be greater than predicted. He will be able to compare his actual trading results with the budget and see if his targets have been achieved.

Example 3: Fixed and flexible budgets

The fixed budget is a forecast on a given target of output. For example, 500 units a month. The flexible budget is designed to allow for changes in output. If a business planned an output of 500 units a month then the costs of labour, materials and overheads would be estimated based on producing 500 units. When the data for the actual figures become available these would be compared to the budget to find what variances, if any, there were.

If sales were 450 units in a particular month then it would make sense to revise the budgeted costs to take account of the fall in output. A flexible budget is prepared on this basis and would provide management with a more realistic comparison of control because it would measure the actual figures at the same level of activity using a flexible budget for this purpose.

The original budget based on an output of 500 units compared with actual figures where sales were only 450 units:

	FIXED BUDGET 500 units	ACTUAL FIGURES 450 units	VARIANCE (50 units)
Sales 500 x £10	5,000	4,350	(650) A
Less			
Variable costs x £4	2,000	1,900	100 F
Variable OH's x 0.80p	400	320	80 F
Fixed costs	1,200	1,190	10 F
Total costs	3,600	3,410	190 F
Estimated profit	1,400	940	(460) A

NOTE: A = adverse variance, F = favourable variance

These figures show that estimated profit is down by £460 (adverse). However, the level of sales had fallen by 50 units in this particular month so that the budget based on an output of 500 units does not correspond directly with the reduced output of 450 units on which the actual results were based.

Comparison of performance is therefore going to be misleading. The favourable variances on variable costs only occur because the actual figures on 450 sales is less than the budget figures based on an output of 500 units.

The Flexible budget based on an output of only 450 units:

	FLEXIBLE BUDGET 450 units	ACTUAL FIGURES 450 units	VARIANCE 0
Sales 450 x £10	4,500	4,350	(150) A
Less			
Variable costs x £4	1,800	1,900	(100) A
Variable OH's x 0.80p	360	320	40 F
Fixed overheads	1,200	1,190	10 F
Total costs	3,360	3,410	(50) A
Estimated profit	1,140	940	(200) A

By using the flexible budget you can see that the total profit is only £200 adverse in comparison to £460 adverse when compared with the original budget. The main reason of course is that actual sales were only £150 less than expected and not £650 less. The variance on the variable costs were in effect greater when compared to the flexible budget because these were adjusted to take the lower output of 450 units into account.

By using the flexible budget against actual costs, the level of activity is the same and this gives much better credence to the comparison of figures and a better basis for management to take any corrective action they feel may be necessary.

KEY POINTS OF CHAPTER

Budget:	A forecast or plan of future activity in monetary terms
Budgetary control:	The monitoring of budget with actual result
Cash budget:	A major budget comparing planned receipts against planned expenditure
Schedule of payments:	A forecast of all planned costs
Operating budget:	A forecast of the profit & loss account
Budgeted balance sheet:	A forecast-of the balance sheet
Fixed budget:	A planned budget of so much per month in either value or units.
Flexible budget:	A planned budget is adjusted to take account of the actual level of activity for better comparison of results

QUESTIONS

1.A new client, Janet Smith, who runs a small tourist office in town, has submitted her proposed budget figures with you.

The business will take effect from 1 March this year and Janet is anxious to know whether she will have sufficient cash to keep her afloat for the first six months of trading .
The data she has supplied is estimated for the six month period, ending 31 August.

Janet is to put £50,000 into the business bank account on 1 March.

- She is to borrow a further £50,000 from the HSBC Bank plc at 8.5% per annum rate of interest with effect from 1 March. First quarterly payment on 1 June.
- The forecast of her monthly sales commission is estimated to be as follows:

	£		£
March	6,500	June	13,500
April	12,500	July	14,000
May	12,500	August	12,500

- All clients are expected to settle their accounts one month *after* the sales go through.
- Janet will draw £1500 per month for personal use, but this will commence from 1 April.
- Staff salaries are estimated to cost £1850 per month, payable in the month.
- Light and heat is estimated to cost £140 quarterly, paid by direct debit, the first quarter being due on 1 June.
- Premises are to be purchased for £105,000 and paid for by 5 equal monthly instalments, the first 4 with effect from 1 March with a final instalment payable in August.
- A motor vehicle for £12,600, to be paid for over 3 equal instalments commencing in March. Depreciation on the vehicle is at 30% per annum. Computer equipment valued £2,500 is to be purchased in March with a 10% deposit followed by 5 equal monthly instalments. The equipment is to be depreciated at the same rate as the vehicle.
- An advertising and promotional campaign is expected to cost £1,500 per month for the first 4 months and £1,250 for the final 2 months.
- Motor expenses are expected to be £250 per month, payable in the month.
- General overhead expenses are estimated to be £400 per month, payable one month *in arrears*.
- Rates, water, insurance and other various costs are estimated to be £1400 per month for the first 4 months of business, rising by 20% thereafter. All these costs are payable one month *in arrears*.

Required:
a) Prepare a cash budget to cover the 6 month period commencing from 1st March.
b) Prepare a profit & loss statement for the 6 month period ending 31 August.
c) Prepare a memorandum to your client Janet Smith, commenting on the monthly cash flow of the business and the profit and loss statement and their significance to the success of the enterprise.

2. Mr Ben is to open a retail shop on 1 July. He will put in £70,000 cash as capital. His plans are as follows:
    - On 1 July to buy and pay for premises £50,000, shop fixtures £7,000 and a motor van £4,000.
    - To employ two sales assistants, each to get a salary of £350 per month, payable at the end of each month (ignore tax and NI).

    - To buy the following goods:

	July	Aug.	Sept.	Oct.	Nov.	Dec.
Units	500	540	660	800	900	760

    - To sell the following goods:

	July	Aug.	Sept.	Oct.	Nov.	Dec.
Units	345	465	585	705	885	945

    - Units will be sold for £25 each. One-third of the sales are for cash, the other two-thirds being on credit. Customers are expected to pay their accounts in the month following that in which they buy the goods.
    - Units will cost £16 for July to September inclusive and £18 thereafter. Suppliers are to be paid in the month of supply.
    - Mr Ben will withdraw £700 per month as drawings.
    - His other expenses are estimated at £400 per month payable in the month following.
    - Stock at 31 December is to be valued £18 per unit.
    - Provide for depreciation on shop fixtures at 10% p.a. and 25% p.a. on the motor van.

    Required:
    a) Prepare a schedule of payments for July to December inclusive.
    b) Prepare a cash-flow budget for the period July to December inclusive, showing the balance at the end of each month.
    c) Prepare a budgeted profit statement for the 6 months ending 31 December.
    d) Prepare a budgeted balance sheet as at 31 December.
    e) Comment on the expected results of the business. Make use of any financial indicators you may wish to illustrate your comments.

3. Smith & Jones wish to form a new private limited company in the name of S & J Co Ltd. The new company is to commence its operations with effect from 1 July. The data estimated for the period from 1 July to 31 December is as follows:

    - Smith is to put £50,000 into the business bank account on 1 July, and will be issued with 50,000 £1 ordinary shares. Jones will put £100,000 into the business bank account on the same date and will be issued with 50,000 £1 ordinary shares and £50,000 of debenture stock at 12% interest.
    - The sales will be on a credit basis and are estimated to be:

        July £25,000   Oct. £50,000
        Aug. £45,000   Nov. £45,000
        Sep. £65,000   Dec. £60,000

        All debtors are expected to settle their accounts *two months* after the month in which the goods are bought.
    - Purchases, all on credit, are estimated to be:

July	£65,000	Oct.	£45,000
Aug.	£35,000	Nov.	£30,000
Sep.	£50,000	Dec.	£45,000

Creditors' payments have agreed to be paid in the month following the purchase.

- Wages and salaries are estimated to be £1,750 per month payable on the last weekday of each month.
- Smith and Jones will each draw director's fees of £1,000 per month payable on the last weekday of each month.
- Debenture interest is to be paid 1/2 yearly, the first payment is due in December.
- Premises are to be purchased for £85,000 and paid for in August.
- Fixed costs are estimated to be £1,500 per month for the first four months of business and then increase by 20% thereafter. These costs are payable one month in arrears.
- Equipment is to be purchased on 1 July for £30,000, half of which is to be paid in July and the other in October.
- Equipment is also to be depreciated by 20% per annum on the straight-line basis.
- Stock is estimated to be valued at £40,000 on 31 December.

Required:

a) Prepare a cash-flow budget for the period July to December (inclusive).

b) Prepare a budgeted profit and loss account and a balance sheet for the half year to 31 December.

c) Prepare a draft report to Smith and Jones concerning the importance of budgetary control. Include aspects such as purpose, functions and problems involving the preparation of budgets.

[Higher National Diploma]

4. You work for a small manufacturing company that is developing a system of budgetary control and the following data is available:

Balance Sheet as at 31 May

	£	£	£
Fixed Assets			
Premises			50,000
Plant (orig. cost £10,000)			6,400
			56,400
Current Assets			
Stock	18,800		
Debtors	11,200		
Bank	600	30,600	
Current Liabilities			
Creditors	18,600		
Proposed dividend	2,000	20,600	10,000
			£66,400
Capital and Reserves			
£1 Ordinary Shares			50,000
Profit and loss account balance			16,400
			£66,400

Month	Credit sales	Cash sales	Credit purchases
May (actual)	£11,200	£5,600	£18,600
June (budgeted)	13,400	8,000	19,000
July (budgeted)	16,400	9,000	20,000
Aug. (budgeted)	16,000	9,000	10,400

- All trade creditors will be paid in the month following receipt of the goods and all trade debtors will take one month's credit
- On 1 June plant costing £5,000 is to be purchased (depreciation is charged on the straight-line basis of 10% pa. on cost)
- The following monthly expenses, to be paid monthly, are estimated as: wages £1,800; general expenses £700
- Rent is £3,600 per year, payable in full in June, for the year to 30 June the following year
- The proposed dividend will be paid in July
- The sales margin is estimated at 20%

Required:
a) Prepare a schedule of payments for June-August inclusive.
b) Prepare a schedule of receipts for June-August inclusive.
c) Prepare a cash-flow budget for June-August inclusive clearly showing the balance at the end of each month.
d) Prepare a budgeted trading and profit and loss account for the three months, and a balance sheet as at 31 August.
e) Comment upon the resulting profitability and liquidity position.

5. The following information relates to a businessman, P Jackson, who will be starting his enterprise on 1 July, with £5,000. He has made a forecast for the next six months concerning his cash flow:
   - Production will concern the making of an electrical component for the computer industry. His plan is to produce 500 units per month in the first six months.
   - Sales: each unit has a selling price of £12.50. The sales estimate for 6 months to 31 December is:

July	August	September	October	November	December	
400	480	480	560	640	400	(Units)

   - Variable overheads (based on output) will be £1.50 per unit, payable in the month of production.
   - Fixed costs will be £1,000 per month payable after the month of production.
   - Production wages (direct) will be £3 per unit payable in the month of production.
   - Salaries will be £500 per month until October but expected to rise by 10% in the months following.
   - Equipment, to cost £8,000, will be purchased in September. 25% deposit will be paid in September with the balance to be paid equally in October and November.
   - Materials will cost £2 per unit and suppliers will be paid in the month *after* the purchase.

All unit sales are on credit. Debtors are expected to pay in the month *following* their purchase, £5,000 was deposited in the business bank account on 1 July.

Required:
a) A schedule of payments for the 6 months ending 31 December and a cash budget to cover the same period.
b) An operating budget which will show the trading and profit and loss forecast for the 6 months ending 31 December and a forecast balance sheet as on 31 December (Note: closing stock to be valued at £6.50 per unit.)

[Higher National Diploma]

6. You work as an assistant to a firm of accountants who deal with a variety of financial and management accounts. One of their new clients is a partnership called Johnston & Buckley who have submitted their proposed budget figures to you. The new partnership takes effect from 1 July and its business is an estate agency. The data below is estimated for a six-month period, ending 31 December:

- Johnston and Buckley are to put £50,000 each into the business bank account on 1 July.
- The goodwill of the new business is estimated to cost a total of £24,000, payable in two instalments, 1 July and 1 October. Initially, this is to be treated as an intangible asset before eventually being written off.

The forecast of sales commission is estimated to be as follows:

	£		£
July	12,500	Oct.	9,000
Aug.	13,000	Nov.	4,000
Sep.	12,000	Dec.	2,500

All clients are expected to settle their accounts one month after the sales go through.
- Johnson & Buckley will each draw £1,800 per month, but this will commence from August.
- Staff salaries are estimated to cost £1,650 per month, payable in the month.
- Light and heat is estimated to cost £140 quarterly, paid by standing order, the first quarter being due on 10 October.
- Premises are to be purchased for £75,000 and motor vehicles for £10,000, both to be paid for in August.
- Motor expenses are expected to be £200 per month, payable in the month.
- General expenses are estimated to be £350 per month, payable one month in arrears.
- Rates, water, insurance and other various costs are estimated to be £1,500 per month for the first 4 months of business, rising by 20% thereafter. These costs are payable one month in arrears.
- Equipment is to be purchased on 1 July for £30,000, half of which is to be paid immediately and the balance in October. It is to be depreciated by 20% per annum on the straight-line method. The motor vehicles are to be depreciated by 25% per annum on the reducing balance method.
- Advertising is to cost £2,000, the first half is due for payment on 1 September, the other on 1 December.
- Accounting fees are £390 to be paid for in August.
- It is estimated that the interest on bank overdraft and bank charges will accrue by £2,000 and be paid on 31 December.

The partnership agreement indicates that 10% interest per annum is to be paid on capital and that profits are to be shared on a ratio of 60:40 in favour of Johnston.

Required:
a) Prepare a cash budget for the six-monthly period July to December, inclusive.
b) Prepare a budgeted profit and loss account* and a balance sheet for the half year to 31 December.
*There is no need for a trading account because this is an estate agency.
  Sales commission less expenses to arrive at net profit will be acceptable.

(Higher National Diploma)

7. A manufacturer planned to produce 5000 units a month. The operating budget figures were calculated as follows:

sales	£20 per unit
direct labour	£4 per unit
direct materials	£5 per unit
factory overheads	£7,500 of which 50p per unit is variable, rest fixed
distribution overheads	£16,500 of which £1 per unit is variable, rest fixed
administration costs	£15,000 fixed

The *actual figures* for one month were recorded as:

sales 4,500 units	£87,500
direct labour	£18,500
direct materials	£23,500
factory overheads	£7,250
distribution overheads	£16,250
administration cost	£15,500

Required:

a) Prepare the fixed budget and compare it with the actual figures noting any variances that arise.

b) Prepare a flexible budget and compare it with the actual figures noting any variances that arise.

c) Make appropriate comments on the findings from a) and b) above.

(Higher National Diploma)

Chapter 38

Capital Investment Appraisal

INTRODUCTION

In many business organisations management need to make financial decisions concerning various investment proposals or opportunities. Capital investment appraisal is an approach whereby a business can decide how best to invest its money for long-term capital projects and to try and ensure that the total funds coming into the business are greater than the cost of these funds going out.

For example, if a business had £100,000 to invest to replace some of it's fixed assets, which would they buy and why? Or, if it wished to invest these funds in some portfolio of stocks and shares over a number of years, what criteria could be used to measure which plan would be the best for the business?

Often, when large sums of money are to be invested, it will be essential to investigate the market and find out the kind of returns that are available so that management can make its best choice. Decisions concerning long-term future investments are often made on the basis of:

- the sum to be invested in a capital project
- the estimated returns from the projects
- the length of time the project is expected to last
- the economic conditions prevailing at the time, for example, the rates of bank interest to borrow money.

There are three major methods of capital investment appraisal:
The 'pay-back' method
The return on investment method (RDI) (or accounting rate of return)
The discounted cash flow method (DCF), including the internal rate of return (IRR).

The Pay-Back Method

This method approaches capital appraisal from the point of view of how long it would take a project to pay back the original cash sum invested. Note that in most cases, the calculations are at best, only estimations and what may look a good and safe bet at the time of investment may turn out to be a disaster. Cash flow refers to the actual movement of cash. Cash flow in is the cash received, the cash flow out is the cash paid. Net cash flow is the difference between these two flows.

When using this method of capital appraisal, the project with the fastest pay-back time in terms of net cash flow will be taken as the best, although each of the three methods ought to be applied before making the final decision.

Example 1

A business has £70,000 to invest and the estimated net cash returns (NCR) from each project over a given time of six years are as follows:

Year	Project A	Project B	Project C
	£	£	£
1	25,000	16,000	15,000
2	23,000	18,000	17,000
3	18,000	18,000	17,000
4	14,000	16,000	16,000
5	10,000	16,000	15,000
6	8,000	12,000	10,000
Total returns:	98,000	96,000	90,000

Which of these projects pays back its original £70,000 the fastest?

Project A   3 years 4.8 months (25,000+23,000+18,000+ 4/10,000 of 1 year)
Project B   4 years 1.5 months (16,000+18,000+18,000+16,000+ 2/16,000 of 1 year)
Project C   4 years 4 months   (15,000+17,000+17,000+16,000+ 5/15 of 1 year)

Project A is the fastest of the three although each project is estimated to pay back the original investment (in cash terms) taking 3 years and 4.8 months. The other two projects both take longer than 4 years to repay the investment.

Nothing is certain of course and it is difficult to calculate anywhere near a 100% degree of accuracy the net returns for each of these years. The fickle business of the economy could well put some of these calculations wildly astray. Interest rates could fluctuate between high, moderate or low over a period of time. Although only the first 6 years were estimated, it would be an advantage to forecast the returns over a longer period of time to see if there were any significant changes to net cash inflows.

The Return On Investment Method (ROI)
The ROI is the average profit for the project expressed as a percentage of the capital invested. This method is also referred to as the *'accounting rate of return'* (ARR). Note that this refers to profit rather than net cash returns so that depreciation would be a factor to take into consideration. If we were to use the same projects as above and take into account 50% depreciation for each of the total returns, what ROI would result?

Example 1 (Continued)
From the figures derived in example 1 above, and taking into account depreciation of 50% for each of the three projects, calculate the average ROI.

	Project A	Project B	Project C
	£	£	£
Total returns: (over 6 years)	98,000	96,000	90,000
less 50% Depreciation	49,000	48,000	45,000
Net profit	8,167	8,000	7,500
Average profit: (divide by 6 years)	11.67%	11.43%	10.71%

ROI is calculated for Project A as: $\dfrac{\text{Average profit} \times 100}{\text{Average investment}}$

$$\frac{8,167 \times 100}{70,000} = 11.67\%$$

Alternatively the average investment could take into account its residual value (if any) at the end of the appraisal period.

For example, if in year 6, its value was £10,000, then the average investment could be seen as £70,000 + £10,000 divided by 2 (beginning and closing values) = £40,000. Project A would then have a return of 20.4%. Whichever figure for the average investment is chosen, the concept of *consistency* must be adopted in that once applied, the same method is used for all projects.

The ROI is straightforward like the pay-back method but both these tend to ignore the fact that any money received in the future will be worth less than it is today. For example £100 spent in 1990 was worth far more than it is in today's money. This introduces the third method of appraisal, the *discounted cash flow* (DCF). Check that the ROI for Projects B and C are correct.

Discounted Cash Flow (DCF)
The discounting of future earnings is really the opposite in meaning to compounding interest rates. For example, what will a sum of £100 amount to in 3 years' time if the interest rate was 8% per annum?

$$PI = P(1+R)^n$$

PI   = sum + compound interest
P   = principal invested
R   = rate of interest
n   = number of years invested

$$PI = 100(1.08)^3$$
$$= £125.97 \text{ (compound interest} = £25.97)$$

Therefore, we could turn this around and say that a sum worth £125.97 in three years time, will only be worth £100 in today's money, given that the current rate of interest is 8%. If we invested £100 in some project now and in three years' time we received *less than* £125.97 then it would appear as negative and unprofitable if the interest rate was at 8% per annum. Alternatively, if the return was more than £125.97 then the project would look positive and profitable.

We can now look at the problem of future earnings at the going rate of interest on borrowed capital and calculate what these earnings are worth in today's value of money, that is, the present value of any future earnings.

The net present value (NPV) converts the future net cash flows into present values after deducting the original investment from the total. Discounted cash flow is a most useful method when trying to evaluate alternative investment plans on capital expenditure projects. The project which reveals the most favourable net cash flow at present values, would be seen as the most profitable.

Conversion Tables to Present Values
[see tables after questions section]

To find the present values of any future earnings it is found by looking them up using present value tables for a range of different interest rates. Each future net cash flow is multiplied by the appropriate interest rate known as the 'discount factor'. Note that this technique looks at net cash flow and not actual profit because it is cash that can earn interest, not profits. The selection of the interest rate to be applied will depend on the *cost of capital borrowed* to a business and this will determine the conversion of future values to current values.

Example 1 *(Using Discounted Cash Flow (DCF) Tables, Interest Rate 12%*
If we continue with our example of using an investment of £70,000 on the three projects where the business plans to borrow capital at a rate of 12% per annum, we can convert the estimated future values to present values.
By using DCF tables for each year's returns the results are shown below. To calculate the present value (PV) the net cash flow is multiplied by the year's discount factor at 12%:

Project A

	Net Cash Flow	Discount Factor 12%		Present Value (PV)
Year 1	£25,000	x 0.893	=	£22,325
Year 2	£23,000	x 0.797	=	£18,331
Year 3	£18,000	x 0.712	=	£12,816

This means that in year 1 a net cash flow of £25,000 will be worth only £22,325 in a year's time if the interest rate was 12% per annum.

Discount Factor: 12%

PROJECTS		A		B		C	
	Discount Factor	Net Cash Flow	PV	Net Cash Flow	PV	Net Cash Flow	PV
		£	£	£	£	£	£
Year 1	0.893	25,000	22,325	16,000	14,288	15,000	13,395
Year 2	0.797	23,000	18,331	18,000	14,346	17,000	15,181
Year 3	0.712	18,000	12,816	18,000	12,816	17,000	12,104
Year 4	0.636	14,000	8,904	16,000	10,176	16,000	10,176
Year 5	0.567	10,000	5,670	16,000	9,072	16,000	9,072
Year 6	0.452	8,000	3,616	12,000	5,424	10,000	4,520
		98,000	71,662	96,000	66,122	90,000	64,448
Less original capital			(70,000)		(70,000)		(70,000)
Net present value (NPV)			1,662		(3,878)		(5,552)

Note:
If you wanted to calculate the discount factor for any particular rate of interest or any given number of years, for example, at 12% for a period of 3 years, the formula to use is:

Discount factor:

$$\frac{1}{(1+R)^N}$$

$$= \frac{1}{(1.12)^3} \qquad = 0.712 \text{ (as indicated above)}$$

Results: Projects A, B and C

We can see at a glance that Project A is the only one of the three that has a positive NPV of £1,662 and is the best. The other two have net present values that are negative, that is, after the original investment has been deducted from total net cash flows, the value of money is less than at present values. The negative cash flow of Project B is (£3,878) and of Project C it is (£5,552) therefore these are seen as far less favourable than the first project.

Another way of looking at this is to say that if the business were to borrow £70,000 at a rate of 12% per annum, the initial outlay would not be covered by the net cash returns of both Projects B and C. The loan would not be paid off because there would still be a shortfall in value.

If the investment of £70,000 was on capital expenditure spent on plant and machinery, there could be some residual or scrap value to be considered. If the residual value of Project A was say £5,000 in the final year, then there would be an inflow of £5,000 x 0.452 = £2,260 in year 6, increasing the inflow by £2,260 to a total of £3,922 (1,662+2260) that becomes a better investment bet.

The Internal Rate of Return (IRR)

This is a further aspect of net present value in that the object is to find the discounted rate required which provides an investment with a net present value of a project that is equal to zero. To find this rate, a trial and error procedure may be followed in order to find the interest rate that returns to the business a net present value of nil, that is, providing neither a profit nor loss on the return.

If the IRR value is less than zero then the return is negative and means that the investment does not equal the desired discount rate of borrowed capital. If it is positive, then the return exceeds the discount rate and the project looks more favourable. Only Project A has a positive NPV at a rate of 12% the other two projects have returns that are negative therefore their IRR must be less than 12%.

For an investment of £70,000 at 12% per annum Project A would have shown a 'profit' of £1,662. Its IRR must be marginally more than 12% if its NPV is to be at 0. The internal rate of return is also referred to as the discounted yield method. We can calculate the IRR of Project A using the example below:

Example 1 using IRR: insert the following:

Calculate the interest rate when the NPV will be zero.

$$
\begin{array}{lll}
\textit{Project A} & & \\
\text{Net present value at 12\%} & & \text{£1,662} \\
\text{at } \underline{14\%} & & \underline{(£2,254)} \\
\textbf{Range} & \textbf{2\%} & \textbf{£3,916} \\
& & \\
\text{IRR} \quad = & & 12\% + \dfrac{1,662 \text{ X 2\%}}{3,916} \\
= & & 12\% + 0.85 \\
= & & 12.85\%
\end{array}
$$

The IRR for Project A is 12.5% where its NPV = 0. It can therefore be satisfactory
To borrow capital up to this rate before a negative value occurs. For example, if it borrowed at 14% we know that the NPV would be negative by £2,254.

Example 2

The net present value of Project D at a discount factor of 16% is £14,130 positive and at 20% it is (£5,840) negative. Calculate the IRR:

	Project D	
	Net present value at 16%	£14,130
	at 20%	(£5,840)
Range	**4%**	**£19,970**

$$\text{IRR} = 16\% + \frac{14{,}130 \times 4\%}{19{,}970}$$

$$= 16\% + 2.83$$

$$= 18.83\%$$

This project could therefore afford interest rates to be just over 18% where the returns would adequately cover the cost of borrowing, the NPV being at 0 at a rate of 18.83%

Conclusions:

If we take the results of the three projects:

	Project A	Project B	Project C
Pay-back	3 years 4.8 months	4 years 1.5 months	4 years 4 months
ROI	11.67%	11.43%	10.71%
NPV	£1,662	(£3,878)	(£5,552)
IRR	12.85%	less than 12%	less than 12%

It is clear that Project A would be the less risky of the three, receiving back its original £70,000 investment with net cash flows in just 3 years and 4.8 months. It would also earn marginally more average profit at 11.67% than the other two projects. It is also the only project that has a positive NPV and its IRR is greater than 12%. The other two projects suffer negative NPV's with IRR's that fall below the 12% rate for borrowed capital.

Note: DCF Tables are at the end of the questions.

KEY POINTS OF THE CHAPTER

Capital investment appraisal:	Investigation into long-term investment projects
Pay-back:	A method used to find out how long it takes to repay the original sum.
ROI:	Return on investment, the average profit per annum expressed as a % of the original sum invested
ARR:	Accounting rate of return (as above, the ROI)
DCF:	Discounted cash flow, a method that discounts future earnings to present values (PV)
NPV:	Net present value, when the original investment is deducted from the total present value
DCF tables:	Tables used to convert projected cash flows to their annual present values
IRR:	The internal rate of return (or investment yield) which should make the NPV of a project equal to 0.

QUESTIONS

1. A business owner has a choice of two investment projects. The estimated costs and returns are as follows:

	Project A £000	Project B £000
Cost	385	298
Year 1 Cash inflow (net)	228	-35
Year 2 Cash inflow (net)	123	53
Year 3 Cash inflow (net)	88	158
Year 4 Cash inflow (net)	70	245

Required:
a) Calculate separately for each project the payback period. The project chosen must earn a return of at least 14%.
b) Calculate separately for each project the net present value, given the table below:

Discounting factor:	14%
Year 1	0.877
Year 2	0.770
Year 3	0.675
Year 4	0.592

c) Advise the business owner which project is the better investment.

(LCCI)

2. A business owner has a choice of two investment projects. The estimated costs and returns are as follows:

	Project A £	Project B £
Cost	400,000	320,000
Year 1 Cash inflow (net)	-20,000 (loss)	25,000
Year 2 Cash inflow (net)	270,000	190,000
Year 3 Cash inflow (net)	360,000	315,000

Required:
a) For Project A calculate the payback period. Give your answer in years and months.
b) The payback period for Project B is two years four months.
   Advise the business owner which project is the better investment. Give a reason.
c) Using a discount factor of 16%, and the following table, calculate the net present value for Project A:

Discounting factor	16%
Year 1	0.862
Year 2	0.743
Year 3	0.641

At a discount factor of 18% the net present value of Project A is (£3,840) ie. negative.
d) Using this information and your answer to (c), estimate the internal rate of return.

(LCCI)

3. The directors of a company are considering the purchase of a machine for improving efficiency of production. The following data are available.

New machine

Purchase price	£175,000
Annual cost savings	£ 50,000
Estimated useful life	5 years

Required:

a) Calculate for the new machine the net present value corresponding to each of the two discount rates 12% and 16%, given the table of discount factors below:

Discount factors

		12%	16%
Year	1	0.893	0.862
	2	0.797	0.743
	3	0.712	0.641
	4	0.636	0.552
	5	0.567	0.476

b) Estimate the internal rate of return. The new machine must earn a return of at least 13%.

c) Interpret your answer to (b) and advise the directors.

(LCCI)

4. A business owner has a choice of two investment projects. The estimated costs and returns are as follows:

	Project 1 £	Project 2 £
Cost	88,000	155,000
Year 1 Cash inflow (net)	16,000	(10,000)
Year 2 Cash inflow (net)	40,000	140,000
Year 3 Cash inflow (net)	48,000	60,000
Year 4 Cash inflow (net)	30,000	30,000

Required:

a) For Project 2 calculate the payback period. Give your answer in years and months.

b) The payback period for Project 1 is two years eight months.
Advise the business owner which project is the better investment. Give a reason. The project chosen must earn a return of at least 15%.

c) Using a discount factor of 15%, and the following table, calculate the net present value for Project 2:

Discounting factor	15%
Year 1	0.870
Year 2	0.756
Year 3	0.658
Year 4	0.572

Using the same discount factor, the net present vale for Project 1 is £1,729.

d) Both Project 1 and 2 are expected to depreciate by 30% per annum. Calculate the annual rate of return for both projects. Use your answers to c) and d) to advise the business owner further, with reasons.

(LCCI)

5. A business owner has a choice of two investment projects. The estimated costs and returns are as follows:

	Project 1	Project 2
	£	£
Cost	70,000	75,000
Year 1 Cash inflow (net)	13,000	-11,000 (loss)
Year 2 Cash inflow (net)	32,000	50,000
Year 3 Cash inflow (net)	30,000	48,000
Year 4 Cash inflow (net)	34,000	34,000

Required:

a) For Project 2 calculate the payback period. Give your answer in years and months.

b) The payback period for Project 1 is two years 10 months.
Advise the business owner which project is the better investment. Give a reason. The project chosen must earn a return of at least 13%.

c) Using a discount factor of 13%, and the following table, calculate the net present value for Project 2.

Discounting factor	13%
Year 1	0.883
Year 2	0.783
Year 3	0.693
Year 4	0.613

d) The net present value for Project 1 is £8,193.
Use this and your answer to (c) to advise the business owner further, with reasons.

(LCCI)

6 A business owner has a choice of two investment projects. The estimated costs and returns are as follows:

	Project 1	Project 2
	£	£
Cost	215,000	154,000
Year 1 Cash inflow	44,000	(18,000)
Year 2 Cash inflow	96,000	115,000
Year 3 Cash inflow	90,000	76,000
Year 4 Cash inflow	70,000	57,500

Required:

a) For Project Two calculate the payback period. Give your answer in years and months.

b) The payback period for Project One is two years ten months.
Advise the business owner which project is the better investment. Give a reason. The project chosen must earn a return of at least 15%.

c) Using a discount factor of 15%, and the following table, calculate the net present value for Project Two:

Discounting factor	15%
Year 1	0.870
Year 2	0.756
Year 3	0.658
Year 4	0.572

d) Using the same discount factor, the net present value for Project One is (£4,884) and at a discount factor of 10% it has a positive value of £19,692.
Calculate its internal rate of return and then use this and your answer to (c) to advise the business owner further, with reasons.

(LCCI)

DCF TABLES:

% Interest rates (1 to 15%)

Future Years (n)	1	2	3	4	5	6	7	8	9	10	11	12	13	14	15
1	0.9901	0.9804	0.9709	0.9615	0.9524	0.9434	0.9346	0.9259	0.9174	0.909	0.9009	0.8929	0.8850	0.8772	0.8696
2	0.9803	0.9612	0.9426	0.9246	0.9070	0.8900	0.8734	0.8573	0.8417	0.8264	0.8116	0.7972	0.7831	0.7695	0.7561
3	0.9706	0.9423	0.9151	0.8890	0.8638	0.8396	0.8163	0.7938	0.7722	0.7513	0.7312	0.7118	0.6931	0.6750	0.6575
4	0.9610	0.9238	0.8885	0.8548	0.8227	0.7921	0.7629	0.7350	0.7084	0.6830	0.6587	0.6355	0.6133	0.5921	0.5718
5	0.9515	0.9057	0.8626	0.8219	0.7835	0.7473	0.7130	0.6806	0.6499	0.6209	0.5935	0.5674	0.5428	0.5194	0.4972
6	0.9420	0.8880	0.8375	0.7903	0.7462	0.7050	0.6663	0.6302	0.5963	0.5645	0.5346	0.5066	0.4803	0.4556	0.4323
7	0.9327	0.8706	0.8131	0.7599	0.7107	0.6651	0.6227	0.5835	0.5470	0.5132	0.4817	0.4523	0.4251	0.3996	0.3759
8	0.9235	0.8535	0.7894	0.7307	0.6768	0.6274	0.5820	0.5403	0.5019	0.4665	0.4339	0.4039	0.3762	0.3506	0.3269
9	0.9143	0.8368	0.7684	0.7026	0.6446	0.5919	0.5439	0.5002	0.4604	0.4241	0.3909	0.3606	0.3329	0.3075	0.2834
10	0.9053	0.8203	0.7441	0.6756	0.6139	0.5584	0.5083	0.4632	0.4224	0.3855	0.3522	0.3220	0.2946	0.2697	0.2472
11	0.8963	0.8043	0.7224	0.6496	0.5847	0.5268	0.4751	0.4289	0.3875	0.3505	0.3173	0.2875	0.2607	0.2366	0.2149
12	0.8874	0.7885	0.7014	0.6246	0.5568	0.4970	0.4440	0.3971	0.3555	0.3188	0.2858	0.2567	0.2307	0.2076	0.1869
13	0.8787	0.7730	0.6810	0.6006	0.5303	0.4688	0.4150	0.3677	0.3262	0.2862	0.2575	0.2292	0.2042	0.1821	0.1625
14	0.8700	0.7579	0.6611	0.5775	0.5051	0.4423	0.3878	0.3405	0.2992	0.2633	0.2320	0.2046	0.1807	0.1601	0.1413
15	0.8613	0.7430	0.6419	0.5553	0.4810	0.4173	0.3624	0.3152	0.2745	0.2394	0.2090	0.1827	0.1599	0.1401	0.1229
16	0.8528	0.7284	0.6232	0.5339	0.4581	0.3936	0.3387	0.2919	0.2519	0.2176	0.1883	0.1631	0.1415	0.1229	0.1069
17	0.8444	0.7142	0.6050	0.5134	0.4363	0.3714	0.3168	0.2703	0.2311	0.1978	0.1696	0.1456	0.1252	0.1078	0.0929
18	0.8360	0.7002	0.5874	0.4936	0.4155	0.3503	0.2959	0.2502	0.2120	0.1799	0.1528	0.1300	0.1108	0.0946	0.0808
19	0.8277	0.6864	0.5703	0.4746	0.3957	0.3305	0.2765	0.2317	0.1945	0.1635	0.1377	0.1161	0.0980	0.0829	0.0703
20	0.8195	0.6730	0.5537	0.4564	0.3769	0.3118	0.2584	0.2145	0.1784	0.1486	0.1240	0.1037	0.0868	0.0728	0.0611
25	0.7795	0.6095	0.4776	0.3751	0.2953	0.2330	0.1842	0.1460	0.1160	0.0923	0.0736	0.0588	0.0471	0.0378	0.0304
30	0.7419	0.5521	0.4120	0.3083	0.2314	0.1741	0.1314	0.0994	0.0754	0.0573	0.0437	0.0334	0.0256	0.0196	0.0151
35	0.7059	0.5000	0.3554	0.2534	0.1813	0.1301	0.0937	0.0676	0.0490	0.0356	0.0259	0.0189	0.0139	0.0102	0.0075
40	0.6717	0.4529	0.3066	0.2083	0.1420	0.0972	0.0668	0.0460	0.0318	0.0221	0.0154	0.0107	0.0075	0.0053	0.0037
45	0.6391	0.4102	0.2644	0.1712	0.1113	0.0727	0.0476	0.0313	0.0207	0.0137	0.0091	0.0061	0.0041	0.0027	0.0019
50	0.6080	0.3715	0.2281	0.1407	0.0872	0.0543	0.0339	0.0213	0.0134	0.0085	0.0054	0.0035	0.0022	0.0014	0.0009

Fig. 35.1   DCF tables 1% to 15%

Chapter 39

Legal Aspects: the Law of Contract

INTRODUCTION

A contract is an agreement between two or more parties that is legally binding as long as
it fulfils certain conditions. For example, if an invoice is sent to a customer, a contract can exist
between the buyer and the seller. The seller *offers* goods, the buyer *accepts* the goods at an agreed
price. Both parties need to benefit in some way and this is known as *consideration.*
The conditions that make a contract legal are:

- All parties have intended the contract to be legally binding
- All parties must have been eligible by law to enter the contract. No person under 18 or who is
  mentally ill or drunk can enter a contract legally unless it is for necessary items like food or
  clothing
- Neither party can have made a false statement in order to *trick* the other party into making a
  contract
- All parties must have entered the contract of their own free will there should not have been any
  force behind one party to secure a contract
- The object of the contract must not be illegal, for example, to defraud the tax office.

There are two types of contract:
1 Simple (such as when you send out an invoice to a customer).
2 Deed, special contracts that must be in writing and signed (such as a Deeds of Partnership).

Contract requirements
To make a valid contract there are **four** requirements:

1 One party must *offer* something to the other.
2 The other party must *accept* the offer.
3 Both parties must give something in return for what they receive known as the
   consideration.
4 There must be *intention,* that is, it should be legally binding for both parties.
   Business contracts are presumed to have intention.

Example:
A builder offers to build you an extension to your property at an agreed price on an agreed date of
completion. You accept the offer, the price is the consideration. Both parties have the intention that
it will be built. A contract exists.

Contracts are not always this clear-cut. Any of the stages can be implied by one or both of the
parties conduct. This means that nobody has to say specifically that they are offering or accepting
anything if they don't wish to do so.

The Offer
When an offer is made you can specify the date the offer expires and the way in which the
acceptance must be communicated. You could state that the offer you make will close at the end of
the day or the end of the week or end of the month. If you change your mind about this, once the
offer has been made, you still have the right to issue a revocation of the offer. That is, to withdraw

it as long as no one has accepted the offer in the meantime, or paid for an option, for example, to keep an offer open.

Do not confuse an offer with *an invitation to treat*. This means that where a person holds himself out as ready to **receive** offers that he may either accept or reject. For example, when a shop displays its goods for sale, this is not an offer, the shop invites you to make an offer. The display is only an invitation to treat. The shop can refuse to sell you the goods if it wishes to do so, by simply refusing your offer.

The Acceptance
There are a number of ways in which you can accept an offer, for example, orally, by letter, fax, e-mail, telephone, etc. The only time when you cannot choose is when the person making the offer has specifically stated the method he or she wants.
An acceptance maybe made by the following:

- Post - by post becomes effective as soon as it is posted (as long as it is properly
  addressed and stamped). Even if the person making the offer never receives the letter
  of acceptance, the contract still holds. This is known as the *postal rule* and only applies
  to acceptances.
- Telephone, fax, e-mail to the person who has made the offer.
- Conduct, for example, if you buy something by mail order and they send you the goods
  and you accept them.

Note that there cannot be a contract until the person who offers knows that his offer has been accepted (unless the postal rule applies). The person making the offer cannot say that silence will be interpreted as an acceptance. For example, if you find that a business has sent you goods that you have **not ordered** you are under no obligation to pay for them or even return the goods. The firm sending the goods needs to make their own arrangements to retrieve the goods.

The Counter-Offer
The rejection of an offer can be made in two ways:

- By simply rejecting an offer outright.
- By making a counter-offer.

For example, Alan offers to sell his bike to Annie for £25 but Annie rejects this and makes a counter-offer of £20. Alan then decides to sell his bike to Peter for £25 and refuses to sell it to Annie even though she has now offered to by the full £25. Has Annie got a contract?
No, because she first made a counter-offer that had been refused.

The Consideration
For a simple contract to be valid, each party must give and receive a benefit. For a simple contract to be valid, the conditions below apply:

- Both parties must give and receive consideration.
- The consideration must have some real value, although this may be a trivial sum.
- Both parties must commit themselves to provide something extra or new under the contract. In
  most cases the consideration is normally given after the contract is made.

Misrepresentation

If any statement is false or misleading in any way it is called *misrepresentation*.
This may have been done innocently or by negligence or by fraud. The remedy for any misrepresentation could be to apply for damages and or the rescission of the contract, that is, to cancel it.

Examples of offer and acceptance:

A Company sends a quotation to a customer offering to sell goods. The customer says he would like to accept the offer but not until a couple of months. Does a contract exist?
NO. For it to exist, the acceptance must be unqualified. The customer stated not until later which in fact becomes a counter-offer. The company did not make an offer on the grounds of a couple of months later.

Another company places an advert in a journal offering jeans at £8.50 each. An error had been made because the jeans should have read £18.50 each. A number of replies stated they would buy at £8.50. Does the company have to sell at the price advertised?
NO. The advert is only an invitation to treat and is therefore not a legal offer.

On 16 November a company sends a quotation to a customer offering to build a garage at a certain price. The customer accepts by post sending it on the 19 November. The company does not receive the letter until 28 November by which time they have increased the price with effect from that date. Is there a contract? Explain.
YES. Offer and acceptance and consideration all apply. The contract date is 19 November because postal rules apply and the price cannot increase.

The Sale of Goods Act 1979 (amended 1994)

All traders need to have some awareness of their rights when purchasing goods. The Act requires that goods correspond with the description and are *fit for the purpose* which mean s that they are of satisfactory quality and fit for the purpose they were intended for.

For example, if you purchased some new shoes and found that a month later that the heals had dropped off, you would have every right to be compensated by your money back or a new pair of shoes or at least have them satisfactorily repaired. Other Acts like the *Consumer Protection Act 1987* protect the consumer against goods that fail to meet certain safety standards, particularly electrical goods and toys for children.

Data protection

In July 1984 the *Data Protection Act* received Royal Assent and was the first piece of legislation in this country to protect information concerning individuals. The Act met two concerns:

- One, arising from the threat that misuse of the power of computer data might pose to individuals coming from the fact that computer systems have the capability of storing huge amounts of data and also the access of it from a wide variety of sources;
- Two, arising from the possibility that our international trade could be damaged if the United Kingdom were not to ratify the Council of Europe Convention of Individuals with the regard to Automatic Processing of Personal Data.

Personal data consists of information concerning individuals including expressions of opinion but excluding any indication of the intentions of the *Data Users* in respect of that individual. Personal data includes all businesses that keep records of their customers and suppliers, usually that retained on computer or manual records.

Data Users must be careful that the information they are asked for by other users does not suffer distress suffered by an individual's subject data. Data users may be taken to court to pay compensation for damages associated with any distress arising from the:

- loss or destruction of an individual's personal data;
- disclosure of or access to data without the appropriate authority to do so;
- inaccurate data that could be incorrect or misleading about the facts of an individual.

The Data Protection Act 1998 established rules for the processing of personal data and clarified the conditions under which processing is to be seen as lawful. All organisations concerned with the processing of personal data should register with the Data Protection Commission and be obliged to follow the principles laid down by the Data Protection Act 1998. Personal data must be handled correctly and information should not be processed unless it is:

- legally and fairly processed;
- accurate, relevant and not excessive;
- retained for a limited period of time and not longer than necessary;
- within the individual's rights and whose vital interests are protected;
- retained securely;
- not transferred to countries outside the European Community unless the data is adequately protected in those countries.

Any data that is deemed to be of a sensitive nature such as racial origin, religious beliefs, physical or mental health, should not be processed unless a person has given their consent freely. Persons have the right to know what personal data is being held by an organisation about them and have the right of access to it.

The Data Protection Act also reinforces the right of confidentiality and an organisation should not reveal to others without permission, personal information about its employees or its customers.

Chapter 40

Exams and Examination Success

INTRODUCTION

Many candidates go into examinations inadequately prepared. They have little idea what the questions are likely to be about and they may not have studied all of the syllabus.

Every candidate must know the full extent of the subject they are undertaking and they should have experienced a number of typical past examination questions in order to know what to expect, both in the coverage of the questions and the depth of knowledge required.

All major aspects of the syllabus should have been studied. It is always too much of a risk to think that a section of work won't be needed because there were questions on it in the previous year.

Exam revision

You should make a list of topics which covers all major areas of an examination. Revise each topic carefully and ensure you understand its basic underlying principles. For example, if you were revising financial statements:

- What are they used for?
- How are they prepared?
- How are adjustments such as accruals, pre-payments and depreciation treated?
- What accounting ratios could be used with the profit and loss account and the balance sheet?

Once a check list has been completed, questions concerning the topic, preferably from previous exam papers, should be attempted and mastered.

You will need to organise and manage your time carefully, to ensure you are fully prepared for the exams you wish to take. If you are attempting a number of exam papers, try to organise certain days of the week so that you spend adequate time on each subject: for example, Monday evenings, Accounting; Wednesday evenings, Economics: etc. Ensure you have sufficient exam questions to practise on and always try to obtain the recommended answers so that you can check your progress.

Wherever possible, nearer the exam time, try to set up your own 'mock exam' at a week-end and attempt to do four or five different questions within the time limits. Many examinations are of a 3-hour duration, so set yourself the requisite number of questions and a time to complete them. It is of essential importance to know how long you have to complete a question.

The examination

Always get to the examination room in plenty of time. Choose a desk where you think you will be comfortable (for example, at the back, front, or side) and make sure you have a watch or can easily see the clock in the room. Relax, breathe soundly and concentrate. The papers may already be face downwards on the desks. When you are allowed to turn the papers over:

- Read the paper briefly but carefully to get the general idea of it.
- Check how many questions you need to do and whether you need to attempt some questions that are compulsory and others where you are given a choice. You may be asked to do questions from different parts of the paper (for example, two from Section A and two from Section B).

- If you have to do *five questions* from a paper in 3 *hours,* this means that you should not spend more than about 35 minutes per question.
- Whilst you go through the Paper, try to make a choice of the questions you would like to attempt. This stops you rereading the exam paper over and over again.
- Attempt what you consider to be the easiest question first to give you some early confidence and help you get on your way.
- Although you will need to write rather quickly, try not to sacrifice presentation altogether. You still need to present your accounts legibly and allow yourself plenty of space for each question. The examiner is not impressed with small print crammed into limited space.
- Try to remember to use a fresh page for each question. If you need to alter some figures or add more material to a question, it can be done more easily if each question is on a separate paper.
- Use a ruler to draw lines rather than doing it freehand. Major totals should always be underscored. It improves presentation and makes your work look more organised.
- Try to finish the number of questions you are set. *Do not spend all your time completing just half of the questions.* The chances of you succeeding would be minimal, particularly if the pass mark were 50%.
- If you do have any time left at the end, always go over the questions again, checking to see if there are any obvious errors. If you do alter anything, strike out the error in pencil and insert the correction. Do so as neatly as possible.
- Ensure that you have your name and candidate number on the examination booklet and also on any extra pages that you may have used.

Finally, make sure that you prepare for your exams thoroughly, leaving adequate time for good revision. Whether you want to revise up to the very last minute or would rather have a pleasant evening off before the day of an exam is simply a matter of choice; but you need to work hard!

All best wishes with all your examinations but have a go at the foundation level below.

AAT Foundation Level Exam

SECTION 1

DATA

Julie Rogers is the owner of Rogers Fashion-wear. You are employed as her bookkeeper and you run a manual accounting system. The double entry takes place in the main (nominal) ledger and individual accounts for debtors and creditors are recorded in the subsidiary (or memorandum) ledgers.

The following balances were available at the start of the day on 1 May 20-3

Credit Customers:	£	
James & Dingle	1,080	
Harris & Co	8,198	
Jess Street & Sons	6,740	
Alan Jones	3,220	
Other debtors	9,307	28,545
Credit Suppliers:		
Nash Brothers Ltd.	9,455	
Brian Matthews Ltd.	7,945	
Other creditors	26,231	43,631

Nominal accounts:	£
Sales	133,856
Purchases	128,943
Sales returns	1,044
Equipment	2,900
Heat, light	1,444
Rent, rates	4,870
Stationery	877
VAT (credit)	2,485
Debtors control	28,545
Creditors control	43,631

Task 1.1

Enter these opening balances as on 1 May in the appropriate ledger accounts.

Transactions

The following transactions took place on 1 May in the books of prime entry as shown below. No entries have yet been made into the ledger. VAT is at the standard rate of 17.5%

Sales Day Book

Date	Customer account	Invoice	Total	VAT	Net
1 May	James and Dingle	2344	940	140	800
1	Jess Street & Sons	2355	2,162	322	1,840
1	Alan Jones	2356	1,410	210	1,200
1	Harris & Co	2357	2,303	343	1,960
			6,815	**1,015**	**5,800**

Purchases Day Book

Date	Supplier account	Invoice	Total	VAT	Net
1 May	Nash Brothers Ltd	6673	4,230	630	3,600
1	Brian Mathews Ltd	19934	4,136	616	3,520
			8,366	**1,246**	**7,120**

Sales Returns Day Book

Date	Customer	Credit Note	Total	VAT	Net
1 May	Jess Street & Sons	C122	**517**	**77**	**440**

Cash Book

Date	Details	VAT	Bank	Date	Detail	VAT	Bank
1 May	Balance b/d		2,890	1 May	Rent		705
1	A Jones		1,610	1	Nash Bros Ltd		3,500
1	Harris & Co		4,200	1	Light, heat	42	282
				1	Stationery	14	94
				1	Equipment	70	470
				1	Balance b/d		3,649
			8,700				**8,700**

Task 1.2

From the prime books above, make the relevant entries into the subsidiary and nominal ledgers. Balance the accounts and bring down balances as at 2 May. Check that the two control accounts match the schedule of debtors and creditors in the sales and purchase ledgers..

Further information

Other balances to be transferred to the trial balance:

	£
motor vehicles	8,435
o/stock	7,800
petty cash	250
purchases returns	2,972
wages	22,140
insurance	890
telephone	1,344
motor expenses	2,475
general expenses	1, 890
capital	37,433
drawings	3,640

Task 1.3

Transfer the balances from the accounts you have prepared and the bank balance to the trial balance and include the remaining balances above and total up the debit and credit entries. Prepare the trial balance.

SECTION 2

Task 2.1

A remittance advice has been received by Rogers Fashion-wear, for £385 payment being made by BACS. What will be the entries in the nominal ledger?

Provide two advantages of being paid by using BACS transfer.

Task 2.2

A cheque is paid to a supplier. Explain the three parties to a cheque, the payee, the *Drawee* and the *Drawer*. Provide two advantages that a current account has over the deposit account.

Task 2.3

A supplier of Rogers Fashion-wear has given the business a discount of £25. What will the accounting entries be in the nominal ledger?

Task 2.4

In which primary records would the following documents be entered?

a) invoices issued from suppliers
b) credit note received from suppliers
c) bad debts written off
d) petty cash voucher for a receipt of payment

Task 2.5

Provide three reasons why a creditors control account should be maintained.

Task 2.6

Rogers Fashion-wear maintains a petty cash book and a cash control account. Provide two details that would be shown in the petty cash book but not in the control account.

Task 2.7
Rogers Fashion-wear is considering changing from a manual to a computerised accounting system. Give three advantages this would bring.

Task 2.8
The following errors have been made in the nominal ledger:
a) A sum of £30 discount allowed has been credited to the bank interest received account.
b) receipt from cash sales of £300 (ignore VAT) has been incorrectly credited to the bank account and debited to sales.
c) A telephone bill of £105 has been entered in the cash book as £150 and posted as this sum.
d) The purchases account has been overstated by £200.

You are to prepare journal entries to correct the above errors. Note that the *suspense account* has a credit balance of £140.

2.9
The following is a summary of sales activities during the month of May:

	£
1 May balance of debtors	18,545
31 credit sales	19,550
received from debtors	15,125
credit notes to debtors	700
discount given to debtors	80
journal debit to correct error	140
bad debt written off	300

The following balances (debit) were in the sales ledger on 31 May:

	£
James & Dingle	3,120
Harris & Son	2,260
Jess Street and Sons	955
Alan Jones	3,488
Robertson's Co.	10,025
Browns	2,482

a) Prepare the debtors control account for 31 May.

b) Compare the control account balance with the list of debtors. If there is a discrepancy, what may have been the cause of it? Provide two reasons.

2.10 On 25 May, Rogers Fashion-wear received the following bank statement:

NATWEST BANK PLC
PO BOX 3
BOURNEMOUTH

To: Rogers Fashion-wear   Account No. 44432111   25 May 20-
STATEMENT OF ACCOUNT

Date	Details	Payments	Receipts	Balance
3 May	balance b/f			5,020 Cr
4	111605	3,500		1,520
4	111606	1,200		320
6	giro credit		2,500	2,820
11	111608	1,850		970
11	Direct debit (insurance)	440		530
16	Direct debit (electricity)	670		140 Dr
22	Standing order (rates)	300		440
24	giro credit		2,800	2,360 Cr
25	bank charges	85		2,275

The cash book on the 25 May is shown as:
Cash Book

		£			£
1 May	balance b/d	5,020	3 May	Nash Bros	3,500
3	A Jones	2,500	3	Matthews	1,200
20	Harris	2,800	5	Harrison's	1,850
25	sales	475	14	motor expense	45
			20	telephone	138
			23	petty cash	88
			25	Johnson's	422

Required:
a) Up-date the cash book with items from the bank statement
b) Total up the cash book and bring down the balance.
c) Prepare the bank reconciliation statement for the period to 25 May.

PAPER 2 FINANCIAL RECORDS AND PREPARING ACCOUNTS (FRA)

Intermediate level

SECTION 1
You work for a local group of accountants as an assistant specialising in small business accounts. A client, Harry Jones is a retailer who does not keep all the appropriate accounting books although he has a summarised bank account. At the beginning of the financial year, 1 January, 20-3 his accounts had the following balances:

	Debit £	Credit £
premises	50,000	
equipment	10,000	
provision for depreciation of equipment		4,250
motor vehicle	3,500	
debtors, creditors	2,750	2,600
stock	4,780	
bank loan		40,400
rates in advance	70	
wages accrued		100
capital		25,750

His summarised bank account for the year:

Receipts		Payments	
balance (1 Jan)	2,000	to suppliers	38,550
cash & customer sales	47,250	light, heat	295
rent received	1,510	advertising	300
		wages	1,550
		drawings	2,375
		rates	250
		motor expenses	750
		new equipment	3,000
		general expenses	505
		balance c/d	3,185
	50,760		50,760

Note:
Discounts to customers £225; discounts from suppliers £550

Further information at 31 December 20-3:
- debtors £1,800, Creditors £2,465
- the motor vehicle is to be re-valued to £3,000
- during the year Harry part-exchanged some of his equipment originally costing £3,000 in 20-0
- for new equipment (shown in payments). Trade in value was £800. Depreciation is 25% per annum reducing balance method. A full years depreciation is charged on acquisition, but none on disposal.
- motor vehicle insurance (part of motor expenses) was paid in June 20-3 £240 for the year

Task 1.1
Prepare the sales ledger and purchase ledger control accounts for the year ended 31 December, 20-3

Task 1.2
Calculate the net book value of the equipment that was part-exchanged during the year.

Task 1.3
Prepare the fixed asset disposal account for the year ending 31 December, 20-3

Task 1.4
Calculate the cost of the replacement equipment purchased during the year.

Task 1.5
Calculate the revised total equipment cost as on 31 December, 20-3

Task 1.6
Calculate the depreciation charge for the year ending 31 December, 20-3

Task 1.7
Calculate the updated accumulated depreciation as at 31 December, 20-3

Task 1.8
Calculate the adjustment necessary as at 31 December, 20-3 for the motor vehicle insurance paid for in June of that year. Name the appropriate accounting concept and the relevant FRS that applies.

Task 1.9
Prepare a trial balance as at 31 December, 20-3, taking into account your answers to all the above tasks and all other information you have been given (this will include depreciation and the adjustment in Task 1.8 above).

Task 1.10
Harry has a constant 20% mark-up on all his purchases. Using the answers to your control account figures, recalculate the sales for the year and note down any difference arising in your answer. Offer a possible explanation of any discrepancy.

SECTION 2
Jack and Jill are the owners of a business that sells computer parts to large retailing organisations. The business uses an integrated computerised accounting system consisting of the ledgers and stock control. You work as an accounting assistant in a local accountant's business and you have been asked to prepare the financial statements of the partnership.
The trial balance for the year ended 31 December 20-3 was taken from the computerised accounting system:

Trial Balance of Jack & Jill as at year ended 31 December, 20-3

	Debit £	Credit £
sales		248,400
purchases	124,800	
advertising	1,085	
accounting fees	870	
office expenses	2,100	
rent, rates	19,000	
telephone	2,655	
wages	49,200	
light, heat	1,315	
general expenses	490	
capital account: Jack		20,000
Jill		25,000
current account: Jack		850
Jill	220	
drawings: Jack	9,520	
Jill	14,200	
equipment (at cost)	32,000	
provision for depreciation		8,000
motor vehicle	10,500	
provision for depreciation		3,500
premises	31,000	
opening stock (1 January)	9,100	
debtors	2,500	
bank	8,170	
prepayments	345	
creditors		7,215
VAT		2,980
accruals		3,125
	319,070	**319,070**

NOTES:

a) Closing stock value at stocktaking, 31 December, 20-3 was £12,420
b) Depreciation is to be charged as follows:
   both on the motor vehicle and the equipment at 25% reducing balance
c) The closing stock balance taken from the computerised system did not include some
   items listed below that had been reduced in value at the year end:

Code No.	Stock Quantity	Cost (per unit)	Net Realisable Value (per unit)
1125	100	£10	£5
1180	10	£80	£20
1190	85	£12.50	£15.50

d) An electricity bill still due to be paid at the year end £125.
e) Rent and rates cost £1,500 per month throughout the year.
f) In the office expenses account there was a bill £150 that was paid for advertising in the
   local paper.

Task 2.1
Prepare suitable journal entries to record the above adjustments required to the accounts. Narratives not required.

Task 2.2
Prepare a profit and loss account for the partnership of Jack and Jill for the year ending 31 December, 20-3 clearly showing both gross and net profit.

Additional data:

The partnership agreement between Jack and Jill has allowed for the following:

a) partnership salaries awarded to Jack£8,500 and to Jill £12,000
b) interest allowed on capital accounts at 5% per annum
c) share of remaining profits effective to 30 June 20-3
   Jack 40% and Jill 60%
d) share of profits effective after 30 June 20-3 to be shared equally.

Task 2.3
Prepare the profit and loss appropriation account for the year ending 31 December, 20-3

Task 2.4
Prepare the partners current accounts for the year ending 31 December, 20-3

Task 2.5
Jack asks you some questions relating to goodwill because he is not sure what it actually means. In a memo to Jack, explain as briefly as possible what goodwill is and how it is normally treated in the accounts including the possible effect on the profit sharing ratio between partners.

GLOSSARY

ABSORPTION COST	A cost that has both direct and indirect costs charged to a unit and is linked to cost plus pricing.
ACCOUNT	A formal record of one or more business transactions expressed in monetary terms and recorded in a ledger. It also refers to the financial statements, that is, the profit & loss account.
ACCOUNTING	The recording of business transactions to enable information to be reported in various forms. Branches include financial, cost and management accounting.
ACCOUNTING BASES	Various methods applied to accounting concepts to use in practice, for example, using either the straight line or reducing balance method of depreciation or using FIFO to value stocks of raw materials. The base a business adopts will form the accounting policies it chooses.
ACCOUNTING CONCEPT	The ideas/rules used in standard accounting practice under FRS18, that is, going concern, accruals, consistency and prudence.
ACCOUNTING EQUATION	Assets = capital plus liabilities and is the basis for the balance sheet.
ACCOUNTING SYSTEM	The model or process whereby business transactions are recorded through documents that are fed into journals and ledgers, trial balance and financial statements.
ACCRUAL	The accounting treatment of expense incurred but not ye paid in one financial year but paid in the next financial year.
ADVICE NOTE	Note that advises the buyer when and where a delivery is to take place.
AMORTISATION	A form of depreciation applied to a lease losing its value over a period of time, the straight line method adopted.
ANNUAL REPORTS	Limited companies are required by law to submit their annual reports, that is, their financial statements, including Auditor's, Director's and Chairman's statements.
APPORTIONMENT	Overheads divided between cost centres using the relevant basis such as floor area or number of employees.
APPRECIATION	Opposite to depreciation whereby a fixed asset could increase in value, for example, land and buildings.
APPROPRIATION A/C	An account that shows how profit or loss is to be divided. Used in partnership and company accounts.
ASSET	Any resource owned by a business, tangible or intangible, for example, premises, equipment, stock, cash. Divided into the two basic categories of fixed and current assets.
AUDIT	An examination of the accounts and supporting records by an independent accountant. Maybe employed internally to check accounting figures or externally by auditors, to provide in their opinion, 'a true and fair view' of a business's performance.
AUDITOR	The person who carries out the audit.
BAD DEBT	An amount receivable but deemed to be not collectable and written off.
BAD DEBT PROVISION	A charge to profit & loss to cover any doubtful debts that maybe written off at a later date in the financial period
BALANCE	The difference between the debit and the credit entries in an account.
BALANCE SHEET	A statement of assets, liabilities and capital held in a business at a particular time – the Position Statement.
BANK RECONCILIATION	A statement explaining the difference between the Cash Book and the statement issued from the bank.
BANK STATEMENT	The bank's position of all receipts and payments received on behalf of a business.
BOOK VALUE	The original cost of an asset less the cumulative depreciation.
BOOK-KEEPING	The process of recording financial transactions in the ledger/journal.
BOOKS OF PRIME ENTRY	Books into which transactions are first recorded before transfer to the ledger.
BREAK-EVEN	The point where a business's income equals its total cost and neither profit or loss is the outcome. It is calculated by the total fixed costs divided by the contribution (selling price - variable cost).
BUDGET	The expression of a business plan in money terms. It is a forecast for a period of time, the most significant being a cash flow budget that forecasts the bank position over the months that follow, usually six or twelve months ahead.
BUSINESS ENTITY	The business is a separate entity from its owners and private expenses of owners must be excluded from that of the business, that is drawings.

BUSINESS PLAN	A plan that outlines what a business intends and includes a cash flow forecast and marketing plan, often presented to a bank to obtain loans.
CAPITAL	Usually refers to the owner's net worth: that is, assets less liabilities.
CAPITAL EMPLOYED	Usually all assets less current liabilities.
CAPITAL INVESTMENT APPRAISAL	Methods used to make decisions when buying fixed assets, example payback, accounting rate of return, DCF and internal rate of return.
CAPITALISATION	Where some costs such as solicitors' and agents' fees are treated as part of the purchase of fixed assets and entered in the balance sheet.
CASH BOOK	A book in which all the cash/bank receipts and payment are recorded.
CASH DISCOUNT	An amount allowed for prompt settlement of an invoice.
CASH FLOW	Cash in and out of a business and could be expressed as the cash flow forecast or cash budget.
CASH FLOW STATEMENT	A statement prepared for limited companies which identified the inflow and outflow of funds, replacing the funds flow statement.
COMPANY ACCOUNTS	Controlled by the 1985 and 1989 Companies Acts, the shareholders are protected by limited liability. Accounts must be submitted annually to Companies House.
CONTINGENT LIABILITY	A liability (debt) that is dependent on what may happen in some future event such as a court case where money could be paid out.
CONTRA	The setting-off of matching debit with credit against each other.
CONTRIBUTION	The difference between the selling price and the variable cost. It can be used in marginal costing to calculate break-even or profit or loss.
CONTROL ACCOUNTS	Used to cross-check sales and purchase ledgers or stock control.
CORPORATION TAX	Calculated on limited company profits and due to be paid to the Inland Revenue.
COSTING	The calculation of costs in terms of labour, materials and overheads to find the unit or product cost and includes techniques of absorption, marginal and standard costing.
CREDIT NOTE	The document that shows the amount and other particulars regarding the reduction or cancellation of the amount originally invoiced.
CREDIT CONTROL	Monitoring and checking a business's customers to ensure they are adequately reliable and they pay their debts on time.
CREDITOR	A supplier to whom money is owed.
CURRENT ACCOUNTS	Used in partnerships by the owners to show their personal finances in the business including their share of profit and drawings.
CURRENT ASSET	An asset held for less than one year which can be converted to cash, such as stock, work in progress or debtors.
CURRENT LIABILITY	A short-term debt which must be repaid within the next financial year.
CURRENT RATIO	The working capital ratio expressed as current assets divided by current liabilities, testing the short-term solvency of a business.
DAY BOOKS	The journals or cash book, or books of prime entry used before posting to ledgers.
DEBENTURES	Long term loans normally secured on a company's assets.
DEBTOR	A customer who owes money to the business.
DEPRECIATION	The estimated loss in value of a fixed asset as a result of wear and tear or obsolescence treated as an expense in the profit & loss account and the cumulative depreciation deducted from assets in the balance sheet.
DIRECT COSTS	Those directly traceable to a unit cost such as direct labour or direct materials and also represent variable costs.
DCF	Discounted cash flow, a method used in capital investment appraisal to bring future values to present day values, using a discount rate.
DIVIDENDS	Received by shareholders from company profits, normally as so many pence in the pound.
DOUBLE ENTRY	The principle used in recording transactions whereby for each one there is a debit entry and a corresponding credit entry of equal value.
DRAWINGS	Any value taken from the business by the owner or owners and includes cash, stock, motor expenses or anything else for personal gain.
EQUATION	The accounting equation where assets = capital plus liabilities or capital = assets less liabilities.
EQUITY	The amount of money or resources invested by the owners. Ordinary shares are known as equities.
FINAL ACCOUNTS	The profit and loss account and balance sheet drawn up at the end of the financial year.
FINANCE	The earning and using of financial resources or the borrowing of finance through a bank or other institution.

FINANCIAL STATEMENTS	The profit & loss account and balance sheet
FIXED ASSET	An asset held for more than one year, such as land, building, plant and machinery, office equipment.
FIXED COSTS	Indirect costs or those that do not vary with output levels, such as rent rates and insurance
GEARING	The ratio of long term debt to capital employed that identifies risk. High gearing has a larger proportion of long term debt to equity where low gearing has a larger proportion of equity to long term debt.
GOODWILL	The excess paid for a business over the book value of assets minus liabilities being acquired on purchase.
GRN	Goods received note that records the receipt of goods.
INDIRECT COSTS	Those that do not relate to the level of output and are normally identified as fixed costs or overheads.
INSOLVENCY	Where a business is not in a position to meet its debts If the current ratio is less than 1, the business is technically insolvent.
INTANGIBLE ASSET	An asset which has no physical substance but possesses a value, such as goodwill, patents or development costs.
IMPREST SYSTEM	Most usually associated with petty cash, whereby a fixed amount of money is advanced to the Petty Cashier who is reimbursed on a regular basis for the amounts paid out on petty cash vouchers.
INVOICE	The document which shows the quantity, price, terms and other particulars regarding goods or services provided. The bill of sale.
LEDGER	The main book of account in which entries are recorded and divided into the purchases, sales and nominal ledgers. The cash book is also identified as a form of ledger recording cash and bank entries.
LIABILITY	Amount owing by a business to its creditors. These can be short term (less than 1 year to repay) or long term (more than 1 year to repay).
LIQUIDITY	The ability of a business to repay its short term debts from its cash or near cash resources that is, its current assets.
MARGIN	Profit expressed as a percentage of selling value.
MARGINAL COSTING	The extra cost of producing one more unit, or the focus on variable costs and contribution to estimate profit or loss.
MARGIN OF SAFETY	The difference between the break-even point and output level.
MARK-UP	Profit expressed as a percentage of cost value.
MATERIALITY	The idea that small items of fixed assets are not worth capitalising.
MONEY CYCLE	Cash flow from sales and other resources coming in and going out on the purchasing of goods and other expenses.
NET ASSETS	The total assets less the total liabilities of a business.
NET BOOK VALUE	Fixed assets less the cumulative (total), depreciation.
NRV	Net realisable value, the value of stock sold less any expenses in disposing it. Stock valued at cost or NRV, if lower than cost.
OVERHEADS	These are the indirect costs and can be identified as factory, distribution or administration overheads and note related to output.
PAR	The nominal or face value of a security.
PETTY CASH BOOK	A book kept by the Petty Cashier in which small cash disbursements are recorded. It's a subsidiary of the Cash Book.
PETTY CASH VOUCHER	Document supporting an entry in the Petty Cash Book
PACIOLO	An Italian thought to have arrived at using the double entry system first in order to assist merchants in their trading.
POSTING	The act of transferring entries from the books of prime entry to their separate accounts in the ledger or Cash Book.
PREPAYMENT	The accounting treatment of expenses incurred in the current financial year which relates to the next financial year.
PRICE	The amount charged to customers for goods/services.
PROFIT	The difference between revenue and expenses expressed as gross profit or net profit.
PROFIT AND LOSS ACCOUNT	A summary account which nets off all revenue expenditure against income showing as its balance the net profit for the accounting period.
PROVISION	An amount to be charged to profit & loss account to provide for depreciation or bad debts or contingent liability.
RECEIPT	A written acknowledgement of payment for goods or services received.
RESERVES	The retained profits of a company (revenue reserves) or other capital reserves (premium account or revaluation of fixed assets).

SHARE CAPITAL	The amount of money invested by the shareholders of a limited company and could be either ordinary or preference shares.
STATEMENT OF ACCOUNT	A statement prepared to show the amount due from a supplier to a buyer, normally sent on a monthly basis.
STATEMENT OF AFFAIRS	A report, usually prepared from incomplete records, that shows the assets, liabilities and net worth of the owner of a business.
STOCK IN TRADE	Goods held for subsequent sale in the ordinary course of business.
SUSPENSE ACCOUNT	A temporary account to make the trial balance totals equal until the error(s) have been located and corrected, clearing the suspense.
TANGIBLE ASSET	Assets that are real such as premises, equipment, motor vehicles, normally refers to tangible fixed assets.
TAX	Income tax, corporation tax, or VAT.
TRADE DISCOUNT	A reduction that is allowed to certain customers on a list price. Usually the greater the quantity of items purchased the higher the discount. (Bulk discount)
TRIAL BALANCE	A list of all the balances in the ledgers of a business to prove the arithmetical accuracy of the debit and credit balances before preparing final accounts.
TURNOVER	Net sales, that is, sales less returns inwards.
VALUED ADDED TAX	Tax levied by HM Customs & Excise on the supply of the majority of goods or services in the UK at the standard rate. Some goods and services are exempt tax or zero rated.
VARIANCE	The difference between an estimated figure and an actual figure. Used in budgeting to show variance analysis, that is, those that are favourable or adverse (worse than the budget).
WIP	Work in progress the value of goods that are only partly finished.
WORKING CAPITAL	Current assets less current liabilities (net current assets). If working capital is negative it can be identified as net current liabilities.

PART VI   SOLUTIONS TO QUESTIONS

Chapter 1 What is accounting?

1. Finance concerns the control and management of money, where it comes from and where it   goes and how it can be raised, for example, to start a business.
2. Bookkeeping is the first stage of accounting and involves the keeping of financial records taken from documents and written into accounts such as sales or purchases.
3. Without bookkeeping there would be no accounts for accounting to use and it would be difficult to prepare financial statements.
4. Financial statements refer to the profit and loss account and the balance sheet. They are prepared periodically for all interested parties in business.
5. a) All parties want to know whether a business is profitable, especially owners, managers, employees, government and banks.
    b) The government: HMRC for VAT and taxation.
    c) To help them organise and control the business and to enable them to make better, more informed decisions.
    d) To check that a business can meet its repayments, including interest charges.
6. Customers (debtors) want to know how much they owe and what a business can supply. Suppliers (creditors) want to know how much a business owes them and how creditworthy it is.
7. The profit and loss account informs about profit/loss and trading performance. The balance sheet indicates the business's financial position in terms of assets, liabilities and capital.
8. Financial accounting is concerned more with the bookkeeping side of business and preparing the profit and loss account and balance sheet. Cost and management accounting seeks to analyse, evaluate and interpret data to improve management decision making. It is aimed at internal management for the purpose of planning, controlling and making decisions, rather than for external users.

Chapter 2 Business Organisations and Sources of Finance

1. Bookkeeping's main function is the recording of financial information on a day-to-day basis and to classify and group this information into sets of accounts.
    Accounting needs bookkeeping records for the purpose of preparing financial statements (such as profit and loss account, balance sheet) to provide the interested parties with essential information about the financial aspects of the organisation.
2. The size of capital relates to the size of an organisation because the potential to raise capital depends on either one or more persons subscribing the initial finance. A sole trader has only his own resources while a Plc can raise vast sums because it can invite the public, through its prospectus, to buy shares.
    Other factors: the size of market available, the nature of the goods or services provided, the personal wealth of the entrepreneur.
3. a) Personal wealth, resources available, such as bank loan.
    b) Share capital, debentures, retained profits and loans.
4. The private sector refers to economic activity in the hands of private individuals, providing goods and services in order to gain individual benefit.
    The public sector refers to economic activity in the hands of the state, providing goods and services for the benefit of the nation.
5. Council Tax and borrowing from various sources, but mainly from the Government's Works Loan Fund.
6. By imposing taxes and by borrowing money if there is a budget deficit.
    PSBR – Public Sector Borrowing Requirement. PSDR – Public Sector Debt Repayment.
7. Government revenue: direct and indirect taxation.
    Government expenditure: Social Security, Health, Education, Defence and other government departments, such as Environment.
8. To regulate the economy, mainly by using taxation as a means of influencing demand for goods and services. To keep inflation under control; to invigorate the economy by providing subsidies and incentives for growth and investment; to stimulate employment through training programmes or financial initiatives; to direct the economy which will respond to the needs of the market.
    Direct tax – taxes on income, such as income tax, corporation tax.
    Indirect tax – taxes on goods and services, such as VAT, Customs & Excise tax.
9. Ordinary shares: true shares, voting rights, no fixed dividends. Preference shares: priority of dividends at fixed rates, no voting rights. They are less risky than ordinary shares.
10. Leasing maybe a sound idea if there is insufficient money to fund fixed assets or it may wish to use its resources for alternative purposes. With leaseback, money will be obtained by selling an asset such as property, then leasing it back at an agreed rental for a specific period of time.
11. Spending: education £78 billion, law £36 billion; revenue from VAT and excise duty £126 billion.
12. Control of interest rates and also keeping the Exchequer account.

Chapter 3 Introducing Financial Statements

1. Revenue and expense accounts are matched in the profit and loss account leaving capital, assets and liabilities to make up the balance sheet.
2. a) To match revenue and expense accounts in order to calculate profit or, loss.
   b) Gross profit = sales - cost of sales; net profit = gross profit - expenses + other income.
3. Gross profit £1,000, net profit £500.
4. a) Gross profit £16,430, expenses £15,640, net profit £790.
   b) Net profit added to capital in the balance sheet.
5. J Smith
   Assets: fixed £10,400, current £1,550, total £11,950.
   Liabilities: deferred £7,500, current £115, total £7,615.
   Capital £4,335.
   a) $\quad$ C $\quad$ = $\quad$ A $\quad$ - $\quad$ L
   $\quad$ £4,335 $\quad$ = $\quad$ £11,950 $\quad$ - $\quad$ £7,615
   b) Mortgage £7,000.
   c) Bank £5 Creditors NIL.
   d) On credit: stock £125, creditors £125.
   e) $\quad$ C $\quad$ = $\quad$ A $\quad$ - $\quad$ L
   $\quad$ £4,335 $\quad$ = $\quad$ £11,960 $\quad$ - $\quad$ £7,625
6. M Crooks
   a) Assets: fixed £53,200, current £16,375, total £69,575.
   b) Liabilities: deferred £33,500, current £16,075, total £49,575.
   $\quad$ Capital £20,000.
   c) $\quad$ C $\quad$ = $\quad$ A $\quad$ - $\quad$ L
   $\quad$ £20,000 $\quad$ = $\quad$ £69,575 $\quad$ - $\quad$ £49,575
   d) Just; by £300.
   e) Sell stock.
7. R David
   Fixed assets £16,000, Current £12,115 = £28,115
   Deferred liabilities £11,500, Current = £4,630 = £16,130, Net assets = £11,985
   Capital £13,985 less Drawings £2,000 = £11,985.
8. H Smith
   a) Balance Sheet: Assets: fixed £34,050, current £7,370 = £41,420 Liabilities: current £6,420. Deferred £24,000 = £30,420, Net assets £11,000. Capital £12,000 less drawings £1,000 = £11,000 b) Liabilitiesof £30,420 against £11,000 of capital. A strain to repay debts within 5 years.
   c) No. Only £100 cash available. d) Most of resources tied up in fixed assets
   d) e) C $\quad$ = $\quad$ A $\quad$ - $\quad$ L
   $\quad$ £11,000 $\quad$ = $\quad$ £41,420 $\quad$ - $\quad$ £30,420
9. R James
   Fixed assets £44,000, Current £12,000 = £56,000
   Less deferred liabilities £26,000, Current £6,250 = £32,250, Net = £23,750
   Capital £20,000 - Drawings £4,500 + Profit £8,250 = £23,750.
10. a) The profit and loss account indicates the trading performance of a business in terms of making a profit or loss in a financial period. The balance sheets indicates the financial position of a business in terms of what it owns (assets), what it owes (liabilities) and the net worth of its owners (capital).
    b) The profit or loss.
    c) C $\quad$ = A $\quad$ - L
    $\quad$ 23,750 $\quad$ = 56,000 $\quad$ - 32,250

Chapter 4 The Role of the Accountant

1. A wide variety of work that can be stimulating, challenging, absorbing and even exciting.
2. Auditors examine the accounting books to see that recording is as it should be and whether, in their opinion, the figures represent a true and fair view as to the state of a business's affairs at the end of the financial year.
3. Private practice can open up a wide range of financial services for different clients, whereas an accounts office will have more specialised work concerning its own affairs.
4. The day-to-day recording of financial information.
5. Her Majesty's Revenue & Customs; Pay As You Earn; National Insurance Contributions. Any tax or National insurance outstanding must be paid to HMRC.
6. The same type of information such as sales, purchases, stock, wages, etc., can be fed into a program and be automatically up-dated, analysed and printed out at the touch of a key.

Chapter 5 The Ledger System and Trial Balance

1. a) The ledger holds records of all the accounts of a business.
    b) To keep a record of accounts of individual customers and suppliers.
    c) The principle of double entry recording in that for every transaction one account will be debited, the other side credited. The trial balance would fail to balance and there would be incomplete information of accounts in the ledger.
2. a) A trial balance is an arithmetical check on the double entry system where total debit balances = total credit balances.
    b) An error or errors had been made in the ledger which need to be found and corrected.
3. Trial balance totals £8,485. Sales £3,135, returns out £100, capital £3,500, creditors £1,750 credit balances. Purchases £3,150, advertising £320, rent £480, drawings £500, bank £2,000, debtors £735 debit balances.
4. Green a/c £0, bank £135 Dr. purchases account £1,600 Dr.
5. Trial balance totals £13,800.
6. Titchmarsh: trial balance totals £10,420. Debits: returns in £35, rent £320, purchases £5,750, drawings £80, equipment £950, stock £2,500, James £785, credits: sales £3,535, returns out £130, capital £4,000, Smith £2,350, bank o/d £405.
7   Trial balance totals £7,318. Debits: bank £64, Jones £148, Belafonte £1,175, purchases £632, stock £2,150, van £2,750, equipment £399, credits: Diamond £100, Jake £2,475, Manilow £584, capital £4,159.
8. Trial balance totals = £1,260: Smith £415, Lillee £201, Thomson £156, Purchases £345, Bank £143 all Dr. Capital £18, May £195, Cowdrey £152, Sales £895 all Cr.

9.* **Ledger of Mrs J Boddy**
On 1 May: Assets £4,000, Liabilities £1,000, Capital £3,000.

Capital Account

		1/5 Assets	3,000

Van Account

| 1/5 Capital | 1,500 | |

Cash Account

1/5 Capital	2,500	1	Bank	2,000
10 Sales	120	4	Purchases	300
		7	Stationery	40
		26	General Exp.	80
		31	Balance c/d	200
	2,620			2,620
Balance b/d	200			

J Smith Account

12 Sales	180	27 Bank	90
		31 Balance c/d	90
	180		180
Balance b/d	90		

D Wheelbarrow Account

28 Sales	330	30 Returns In	33
		31 Balance c/d	297
	330		330
Balance b/d	297		

Rent Account

| 2 Bank | 250 | |

Stationery Account

| 7 Cash | 40 | |

Motor Expenses Account

| 16 Bank | 30 | |

General Expenses Account

| 26 Cash | 80 | |

Equipment Account

| 20 LS Ltd | 1,800 | |

Returns Inward Account

| 30 Wheelbarrow | 33 | |

Bank Account

1/5 Cash	2,000	2 Rent	250
17 Sales	23,524		
Sales	130	16 M/Expenses	30
27 Smith	90	19 H/P	100
31 Sales	225	20 LS Ltd	450
		31 Steele	500
		LS Ltd	270
		Balance c/d	1,080
	2,680		2,680
Balance b/d	1,080		

	Trial Balance Debit	Credit
Capital		3,000
Van	1,500	
Cash	200	
Bank	1,080	
H/P		900
Smith	90	
Wheelbarrow	297	
Motor Expenses	30	
Stationery	40	
Rent	250	
Purchases	1,600	
Sales		1,220
Daley		400
Steele		250
LS Limited		1,080
General Expenses	80	
Returns In	33	
Returns Out		150
Equipment	1,800	
	7,000	7,000

H/P Account (Van)

19 Bank	100	1/5 Capital	1,000
31 Balance c/d	900		
	1,000		
		1,000	
		Balance b/d	900

Purchases Account

4 Bank	300	
5 Daley	550	
14 Steele	750	
	1,600	

Sales Account

	10 Cash	120
	12 Smith	180
	17 Bank	235
	24 Bank	130
	28 Wheelbarrow	330
	31 Bank	225
		1,220

A Daley Account

18 Returns	150	5 Purchases	550
31 Balance c/d	400		
	550		550
		Balance b/d	400

D Steele Account

31 Bank	500	14 Purchases	750
Balance c/d	250		
	750		750
		Balance b/d	250

Land Supplies Limited Account

20 Bank	450	20 Equipment	1,800
31 Bank	270		
Balance c/d	1,080		
	1,800		1,800
		Balance c/d	1,080

Returns Outward Account

	18 Daley	150

Chapter 6 The Running Balance Method of Recording Accounts

1. S. Jameson. Trial balance total: £3,275. Sales £925, Capital £650, creditors: Robinson £450, Arthur £650, Brown £600 all credits. Purchases £1,450, returns in £50, wages £125, rent £300, overheads £70, drawings £250, bank £200, equipment £750, debtor Jackson £80 all debits.

2. R Lee: Trial balance total: £3,852.
Purchases £2,585, Jackson £250, Fanshawe £300, Bank £717 all Dr. Capital £221, Sales £3,198, Newman £433 all Cr.

3. F Smith: Trial balance totals: £29,051, Premises £20,000, MV £1,875, Stock £1,900, Bank £1,277, Rollin £500, Vines £450, Purchases £2,850, General expenses £115, Insurance £84, all Dr. Capital £6,263, Mortgage £16,750, Boston £2,950, Turner £600, Sales £2,488 all Cr.

4. J Briggs: Trial balance totals: £26,380, Bank £265, Premises £17,000, Fixtures £1,000, Cash £595, Collins £2,850, Smith £720, Purchases £1,870, Salaries £600, Repairs £260, Stock £1,200, Drawings £20 all Dr. Capital £20,000, Jones £1,055, Sales £5,325 all Cr.

5. G Harrison: Trial balance totals: £3,605. Cash/Bank £1,226, Lloyd £250, Jones £268, Purchases £1,195, General Expenses £57, Salaries £165, Insurance £54, MV £350, Drawings £40, all Dr. Capital £1,860, Bloggs £250, Sales £915, T Jones £580 all Cr.

6. L Dawson: Trial balance totals £44,980.
Debits: Bank £14,258, Cash £2,658, Purchases £9,500, F + F £6,200, Advertising £56, Rent £6,000. Wages £170, Insurance £400, P + S £38, Drawings £500, Redhill £3,100, Shaw £2,100.
Credits: Capital £30,000, Sales £11,480, Green £3,500.

7.* Jack Jones – Ledger On 1 March: Assets £3,350, Liabilities £1,150, Capital £2,200

Capital Account

	1/3 Assets	2,200

Equipment Account

1/3 Capital	550	
31 Rawlings	1,200	
	1,750	

Van Account

| 1/3 Capital | 1,800 | |

H/P Account

| | 1/3 Capital | 1,150 |

Bank Account

1/3 Capital	1,000	4 Furniture	150
8 Sales	125	12 Purchases	220
26 Sales	190	19 General Exp.	115
29 Taylor	150	29 Overheads	135
30 Sales	400	30 Drawings	200
31 Bright	225	Purchases	480
Balance c/d	50	31 Rawlings	240
		Guest	350
		Good	250
	2,140		2,140
		Balance b/d	50

Office Furniture Account

| 4 Bank | 150 | |

Purchases Account

3 Guest	350	
Good	245	
10 Good	300	
12 Bank	220	
30 Bank	480	
	1,595	

Sales Account

	5 Bright	180
	8 Bank	125
	11 Bright	85
	14 Taylor	300
	22 Bright	125
	26 Bank	190
	30 Bank	400
		1,405

Rawlings Account

31 Bank	240	31 Equipment	1,200
Balance c/d	960		
	1,200		1,200
		Balance b/d	960

D Guest Account

| 31 Bank | 350 | 3 Purchases | 350 |

J Good Account

20 Returns Out	60	3 Purchases	245
31 Bank	250	10 Purchases	300
Balance	235		
	545		
	545		
		Balance b/d	235

M Bright Account

Dr			Cr		
5	Sales	180	27	Returns In	40
11	Sales	85	31	Bank	225
22	Sales	125		Balance c/d	125
		390			390
	Balance b/d	125			

C Taylor Account

Dr			Cr		
14	Sales	300	29	Bank	150
		___	31	Balance c/d	150
		300			300
	Balance b/d	150			

General Expenses Account

Dr		
19	Bank	115
		135
		250

Returns Outward Account

	Cr		
	20	Good	60

Returns Inward Account

Dr		
27	Bright	40

Drawings Account

Dr		
30	Bank	200

J Jones
Trial balance as on 31 March

	Dr	Cr
Capital		2,200
Van	1,800	
Equipment	1,750	
Bank (o/d)		50
H/P		1,150
Purchases	1,595	
Furniture	150	
Sales		1,405
Rawlings		960
Good		235
Bright	125	
Taylor	150	
General Expenses	250	
Returns In	40	
Returns Out		60
Drawings	200	
	6,060	6,060

Chapter 7   The Sales Day Book

1. a) A bill of sale sent from a supplier to a customer.
   b) Each copy has a function, example, accounts copy, delivery note, etc.
2. a) Trade discount is given to traders usually for bulk purchases, cash discount is given for prompt settlement of account.
   b) On the net value of the invoice, that is, after any trade or cash discounts.
3. a) Sales £751.68, VAT £131.54, total invoice £883.22.
   b) Yes, the invoice is correct.
   c) The debtor (M Jones) is debited £883.22 [and the sales control account], sales is credited £751.68 and VAT credited £131.54.
4. a) R Carlton: SDB totals: sales £1,690, VAT £295.75, total £1,985.75.
   b) Sales ledger, Dr.
   c) Nominal ledger: sales and VAT Cr. Debtors total Dr.
   d) To cross-check accuracy of sales ledger. Double-entry already completed.
5. a) Sales £890.
   b) Arthur £450, Brian £160, Colin £280 all Dr. Sales account £2,130 Cr.
6. a) Sales £2,460, VAT £430.50, total £2,890.50.
   b) Debtors: Bremner £1,691.25, Gray £429, Lorimer £1,195, Jones £637.75, Giles £117.50 all Dr. in the Sales Ledger. Sales ledger control £1,180 + £2,890.50 = £4,070.50Dr.
7. Totals: Total amount £1,109.55, bats £755, balls £111.75, pads £242.8.
   Debtors: Brearly £420.46, Botham £99.75, Boycott £415.85, Bailey £188.38, Benaud £335.5 all debits in the sales ledger. Debtors control: £1,459.94 Dr.
8. a) Grant: sales journal, Sales £1,240, VAT £217, total £1,457
   b) Sales ledger: Debits, Goldney £423, Capel £399.5, Carlton £352.5, Wood £432, total £1,607.
   Nominal ledger: Sales £1,240, VAT £217 credits, S/l control £1,607 debit.
9.* Totals: Sales £5,930, VAT £1,037.75, Total Debtors £6,967.75, Jackson £657, Thomson £1,520, Illingworth £901, Rocastle £2,803, James £1,710 all debits, total = £7,591, equals S/L control account.
* Full Answer Provided
10. a) Totals: S161 = £840, S162 = £200, S163 = £560, VAT £280 = £1,880.
    b) Davies £575.50, Smith £352.50, Forbes £508, S/L Control £1,436.
    c) VAT account and each sales account would be credited.

9.*

Dawson's Ltd

	Sales	VAT	Debtors
Jackson	780	136.5	916.5
Thompson	990	173.25	1,163.25
Illingworth	660	115.5	775.5
Rocastle	1,500	262.5	1,762.5
James	2,000	350	2,350
	5,930	1,037.75	6,967.75

Schedule of debtors account:

Jackson	657	
Thompson	1,520	
Illingworth	901	
Rocastle	2,803	
James	1,710	7,591

Sales Ledger control account

	Debit	Credit	Balance
Balance c/d			3,623.25 Dr
Sales, VAT	6,967.75		1,059.1
Bank		3,000	7,591

Chapter 8 The Purchases Day Book

1. Value £917, carriage £35, VAT £166.59, total = £1,118.59.
2. The GRN records incoming goods that must be checked in and signed for. The driver's delivery note is also signed as proof that goods were delivered.
3. The control grid is stamped on incoming invoices to ensure a thorough check is completed and initialled by those authorised to do so.
4. Net value £945.00, VAT £157.11, total = £1,102.11.
5. a) Purchases day book of R Jones.
   b) Net purchases £157.87.
   c) VAT £26.94.
   d) Total £184.81.
   e) Purchases and VAT Dr. purchase ledger control Cr. Also Cr. Harrison's account in the purchases ledger.
6. a) Purchases day book £4,497.5, sales day book £2,420.
   b) Purchases ledger: ABC £3,937.5 XYZ £560 Cr.
   Sales ledger: Green £1,575, Jones £495, Smith £350 Dr.
   Sales account £2,420 Cr. Purchases account £4,497.5 Dr.
7. Purchases day book. Purchases £1,605, VAT 280.88, total £1,885.
   Purchases ledger: Mellows £646.25, Hudson £652.13, Paterson £470. Moorcroft, £117.50 all Cr.
   Purchases ledger control account £1,885.88, Cr.
8. a) Purchases journal: purchases £2,780, VAT £486.5, total £3,266.5
   b) Purchase ledger: Metro £1,210, Auto £1,004, Dunlop £352.5
   c) P/l control £2,566.5, purchases £2,780, VAT £486.5 debits.
9. a) Tom: Sales journal, sales £1,360, VAT £238, total £1,598. Purchases journal, purchases £2,680, VAT £469, total £3,149
   b) Sales ledger: Green £329, Smith £2,501, Jones £215 debits, total = £3,045
   Purchase ledger: ABC Co. £1,974, Hollins £1,363, Jenkins £235 credits, total = £3,572
   c) Nominal ledger: sales £1,360, p/l control £3,572 credits, purchases £2,680, VAT £231, bank £56, s/l control £3,045 all debits.
10. Total VAT £732.56, Footwear £1,862, Leisure £1,094, Sports £1,230 = Total £4,918.56. Debit each purchase account and VAT account. Purchases ledger control account £4,918.56 Credit.

11.

Date	Supplier	Invoice	Purchases	VAT	Total
4	Fox	3345	520	91	611
10	Skene	21219	740	129.5	869.5
12	Poynton	98942	180	31.5	211.5
14	Holliday	104	1,240	217	1,457
			2,680	469	3,149
18	Fox (returns)		(40)	(7)	(47)
			2,640	462	3,120

Purchase Ledger

Fox Account

18	Returns	47			
28	Bank	315	1	Balance	315
	Balance	564	3	Purchases, VAT	611
		926			926
				Balance	564

Skene Account

28	Bank	640	1	Balance	1,040
	Balance	1,269.5	3	Purchases, VAT	869.5
		1,909.5			1,909.5
				Balance	1,269.5

Poynton Account

			1	Balance	220
			12	Purchases, VAT	211.5
					431.5

Holiday Account

14	Bank	100	1	Balance	100
	Balance	1,457	14	Purchases, VAT	1,457
		1,577			1,577
				Balance	1,457

Schedule of creditors:

	Fox	564.0
	Skene	1,269.5
	Poynton	431.5
	Holiday	1,457
		3,722

P/L Control Account

28	Bank	1,055	1	Balance	1,675
	Balance	3,722	3	Purchases, VAT	3,102
		4,777			4,777
				Balance	3,722

Purchases Account

18	Creditors	2,640			

VAT Account

18	Purchases	462			

Bank Account

			28	Creditors	1,055

Chapter 9 The Returns Day Book

1. Returns inward day book. Returns inward £130, VAT £22.75, total £152.75.
    Sales ledger: Arthur £76.5, Brian £49.5, Colin £91.25 all Dr.
    Nominal ledger: Returns Inward a/c £387 Dr, VAT a/c £147.75 Dr.
    Sales ledger control a/c £217.25 Dr.

2. Returns outward day book. Returns outward £188, VAT £32.9, total £220.9.
    Bought ledger: Dick £186, Eric £43.6, Fred £49.5 all Cr.
    Nominal ledger: Returns outward a/c £540 Cr, VAT £92.1 Dr.
    Bought ledger control a /c £279.1 Cr.

3. Purchases day book: Total £9,605.92.
    Returns outward day book: Total £991.41.
    Dunlop's a/c £3,087.9, Metre a/c £3,395.75 Cr.
    Sondico's a/c £2,130.86 Cr. Purchase ledger control account £8,614.51 Cr.

4. Purchases day book: Purchases £2,580, VAT £393.75, total £2,973.75.
    Returns outward day book: Returns out £96.30, VAT £16.85, total £113.15.
    Purchase ledger: Trueman £1,771.50, Statham £580, Tyson £1,292.25, Snow £951,
    Illingworth £659.35, Old £861.50. All credit balances. P/L control a/c = £5,935.60.

5. Sales day book: Sales £510, VAT £76.5, total £586.5.
    Purchases day book: Purchases £370, VAT £55.5, total £425.5.
    Returns outward day book: Returns out £200, VAT £30, total £230.
    Sales ledger: Hunt £149.5, Speedie £247, Milton £230. All debits.
    Purchase ledger: Ball £287.5 Cr, Carlson £230 DR, Smith £138 Cr.
    S/L control a/c £626.5. P/L control a/c £195.50.

6. **J Smith: Sales ledger**

	Dr	Cr	Balance
Appleby a/c			
1 Balance			150 Dr
12 Sales	240		390
15 Returns in		10	380
25 Bank		150	230
Shuttleworth a/c			
1 Balance			210 Dr
3 Sales	150		360
9 Bank		360	0
12 Sales	160		160
29 Sales	160		320
Vincent a/c			
1 Balance			145 Dr
4 Sales	210		355
26 Sales	310		665
30 Returns in		14	651

Purchase ledger

	Dr	Cr	Balance
Morton a/c			
1 Balance			175 Cr
8 Purchases		470	645
8 Bank	175		470
12 Returns out	10		460
Pierce a/c			
1 Balance			184 Dr
8 Purchases		197	381
15 Returns out	15		366
19 Bank	184		182
29 Purchases		180	362
30 Bank	182		180

Chapter 10 VAT and VAT Returns

1. a) At monthly intervals payment by direct debit.
   b) Usually the invoice date or it a cash transaction, at point of sale.
   c) On form VAT 100 as inputs.
   d) The debit must be owing for at least 6 months.
   e) No, only those for business purposes allowed by the VAT office.
   f) As part of the expense, VAT is not separated.
   g) VAT recorded in VAT a/c as an input.
1. Sales £60,000 Cr, purchases £40,000 Dr, general expenses £800 Dr, VAT £3,360 Cr
3. VAT credits £9,875, sales £58,590, debits bank £9,875, purchases £41,860, balance £16,730 Cr.
3. a) VAT a/c, debits: purchases £1,687, returns in £140, equipment £147, expenses £126, o/payment £62, credits: sales £2,170, returns out £119, balance £127.
   b) Sales £11,600, (12,400-800) purchases £8,960 (9,640-680).
   c) Equipment £840, MV £8,850, expenses £720 all debit.
5. VAT a/c, debits: £787.5, £1,830.5, credits: £2,165, £997.5, balance b/d £544.5.
6. a) VAT inputs claimed 5/6 of £292,000 = £243,333.
   b) VAT a/c: sales £87,500, expenses £42,583, balance £44,917 credit.
7 Purchases £17,500 Dr, sales £25,000 Cr, VAT due £1,312.5, debtors £11,125 Dr, creditors £8,562 Cr, VAT a/c nil (paid)

Chapter 11 The Banking System

1 To keep money for safe-keeping, to lend money for overdrafts and loans; in the middle between savers and borrowers, provides a wide variety of services.
2. Deposit account is an investment earning interest.   Current account is a business account, using cheques for payment.
3. Cheque to be paid into a bank account.
4 Cash £480.41, other £165.92, total = £646.33.
5. Safety. Regular trips can be observed with criminal intent.
6 DD suitable for irregular payments which may differ in amount and at intervals which may vary. SO for regular fixed sums paid.
7 BGC (credit transfers) convenient for payments through the bank to pay bills, wages, suppliers. The payee is credited, the drawer debited.
8 Allows cheques to be paid using the bank's money as credit and can temporarily assist working capital difficulties.
9. Bank is free to decide how to use customers' money and has a duty to honour cheques and also act with discretion.
10. BACS and CHAPS are both electronic entries by computer transfer to make various payments to creditors. CHAPS is used for the more high value payments eg. Payment of a motor vehicle.
11. Debit cards directly debit the customer's bank account whereas a credit card allows a time of credit before payment is made to the credit card company.
12. Computer hackers can obtain customers' names and credit and debit numbers from web sites and can go on a criminal spending spree charged against these customer accounts.

Chapter 12 The Cash Book

1. To serve the need of different businesses, some wanting analysed columns, others more basic with single columns for receipts and payments.
2. The double entry has already been completed, the n/l used simply to total up discounts allowed and received.
3. a) Sales ledger: Cr customer's a/c £608 bank, discount £32. Nominal ledger: Cr s/l control £608 and £32 and Dr Discount allowed £32 (bank and discount Dr in cash book).
   b) Purchase ledger: Dr supplier's a/c bank £195, discount £5.
   Nominal ledger: Dr p/l control £195 and £5 and Cr Discount received £5 (bank and discount   Cr in cash book).
4. Cash a/c £661, Bank £1,597 Dr, Discount allowed £6, Discount received £40.
5. Cash a/c £369.81, Bank £932.50 Dr, Discount allowed £50.65, Discount received £28.
6. Cash a/c £388, Bank £336.80 Dr, Discount allowed £15.20, Discount received £7. Personal a/cs all Nil balances.
7. Cash a/c £62, Bank £101 Dr, Discount allowed, £13, Discount received £9.
8. Bank a/c £62.85 Dr, Discount allowed £22.5 Debtors £502.5, Record Sales £225.36. Other sales £901.44. Discount received £15, Creditors £1,435, Wages £280, Other £427, Drawings £275.

9.

R Lees: Cash book

Date	Details	Wine	Beer & larger	Sprits	Other sales	Total sales	VAT	Bank
2	Sales	200	250	80	30	560	84	644
3	Sales	50	200	50	20	420	63	483
4	Sales	180	240	60	24	504	75.6	579.6
5	Sales	300	340	100	60	800	120	920
	Week's	830	1,030	290	134	2,284	342.6	2,626.6

e)   All individual sales totals and vat are posted to their respective accounts on the credit side in the nominal ledger; for example:

Sales a/c – Wine	Dr	Cr	Balance	
5 Sundries		830	830	Cr
Sales a/c - Beer/Lager				
5 Sundries		1,030	1,030	Cr
VAT a/c				
5 Sales		342.6	342.6	Cr

c) This information assists management in the buying, selling and control of stocks.

10. Nominal ledger: all debits – advertising £20, telephone £100, motor expenses £15.75, rent £188, bank Charges £18.75, insurance £224..25, pc control £50. Credits – VAT £98.75, sales £700.

Chapter 13 The Bank Reconciliation Statement
1. Bank a/c £253 Dr. BRS: £420 + £90 - £257 = £253.
2. Bank a/c £699 Dr. BRS: £864 + £205 - £370 = £699.
3. Bank a/c £2,791 Dr. BRS: £3,084 + £404 - £697 = £2,791.
4. Bank a/c £206.35 Dr. BRS: £625.15 + £156.20 - £575 = £206.35.
5. Bank £630 Cr (Overdrawn). BRS: £893 (Overdrawn) - Deposits Cr £1,215 = £322 Cr
    – Un-presented cheques £952 = £630 (overdrawn). Cash Book errors: Debit £426, £500.
    Credit £840, £19, £23, £215, £99, £1,700.
6. Cash Book: Debits: £600, £420, £122. Credits: £79, £1,353, £90, £200, £70. Balance £2,200.
    BRS: £1,935 + £1,800 - £1,535 = £2,200.
7. Bank b/d £106, BRS: £602.5 + £345 - £841.50 = £106
8. Cash book: debits £142, £8, credits £1,689, £164, £310, £144, £46 = balance b/d £2,203.
    BRS: £1,784 overdrawn add deposits £800 = (£984) – un-presented cheques £2,259 = (£3,243 – error £1,040 = £2,203 cash book balance.

Chapter 14 The Petty Cash Book
1. It is a subsidiary of the cash book, required for small payments of cash and is separated from the mainstream of larger payments.
2. Use of vouchers, cash under lock & key and spot checks by a supervisor matching vouchers used with balance of cash.
3. Given responsibility for handling cash and recording and balancing accounts in the petty cash book and nominal ledger.
4. Petty Cash balance £23.15, Cleaning £27.59, Stationery £31.31, Postage £8.35, Sundries £9.60, No VAT, Reimbursement £76.85, Cash float £100.
5. Petty Cash balance £13.93, VAT £4.80, Cleaning £24.32, Stationery £37.65, Postage £17.80, Sundries £19.50, Packing Materials £32, Reimbursement £136.07, Cash float £150.
6. Petty Cash balance £39.26, VAT £4.30, Travel £8.35, Cleaning £16.30, Postage £13.28, Stationery £12.40, Refreshments £3.76, Sundries £2.35, Reimbursement £60.74, Cash float £100.
7. Petty Cash balance £9.80, VAT £4.19, Travel £13.27, Stationery £10.53, Cleaning £4.36, Refreshment £4.85, Postage £3, Reimbursement £40.20, Cash float £50.
8. Petty Cash balance £22.16, VAT £8.20, Post £29.61, Travel £32.80, Cleaning £31.50, Refreshments £23.49, Stationery £18.04, Sundries £34.20 £177.84.

Chapter 15   Capital and Revenue Expenditure
1. a) capital   2   a) capital
   b) revenue   b) capital
   c) revenue   c) capital

d) capital	d) capital
e) revenue	e) capital (or revenue if new system)
f) revenue	f) revenue
g) revenue	g) revenue
h) capital	h) capital
i) revenue	i) capital
j) revenue	j) revenue
k) revenue	k) capital
l) revenue	l) revenue.

3. a) So that profits are not distorted and fixed assets are correctly valued.
    b) Profit and fixed assets are under-stated by £2,320.

Chapter 16 The Trial Balance, Journal and Suspense Accounts

1. a) In most case yes but it is not fool-proof, errors can occur, where the trial balance fails to disclose, example, error of omission.
    b) It is convenient with its Dr and Cr columns to record the double entry required to correct errors.
2. a) Those that make the trial balance fail to balance, eg recording only one side of the double entry and not the other.
    b) Errors in documents example, the invoice, where the double entry is automatic. The type of errors the trial balance fails to disclose.
3. Journal entries:
    a) Drawings Dr, Salaries Cr.
    b) R Smith Dr, P Smith Cr.
    c) Office Equipment Dr, Purchases Cr.
    d) Rates Dr, Wimborne DC Cr.
4. Journal entries: Premises £20,000, Vehicle £500, equipment £2,100, Stock £1,860, debtors £675, all debit entries. Mortgage £15,000, Bank O/D £450, Creditors £1,155 and capital - T Jones £8,530 all credit entries.
5. Journal entries:
    a) R Smith Dr, J Smith Cr; Sales £600 Dr, equipment £600 Cr; Discount allowed £8 Dr, Suspense a/c £8 Cr; Suspense a/c £200 Dr, Sales £200 Cr; Suspense a/c £55 Dr, Salaries £55 Cr; Debtors a/c £275 Dr, Sales £275 Cr.
    b)

Suspense a/c Dr	Sales	£200	T Balance	£247	Cr
	Salaries	£55	Disc. All.	£8	
		£255		£255	

6. a) Suspense a/c Dr. Bank £2,490, Cr. T Balance £2,275 Discount £160, Cash £55.
    b) Corrected Trial Balance: Bank £1,245, Capital £34,900, Sales £21,900 and Creditors £4,230, all Credit balances. Stock £3,400, Premises £23,000, Furniture £900, Wages and Salaries £13,000, Office Expenses £860, Purchases £14,300, Drawings £4,000, Debtors £2,600, Discount All. £160, Office cash £55, all Debit balances. Totals: Trial Balance £62,275.
7. Underwood:
    a) Suspense a/c £248 Dr, Returns Out. £248 Cr; Purchases £200 Dr, Biggs £200 Cr; Vehicle Repairs £2 Dr, Suspense £2 Cr; Bradford £54 Dr, Suspense £54 Cr; Sales £100 Dr, Office equip. £100 Cr; Drawings £230 Dr, Purchases £230 Cr; Purchases £92 Dr, Suspense £92 Cr.
    b) Suspense a/c £248 Dr Credits: £100, £2, £54 and £92. c)   £10,584.
8. Hawkins:
    a) Suspense a/c £300 Dr, Pitman £300 Cr; Suspense £450 Dr, Sales £450 Cr; Discount Allowed £242 Dr, Suspense £242 Cr; F & F £90 Dr, Suspense £90 Cr; Knight £730 Dr, Sales £730 Cr; Heat and Light £233 Dr and Suspense £89 Dr, Motor Expenses £322 Cr; Stationery £180 Dr, Equipment £180 Cr.
    b) Suspense a/c Dr £300, £450, £89. Credits: £507, £242, £90. c) £22,878.
9. Suspense a/c: Debits: Trial balance £1,352, Stanley £8, Credits: disc. £100, sales £900, purchases £360. Profit £13,564 less: £100, £900, £9, £360, £15; add £20 = adjusted profit £12,200.
10 a) Journal: Equipment £500 Dr, Purchases £500 Cr, Light, heat £85 Dr, Bank £85 Cr, Discount allowed £68 Dr, Suspense £68 Cr, Suspense £800 Dr, Sales £800 Cr, Suspense £45 Dr, Smith £45 Cr, Returns In £87 Dr, Suspense £87 Cr.
    Suspense a/c: Debits: Sales £800, Smith £45; Credits: Balance £690, Discount £68, Returns In £87.
    b) Trial balance totals = £50,745.
    c) Those entries that exclude the suspense account would not be affected. The trial balance would still balance because the double entry is completed with an equal debit and credit.

AAT REVISION SECTION

1   Capital = assets - liabilities (or assets = capital + liabilities)
2   For every transaction there is a debit entry and a corresponding credit entry of equal amount
3   Dr bank, Cr sales; Dr purchases, Cr XYZ Ltd.; Dr drawings, Cr bank; Dr bank, Cr debtor
4   Those on credit are entered in the day books; those by cash are entered in the cash book. These are the prime books of entry. Posting from the prime books go to the sales, purchase and nominal ledgers. The trial balance is used to check the accuracy of the double entry.
5   Posting from sales journal: Dr customer's account, credit sales, credit VAT; also Dr s/l control.
6   Posting from the returns out journal: Dr supplier's account, credit returns out, credit VAT and also Dr the p/l control.
7   £560 + VAT £98 = £658
8   £900 - 5% = £855 (to calculate VAT) VAT =£149.62 + £900 = £1049.62
9   Opposite sides rule: the debit cash book entries are posted to the credit side of their relevant ledger accounts and the credit side of cash book to the debit side of ledger accounts. Exception to rule: discount accounts are posted to the same sides in the ledger.
10 Dr p/l control account £1860 and £50. Discount received account Cr £40
11 Returns in, -R, returns out, -E, drawings, -C, discount received, R, discount allowed E, cash, A.
12 Timing differences when transactions are recorded, particularly for unpresented cheques. Also the bank may make a number of direct payments through the bank like direct debits, standing orders and bank giro credits.
13 Tick the items that are the same on both sets of records (including any from the previous reconciliation) Those items left unticked must be actioned. The cash book is then brought up to date and the reconciliation prepared. On the debit side of the bank statement but on the credit side of the cash book.
14 To provide more analysis of data so that management can have better information about how stocks are moving and the type of costs being incurred. Also facilitates ledger posting of totals.
15 To correct errors; to write off bad debts and to make adjustments to the accounts.
16 Principle: an error where the wrong group of account is entered; example, equipment posted as a purchase of goods instead of a fixed asset. Commission: where the wrong account is entered but within the correct group, example, a gas bill posted to the telephone account. Compensation: a same error is posted to both the debit and credit account example, a cheque for £292 posted as £229. Original entry: where an error has not been detected on a document such as an invoice and posting has gone through with the error.
17 Control accounts such as s/l and p/l control can cross-check the accuracy of the sales and purchase ledgers with the control accounts. Also the total control accounts indicate the total debtors and total creditors that are used for the trial balance.
18 Credit cash book with sum to be reimbursed and debit the petty cash book. The petty cash control account can also record the reimbursement on the debit side.
    Analysis columns posted to the debit side of the ledger accounts because they are all expenses. Evidence: petty cash voucher, receipts from purchases, authority from supervisor.
    Petty cash is a current asset, petty cash expenses are expenses.
19 Usually at stock taking time when the closing stock value of one period (example, at the end of the accounting year), then becomes the opening stock in the new period.
    Purchases account when buying stock and sales account when selling stock.
20 Debit bad debts account, credit the customer's account and also the s/l control.
21 Its function is to check the arithmetic accuracy of the double entry system to ensure that for every debit entry there is a corresponding credit. However, it is not a fool-proof system because some errors as in Q16 are not detected by the trial balance.

AAT PROCESSING QUESTION

Sales ledger: Auto £30109, Salfords £44957, Ford Motors £31562, Other customers £648587 all debit balances. Total = £755,215
Purchase ledger: Carmart £36784, Lombards £61756, Lucas £39612, Other suppliers £504079 all credit balances. Total = £642,231

Trial Balance as at 1 June

	Debit	Credit
Sales		3,154,905
Sales returns	6,368	
Discount received		15,335
Interest received		225
Purchases	2,682,795	
Bank charges	471	
Discount allowed	21,486	
Debtors control	755,215	
Bank	1,324	
Other debit balances	1,431,500	
VAT		71,329
Creditors control		642,231
Other credit balances		1,015,134
	4,899,159	**4,899,159**

Chapter 17 Costing Principles

1. To assist management to make better, informed decisions concerning how much things cost to produce.
2. Absorption takes into account the total cost per unit in terms of fixed and variable cost. It ensures that a fair proportion of fixed costs are charged to the unit cost of a product. Fixed costs are seen as a significant part of the unit cost. Marginal costs focuses on variable costs and the volume of output and its effect on fixed costs. The cost of a product is linked to the variable cost per unit as the key elements of cost. It seeks to answer 'how much extra cost is involved in producing one more unit'.
3. Budgetary control assists management in the monitoring & control of costs comparing pre-planned costs against actual costs.
4. Establishing predetermined costs so that they can be compared with actual costs and any differences evaluated between the standard costs and the actual costs.
5. a) £16 per unit.
    b) direct wages, direct materials.
    c) £28,000.
7. Contract costing usually concerning long term projects such as building an office block. Job costing refers to the cost of a specific unit or group of units, eg a TV set.
7. Computerisation requires coding of products/components for proper control and analysis of stock: eg code 01334402, 01 (buying – shop 1) 33 (motors) 44 (electric) 02 (stock-components).
8   a) direct materials b) indirect labour c),d) direct labour e)indirect expense f) g) p & l expenses
    h) indirect materials i) p & l expenses j) indirect expense k) p & l expense.
9   a) so that costs can be identified into certain significant categories such as direct and indirect   costs.
    b) all direct costs - labour, materials and direct expenses
    c) direct labour, direct materials and all overheads (factory, distribution and administration)
10 a) £3.10 b) 0.84p c) £3.94 d) £6.12 e) £7.34 f) contribution £4.24, break-even 3561 units.

Chapter 18 The use of cost centres and coding of costs

1   A cost centre is defined as a location, function or activity where costs can be attributed to it.
2   A cost code is a system of letters or numbers or symbols used to represent a specific cost. They can be alphabetical and or numerical or both together.
3 Good management information is reliable, relevant and up-to-date.
4   It provides management with information about how and where costs are located that will help to identify and control costs in different areas of a business.
5   Because they often benefit two or more cost centres and a system of apportioning must take place so that a true and fair charge can be made to those cost centres.
6 a) To find out the value of sales for each product and which products are the most and
     least popular.
  b) So that any relevant analysis can be obtained and any account called up by its
     relevant number in the system
  c) All items coded with a cost centre's code can then be immediately attributed to that
     centre.
7 Centre A £120,000, B £60,000, C £20,000, D £40,000
8 Order No. 238: sales £800 - £80 = £720 + £8 + VAT £127.40 = £855.40
   Order No. 239   sales£740.60 - £74.06 = £666.54 + £8 + VAT £118.04 = £792.58

Chapter 19 Providing comparisons on costs and income

1 A budget is a forecast or plan of action about where resources come from and where resources go.

2 A key aspect of control is to monitor the budget figures against actual figures to see any variances that may arise and to take any corrective action that might be necessary.

3 Variance is simply the difference between budget figures and actual figures. A favourable variance means that costs are less than anticipated whereas an adverse variance means that costs are more than anticipated. A favourable sales variance means that sales were higher than forecast whereas an adverse variance would put sales lower than forecast.

4 Comparisons includes previous periods, or with forecasts, with competitors or even internally with other cost centres.

5 Only those variances which exceed a certain amount or percentage.

6 External factors could include shortages of supply for materials or energy or the Government may introduce some form of legislation or increase VAT, or demand for goods could suddenly either increase or fall.

7

	Budget	Actual	Variance
DL	4.8	4.87	7p adverse
DM	6.5	6.45	5p favourable
Overheads	5.7	5.65	5p favourable

The budget and actual figures did not vary by too much. The adverse labour cost could have been due to a higher rate of pay or more time could have been taken to produce 1 unit. The 5p favourable items for materials and overheads could be interpreted as cheaper materials or less wastage of them and overheads more efficiently used.

8 Little Ltd has better profits (£22,000 net against £17,000) although both net profit %'s show little difference. (5.6% Big with 6.1% Little). Interest charges for this company is much higher but other costs more in line with output. Overall, Little Ltd. has the better performance but if interest charges were less this could be improved.

Chapter 20 An introduction to wages

1 Harry £162, Jack £134.40, Fred £123.90

2 Tom £126, Dick £119.25, Harry £148.50

3 Charlie £52.50 + £43.12 = £95.62

4 Sales representative £885

5 Pamela gross £188, net £141.75

6 No.10 £198.45, No.11 £176.40, No.12 £222.60

7 Arthur: gross pay £226.80 less tax £17,40, pension £14, NIC £16.34, TU £1.10 = total deductions of £48.84, net pay = £177.96

8 Wages a/c Dr gross £138,815, NIC (employer) £13,000.55; HMRC a/c Cr tax £18,981.55, NIC (employer) £13,000.55, NIC (employee) £12,500.40; Pensions a/c Cr £1,055, Bank a/c £106,278.05, Wages control a/c Dr tax £18,981.55, NIC £13,000.55, NIC £12,500.40, pensions £1,055, bank £106,278.05, Cr wages £138,815, NIC (employer) £13,000.55, totals = £151,815.55.

9 Statutory deductions refer to those legally deducted on the authority of Government; that is tax and NIC.

10 Julie Harris - basic pay £182.40, overtime £82.80, total pay £265.20.

Chapter 21 Control accounts: sales & purchase control

I. F Smith: Sales ledger,control £4,820 Dr. A discrepancy of £260 with sales ledger. Purchase ledger control £2,240 Cr. Agrees with purchase ledger balance.

2. H Jones: Sales ledger control £11,501 Dr. purchase ledger control £8,991 Cr.

3. G Harrison: Sales Ledger Control £16,977 Dr. A discrepancy of £19 with sales ledger.

4 a), b) Rock Ltd:

Sales Ledger Control account

Balance b/d	51,400	bad debts	420
Sales	74,900	returns in	1,480
Bank (dishoured)	140	bank	47,360
		Contra (p/l)	800
		Discount allowed	1,840
		Balance c/d	74,540
	126,440		126,440
balance b/d	74,540		

Purchase Ledger Control account

Returns out	510	balance b/d	26,100
Bank	24,270	purchases	37,590
Contra (s/l)	800	bank receipt	460
Discount received	960		
Balance c/d	37,610		
	64,150		64,150
		balance b/d	37,610

Note that both cash sales and cash purchases are omitted from the control accounts because they are not associated with debtors or creditors.

The bank reconciliation statement would be another internal check, that is, the cash book with the bank statement entries. The sales ledger agrees with the s/l control account but there is £100 discrepancy that needs to be investigated between the p/l control account and the purchase ledger.

5   Zarak Ltd.

Sales Ledger Control account

Balance b/d	48,000	discount allowed	760
Sales	61,740	returns inward	1,750
Bank (dishonoured)	880	bank	51,720
		Contra (p/l)	750
		balance c/d	55,640
	110,620		110,620
balance b/d	55,640		

Purchase Ledger Control account

Discount received	980	Balance b/d	24,200
Returns out	430	purchases	34,720
Bank	23,890		
Contra (s/l)	750		
Balance c/d	32,870		
	58,920		58,920
		balance b/d	32,870

The control account help to verify balances in the sales and purchase ledgers with the control accounts in the nominal ledger to ensure totals agree. In the above example, the purchase control account agrees with the purchase ledger but the sales control has a discrepancy of £150 with the sales ledger that needs to be investigated and errors located and corrected.

Chapter 22 Financial Statements: Calculating Profits
1.   Gross profit £1,250, net profit £550.
2.   Gross profit is selling price less cost price of goods without the deductions for all other expenses which net profit takes into account.
3.   Working capital is required to finance day to day business in order to trade comfortably and to keep creditors satisfied.
4.   a) £88,000 b) £24,000 c)   £89,800 d) £2,400 e)£1,100.
5.   Wright: Gross Profit £8,350, Net Profit £5,975. Fixed Assets £25,325, Working Capital £3,900. Capital employed £29,225.
Capital £25,000 - Drawings £1,750 + Net Profit £5,975 = £29,225.
6.   Armstrong: Gross Profit £31,950, Net Profit £9,100. Fixed Assets £34,300, Working Capital £1,800. Capital employed £36,100 - Deferred liabilities £20,000 = £16,100. Capital £7,000 + Net Profit £9,100 = £16,100.
7.   F Smith: Gross Profit £3,280, Net Profit £2,000.   Fixed Assets £2,700 + Working Capital £1,300. Capital employed £4,000. Capital £2,000 + Net Profit £2,000 = £4,000.
8.   White: Gross Profit £6,057, Net Profit £3,128. Fixed Assets £14,410, Working Capital £248. Capital employed £14,658. Capital £12,730 - Drawings £1,200 + Net Profit £3,128 = £14,658.
9.   Robert: Gross Profit £15,820, Net Profit £6,780.   Fixed Assets £18,100, Working Capital £3,880. Capital employed £21,980. Capital £18,000 - Drawings £2,800 + Net Profit £6,780 = £21,980.

Chapter 23 Adjustments: Accruals, Prepayments and Drawings

1. The accounts would not correctly match revenue and expenses and profit (or loss) would be distorted.
2. Each of them would require a double entry, one in the p & l a/c, the other in the balance sheet, example, wages £150 accrued. Wages increased by £150 in p & l a/c and a c/liability in the balance sheet.
3. 2 months at £120 a month is accrued in the p l a/c and £240 is a c/liability in the balance sheet. L & h a/c: Dr £1,855, £360, £240, Cr p & l a/c £2,455, totals £2,455. Cr balance b/d £240 (accrued).
4. Wright: Gross Profit £7,770, Net Profit £1,373. Fixed Assets £15,010.
   Working Capital (-£1,837) insolvent. Capital employed £13,173. Capital £16,000 - Drawings £4,200 + Net Profit £1,373 = £13,173.
5. Rent a/c: Dr Bank £1,800, accrued £600, Cr p & l £2,400, totals = £2,400, accrued b/d £600 Cr.
   Insurance a/c: Dr bank £2,100, Cr, prepaid £550, p & l £1,550, totals = £2,100, prepaid b/d £550 Dr.
6. Insurance a/c: Dr bank £3,000, Cr prepaid £533, p & l £2,467, totals = £3,000, prepaid b/d £533 Dr.

7.* Jackson: Gross profit £20,490, net profit £14,853 (accrued revenue £240). FA £22,100, CA £5,580, CL £3,402, WC £2,178, CE £24,278 - £4,925 = Net assets £19,353. Capital £4,500 + profit £14,853 = £19,353.

8.* Andrews: Gross profit £26,418, net profit £18,353. FA £33,002, CA £16,910, CL £14,937, WC £1,973, CE £34,975 - £6,160 = Net assets £28,815. Capital £18,860 + profit £18,353 - drawings £8,398 = £28,815.

7.* **Jackson Trading & profit & loss a/c y/e 30 June**

Sales	77,615	
returns in	(205)	77,410
Cost of Sales		
o/stock	3,345	
purchases	56,470	
returns out	(315)	
o/stock	(2,580)	56,920
Gross profit		20,490
Less Expenses:		
insurance, telephone	430	
accrued	95	
prepaid	(105)	420
light, heat	446	
accrued	182	628
postage & stationery	450	
prepaid	(55)	395
discount		75
motor expenses		1,060
wages	4,785	
accrued	145	4,930	7,508
	12,982	
Add other revenue:		
rent received	1,545	
accrued	240	1,785
discount received		86	1,871
Net profit		14,853

Balance sheet as at 30 June

FIXED ASSETS			
Premises	20,000		20,000
Equipment	1,600		1,600
Motor vehicle	500		500
CURRENT ASSETS			22,100
Stock	2,580		
Debtors	2,400		
Cash	200		
Prepaid	160		
Accrued rev.	240	5,580	
CURRENT LIABILITIES			
Creditors	2,560		
Overdraft	420		
Accrued expenses	422	3,402	
Working capital			2,178
Capital employed			24,278
LONG-TERM LIABILITIES			
Loan			4,925
			19,353
CAPITAL	4,500		
Profit	14,853		19,353

8.* **Andrews Trading & profit & loss A/c y/e 30 November**

Sales		57,615	
returns in		(1,205)	56,410
Cost of Sales			
o/stock		2,355	
purchases		36,470	
returns out		(1,315)	
carriage in		442	
stock drawings		(4,160)	
c/stock		(3,800)	29,992
Gross profit			26,418
Less Expenses:			
main. & repairs		998	
insurance, telephone	334		
prepaid	(80)	254	
light, heat	546		
accrued	190	736	
postage & stationery	350		
prepaid	(110)	240	
discount		175	
motor expenses		560	
wages	6,285		
accrued	185	6,470	9,433
			16,985
Add other revenue:			
comm. received	1,520		
prepaid	(152)		1,368
Net profit			18,353

Balance sheet as at 30 November

FIXED ASSETS			
Equipment		30,502	30,502
Motor vehicle		2,500	2,500
CURRENT ASSETS			33,002
Stock		3,800	
Debtors		12,400	
Cash		520	
Prepaid		190	16,910
CURRENT LIABILITIES			
Creditors		12,560	
Overdraft		1,850	
Accrued expenses		375	
Prepaid revenue		152	14,937
Working capital			1,973
Capital employed			34,975
LONG-TERM LIABILITIES			
Loan			6,160
			28,815
CAPITAL		18,860	
net profit		18,353	
drawings	4,238		
stock	4,160	(8,398)	28,815

[

Chapter 24 Adjustments: Bad Debts and Provisions for Debtors

1.   A bad debt creates an expense to a business (Dr) whilst crediting the debtor's a/c (asset reduced) because the asset is lost.

2.   No. If the bad debt is transferred to the provision a/c (Dr), the overall sum to p & l a/c is the same as if the bad debt was transferred to the p & l a/c separately.

3.   Half the sum lost is reinstated by Dr the debtor and Cr the provision for bad debts a/c. The sum received is Dr bank and Cr the debtor, thereby zeroing the debtor's a/c. (The s/l control a/c is also Dr and Cr the same as the debtor).

4.   To be cautious in the event that some debtors might fail to pay.
      Calculations can be made on a per cent basis, higher % on older debts, less on more recent debts.

5.   Hunt: Gross Profit £4,950. Net Profit £403. Fixed Assets £1,900.
      Working Capital £4,003. Capital employed £5,903. Capital £8,000 Drawings £2,500 + Net Profit £403 = £5,903.

6.* Waugh: Gross Profit £150,100, Net Profit £57,400. Fixed Assets £89,000, Current Assets £52,740, Current Liabilities £14,340, Working Capital £38,400, Capital employed £127,400, LTL £25,000 = £102,400.

* Full Answer Provided

7.* Farney: Gross Profit £57,600, Net Profit £28,834. Fixed Assets £66,500, Current Assets £47,124 (debtors £20,974), Current Liabilities £7,550, Working Capital £39,574, Capital employed £106,074, LTL £10,000 = £96,074.

* Full Answer Provided

8.* Charcoal: Bad debts £6,370, Provision for bad debts £8,418 (75% = £2,558, 50% = £3,780, 10% = £2,080). P & L a/c: Bad debts provision £8,388. Balance Sheet: debtors £88,210 - £8,418 = £79,792.

9.* Bradshaw:

* Full Answer Provided

6. **Waugh: Trading and profit and loss account y/e ended 28 February**

Sales	319,200		
returns in	(1,200)		318,000
Cost of Sales			
o/stock	26,500		
purchases	173,200		
	199,700		
returns out	(800)		
	198,900		
- stock	(31,000)		167,900
Gross profit			150,100

Less EXPENSES

carriage out		4,000	
discount allowed		4,000	
motor expenses		9,200	
bad debts prov.		856	
rent & rates	12,400		
prepaid	(850)	11,550	
postage & tele.		3,100	
wages		49,800	
insurance		6,100	
interest	2,000		
accrued	140	2,140	
advertising	4,200		
prepaid	(146)	4,054	94,800
			55,300
+ discount received			2,100
Net profit			57,400

Balance sheet as on 28 February

FIXED ASSETS			
premises	39,000		
fixtures	15,000		
motor vans	35,000		89,000
CURRENT ASSETS			
stock	31,000		
debtors	21,400		
provision bad debts	(856)		
bank/cash	200		
prepaid	996	52,740	
CURRENT LIABILITIES			
creditors	14,200		
accrued	140	14,340	
Working capital			38,400
Capital employed			127,400
LTL			
loan			24,250
			102,400
Capital	60,000		
net profit	57,400		
	117,400		
drawings	(15,000)		102,400

[ICM]

8. **Charcoal:**   **Bad debts a/c**

Balance b/d	6,420	Bad debts rec.	850
Debts w/o	800	Balance c/d	6,370
	7,220		7,220
Balance bld	6,370	Provision for b/debts	6,370

Provision for bad debts a/c

Bad debts	6,370	Balance b/d	6,400
Balance c/d	8,418	P & l a/c	8,388
	14,788		14,788
		Balance b/d	8,418 *

* Calculated total 8,418:
   3,410 x 75% = 2,558
   7,560 x 50% = 3,780
   20,800 x 10% = 2,080

Extract from profit & loss a/c:
   Provision for bad debts   8,388

Extract from balance sheet:

Debtors	88,210	
- Provision	(8,418)	79,792

8. **Farney: Trading and profit and loss account y/e 30 November**

Sales		78,350
Cost of sales		20,750
Gross profit		57,600
Less expenses:		
Rent, rates	1,100	
Light, heat	700	
Carriage out	350	
Office salaries	25,800	
Bad debts	400	
Provision for bad debts	500	
Provision for discounts	266	
Interest accrued	1,000	30,116
		27,484
Add other revenue:		
Commission		1,350
Net profit		28,834

Balance sheet as at 30 November

FIXED ASSETS			
Land & buildings		46,000	
Furniture, fittings		8,000	
Motor vehicle		12,500	66,500
CURRENT ASSETS			
Stock		19,500	
Debtors	23,600		
- provision	(2,360)		
- provision	(266)	20,974	
Bank/cash		6,500	
Prepayments		150	47,124
CURRENT LIABILITIES			
Creditors		5,650	
Accrued expenses		1,900	7,550
Working capital			39,574
Capital employed			106,074
LONG-TERM LIABILITIES			
Bank loan			10,000
			96,074

CAPITAL		75,740	
Profit		28,834	
-Drawings		(8,500)	96,074

[ICM]

9. **Bradshaw**
Calculation of provision for bad debts:

	20-4	20-5
3 months	2,000	1,000
2 months	3,000	2,500
1 month	600	1,200
current	250	450
	5,850	5,150

Provision for bad debts a/c

		1/1	Balance b/d	4,900
Balance c/d	5,850	31/12	P & L	950
	5,850			5,850
P & L	700	1/1	Balance b/d	5,850
Balance c/d	5150			
	5850			5850
			Balance b/d	5150

[ICM]

Chapter 25 Depreciation of Fixed Assets

1. a) Depreciation by time, wear/tear depletion and obsolescence.
   b) i) obsolescence ii) wear/tear iii) depletion iv) not applicable v) time.
2. a) A prime entry to record the sale or purchase of fixed assets on a credit basis, including disposals and annual depreciation charged on fixed assets.
   b) To record various details concerning cost, depreciation, location and improving the control of fixed assets including any disposals.
3. a) Depreciation per annum £680,000. NBV year 1 £2,820,000, 2 £2,140,000, 3 £1,460,000, 4 £780,000, 5 £100,000. b) 97.1% c) year 1 £1,715,000, 2 £840,350, 3 £411, 772, 3 £201,768, 4 £98,866.
4. a) 96.7% b) £43,500, c) year 1 £181,500, 2 £138,000, 3 £94,500, 4 £51,000, 5 £7,500 d) 49% e) £15,222
5.* Jones: Gross Profit £37,500, Net Profit £11,125. Fixed Assets £75,600. Working Capital £5,725. Capital employed £81,325. Capital £71,000 Drawings £800 + Net Profit £11,125 = £81,325.
* Full Answer Provided
6. ABC Co: Gross Profit £9,700, Net Profit £4,022. Fixed Assets £31,350. Working Capital £4,072. Capital employed £35,422 Deferred Liabilities £15,500 = £19,922. Capital £18,000 - Drawings £2,100 + Net Profit £4,022 = £19,922.
7. Mavron: Ledger: Motor Vehicle a/c Dr. £27,000; Provision for depreciation a/c Cr. £6,025, Disposal a/c £200 loss; Journal: Motor Vehicles Dr. £15,000, Cr. Vehicle disposal £5,000, Bank £4,000, Pinot £6,000; Disposal Dr. £8,500 Cr. Vehicles £8,500; Provision for depn. Dr. £3,300, Disposal Cr. £3,300; P& I Dr. £200, Disposal Cr. £200; P & L Dr. £3,825, Provision for depn. Cr. £3,825.
   P & L account: Depreciation of vehicles £3,825, Balance Sheet, NBV of vehicles £20,975
8. Gallagher: Gross Profit £13,153, Net Profit £247. Fixed Assets £18,880, Current Assets £16,207 (debtors £11,622), Current Liabilities £15,840, Working Capital £367, LTL £3,500 = £15,747. Capital £18,860 + Profit £247 - Drawings £3,360 = £15,747.
9.* Barlow: Full answer provided
   b) The statement is untrue because depreciation does not set cash aside for replacement, although profits are reduced due to the expense which depreciation creates.
10. Jackson, Jackson & Walker: Task 1
   Equipment account balance b/d £28,000; Provision for depreciation account at
   1/1/03 balance b/d (credit) £13,555 credit, 31/12 p& l account (W2500) £850,
   (W2431) £1,520, (W3010) £1,600, (W325) £700 all credit. Debit 2/7 disposal £5,525, totals =
   £18,225, balance b/d £12700. Insurance account debit £720, credit prepaid £360, p& I £360.
   Disposal account: debit £10,800, credit depreciation £5,525, trade in £5,000,
   balance £275 (loss).
   Rothwell account: balance b/d £5,810 credit. VAT account £1,610 debit.
   Task 2 Journal: Dr equipment £9,200, VAT £1,610, Cr Rothwell £10,810; Dr Disposal
   £10,800, Cr Equipment £10,800; Dr Depreciation provision £5,525, Cr Disposal £5,525; Dr
   Rothwell £5,000, Cr Disposal £5,000; Dr p&l £4,670, Cr provision for depreciation £4,670; Dr
   p&l £275, Cr Disposal £275. Profit & loss account: depreciation of equipment £4,670, loss on
   disposal £275. Balance sheet: cost £28,000, depreciation £12,700, net book value £15,300.

Task 4

Register:	cost	depn	cum.depn	NBV	sale of FA	Gain/loss
W2431	8,400	1,520	7,600	800		
W2500	(10,800)	850	(5525)	(5275)	5,000	(275)
W3010	10,400	1,600	4,400	6,000		
W3250	9,200	700	700	8,500		
Totals:	**28,000**	**4,670**	**12,700**	**15,300**		

5. **Jones Trading & profit & loss a/c y/e 31 December**

Sales		66,600	
returns in		(700)	65,900
Cost of Sales			
o/stock		8,300	
purchases		30,800	
returns out		(900)	
carriage in		500	
stock drawings		(800)	
c/stock		(95,000)	28,400
Gross profit			37,500
Less Expenses:			
carriage out		400	
bank interest		350	
light & heat		1,650	
postage & stationery	600		
prepaid	(95)	505	
insurance		1,200	
telephone		500	
wages	16,500		
accrued	550	17,050	
bad debts		450	
discount		100	
provision for bad debts		700	
depreciation of van		1,500	
depreciation of equipment		3,400	27,805
			9,695
All other revenue:			
rent received	750		
accrued	180	930	
commission		500	1,430
Net profit			**11,125**

Balance sheet as at 31 December

FIXED ASSETS				
Premises		57,500		57,500
Equipment		23,000	9,400	13,600
Motor vehicle		8,000	3,500	4,500
CURRENT ASSETS				75,600
Stock		9,500		
Debtors	7,000			
- prov.	(700)	6,300		
bank/cash		1,950		
prepaid		95		
accrued rev.		180	18,025	
CURRENT LIABILITIES				
Creditors		11,750		
Accrued expenses		550	12,300	
Working capital				5,725
Capital employed				81,325
CAPITAL		71,000		
Profit		11,125		
- drawings		(800)		81,325

9. a)

Depreciation:	Ford	Toyota
Year 1	1,000	
Year 2	900	800
Year 3	810	720
	2,710	1,520

Value of Ford 7,290 (10,000 - 1,710)
Value of Toyota 6,480 (8,000 - 1,520)

b) **Journal**

	Debit	Credit
Disposal	10,000	
Motor vehicles		10,000
Provision for depn.	2,710	
Disposal		2,710
Motor vehicles	15,500	
Disposal (trade)		6,000
(bank)		9,500
P & L (depn.)	2,198	
Provision for depn.		2,198
P& L (loss)	1,290	
Disposal		1,290

Motor vehicle a/c

	Debit	Credit	Balance	
Bank (Ford)	10,000		10,000	Dr
Bank (Toyota)	8,000		18,000	
Disposal		10,000	8,000	
Bank & TI (Mercedes)	15,500		23,500	

Provision for depreciation of motor vehicle a/c

Yr 1	P&L (Ford)		1,000	1,000	Cr
Yr 2	P & L (Ford)		900		
	(Toyota)		800	2,700	
Yr 3	P&L (Ford)		810		
	(Toyota)		720	4,230	
	Disposal	2,710		1,520	
Yr 4	P&L (Toyota)		648		
	(Mercedes)		1,550	3,718	

Disposal a/c

Motor vehicle	10,000		
Provision for depn.		2,710	7,290
Trade-in		6,000	1,290
P & L (loss)		1,290	0

Extract from p & l account 30 June:

Depreciation of motors	2,198
loss on sale	1,290

Extract from balance sheet 30 June:

Motor vehicles	23,500	
-Depreciation	3,718	19,782

c)

Depreciation:	Ford	
Year 3	2,710	
Year 4 (4 months)*	243	2,953
*(729/3)		

Disposal a/c

	Debit	Credit	Balance
Motor vehicle	10,000		10,000 Dr
Provision for depn.		2,953	7,047
Trade-in		6,000	1,047
P & L (loss)	1,047		0

Provision for depreciation of motor vehicle alc

		Debit	Credit	Balance
Yr 3 Balance				4,230 Cr
Yr 4 Disposal		2,953		1,277
Yr 4 P & L	(Ford)		243	
	(Toyota)		648	
	(Mercedes)		1,033	3,201

Extract from P & L account 30 June:

Depreciation of motors	1,924	
Loss on sale	1,047	

Extract from balance sheet 30 June:

Motor vehicles	23,500	
-Depreciation	3,201	20,299

Chapter 26 Partnership Accounts

1. * Full Answer Provided
2. Lee and Crooks: Gross Profit £14,565, Net Profit £5,097. Appropriation a/c: Net Profit £5,097 - Salaries £2,500 + Interest on Drawings 549 = £3,146. Profit Share £1,573 each partner. Current Accounts Lee £626 Dr. Crooks £955 Dr. Balance Sheet: Fixed Assets £20,680, Working Capital £5,738. Capital employed £26,418. Capital a/cs £28,000. Current a/cs £1,582 Dr. = £26,418.
3. a) Jones, Smith & Brown: Gross Profit £60,970. S & D costs £6,767. Admin. costs £17,202. Net Profit £37,001.
   Appropriation a/c: Net Profit £37,001 - Salary £2,750 - Interest on capital £3,000 + Interest on Drawings £550 = £31,801. Share of Profit 5:4:1. James £15,900.5, Smith £12,720.4, Brown £3,180.1 Total £31,801.
   b) Current a/cs Jones £12,342.5, Smith £14,085.4, Brown £2,393.1 all Cr.
   c) Balance Sheet: Fixed Assets £72,800, Working Capital £33,021. Capital employed £105,821 - Deferred liabilities £27,000 = £78,821 (net assets). Capital a/cs £50,000. Current a/cs £28,821 = £78,821.
4.* Smith, Jones & Rogers: * Full Answer

5. French & Saunders:
   a) Appropriation a/c: Net Profit £19,800 - interest on capital £3,600 + interest on drawings £800 = £17,000. Profit share £8,500 each partner. Current a/cs: French £2,100 Cr. Saunder (£7,160) Dr. Fixed Assets £61,000, Working Capital (£1,060), Capital employed £59,940 - Loan £20,000 = £39,940. Capital £45,000 + Current a/cs (£5,060) £39,940. WC ratio 0.87 (insolvent).
   c) Reduce the Drawings of £27,000.
   d) Dr P + L a/c, Cr French's current a/c.
6. Wooldridge & James: Approriation a/c: Net Profit £38,650 - salary £21,000 - interest on capital £8,300 + interest on drawings £1,550 (W £650, J £900), = £10,900. Profit share: Wooldridge £6,540, James £4,360. Current a/cs: Wooldridge £7,990, James £2,660, both Cr.
   Fixed Assets £114,000, Working Capital £5,650, Capital employed £119,650, - Deferred Liabilities £29,000 = £90,650. Capital £80,000 + Current a/c's £10,650 = £90,650.
7. A & B: Appropriation a/c: Net Profit £14,680 - Salaries £6,000 - Interest on Capital £1,200 + Interest on Drawings £460 = £7,940. Profit Share £3,970 each partner. Balance Sheet: Capital   a/cs   £24,000. Current a/cs A £3,470, B £2,245, both Cr.
   Balance Sheet: Capital a/c A £15,000, B £15,000, C £10,000, Total £40,000. Profit Sharing Ratio 3:3:2.
8. A, B & C: Appropriation a/c: Net profit £81,500 – salaries £40,000, interest on capital £8,100, share of profit: A £12,525, B £12,525, C £8,350. Current a/c's: A £3,125 Cr, B £3,365 Cr, C £3470 Dr. Capital accounts: A £63,750, B £53,750, C £27,500, D £20,000. Goodwill a/c Dr. £90,000, Cr. £90,000.
   Balance sheet: FA £142,000 + net current assets £26,020 = capital employed £168,020. Financed by; capital accounts £165,000, current accounts £3,020.

1. **Smith and Jones:**
   Trading and Profit and loss account y/e 31 December

Sales	21,429		
returns in	(288)		21,141
Cost of sales			
o/stock	3,865		
purchases	11,665		
returns out	(343)		
carriage in	142		
stock (31/12)	(4,200)		11,129
Gross profit			**10,012**
EXPENSES			
bad debts provision		135	
depreciation of fix. & fit.		550	
depreciation of van		200	
salaries		5,055	
discount		199	
rates & insurance	645		
prepaid	(30)	615	
light. heat	162		
accrued	66	228	6,982
			3,030
+ discount received		146	
rent received		2,514	2,660
Net profit			**5,690**

Appropriation account y/e 31 December

Net profit		5,690
Salaries		
Jones	1,000	(1,000)
		4,690
Interest charges		
Smith	210	
Jones	160	370
		5,060
Share of profit		
Smith	3,036	
Jones	2,024	5,060

Current Accounts	Dr	Cr	Balance	
Smith				
31 balance			625	Dr
profit		3,036	2,411	Cr
drawings	2,303		108	
interest charges	210		102	Dr
Jones				
31 balance			540	Dr
salaries		1,000	460	Cr
profit		2,024	2,484	
drawings	1,500		984	
interest charges	160		824	

Balance sheet as at 31 December

FIXED ASSETS			
Premises	23,500		23,500
f & f	2,750	550	2,200
van	2,000	200	1,800
	28,250	750	27,500
CURRENT ASSETS			
Stock	4,200		
Debtors	2,355		
Provision bad debts	(250)		
Bank	522		
Prepaid	30	6,857	
CURRENT LIABILITIES			
Creditors	3,569		
Accrued	66	3,635	
Working capital			3,222
Capital employed			30,722
Capital accounts			
Smith	18,000	30,000	
Jones	12,000		
Current accounts			
Smith	(102)		
Jones	824	722	30,722

4. **J & R: Appropriation account y/e 31 May**

Net profit		7,300	
Salaries			
Jones	900		
Interest on capital			
Smith	510		
Jones	480		
Rogers	450	2,340	
		4,960	
Interest charges			
Smith	65		
Jones	55		
Rogers	45	165	
		5,125	
Profit share			
Smith (2)	2,050		
Jones (2)	2,050		
Rogers (1)	1,025	5,125	

Current accounts

Smith a/c

1	Balance		600	Cr
31/5	Int. on cap.	510	1,110	
	Profit	2,050	3,160	
	Drawings	2,000	1,160	
	Int. on drawings	65	1,095	

Jones a/c

1	Balance		400	Dr
31/5	Salary	900	500	Cr
	Int. on cap.	480	980	
	Profit	2,050	3,030	
	Drawings	1,900	1,130	
	Int. on drawings	55	1,075	

Rogers a/c

1	Balance		300	Dr
31/5	Int. on cap.	450	150	Cr
	Profit	1,025	1,175	
	Drawings	1,500	325	Dr
	Int. on drawings	45	370	

Balance sheet as on 31 May

FIXED ASSETS			30,700	
CURRENT ASSETS				
Stock	12,750			
Debtors	4,655			
Cash	500	17,905		
CURRENT LIABILITIES				
Creditors	14,560			
Accruals	300			
Overdraft	2,995	17,855		
Working capital			50	
			30,750	
LTL				
Loan			4,950	
			25,800	
Capital a/c's				
Smith	8,000			
Jones	8,000			
Rogers	8,000	24,000		
Current a/c's				
Smith	1,095			
Jones	1,075			
Rogers	(370)	1,800	25,800	

[ICM]

Chapter 27 Company Accounts

1. XYZ Co Ltd:
    a) Net Profit (before tax) £15,500 - Provision for tax £3,760 = Net Profit (after tax) £11,740
    Less provision for dividends £11,750 and Reserves £2,000 = (£2,010) + P & L balance
    £5,000 = P & L balance (31/12) £2,990.
    b) Balance Sheet. Fixed Assets £144,000. Current Assets £13,000 current liabilities £22,010.
    Working capital (insolvent) £9,010 Capital employed £134,990. Capital £130,000, Reserves £2,000,
    P & L a/c £2,990 = £134,990.
2. ABC Ltd: Net Profit (before tax) £18,750 - Provision for tax £1,500, Net Profit (after tax)
    £17,250 less Provision for dividends £9,000 and reserves £10,000 = (£1,750) + P & L balance
    £5,460 = P & L balance 31/12 =£3,710.
    Balance Sheet: Fixed Assets £94,250, current assets £27,670 - current liabilities £18,210 =
    working capital £9,460. Capital employed £103,710. Capital £60,000, Reserve £40,000, P & L
    a/c £3,710 + £103,710.
3. Bournemouth T Co Ltd: Gross Profit £31,310, Net Profit (before tax) £9,505 - Provision for tax £500 =
    Net profit (after tax) £9,005, less Provision for dividends £9,000, Reserves £600 = (£595) + P & L
    balance £1,300 = P & L balance (31/12) £705.
    Balance Sheet: Fixed Assets £53,900, current assets £33,931 - current liabilities £15,526 =
    working capital £18,405, capital employed £72,305 - Deferred liabilities £5,000 = £67,305.
    Capital £60,000, Premium a/c £6,000, Reserve £600, P & L a/c £705 = £67,305.
4.* Full Answer Provided
5 G Chappell & Sons Ltd: Gross Profit £19,324. Net Profit (before tax) £6,305. Provision for tax £1,250.
    Net Profit (after tax) £5,055 less Dividends £4,125, Reserves £2,000 = (£1,070) + P & L balance £1,170
    = P & L balance £100.
    Balance Sheet: Fixed assets £113,000, current assets £28,567 - current liabilities £9,967.
    Working Capital £18,600. Capital employed £131,600. Capital £125,000, Premium a/c £2,500,
    Reserve £4,000, P & L a/c £100 = £131,600.

6   Harrison Ltd: Gross Profit £94,225, Distribution cost £40,414, Admin. expenses £40,595. Operating
    profit £13,216 less Interest payable £5,000, Net Profit (before tax) £8,216. Provision for tax £3,750. Net
    Profit (after tax) £4,466 - Provision for dividends £3,750 = P & L balance (31/ 12) £716.
    Balance Sheet: Fixed assets £101,300, current assets £52,160, Current liabilities £60,744.
    Working capital (insolvent) - £8,584. Capital employed £92,716. - Deferred liabilities £40,000
    = £52,716 (net assets). Capital £50,000, Reserve £2,000, P & L a/c £716 = £52,716.

7. * Full Answer Provided
8. *Full Answer Provided

9. J P Davies, plc: Appropriation a/c, Operating Profit £80,000 less interest £12,500 = Net profit (before
    tax) £67,500 - tax £20,000, net profit (after tax) £47,500, less Dividends £15,000, £40,000, Reserves
    £25,000 = (£32,500) + P & L balance £40,000 = P & L balance 30/6 = £7,500
    Balance sheet: Fixed Assets £355,000, current assets £419,000, current liabilities £296,500, Working
    Capital £122,500, Capital employed £477,500 Deferred Liabilities, £100,000 = £377,500. Share Capital
    £300,000 + Reserves £70,000, P & L a/c £7,500 = £377,500.

4. **Robertson and David: Trading and Profit and loss a/c y/e 31 December**

Sales		696,500	
Returns in		(500)	696,000
Cost of sales:			
Stock	49,600		
Purchases	535,600	582,200	
Returns out		(1,600)	
		583,600	
Stock (31/12)		(39,400)	544,200
Gross profit			151,800
Expenses:			
Wages	68,820		
Rates, W and Insurance	2,600		
General expenses	22,566		
Depreciation vehicle	5,440		
Depreciation plant	4,220		
Bad debts	2,150		
Provision bad debts	49		
Discount	122		105,967
Operating profit			45,833
Interest accrued			2,800
Net profit before tax			43,033
provision for tax			19,200
Net profit after tax			23,833
-Provision for dividends:			
Preference (paid)		3,200	
Preference		3,200	
Ordinary		16,000	(22,400)
			1,433
Reserves			(4,000)
			(2,567)
P & I balance (1/1)			7,780
P & I balance (31/12)			5,213

Balance sheet as on 31 December

FIXED ASSETS			
Premises	287,910		287,910
Plant, equipment	16,880	4220	12,660
Vehicles	32,000	10,240	21,760
			322,330
CURRENT ASSETS			
Stock		39,400	
Debtors	63,380		
Provision for bad debts	(3,169)	60,211	
Cash		1,558	
Prepaid		1,000	102,619
CURRENT LIABILITIES			
Creditors		53,944	
Accruals		3,390	
Interest		2,800	
Dividends		19,200	
Taxation		19,200	
Overdraft		11,752	110,286
Net current liabilities			(8,117)
			314,213
LTL			
Debenture stock			40,000
			274,213
CAPITAL AND RESERVES			
Ordinary shares	160,000		
Preference shares	80,000	240,000	
Reserves		29,000	
P and L a/c		5,213	274,213

Note: An interim dividend is normally a part payment of a dividend usually paid at some mid-point in the year. It is not therefore a current liability.

[ICM]

7. **Jason Ltd: Appropriation a/c y/e 30 November**

Net profit (before tax)		40,600
Provision for taxation		8,400
Net profit (after tax)		32,200
-Provision for dividends:		
Preference	2,400	
Ordinary	9,000	(11,400)
		20,800
Reserves		(40,000)
		(19,200)
+ P & I a/c balance (1/12)		19,200

Balance sheet as on 30 November

FIXED ASSETS			
Premises	140,000		140,000
Plant, equipment	50,000	30,000	20,000
			160,000
CURRENT ASSETS			
Stock	38,340		
Debtors	5,800		
Cash	40		
Prepaid	820	45,000	
CURRENT LIABILITIES			
Creditors	1,120		
Accruals	880		
Taxation	8,400		
Dividends	11,400		
Overdraft	8,200	30,000	
Net current assets			15,000
			175,000

CAPITAL AND RESERVES
Ordinary shares	100,000	
Preference shares	30,000	130,000
Reserves		45,000
		175,000

[ICM]

8. **Compton Ltd: Appropriation a/c y/e 31 March**

Net profit (before tax)		108,000	
Provision for taxation		30,000	
Net profit (after tax)		78,000	
less			
Provision for dividends:			
Preference	16,000		
Ordinary	48,000	(64,000)	
Reserves		(20,000)	
		(6,000)	
P & L balance (1/4)		22,000	
P and L a/c balance (31/3)		16,000	

Balance sheet as on 31 March

FIXED ASSETS
Premises	300,000		300,000
Plant, equipment	310,000	140,000	170,000
Vehicles	200,000	116,000	84,000
			554,000

CURRENT ASSETS
Stock		98,000	
Debtors	87,000		
Prov	(4,000)	83,000	
Bank		4,000	
Prepaid		2,500	
		187,500	

CURRENT LIABILITIES
Creditors	74,000		
Accruals	3,500		
Taxation	30,000		
Dividends	64,000	171,500	
Working capital			16,000
			570,000

CAPITAL AND RESERVES
Ordinary shares	400,000		
Preference shares	100,000	500,000	
Share premium account		20,000	
Reserves		34,000	
P & I account		16,000	570,000

[ICM]

Chapter 28 Cash Flow Statements

I.   ABC Co: Operating activities: Operating profit £44,150 + depn £8,000 + WC changes £5,125 = £57,275; Tax (£12,500); FA (£63,000), Dividends (£8,000) = (£26,225); Financing: shares £10,000, debentures £15,000 = net outflow (£1,225), Bank balance (£1,225).

2.   Bishop: Operating activities: Operating profit £147,450 + depn £24,000 + WC changes £15,375 = £186,825; Interest payable (£15,000); Tax (37,500); 4, FA (£189,000), Dividends (£24,000) = (£78,675); Financing: shares £30,000, loan £45,000 = net cash outflow (£3,675), Bank balance = (£3,675).

3.* Jackson: Operating activities: Operating profit £12,750 + depn £3,500 - WC changes (£7,070) = £9,180; Tax (£5,100); FA (£16,000) + sale £1,500 = (£10,420); Financing: shares £10,000 = net cash outflow (£420), Bank balance = (£420).

* Full Answer Provided

4.   Jones & Rodgers: Operating activities: Operating profit £30,000 + depn £20,000 - WC changes (£26,000) = £24,000; Tax (£16,000); 4, FA (£80,000) + sale £9,000, Dividends (£12,000) – (£75,000); Financing: shares £33,000, debentures £50,000, = net cash inflow £8,000, Bank balance = £8,000.

5. Fox: Year 1 FA £28,904, WC £2,000, LTL £5,000 = £25,904. Year 2 FA £38,244, WC (£1,500) LTL £2,500 = £34,244.
   Operating activities: Operating profit £21,590 + depn £4,500 - WC changes (£5,276) = £20,814; Tax (£5,100); FA (£13,840), Dividends (£6,500) = (£4,626); Financing: shares £5,000, loan (£2,500) = net cash outflow (£2,126), Bank balance = (£2,126).

6.* XYZ: Operating activities: Operating profit £7,500 + depn £3,800 - WC changes (£800) = £10,500; Tax (£6,000); 4, FA (£9,000) + sale £3,500 = (£1,000); Financing: £0, = net cash outflow (£1,000), Bank balance = (£1,000).

* Full Answer Provided

7.* Aspen: Operating activities: Operating profit £49,160 + depn £20,300 - WC changes (£4,140) = £65,320; Interest payable (£1,000), Tax (£17,120); FA (£70,400), Dividends (£10,000) = (£33,200); Financing: shares £20,000, = net cash outflow (£13,200), Bank balance = (£13,200).

* Full Answer Provided

3. **Jackson**

		£
Operating profit		12,750
Depreciation		3,500
		16,250
Working capital:		
Stock	(5,580)	
Debtors	(3,925)	
Creditors	2,605	
Accruals	(170)	(7,070)
		9,180
Tax		(5,100)
Fixed assets (mach + premises)		(16,000)
add sale of fixed assets		1,500
		(10,420)
Financing:		
Share capital		10,000
Decrease in net cash flow		(420)

6. XYZ Ltd

Operating profit		7,500
(£10,000 – profit £2,500)		
Depreciation		3,800
		11,300
Working capital:		
stock	(1,400)	
debtors	(400)	
creditors	1,000	(800)
		10,500
Tax		(6,000)
Fixed assets		(9,000)
Disposal of FA		3,500
Dividends		0
		(1,000)
Financing:		
Shares		0
Decrease in net cash flow		(1,000)

7. **Aspen Ltd**

Operating profit		49,160
Depreciation		20,300
		69,460
Working capital:		
stock	2,320	
debtors	(2,100)	
creditors	(4,360)	(4,140)
		65,320
Interest payable		(,1000)
Tax		(17,120)
Fixed assets		(70,400)
Dividends		(10,000)
		(33,200)
Financing:		
Share capital		20,000
Decrease in net cash flow		(13,200)

Accounting ratios:	Year 1	Year 2
Current ratio:	2.67	2.7
ROCE		17.6%

Chapter 29 Accounts of Clubs and Societies

1. a) A club has the same type of statements example, the income & expenditure a/c is the p & l a/c.
   b) The accumulated fund is the net worth of a club, its capital calculated from A - L.
2. Subscriptions a/c: Dr balance b/d £200, £150, balance c/d £2,600, Cr balance b/d £75, £2,650, £225 totals £2,950, balance b/d £2,600, t/f to income & expenditure a/c.
3. Revenue £15,175, Expenditure £7,878, Surplus £7,297. Fixed assets £13,500, Working capital £5,397. Capital employed £18,897. Accumulated funds £11,600 + Surplus £7,297 = £18,897.
4. Bank Account (31/3) £4,115. Revenue £7,827, Expenditure £3,842 Surplus £3,985. Fixed assets £8,550. Working capital £3,735. Capital employed £12,285. Deferred liabilities £5,000 = £7,285. Accumulated funds £3,300 + Surplus £3,985 = £7,285.
5. a) Refreshment surplus £1,640.
   b) Revenue £4,715, Expenditure £3,496 = surplus £1,219. Fixed Assets £19,299. Working Capital (£1,625), Capital employed £17,674, - Loan £5,955 = £11,719. Accumulated funds £10,500 + surplus £1,219 = £11,719.
6. Bank a/c £2,825. Refreshment surplus £515. Revenue £3,980. Expenditure £1,953 = surplus £2,027. Fixed Assets £17,750, Working Capital £2,827, Capital employed £20,577 - Loan £2,000 = £18,577. Accumulated funds £16,550 + surplus £2,027 = £18,577.
7. Bank balance = £65. Surplus £43 (subs £160, depn £11, loss on sale £7). Fixed Assets £1,099, Working Capital £58 = £1,157. Accumulated Fund £1,114 + surplus £43 = £1,157.
8. Bar a/c surplus = £318. Surplus on I & E = £5,577 (subs £17,670). Fixed Assets £106,200, Current Assets £19,465, Current Liabilities £2,088, Working Capital £17,377 = £123,577. Accumulated Fund £118,000 + surplus £5,577 = £123,577.

Chapter 30 The Extended Trial Balance

1. Gross Profit £34,150, Net Loss (£1,252). Fixed Assets £163,048, Current Assets £14,040, Current Liabilities £17,040, NCL (£3,000), Capital Employed £160,048, LTL £91,300 = £68,748. Capital £70,000, loss (£1,252) = £68,748.
2. Gross Profit £110,615, Net Profit £16,667. Fixed Assets £104,400, Current Assets £54,340, Current Liabilities £26,020, Working Capital £28,320, = Capital Employed £132,720. Capital £131,653 + Profit £16,667 - Drawings (£15,600) = £132,720.
3. Gross Profit £55,141, Net Profit £5,888. Fixed Assets £30,300, Current Assets £27,560, Current Liabilities £6,681, Working Capital £20,879, = Capital Employed £51,179. Capital £53,091 + Profit £5,888 - Drawings (£7,800) = £51,179.
4. Gross Profit £22,258, Net Profit £3,250. Fixed Assets £20,880, Current Assets £16,670 Current Liabilities £16,000, Working Capital £670 = Capital Employed £21,550 – LTL £6,000 = £15,550. Capital £14,860 + Profit £3,250 - Drawings £2,560 = £15,550.
5.* * Full Answer Provided
6.   * Full Aswer Provided

7. Gross profit £23,245, net profit £997 [expenses £22,623], fixed assets £61,500, current assets £32,827, current liabilities £8,740, working capital £24,087, capital employed £85,587, LTL £28,690 = £56,897. Capital £62,500 + net profit £997 - drawings £6,600 = £56,897.

5. Smith: Extended trial balance

Details	Trial balance Debit	Credit	Adjustments Debit	Credit	Profit and loss Debit	Credit	Balance sheet Debit	Credit
Sales		27,615				27,615		
Returns in	205				205			
Stock	2,355				2,355			
Purchases	16,470				16,470			
Returns out		315				315		
Carriage in	442				442			
Carriage out	580				580			
Wages	5,285		185	185	5,470			185
Main., rates	1,998				1,998			
Insurance, telephone	334		80	80	254		80	
Post, stationery	350		110	110	240		110	
Bad debts	175				175			
Motor expenses	560				560			
Light, heat	546		90	90	636			90
Debtors	2,420						2,420	
Prov for bad debts		65	56	56	56			121
Cash	200						200	
Bank overdraft		2,005						2,005
Equipment	11,600						11,600	
Prov for depreciation			1,160	1,160	1,160			2,320
Motor van	2,500						2,500	
Prov for depreciation		1,500	250	250	250			1,750
Capital		8,860						8,860
Drawings	2,560							2,560
Creditors		2,560					25,600	
Bank loan								4,500
	48,580	49,920						
Closing stock			2,895	2,895		2,895	2,895	
					330,851	30,825		
Net profit (loss)					-26			-26
			4,826	4,826	30,825	30,825	22,365	22,365

6 Jackson Extended Trial Balance

Details	Trial balance Debit	Credit	Adjustments Debit	Credit	Profit and loss Debit	Credit	Balance sheet Debit	Credit
Sales		76,450				76,450		
Returns in	1,800				1,800			
Stock	6,300				6,300			
Purchases	46,000			2,000	44,000			
Returns out		1,500				1,500		
Carriage in	500				500			
Accounts fees	750				750			
Office salaries	16,000		540	540	16,540			540
Discounts		96				96		
Interest paid	938		312	312	1,250			312
Rent, rates	1,400		200	200	1,200		200	
Light, heat	700				700			90
Commission rec.		1,500	426	426		1,926	426	
Debtors	24,700						24,700	
Prov for bad debts		2,000	470	470	470			2,470
Cash	0						0	
Bank overdraft		6,500						6,500
Land and build.	65,000						65,000	
F & F	8,000						8,000	

Prov. Depreciation f & f		2,400	800	800	800			3,200
Motor van	12,500						12,500	
Prov. depreciation		5,000	1,500	1,500	1,500			6,500
Capital		72,450						72,450
Drawings	9,611		2,000				11,611	
Creditors		16,495						16,495
Bank loan		10,000						10,000
Closing stock			5,300	5,300		5,300	5,300	
					75,906			
Net profit					9,270			**9,270**
	194,295	**194,295**	**11,548**	**11,548**	**85,176**	**85,176**	**127,737**	**127,737**

Chapter 31 Accounting Ratios and Preparing Reports

1. Gross Profits £10,000, £12,000, £13,050. Net Profits £3,850, £5,050, £4,675.
   Gross Profit %'s £33.33%, 33.33%, 29%. Net Profit %'s 12.8% 14% 10.4%. Expense %: Distribution 10%, 8.9%, 9.1%.
   Administration 10.5%, 10.4%, 9.5%.
   Stock turnover = 10, 9.6 and 8 times per annum.
   Credit days taken 73 days in Year 1 and Year 2; 89 days Year 3.
   Return on capital 14.5%, 16.8%, 14.7%.

2.

	Co A	Co B
Gross Profits	£4,000	£13,500
Net Profits	£2,450	£6,000
Gross Profit %	44.4%	56.25%
Net Profit %	27.2%	25%
Return oncapital	26.4%	45.3%
WC ratio	2.14	1.9

3.

Harry Smith	Year 1	Year 2	Year 3
Working capital	£8,100	£6,280	£5,470
Working capital ratio	2.25	1.64	1.39
Acid test ratio	1.54	1.01	0.67

Year 1 obviously the most liquid year.

4.

	Year 1	Year 2	Year 3
Gross Profit %	40%	33.33%	40%
Net Profit %	22%	12.33%	17.5%
Return on Capital Inv.	35.5%	19.0%	29.5%
Return on Capital Employed.	22.9%	15.6%	27.3%
Current ratio	2.1	1.3	1.25
Net worth/total assets	72.5%	68%	65.3%

Year 2 inferior in all respects.
Big improvement in Year 3.

5.*

	Ball Bearings Ltd	Rocco Bank Ltd
Net Profit (after tax)	£1,500,000	£1,600,000
Earnings/Share	15p	80p
Dividend/Share	7p	20p
Cover	2.1	4
Current ratio	0.98	0.95
Acid test	0.5	0.95
Capital gearing	75% (high)	6.25% (low)
Net worth/total assets	11%	7.5%

6.		Sales	Cost of sales	Gross profit		Expenses		Net profit	NP%
	Year 1	£36,000	£27,000	£9,000	25%	£8,400		£600	1.67%
	Year 2	£54,000	£40,500	£13,500	25%	£9,500	£4,000		7.4%
	Year 3	£78,000	£58,500	£19,500	25%	£11,500	£8,000		10.3%
	Year 4	£120,000	£96,000	£24,000	20%	£19,000	£5,000		4.2%

7.		Year 1	Year 2	Year 3
	Gross Profits	£36,000	£50,000	£70,000
	Net Profits	£1,600	£7,000	£16,000
	Profit Returns			
	Gross Profit %	30%	331/3%	35%
	Net Profit %	1.33%	4.67%	8%
	ROCE	2.67%	6.67%	10%
	Stock Turnover	10.5	11.8	13

Steady improvement over the 3-year period. Sales and turnover of stock has increased each year to give a ROCE of 10% [still moderate]. Reduction of fixed costs and cost of sales for further improvement in Year 4.

8. a)

	Year 1	Year 2	Year 3
Gross %	33.3	25	20.0
Net %	10.0	4.4	2.6
ROCE %	15.0	8.0	5.8
WC ratio	3.5	2.14	1.73
Acid test	2.3	1.43	1.0
Sales/cap. Employed.	1.5	1.8	2.25
Debt collection	79 days	81 days	74 days
Owner's stake (%)	80.0	74.1	68.6
EPS	24p	12.9p	9.3p

b) Turnover has been achieved but at declining profit and liquidity levels. Difficult to justify increased investment. Problem is the high COS, but variable overheads improved along with asset usage.

Chapter 32 Accounting Standards: SSAP's and FRS's

1. Accounts would be prepared far more subjectively and many more anomalies would occur in the final accounts.
2. a) The owner(s) is separate from that of the business,
   b) transactions with a monetary value can only be recorded, not human or other values.
3. At original cost. at cost less depreciation. at net realisable value (NRV), at present value, etc.
4. The value of future returns from an asset, discounted at the going interest rate, to bring returns to their present value example, £121 earned 2 years from now at 10% pa is worth only £100 at today's present value.
5. SSAP 2 outlines the four basic accounting concepts: going concern, accruals, consistency and prudence, which provides the whole basis of preparing of final accounts.
   FRS 15 continues by stating:
   The concepts of going concern and accruals are seen as 'bedrock' principles and are of prime importance when preparing financial statements. Consistency and prudence are seen as 'desirable' elements and should still play an important part in preparing these statements.
6. Renton: Concepts include: cost price, revaluation of assets, consistency (depn.), prudence (stock and provision for losses), realisation (sales), accruals and materiality (interest), going concern (assumes the company continues).
7. The total cost of purchases and expenses is to include VAT in the final accounts. No VAT account recorded.
8. A registered trader records inputs and outputs of VAT. The income and expenses in the final accounts would exclude VAT charges, any balance of VAT is listed in the balance sheet.
11. In the value of stock, the concepts include: consistency, prudence and accruals and using the lower of cost and net realisable value.

12. a) Two methods which tries to deal with inflation are CPP and CCA. CPP requires recording at cost adjusted by an appropriate index (example, RPI) with the problem that there are other indices to use. With CCA, the profit for the year is calculated after allowing for inflation and changes in net asset values between the beginning and end of a financial period.
   b) In adjusting asset values for the effect of inflation, profit would be lower and distributions to shareholders lower, protecting capital maintenance.
   c) Development costs are treated as capital expenditure if they have potential future benefit of profits.
13. 'Impairment' refers to a fixed assets recoverable value falling below that of its net book value and further depreciation maybe required to meet the recoverable value.
   If an asset is to be re-valued the depreciation is charged on the re-valued sum and the remaining life of the asset.
12. In an attempt to ensure that financial statements are 'true and fair' and that compliance with accounting standards will be necessary in order for this to be purposefully achieved.

Chapter 33 Accounting for Stock
I. As per text: purchase requisition, purchase order, delivery note, GRN, stock requisition voucher, store issue voucher, stock card.
2. To ensure control of stock movements and buying at optimum levels of stock.
3. To check quantities on any given item and to ensure re-orders are made on time.
4.* a) 3,000 b)4,382c) 5,382d) 500.
* Full Answer Provided
5.* a) 1,732 b) 1,800 (600 x 3 weeks) c) 800 d) 3,132.
* Full Answer Provided
6.* a) as per text
   b) 11,200 re-order, 4,000 minimum level, 19,200 maximum level.
* Full Answer Provided
7.* Jack's store: Lower of cost or NRV £525, £140, £900, £750, £149.25, £57.50 and £5. Total stock value = £2,526.75.
* Full Answer Provided
8.* Using FIFO: value of stock 1/7 £715 1/8 £745 1/9 £765 = 100 units x £2.15 = £215.250 units x £2.20 = £550. Total value = £765.
   Using LIFO: value of stock 1/7 £700 1/8 £700 1/9 £700 = 200 units x £2 = £400. 100 units x £1.95 = £195, 50 units x £2.10 = £105. Total value £700.
* Full Answer Provided
9. Stock Card: 12/9 299 reams x £2.5 = £747.5 20/9 Balance 170 reams: FIFO 80 x £2.5 = £200, 90 x £3 = £270. Total value £470.

10. FIFO: 24/1 Balance 100 units x £3.2, 70 units x £3, total 170 units value £530. 28/2 Balance 50 units x £3.40, 50 units £3.50, total 100 units value £345.
   LIFO: 24/1 Balance 150 units x £3, 20 units x £3.20, total 170 units value £514. 28/2 Balance 50 units x £3, 50 units x £3.40, total 100 units value £320.
   LIFO's stock value is £25 less than FIFO. Therefore gross profit would be £25 less if LIFO stock value used.

4.* a) Re-order level: max use (per day) x rnax lead time
                    100   x   30 days
                               = 3,000 units

   b) Re-order quantity: $Q = \sqrt{\dfrac{2AC}{H}}$

                    $= \dfrac{2 \times 24,000 \times 400}{1}$

                    $= \sqrt{1,920,000}$
                    = 4,382 units
   c) Max level:
      Re-order level + re-order qty - (min use x min lead time)
         3,000   + 4,382   - (100 x 20) = 5,382 units

   d) Min level: re-order level - (average use x average lead time)
                    3,000   - (100 x 25) = 500 units

5. Reorder $= \sqrt{\dfrac{2AC}{H}}$ (weeks)
    (REQ)

$$= \sqrt{\dfrac{2 \times 400 \times 50 \times 150}{2H}}$$
$$= 1,732 \text{ kilos}$$

Reorder level = max use x max LT
(REL)

= 600 x 3 weeks
= 1,800 kilos

Min stock level =   ROL - (av.use x av. LT)
= 1,600 - 400 x 2
= 800 kilos

Max stock level = ROL + ROQ - (min use x min LT)
= 1,800 + 1,732 - (400 x 1)
= 3,132 kilos

6. Reorder Q = 12,000 kilos

ROL = 800 per day x 14 days
= 11,200 kilos

Min stock level = 11,200 - 600 per day x 12 days
= 4,000 kilos

Max stock level = 11,200 + 12,000 - 400 x 10 days
= 19,200 kilos

8.

Date	Details	Quantity	Unit	Cost	Issued	Balance (qty)	Unit	Stock value
1/6	Balance					200	2	400
15/6	Purchased	100	1.95	195		100	1.95	595
30/6	Purchased	200	2.1	420		200	2.1	1,015
30/6					150	50	2	100
						100	1.95	295
						200	2.1	715
21/7	Purchased	200	2.15	430		200	2.15	1,145
30/7					200	150	2.1	315
						200	2.15	745
10/8	Purchased	150	2.2	330		150	2.2	1,075
21/8	Purchased	100	2.2	220		100	2.2	1,295
31/8					250	100	2.15	215
						250	2.2	765

FIFO

Date	Details	Quantity	Unit	Cost	Issued	Balance (qty)	Unit	Stock value
					LIFO			
1/6	Balance					200	2	400
15/6	Purchased	100	1.95	195		100	1.95	595
30/6	Purchased	200	2.1	420		200	2.1	1,015
30/6					150	200	2	400
						100	1.95	595
						50	2.1	700
21/7	Purchased	200	2.15	430		200	2.15	1,130
30/7					200	200	2	400
						100	1.95	595
						50	2.1	700
10/8	Purchased	150	2.2	330		150	2.2	1,030
21/8	Purchased	100	2.2	220		100	2.2	1,250
31/8					250	200	2	400
						100	1.95	595
						50	2.1	700

[ICM]

Chapter 34 Accounting for Incomplete Records

1. H Jones: Debtors – to reconstruct sales £53,690. Creditors to reconstruct purchases £43,525. Bank a/c £1,588. Gross Profit £11,915. Net profit £5,708.
Balance Sheet: Fixed assets £2,465, Working capital £7,933. Capital employed £10,398. Capital £7,000 - Drawings £2,310 + Net Profit £5,708 = £10,398.
2. F Smith: Bank a/c £10,625 - Cash Drawings £5,000 = £5,625. Sales a/c £72,767. Purchases a/c £46,960. Gross Profit £27,357. Net Profit £11,707. Balance Sheet: Fixed assets Nil. Current assets £18,672, current liabilities £5,465, working capital £13,207. Capital £6,500 - Drawings £5,000 + Net Profit £11,707 = £13,207. Note: Rates £1,065 in P & L a/c.
3. Jack: Capital = £8,000 (Assets £11,410 - Liabilities £3,410). Sales a/c £59,850, Purchases a/c £41,540. Gross Profit £18,910. Net Profit £7,605. Balance Sheet: Fixed assets £2,500. Working capital £6,580. Capital employed £9,080. Capital £8,000 - Drawings £6,525 + net Profit £7,605 = £9,080. Note: insurance £105 in P & L a/c.
4. F Smith: Bank a/c commence payments with O/D £1,765 and include £1,955 mortgage repayment. Balance on 31/12 = £1,425 overdrawn. Sales a/c £49,695, Purchases £35,570. Gross Profit £15,735, Net Profit £9,261.
Balance Sheet: Fixed assets £30,685, Current assets £6,066, current liabilities £6,305, working capital (insolvent) - £239, capital employed £30,446. Deferred liabilities £13,295. Net assets £17,151. Capital £13,800 - drawings £5,910 + Net Profit £9,261 = £17,151.
5. J Archer: Capital £99,700. Sales a/c £228,600. Purchases £158,950. Gross Profit £110,770, Net Profit £12,850. Fixed assets £14,550. Working Capital £86,000. Capital employed £100,550. Capital £99,700 - Drawings £12,000 + Net Profit £12,850 = £100,550. Note: Depreciation of fixtures £1,900.
6. J Jones: Capital £20,000. Sales £46,525, Purchases £38,965. Gross Profit £9,175, Net Profit £4,225. Fixed Assets £19,300, Working Capital £5,250, Capital employed £24,550 - Loan £4,000 - £20,550. Capital £20,000 + Net Profit £4,225 - Drawings £3,675 = £20,550.
7. D White: Gross Profit £60,898, Net Profit £10,742. Fixed Assets £51,000, Current assets £31,600, Current Liabilities £13,680, Working Capital £17,920, Capital employed £68,920.
Capital £73,078 + Net Profit £10,742 - Drawings £14,900 = £68,920.
8. Justin Harris: Gross Profit £51,200, Net Profit £16,520.
Fixed Assets £43,200, Current assets £53,720, Current Liabilities £13,360, Working Capital £40,360, Capital employed £83,560.
Capital £80,760 + Net Profit £16,520 - Drawings £12,160, £1,560 = £83,560.
9. Murray Ltd: Credit purchases £584,000. Credit Sales £660,000. Sales £820,000 - COS £574,000 = Gross Profit £246,000. Closing stock £308,000 (£882,000 - £574,000).
Stock Loss £126,000. (£308,000 - £182,000).
10.* Full Answer Provided

Patel Trading and profit and loss account y/e 31 October

Debtors a/c

1/11	Balance	19,630	31/10	Receipts	181,370
31/10	Sales	173,770		Bad debts	530
				Balance c/d	11,500
		193,400			193,400

Credit sales	173,770		
Cash sales	61,190	234,960	

Creditors a/c

31/10	Bank	163,100	1/11	Balance	9,440
	Balance c/d	12,700	31,10	Purchases	166,360
		175,800			175,800

Trading and profit and loss account y/e 31 October

Sales*			238,140
Cost of sales:			
Stock	16,100		
Purchases	166,360	182,460	
Stock (31/10)		(23,700)	158,760
Gross profit (33 1/3%)			79,380
Expenses:			
Establishment .& administration		33,300	
Sales distribution		29,100	
Bad debts		5,300	
Depreciation. vehicles		2,920	
Depreciation F & F		1,000	66,850
Net profit			12,530

*Calculation of cash drawings:
331/3% of the sales = 50% of cost

50% of cost:	158 760 x 50%	79,380
	Cost	158,760
	Sales	238,140
	Sales known	234,960
		3,180
	Less float	40
	Cash drawings =	3,140

Balance sheet as on 31 October

FIXED ASSETS			
Fixtures, fitings	10,000	7,000	3,000
Vehicles	20,200	4,720	15,480
CURRENT ASSETS			18,480
Stock	23,700		
Debtors	11,500		
Bank	6,620		
Cash	200	42,020	
CURRENT LIABILITIES			
Creditors		12,700	
Working capital			29,320
			47,800
Capital	30,910		
Net profit	12,530		
New capital	16,000	59,440	
Drawings	8,500		
	3,140	11,640	47,800

[AAT]

Chapter 35 The Manufacturing Account

I. F Smith: Prime Cost £58,925, Factory overheads £10,102, Factory Cost £69,117.   Gross profit £25,578, Net profit £15,384.25.

2.* Harry: Full Answer Provided

3. ABC Co Ltd: Prime Cost £73,185, Factory overheads £11,760, Factory Cost £84,415. Gross Profit £39,299, Net Profit £15,519. Prime Cost/Unit £6.97, Factory overheads/Unit £1.12, prod. Cost/Unit £8.04, Total cost/unit £10.30. Mark-up % 18.1, Margin % 15.3.

4. Fred's Co Ltd: Prime Cost £49,005, Factory overheads £10,470, Factory Cost £59,475. Factory Cost/Unit £5.95. Gross Profit £24,212.5, Net Profit £17,515.

5.* P Jackson: Full Answer Provided. Note: Balance sheet FA £43,025 + WC £10,272 = £53,297 capital employed.

6. XYZ Co Ltd: Prime Cost £198,623, Factory Cost £201,000, Cost/Unit £4.02. Finished goods stock 31/12 £18,090. Gross Profit £12,590, Net Profit £1,802. P & L c/f £1,382, Fixed Assets £91,400. Working capital - £11,018 (insolvent). Capital employed £80,382. Shareholders' funds: £80,382.

2.* **Harry: Manufacturing account y/e 3I December**

Stock (1/1)	6,567		
Purchases	40,875		
Stock (31/12)	(5,583)	42,049	
Direct wages		15,500	
Prime cost			57,549
Rent, rates & insurance	3,664		
Manufacturing expenses	5,945		
Depreciation machinery	2,150		
Factory overheads			11,759
Factory cost			69,308
Market value (wholesale prices)			78,000
Profit on manufacture			8,692

Trading and profit and loss account y/e 31 December

Sales			101,500
Cost of sales			
o/stock	10,560		
factory cost (MV)	78,000		
	88,560		
c/stock	(12,565)		75,995
Trading profit			25,505
Manufacturing profit			8,692
Gross profit			34,197
EXPENSES			
office wages	12,765		
rent, rates & ins.	916		
selling expenses	12,855		
admin expenses	7,400		
depreciation furniture	500		
depreciation office mach.	150		34,586
Net loss			(389)

Direct labour/unit	7.75
Direct materials/unit	21.02
Factory overheads/unit	5.88
Production/unit	34.65
Office overheads/unit	17.29
Total cost per unit	51.94

(Costs too high, business can hardly break-even. Manufacturing profit is inadequate to sustain business).

5. **Jackson Manufacturing account y/e 31 December**

Stock raw materials(1/1)	6,885		
Purchases	55,725		
Stock raw materials (31/12)	(7,432)	55,178	
Direct wages		45,780	
Prime cost			100,958
Factory overheads	14,385		
Prepaid	(240)		
Accrued	600		14,745
Factory cost			115,703

Trading and profit and loss account year ending, 30 June

Sales		180,344	
Returns in		548	179,796
Cost of sales			
Stock finished goods (1/7)	3,500		
Factory cost	115,703	119,203	
Stock finished goods (30/6)		4,200	115,003
Gross profit			64,793
Expenses			
Discount allowed		855	
Salaries		18,346	
Overheads		7,044	
Depreciation vehicle		875	27,120
			37,673
+ discount received			1,044
Net profit			38,717

Chapter 36 Marginal Costing

I. a) Table: Fixed costs £56,000, Variable costs £44,000.
   b) Contribution/Unit £38 (£60 - £22).
   c) Profit on 2,000 units, £20,000.
   d) 2,100 units, £23,800; on 1,950 £18,100.
   e) Break-even 1,474 units. Profit (1 above) £38. Loss (1 below) £38.
   f) Variation: £14,400 profit.
2. a) C/Unit £8.
   b) Profit £1,250.
   c) B/E 344 units, £4,300 revenue.
   d) Profit £10,700.
   e) £1,058.
   f) £1,450 profit first, £1,427.5 profit second, first best.
   g) 96 extra units.
3. a) Table; Fixed costs £63,250, Variable cost £94,750.
   b) C/Unit £2.105.
   c) £1,895 extra cost.
   d) Yes.
   e) B/E 30,048 Units, £120,192 revenue.
   f) Loss £104.2.
   g) £42,000.
   h) £19,897.50 profit.
4. a) B/E 23,500 units.
   b) £17,500 loss.
   c) 16,000 units extra.
   d) £2,250 loss.
   e) £2,500 profit; £36,500 profit; £10,000 extra profit - total profit £42,500. Third is best proposal.
5. a) 9,400 units.
   b) £7,000 loss.
   c) 3,200 units.
   d) Profit £5,500; Profit £17,000; second is best proposal, current profit only £13,000.
6. a) Fixed costs £156,000, Variable costs £204,000.
   b) C/Unit £41, B/E 3,805 units.
   c) 6,500 units = £110,500 profit, 3,500 units £12,500 loss.

7. a) Contribution £60.
    b) Break-even 4,000 units.
    c) Margin of safety 6,000 units, 60%.
    d) Estimated profits £360,000 and £270,000.
    e) Proposals: £360,000 profit; £425,000 profit; £408,000 profit.
    Therefore, second has best profit potential
8   a) Contribution per unit, total contribution, contribution/materials or other cost, c/s ratio are some
    examples. b) Contribution/materials A = £1.20, B = £1.67. Make 34 of A, 80 of B. Total contribution,
    A £1,632, B = £2,000. c) The effect of fixed costs, also morale of workforce, cost of equipment, etc.
9. a) Contrib/DM: X = 0.5, Y = 0.78, Z = 0.55. DM allocated: Y = £1,024,000, Z = £950,000, X =
    £120,000; total £2,094,000. Profit X = £60,000, Y £800,000, Z £525,000 - Fixed Costs £585,000 =
    £800,000.b) Extra contribution £55,000 - £7,500 = £47,500; order accepted.

Chapter 37 Budgeting

1. Cash Budget

	March	April	May	June	July	August	Total
Receipts	100,000`	6,500	12,500	12,500	13,500	14,000	159,000
Payments	29,050	32,550	32,550	29,553	7,100	28,380	159,183
Net cash flow	70,950	(26,050)	(20,050)	(17,053)	6,400	(14,380)	(183)
Balance b/f	0	70,950	44,900	24,850	7,797	14,197	0
Balance c/f	70,950	44,900	24,850	7,797	14,197	(183)	(183)

Sales £71,000 less expenses £37,131 = net profit £34,369
Balance sheet (if required) FA £117,835, net current assets £9,034, capital employed ;£126,869 – loan £50,000 =
£76,869; financed by capital £50,000 + profit £34,369 less drawings £7,500 = £76,869.

2.

Cash Budget (£)	July	Aug.	Sept.	Oct.	Nov.	Dec.
Balance b/f	70,000	2,475	1,660	1,925	1,350	2,475
Receipts	2,875	9,625	12,625	15,625	19,125	22,625
Payments	70,400	10,440	12,360	16,200	18,000	15,480
Balance c/f	2,475	1,660	1,925	1,350	2,475	9,620

Gross Profit £30,910. Net Profit £23,460. Proprietor's capital 31/12 £89,260.

3.

Balances c/f	£131,250	(24,000)	(39,250)	(64,500)	(49,750)	(38,300)

Gross Profit £60,000, Net Profit £21,900.
 Fixed Assets £112,000, Working Capital £59,900,
 Capital employed £171,900 - Debentures £50,000 = £121,900.
 Capital £100,000 + Profit £21,900 = £121,900.

4.

Cash Budget (£)	June	July	August
Balances c/f	(9,900)	(11,000)	(8,100)

Sales £71,800 - COS £57,440 = Gross Profit £14,360.
 Stock value £10,760. Net Profit £5,585.
 (Note: Depreciation £375, Rent £900).
 Fixed Assets £61,025, Working Capital £10,960, Capital employed £71,985.
 Capital £50,000 + P & L a/c £21,985 = £71,985.

5. a) Bank balance December £2,400.
    b) Gross Profit £17,760, Net Profit £7,860.
    Fixed Assets £7,200, Current Assets £7,660, Current Liabilities £2,000, Working Capital £5,660 = Capital
    Employed £12,860.

6.

	July	Aug.	Sept.	Oct.	Nov.	Dec.
Balance b/f	0	71,150	(9,040)	(4,340)	(26,780)	(25,080)
Receipts	100,000	12,500	13,000	12,000	9,000	4,000
Payments	28,850	93,690	8,300	34,440	7,300	10,600
Balance c/f	71,150	(9,040)	(4,340)	(26,780)	(25,080)	(31,680)

Sales £53,000, expenses £31,720, net profit £21,280.
Fixed assets £134,750, current assets £2,500, current liabilities £33,970, working capital (£31,470), capital employed £103,280.   Capital a/c's £100,000, current a/c's Johnson £2,768, Buckley £512 = £103,280.

7. a) Profit: fixed budget £16,000, actual £6,500, variance = (£9,500) adverse largely
        due to sales variance £12,500 adverse
   b)   Profit: flexible budget £11,250, actual £6,500, variance = (£4,750), variance lower
        due to sales units now same.

Chapter 38 Capital Investment Appraisal

1.a) A pays back in less than 3 years, B takes over 3 years.
  b)   NPV Project A £395,506 = £10,506 positive. B £261,805 = £36,195 negative.
  c) A is the better of the two Projects because its NPV is a positive figure.
2.a) Project A pays back in 2 years 5 months.
  b) Project B pays back 1 month faster, therefore better.
  c) NPV Project A £414,130 = £14,130 positive.
  d) IRR = 16% + £14,130/£17,970 x 2 = 1.57% = total 17.57%.
3.a) NPV at rate 12% = £5,250, at rate 16% = (£11,300) negative.
  b) IRR = 12% + £5,250/£16,550 x 4 = 1.27% = total 13.27%.
  c) IRR is more than 13% and is satisfactory.
4.a) Project 2 pays back in 2 years 5 months.
  b) Project 2 pays back faster by 3 months and is better than Project 1.
  c) NPV of Project 2 £153,780 = (£1,220) negative.
  d) ARR for Project 1, 26.6%, Project 2, 24.8%
      Project 1 is positive by £1,729 and earns more than 15% and has a marginally larger ARR
      and therefore is preferred.
5.a) Project 2 pays back in 2 years 9 months.
  b) Project 2 better, pays back 1 month faster than Project 1.
  c) Project 2 NPV £83,543 = £8,543 positive.
  d) Both Projects satisfactory, the difference is very marginal.
6. a) Project 2 pays back in 2 years 9 months
   b) It is faster than Project 1 by 1 month
   c) Project 2 has NPV £154,178 = £178 positive
   d) IRR for Project 1 = 14%, Project 2 has 15% at least. Project 2 would therefore be the better investment.

Chapter 40 Exams and Examination Success

ANSWERS TO FOUNDATION EXAM

Tasks 1.1, 1.2
SL: James & Dingle £2,020, Harris & Co £6,301, Street & Sons £8,385, Jones £3,020 (all debits)
PL: Nash Bros £10,185, Mathews £12,081 (credits)
NL: sales £139,656 Cr, purchases £136,063, sales returns £1,484, heat, light £1,684, stationery £957, rent, rates £5,575, equipment £3,300 (all debits), VAT £2,051 Cr, debtors control £29,033 Dr, creditors control £48,497 Cr

Task 1.3
Trial Balance as at 1 May 20-3

	Debit £	Credit £
sales		139,656
sales returns	1,484	
purchases	136,063	
purchases returns		2,972
wages	22,140	
insurance	890	
heat and light	1,684	
rent and rates	5,575	
telephone	1,344	
motor expenses	2,475	
stationery	957	
general expenses	1,890	
equipment	3,300	
motor vehicle	8,435	
o/stock	7,800	
bank	3,649	
petty cash	250	
debtors control	29,033	
creditors control		48,497
VAT		2,051
capital		37,433
drawings	3,640	
	230,609	**230,609**

SECTION 2
Task 2.1
Dr bank £385, Cr debtors control; BACS provides safety and speed of payment and no documents need to be posted.
Task 2.2
Payee - the party to receive the cheque, drawee - the bank where the cheque is drawn, drawer, the party who signs the cheque. A current account operates the cheque system and allows overdrafts.
Task 2.3
Dr creditors control £25, Cr discount received £25
Task 2.4
a) purchases day book b) purchases returns day book c) journal d) petty cash book
Task 2.5
To verify the purchase ledger, to have a total sum to represent creditors, to enter a single figure to the trial balance.
Task 2.6
Petty cash vouchers used, analysis columns to show expenses
Task 2.7
Automatic double entry system, instant up-dating of accounts, available printouts when required, instant analysis of accounts, unlimited storage of accounts without need of space.

Task 2.8

Journal entries	Debit	Credit
discount allowed	30	
bank interest	30	
suspense		60
bank	600	
sales		600
bank	45	
telephone		45
suspense	200	
purchases		200

Suspense account: Dr £200, Cr £140, £60, (cleared)

Task 2.9
Debtors control Dr £18,545, £19,550, £140, Cr £15,125, £700, £80, £300, balance = £22,030
sales ledger totals = £22,330, discrepancy = £300. This could be the bad debt written off not yet posted to
sales ledger on incorrect balancing of ledger accounts or errors posting from primary books.
Task 2.10
Cash book up-dated with DD's, STO and bank charges, balance = £2,057 debit

Bank reconciliation statement: £
1 balance as per statement   2,275 Cr
2 add deposit   <u>475</u>
    2,750

3 less un-presented cheques
  Nos.   45, 138, 88, 422   <u>693</u>
4 balance as per cash book   2,057 Dr

ANSWERS TO PAPER 2 INTERMEDIATE LEVEL
Section 1
1.1 Sales ledger control account £46,525, Purchase ledger control account £38,965
1.2 Net book value: cost £3,000 less depreciation £1,735 = £1,265
1.3 *Fixed asset disposal account:*

equipment	3,000	depreciation	1,735
		trade-in	800
		p & l	465
	3,000		**3,000**

1.4 Cost of replacement: £3,000 + £800 = £3,800
1.5 Revised equipment cost: £10,000 - £3,000 + new £,800 = £10,800
1.6 Depreciation charge: cost £10,800 - depreciation £2,515 = £8,285 X 25% = £2,071
1.7 Accumulated depreciation: £2,515 + £2,071 = £4,586
Provision for depreciation account:

disposal	1,735	balance	4,250
balance c/d	4,586	p & l	2,071
	6,321		**6,321**

1.8 Adjustment: prepaid insurance half year £120

1.9   **Trial balance as at 31 December**

	Debit	Credit
sales		46,525
rent received		1,510
discount received		550
purchases	38,965	
discount allowed	225	
equipment (cost)	10,800	
provision for depreciation		4,586
motor vehicle (cost)	3,500	
provision for depreciation		500
premises	50,000	
light, heat	295	
advertising	300	
wages 1550 - 100	1,450	
rates 250 + 70	320	
motor expenses 750 - 120	630	
general expenses	505	
depreciation 2071 + 500	2,571	
loss on disposal	465	
bank	3,185	
debtors	1,800	
prepayments	120	
o/stock	4,780	
creditors		2,465
bank loan		40,400
capital		25,750
drawings	2,375	
	122,286	**122,286**

1.10
Mark up on purchases: £38,965 + 20% = sales £46,758, actual sales = £46,525, only a very marginal discrepancy of £233 that could be due to stock theft, owner taking stock but more likely that some sales may have been at a lower price.

Section 2
2.1 Journal entries
a) Dr depreciation p & I £7,750   Cr provision (equipment) £6,000, motor £1,750
b) Dr stock p & I £1,100   Cr stock (balance sheet) £1,100
c) Dr light, heat £125   Cr accruals £125
d) Dr prepayments £1,000   Cr rent, rates £1,000
e) Dr advertising £150   Cr office expenses £150

2.2 Profit and loss account
Gross profit £125,820, Net profit £42,230
Balance sheet (extra if required)
FA £54,250, CA £23,335, CL £13,445, WC £9,890, CE £64,140
Capital £45,000, Current accounts Jack £9,596, Jill £9,544

2.3 Appropriation account
Net profit £42,230 less salaries £20,500, interest on capital, Jack £1,000, Jill £1,250
= £19,480, less profit share to 30/6, Jack £3,896, Jill ££5,844, less profit share to 31/12
Jack and Jill £4,870 each.

2.4 Current accounts
Jack Dr £9,520, Cr £850, £8500, £1,000, £3,896, £4,870, balance = £9,596
Jill   Dr £220, £14,200, Cr £12,000, £1,250, £5,844, £4,870, balance = £9,544

2.5 Memo: Goodwill
Goodwill arises from the reputation or good name of a business and when a new partner
arrives or existing partner leaves, an amount for goodwill maybe calculated to charge a
new partner or pay off an existing one.

It is prudent to write off goodwill (FRS 10) as soon as possible and this is based on the partners profit
sharing ratios.

Any goodwill created is credited to partners capital accounts based on existing profit sharing rate (and
debited to the goodwill account). Goodwill written off is based on the new profit sharing ratio,
debiting the partners capital accounts and crediting goodwill to write it off.

INDEX